THE SEARCH FOR

FOR

JFK

by

Joan and Clay Blair, Jr.

Published by
Berkley Publishing Corporation
Distributed by
G. P. Putnam's Sons
New York

Acknowledgment is gratefully made for permission to reprint from the following:

Doubleday & Company, Inc.: *Times To Remember* by Rose Fitzgerald Kennedy. Copyright ©1974 by The Joseph P. Kennedy, Jr. Foundation.

The New York Times Company: from the marriage of "Kathleen Kennedy to Lord Hartington" © 1944.

Esquire Magazine: excerpt from "Rich, Young and Happy" by Harry Muheim, © 1966 by Esquire Inc.

The Associated Press: story by Leif Erickson.

Yale University Library: from the Paul Palmer Papers.

McGraw-Hill Book Company: *PT-109* by Robert J. Donovan. Copyright © 1961 by Robert J. Donovan.

United Press International: "Somewhere in New Georgia, Aug. 8"

The *Philadelphia Inquirer:* from story by Bob Fensterer of August 15, 1971.

Little, Brown and Company in association with The Atlantic Monthly Press: *Memoirs, 1925-1950* by George F. Kennan.

The New American Library, Inc.: *The Lost Prince* by Hank Searls. Copyright © 1969 by Hank Searls.

Excerpts from *John Fitzgerald Kennedy: As We Remember Him* (edited and produced under the direction of Goddard Lieberson; copyright © Columbia Records, 1965. A Columbia Records Legacy Collection Book; all rights reserved).

To Jean and Paul Rutledge—with love

Contents

8

Part III   TRANSITION

Part IV   BOSTON

Part V   WASHINGTON

Foreword

JOHN Fitzgerald Kennedy captured the fancy of journalists, writers, and publishers as had no other politician in modern times. Not even FDR evoked such a vast, uncritical outpouring—books, magazine and newspaper articles glamorizing Jack, his teeming, energetic family, his elegant and beautiful young wife, Jacqueline, and even his second- and third-echelon political aides. After his assassination in Dallas, the outpouring increased in intensity with eulogies, sentimental memoirs by friends and political associates, and flattering assessments by historians. Robert Kennedy's assassination in 1968 generated yet another wave of Kennedy literature. To this day, Kennedy books continue to roll off the presses in astounding numbers. With two or three exceptions, deliberate and execrable hatchet jobs, all these millions of words have tended to turn Jack Kennedy into a plaster saint.

During Watergate (which revealed to us the real character of President Richard M. Nixon—as opposed to the manufactured Madison Avenue image), our thoughts turned to Jack Kennedy. Neither of us knew him personally, but as editor-in-chief of *The Saturday Evening Post* during the thousand days of the Kennedy Administration, one of us contributed in no small part to the romanticizing of Jack and his family. Like other journalists, we were captivated by what was then called the "Kennedy mystique" and the excitement of "the New Frontier." Now we began to wonder. Behind the image, what was Jack really like? Could one, at this early date, cut through the cotton candy and find the real man?

We set off on a journalistic search with no preconceived bias or scheme other than to see if it could be done. At first we contemplated a full life story, from birth to assassination. But that soon proved overly ambitious in terms of our time and resources. In the end, we narrowed our search to a comparatively unknown, yet extremely interesting and crucial period in Jack's life. This was the twelve-year period from about 1935, when he was graduated from The Choate School, to about 1947, when he made his political debut in the United States House of Representatives. These were years of physical and intellectual growth and character development.

Years of coming to terms with his domineering father. Years of choosing close friends, a life-style, a career. Years of forming the vaunted Kennedy political machine. Years of fun and girl-chasing in Palm Beach, Hollywood, and on the Riviera. Years of war, and testing himself in combat.

We were not, of course, the first writers to explore these years. The noted historian James MacGregor Burns, in his exceptional 1960 campaign biography of Jack, *John Kennedy, A Political Profile*, covered them cursorily. Several authors, notably Robert J. Donovan in his best-selling *PT-109*, reported Jack's naval service in considerable detail. These books and others had set the general outline for those years. Jack was a dedicated and brilliant intellectual with a gift for writing. He was graduated *cum laude* from Harvard in 1940. He turned his honors thesis into a best-selling book, *Why England Slept*. He studied economics and social theory at The London School of Economics and at Stanford University. A robust athlete who played football and swam at Harvard, he entered the U.S. Navy in 1941 and served in PT boats. In 1943 his *PT-109* was rammed by a Japanese destroyer. During the following week, Jack and his surviving crewmen were trapped behind enemy lines. By various brave actions, Jack saved his crew, earned a medal, and emerged from the war a hero. In 1945 he tried his hand at journalism but found it too "passive." In 1946 he launched a political career in Boston, running as a young, idealistic veteran, independent of the old pols and assisted by a group of dedicated amateurs. He won easily and in January, 1947, took his seat in the U.S. House as a freshman Congressman, the beginning of a brilliant political career.

We began our search, which would continue for two years, at the temporary Kennedy Library in Waltham, Massachusetts. There we found thousands of letters and documents on this period which have only recently been released. We were the first Kennedy biographers to have access to them. We continued our search in other archives, where we turned up scores of other letters or documents that had not been utilized by Kennedy researchers. We concluded our search by interviewing in depth over one hundred and fifty men and women who knew Kennedy well during the period 1935-1947. These interviews included two surviving members of the Kennedy family closest in age to Jack: his younger sister Eunice Shriver, and her husband, R. Sargent Shriver.

Early in our research, we were forced to an unsettling conclusion. The standard accounts of these years were enormously incomplete. Many major events and episodes in Jack's life, some of which had to bear crucially on the formation of his character and his decisions about life, were wittingly or unwittingly left out. Many of these events, we discovered, had been deliberately concealed or covered up by the Kennedys. Other major events had obviously been warped and distorted to place Jack in the most favorable light politically. Upon realizing this, we made use of secondary works charily, and only as a last resort. Wherever possible, we employed primary sources (letters, official documents), more or less re-creating the years from scratch. We went to extraordinary lengths to account for Jack's whereabouts and doings during the twelve years to minimize the possibility that we ourselves would unwittingly leave untold some important episode.

We focused especially carefully on Jack's three years of active service in the Navy. This service was, beyond doubt, a vital factor in his rise to political fame. It was apparent to us almost immediately that the Donovan book, while it made certain important new contributions to the standard accounts, was in almost every respect unreliable as history and biography, as were the other Kennedy Navy books, television documentaries, and the movie. Approaching this subject, we were fortunate to have spent the previous five years in intense study of U.S. naval operations in World War Two. We are, we believe, the first experienced naval historians to exhaustively explore Jack's naval career. Our interpretations and conclusions about it are markedly different from the usual accounts.

What follows, then, is often surprising and occasionally sensational. Tens of thousands of words of heretofore unpublished letters, documents, facts, episodes, and new insights into Jack, his family, and his close friends, male and female, during those years. Most of the people who helped us seemed to share our impatience with the omissions, concealments, and distortions of these years. They had known Jack Kennedy as a human being. They wanted to help us to restore the humanity to his portrait in history.

JOAN AND CLAY BLAIR, JR.
Boston-Washington-Key Biscayne
1973–1975

Preliminaries

The Birthplace

W E made a tourist visit to the Kennedy home where Jack was born in Brookline, Massachusetts, a Boston suburb, at 83 Beals Street. It is now a national monument, maintained by the federal government and open, at certain hours, to the public.

The house is quite small. The three teen-age guides in green uniforms sitting on the front porch seemed happy to see us. They said business had been slow that day. On the wall by the entrance to each room there is a button which activates a tape recording of Rose Kennedy's voice. One by one we pushed the buttons and heard how she and her husband came to buy the house (their first), the daily routine, the servants, and a little about the important pieces of furniture. She said the first four Kennedy children had been born in the house: Joseph Junior in 1915, Jack in 1917 (on May 29), Rosemary in 1918, and Kathleen in 1920. By the time the fifth, Eunice, was born in 1921, Rose said, they had moved to a much larger house in Brookline which is still privately owned and not likely to be converted to a monument. Two other children were born while the family lived in the second Brookline house: Patricia in 1924 and Robert in 1925.

We knew that shortly after that the Kennedys left Boston for good, moving first to Riverdale, New York, then to Bronxville, a very fashionable suburb of New York City, where they had a palatial home (since torn down), on six acres of land. The last two of the nine children were born while they lived in New York: Jean in 1928 and Edward in 1932.

The Library

Our real research began at the Kennedy Library. We had seen architectural renderings of the John F. Kennedy Library: a rather grandiose pyramidal structure of steel and glass, designed by the noted architect Ieoh Ming Pei.

We were surprised to find there *is* no Kennedy Library. The building of the Kennedy Library has been delayed, mainly because it was to have included a "museum." The people of Cambridge, Massachusetts, where it was to have been located, next to Harvard University, feared that the museum would invite throngs of tourists to their already crowded town. It will have to be located elsewhere.

Jack's papers and the museum memorabilia are now being stored in a federal warehouse in Waltham, Massachusetts, another suburb of Boston. There are, of course, millions of "Kennedy documents"—his personal papers and letters, Harvard records, Navy records, his official correspondence and other documents from the House, Senate, and White House. Most of these have been collected at the Kennedy Library. Not all of them have been released for public scrutiny. Before a document is released, it must first be approved by a screening committee composed of three advisers designated by the Kennedy family. Further, documents from the White House which bear a government classification stamp ("Top Secret," etc.) must be officially "declassified" by qualified personnel in Washington.

Several archivists are occupied full time in going through the documents, following guidelines set when the library was founded, and preparing them for the screening committee, which meets from time to time. Judgments must be made both by the archivists and the screening committee; generally the library will not release a document which will embarrass the memory of the president, or his family, or any living person. The screening committee samples the documents to be released but generally follows the recommendations of the archivists. The declassification of classified documents is regulated by federal laws which require the downgrading of certain documents after specified intervals of time.

The Kennedy family exerts considerable influence on what is to be released of a personal nature in several ways. In addition to controlling the appointment of screening committee members it can—and does—withhold personal documents from the library. For example, the papers of Joseph P. Kennedy, which would be invaluable to any researchers exploring Jack's life, have not yet been turned over to the library. Nor have Rose's papers. Robert F. Kennedy's papers are in the library but they have not been released to the public (although the family has granted access to them to Arthur M. Schlesinger, Jr., who is writing a biography of Bobby). A very long oral history by Jackie is "locked in the vault" and an archivist told us it would probably not be released for "fifty years." Jack's "childhood" letters have not been released, nor his financial records. Thus, Joe Kennedy's useful discovery of "public relations," and his conviction that it was his or the family's right and responsibility to control what the public is to know and believe about all members of the Kennedy family continues to this day.

By the greatest stroke of luck, the archivists and the screening committee had, after years of work, just released thousands of new personal documents—letters, telegrams, invitations, memoranda, appointment books, scrapbooks, passports, and so on. We were the first investigators to have a look at this material.

In addition, there were countless other documents, already released, that would prove invaluable. These included oral histories (transcriptions of recorded interviews) by people who had known Jack at various times, his office newspaper scrapbooks, his collected speeches and other items. In addition, there were several Kennedy books on file which we had overlooked.

We worked at the library in high spirits for several weeks, distilling information we found onto 4 x 6 index cards or ordering Xerox copies for a small fee. With each new document our knowledge of Jack Kennedy expanded; slowly at first, then in a rush.

Some People

Six people were closest to, and had the most influence on, Jack when he was a young boy growing up in Brookline and, later, Bronxville: his father, his mother, his older brother, his two closest sisters in age, and his maternal grandfather. They will all figure importantly in our narrative as well.

Joseph Patrick Kennedy, Jack's father, was born in Boston in 1888, son of an East Boston saloon keeper and ward politician, Patrick Joseph Kennedy. There are two excellent books on the life of Joe Kennedy: *The Founding Father* by a journalist, Richard J. Whalen, published in 1964; and *Joseph P. Kennedy* by David E. Koskoff, published in 1974. The Koskoff book contained material released after Whalen wrote and more thorough and penetrating research and analysis. For our purposes, both books were indispensable.

Joe Kennedy was graduated from Harvard in 1912, an intelligent, fiercely ambitious young man who did not drink or smoke and who had a consuming interest in baseball and football. By age twenty-five, he had gained control of a small bank in East Boston, the Columbia Trust Company. During World War One and afterward, he speculated heavily and successfully on the New York Stock Exchange, pulling out before the great crash of 1929. In the late 1920s, he moved (without his family) to Hollywood, where he became a motion picture executive and had a highly publicized liaison with Gloria Swanson. He developed a genius for self-promotion. By then fabulously wealthy, he returned East, to New York, and involved himself in national politics. He contributed large sums to the

1932 presidential campaign of Franklin D. Roosevelt and became close friends with Roosevelt's son, James. This association helped Kennedy obtain a lucrative scotch liquor importing concession about the time Prohibition ended. In 1934 President Roosevelt appointed Kennedy chairman of the Securities and Exchange Commission, created to police the New York Stock Exchange.

Joe Kennedy was an immensely complicated character. In business he was shrewd, ruthless, and unscrupulous, believing contemptuously that "all businessmen were sons-of-bitches" (as Jack reported when he was President). He made his money in liquor, cheap movies, racetracks, gambling in the stock market (even rigging stocks on occasion), and real estate. He was a Catholic, yet amoral: his love affairs were conducted almost publicly. Not many people liked Joe Kennedy. Not a few believed he was a crook. The Boston Establishment ostracized him and that was why he moved away.

This exchange from a long conversation we had with his friend, the distinguished journalist Arthur Krock, is a witty and typical example of the sort of reputation Joe Kennedy had:

Q. What's your view of his character? We've heard so many stories that he was amoral.

A. Yes, that's quite true. He was. I think only a Roman Catholic could possibly describe how you could be amoral and still religious. That is, how you can carry an insurance policy with the deity and at the same time do all those other things. . . . Yes, he was amoral. Sure he was.

Q. You had a close relationship with him. We wonder if this particular aspect of his character disturbed you?

A. I never had any idealism from the time I was a young reporter about anybody who touched the edges of politics or big business. So I was not shocked in the least. I expected, and still do, that politicians and big-business men don't have any morals. That is, public morals.

Q. Did the fact that Mr. Kennedy had girls around make you uneasy or did you just accept it?

A. It was a way of the world as far as I knew it and the way of *his* world. I was not concerned about what happened to him in that respect. It never bothered me at all because Rose acted as if they didn't exist and that was her business, not mine. Kennedy was a very able man. He was an informed, intelligent cynic. He knew the human race pretty well and he knew its weaknesses and strengths and pretensions and hypocrisies and he went right to the nut. He would have made a hell of a president. But of course, he was terribly generous to his friends, to those people he liked. I've often reflected since those days that he probably never liked me at all, but found me useful and thought he might be able to make use of me. I'm not aware that he was ever able to do it. I am aware that he tried. I happened to be in a position of value to him. I remember once he called me and said, "I don't want to hear any nonsense from you. You look out the window Christmas morning and you'll see an automobile." I said, "I will see nothing of the kind. I'll have it towed away if it's there." And that was the end of that. That was a pretty coarse kind of bribe. He didn't need it. That's the way his mind worked. . . .

When most of his children were young, he was almost an absentee father—off in New York, Hollywood, Washington. He was not even present for the birth of several of his children. And yet, he took a deep interest in his children. He encouraged them in sports, planned their education, urged them to seize higher social ground. He set up $1 million trust funds for them when they reached the age of twenty-one, then pointed them toward public service. When he was home, he ruled the roost absolutely.

The Kennedys lived at the vanguard of the new and novel. They had one of the first automobiles. When commercial air travel commenced in the United States, and later overseas, they were among the first to utilize it and thereafter embraced it. Their houses were full of new radios and phonographs. Later they had one of the first tape recorders and television sets. When a new spa for the rich opened up, they were soon there. They saw all the new plays on Broadway and the latest movies. The tables at home were laden with the latest best sellers. Kennedy bought a big home—the famous "compound"—on Cape Cod for summer vacations, a home on the ocean in Palm Beach for the winter. Jack grew up traveling between these places, exposed to every new gadget, entertainment, or idea.

There were gaps. For example, none of them had any interest in the fine arts. They never acquired fine paintings. They had no antiques or rare books. The vast record collections contained little serious music. They preferred Broadway musicals to opera, entertainment over art on the stage. Jack grew up aware of that gap, but until he was married to Jacqueline Bouvier, he never attempted to make his own connection to the arts.

Rose Fitzgerald Kennedy, Jack's mother, was born in Boston in 1890, daughter of a fabled Boston politician named John Francis "Honey Fitz" Fitzgerald. Rose grew up in very comfortable circumstances, attending exclusive private convents in Europe, always in the public eye and the newspapers. In 1914 she married Joe Kennedy and began having her nine famous children.

There are two useful books on Rose. The first, published in 1971, is *Rose*, by a journalist, Gail Cameron. The second is Rose's autobiography, *Times to Remember,* which was written with the assistance of the magazine writer, Robert Coughlan, and published in 1974. Rose says that she prefers to remember only the good times in her book. Thus, the book is interesting and entertaining, but offers only a grossly distorted view of her life, her husband's life, and the lives of her children. A good deal of her material on Jack was previously published elsewhere, but we found a few new tidbits which were useful to our project.

Rose was also a complex person. She was petite, gentle, intelligent. When her children were young she was able to devote most of her hours exclusively to them, because there were always plenty of domestics to handle housekeeping chores. She stimulated their interest in history and saw to their religious upbringing. Each was sent away to boarding school at an appropriate age; it was the custom of those who could afford it. She loved to travel and as the children entered boarding school, she traveled almost constantly. She was devoutly religious, a daily communicant, who contributed much time (and money) to various Catholic organizations and causes. She took care of her relatives when they fell on hard times. She was notoriously absentminded, always pinning reminder notes to her dress or leaving them around the house in strategic locations. She took pride in her figure, and her clothes were the latest Paris fashions. Yet she was extremely frugal in mundane matters, such as the household budget, an eccentricity she passed along to all her children. She neither drank nor smoked.

In her reflections Rose had nothing but the kindest words for her husband. She innocently dismisses his notorious affair with Gloria Swanson by describing the relationship as a complicated business deal. She is not critical of his long absences from home in the early years, including the times when she was giving birth, because, she says, he was off working hard for the family. She summed up their relationship as follows:

> There is a time to fall in love, and I did—once and for all, with a charming young man named Joseph Patrick Kennedy. There are not many perfect equations in human affairs and particularly in marriage—as I have observed during a long life—but this was one of them. Joe fell in love with me with the same devotion I felt for him, and this was the beginning of what was to be a miraculous life together.

Very well. Rose is certainly entitled to remember what she wants the way she wants. But our view is that Rose was roughly treated by her husband, who had little or no respect for women. As we see it, she escaped into an intensely religious, near-fantasy life, a life of distracting travel and withdrawals to her private retreats at Hyannis Port and elsewhere. We think it is noteworthy that in her book many of the recollections of the children growing up are supplied by the children themselves; and that when important or tragic family events occurred, she was often off somewhere else.

From his mother Jack acquired an interest in history. At her encouragement he became a voracious reader of books—history, biography, romantic literature. (*King Arthur and the Round Table, The Jungle Book, Kidnapped, Arabian Nights,* and so on). The reading led to his knack for writing. She passed on her religion; Jack kept the Sacraments and attended church on Sundays and Holy Days, though clearly he was not nearly so devout as she. Later, he even considered giving up Catholicism. Finally, we believe, Jack inherited or acquired from his mother her peculiar absentmindedness. He was extremely disorganized, always leaving clothes, briefcases, or papers behind in hotels or airports or on trains. He was late for appointments and often forgot them altogether.

Jack's grandfather, John Francis Fitzgerald, was a legendary political figure in Boston. He was a slightly built man, a nonstop talker and gladhander. He was a mayor of Boston and a U. S. Congressman, and had run unsuccessfully for other offices. Honey Fitz was a constant presence in the Kennedy household during Jack's childhood. He was apparently a powerful influence on Jack, who loved him deeply and was greatly and continually amused by him.
Rose remembers her father this way:

> His vigor, charm, and sheer joy in living were contagious. Many times I saw him walk into a room—a parlor, ballroom, the main lounge of an ocean liner—full of somnolent, inhibited people bored stiff with one another, and within five minutes have them smiling, attentive, active, having fun, perhaps even singing. He took charge of them and they loved it. And he did too. I think he felt it was a challenge to wake them up. Yet he also truly liked people and liked to see them happy.

He remained a source of joy and amusement for the Kennedy children late into life. In Rose's book, Teddy recalled him from the 1940s:

> He was a marvelous storyteller. I heard my first off-color story from Grampa. But he was laughing so hard while he was telling it that I don't think he ever got to the punch line. He enjoyed his own

stories. He would start out telling a story, and start laughing, and pretty soon be laughing so hard he cried. It was very infectious. I can't remember any of them, but that's probably because they weren't such great stories—it was the way he told them.

It is likely that Jack drew more of his outward personality from Honey Fitz than he did from his own father: that is, the charm, wit, and irreverence, and that politician's valuable gift for "turning on" at will.

Jack's older brother, Joseph P. Kennedy, Jr., was the subject of a book, *The Lost Prince*, by Hank Searls, published in 1969.

Joe Junior was the firstborn male, an important figure in an Irish family. He was the heir apparent and as such enjoyed a preeminent position among the children. Both Joe Senior and Rose lavished attention on Joe Junior. He was shaped into a "model" for the other children to emulate. Joseph Dinneen, a Boston journalist and Kennedy family friend who published a book, *The Kennedy Family*, in 1959, quoted Rose on the point: "I always felt that if the older children are brought up right, the younger ones will follow their lead. It was easy for all the children to look up to Joe Junior because he was a good scholar, a good athlete, and popular with girls as well as men in every neighborhood where we lived."

In fact, as Searls and other Kennedy book authors point out, the attention lavished on Joe Junior inevitably created sibling rivalry—especially between Joe Junior and Jack, the second-born male, who was physically smaller than Joe. Stories abound of physical conflict between the two, with Jack defiantly and bravely fighting back, usually the loser.

At some point in Joe Junior's life, Searls writes, his father decided Joe should go into politics. Legend has it that the aim was to make Joe Junior the first Catholic president of the United States and that it was for this reason among others that Joe Junior was sent not to Catholic secondary school, but to Choate and Harvard, where he could meet and become friends with the children of the Establishment. Whatever the truth of that, it is true that at both schools he was an outstanding scholar and athlete. At the suggestion of one of his father's Boston and New Deal friends, Felix Frankfurter, who believed Joe Junior should be exposed to liberal views, he was sent for the year 1933-1934 (between Choate and Harvard) to The London School of Economics, to study under the noted socialist economic scholar Harold J. Laski. Laski had a high opinion of Joe Junior and did not doubt he would achieve his father's goal.

Jack's immediately younger sister, Rosemary, was born retarded. In those days a retarded child in the family was considered a grave calamity, even a scandal, because it tended to indicate that horror of all horrors, "insanity in the blood." In keeping with the custom of the times, the Kennedys concealed Rosemary's condition to the greatest extent possible from friends and neighbors. Later, when Mr. Kennedy was in the public eye, and Jack entered politics, the family lied to the press about Rosemary, saying she had a strong religious bent and had gone away to a convent to teach.

James MacGregor Burns, from whom, we are told, Jack withheld nothing, described Rosemary as "a sweet, rather withdrawn girl, not up to the children's competitive life." Farther along in the book he reports that after she reached maturity, Rosemary went to St. Coletta, a Catholic school near Milwaukee, where she "helped care for mentally retarded children." Of course the opposite was true; the nuns at St. Coletta, as Rose reveals, were caring for Rosemary.

Other books on the Kennedys during the late 1950s contain similar statements. Joseph Dinneen (1959) wrote that Rosemary was "shy and retiring" and that she had devoted her life "to the sick and afflicted and particularly to backward and handicapped children." In another book on the family, *The Remarkable Kennedys*, published during the campaign in 1960 and serialized in *Look* magazine, the author, Joe McCarthy, a journalist who extensively interviewed all the Kennedys, wrote that Rosemary was "teaching in a school for retarded children in Wisconsin." And so on.

The first hint in the press that anything was amiss with Rosemary appeared in a *Time* magazine cover story on the Kennedy family in the issue of July 11, 1960. *Time* wrote, "Rosemary, the eldest of the Kennedy daughters, was a childhood victim of spinal meningitis, is now a patient in a nursing home in Wisconsin. Says Joe Kennedy: 'I used to think it was something to hide, but then I learned that almost everyone I know has a relative or a good friend who has the problem. I think it is best to bring these things out in the open.' "

But Joe Kennedy's candor was, of course, spurious. As Rose writes, without any mention of spinal meningitis, Rosemary was born retarded. It was not until *after* Jack was in the White House that the family conceded the truth about Rosemary, and then only sketchily. Rose's book (1974) contains the first full, honest account to be furnished by a Kennedy.

So there they were, in the small house on Beals Street, with a "touched" child in their midst. Rose writes that it was an extremely difficult situation, that much of her time was taken up with attending to Rosemary, and she worried that the other children might resent it.

We have no writing left by Jack to indicate what it was like for him growing up with Rosemary in the family. Difficult, we suspect, to carry the secret through most of his life. What his young friends may have thought, and how they behaved, is a matter for speculation, for despite Rose's belief that the cover-up was entirely successful, children have an uncanny way of knowing such secrets. And then Jack might very well have felt as most people of that time did about "insanity in the family"—including the possibility that it might conceivably "break out" in himself at any time. In all, Rosemary's affliction must have been a heavy burden for Jack.

Jack's second sister, Kathleen, three years younger, was called "Kick." She grew up to be a pretty, high-spirited girl with a mind of her own. With Joe Junior beating up on Jack, and Rosemary retarded, Kick was a natural playmate and ally for Jack. She is invariably described in the Kennedy literature as Jack's favorite sister. As we shall see, as they grew older and Kick became the most nearly independent of all the Kennedy children, she and Jack remained close allies.

His Health

An aspect of Jack's life and personality that soon began to demand constant consideration was his health. We read in Rose's book that when Jack was growing up he was "frail" and "sickly." Rose writes that "almost all his life, it seemed, he had to do battle against misfortunes of health." She mentions an onset of scarlet fever when Jack was about three years old. At Choate, she reports, he had a virus that led to swollen glands, a bad knee, and fallen arches.

Elsewhere we found a similar, generalized statement by Robert F. Kennedy. It was in a very useful picture book prepared under Bobby's supervision entitled *John Fitzgerald Kennedy, As We Remember Him*, produced and edited by Goddard Lieberson, published in 1965. In a preface Bobby wrote in part, "At least one half of the days that he spent on this earth were days of intense physical pain. He had scarlet fever when he was very young and serious back trouble when he was older. In between he had almost every other conceivable ailment. When we were growing up together we used to laugh about the great risk a mosquito took in biting Jack Kennedy—with some of his blood the mosquito was almost sure to die."

The world knows that Jack Kennedy had a "bad back." All the Kennedy books talk about it. Burns and others say it came from a football injury sustained when Jack was at Harvard, although there is disagreement as to the precise time. According to Burns and others, it was exacerbated during the celebrated *PT-109* incident. It is said that in 1954 he had an operation for the condition that almost killed him. (But what sort of back operation is dangerous to the patient's life?) In the White House he used the famous rocking chair as a therapeutic device for his back. The back had caused him "intense physical pain," Bobby says. But what did Bobby mean by "every other conceivable ailment"?

At the Kennedy Library we routinely requested Jack's medical records. We were told that the medical records were "definitely here," but they were in the category of Jack's financial records—nonreleasable for years, perhaps forever.

We recalled that during our tourist visit to the Brookline house, we had seen on a desk in the upstairs den Rose's famous card file on the children's childhood illnesses. We returned there and asked one of the guides if we could have a look at it. He had no objection, but explained that the file was not the original, only a copy.

We copied down the information on Jack, much of it new but none of it very interesting:

February 20, 1920 (age 2¾) Scarlet fever, whooping cough, measles, chicken pox.

Undated. City Hospital: Dr. Hill, Dr. Reardon took care of ear.

1928. German measles. Schick Test. Bronchitis occasionally.

June 15, 1930. Examined at Lahey Clinic. Tonsils and adenoids O.K.

October to December, 1930. While at Canterbury, weight fell from 99¾ to 95½.

December 31, 1930. Examined by Dr. Schloss. Good condition. Loss of weight attributed to lack of milk in diet.

May 2, 1931. Appendicitis operation. Dr. Verdi of New Haven performed at Danbury Hospital.

March 21, 1931. Glasses prescribed for reading. Dr. John Wheeler.

August, 1933. Boston. Tonsils and adenoids out. Dr. Cahill. St. Margaret's Hospital.

Why had Rose stopped Jack's file in 1933 when he was just sixteen? Had Jack had *no* further illnesses? Or had subsequent cards been removed? And if so, why?

Back at the library we found a letter from the headmaster at Choate, George St. John, to Harvard. He was explaining that Jack had "rather superior mental ability," but had not made the most of it at Choate. He went on: "Part of Jack's lack of intellectual drive is doubtless due to a severe illness suffered in the winter of his fifth form year. Though he has recovered, his vitality has been below par, he has not been allowed to enter into any very vigorous athletics and has not, probably, been able to work under full pressure."

Jack's fifth form year at Choate was his "junior" year, or 1933–1934. Thus, this "severe illness" occurred shortly after the removal of his tonsils and adenoids in August of 1933—as indicated on the last card in Jack's file. Was this not worthy of note? And if it had been "severe," why hadn't Rose alluded to it in her rundown of Jack's medical problems at Choate?

We saw in several of the Kennedy books that in his youth, Jack had been a regular patient at the Lahey Clinic in Boston. Theodore M. Sorensen, in his memoir *Kennedy*, for example, states that a Dr. Sara Jordan of the Lahey Clinic had treated Jack "since he was eleven."

We found the Lahey Clinic in an ugly brick building in downtown Boston. Mr. Thurston Hammer met us and escorted us to an empty office. He was a soft-spoken, cautious man in his fifties.

Mr. Hammer told us that the clinic was founded in 1925 by Dr. Frank Howard Lahey. Lahey had recruited many fine doctors to his staff, built a thriving practice and a formidable reputation in medical circles; in 1953, at age seventy-three, he died of a heart attack, but the clinic survived him and had grown.

Dr. Sara Jordan had been one of his earliest recruits. A woman of very strong personality, she had nonmedical degrees from Radcliffe and the University of Munich, and her MA from Tufts in 1921. When she joined Lahey in 1922 (even before he had established his clinic), he encouraged her to specialize in gastroenterology—indigestion, ulcers, bladders, diseases of the intestinal tract, and so on.

The rich and famous flocked to the Lahey Clinic, among them Joe Kennedy, who had a chronic stomach disorder, believed at one point to be ulcers. Kennedy became Sara Jordan's patient.

Mr. Hammer confirmed Sorensen's report that Jack Kennedy, too, became a patient of Dr. Jordan's. It had been a very long time ago and Hammer had no personal recollection of the Kennedy-Jordan relationship. We asked Mr. Hammer if the clinic could give us any information on Jack's medical history—illnesses, other doctors who treated him, dates of visits, and so on. He said he would take it up with the director. Mr. Hammer telephoned a few days later to say the clinic could not release its records without approval from the family.

Later, back again at the Kennedy Library, we found mention in some of the recently released documents that a Dr. Elmer C. Bartels of the Lahey Clinic had treated Jack for some unspecified illness. A phone call to Mr. Hammer turned up the information that Bartels was indeed alive, retired from the clinic, living in Osterville on Cape Cod.

Bartels, a wiry, restless man, thin and balding, gave us a long and revealing interview—the most important interview on Jack's health we were ever to get.

It turned out that Bartels knew little about Jack's childhood illnesses, except one very important and hitherto unrevealed fact. Jack, he said, was "born with an unstable back."

Bartels went on to explain. "An unstable back is something you are born with and it doesn't maintain itself properly." An unstable back lasts a lifetime. It is a back that can be normal for long periods of time and then go out of whack for no apparent reason. When it goes out of whack, the pain can be excruciating, lasting days or weeks. During the 1920s and 1930s there was not much anybody could do about an unstable back. The standard treatment was: take it easy. Don't do anything rough or violent to aggravate the back. Take hot baths. In some cases, some doctors recommended a type of stiff back brace resembling a corset. A very few recommended surgery. But surgery was considered a "radical" approach. It was not often successful.

To be certain we had understood Bartels correctly, we asked, "You say Jack Kennedy was *born* with an unstable back?"

"Yes."

So Jack had not originally incurred his back injury playing football at Harvard. He had had a bad back all along. Then, and later in PT boats, and still later. All his life, in fact. The Kennedys had concealed this fact, rather in the way they had concealed Rosemary's retardation. As Rosemary had been given as saintly, caring for helpless children, Jack was given as heroic; the "injury" was sustained at football, aggravated on *PT-109*. Later it was widely and repeatedly identified as a "war injury."

We asked Bartels who had been Jack's back specialist at the clinic. He said: "Ned Haggart, now deceased." (This was Gilbert Edmund Haggart, who joined the Lahey Clinic in 1928 as an orthopedic surgeon. He died in Plymouth, Massachusetts, in 1970.)

Dr. Bartels had actually taken Jack on as a patient in 1947; we shall return to this at the appropriate point in the narrative. Indeed, Jack's medical history was to become a very important avenue for further research— research which would uncover very dramatic facts. To begin with, as we considered his early childhood, we had to make a difficult adjustment in our perception. We had begun with the image of a robust, carefree lad on the football field. Now we had to picture another Jack. Thin, often ill, often denied the out-of-doors, perhaps angry and frustrated because his body could not keep pace with his plans and dreams; bedridden, elfinlike (as Rose describes him), reading the heaps of books his mother gave him, eating the special foods she served to fatten him up and build his strength. And yet strictly adhering to his father's prohibition on self-pity. In his preface to *As We Remember Him*, Bobby wrote, "I never heard him complain. I never heard him say anything that would indicate that he felt God had dealt with him unjustly. Those who knew him well would know he was suffering only because his face was a little whiter, the lines around his eyes were a little deeper, his words a little sharper. Those who did not know him well detected nothing."

And more. Jack refused to accept his illnesses. When he was at all well, he'd go on the football field or engage in other sports, unstable back and all. Always trying to keep up with the other boys. "He went along for many years," Rose writes in what we take to be a very revealing passage, "thinking to himself—or at least trying to make others think—that he was a strong, robust, quite healthy person who just happened to be sick a good deal of the time."

Part I

SCHOOL

1

Choate

IN the 1930s The Choate School, founded in 1896 by an Episcopalian judge, William Choate, was an exclusive college preparatory school. Located in Wallingford, Connecticut, a few miles north of New Haven and the Yale campus, and about sixty miles from the Kennedy mansion in Bronxville, New York, it had a spacious, elm-shaded campus, athletic fields, a chapel, gymnasium, infirmary, dormitories, and classroom buildings of various sturdy architectural styles typical of New England schools of the day. The five hundred students lived in the dormitories or in several wood-frame "houses," closely supervised by housemasters who were part of the sixty-man teaching staff. The school was, in every respect, a pleasant, well-equipped establishment with high academic standards. There was a strong Episcopalian flavor; daily attendance at chapel was mandatory for all boys. The school was presided over by a fastidious, conservative headmaster, George St. John, appointed in 1908 when Choate was only eight years old and struggling.

Jack's Choate records are not in the Kennedy Library, nor have they ever been released. We had to piece together the highlights of his tour there from previously published bits and pieces, and our own interviews.

Jack entered his senior (sixth form) year, his fourth year at the school, in the fall of 1934. In the previous three years he had not done well, perhaps because he had been overshadowed by Joe Junior, who seemed to excel almost effortlessly at everything he did, whether in sports or academics. Jack had gamely tried out for football, but he was too frail and sickly to get anywhere with that. He is said to have had a high IQ but he did not apply himself in his studies. His room was a notorious mess. He was always late to classes. He was a charming, devilish cutup, much liked by the other students (who, because of his thin face and protruding ears, called him "Rat Face"), but a trial to the authorities at the school.

In his junior (fifth form) year when, as we know, Jack came down with the "severe illness," he had been especially difficult. That year headmaster St. John wrote Jack's father a letter quoted in *As We Remember Him.* The letter is humorless and not necessarily perceptive, but the impression it gives will be substantially confirmed by the recollections of those who were close to him. In part:

Jack has a clever, individualist mind. It is a harder mind to put in harness than Joe's—harder for Jack himself to put in harness. When he learns the right place for humor and learns to use his individual way of looking at things as an asset instead of a handicap, his natural gift of an individual outlook and witty expression are going to help him. A more conventional mind and a more plodding and mature point of view would help him a lot more right now; but we have to allow, my dear Mr. Kennedy, with boys like Jack, for a period of adjustment. All that natural cleverness Jack has to learn how to use in his life and work, even how to cover it up at times, how to subordinate it and all the rest. I never yet saw a clever, witty boy who at some stage in his early development was not considered fresh. It is only because he hasn't learned how to use his natural gift. We must allow for a period of adjustment and growing up; and the final product is often more interesting and more effective than the boy with a more conventional mind who has been to us parents and teachers much less trouble.

I think all that ought to be said about Jack; and I think we ought to say, also, that Jack is not as able academically as his high IQ might lead us to think. I very honestly think that this is so. I think we overestimate Jack's present academic ability. By and by, when Jack is in college, and especially when he can choose his own subjects, his academic output will correspond more nearly with his high IQ.

In his senior year Jack looked forward to graduating and to following Joe Junior to The London School of Economics. But he got off to a bad start in the first quarter. On December 4, after the grades had been posted, Jack wrote his father a letter reproduced in *As We Remember Him:*

DEAR DAD:

I thought I would write you right away as LeMoyne and I have been talking about how poorly we have done this quarter, and we have definitely decided to stop any fooling around. I really do realize how important it is that I get a good job done this year if I want to go to England. I really feel, now that I think it over, that I have been bluffing myself about how much real work I have been doing. . . .

I really feel that we will get something done this quarter as LeMoyne seems to feel the same way as I do.

Love,
JACK

LeMoyne "Lem" Billings was Jack's roommate in the sixth form, his first very close friend. They would remain friends for life. In J.B. West's book *Upstairs at the White House,* West, who was the chief usher at the White House from 1941 to 1969, writes that Jacqueline Kennedy once said of Lem Billings in mock despair, "Oh, Mr. West, he's been a house-guest of mine every weekend since I've been married."

Billings has done an oral history for the Kennedy Library, but it has not been released. It was immense, we were told, some thirty or forty hours of taping. It had been transcribed, but an archivist told us, "Billings is very fastidious. He's going over every word, rewriting and editing. It may *never* be released."

We arranged to see Billings at his home in New York City, a brownstone in a fine East Side neighborhood. He is big and ruddy-faced. He wears glasses with thick lenses.

"In all the books about Jack Kennedy," he said, "I'm referred to as a roommate from Choate and then dropped. I don't particularly want to be in books, but I resent always being treated as a childhood friend who could then be dropped. You never see me in the last pages and yet I was at his house every single weekend he was president. . . . Jack was the closest person to me in the world for thirty years."

He led us into the house. The walls were covered with fine paintings—Picassos and Chagalls.

"I started collecting these many years ago," Billings said. "a very good investment it turned out to be."

We went to a comfortably furnished den, also crowded with fine paintings. He plopped down on the sofa with a highball. He seemed very bright and quick-witted and laughed a great deal. He was not outwardly emotionally scarred by Jack's death. But Lem Billings had given much of his life to Jack and the Kennedys; as companion, cultural adviser (he helped Jackie redecorate the White House), and political campaigner. He is still on the Kennedy payroll, an employee in the famous "New York office," which Joseph Kennedy established years before as a business headquarters to consolidate his far-flung enterprises and to serve as a bank for the family. The New York office was now run by Stephen Smith, Jean Kennedy's husband. Billings was rather vague about his own duties. "When they want some furniture moved around or something, I take care of it," he said.

What is reported at this point is the portion of our interview that dealt with Choate. We began by asking Billings about his family background. He told us he was born Kirk LeMoyne Billings in 1917, the third child and second son of a Pittsburgh physician who was married into an old and distinguished Pittsburgh family. Billings had grown up in the shadow of an outstanding older brother, Frederic, Jr., who had been president of his class at Choate, editor-in-chief of the yearbook, *The Brief,* a football and crew star who walked off with all the top prizes. He went on to Princeton and more dazzling honors. Billings told us, "He was pretty tough to follow. . . . I think in hindsight maybe my parents shouldn't have sent me to the same schools as he. It was a constant concern to try to keep up with him. It doesn't work well at all. I think people expected more of me than I could give. My father did try very hard to have me live up as well as my brother in every area and was very disappointed that I didn't. . . ."

Jack and Lem must have been kindred spirits. Billings went on to tell us about his first meeting with Jack:

> The spring of 1933 we both heeled—went out for—*The Brief.* He ended up business manager and I was advertising manager. So during the [fifth form] year 1933 to 1934, I got to know him very well. We became close friends and I visited in Florida during the Christmas vacation, 1933, in Palm Beach. And that's when I first met his family. He roomed with me the last year at Choate, 1934 to 1935.
>
> There's no question that Joe Junior had a much more outstanding career at Choate. But Jack was not well at Choate. He was really very, very delicate and really couldn't do a lot of athletics. But he was beautifully coordinated and one of the best natural athletes I've ever seen. He was fantastic. He had this natural coordination. He could pick up a golf club, having never played golf before, and play pretty decent golf. Same with tennis. So he'd catch a football and do all the things that take coordination. But he had very delicate health there. He was lightweight. He played football but for health reasons he didn't do very well.

We asked how it happened that he and Jack Kennedy had become such close friends. He replied:

> I don't know. Jack had the best sense of humor of anybody I've ever known in my life. And I don't think I've ever known anybody who was as much fun. I think our sense of humors must have jibed. We had a hell of a good time together and I think that's what makes two people like each other. I've always thought a good sense of humor was as important as hell. And then your common interests enter into it and the longer you know somebody, the more interests you have in common. I think it's the ability of two people to enjoy each other. And we did.

We asked him if Jack had a one-and-only girl. "No. He had a lot. He was very successful with girls. Very. I'd say if he had any girl it was one—I wouldn't say it was very serious, but one that went through his life as a schoolboy and into college would have been Olive Cawley, Olive Field Cawley, who married Tom Watson."

Billings told us that his father, who had had his money in the stock market, died in 1933, leaving his mother very little. After that, Billings was on scholarship at Choate. "I didn't ever feel it was an actual scholarship," he explained, "because my father had given a great deal of money to Choate. I felt my tuition was being paid by the money he had given. But, anyway, it was called a scholarship."

Billings has an enormous number of photographs of Jack as a young man, dozens of telegrams, and about one hundred fifty letters. He is keeping the letters for himself, perhaps to write a book someday and because "a lot of them are full of juvenile bad language."

We knew that Jack had made another close friend at Choate, Ralph "Rip" Horton, Jr. There is an oral history from Horton on file at the library. It touches on the Choate days, but it is devoted mostly to the 1960 presidential campaign and beyond. We found him in Norfolk, Virginia, where he was working in a government-funded program to help disadvantaged blacks in the Tidewater area.

We met Horton at his office in downtown Norfolk. There was a sign on his door, "New Careers," and a black secretary. Horton greeted us affably and ushered us into a small and somewhat seedy office. He was wearing a black pinstripe suit with broad lapels. A cigarette dangled from his lips. He was slightly-built, florid-faced, and had an exceptionally high forehead.

He told us he was from an old and well-to-do New York City family which had once owned a big dairy, Sheffield Farms, then organized National Dairy (Southern Dairy, Sealtest, Kraft, etc.), now known as Kraftco. He was born in 1916 and raised a Catholic. He entered Choate as a freshman (third form), in the fall of 1931, when he first met Jack. He recalled:

> We were both skinny little guys and went out for the lowest class of football—C team. He was a boy of many interests but he would never stick to anything, give himself enitrely to anything. He liked sports, he liked roughhousing, he liked to be sloppy, he liked to play golf, he liked girls, and he loved to come to New York to see me.
>
> Jack was wealthy but unsophisticated. I, unfortunately, was sophisticated. My family used to take me to all the best restaurants and clubs and they actually gave me cards to some speakeasies. I would take Jack to these clubs in New York. He liked that—he liked to go twenty-four hours a day. We would go to hear people like the *Show Boat* singer Helen Morgan. I can remember us send-

ing a note to Helen Morgan to join us at our table for a bottle of champagne. She came to the table but said she didn't drink. An aunt of mine who knew her said, "No, she doesn't drink—just a bottle of brandy a day!"

As far as girls were concerned, our dating was largely confined to the big spring dance at the end of the year. I remember Jack dated Olive Cawley. She was a magnificent-looking girl, really beautiful. But I can remember clearly that we were not particularly effective with girls. I remember once about ten of us came down to New York to go tea dancing. Well, we managed to scrape around and find *two* girls! We went to the Hotel Pierre. We started kidding around—boys dancing with boys—and they threw us out.

Another time I remember, when Jack first got laid. What a night! I had had *slightly* more experience, I mean, you know, we were seventeen, right? Jack and another friend came down to see me and they had to do this thing, right? So they got in a cab and went to a whorehouse up in Harlem. They told me that first there was a kind of dirty show, then they took these girls—they were white girls of course—to their rooms. It all cost about three dollars. Not long afterwards, they came back to my family's apartment in a total panic. They were frightened to death they'd get VD. So I went with them to a hospital—can you believe this?—where they got these salves and creams and a thing to shove up the penis to clean it out. They came home, still sweating. They couldn't sleep. It was a scene. Finally, in the middle of the night, Jack thought they ought to see a doctor. So we woke this doctor up and they went over.

There was another whorehouse in West Palm Beach we used to go to a couple of times at three dollars a shot—The Gypsy Tea Room.

I used to visit Jack in Palm Beach and at the Cape. The stories are true: you'd sit down at the table and Mr. Kennedy, the leader, would direct the talk to current events. Jack and Joe Junior would ask questions and Mr. Kennedy would answer in great detail. But if I asked a question, he'd treat me like a piece of dirt. He'd ignore me. He was only really interested in his own family.

We used to play a lot of golf. I was captain of the Choate golf team and played number two. In Florida we'd play golf with Mr. Kennedy. Now, when we got on the golf course, Mr. Kennedy would always point out what an outstanding character I was. That was because I was a good golfer. He wanted to goad Jack into playing a better game, so he built me up and belittled—and irritated—Jack. He didn't mean it, of course. He was simply using me for the moment.

There was a radio program called "Information Please." Jack

would amaze me with the high percentage of answers he got. Very quick. I asked him how he had learned so much, or why he had such a retentive memory. He told me that every day he read something—a magazine or the *New York Times*—and he'd *force* himself to sit down and think about one or two items and analyze them. His grades were mediocre but he had an extremely keen wit. He liked to bug people—just to see their reactions. He wrote little ditties. There was a guy in our group, Maurice Shea, who was quarterback of the football team. The wife of one of the assistant headmasters used to have him over for tea a lot. She was really beautiful. We called her Queenie. Every time we saw her we were kind of popeyed. We were jealous of Maury Shea, and Jack wrote this ditty:

> Maury Shea, Maury Shea,
> Drinking tea every day,
> Maury Shea, what's your appeal?
> Queenie, we want a new deal.

Well, damned if she didn't find out about it. Then one day she saw us sitting on the steps. She *made* us sing the song. We almost died.

Jack had an excellent mind. I remember once one of our English teachers, Harold Tinker, called Jack aside and told him that when he graduated from college he ought to go into journalism or writing because his essays showed a very fluid mature style for somebody his age. But he hadn't matured yet.

We shall refer to other parts of this interview later, of course, although not so frequently as to that with Lem Billings. After Choate, Rip and Jack were not so close as Lem and Jack. After the war they saw each other only occasionally in New York or Washington. In 1953 Jack asked Rip to be an usher in his wedding but Rip couldn't make it. When Jack began his Presidential race, the friendship resumed. Horton organized a Kennedy for President Club in New York; then in 1960 managed the campaign in Nebraska. After the election Horton came to Washington with the New Frontier. Jack assigned him to a high-level job in the Department of Defense to make sure defense contractors hired blacks. He saw Jack in the White House for private dinners. He remained with the Defense Department until 1967, then moved to Norfolk.

The halcyon days at Choate drifted by through winter into spring. Jack pulled his grades up—some. But then the roof fell in on Jack, Lem, and Rip. They and ten other boys (mostly athletes) had organized a secret club which met nightly in Jack and Lem's room. They called themselves "the Muckers" and bought little gold charms in the shape of a shovel with

"CMC" (Choate Mucker Club) engraved on them. "Mucker" was a word the headmaster often used in chapel to describe errant boys at Choate who were not living up to the school's high standards. In adopting that name for the club, Jack and his cohorts were deliberately mocking George St. John, a reckless course. Inevitably St. John found out. Jack and the rest came very near being expelled.

In *As We Remember Him,* Headmaster St. John recalled that Jack was the "chief mover" in the group and that

> . . . they gave themselves purposely a wrong title, which I wouldn't like to repeat. I don't think it would be quite fair to Jack. They were kids. They weren't wicked kids, but they were a nuisance. At one time, it came to the point where I was saying to myself, "Well, I have two things to do, one to run the school, another to run Jack Kennedy and his friends." And they weren't bad, you know, but they had to be looked after. In other words, they just weren't maturing. So I wrote Mr. Kennedy, and I said, "I think you and Jack and I ought to have a three-cornered talk, Mr. Kennedy. Could you come up here. . . . " We held nothing back. I was angry. Let's say I was—there's a better term for it than anger—I was—I can't get just the right word. I was enormously interested. Psychologically I was enormously interested. I couldn't see how two boys from the same family could be so different. But Mr. Kennedy and Jack and I sat together, in my study, and I rehearsed the chapter and verse of things that had happened. I've forgotten what they were; most of them were just peccadilloes.
>
> Well, we reduced Jack's conceit, if it was conceit, and childishness, to considerable sorrow. And we said just what we thought, held nothing back, and Mr. Kennedy was supporting the school completely. I've always been very grateful to him.
>
> There are lots of boys who go through a period like that, and the greatest kindness is some severity. Jack's father didn't hold back. In fact, he spoke very, very stongly, and also with some Irish wit. You know, in dealing with Jack, you needed a little wit as well as a little seriousness. Jack didn't like to be too serious; he had a delightful sense of humor, always. His smile was, I think, as a young boy, when he first came to the school—well, in any school he would have got away with some things, just on his smile. He was a very likeable person, very lovable.

Horton told us:

> The Muckers thing was a serious affair. Why we weren't thrown out of school, I'll never know. I think the headmaster wanted to

dismiss us all from school. He got up in chapel and publicly referred to us as bad apples in the basket. I think Jack was public enemy number one, Lem Billings was number two, and I was number three. Mr. Kennedy came up. There must have been some kind of financial consideration. This was during the darkest days of the Depression. Maybe I just invented this later, but it seems to me that right after we disbanded the club, Mr. Kennedy donated two very fine movie projectors for the Saturday night movie. We never did anything really *bad*. It was more of an antiestablishment thing. Roughhousing. Sneaking out at night to get a milkshake. Maybe we didn't like to be structured. We were just nonorganization in some ways. A little zany. . . .

We were kept over Easter vacation for three or four days and not allowed to go home with the rest of the students.

But they were graduated in June, Jack standing sixty-fourth in a class of 112. He was voted "most likely to succeed"—not necessarily because his peers devoutly believed it. In his oral history, Horton explained:

In our senior year we had elections for the handsomest, the best dancer, the wittiest, and so on. Jack wanted to be voted the most likely to succeed. So we campaigned and traded votes back and forth. I was accepted as most generous. Jack secured approximately fifty percent of the vote for most likely to succeed. There was nobody near him. Word got around that Jack Kennedy was most likely to succeed. But it wasn't a hardship on any person at that particular time to vote for him for that office. None of us was too concerned about the future.

At Choate, Jack had begun to display several traits that would continue to be characteristic of him. First, his strong interest in athletics. He was sickly—but he had tried like a tiger.

Secondly, the quickness and also the restlessness of his intellect. He had little tolerance for, or success with, routine classwork on subjects that did not interest him; no amount of threats or discipline could move him to work at what he did not want to work at; but all who knew him, faculty and peers, took him to be very bright.

Thirdly, his best-remembered achievements at Choate were political. He had demonstrated a great capacity for making friends. Everybody at Choate liked Jack Kennedy; he had little trouble getting his classmates to cast the vote he sought in the class elections. The formation of the Muckers—with Jack as the "chief mover"—was a political act. The Muckers had no legitimate goals; indeed, the opposite was the case, but it was a close-knit society that, as Horton explains in his oral history, was competititve for prestige with the existing student council. Forming the Muckers can be thought of as not utterly different from forming his own political machine, separate from the Democratic Party establishment. Horton told us that when he and Jack exchanged photographs at graduation, Jack wrote on his: "To Boss Tweed from Honest Abe, pray we room together at Sing Sing."

2

A Year Out

Ix attempting a complete, detailed biography of these years, we were inevitably stumped occasionally, and left with guesswork. Unfortunately, such a point occurs this early in our narrative. One important fact that has been confusingly reported until now has been cleared up, and we shall present it first; then the reader must be asked to forgive some uncertainty and speculation about this not unimportant summer in Jack Kennedy's life.

Most of the Kennedy literature of the 1950s and 1960s—books, newspaper profiles, magazine articles, and so on—contain the information that following his graduation from Choate, Jack went to London to study under Harold Laski as Joe Junior had done in 1933–1934. For example, in the first major national magazine profile on Jack in *The Saturday Evening Post,* June 13, 1953, Paul F. Healey, a Washington journalist, wrote, "He had rounded out his education by taking a look at the radical theories of Prof. Harold Laski at The London School of Economics during 1935–36." In *Who's Who* of 1950–1951, probably the source for many of the statements, Jack listed it this way: "Student London Sch. Economics, 1935–36."

Writing in 1959, James MacGregor Burns discloses that this was not entirely accurate. Based on his help from Jack, Burns writes, "His father, determined that Jack should make good use of his summer before college, packed him off the The London School of Economics to study under the noted Socialist professor Harold J. Laski. . . . Jack had little contact with Laski, for he fell ill with jaundice in London, left the London School, but was not well enough to enter Princeton until several weeks after classes began. . . ."

Rose Kennedy's version, written in 1974, is only slightly different. She says that in September (not precisely summer) of 1935, she and her husband, who had just completed an intense fourteen months in Washington as chairman of the SEC, sailed for a European vacation, taking Jack and Kick along. It was Jack's "time," she said, to study under Laski. She had decided to enroll Kick, then fifteen, in a French convent. Jack entered The London School of Economics, she says, but "after only a month,"

Jack came down with "jaundice" or "hepatitis" and had to withdraw. He returned to the United States and enrolled in Princeton University.

Thus we approached this subject with these extant versions of Jack's tour at The London School of Economics: (first) Jack's own—that he was there for the full year 1935-1936, published by almost everybody until (second) the 1959 Burns version—placing Jack there in the "summer" of 1935, then withdrawing because of illness. And (third) Rose's version, placing him there in September for one month, then withdrawing because of illness.

The London School of Economics (now The London School of Economics and Political Science), in the person of its registrar, G. Ashly, responded to our inquiry with what we take to be the fact of the matter: "John F. Kennedy registered at this school in October 1935 with the intention of attending a general course of lectures. In fact he returned to America in November 1935 after being taken ill and took no part in the course."

At the Kennedy Library we examined Jack's passport for 1935 (his first). The old immigration and customs stamps on the passport were hard to read and decipher. One stamp clearly shows that Jack entered Germany on August 16, 1935—and that conflicts with other evidence as to his movements.

Rose Kennedy in *Times to Remember* writes that Jack sailed with the family in September. In the United Press International photographic library in New York, there is a picture of Joe and Rose "sailing for Europe" on September 25. In the picture are seven of the nine Kennedy children, identified as Kathleen, Eunice, Robert, Jean, Patricia, Edward, and John. And yet Jack's passport clearly indicates that he entered Germany on August 16.

What to make of this? We do not know. The passport entry is clear. And yet it is also clearly Jack in the photograph taken in New York. The best possible conclusion we can draw is that earlier in the summer, Jack sailed alone to Europe on a heretofore undisclosed visit, then sailed back to the U.S. in time to sail again for Europe with his parents and Kathleen. In any case, it is clear that Jack and his parents were in London in October. Kick had probably entered the convent school in France. In London, while Joe Kennedy did business with his liquor distillers (primarily Haig & Haig), Jack registered at The London School of Economics. Then he became ill and returned to the United States.

At the Kennedy Library there is a letter from Jack's father to the Harvard authorities which says in part: "I took him abroad last year but he had a recurrence of a blood condition and I brought him home to be near his doctors." The words "blood condition" could have been a way of describing hepatitis or jaundice in those days. The use of the word "recurrence" led us to speculate that the "serious illness" in Jack's fifth-form year at Choate—winter of 1933–1934—had been hepatitis or jaundice. But with the medical records denied us, there was no way to check.

Now headed home, what was Jack to do? One would think that a young man recovering from hepatitis would avail himself of his family's Florida retreat to relax in the sun for some months. But Jack insisted on entering college, even though he would be entering weeks late. This might be taken as a sign that there was nothing seriously wrong with him; or it might not. We have seen a boy who had no business whatever playing football stubbornly and recklessly attempting to do just that, and we will later see the same young man of unstable spine standing, by his own choice, on the deck of a bone-crushing PT boat. Clearly, no conclusion may be drawn.

The question remained, which college? The answer created a controversy between Jack and his father. Rip Horton had told us that Joe Kennedy was dead set on Jack going to his alma mater, Harvard, where Joe Junior was then enrolled. "Jack had not done well at Choate," Horton said, "and I believed Mr. Kennedy blamed that, in part, on Lem Billings and me. We had both enrolled in Princeton. Jack wanted to go to Princeton with us. But Mr. Kennedy wanted us separated."

There is some evidence to support this at the Kennedy Library—letters showing that in early 1935 Jack applied to both Harvard and Princeton, as though the matter were not yet settled.

Now the matter came to a head rather quickly and Jack won. According to Koskoff, his father made contact with an influential Princeton alumnus, Herbert Bayard Swope, the editor of the *New York World,* who in turn helped persuade the Princeton authorities to accept Jack, even though it was late. Based on some Princeton records at the Kennedy Library, we estimate that he entered Princeton in late October, five or six weeks behind his freshman classmates.

Jack moved in with Lem Billings and Rip Horton. Billings had recalled in our interview:

> I had a tuition scholarship the whole four years I was in Princeton. My mother was very hard up then and I had to do student employment, like the student furniture exchange, which I was involved in. You would buy furniture from the outgoing seniors, store it in the gym in the summer, then sell it to incoming freshmen for a big profit. Ninety percent of the profits went for scholarships, ten percent to the leaders of the exchange. I was rooming with Rip Horton from Choate when Jack came back from London. It was the cheapest set of rooms on campus, seventy-five steps up in South Reunion Hall, an old place now torn down. When Mr. Kennedy came to visit, he climbed those seventy-five steps and said

there must be someplace better his son could stay. But Jack stayed with us. So there were the three of us, Jack, Horton and I. We had two bedrooms and a living room. The bathroom was down a couple of flights.

In his oral history, Rip Horton recalled:

> I can remember one day very well when Mr. Kennedy pulled up there in a chauffeur-driven Cadillac. We were up four flights, on the top floor of South Reunion Hall. He had on a very heavy coat because he was going to a football game. After he had climbed two flights of stairs he was so fatigued that he stood out on the fire escape, took off the coat, and threw it down to Dave, the chauffeur. He was overheated and overexerted on that trip up to our room!

In our interview with Horton, he could remember very little about Jack's Princeton days:

> I remember at least three occasions—weekends—when he came up to my apartment in New York. I think we had dates. But the big thing was that I was in a boxing tournament at the New York Athletic Club and Jack was my manager. I boxed at one hundred and thirty-five pounds. He'd make me work out at Princeton, then he'd sit in my corner at the NYAC ring. What a team! I made it to the finals and then some guy knocked my brains out.

Jack was still quite ill, but gamely hanging on, as shown in a letter Rose published. It was from Joe Kennedy to Jack, undated, but probably early November:

> DEAR JACK,
> I had a nice talk with Doctor Raycourt . . . and we have decided to go along on the proposition as outlined by Dr. Murphy and see how you get along until Thanksgiving. Then, if no real improvement has been made, you and I will discuss whether or not it is best for you to lay off a year and try to put yourself in condition.
> After all, the only consideration I have in the whole matter is your happiness, and I don't want you to lose a year of your college life (which ordinarily brings great pleasure to a boy) by wrestling with a bad physical condition and a jam in your studies. A year is important, but it isn't so important if it's going to leave a mark for the rest of your life. So let's give it a try until Thanksgiving and see if you are showing any improvement, then you and I will discuss what's best to do.

You know I really think you are a pretty good guy and my only interest is in doing what's best for you.

Love,
DAD

Jack lagged in his studies. In a letter to Harvard in the following year, Jack would write: "I made up and passed English, History, Military Science, French, but failed trigonometry." In early December he gave it up. He went to the Peter Bent Brigham Hospital in Boston, according to that same letter. He remained in the hospital two months under care of Dr. William P. Murphy. Then he went to the Kennedy home in Palm Beach.

In his biography of Joe Junior, Hank Searls writes that about this time (March 1936), Arthur Krock suggested to Joe Kennedy that he send Jack out to a ranch in Arizona which was operated by a friend of Krock's. Krock was working with Joe on a book to be published over Joe Kennedy's name. From our Krock interview:

Q. Is it true that you helped him write his book, *I'm For Roosevelt*, in 1936?

A. Yes. He had the idea. He honestly believed Roosevelt had saved the capitalistic system. So did I. I gave him the title for the book. I wrote a good deal of it and edited the rest. I took no pay for this.

We asked if it were also true that he had proposed that Jack be sent to a ranch in Arizona. He said yes. It was the Jay Six Ranch near Benson, Arizona, a cattle spread operated by a friend of his from Long Island, John G. D. Speiden. But, Krock said, Speiden and everyone else concerned with the ranch was now dead and that it would be "impossible" to find out any details of Jack's stay there.

Hank Searls, in *The Lost Prince*, has a few details obtained from Speiden before he died. Searls explores this because Joe Junior was with Jack at the ranch for a time. He writes:

The Jay Six ranch reclined along a great watershed between the San Pedro and Santa Cruz rivers, halfway between Tucson and Naco on the Mexican border. It sprawled over forty-three thousand acres on the topographical map on the wall of the main house, but maps are bird's-eye views and a great many of the actual acres, being straight up and down, were not accounted for on the wall. Visible or not, the whole spread had to be contained in barbed wire, and in the maintenance of the wire even the vertical planes had often to be traversed, usually by horse but sometimes in the last resort by foot. Tending the wire, Joe and Jack found that actual life as ranchhands in the Old West bore little relation to that portrayed on the screen. . . .

There was plenty of riding—out to fences and back—and Speiden's ambiguous verdict of the boys' horsemanship was that it was "completely adequate."

They had arrived at a propitious time—for Mr. Speiden. He intended to carry out the suggestions of his old newspaper friend to the letter. (Krock had advised Speiden to "work hell out of them.") He was building permanent ranch offices, and he was building them in the old way, of indigenous adobe mud and strong backs, a method which, when employed by the Spanish priests, had effectively wiped out the more devout of the aborigines of Arizona, New Mexico, and California.

John Speiden, a quiet man given to understatement in a deep gravelly voice, found them "philosophical." They lived in the bunkhouse with the other ranchhands, who never knew of their wealth. They ate enormously. They were hauling adobe each day before the sun was baking the eastern flanks of the Galiuros, broke for midday dinner, and worked until it sank behind Apache Peak to the west. With a Mexican, an alcoholic Scotsman named Mac and Speiden himself, they erected an adobe complex to house the ranch offices. They worked six days a week. On Saturday nights they would bump in a ranch truck to the border town of Nogales . . . [they] made one dollar a day. . . .

There may be minor errors in the Searls account. We wonder how much adobe mud Jack lifted with his bad back. Searls says Joe Junior went out at the same time Jack did (March?) and remained there four months. But if that's true, then Joe Junior withdrew from the spring term at Harvard and missed spring football practice—unlikely. (Elsewhere Searls says that Joe Junior did go out for spring football practice.) In any case a letter from Jack to Harvard indicates that by July 1, Jack was back at Hyannis Port. We speculate that Jack probably went out in March and Joe Junior came in late May, after football practice, classes, and exams. Most likely Joe Junior was in Arizona with Jack for only the month of June. A letter in Rose's book—from Eunice to her mother—indicates that during his stay in Arizona, Jack joined his father in Hollywood at least briefly, perhaps on his nineteenth birthday (May 29). This was Jack's first visit to Southern California, a place he liked and would return to often.

To recapitulate: Jack arrived in London in October, 1935, registered at The London School of Economics, probably saw little or nothing of Laski, became ill with hepatitis or jaundice or a "blood disease," returned to the United States, enrolled at Princeton, left Princeton, and entered the Peter Bent Brigham Hospital in Boston where he spent two months, then went on to Palm Beach, then to Arizona (and California) for four months. In sum, he was ill for most of this academic year.

Why then had Jack for years encouraged everyone beginning with *Who's Who* to believe that he spent the academic year 1935–1936 in London studying under Laski? At first we speculated that the error had been allowed to stand simply because it gave Jack another academic—and also another liberal—credential. Later, as we uncovered more and more dissimulation in his and the family's public posture as to his lifelong health, we entertained the theory that it was instead another aspect of this medical cover-up, meant to conceal the fact that Jack had been ill for virtually the entire year. That it also tended to give Jack a liberal image and more academic credits than he had actually accumulated may have been merely a fortuitous byproduct. This question was not, of course, ever resolved for certain.

3

Harvard—
Torby, Ben, and Charlie

O N July 6, 1936, Jack wrote to Harvard to apply for enrollment in the fall, with the class of 1940. In this letter, on file at the Kennedy Library, he mentions the decision to attend The London School of Economics, his "sickness," and his enrollment in Princeton. Perhaps to soft-pedal his defection to Princeton, he states that he went there "due to its proximity to New York where the doctors who were treating my illness were located." He concludes by saying his doctors now believe he is physically fit to attend college. His father followed up with a letter, written August 28, explaining the whole complicated year again, concluding: "He seems to have recovered now and is in very good health."

In a Harvard entrance examination taken that summer (or the previous summer) Jack scored as follows: English 85, History 85, French 55, Physics 50. The scores in English and History were considered "honors." The French and Physics grades were considered "unsatisfactory." Nonetheless, he was accepted. He began his studies as a freshman in the fall of 1936, a year behind his Choate classmates. Joe Junior was then a junior at Harvard and a big man on campus. It was election time. Joe Kennedy Senior was busy promoting his book and making speeches urging Roosevelt's reelection to a second term.

When Jack entered Harvard in the fall of 1936, he went out for, and made, the freshman football squad. The freshman team was the training ground for the varsity. In sophomore year, those who made good on the freshman team were eligible to try for a varsity position. The freshman squad on which Jack played had a miserable record: no wins, four losses, a tie. According to his Harvard records, Jack had played left or right end in three of the games: Andover, Dartmouth, and Yale.

There is an oral history by James Farrell in the library. Farrell is described as a "Harvard sports equipment man." He said, "Jack was a big, tall stringbean. He didn't look much like an athlete. You could blow him over with a good breath. He didn't have the physique for football. The game was too much for his build. . . ."

It was during his time on the football team that Jack is said to have hurt his back. The books and magazine articles differ about the date this happened and in their descriptions of the injury. Burns describes it as occurring in his freshman year. But William Manchester, in his *Portrait of a President, John F. Kennedy in Profile,* a slight, flattering biography published in 1962, places the injury in Jack's sophomore year, when Jack, who failed to make the varsity, was playing on the junior varsity team. Burns says only that he "injured" his back. Manchester says he "sprained" it.

In her book, Rose Kennedy says that the injury occurred in the sophomore year and describes it in specific terms: "He dropped back to the junior varsity and was doing a good job there until one day in practice he was hit by a hard block or tackle and landed at the wrong angle and ruptured a spinal disc. This injury ended his football days and marked the beginning of troubles with his back that were to haunt him the rest of his life."

One member of the freshman squad that year was Torbert Macdonald. In time, he would become Jack's roommate and "best friend," as Lem Billings put it to us. He also became an all-American running back for Harvard and the team captain. In *As We Remember Him,* Macdonald recalled:

> I weighed maybe one seventy-five when I was a freshman, and Jack couldn't have weighed more than one fifty or one sixty. In those days, you had to play both ways, and he was great on offense and could tackle very well on defense, but as far as blocking and that sort of thing, where size mattered, he was under quite a handicap. Guts is the word. He had plenty of guts. . . .
>
> I had just finished Andover Academy and come down to live roughly seven miles from the center of Harvard, the Yard as it's called, so I didn't have a preference for a roommate or make any preparations. Jack got assigned to a room in Weld Hall, in the Yard, and it was after a series of months in which we both played football on the same squad and sometimes team, that I got to know him that well. During those months, we decided it was time for him to have a roommate. We roomed together throughout the rest of our term in college. . . .

Torbert Macdonald is now a Congressman representing the Malden area of Massachusetts. He had no oral history on file at the library, nor had he written a book. Early in our research we wrote him, giving the background on our project, requesting an interview. With much difficulty, including a broken appointment and a dozen phone calls, it was arranged. An aide told us we were lucky. Torbert Macdonald did not like to give interviews on Jack Kennedy.

The Macdonald interview was disappointing. Being very much in the public eye, and a Democratic Congressman in Senator Edward M. Kennedy's bailiwick, he was under considerable constraint. He seemed to us evasive, defensive, and simplistic. Later we followed up our interview with a letter, asking him to expand on a couple of points. He called to do so, but when we sent another letter inquiring about an aspect of Jack's health, we never heard from him again.

Torbert Hart Macdonald has served in the U.S. House of Representatives since 1954. On the Hill he has a reputation as conscientious though not brilliant. He is one of those men who serve in the House year after year without showing any sign of higher ambition. He has sponsored many workmanlike bills but few have brought him notice—the most famous was his bill which forced the National Football League to lift the TV blackouts on home games in cities where tickets were sold out in advance.

We met Macdonald in his office in the Cannon Building, opposite the Capitol. He was big (like Billings) and craggy-faced and blue-eyed. He was cold (or shy) in his greeting and appeared wary. He was fastidiously dressed in blue suit, vest, striped tie. He had straight black hair and almost no neck. He spoke slowly and very softly with a Boston accent.

"Are you going to use a tape recorder?" he asked when he had taken a seat opposite his cluttered desk.

"Yes, if you don't mind."

"So am I," he said, bending down behind his desk, opening a drawer.

Later, an aide in Macdonald's office would telephone to ask us for a duplicate of our interview tape. Macdonald had let his tape run out. In complying with this request, we discovered our tape had also run out for a brief period! There were gaps during the interview. We had a tough time convincing Macdonald's aide that this had really happened. Fortunately, we had made extensive and detailed notes, and between the tapes we did have and the notes, we were able to reconstruct the entire interview—of which only the part that relates to Harvard is reported at this point.

We began as we had begun with the others, by asking Macdonald about his background. He seemed surprised that we would want to know anything about *him*. His replies came slowly—and cautiously.

I have Irish and Scotch blood, but I feel more Irish than Scotch and I am a Catholic. My father was born in Boston, my mother in Everett, Massachusetts. My father went to Brighton High School, Boston Latin, then Holy Cross College. He played football at Holly Cross, was a letterman. Before I was born, my father was a football coach at Beverly High School, Watertown High School, and Boston University. He ended his career in Malden. He was athletic director at Malden High School. The stadium is named Jack Macdonald Stadium. I was born at the Boston Lying-In Hospital in 1917, the youngest of my family. I had an older brother, John Junior, who died at fourteen or fifteen of spinal meningitis. I have two older sisters. Margaret married John Prior, who was athletic director at Medford High School in Massachusetts.

I grew up in Malden. I went to Malden High School, graduating in 1935. I played football, basketball, baseball, track. My father did not encourage football; he thought I was too small and too thin. But I played defensive end and safety, and halfback on offense. I had no academic interests except staying eligible for football. Then I went to Phillips Andover Academy for one year. I loved that school. It stimulated my dormant intellect. I went on to Harvard in the fall of 1936 and made the freshman team, playing quarterback. Yale beat us that year, twenty-six to fourteen, but I ran for the two touchdowns we got. One was for about eighty yards, the other for twenty yards. Then I went on to play varsity football. I was a halfback, actually a tailback—the running back in the single-wing formation. I was captain of the Harvard varsity in my senior year and all-American. In October 1973, I was voted into the Harvard Football Hall of Fame.

Macdonald had met Jack before they both arrived at Harvard. Macdonald had been taking out a girl in West Medford. The girl's cousin was going out with Ted Reardon, a classmate and best friend of Joe Junior, and later one of Jack's political aides. Macdonald met Joe and then Jack through Ted Reardon. He also met Kathleen and Eunice and the younger children. He had a deep crush on Kathleen and kept her picture on his bureau at Harvard. He talked about Jack:

There was no question that Jack was my best friend. All my life. Jack and I were very alike. I was born June sixth, so we were both Geminis. We had the same interests. He was very humorous, very bright, very unassuming. It just grew. We had many similarities, both in taste in people and just general outlook on things. There was no meshing of ambitions about running the country or anything like that. I thought he'd end up in some field, while if not as writer-author, something that would call on his interests and talents in literature, per se. I didn't see him as writing the Great American Novel but I felt that whatever he went into, he would be a great success at it. He was a man of multiple talents.

Macdonald is not a man much given to analyzing the character of other people or his own character. We kept the interview focused on facts and dates and events, hurrying from one topic to another, frequently interrupted by the bell that called Congressmen to the House floor for a roll-call vote.

We asked Macdonald about the condition of Jack's back when he was at Harvard. He said, "If Jack had a weak back, I never saw any sign of it. I think of his back problems as being more of PT thing than football. He was on the swimming team after football and I don't know if you can swim with a bad back. He never complained about his back in college; he never *discussed* his back. I put it down directly to the PT's. They'd put a guy with a *good* back in trouble. If you didn't know how to ride them, they'd pound the hell out of your legs and back."

In their sophomore year Torby and Jack had taken a room in Winthrop House. The room, Torby told us, was one of the least expensive—tailored to Torby's budget, not Jack's. During the fall semester of their junior year, 1938, they moved to a larger room in Winthrop House and brought in two more roommates, Ben Smith and Charlie Houghton—both varsity football players.

From the Kennedy books, we knew a little about these men. Ben Smith and Jack had remained close friends. Smith had been an usher at Jack's wedding in 1953. In 1960, when Jack was elected president, he chose Smith to fill out his Senate term. Then, when Teddy replaced Smith in a special election in 1962, Smith disappeared from public life. Charlie Houghton had been a close friend in college, but the friendship had petered out. Torby blamed it on geography. Houghton had married a St. Louis girl and settled in the Midwest. After that, his path and Jack's seldom crossed.

The Kennedy Library had released no oral history from either Smith or Houghton. We sought them out for interviews. Ben Smith lives in Gloucester, Massachusetts, once a commercial fishing port, now mostly a bedroom for Boston businessmen and a summer resort. It is old Yankee and Republican territory.

Ben Smith, too, is a big man—bigger than Lem Billings or Torby Macdonald—handsome, with brilliant blue eyes and a deep suntan.

His summer house on Ipswich Bay is rambling and nautical in flavor, full of photographs and prints of sailing vessels, and silver trophies that Smith and his father and grandfather had won in sailing regattas.

He told us he was born Benjamin Atwood Smith II in Gloucester in 1916, descendent of an English family who came to America in 1776. His mother was from Boston—daughter of an Irish immigrant. Smith was raised a Catholic. He said:

I grew up and went to school here, graduating from Gloucester High in 1934. I played varsity football—end—and was on the stu-

dent council and from age two or three always sailed a lot, cat-
boats, then larger boats. I spent a year at Governor Dummer
Academy in Byfield, Massachusetts, prepping, then went to Har-
verd in the fall of 1935, a year ahead of Jack. I went out for the
freshman team. We had a good season, but lost to Yale, twenty-
one to nineteen. I made the varsity squad my sophomore year.
That's when I met the Kennedys. Joe Junior, a year ahead of me,
was competing for the same position on the team—end. Neither of
us made first string, but we played a lot and got to be friends.

The summer after my freshman year, I ran into Joe at the Edgar-
town Sailing Regatta on Martha's Vineyard. He was with Ted
Reardon and his kid brother Jack. The following fall Jack came to
Harvard and went out for football with Torby on the freshman
team. We all got to know each other pretty well. Charlie Houghton
was a football player too. He was a good tackle. In his second
year, the coach, a dumb bastard, shifted him to halfback. Charlie
was no halfback. His senior year, he finally quit. Jack hurt his back
a couple of times and finally had to give it up.

Jack was a real battler. He used to take an awful beating. I think
he was playing on the JV's and had a series of injuries. So Jack and
Charlie weren't playing, Torby and I were playing. I had been
shifted to fullback; Torb was a halfback and captain of the team.
Joe Kennedy Junior did not play in the Yale game so he never did
get a letter. His father was really mad about that.

Smith's wife, Barbara, whom he called Sis, had come into the living
room. She was tall, blond, blue-eyed, and slim, and looked far younger
than her age. She joined the interview—reluctantly—and said in a voice
so soft we had to put the tape recorder mike almost in her lap, "I came to
Gloucester that summer of 1939 and helped Ben campaign for the school
committee. Then, about six months later, in February, 1940, we were
married in Lake Forest. Jack was in the wedding. He was a fantastic guy,
he really was. He had that *great* charisma. . . ."

Ben and Sis told us they had married early and quickly became busy
raising children. They had not seen much of Jack during his bachelor
days, 1940 to 1953. Nor had they seen much of Charlie Houghton over the
years. They heard he'd been divorced and remarried. As we were leaving,
Ben Smith said to Sis, "Damn! I've got to call old Charlie. It bothers me
to lose touch like this."

Charles Gilbert Houghton works in a St. Louis brokerage firm. We arranged to meet him at his private club in Florida, just south of Palm
Beach. He met us on the beach, wearing a bathing suit, complaining about

the weather. He is big, blue-eyed, slightly balding. He had been on vacation for a week. In spite of the uneven weather, he was tanned. He told us he spent most of the day on the beach or in the club bar.

Houghton suggested we have lunch outside by the pool. The sun beat down but there was a strong, chilly wind. Houghton warmed his insides with a martini and told us about his background. He was born in Boston in 1915, son of an investment banker whose family owned a downtown department store, Houghton-Dutton. Charlie attended private secondary schools around Boston. Then:

I wanted to go to Princeton, but all the family had been to Harvard so they persuaded me to go there. I was a good athlete: tackle in high school, but hockey was my best game. I met Jack through Joe Junior, who was out for football. I was a good tackle, but then the coach, Richard C. Harlow, who came to put Harvard back in big-league football, made a halfback out of me. I couldn't do that. I didn't like the coach and he didn't like me. Joe Junior was a hell of a guy. I really liked him. He had a much more natural flair for politics than Jack. It came easier. He had a lot of stamina. He never missed a day's football practice in three years. He didn't get his letter and it was terrible. I think that's one reason Mr. Kennedy never gave a penny to Harvard. The week before the Yale game, we played Dartmouth. It was a terrible rainy day. The field was a mess. Ben Smith scored a couple of touchdowns, I think, and Ted Husing, the radio announcer, picked Ben for his all-star team.

I'm sure Torby feels differently about Dick Harlow because Harlow threw his weight behind Torby to be elected captain of the team. It was all politics. Torby had terrible knees, like Joe Namath. Harlow used to give him Novocain shots to deaden the pain. In those days, you just didn't do things like that in college football.

Anyway, I wound up rooming with Jack and Ben and Torby, the only Protestant and Republican in with three Catholic Democrats. I am probably the only man in history who can say of his college roomates that one was a congressman, one was a senator, and the other was the president of the United States!

Jack was a very stimulating person to live with. Very argumentative in a nice way. He questioned everything. He had a great intellectual curiosity and the best sense of humor of any of the Kennedys. When Ben and Sis got married in Lake Forest, Jack and I were ushers. We were staying in a friend's house and they had just redecorated it. Jack took a bath and left the water running all night. In the morning, the plaster was all falling down. We wrecked the

house. It was awful. But they loved him. We went away with them
hating me but loving Jack—and *he* did all the damage!

In 1961 Houghton had told *Coronet* magazine interviewers: "They put
Jack and me up with someone called 'Fighting Tom' Cassidy who lived
across the street. Jack busted a chair before he even got upstairs. Then
the tub overflowed when he was taking a bath and we cracked up their
car. But Fighting Tom was still talking to us when we left. Jack could always get anyone on his side."

Torby Macdonald had told the *Coronet* writers about how sloppy Jack
was in his living habits at Harvard. "One time he was changing his clothes
to go out, heaving his things into a heap in the middle of the floor. I told
him to watch the way he was throwing things around our room because it
was getting to look like a rummage sale. 'Don't get sanctimonious with
me,' Jack warned me. 'Whose stuff do you think I'm throwing mine *on
top of?* Yours!' "

We asked Houghton about that. He rolled his eyes in mock horror.

Jack was the sloppiest of us all. He never hung up *anything.* He
just dropped his clothes where he was, or strewed them all over the
suite. But we were lucky in one respect. Jack had a kind of part-
time colored valet he inherited from Joe Junior, a man named
George Taylor, who worked in a cleaning joint on Harvard Square.
George would come by once a day or so and pick everything up
and take away what had to be pressed. I don't think Jack ever gave
any of that a second thought. He'd been raised with maids and people running behind him picking up—all the Kennedy kids had—so
it was a kind of habit.

Living with Jack was the first time I ever heard about PR—public relations. His father *hired* PR men to promote himself and the
family. He had a big in with the *New York Times.* I remember once
we were sailing in a race down at the Cape. I raced one boat, Jack
raced one boat, and Joe Junior raced one. Joe won the race. And it
got on the front page. I asked why and they said because it's good
PR. If there hadn't been two Kennedys in the race, I don't think it
would have received any publicity. I was amazed by the whole
thing.

In a 1961 *Parade* magazine article on Jack's college days, the author,
Lawrence Lader, who knew Jack at Harvard, wrote: "In his sophomore
year, shortly before Jack was slated for the runoff trial for No. 2 backstroke spot against Tregaskis [Richard Tregaskis, later author of *Guadalcanal Diary* and other books] he went to the infirmary with grippe. To

keep up Jack's strength, roommate Torbert Macdonald . . . smuggled milkshakes and small steaks to his bedside. The myths of fame have gradually amplified this incident to the point where Jack sneaked out of the infirmary to practice in the indoor pool. One story even says he beat out Tregaskis for the team and made his letter. The less romantic facts are that Jack won neither the runoff nor his letter."

We asked Houghton if he could remember anything about that, Jack's health in general, the back injury in particular. Furrowing his brow, he appeared to be thinking long and hard. He said:

Jack was sick a lot. Yes, I remember the swimming team tryouts. He got very sick and had to go to the infirmary. He was supposed to try out for the team but the doctors wouldn't let him out. I remember Torby taking him chocolate milkshakes and hamburgers. Jack wasn't supposed to eat that kind of stuff. Then Torby sneaked him out of the infirmary for the tryouts. Jack couldn't possibly have won. He just wanted to be there. It showed a determination—and what kind of friend Torby was. I'd never have thought of it. I'd have done it if Jack asked me to, but I didn't think it was that important.

He had a bad back when he was at Harvard. He wore a corset all the time to brace it. It was real bad. If I'd been anywhere near the shape he was in, I wouldn't have gone out for football or anything else.

One other thing, sort of funny. You know Jack never had any money? Any cash on him? That year we roomed together, the telephone was in my name and Torby was going with Jack's sister Kathleen, who was in London. Ben was going with Sis, who was in Chicago, and Jack was always calling his family in London. My longest call was probably to Newton Center. The bills would come in each month and they were staggering. I used to tell them they owed me this and that and they'd give me ten or fifteen and say they'd pay me *next* month. I came out way behind on the phone bill—it got to be a big joke. Some joke! But that was typical of Jack. He never had any cash.

Houghton had a second martini. Then his wife, Carol, a stunningly beautiful young woman, joined us at the table for lunch. This was Houghton's second wife. While Carol listened with rapt attention, almost as though she were hearing a part of her husband's life for the first time Houghton told us the rest of the story. After college, he said, he saw Jack several times in the Navy; attended Jack's wedding (but not as part of the wedding party); helped raise funds for him in Milwaukee, Wisconsin, dur

ng the 1960 presidential campaign; then visited him once or twice when
1e was president. He recalled:

> When I graduated from Harvard I might have gone into invest-
> ment banking, but I saw so many of my father's friends turn on the
> gas during the Depression, I looked for something else. I went to
> work for Pittsburgh Plate Glass Company and then I got called up
> in the Navy. . . . After the war, I had in mind getting a liquor dis-
> tributorship for Haig & Haig in St. Louis. I called Jack and he fixed
> me up with an appointment in New York with his old man, who
> had Haig & Haig. Mr. Kennedy sent me to see some people, but
> nothing ever came of it.
>
> Anyway, Jack wrote me and advised me *not* to get into the Haig
> & Haig thing. He said, what the hell, you married a rich gal and
> you've got all the influence you need and, after all, from every-
> thing I hear about St. Louis, they're all rich and slow thinkers and
> you'd do damn well out there. . . . As it turned out, it was all for
> the best. About that time, Mr. Kennedy sold out of Haig & Haig.

So Jack had chosen football stars as his college roomates. His father
1ad roomed with the football captain at Harvard, and so would Robert
Kennedy in turn. Simple machismo (insofar as machismo is simple, or ex-
4lains anything) can surely be assumed as a factor in this pattern; the
Kennedy men, most assuredly including Jack, were concerned with
"manliness" to an extent that would be called sexist today. Football stars
vere the elite of campus life (even at Harvard) and it was a form of social
limbing for young men who were not equipped to play to make it their
1usiness to associate themselves with stars. But Jack's love of the game
asted through his life, and two of these roommates would remain close
1iends through his life—long past the point when he had gained celebrity
ar surpassing that of any all-American halfback.

4

Harvard—Traveling

IN all, during Jack's Harvard years he made three trips to Europe: One
in the summer of 1937, another in the summer of 1938, and the third in
1939, after his father was appointed ambassador to England, a very long
one: seven months. During the forty-eight months that passed while Jack
was enrolled at Harvard, he spent twelve months abroad. The trip provid
ed him another kind of education: a broad and substantial knowledge o
European geopolitics, society, and customs. He made many close friend
there and, like his mother, became an Anglophile. He was a witness to
some stirring moments of history.

The first trip to Europe in the Harvard years came in the summer o
1937 after Jack completed his freshman year at Harvard. Lem Billings
who had finished his sophomore year at Princeton, went with him. During
our interview with Billings we had asked about the trip. He put a serious
face on it, telling us that in his sophomore year he had cultivated an in
tense interest in architecture and was considering making a career of it
He was eager to see the cathedrals and museums of Europe. We asked
how, since his family had no money, he could afford a trip to Europe. H
said, "Jack wanted me to go with him and Mr. Kennedy *asked* me to g
with him. He would pay my expenses. My mother didn't like that. M
grandmother had left me one thousand dollars which I was to collect a
the end of my education. So Mr. Kennedy and my mother made a dea
Mr. Kennedy would pay half my trip and I would pay half my trip and
would repay Mr. Kennedy when I finished college."

When we saw Billings, we had with us a *New Yorker* piece from th
May 1, 1961, issue, an interview with Billings in "Talk of the Town." Par
of the interview dealt with the 1937 trip to Europe. When we showed hir
the copy he said, "Oh, my! I never even *saw* that. Will you make a cop
and send it to me?" Then he rushed off to another room and returned wit
a thick photo album. He laid it on the coffee table and invited us to pe
ruse. It was filled with pictures of Jack and Billings in Europe. Besid
each picture, Billings had written a long caption in an elegant hand, ex
plaining where they were and what they had seen.

The first picture in the album showed a car being lifted off the deck of ship by a crane. It was captioned "Le Havre." The car was a 1936 four-door Ford convertible.

"That was Jack's new car," Billings said. "We shipped it over and back on the boat."

The New Yorker quoted Billings:

We went over on the *Washington*, landed at Le Havre and drove through the cathedral country in the north of France. We visited churches and museums and spent a lot of time interviewing French peasants in schoolboy French. We wanted to see what they thought of the Germans. They were so confident of the Maginot Line! Jack wrote down his thoughts and ideas about everything; he sent his father long letters. We based our living on what we could afford to spend which wasn't much. In Paris, we stayed at a small hotel near the Gare du Nord; we paid eighty cents for a walkup room for two. . . .

Billings expanded: "Actually, we always stayed in the cheapest places we could find—to fit my stringent budget. About five years ago I was in Paris and I looked up that hotel. It was the Montana."

Billings in *The New Yorker* : "We covered all the museums and sight-seeing spots and then went on to the chateau country in the Loire Valley. In Biarritz we went to a bullfight, which we thought was extremely cruel. We stayed a week in Saint-Jean-de-Luz with a Harvard classmate of Jack's whose family had a house there. We met a lot of refugees from Spain. They had terrible stories to tell. . . . "

Billings expanded: "The classmate was Count Alexis de Pourttes. He was Swiss. His family had a house there. Do you know Saint-Jean-de-Luz? It's a resort on the Bay of Biscay very close to the France-Spain border. It's where Louis XIV met his bride: he was married there. When we were there, it was a refugee place for Francoists, I think. It was in the middle of the Spanish Civil War and we heard all the atrocity stories. We wanted to go to Spain but we couldn't get in."

We remembered that James MacGregor Burns had quoted excerpts from a letter written by Jack "from Spain." (Other books had carried it a step further: "from Madrid.") The excerpt was included in Burns to confirm that Jack always did, in fact, send detailed reports to his father on the political situation in the countries he visited. The excerpt of the letter "from Spain"—four or five lines—had not been impressive in its facts, ideas, or opinions. We now concluded that Jack must have picked them up in Biarritz, France, and written the letter from there, not from Spain.

Billings went on: "I'll tell one bad thing we did. We went to Lourdes, which is very funny because we were terrified that we would catch some horrible disease. And I did. I was sick as hell for about four or five days after our visit to Lourdes.''

Leaving Lourdes, Billings told us, they drove across southern France to the Riviera—Monte Carlo. They found a double room in a seedy hotel for sixty cents a day. They were turned away from the main casino because they were both under twenty-one, but they evidently gambled elsewhere. Burns quotes an excerpt from a letter Jack wrote his father—the one hint in Burns that Jack's trip might have included any frivolous activity at all: "Played with five-Franc chips next to a woman who was playing $40 chips and she was quite upset by my winning $1.20 while she lost about $500."

After that, Billings told us, they went on to Italy. They climbed Mount Vesuvius, visited Naples, Capri, Milan, Pisa, Florence, Venice, and Rome. Billings said, "We had a small audience with Cardinal Pacelli, who was then secretary of state at the Vatican (and an acquaintance of Jack's father) and saw Pope Pius XI at his summer home with about five thousand other people. He was brought out on a litter and died shortly after that. We went to a fantastic Mussolini rally, a very exciting experience. I can remember it terribly well. He was such an, er, unusual speaker. You know—he'd talk and then he'd jut out his chin, like this."

From Italy they turned north and went to Germany. *The New Yorker* quoted Billings: "We picked up hitchhikers in Germany so that we could compare their way of life with ours. We slept in youth hostels at ten cents a night. Most of the Germans we met were students and they could speak some English. They were very sure of themselves. We spent a lot of time in museums and churches."

Billings expanded to us: "And the dumbest thing we did was that when we were in Germany, Hitler was going to speak at a rally in Nuremburg and we'd have had to wait three days. So we didn't go. Can you believe it? But the Germans were so anti-everything and so snotty and so awful then. They were insufferable, so haughty and sure of themselves. We had awful experiences. The German people were going through a very strange period."

They ended this grand adventure in London. There was a picture in the album showing Jack lying in bed. He looked ghastly. We asked Billings what had happened. He said: "Jack got desperately sick in London. His face all puffed up and he got a rash and we didn't know anybody to even get a doctor. He had terrible allergies. We had a dog we bought in Amsterdam or Germany. We didn't know he had a *dog* allergy. He'd had dogs around before but never knew it. He got terrible asthma. We had to get rid of the dog."

In early 1938 President Roosevelt appointed Joe Kennedy ambassador to the Court of St. James's in London. The Kennedy family life took on an even more complex aspect. For the next two years Joe and Rose and the children were constantly on the move between London and the States, London and the Riviera, London and the capitals of Europe.

According to Whalen, Joe Kennedy sailed for England on February 23, 1938. Rose did not see him off. She was in the hospital with appendicitis. She sailed over in early March, she writes, with Kick, Pat, Bobby, Jean, and Teddy. Eunice, who was enrolled in a Catholic school in Noroton, Connecticut, remained behind, as did Jack and Joe Junior, both still at Harvard. The other Kennedy child, Rosemary, who was retarded, also remained in the States for a time, just where we do not know. Nor do we know when or how she got to London. But Rose says she was there by May.

At this time Jack became ill again. Whalen writes that he was confined to the Harvard infirmary with "flu," but we were not able to confirm that from any other source. In Jack's Harvard records there is a note that he had "cuts" from classes February 23 to March 4, 1938, and from March 13 to April 11, and that he was under the care of a Dr. Bock. Another note dated 1938 says "Kennedy was ill during part of the year and did no very large quota of tutorial work. . . . " Yet another note states that "Kennedy was out about one month" on account of an illness. This may have been the time when Torby sneaked him into the swim team trials against Richard Tregaskis. In the UPI photo library, we found a picture of Jack dated March 24, 1938. The caption stated that he was en route "south" (evidently to Palm Beach) "for his health." He does not look well.

That summer, 1938, Jack again went to Europe. A picture story in the September 1961, issue of *Esquire* , showing Jack, Kick, and other young people at an embassy party, gives the impression that Jack was in London on May 29 for his twenty-first birthday. But that is undoubtedly an error—an error which has been carried forward into some of the Kennedy books. Whalen and Koskoff both write that the ambassador came back on the *Queen Mary* for Joe Junior's graduation ceremony on June 20. According to an Associated Press picture, he arrived on June 20. Then he, Joe Junior, and Jack sailed back together to England on the *Normandie* on June 29, arriving in London in time for the traditional Fourth of July party at the embassy. Arthur Krock (and his good friend Bernard Baruch) sailed with them. Krock recalled in his *Memoirs* , published in 1968:

> There were the usual exceptions, however, to this devotion of the boys to their father and their obedience to his rules. One of the most amusing recollections I have of the latter occurred when I was crossing with Joe, Jr., Jack, and their father on the *Normandie* to England, while Joe, Sr.was still Ambassador. The ship's company was gay, and there was a beautiful actress aboard to whom young Joe was very attentive. This annoyed his father, because he thought that the boy might perhaps be a little too impulsive and the

girl be making a play for a youth of his prominence and wealth. Jack was also staying up late at night, with a girl I think his father didn't know about. So he imposed a curfew on the young men: they would have to be in their quarters in his suite by midnight or thereabouts. They made the first deadline. But the suite had a service door, distant from the bedrooms. So when thereafter I saw them as my fellow-conspirators, enjoying themselves in the ship's salons in the small hours of the night, I assumed they must have used this facility to elude the curfew.

By this time the Kennedys were celebrities in England. The press appeared to be mesmerized by the teeming, energetic family. Almost every day, Koskoff and Whalen report, one newspaper or another carried stories about them, usually including a pithy quote from the ambassador. Kick and Rosemary (how the Kennedys managed to keep her retardation concealed from the press is a mystery) made their debut along with the daughters of London's elite. Rose, Kick, and Rosemary were presented at court.

We were unable to learn very much that was definitive on Jack's visit to Europe in the summer of 1938. We assume the party depicted in *Esquire* occurred in July sometime, and that Jack and Joe Junior were deep in the London social whirl. In late July, Rose writes, the family took a house on the French Riviera. According to a diary Rose kept that summer, Jack was on the Riviera in "early August." An entry for August 5 indicates that Rose was still trying to fatten up Jack—with European milk. But Jack was resisting: "Joe had told Jack that though the milk has a peculiar, to us, sour taste, it is really the flavor that milk has which is not pasteurized. He says he drank that sort of milk in Wales for three or four days—at Mr. Heart's castle. Jack is more resigned."

It was a dark summer politically. Hitler occupied Czechoslovakia. Neville Chamberlain went to Munich to obtain "peace in our time." Whalen and Koskoff report that Joe Kennedy approved of the course Chamberlain took. England was militarily weak, he felt, and Chamberlain had no alternative.

According to a photograph in the Associated Press library, Jack sailed home on the German steamer *Bremen*, arriving in New York on September 8, 1938. After reentering Harvard, he sent a letter to his father, the text of which appears in *As We Remember Him* , indicating that he had been ill again. He wrote in part, "Things have been going pretty well. Feeling much better. . . . The papers have been a little sour on Torb [Macdonald] this fall as he had some tough times with Cornell, Dartmouth, etc. But he got three touchdowns and ran all over the field [in the Princeton game]. . . . Ben Smith played very well and is now first string. Our good friend Dick Harlow only put him against Dartmouth for 5 minutes and he scored a touchdown, which pleased us all, as it made Gentleman Dick look a little sick.''

The third trip to Europe—the longest and most important—came in the middle of Jack's junior year. He withdrew from Harvard for the spring semester of 1939 and remained in Europe until the following fall—a period of seven months. He served as a kind of secretary to his father, traveling through Europe, gathering political information, and sending reports to his father in London. These reports, we gather, were designed more to educate Jack than his father.

The trip was planned well in advance. Only a few days after Mr. Kennedy had been appointed ambassador in 1938, Jack applied for a "leave of absence" to work for his father the following year. He would carry extra courses in his senior year to make up the lost credits, he said. Harvard approved the idea. When the ambassador came home for the Christmas holidays—December 15, 1938—Jack met his ship, the *Queen Mary,* and traveled to Palm Beach with him. Rose, Joe Junior, and others were skiing at St. Moritz, Switzerland. Then, on February 25, the ambassador and Jack sailed back to London together on the *Queen Mary.* Jack described his forthcoming duties to an inquiring reporter as "glorified office boy.''

Joe Junior had been working for his father in the embassy since his graduation from Harvard. When Jack sailed, Joe Junior was in Spain, traveling as a journalist. He was gathering material on the final days of the Spanish Civil War, which was later shaped into an article published in *Atlantic* magazine. Hank Searls reports that Joe Junior wrote a friend, rather patronizingly, that "Jack comes over in February to *begin* his education.''

Jack had no sooner arrived than he was swept up in a big diplomatic event. The new Pope, Pius XII, was to be crowned on March 12. President Roosevelt had named Ambassador Kennedy official representative for the event. All the Kennedys (except Joe Junior, still in Spain) journeyed to Rome for the ceremony. At the Kennedy Library there is an oral history from the then Cardinal Giovanni Batista Montini, now Pope Paul VI, who recalled the Kennedy visit:

It happened that the ambassador of the United States to London, Mr. Kennedy . . . arrived punctually but bringing with him . . . children who proceeded to occupy places that were reserved for members of the official missions with the result that the arrangement of places was altered; and when there arrived the Italian minister of foreign affairs, Count Ciano, the son-in-law of Mussolini, he found his seat in the gallery of the official missions was occupied and he began to protest, threatening to leave the Basilica

and to desert the ceremony. The situation was immediately resolved, but there remained in our memory the procession of the
children of Ambassador Kennedy.

After the coronation of the pope, Jack got down to a serious work-
study-travel program, supervised by his father. During this time he also
got to know Professor Harold Laski. According to Burns, Jack went from
one European country to the next, studying the economic and political situations, and wrote analyses for his father in London. Burns, who evidently had access to all these letters, said the "literary quality of his reports
was not the highest and the spelling was . . . atrocious, but they showed
a cool detachment."

Jack's passport for this period was not among the documents at the library, so we cannot precisely detail his itinerary. We guess that he probably began his travels in Paris, where a good friend of Joe Kennedy, William C. Bullitt, was ambassador. Here, and elsewhere on the trip, Jack
made good use of the research facilities of the U. S. Foreign Service in
preparing his reports. There was a note in Koskoff quoting Ambassador
Bullitt's assistant, Carmel Offie, about Jack's visit to his office in Paris.
Offie recalled Jack "sitting in my office and listening to telegrams being
read or even reading various things which were actually none of his business but since he was who he was we didn't throw him out."

From Paris, we surmise, Jack went on to Germany and Poland, where
he stayed several weeks. At that time, Hitler was demanding the right to
have a "corridor" to the Polish port of Danzig. The Poles, of course, took
a dim view of this. According to Burns, Jack wrote his father a 2,500-
word report on the Polish situation which concluded, "Probably the
strongest impression I have gotten is that rightly or wrongly the Poles will
fight over the Question of Danzig."

From Poland, we believe, Jack crossed the Russian border into Lith-
uania, Latvia, and Estonia. There he was aided in his studies and interviews by a career foreign service officer, John Cooper Wiley. Many years
later, Wiley's wife, Irena, wrote a book, *Around the Globe in Twenty
Years*, in which she recalled Jack's visit. A sculptor, she was then in the
process of creating an elaborate altar for a church in Belgium and had
chosen Sainte Thérèse of Lisieux as her motif. The altar consisted of a
life-size statue of Sainte Thérèse and twelve panels depicting various
highlights of her life.

"I needed a model for the angel in one of the panels," Mrs. Wiley
wrote. "Jack with his curly hair and youthful serenity of expression was
literally Godsent." During the week of his visit, Jack posed for Mrs. Wiley. By the time the work was complete, the Nazis had overrun Belgium,
so Mrs. Wiley sent the altar to the Vatican where it remains today with
Jack Kennedy's likeness in one of the panels.

After that, Jack extended his tour of Russia to Leningrad, Moscow, and the Crimea. He was helped along in Russia by another Foreign Service officer in the Moscow Embassy, Charles "Chip" Bohlen. According to Burns, Jack covered much of this vast territory by airplane—Russian transports, which had broken windows and few comforts. Burns included a brief extract from a letter Jack wrote his father, concluding that Russia was a "crude, backward hopelessly bureaucratic country."

If our guesses about the itinerary are correct, Jack took a steamer from the Crimea to Istanbul, then went on to Palestine and Egypt. The Kennedy Library has released Jack's report on Palestine. It is a quite sophisticated analysis in a typed letter of about 1,500 words. The typing, spelling, and grammar are perfect. Perhaps in the preparation of this report Jack was assisted by a stenographer, or perhaps at a later time his report was spruced up and retyped and released for some purpose. It begins with a long historical account of how the "problem" came to be, then deals with the then current conflicts. Jack found the conflicts extremely complex—a tougher problem than Danzig. The Jews and Arabs were at one another's throats—the Jews seeking to found a permanent homeland, the Arabs unalterably opposed. The British, Jack pointed out, had made conflicting promises to both sides which further muddled the problem. His conclusion was pessimistic: there was probably no solution.

He added, "Incidentally, I have become more pro-British down there than I have been in my other visits to England as I think that the men on the spot are doing a good job. . . . "

From the Middle East, Jack probably went up to the Balkans, stopping next in Bucharest, Romania. The itinerary becomes even more obscure at this point, but by June 16, according to a note in Koskoff, he was headed for Belgrade, Yugoslavia. Koskoff says that on that date his father sent a wire to the U. S. ambassador in Belgrade, Arthur Bliss Lane: WILL APPRECIATE ANY COURTESY MY SON ARRIVING TODAY. From there the trail peters out. We think that after Belgrade, Jack returned to London for some socializing and good times. According to Rose, Eunice had her coming-out party on June 22, and Jack was on hand for a June 27 reception given by Prime Minster Chamberlain at Ten Downing Street. Right after that, Torby Macdonald arrived. He had said in his interview with us:

Harvard and Yale formed a joint track team to compete against a joint team formed by Oxford and Cambridge. The best players from all the schools. I went over June ninth on the French liner *Champlain*. We competed at the White City Stadium in London. I met Jack in London in late June or early July. I remember I was at the embassy for the traditional July Fourth party. I lived in the embassy about two weeks. Then Jack and I took off on a trip. We went from London to Paris to Germany to Italy and back to Paris.

During that time we worked fairly seriously, gathering information, interviewing people. . . .

In Germany, Jack and Torby met the famous all-American football player, Byron Raymond ("Whizzer") White, whom Jack would meet again in the South Pacific in the PT boats and whom as president, he would appoint to the Supreme Court. Justice White's office informed us that the justice no longer grants interviews. We were referred to the last he had given, an exhaustive article in *Sports Illustrated* by Alfred Wright published in the December 10, 1962 issue.

There were only a few vague details on his days in Germany and his encounter with Jack Kennedy and Torby Macdonald in the summer of 1939:

> That summer I borrowed a car from a South African fellow and toured around France and Germany and then settled down for a couple of months in Munich, where I rented a room from an old German woman. I spent those months studying Roman law and trying to improve my German, reading the newspapers and talking to the Germans. . . . The first time I remember meeting President Kennedy was that summer in Munich. He was traveling around with some friends of his and I think we had a couple of evenings together. . . .

Torby Macdonald had given the authors of the *Coronet* article a more vivid recollection of the White meeting. During our interview, he had confirmed the substance:

> We went to Berlin and Munich and Whizzer White was there. . . . Jack had met him and introduced me to him. We got along very well, all three of us, so we decided to take a tour of the city. Whizzer had a car that some guy loaned him: we got in it. We went by a monument to Horst Wessel and we slowed down to take a look. Some Stormtrooper-types had a flame burning outside and they started to yell. At that time I didn't know who Horst Wessel was—frankly, I thought just a guy who was some sort of local hero—so we stopped. They started getting rough: we were yelling back, and they started throwing bricks at the car. As we drove the car away I turned to Jack and said: "What the hell is wrong with them? What's this all about? We weren't doing anything." And Whizzer explained it: the car we were driving had English plates on it.

Macdonald told us that after they traveled from Germany to Italy, they returned again to Paris and that "then the work was all over . . . it was pure vacation for about a month." He confirmed another anecdote in the *Coronet* article:

> We'd rented a rickety heap of a car to drive from Paris to the Riviera for a party. Jack wasn't the world's most conservative driver, and he was at the wheel when we slipped off the right shoulder of the road, skidded on our top for thirty feet and ended upside-down with our baggage strewn all over the landscape. There was a big silence. We were literally standing on our heads in the overturned car. Jack looked over at me. 'Well, pal,' he said. 'We didn't make it, did we?'

Torby told us he and Jack were on their way to the Kennedy villa near Cannes to spend the vacation on the beaches. As she had the previous summer, Rose had moved the family down from London. The ambassador came down from time to time. "Kathleen was down there," Macdonald recalled, "and, of course, Jack. But Joe wasn't. I don't remember where Joe was."

After a good time at the beach, Jack and Torby became restless and began traveling again. An entry in Rose's diary, dated August 12, 1939: "Jack and Torby Macdonald leave for Germany. They would like to go to Prague but are told no one is allowed to go there."

Macdonald told us, "We went up to Vienna, Austria. But we split up there. I had always wanted to go to Budapest, Hungary. I went there—Jack went on to Czechoslovakia and Germany. In spite of the rules against visiting Prague, Jack got in—with the help of a Foreign Service Officer, George F. Kennan."

In his book, *Memoirs, 1925–50*, published in 1967, Kennan recalled the episode:

> In those days, as the German forces advanced like encroaching waves over all the borders of Bohemia, no trains were running, no planes were flying, no frontier stations existed. Yet in the midst of this confusion we received a telegram from the Embassy in London, the sense of which was that our Ambassador there, Mr. Joseph Kennedy, had chosen this time to send one of his young sons [John] on a fact-finding tour around Europe, and it was up to us to find a means of getting him across the border and through the German lines so that he could include in his itinerary a visit to Prague.
>
> We were furious. Joe Kennedy was not exactly known as a friend of the career service, and many of us, from what we had heard about him, cordially reciprocated this lack of enthusiasm. His son had no official status and was, in our eyes, obviously an upstart and ignoramus. The idea that there was anything he could

learn or report about conditions in Europe which we did not already know and had not already reported seemed (and not without reason) wholly absurd. That busy people should have their time taken up arranging his tour struck us as outrageous. With that polite but weary punctiliousness that characterizes diplomatic officials required to busy themselves with pesky compatriots who insist on visiting places where they have no business to be, I arranged to get him through the German lines, had him escorted to Prague, saw to it that he was shown what he wanted to see, expedited his departure, then, with a feeling of "that's that" washed my hands of him—as I thought.

From Prague, the Kennedy books say, Jack went on for a second visit to Berlin. Macdonald thought he might also have revisited Danzig, Poland—but he was not certain. The Nazis invaded Poland on September 1. Britain and France declared war on September 3. Chamberlain gave his famous tearful speech to Parliament on September 3. Rose says that Jack, Joe Junior, and Kathleen were in the visitors' gallery when he gave it.

By then, Torby had already left for the States. There is a recollection of his departure in *As We Remember Him:* "I left in September and we were at sea when they declared war. I came back on the last trip the *Normandie* made. We were blacked out all the way home. The ship was zigzagging."

So the long nightmare that would envelop Europe for the next five years had begun. American citizens began to flee, booking passage in any ship in which they could find space. Some of them were on the liner *Athenia*, sunk off Scotland by Nazi U-boats. According to the Kennedy books, Ambassador Kennedy sent Jack to Scotland for a few days to help the American survivors find other passage home—giving Jack his first experience with the victims of war. About that time, the Kennedys were departing England—all but the ambassador and Rosemary, who had been enrolled in a good, safe school Rose especially liked. Rose, Kick, Eunice, and Bobby left on the crowded liner *Washington*, Rose reports. Joe Junior, who was returning to the States to enter Harvard Law School, sailed on the *Mauritania*. How Pat, Jean, and Teddy got home, we do not know. After he finished his *Athenia* work in Scotland, Jack flew home on a Pan American clipper, the *Dixie*. According to a captioned photograph we found in the National Archives, he arrived in Port Washington, Long Island, New York, on September 21, 1939. Torby recalled that he shipped his 1936 Ford home on a steamer.

Jack Kennedy must have been profoundly influenced by all these experiences in Europe at such a momentous time. He was seeing history made close up, on the highest level. As the letter to his father from Palestine indicates, he became more and more pro-British. He and Kick had made many very close friends among the scions of England's ruling class—Hugh Fraser, David Ormsby-Gore, and others—whom he would continue to see the rest of his life. He became an admirer of Winston S. Churchill and his speeches and writings; he would often quote Churchill in later life. His favorite book, he would tell people later, was John Buchan's *Pilgrim's Way*, an autobiographical account of Buchan's life among the English aristocracy and their institutions in war and peace.

5

Harvard—
Two Courtships

FROM our interviews with Billings, Horton, Macdonald, Smith, and Houghton, we knew that Jack dated many girls while in Harvard and abroad. Two were mentioned in the interviews significantly more often and more prominently than others. These were girls whom Jack probably considered marrying. One, Frances Ann Cannon, was the daughter of the Cannon Mills family—extremely wealthy, prominent, and powerful in North Carolina. Rip Horton had told us:

> I can remember going out with Jack and Frances Ann in New York. She was a tremendously attractive girl. I thought she was the most attractive girl he ever went out with. Good looking, good mind, good wit, provocative. A *great* girl. I can remember thinking, my God, why doesn't Jack marry this girl? I don't think the fact that she was Protestant would have made much difference to him. I just don't think he was ready for marriage. He liked to play—and not with just one girl. His mind kept developing so much and his interests were so tremendously varied that nobody could hold his attention for any period of time without his becoming slightly bored by them. . . .

Jane Suydam, born Jane Gaither Eustis in New Orleans, was a good friend of Jack Kennedy's during his presidency. A strikingly beautiful dark-haired woman with a fine mind, she told us:

> I first met Jack in about 1938 or 1939, I can't remember which, in New Orleans. It was during Mardi Gras. Jack was down there chasing Frances Ann Cannon. He was staying with Robert Walmsley, a Princeton boy. I was making my debut that year. I first saw Jack at the Comus Ball. He was standing there in the call-out section, very tanned, wearing white tie and tails. He was unbelievably handsome. He had this remarkable animal pull. The impact on me was overwhelming. Well, I had long talks with Frances Ann about

68

Jack. She said it was a great romance, but her father didn't want her to marry a Catholic.

Robert Walmsley told us:

It was not in 1939. It was 1937 or 1938. I'd known Jack because we were all kind of traveling in the same group in the East. We were in the same class at Princeton—1939—until he dropped out. I was a friend of his sister Kathleen, who was very warm, very entertaining, and had a good mind. Jack came down here to New Orleans, hot after Frances Ann Cannon. He didn't stay with me; he stayed at a hotel. I knew Frances Ann. She asked me if I would take her out to the airport to meet Jack, which I did. Not many people flew in those days. I had him in tow because I was the only guy he knew around here. He didn't bring tails, which are obligatory down here. I loaned him a pair of my brother's, who was five feet four and a half inches tall and weighed one ninety, so Jack really cut quite a figure in those.

One night we went to a party. Jack cut his finger on an automobile door and I had to take him to Charity Hospital. He was very impressed by how well it was organized. I don't remember one other thing about the visit, except the general impression that Jack—as Jane said—was certainly chasing Frances Ann hard.

The end of this courtship occurred precipitously and possibly painfully for Jack. Rose has a letter from Kick dated September 26, 1939 (shortly after Jack arrived back in the United States from London), in which Jack's favorite sister says, "Jack is taking out Frances Ann Cannon this weekend so we can hardly all wait." It sounds as though Kick expected a momentous outcome of this date.

But Charlie Houghton had told us he was along on that same date. He said:

Frances Ann Cannon was a very, very attractive and brilliant girl. She had a hell of a good mind. She wanted to do things with her life. I don't know who found Ann first. I did or Jack did. I was in hot pursuit, I'll tell you. We both went out with her. Then in the summer of 1939, she went to Europe. She came back on a boat and when it docked in New York, both Jack and I were there to meet her. The boat was late, so we had dinner at "21," then met her and took her to a nightclub—the Belgium Village at the World's Fair—for dinner. There was some guy playing an organ and they had waterfalls going up and down in time with the music. We were both very bad and showing off terribly. We hoped that she would get engaged to one of us. She invited us over to her mother's apartment the next day, Sunday, and there introduced us to her new fiancé, John Hersey.

Shortly thereafter, Jack wrote his father a letter, reproduced in *As We Remember Him,* which says, "Cannon and I have cooled a bit, but am looking around sharply for a substitute. . . ."

"Cooled a bit" indeed; the bravado, if that's what it is, is amazing and quite touching.

We asked John Hersey about all this during an interview principally about another aspect of Jack's life to which we shall return. About Frances Ann Cannon, he said:

> Frances Ann Cannon was five years younger than I. She went to Sarah Lawrence. I met her when she was there, at a friend's house, a social occasion. We were married on April 29, 1940. I met Jack through my wife, in 1939, in New York. I think we were engaged at that time. She'd known Jack before. We liked to party and go to nightclubs and I was in a phase of my life when some of that was going on. I met him first with Torby Macdonald one evening in the Ambassador Hotel. I think this was a chance meeting. Jack recognized my wife. We sat down and had some drinks and talked and got acquainted.

Hersey told us that he and Frances Ann had been divorced in 1956; that she had since married Frazer Dougherty; and that she now lived in New York City. When we called her she said to us, courteously but quite finally, "I never give out interviews about my relationship with Jack Kennedy. Sorry."

In a full-page account in the Charlotte *Observer* of the wedding of Frances Ann Cannon to John Hersey, April 29, 1940, it is reported that "Guests from a distance included John Kennedy, of Bronxville, N.Y. . . ."

Finally, Rose has a letter from Kick to her father, dated May 21, 1940, a month after the wedding, in which she says, "He still misses Cannon quite a bit." And a 1961 *McCall's* magazine article on Rose, by Marguerite Higgins, contains a letter from Rose to the ambassador in London written about the same time as Kick's letter. Rose says, "Jack seems depressed that he let his girl get away. He says she is the only one he really enjoyed going out with. And yet he admits that he did not want to get married."

In a letter from Jack at Harvard to his father in London, probably mailed in November of 1939, reproduced in *As We Remember Him*, Jack wrote:

> Torb has been out with a bad leg. Played part of the Penn game with a quart of Novocain in his leg and sprained it again. So now he is out for a couple of more weeks. I seem to be doing better with the girls, so I guess you are doing your duty out there so before resigning give my *social career* a bit of consideration as it looks now as though I will have to carry Torb also if his leg doesn't get better. . . . Am taking Kick's friend, Charlotte Macdonald out to the Princeton game which will be my first taste of a Catholic girl so will be interested to see how it goes. . . .

This last seems astonishing, if true. Jack is usually said to have been "casual" about his religion, but he was now twenty-two years old and we know he had dated very actively; had the law of averages never produced one Catholic date? Or had he deliberately avoided them?

However that may be, this historic first was Charlotte McDonnell (not Macdonald), the daughter of a wealthy New York stockbroker, James Francis McDonnell. That family has been described in some detail by Stephen Birmingham in a book published in 1973 entitled *Real Lace, America's Irish Rich.*

The most famous of the children of James and Anna Murray McDonnell was a daughter, Anne, who married Henry Ford II on July 13, 1940, in a social event that is sometimes called (as it is by Birmingham in a chapter title) "The Wedding of the Century." Ford, a student at Yale and an Episcopalian, converted to Catholicism in order to marry Anne. Among the bridesmaids were Kathleen Kennedy and Anne's younger sister Charlotte. Birmingham writes:

> Still another rumor [at the time of the Ford-McDonnell wedding] was the engagement of Anne McDonnell's sister Charlotte to young John Fitzgerald Kennedy. This engagement, which lasted only briefly, was thoroughly disapproved of by the Murrays and the McDonnells, particularly Uncle Tom Murray, who considered the Kennedys upstarts. They regarded Jack Kennedy as a "moral roustabout" and his father as a "crook and thorough bounder." Needless to say that marriage did not take place. "If he had married me," Charlotte McDonnell says today, "I'm sure he would never become President," meaning that her own freewheeling and party-loving style of life would have perhaps not been an asset to the White House. Several years later, the then Senator Kennedy was riding up an elevator in New York with Mrs. James Francis McDonnell to attend some Catholic function. "Did you know I al-

most married your daughter?" he asked pleasantly. "I did," said Mrs. McDonnell, "and I'm happy you didn't."

Further on in the book, after describing Joe Kennedy's affair and breakup with Gloria Swanson, Birmingham adds:

The association with Gloria Swanson might be over, but not Joe Kennedy's reputation as a rake. In Catholic circles in New York, it was inevitable that the Kennedy children should meet and mingle with the children of the older-established Murrays and McDonnells, and pretty Charlotte McDonnell became a close school friend of Kennedy's daughter Kathleen "Kick" Kennedy. In the days when both girls were of debutante age, Charlotte . . . recalls an instance when Mr. Kennedy was staying in his Waldorf-Astoria apartment and Mrs. Kennedy was ensconced in a suite at the Plaza. One evening before a party, Charlotte called for her friend at the Waldorf apartment and was met by Mr. Kennedy. After a few pleasantries, Mr. Kennedy jogged her arm, winked mischievously and said: "Leave your coat here. Will Hays is coming by in a little while, and I want him to think I've got a girl in the bedroom."

Charlotte McDonnell married Richard Lewis Harris of Rye, New York, in 1943, and now lives in New York City. We had a pleasant talk with her:

I was quoted by Stephen Birmingham on things I never said. Never in a million years would have said. In other words, he pitted us against the Kennedys. There was no way. That was an absolute lie. There was no animosity between the families. We didn't look down on the Kennedys. We were all friends. You know, essentially, they are a marvelous family. They really are. I hate to see them being dragged through the mud. Kick was my best friend and the Kennedys were my second family.

Q. There's a story about your mother meeting Jack on an elevator . . .

A. That's nonsense. Absolute nonsense.

Q. And there are quotes that everybody considered Joe Senior a kind of crook.

A. Well, I'm afraid that's kind of true.

Q. What about this curious story about you going up to the Waldorf to meet Kick?

A. That's the only story I told Birmingham. That was true. I was about sixteen at the time and pretty shook up. I could not imagine *my* father walking into the room and saying, "Hey, would you believe it? Will Hays thought I had a girl in the bedroom.'' When you're sixteen years old and you've been born and bred in the convent and you've got a very strict father who never deviated from any line, morally or ethically—it did shake me up. But Kick and Jack didn't seem to care. I think maybe they were so used to it.

Q. You mean they were used to their father having women around?

A. Yes. I found that very putting off. They just didn't seem to have the same, for lack of a better word, moral values. Although that is not really the proper word. Respect for women.

Q. Was that also true of Jack?

A. Yes. . . . I went out with Jack lots of times. But he was never in love with me. He liked to think he was, when things were going bad and he didn't have anyone else, but he really wasn't. He'd come down and talk to his friends. He'd talk to Lem and he'd talk to Torby and he'd say, "Hey, what would you think if I married Charlotte?" And they'd have a big pow-wow. But when it comes right down to the nitty-gritty, did he ever ask me to marry him? No, he did not. The two people that Jack was really in love with were Olive Watson—now Tom Watson's wife—and Frances Ann Cannon. We just had a good time together.

He loved the theater. We'd go there or to a restaurant. Up at the Cape, we'd walk on the beach. What do you do at that age? No sex or anything. He was such fun. If you wanted to go to Times Square to see New Year's Eve in, he'd go to Times Square to see New Year's Eve in. I've never done it before or since then. He was bright, very bright. Always interesting to talk to, I don't care what you talked about. He was a very special human being. I was terribly fond of him.

Would I have married him? I don't know. How do you know when you're nineteen, twenty, twenty-one? It's hard to look back that many years and say you were either in love or you weren't. To me, it's just pot luck. If you hit the right one, okay.

He arrived late very often, or he might send one of his friends up to get me, which drove me up the wall. But he was such good company that once you got with him you forgot all that.

I'll tell you one thing. He'd never have been President if he had married me. He might have been a dogcatcher, but that's about it. I don't have any political ambitions. If I'd have gotten into the White House we'd have been at war with the whole world.

In 1943, Dick [Richard L. Harris, her husband] was in the Army—the First Infantry Division—and he wrote me, "You've just

got to make up your mind.'' I made up my mind—we got married—
and thirty-one years later I don't regret it.

The more important relationship of the two, probably by miles, was
that with Frances Ann Cannon. Jack pursued her ardently, then, as Rose
wrote, let her "get away" because he wasn't ready to marry. That may
have been the way the Kennedy family saw it, but we doubt that Frances
Ann had any real intentions of marrying Jack. He was Catholic, Irish, still
a college boy with few serious thoughts in his head and showing no sign of
settling down. In those days, the very eligible John Hersey, then well on
the road to becoming a noted journalist and novelist, must have seemed a
much better mate to a serious-minded girl.

6

Harvard—
The Work of Many Hands

JACK'S academic record at Harvard seems to reflect that era's languorous tradition of the "gentleman's C." In his freshman year, the records show, Jack received a B in Economics, C's in English, French, and History. In his sophomore year he managed one B, four C's and, and a D. But in his junior year—half of it spent abroad—when he brought his research and writing talents to bear in political science, he began to blossom. And in his senior year, with his father's considerable help, he turned these talents to the production of a thesis which enabled him to graduate with honors in political science. With assistance from several of his father's friends, the thesis was turned into a best-selling book, *Why England Slept.*

What first engaged Jack's interest was a course in political science taught by Professor Arthur Holcombe in the first half of his junior year. In *As We Remember Him*, Holcombe recalled:

> The purpose of this upper class course of mine, Government 7, was to answer some definitive questions: What could an intelligent citizen expect to learn about the work of his representative in Congress from the official publications available to the public in public libraries? Jack Kennedy came from Boston. Well, there were a good many Boston boys in the class, and he being a Democrat, I figured he'd learn more if he studied a Republican. I assigned him an upstate New York Congressman who came from Potsdam, as a matter of fact, and was an influential member of the electric power interests of upper New York. His name was Bertram Snell. He had no national reputation, but he was outstanding among upstate Republicans in New York. And an influential member of the Republican leadership in the House in Washington.
>
> Well, the method of conducting the course was to assign a particular question each week. First week, how did your Congressman vote? That you can find out from the *Congressional Record*. Takes a little digging, but the fact is there. Second week, what did he have to say? Third week, what did he do in his committee, and

so on—a series of specific questions that would carry through the term. The object was, in the first place, to get a line on the Congressman's purpose. Did he create the impression of trying to serve the public interest? Or some local or private interest? This particular Congressman was interesting from that point of view. Then the process: What was his method? Did he talk a good deal? Did he have little to say but apparently accomplish his purpose in his committee work, or otherwise out of sight? And, finally, the performance: What was the character of the performance? Did he seem to accomplish his purpose? Did he get some private bills through? Did he influence the form of any measure coming out of his committee? Did he vote?

If you get a fair sample of the whole of Congress, you're going to get a group of findings which should throw a great deal of light on the nature of Congress as a political institution. I tell the boys that when they are discussing public affairs, others offer opinions. You don't simply contradict the man if you hold a different opinion. You ask him, "What's the basis of your opinion? What are the facts upon which these conclusions of yours rest?" Asking the other man questions about the method by which he reached his opinion is the effective way of dealing with a man who differs with you. When Jack took that course, we had a sample of Congress consisting of about one-fifth the total number of districts. It wasn't a perfect sample, but it was not a bad sample. In an hour's discussion of the findings of all the students, you get a pretty good line on the character of the sample, and by implication you get a basis for judgment about the institution.

Jack was very much interested in that. He did a very superior job of investigating, and his final report on his Congressman was a masterpiece. He got so interested that when Christmas vacation came, he went down to Washington, met some of his father's friends, and got a further line on his Congressman and on Congress. Well, that was the method of the course. And Jack was interested in it, did a superb job.

In the postwar years, when Jack was in Congress, he maintained close relations with Holcombe, often going to Harvard for off-the-record seminars, valuable to Holcombe and his students. Jack may have done him other favors such as assisting in getting other politicians to visit Holcombe's seminars. We tried to find Jack's "masterpiece" on Congressman Snell at the Kennedy Library to make an independent judgment. It has either not been released or it may have been lost. However, we see no reason to doubt Holcombe's general assessment: in this class, Jack shone.

The good work Jack did for Holcombe helped earn him a B+ average and put him on the Dean's List for the first semester of 1938, and that made him eligible to graduate with honors. To earn the honors, it was necessary to write a thesis. We spent no little time at the library tracing the evolution of the thesis, reading the original text, and then gathering information on how it was turned into a best-selling book. Jack had, of course, resources beyond those available to most college students, and of course he used them.

The idea for the thesis began to take shape in Jack's mind shortly after he returned from London in September of 1939. He wrote his father a letter, reproduced in *As We Remember Him*, which said in part: "I am taking as my thesis for honors England's Foreign Policy Since 1931, and will discuss the class influence in England. Will get in touch with Jim Seymour if I want him to send me stuff. . . ."

James Seymour was Ambassador Kennedy's personal secretary in London. He had been associated with Joe Kennedy for many years, since the Hollywood days. We could find no indication of how much "stuff" Seymour sent along to Jack. Our surmise was that it was considerable. Later, the ambassador and others in the embassy pitched in to help Jack with his research.

Burns reports that in the winter of 1939–1940, Jack "toiled" at Harvard's Widener Library "studying parliamentary debates, Foreign Office minutes, issues of the *Times* of London and the *Economist*." His mentors on the project were two Harvard political scientists, Bruce Hopper and Payson Wild. Both men have oral histories at the Kennedy Library, but these were among the least instructive there. There was no detail about the thesis, merely some trifling and seemingly unreliable and contradictory recollections. For example, Hopper recalled Jack as a "deep thinker and genuine intellectual." Wild, who was attached to Winthrop House and knew both Joe Junior and Jack much better, seems to argue the opposite. He compared the two brothers, finding Jack inferior to Joe Junior, and quoting Jack as saying on their first meeting: "Dr. Wild, I want you to know that I'm not bright like my brother Joe. . . ."

By early February, Jack was well along with the writing of the first draft, which must have been a nearly full-time occupation. Since he was a poor speller and typist, he decided to hire a secretary to type the manuscript. This decision led to an amusing episode which, though unimportant in itself, sheds some light on Jack's extracurricular record and reputation at Harvard.

In the *Coronet* article on Jack's Harvard days, Torby Macdonald said Jack, who was "leaving for Christmas vacation," asked him to put an ad in the paper and then follow up with interviews. The ad: "WANTED. Stenographer, young, to furnish typewriter, assist on thesis; capable taking shorthand. $20. Apply Wednesday, F-14 Winthrop House Harvard College."

He does not explain why Jack had specified that the stenographer be "young." He says, "I took care of it all right except for one thing. I forgot to give the paper a cutoff date and the ad ran for ten days. On the day I'd set for interviewing applicants, I spent an uncomfortable half hour in the office of one of the college administrators trying to explain the presence of sixty clamoring females outside our dormitory at nine-thirty A.M."

It was February, so Torby's recollection that Jack was leaving for Christmas vacation is clearly in error. In fact, it was the weekend of Ben and Sis Smith's wedding in Chicago. The ad actually ran for three days— Sunday, Monday, and Tuesday. However, it obviously did attract a large number of young females because there was an official investigation of Jack and Torby. A Dr. Else, evidently a disciplinarian in Winthrop House, called Jack on the carpet, then submitted this third-person report:

> Else pointed out the nuisance the whole thing had caused and the doubtful publicity the House had got. One of the Houses had already asked what were our receiving hours here. Else also said that the Dean's office had learned of it, though he did not tell Kennedy how. Else asked how often the secretary was to come to work. Kennedy said he had not thought of having her work in the room except for a few days near the end. The thesis was due March 15. In the beginning he proposed to take the girl to Widener.

One reason for the official investigation was that this was not the first time Jack and Torby had been in trouble for having girls in Winthrop House. On the night of the previous November 25 (the date of the Harvard-Yale game), Jack and Torby had been found "entertaining" girls in their room in violation of house rules. Dr. Ronald Ferry, headmaster of Winthrop House, had investigated and on December 1 he submitted a report indicating that Jack and Torby had gotten out of that by blaming everything on Joe Junior. They said Joe Junior brought the girls up to Jack and Torby's room and then refused to make them leave!

The Dr. Else report on the second incident continues:

> Although neither case was terribly serious in itself, they were beginning to add up and we would deal with any more seriously. Else said that he *might* be allowed to have the secretary in in March, but it was not at all sure and that Dr. Ferry would have to decide that. Else did not threaten him with any immediate punishment, for he thought that Dr. Ferry would want to talk with him

first. Dr. Else's feeling about the whole thing is this: We should make it clear to him that from now on any women in his room for any purpose have to be duly signed for and arranged for. There should be no slip in the technicalities of the rule anymore, and Kennedy should stick close to the proper procedure. Kennedy agreed.

Postscript: After Dr. Ferry had seen Kennedy about the ad which he had put in the paper, he told Kennedy that he was not to have the secretary in his room until perhaps 5 or 6 days toward the end, but no more.

These documents had been released by the Kennedy Library in 1971. A sharp-eyed reporter found them and the story was widely published. Shortly after the story broke in the newspaper, an enterprising Philadelphia *Inquirer* reporter, Robert Fensterer, located the stenographer Jack finally hired and interviewed her. His story, published in the *Inquirer* August 15, 1971, in part:

JFK'S FIRST SECRETARY
RECALLS HIS STUDENT DAYS

Mrs. Marie B. Baker, a lively 58-year-old secretary who lives in Huntingdon Valley, said she couldn't care less whether the late President John F. Kennedy had girls in his room when he was an undergraduate at Harvard College.

"After all," she said, "that was back in 1939, so who should care about that now?"

But then when Mrs. Baker read some newspaper accounts of some incidents based on the recently released Kennedy Papers, she perked up her interest.

"Golly!" she said. "They are talking about me! And it never happened! I was never in Jack Kennedy's room at Harvard or anywhere else. . . ."

For the several weeks that she worked on the paper, she said, she did all her work with Kennedy in the college library.

"Except for the final meeting when we worked on the final draft," Mrs. Baker said. "That was in my mother's home on Commonwealth Ave. in Boston. I assure you that was all very proper."

That summer Kennedy invited her to Bronxville, N.Y., where the family had a home. [To type the manuscript as revised for book publication.]

"They put me up in the Gramatan Hotel in a very luxurious room," she said. "Every morning the family chauffeur would call for me and take me to the Kennedy home where I worked on the manuscript. . . ."

Jack apparently made his March 15 deadline by a whisker. In the Hank Searls book, *The Lost Prince*, there is a letter from Joe Junior to his father which says: "Jack rushed madly around the last week with his thesis and finally with the aid of five stenographers the last day got it under the wire." Joe Junior read the thesis but didn't think much of it. In another letter to his father in *The Lost Prince* he says, "It seemed to represent a lot of work but did not prove anything."

In *As We Remember Him*, there is a letter from Jack to his father: "Finished my thesis. It was only going to run about average length, 70 pages, but finally ran to 150. Am sending you a copy. It is the third carbon, as the other two had to be handed in. . . . Thanks a lot for your wire. Worked it in. I'll be interested to see what you think of it, as it represents more work than I've ever done in my life. . . ."

The focus of the thesis had narrowed considerably, to a study of why and how the British remained so weak militarily in the 1930s in the face of an increasingly aggressive Hitler and his swelling military machine. It was entitled "Appeasement at Munich: The Inevitable Result of Slowness of the British Democracy to Change From a Disarmament Policy."

As we see it, the thesis was, among other things, a whitewash of the British ruling class for the disaster at Munich—for caving in to Hitler. Jack argues that it was not the fault of the rulers—Prime Ministers Stanley Baldwin and Neville Chamberlain—but rather of the democratic system, which has trouble gearing up and responding to an ambiguous threat. In peacetime few people in a democracy want to pay taxes for armaments (in those days, anyway). Furthermore, in the early days, Hitler rearmed in secret and did not seem to have direct designs on Britain.

The argument is by no means silly, but does seem to be stretched rather thin. Why did Jack take this tack? We surmise that it grew out of Jack's newly developed admiration for the British and his friends there. Or perhaps he felt a need to rationalize Munich because his father had supported Chamberlain. At one point, Ambassador Kennedy asserted that it was he who gave Jack his focus. The ambassador came to the United States for Christmas, 1939–1940, and had some long talks with Jack. George Bilainkin, a distinguished journalist who knew the ambassador well in London, writes in his book *Diary of a Diplomatic Correspondent*, published in 1942, that the ambassador said to him in August, 1940: "When I was in the States with Jack and heard some professors talking about Munich, I realized they knew nothing about it. I said to Jack: 'You get down to it and tell them all about it.' "

The faculty voting, on file in Jack's Harvard records:

First vote: "Badly written; but a laborious, interesting and intelligent discussion of a difficult question. MAGNA CUM LAUDE."

Second vote: "Fundamental premise never analyzed—much too long, wordy, repetitious. Bibliography . . . spotty. Many typographical errors. English diction repetitive. CUM LAUDE PLUS."

After he turned in the thesis, Jack went down to Palm Beach for Easter vacation. There, according to some accounts, Jack ran into his father's friend, Arthur Krock. In any event, Jack soon wrote his father a long letter, the text of which is reproduced in *As We Remember Him*:

> I am sending my thesis. The delay has been that it had to be retyped as the first two copies had to be handed in and this copy isn't too clear. Arthur Krock read it and feels that I should get it published. He thinks that a good name for it might be "*Why* England Slept," as sort of contrast to Churchill's "*While* England Slept." The conclusion I have now was done for college and can and should be changed, although I can keep some of the ideas. Krock felt it should be brought out in the spring—May or June—but it would depend on
>
> 1st When you resigned and
> 2nd If you thought it was worth it—
> 3rd If you stayed on later than summer whether it
>   could be published while you are in office.
>
> You can judge that after you've seen it. As I get finished on May 10th with my [classes?] I thought I could work on rewriting it and making it somewhat more interesting for the average reader—as it stands now it is not anywhere polished enough although the ideas etc are O.K. I think Jack Daly [a neighbor in Hyannis Port] also read it and thought it should be done. Whatever I do, however, will depend on what you think is the best thing. Jim Seymour might be able to assist me in some way on the English if I went ahead. . . . Please let me know what you think about the thesis as soon as you can. Am sending it to an agent Krock gave me—and see what he thinks—the chief questions are:
>
> 1 Whether it is worth publishing if polished up.
> 2 If it can be published while you are still in office.

Joe Kennedy told Jack to go ahead. The agent Krock had proposed, Gertrude Algase, began shopping for a publisher. Between sessions with his stenographer in Bronxville, Jack went down to Washington to enlist Krock's help in rewriting. Krock told us, "Gertrude Algase used to write me letters referring to 'this boy.' Fascinating to look at them now. So, in my library in Georgetown—on P Street—he brought the stuff to me and we worked over it. I gave him a title. . . . I was an editor, yes, an adviser, and I may have supplied some of the material as far as the prose is concerned, but it was *his* book. . . ."

Then, on May 20, the ambassador sent Jack a long letter about the thesis. The letter is on file at the Kennedy Library. Interestingly, the father thought Jack had gone overboard in whitewashing the ruling class. He wrote:

> I have shown your thesis to various people around here. Everyone agrees that it is a swell job, and that you must have put in some long hard hours assembling, digesting and documenting all of this material. Most people, I believe, will agree with the fundamentals of your thesis. However, one or two of those who have read it complain that you have gone too far in absolving the leaders of the National Government from responsibility for the state in which England found herself at Munich. These people agree that no good purpose can be served by making scapegoats out of Baldwin and Chamberlain; on the other hand, they feel that you have gone too far in putting the blame on the British public. . . . I am having a mimeographed copy edited here and will get it on the next Clipper. You might also be trying to improve the writing. After you are satisfied with it, ask Krock to go over it again. . . . Check your references. We have found several misspellings of names and a couple of wrong dates.

Burns reports that Jack then replied to his father: "Will stop whitewashing Baldwin," but we could not find that letter.

In his May 20 letter the ambassador had also suggested some specific textual changes, and included some research to buttress his point. Jack incorporated the material almost verbatim into his book as can be seen by this comparison:

Ambassador's letter	*Jack's book*
Germany got a head start on the Allies before they were able to comprehend what she was about. She probably got this head start not so much through the manufacture of actual implements of war, but through the laying a foundation for their manufacture. The German lo-	The truth is that Germany got a head start before the Allies grasped what she was about. This was accomplished not so much by the manufacture of actual implements of war, as by laying a foundation for their manufacture. The German locomotive industry, for ex-

comotive industry, for example, was turned over to the manufacture of tanks instead of rolling stock for the deteriorating German railways. Germany was especially smart in getting tooled up for aircraft production. It takes a couple of years to get factories organized for the munitions on a large scale. Germany got the jump principally through getting everything set for a large-scale output rather than through the output itself, even though the latter certainly was considerable. It was easy for the Allied leaders to overlook this preliminary preparation, as it is difficult to keep track of manufacturing in a foreign country and to know whether an automobile plant is being tooled to produce engines for the "people's car" or to produce engines for planes.

ample, was assigned to the manufacture of tanks instead of rolling stock for the deteriorating German railways. Germany was shrewd in getting tooled-up for aircraft production . . . it takes more than a year to get factories organized for the production of munitions on a large scale. Germany got the jump principally by getting everything set for a large-scale output rather than actual output itself, though its output was considerable.

It is difficult to keep track of manufacturing in a foreign country like Germany where all the preparations are guarded in totalitarian secrecy. . . . During this period, it will be remembered, there was considerable talk about a new, cheap car that would make an automobile available for everyone in the Reich. But it was almost impossible to discover whether an automobile plant was being tooled to produce engines for "the people's car" or to produce engines for planes.

Finally, Jack adapted a portion of his father's letter as the conclusion of his book:

Ambassador's letter	*Jack's book*
You might point out the difficulties our own President has in seeking to awaken the country to the dangers of aggression. To say that democracy has been awakened by the horrible events of the past few weeks	I say therefore that we cannot afford to let England's experience pass unnoticed. Now that the world is ablaze, America has awakened to the problems facing it. But in the past, we have repeatedly refused to ap-

does not prove anything: any system of government would awaken at a time like this. Any person will wake up when the house is burning down. What we want is a kind of government that will wake up when the fire starts or, better yet, one that will not permit a fire to start at all. The American Congress has repeatedly cut the president's request for defense appropriations. And Roosevelt was strong. The English leaders didn't fight for rearmament. Roosevelt fought but Congress resisted and sometimes licked him. Now that the world is ablaze Congress may give him the treasury but we can't escape that democracy in America, like democracy in England, has been asleep at the switch. If God hadn't surrounded us with oceans three and five thousand miles wide, we ourselves might be caving in at some Munich of the Western World. We should profit by the lessons of England and make our democracy work. We must make it work right now. Any system of government will work when everything is going well. It's the system that functions in the pinches that survives.

propriate money for defense. We can't escape the fact that democracy in America, like democracy in England, has been asleep at the switch. If we had not been surrounded by oceans three and five thousand miles wide, we ourselves might be caving in at some Munich of the Western World. To say that democracy has been awakened by these events of the last few weeks is not enough. Any person will awaken when the house is burning down. What we need is an armed guard that will wake up when the fire first starts or, better yet, one that will not permit a fire to start at all. We should profit by the lessons of England and make our democracy work. We must make it work right now. Any system of government will work when everything is going well. It's the system that functions in pinches that survives.

In his *Memoirs*, Arthur Krock, who had worked long and hard on *Why England Slept*, writes that he had expected to write a foreword for the book, but he was upstaged. Joe Kennedy telephoned Henry Luce from London and asked *him* to write the foreword (as Luce recalled in his oral history at the library). With that neat stroke, Joe Kennedy had got both the *New York Times* and the *Time-Life* organization on Jack's side. The agent, Gertrude Algase, made a deal with the firm of Wilfred Funk, Inc. Funk went into a crash program for July publication.

In early June the ambassador wrote Jack a letter which Rose reproduced in her book:

> I am very anxious to read the final copy. I am sure if it reaches the problem as they now visualize it in England, the book will have quite a sale. Chamberlain, Halifax, Montagu Norman, and Harold Laski have all asked me about it. So, whether you make a cent out of it or not, it will do you an amazing amount of good, particularly if it is well received. You would be surprised how a book that really makes the grade with high-class people stands you in good stead for years to come. I remember that in the report you are asked to make after twenty-five years to the Committee at Harvard, one of the questions is "What books have you written?" and there is no doubt you will have done yourself a great deal of good.

When the book was published, it received many excellent reviews. What seemed to impress reviewers most was the fact that the book had been created by such a young man—a college senior! There was no mention of the fact that this young man had rather high-powered help.

Not everybody was pleased with it. Harold Laski, at The London School of Economics, wrote the ambassador a letter, reproduced in Koskoff:

DEAR JOE,

The easy thing for me to do would be to repeat the eulogies that Krock and Harry Luce have showered on your boy's work.

In fact I choose the more difficult way of regretting deeply that you let him publish it. For while it is a book of a lad with brains, it is very immature, it has no real structure, and it dwells almost wholly on the surface of things. In a good university, half a hundred seniors do books like this as part of their normal work in their final year. But they don't publish them for the good reason that their importance lies solely in what they get out of doing them and not in what they have to say. I don't honestly think any publisher would have looked at that book of Jack's if he had not been your son, and if you had not been Ambassador. And those are not the right grounds for publication.

I care a lot about your boys. I don't want them to be spoilt as rich men's sons are so easily spoilt. Thinking is a hard business and you have to pay the price for admission to it. Do believe that these hard sayings from me represent much more real friendship than the easy price of "yes men" like Arthur Krock.

We must add that our reading of the book—as well as two typescript versions of the thesis—supports Laski's view of the project. The book is a vast improvement over the thesis, but still its popular success can only be accounted for by its timing. As evidenced by best-seller lists of the time, the American book-buying public was starved for information on the war and its beginnings in Europe; *Why England Slept* was one of the first books to promise to satisfy that hunger.

In June 1940, Jack was graduated from Harvard *cum laude*. He was twenty-three, a year behind his contemporaries. Rose writes that she, Rosemary (who had come home from England), Eunice, and Bobby attended the ceremony. (Joe Junior was off on a boating trip; we do not know where Kick was.) Burns reports that the ambassador sent Jack a cable from London that concluded: TWO THINGS I ALWAYS KNEW ABOUT YOU ONE THAT YOU ARE SMART AND TWO THAT YOU ARE A SWELL GUY.

In thinking back over Jack's years at Harvard, ages nineteen to twenty-three, we came to the inescapable conclusion that during this period of his life Jack was completely dominated by his father. He attended Harvard instead of his first choice, Princeton, because his father insisted on it. For twelve months of the elapsed forty-eight months, he was actually working in close concert with his father in Europe. As we have seen, he kept his father posted on the girls he was dating. Finally, the ambassador influenced his son in the choice of his thesis—Jack's most notable achievement at Harvard—and then devoted considerable time to shaping Jack's ideas and the final product.

We searched in vain for some sign that Jack might be rebelling or striking out on his own, emotionally or intellectually. Burns writes that the Harvard campus was then "boiling with ideas, fads, stunts—a ferment of protest against parents, deans, and more in the 1930s than ever before, politics. . . ." But, as Burns goes on to say, Jack "took no part in this." He was conservative in outlook; cautious in commitment: his father's son.

7

A Lark

THE summer of 1940 was a time of grave uncertainty for everybody, and not least for a young man trying to plan a future. In the spring, Hitler's armies had occupied Denmark and Norway. Then, in May and June, he occupied Belgium, Luxembourg, the Netherlands, and France. Mussolini brought Italy into the war on Hitler's side. On the other side of the world, Japan stepped up her military conquest of China.

Domestic politics ranked side by side with the calamitous international situation in Kennedy family dinner-table discussions. As Krock told us and as others have said (Koskoff details it at length), Ambassador Kennedy had presidential ambitions for 1940. He thought that Roosevelt would step aside, as had his predecessors after two terms, and might support Kennedy's bid for the nomination at the Democratic National Convention. But Roosevelt declared for a third term, leaving Kennedy high and dry—and angry. As Koskoff reports, Kennedy felt Roosevelt had betrayed him.

The "betrayal," we gather, cast Ambassador Kennedy into a depression. He remained in London that summer of 1940—missing his family—and into the fall, when the Nazis began the bombing of London and other English cities. But he was increasingly pessimistic and defeatist. He didn't think the British Isles could survive Hitler's onslaught—and freely gave vent to his feelings in public. The British press, which had fawned over Kennedy and his family, turned against him. Roosevelt, then actively working out secret agreements to help the British, became increasingly annoyed with him.

It appears that originally Jack and Kick had planned to spend the summer of 1940 in London with their father. There is a letter from Jack to his father, written about June 1 and published in *As We Remember Him*. By then Jack seems to have lost interest in the trip, but he makes a strong pitch for Kick. Interestingly, Jack seems mindful of the criticism that had been leveled at the Kennedy family for fleeing Britain at the outbreak of the war: "I gather from your last letter to mother that you did not think it too advisable for us to come over this summer. I should like to come very much if there is anything of interest going on—otherwise I shall stay at

87

the Cape. Kick is very keen to go over—and I wouldn't think the anti-American feeling would hurt her like it might us—due to her being a girl—especially as it would show that we hadn't merely left England when it got unpleasant. . . ."

Jack's book came out in July. Henry Ford and Anne McDonnell were married in July in New York City and the Kennedys were very much involved in those festivities.

Jack did not see much of his close friends that summer. Billings was working for the Coca-Cola Company in Bridgeport, Connecticut. Torby, who planned to go to Harvard Law School that coming fall, spent the summer playing professional baseball with a New York Yankees farm team in Newark, New Jersey. Rip Horton, who had also got sick, dropped a year, and was graduated from Princeton in June, 1940, was working for Continental Can Company in New Jersey. Ben Smith, now a married man, joined the family seafood business in Gloucester.

That summer at the Cape, Jack made a new friend who would become and remain one of his closest. He was Charles F. Spalding (often misspelled "Spaulding" in the Kennedy books). We located Spalding in New York City, where he works for a large investment banking firm. He invited us to his office for lunch, taking our sandwich orders in advance.

We were met by a striking figure: 6 feet 4½ inches tall, thin as a rail. He reminded us of a beardless Lincoln, even to the somber and brooding expression. But as we talked his green eyes glinted happily and he proceeded to give us one of our finest interviews: candid, deeply thoughtful, and amusing. About his background, he told us he was born in 1918 in the Chicago suburb of Lake Forest, son of a stockbroker who had married into the Cudahy (meatpacking) family. Chuck attended private schools in Chicago, then went on to The Hill School and, like his father and others in the family, Yale University. He said:

I was always very thin, almost comically thin, and I grew very tall, very suddenly. I read a great deal. I was pulled out of Yale at Christmastime my first year—1936. Just like Jack at Princeton. I was a little too fragile. I had a lot of bronchitis. I suppose it was the culmination of being too thin too long. I started to play a lot of tennis. My mother took me abroad in the spring and summer of 1937 and I played tournament tennis with some European stars at Cannes and Monte Carlo. When I reentered Yale that fall, I joined the Yale tennis team and stayed on it. And I started to write—for the *Alumni Weekly* and a satirical column for the *Yale Daily News*. In the summer of 1940, between my junior and senior years, I met Jack Kennedy through a close friend at Yale, George Mead, who had a summer home on Great Island in Hyannis. During summers we'd visit back and forth.

We had heard from others that George Mead had been another of Jack and Kick's close friends. Mead had been killed in the war, on Guadalcanal, Spalding told us. From various sources, including his mother, Elsie T. Mead, and George's best friend, Paul Moore, now the Episcopal Bishop of New York, we later shaped a portrait: He was the son of George Mead, founder and principal owner of the huge Mead Paper Company in Dayton, Ohio. He attended Hotchkiss School, then Yale, where he managed the varsity football team, played hockey and polo. Bishop Moore (who named one of his nine children for George) told us George had been an exceedingly friendly, popular, and decent young man. He joined the Marines early and was killed. Of that tragedy, more later.

Chuck Spalding had given the Kennedy Library an oral history on his first meeting with Jack and his impressions. In addition, he had supplied Rose a letter for her book, similar in content. We had made notes of these sources and brought them to the interview:

> One day George Mead and I were golfing at the Cape. On the way home, about suppertime, we stopped off at the Kennedys'. I remember all the kids hanging out the windows taunting George. They told him to go home; there was not enough food for us. Jack was in the living room with a big pile of his book, *Why England Slept.* He was promoting the book. There were letters from all over—one from a prime minister under a bathing suit. The whole family was in turmoil, moving in every direction, vitally involved and interested in what was going on.

He expanded on this account of his first meeting with the Kennedy family for us, describing his own reactions:

> Right then it seemed to me that this was something special. I was just going along, a guy who grew up during the Depression when life really seemed to stop. It was still the Depression, really. It had taken so much wind out of the sails of the Cudahys and Spaldings. I wasn't a Depression child in the sense that I knew the real hardships of the Depression . . . but I didn't have any aims. What struck me was the very strong sense of direction that had been implanted in this house by Mr. Kennedy. And thoroughly subscribed to by everybody else. It was terribly exciting and had all the elements I was looking for. . . . It is a very startling thing to run into. You can go your whole life without finding that kind of excitement. My father's friends and contemporaries hadn't managed to survive the Depression the way Mr. Kennedy had. He really had been able to capitalize on the Depression. And here it all was, located in the Kennedys. It really startled me and gave me a terrific lift.

In his oral history, Spalding had said of Jack, "There were times when his health put him out of commission, but in other times he was euphoric, the greatest company. He was so bright, so restless, and so determined to use every last minute that he set a pace that was abnormal. He had the sense of not being well—and how much time is there? I think I'd only seen a couple of people in my life who gave that heightened sense of being—a pleasant heightened sense of being."

Our interview with Chuck Spalding went on for three or four hours; we shall return to it again in this narrative. He was quite different from Torby Macdonald, Ben Smith, and Charlie Houghton. He was not a football player; he was the closest thing to an intellectual we found among Jack's close friends. His sense of humor—and irony—was sharply developed.

Before Jack was graduated from Harvard he had toyed with the idea of going to law school. In the spring of 1940 he asked Harvard to send a transcript of his records to Yale Law School. One of his teachers, Bruce Hopper, thought that Jack was thinking of specializing in international law. How serious his interest really was is a matter for speculation; it does not seem to us that he had the temperament for the highly disciplined, rigidly structured regimen of a law school. However, as we shall see, the idea came up again the next spring.

Lem Billings had told us:

> I think he played with the idea of going to law school, but he didn't go to law school. Jack wrote very well. There was no question about it; he knew he had intellectual interests. I don't think there was any question but that he was thinking he would go into journalism and teaching. You've got to realize there was an awful vacuum there in 1940, a very uncomfortable period for a guy who was graduating from school. I mean, what to do? We were so damn close to going to war. There was no depth in the future. You didn't know what you were going to do so what was the point of getting into any lifelong thing? I think every boy at that time was just sort of marking time. . . .

And besides that, Jack was afflicted by still another ailment. There is a prescription in the 1940 files at the Kennedy Library from Dr. Sara Jordan, one of the few official documents on Jack's health we found. It is written in a spidery hand, very difficult to read. Our deciphering: "Continue care in diet. Take a Trasentin [?] tablet before each meal & in early morning. Take a Trasentin [?] tablet on first awakening. Apply heat to abdomen on first awakening for fifteen minutes before arising. Take no Ampliozel [?] except for distress. Continue using Ceritraine acid tablets and vitamin B complex *faithfully*."

We consulted a physician for guidance. He said the prescription indicated stomach trouble: a serious gastrointestinal disorder, perhaps even ulcers.

And then there was a note from former Ambassador William C. Bullitt which indicates in passing that Jack had been to the Mayo Clinic in Rochester, Minnesota. Bullitt wrote that his aide, Offie, had told him "that you recently made a trip to Rochester. I hope they told you there is absolutely nothing wrong with you. I am still convinced you are in perfect order."

At the Library of Congress we found a letter in the papers of James M. Landis, one of Joseph Kennedy's Harvard Law School friends whom Kennedy had recruited to help at the SEC, and who was then dean of the Harvard Law School. The letter was dated August 6, 1940, from the ambassador in London to Landis. In part: "Jack also intended going to Law School this year, although he thought he would go to Yale, principally because he felt it would be better not to be constantly in direct competition with his brother, and I rather sympathize with him in that point of view. However, Jack has been having trouble for a number of years with his stomach and I now hear that the doctors advise him to take a year off. I hate to see him lose a year in these crucial times, but, after all, his health is more important."

This was a new light on Jack's health. Some of the Kennedy books say that Jack's stomach gave him trouble in his House and Senate days. But there is no hint that this trouble extended back to his college days, or perhaps before. Some Kennedy books ascribe the stomach trouble—like the back injury—to the stress of the *PT-109* incident. One political aide said to us, "It was the *PT-109* thing. He swallowed a lot of gasoline."

Toward the end of the summer, Jack arrived at what seemed a somewhat mystifying decision as to what he would do in the immediate future: he would enroll at Stanford University in Palo Alto, California. Torby told us he thought it was because Stanford had a good school of journalism and Jack wanted to develop his writing skills. But Rose has a different explanation. She writes: "He had thought of law school. Then, perhaps because Joe Junior was to be a lawyer, he thought of becoming a businessman. Jack evidently figured that if the life of a businessman and financier was interesting enough for his father it would be interesting for him. Consequently in the fall of 1940, he had enrolled in courses in economics, finance, and business administration at Stanford University."

Maybe so; certainly, as we have seen, he was his father's son; but it is difficult to picture Jack as a businessman. And if that were his aim, why Stanford? Why not the Harvard Graduate School of Business? We looked for some other reason—or reasons—for Jack's going to Stanford. The inquiry soon led us to Tom Killefer, now a vice-president of the Chrysler Corporation, then in Harvard Law School, and a close friend and roommate of Joe Junior's. Killefer, whom Jack knew well, told us: "I was probably a big influence on Jack going to Stanford. I talked to him a lot about Stanford that previous Christmas [1939] when I was visiting the Kennedys at Palm Beach. That summer—1940—Joe Junior came out for a long visit at my house in Hermosa Beach, California, so maybe he helped put the bug in Jack's ear. From all I heard, Jack had a very good time at Stanford. Maybe too good a time. He was really bombing around that place and he was on the town a great deal. I think he had a much better time than he deserved to have. . . .'

We knew that Jack's sister Eunice had followed him to Stanford. In a wide-ranging interview with her (to which we shall, of course, return later) we asked her about Jack's reasons for going there: "I think it was because he wasn't feeling terribly well. He had back and stomach problems. He had nothing very pressing to do, but he wanted to continue his education. I think the climate had a lot to do with it. At Stanford he'd be able to swim and exercise and be healthy, which he wanted to be, and he'd be able to proceed with his intellectual interests. Jack never liked the cold. He always liked the warm, the heat. He loved to swim. He always went where the sun was. . . ."

And that is probably the solution to the Stanford mystery—not much of a mystery, really. Facing the uncertainty of the times, Jack was not sure what he wanted to do. He sought the sun, a good climate. Having heard about Stanford from Tom Killefer (and perhaps Joe Junior), he enrolled there to continue his studies, as Eunice said, and, as Killefer said, to "bomb around" and have a good time. Most assuredly he had not, as Rose puts it, gone to Stanford "with the thought of being a businessman."

The publicity director at Stanford provided us with a variety of material from which we distilled this history:

Jack enrolled at Stanford in the fall of 1940 under a "permit to attend"; that is, with permission to audit graduate school classes without credit. Stanford was then on the quarter system; Jack did not spend a semester at Stanford (as Burns, Rose, and others wrote) but only ninety days in the fall quarter, September to December. Professor Theodore Kreps remembered Kennedy attending a graduate class in business administration and government. Jack also audited two political science courses offered by Professors Thomas S. Barclay and Graham S. Stuart. He lived in a cottage on campus owned by the late Miss Gertrude Gardiner, 624, Mayfield Avenue. Rent: $60 per month. Miss Gardiner remembered Jack "sunning himself" on the cottage terrace. In October, 1940, Jack had registered for the draft. There was a photograph in the packet of a very young, earnest-looking Jack wearing a black-knit tie and a windbreaker, apparently signing his draft papers, with some other Stanford students.

Among the material was an undated copy of a story in *The Stanford Daily*, written by Jean Nowell. The headline: AUTHOR KENNEDY FOLLOWS KILLEFER RECOMMENDATION. There was a photograph of Jack, smiling wanly. The story began: "When Jack Kennedy, late of The London School of Economics and Harvard. . . ." It was mostly about Jack's book, *Why England Slept*. Nowell wrote that Jack planned to spend a year at Stanford concentrating on economics courses, after which he would return East to Yale Law School. She quoted Jack on his reasons for choosing Stanford: "I picked Stanford principally because of your ex-student body president and student manager Tom Killefer. He was my brother's roommate at Harvard and he sneered so at the Florida climate when he was staying with us there that I had to find out if it is really the climate or just Killefer. So far he's right, but wait until I see that first cloud. . . ."

Also in the Stanford material was a press release referring to an article in *Esquire*, August, 1966, about Jack's days at Stanford. The title: "Rich, Young and Happy." The author was Harry Muheim, a Stanford graduate who was described as a "television writer." Excerpts:

I first met Mr. Kennedy in late September of 1940. It was the twilight of a fine California day on the Stanford campus when he and Bruce Jessup, the new student-body president, pulled into the unkempt driveway of the Kappa Alpha house to pick me up. I had expected Jessup alone and on foot, so I was surprised to see him sweep up as the passenger in a brand-new cactus-green 1941 Buick convertible. The top was down, a laughing stranger was at the wheel, Jessup was laughing too, and like many young men on the Stanford campus, they looked healthy and happy and rich. I looked that way myself.

As the car crunched to a halt, I glanced into the back seat where six identical new books were slewed across the green leather. On each jacket, the title *Why England Slept*, was superimposed on the British flag, and I knew immediately who the driver was. A week or so before, there had been an article in *The Stanford Daily* about Jack Kennedy's arrival on campus, about his book, *Why England Slept*. . . . He said he was glad to meet me. . . . We swung down The Row, purring past fraternity houses at a good clip. . . . . I don't know how he drove when he got older, but in September of 1940, Kennedy drove too fast with no effort at all. . . .

The three young men, Muheim wrote, were bound for a dinner party for faculty and students at the home of a Stanford professor. Muheim continues:

Even when you didn't care much about the conversation, Jack
Kennedy was compelling. He was quick to explain, to ask, to consider. His sentences flowed spontaneously. Gags were naturally in-
terspersed with the straight material. Illustrations and examples
were brought in without effort from several locations and several
centuries. I had never before heard one of my contemporaries *al-
lude* to so many things. . . .

At the party, Muheim was impressed by the deference and respect
shown Kennedy by the faculty members. He was also struck by Kennedy's earnestness, facile mind, and powers of persuasion.

Jack Kennedy's message for the remote Westerners was that
there was a war on, that it had been on for a year, and that we were
going to get into it. I had heard the same thing before from other
people—in various veiled ways from President Roosevelt himself
on the radio—but it was not until that night that I believed it. . . .
Jack Kennedy did not seem depressed by the news that he brought
us. Even though the subject was solemn, he kept tossing bright humor into the exchange and several times he had the place roaring
with laughter. . . . The faculty members were laughing too.

Muheim wrote that he saw Kennedy again about a week later. He was
parked illegally in front of the Stanford bookstore, with the convertible
top down.

He was . . . chatting with a strikingly beautiful co-ed named
Harriet Price. She stood on the curb next to the car . . . laughing
delightedly at something Jack Kennedy had said. She was also
pushing back a wisp of her long honey-colored hair with the thumb
of her right hand, and at the same time dexterously holding a light-
ed cigarette between the first two fingers of the same hand. . . .
Kennedy sat beaming up at her expansively, thoroughly enjoying
the moment, one arm hooked over the top of the car door, the other stretched along the top of the green leather seat.

We located Harry Muheim living in a suburb of Washington; from him
and others we compiled a list of people who had known Jack at Stanford.
All lived on the West Coast. We flew to California to have a look at Stanford and to interview the people on our list.

The university lies about thirty miles south of downtown San Francisco
in a beautiful valley. On the west side there is a low coastal mountain
range, and beyond it the Pacific Ocean. The campus itself is enormous,
over 8,000 acres. The buildings are neo-Spanish: low, tan in color, with

red tile roofs. The school was founded in 1891 by Leland Stanford in memory of his son, Leland, Jr., who died at age fifteen of typhoid fever. It attracted the sons and daughters of the Far West's rich, social families. When Jack enrolled in 1940, there were about 5,000 students. It was an exclusive, conservative, Establishment institution.

We had heard from several sources that Jack had dated Nancy Burkett. One, Charles F. Bulotti, Jr., told us Nancy had been one of the best-looking girls on campus. She came from an old, social San Francisco family. Bulotti said: "Nancy was conservative, almost prim—Miss Straight Arrow. She always drank milk. It was really something to see her in the Mark Hopkins bar at one in the morning ordering a glass of milk."

Nancy, now Mrs. Robert S. Morse, met us in San Francisco. She has hazel eyes and brunette hair and is very slim and pretty. She recalled:

> I was in Europe in 1939. My mother and sister and I went to the Fourth of July party at the embassy in London. I saw Jack then, but we didn't meet. When the war broke out we were in Italy and got a boat home. I returned to Stanford. I was a Kappa Kappa Gamma and lived in the Kappa house with thirty or forty girls. . . . A girl in our house, Molly Moser, I think, had a letter from somebody back East saying Jack was coming. He looked her up and I met him at the Kappa house. He created a stir. He was a glamorous arrival, in my eyes anyway. Everybody knew who he was—son of the ambassador. He drove a navy blue—I think— Buick convertible with red leather seats. He wore casual Ivy League clothes—polo shirts and sneakers. He had a big mop of blond hair. He took me to San Francisco to the opera and around Palo Alto to various eating places. On one of our first dates we went to L'Omelette, a favorite hangout for Stanford students. We took a back road and came to a ninety-degree turn. Jack wasn't expecting it. He turned too sharply. The car went up on a bank and I was thrown down on top of him. He shoved me back and we got the car stabilized. I really thought this big, open car was going to fall on top of us. That's the closest I ever came to being crushed in a car.

We asked about Jack's health.

> I know he had back problems because driving the car a lot made it hurt. I heard him mention it several times. I don't remember that he was a picky eater. He wasn't the most tidy eater. He didn't worry too much about his manners. He was just casual. I think he had other things on his mind. He was too interested in conversation.
>
> He autographed one of his books for me—"To Nancy who's

heard it all before." But he misspelled "who's," writing "whose."
I corrected it with an eraser. I wish I hadn't now. He liked to talk
about his father, I think he had great respect for his father. When
we went to dinner, Jack never drank anything and he didn't smoke.
It was really unusual to know a boy who didn't even drink beer. He
said he didn't drink because he had promised his father he
wouldn't. I felt there were very close ties between Jack and his father. His father came here. Jack wanted me to go to lunch with
them at L'Omelette. I had a biology lab and exam and couldn't go.
Jack said: "Just this once?" I said no. So I never did meet his father. Nor his mother, who was also here about that time.

In the fall of 1940, while Jack was at Stanford, the ambassador finally
resigned and came home. There had been speculation in the press that he
might oppose Roosevelt for election and declare in favor of Wendell
Willkie, but Kennedy supported the president. Afterward he launched his
own personal campaign to try to keep America out of the war. In mid-
November he had come to California for that purpose and he and Rose
stopped for a few days at Stanford. We found photographs of Jack meeting his father at the San Francisco airport in both the AP and UPI photo
libraries. Jack looks unusually dapper in a dark pinstripe suit.
　We asked Nancy how serious she and Jack had been and what finally
happened. She said:

　　I went out with him quite a bit, but I dated other boys, too. I had
　a crush on Jack. I didn't get to know him well enough to be in love
　with him. I was certainly fascinated with him. I guess he liked me
　or he wouldn't have kept asking me out. Then came the weekend
　of the Big Game against our rival, California at Berkeley. That's a
　very special occasion at Stanford. It's in November and it's always
　followed by a big weekend party down on the Monterey Peninsula.
　That year we had a fabulous football team and it was extra special.
　Jack asked me for a date. . . . But, you see, the previous August
　a boy I had known since I was sixteen, Bradford Young, asked me
　to go to the Big Game and I had said yes. So I had to tell Jack no.
　That plus not going to lunch with his father did it. But I saw him a
　couple of times later in the war and after. . . .

Knowing of Jack's deep interest in football, we took pains to confirm
that Stanford had fielded a "fabulous" team that year. It was in fact one
of the greatest teams in Stanford history—undefeated, winner of the Rose
Bowl game, and ranked second in the nation, after Minnesota. Jack had
been caught up in the excitement. Jean Nowell's *Daily* story of 1940 quot-

ed him as saying, "You have no idea how it feels to yell for a winning team," and went on: "He was amazed at the rooting section's spirit and thinks the women probably have something to do with it. . . . 'At Harvard whenever they ask for undergraduate opinion on what would improve the school, about 80% of the suggestions are to make the school coeducational. . . . I think I'll have one of my sisters come here.' "

Jeanne Bouchard had been a sorority sister—a Pi Phi—of the girl Harry Muheim mentioned in the *Esquire* piece, Harriet Price, who was nicknamed "Flip." Jeanne's younger sister Patricia had also been a Pi Phi and a good friend of Flip's. All three had lived at the Pi Phi house at the same time. Jeanne said:

It was an old brown shingle house. Thirty girls lived there. The boys would come in and yell up the stairs for their dates, then wait in the living room. I remember meeting Jack there when he was dating Flip. Flip was actually two years behind me. She was most attractive. She had wide-apart eyes and a rather broad face. She had a sexy figure and kind of slunk around when she walked. The boys were just crazy about her. It was natural that Jack should be attracted to her. She was lots of fun and very vivacious. If you had a big date, you always went to San Francisco. To the hotels which had orchestras. The St. Francis and the Mark Hopkins were the most popular. Or there were restaurants here—L'Omelette and Dinah's. Then there were two bars—sort of roadhouses—Autens and Ethans, which were not so elegant. On Big Game weekends we all went down to Del Monte—to the Del Monte Hotel to spend the weekend. Everybody would get all dressed up and go to a dinner dance. The next day you'd get up, have breakfast, and sit around the hotel, then, if the weather was good, go to the beach at Carmel for a while. Then you'd drive back in time for the midnight lockout Sunday night.

One weekend my sister Patty and Flip and some other Pi Phi's went down to Los Angeles for the UCLA game. Jack went down for the weekend with a blond boy from the East nicknamed Hank the Tank. The game was played on Saturday, November 2, 1940. The girls stayed at our house. My mother invited the boys for dinner. She served pot roast—my sister's favorite dinner. My mother told me later that neither Jack nor Hank the Tank took *any* food that was passed. They ate absolutely nothing! My mother thought maybe it wasn't fancy enough for those Easterners. Later someone told her that both of them had ulcers. When he was there, Jack talked to my father—who was a lawyer—about world affairs and gave the family one of his books. It was inscribed to Patty and me.

Hank the Tank was Henry James, Jr. We reached him by telephone at Sweet Briar College in Virginia, where he is a librarian. He told us that he grew up in New York City and Southampton, Long Island. He had met Kathleen Kennedy at the McDonnell place in Southampton. He was in graduate school at Stanford. He said:

> I saw an article about Jack in the *Daily* and looked him up. We were not close friends but went around in the same groups. He gave me the nickname Hank the Tank. A joke. I didn't even drink! I had ulcers and it would have killed me. I didn't take offense. Jack was so irresistibly charming you couldn't. He was in frail health out there. He had come to Stanford because of the mild climate, I think. He wasn't excited by Stanford academically. He had the Harvard view, of course.
>
> I remember Flip well. Jack took her to all the best places in San Francisco. . . . After Stanford, Jack and I more or less drifted apart. I saw him once in Palm Beach during the war, 1942. The military wouldn't take me, but Jack—who was prime 4-F material— got in the Navy somehow. I didn't see him after the war.
>
> I kept a diary at Stanford. In 1970 some burglars broke into my house in New York and stole it and some jewelry. They caught the men, but never recovered the diary. Too bad. I think I had a lot about Jack at Stanford in it.

Harriet Price, now Mrs. James Davis Fullerton, talked with us in her large, elegant home in Pasadena. Flip is, as she has been described, quite beautiful—slim and brown-eyed. She seemed a trifle shy. She told us:

> I liked Jack immediately. He was very attractive, tall and slim, sparkly and, I guess, Irish-looking. And fun. But he always had a serious side, too. His book was out. He gave me a copy. We used to go to L'Omelette, a French place, and Dinah's Shack, a steak house and bar with a fireplace. Or to the hotels in San Francisco for dinner and dancing. One night we were driving by the Mark Hopkins in Jack's Buick convertible and all of a sudden he slammed on the brakes, jumped out of the car and ran across the street and threw his arms around a woman. It turned out to be an old nurse of his. I don't think he had seen her for about ten years. It was just out of the blue. .. . .
>
> We always went out alone. He was a loner. Photographers were always taking his picture at the St. Francis and elsewhere. He was sort of a minicelebrity. I was in love with him. I was wildly in love with him. I think Jack was in love with me. We talked about the

possibility of marriage—a little bit, but not seriously. Jack took me to the Big Game—Stanford versus Berkeley. He had a bad back—slept on a board. After the game his back hurt him a lot. It had been a long day on hard benches. We went Dutch from the game—as was the tradition—to the old Del Monte Lodge for the weekend. It was six dollars apiece for the room, dinner, dancing, breakfast—the works. He was tired so I drove the Buick with the top down. He was lying on the back seat and I was driving pretty fast and I had to slam on the brakes. He fell on the floor and cursed a blue streak. I learned a lot of words I never heard before from Jack Kennedy. Now it would be nothing, but then it was rather startling. . . .

I met his mother when she came out to visit him. She came to the Pi Phi house for lunch. It was a big occasion for all of us—the wife of the ex-ambassador and all that, so we girls put on our best finery, including, I think, white gloves. But Mrs. Kennedy came with her hair up in curlers! We were really shocked. No one could believe it or understand it. . . .

Jack was never a drinker. I was surprised, but he never seemed to miss it. He didn't need it and I don't think he'd have liked the blurring of the mind. World affairs were very important to him. I think he was thinking about politics all along—and himself in politics. Listening to the news was terribly important to him. He listened to *every* radio news broadcast. When we were driving around San Francisco one time, I turned it off. He was furious. We had one of our worst fights. He had a wild temper. He was really angry. Once he went down to spend a weekend with the Hearsts—at the Hearst ranch on the coast. I think Marion Davies was there. He came back and told me—I remember this clearly—that on this sumptuous, huge dinner table in the banquet hall or whatever, he saw a *bottle* of catsup!

We asked Flip—as we had asked Nancy Burkett—what happened in the end? She looked somewhat uneasy and her memory seemed to fail. She went upstairs and brought down several letters Jack had written her in 1941 and 1942 and a postcard from Palm beach signed "H the T." She also had a photograph of her and Jack taken, she said, at the Glendale Railroad Station. After she read the letters into the tape, she said vaguely: "The whole thing just fizzled out. . . . The war came. . . . He went away. . . ."

We pressed for further details. She could not remember when Jack had left Stanford or why. She recalled that Jack had left the Buick with her but could not remember what she had done with it. Nor could she remember what the occasion was when the picture was taken at Glendale station. We had the feeling that we were invading private territory, so we broke off the interview.

We called on Professor Thomas S. Barclay, whose political science course Jack had audited. He is now retired and getting on in years. He gave us the impression Jack had been more interested in political science than in his business school courses:

> For many years Stanford was one of the two leading institutions of higher learning in the West, along with [the University of California at] Berkeley. The professional schools—medical, law, engineering—were small but adequate. The graduate school of business was second in the U.S.—after Harvard. The majority of the faculty regarded themselves as members of the Republican Party. There were no radical students here then. I went to the 1940 Democratic convention and when I got back here, Miss Gardiner, who owned the apartment where I lived on Mayfield Avenue, told me that Jack Kennedy had rented the cottage out back, where I had once lived. I met him right away and saw him almost every day for the next three months. He was a careless housekeeper, but he paid his rent. I didn't ask him why he was here. He had graduated from Harvard, attended The London School of Economics in England, and I don't think he knew what he wanted to do. . . . He was shopping around. He attended my classes occasionally, especially my seminar in politics in which we discussed the 1940 campaign and other things. It was a small group of seven or eight students. Jack was exceedingly attractive and had a charming manner. He was well-informed and intelligent in the field of politics and international relations.

Michael Levee, who was a student at Stanford in 1940, is now a motion picture producer in Los Angeles. He recalled:

> I was a Jew and a Democrat at Stanford. Being a Democrat was a rarity, but being a Jew was even rarer. They had only a small quota of Jews. I was co-chairman of the Stanford chapter of the Fight For Freedom Committee, a nationwide organization which backed Roosevelt's support of Britain and France against Germany. During the 1940 presidential election I had a Roosevelt sticker on my car and people I thought were my friends—girls as well as boys—would not ride in the car with me because of the Roosevelt sticker. But Jack would ride in the car with me, maybe *because* I

had a Roosevelt sticker. Jack had written that book and he was
very committed to this kind of position. . . . But he was not actually a member of the committee.

William Lyng Turner, Jr., was one of the boys with Jack in the draft
registration photograph. He is now president of a paint company in Oak-
land. He remembered registering for the draft with Jack. In fact, he had
only recently written a small piece about it for a local magazine, *Architect
and Contractor.* He later sent us several pages from his scrapbook. From
our talk and the scrapbook and other sources, we were able to construct
this outline of what had happened.

In the summer of 1940 Congress had passed the Selective Service and
Training Bill—the first peacetime draft in the nation's history. The isolationists (Senator Burton K. Wheeler, the *Chicago Tribune*, etc.) were
fiercely opposed to the draft, but a Gallup poll in mid-August disclosed
that 71 percent of the nation was behind it. The bill became law on September 16, about the time Jack left for Stanford.

Draft boards were established and all men between the ages of twenty-
one and thirty-five were required to register on October 16, 1940. This
was the date of the photograph. In late October the draft officials would
draw numbers in a lottery. College students would be deferred until the
end of the school year—June, 1941. Some would be eligible for call-up in
July, 1941.

Bill Turner said:

> The draft was a very unpopular cause on campus. I was a com-
> mitteeman, active in campus affairs, and knew the president of
> Stanford, Ray Lyman Wilbur. He had put the finger on me in the
> past for help—for one thing, Young America Wants to Help [a stu-
> dent organiation supporting Roosevelt's support for Britain]. I
> went to Washington on that, and met FDR with a lot of other stu-
> dents. So when the draft thing came up, I was appointed head of
> the National Emergency Committee, a group of students on the
> Stanford campus to liaison with the draft board. Jack Kennedy be-
> came a member of that committee through the same pres-
> sures. . . .
>
> Q. They enlisted you, as a popular figure on campus to put your
> weight behind the unpopular draft?
>
> A. I think that's right. And Jack Kennedy, too. . . . That was
> the origin of the photograph. It appeared in the San Francisco pa-
> pers. . . .

Jack had lent himself to other pro-draft publicity, Torby Macdonald had told us in his interview: "The first I knew about his being called up was when I was at the movies and saw a newsreel of Jack being drafted. I called him up and we talked about it. . . ."

Rip Horton saw the same newsreel. In his oral history at the Kennedy Library, he recalled, "I can remember clearly one time being in a movie and watching the news. It was just at the time the draft was put into effect—drafting men into the Army. Young Jack Kennedy had one of the lowest draft numbers. This picture was flashed on the screen and I remember getting quite a kick out of it, thinking in terms of him being drafted into the service. He was out on the West Coast at the time. What was particularly odd about it at that time was the fact that his father was so opposed to our getting involved in any foreign commitments."

Did this mean, as Horton suggests, that Jack was out of agreement with his father? We doubt it. Clearly Ambassador Kennedy opposed "foreign entanglements" and wanted the United States to keep clear of "Europe's war." But he also advocated "preparedness" so the United States would not find itself defenseless, as Britain had. Ambassador Kennedy was probably not opposed to the draft per se.

What happened after Jack registered for the draft, we wondered? Was he drafted at Stanford? His White House naval aide, Tazewell Shepard, had written in his book, *Man of the Sea*: " . . . at the end of October 1940 John F. Kennedy was Number Eighteen on the draft-board rolls in Palo Alto, California. His serial number was 2748. He was among the first in the country to be called, but because of an injury to his back incurred in football at Harvard, he was rejected. . . ."

We asked Shepard for the source for his statement and asked if he knew positively that Jack was drafted at Stanford. Shepard replied that in moving about, his records had been so scattered that he did not think he could find his notes and could not help further.

Harry Press, of the Stanford publicity office, very kindly searched the back issues of the *Daily* for us and found the story that cleared up most of the mystery. The story was published on the front page of the *Daily* on October 30, 1940, under the headline NATIONAL LOTTERY DRAWS THE NAMES OF 24 STANFORD MEN, TWO PROFESSORS . . . KENNEDY, STANLEY, GLIKBARG, HISLOP GET FIRST CALL. There was the same photograph of Jack used in the first *Daily* story.

According to an accompanying Associated Press story, President Roosevelt, Secretary of War Henry L. Stimson, and other high government officials gathered at noon on October 29 in Washington for the lottery. There were 9,000 capsules in a ten-gallon jar (called a fishbowl), each bearing the serial number for a group of draft registrants. At 12:18, Stimson, blindfolded with a strip of linen, reached into the jar and began drawing capsules. On the eighteenth draw, he pulled out a capsule bearing the serial number 2748. The story said: "The holder of 2748 for the Palo Alto area was Jack Kennedy . . . student at the Stanford Business School."

The Associated Press continued, "Though these students are exempt from induction until after the end of the present university year, they will become eligible July 1, 1941, if found physically fit and without further deferment granted them because of further university work, employment in a 'necessary position,' dependents or other reasons." Those whose numbers were drawn would fill out a questionnaire, then they would be "'classified''—given a draft status.

Jack had not, then, in the technical sense, been "drafted" at Stanford. He had registered on October 16, along with 17,000,000 other Americans between the ages of twenty-one and thirty-five. He had engaged in publicity supporting the draft. On October 29 Stimson had drawn the serial number that covered Jack. Sometime after that, Jack must have filled out the required questionnaire to determine his draft status. He probably stated that he intended to continue with his studies in graduate school which, under certain circumstances, entitled him to a deferment. At very best he did not have to face being called up until the following July—1941.

We had seen a letter to Jack from Charles E. Martin, University of Washington in Seattle, regarding an "Institute" Jack attended while at Stanford. Martin had said in his letter, "I appreciate very much your comment on the work of the Institute and your feeling that your experience there was worthwhile. I shall be writing you more formally in regard to your services as a reporter. . . ."

We found Professor Martin living in Seattle. He is now retired from the university. Professor Martin told us in a letter that from December 8 to December 13, 1940, the Institute of World Affairs, a group of West Coast political scientists and academicians, had held a meeting at Riverside, California. Martin said that Kennedy had attended the conference and had been appointed a "rapporteur," responsible for drafting a summary report of the discussions. By separate mail he sent us the published proceedings of the meeting—a collection of the papers given and summaries of the discussions prepared by the reporters—in a 296-page, soft-back book.

Kennedy had served as reporter for four sessions:

1. War and the Future World Economy (on this one he was assisted by two other "rapporteurs," Ross N. Berkes, editor of the reports, and Marjorie Severyns).

2. The Americas: Problems of Hemispheric Defense & Security.

3. War and the Preservation of European Civilization (Jack reported the section, British Civilization).

4. Proposed Plans for Peace.

Jack's reports comprised, in sum, about twenty-one pages of the book.

The one on the Americas began, "Dean Mears opened the discussion by summarizing briefly the economic factors and problems to be met in trying to achieve hemispheric cooperation. . . ." By the end of that sentence, we had to fight to maintain interest. We noted an error in his byline. Someone had written John *L.* Kennedy. The other three reports were similarly solemn and dense.

Dr. Martin, who was director of that meeting of the institute, said in his letter to us:

> He was kept busy, reporting four round tables in five day sessions. I understand that he authored all the reports from the tables he served. He was meticulous on attending the staff meetings and was interested in doing a good technical job. You see the diversity of his interests in the round tables he served. I often encountered him in administering the affairs of the Institute from day to day.
>
> From the titles of the papers and the tables and the personnel of the program, you can get an idea of the quality of the conference and its importance to the people of the Pacific Coast. It shows, I believe, that young Kennedy was on the alert to get the best he could from anything in the area of his current operations at any given time. I can remember his questioning many of the leaders of the Institute and taking an active part in the substance of the conference as well as its procedure.

Dr. Martin did not exaggerate as to the quality of the conference, judging from the credentials of the participants. Their papers covered in detail an extremely broad range of subject matter in foreign affairs. We concluded that if Jack had absorbed all that material in December, 1940, he must have been a well-informed young man.

But we should point out that the institute was not all dull grind. In the Kennedy Library photographic archives, we found a picture of Jack visiting Universal Studios in Hollywood. The picture was dated December 12, 1940, one day before the conference adjourned.

In sum, Jack's quarter-year at Stanford was mainly a lark. He seems to have enjoyed some political science classes and he did participate as a reporter in the serious conference we have just discussed, but his own contribution as a scholar was nil.

In spite of his stated intention to spend a year at Stanford, he left after only a quarter. Illness may (yet again) be the reason. Following the institute, we believe that Jack returned East for Christmas, stopping briefly at Palm Springs, California. When he returned East, as we saw from three items at the Kennedy Library, he consulted doctors in New York and Boston, and went back in the hospital.   .

First, a telegram from Jack's literary agent, Gertrude Algase, dated

December 19, 1940, was addressed to Jack in care of Dr. Sara Jordan at the Lahey Clinic in Boston. Second, a letter from Arthur Krock to Jack, dated December 31, 1940, said in part, "When I say, in return, Happy New Year, I mean every good wish that your expedition to New York will prove a turning point in the record of your health. You deserve the best of life and I hope you will have it from now on. . . ." Third, another telegram from Gertrude Algase to Jack, dated January 9, 1941, was addressed to Jack in care of the New England Baptist Hospital in Boston.

In her second telegram, Algase had asked Jack if he would be willing to write an article about the controversial debate over Britain's demand for military bases in neutral Ireland. Jack did. It was published February 2 in the Hearst-owned New York *Journal American* under the headline: IRISH BASES VITAL TO BRITAIN. As far as we could determine, it was (except for his contribution to the proceedings of the Riverside conference) the first writing Jack had published since his book. It would be the last for many years. It was an indication that though Jack was confined to a hospital, he was well enough to write.

Lacking Jack's medical records, or other evidence, we have no idea what was wrong with him now. Yet another recurrence of hepatitis? A continuation of the stomach disorder? Ulcers? Something entirely different?

Jack had been ill a great deal with his back and various other problems since at least his fifth-form year at Choate, 1933–1934. He had by now been treated by a small army of doctors in Boston, New York, at the Mayo Clinic, and elsewhere. This history nags at us as it grows longer. Increasingly it seems that no definitive biography can be written, and no full understanding of the man achieved, until the Kennedy family releases those medical records. And more: the secrecy in which they are being held cannot help but arouse suspicion. That his medical history was effectively falsified for public consumption during his political career is now known; members of his family and close friends began speaking more candidly about it not long after his death (*e.g.*, Robert Kennedy's account of Jack's pain in "at least half of the days that he spent on this earth"). Whatever scandal may be attached to the fact of concealment, then, is now public. One cannot resist asking why the continued secrecy: is something sordid being concealed? In fact, we doubt it; more likely it's simply inertia. This is, as we have said, a family that is used to controlling what the public believes about it. It may even be that this is what the family supposes Jack would have wanted. His own stubbornly held sense of himself might well have been damaged—and not only his political career—if this whole history had become known during his life. His lifelong behavior is certainly understandable as that of one who believed himself, as Rose said, to be "a strong, robust, quite healthy person who just happened to be sick a good deal of the time." Whatever the reason, the policy is frustrating to a researcher at best, and at worst encourages speculation of all sorts.

It must be said in any event that Jack's progress through life bearing this burden bespeaks, among other things, a truly awesome indomitability. He had unlimited alternatives to the pursuit of an active and demanding career. A life of drink and indolence would not have been an astonishing choice for a healthy young man of his inherited wealth and power. For one of Jack's frailty (and pain—Bobby's statement, it is clear, cannot have been much of an exaggeration and may have been an understatement), it would have been not merely forgivable but almost natural. His refusal to surrender is surely a choice of positive heroism.

8

Pulling Strings

W HEN Ambassador Kennedy and Rose returned from their West Coast trip, Whalen reports, they decided to sell the huge house in Bronxville and make their legal residence in Florida, which had no income or inheritance taxes. The house was sold in early 1941, and thereafter when the ambassador was in New York, which was often, he took a suite at the Waldorf-Astoria. The real estate broker who handled the deal, John J. Reynolds, subsequently interested the ambassador in real estate speculation in New York City. For the next half dozen years, the ambassador bought and sold, riding wartime inflation. Whalen says that these deals made Kennedy "enormously richer."

When Jack left the New England Baptist Hospital in February, 1941, he went to Palm Beach, where he found his father involved in a new project. He wanted to write his memoirs, and he enlisted Jack's help in locating a suitable ghostwriter and editor. Jack wrote Frances Ann Cannon's husband, John Hersey, at *Time* magazine. We found his letter, dated February 22, at the Kennedy Library. It indicated, among other things, that Jack had been in the Bahama Islands and in Frances Ann's hometown, Charlotte, North Carolina.

DEAR JOHNNY,

I was sorry to miss you when I was last in New York, but was only passing through after my weekend in Charlotte.

My father has decided to get his papers, for the last three years, in shape for eventual publication. He has been looking around for someone who could help with the job and it was in connection with this that I am writing. When I was down in Charlotte I met a friend of Frances Ann's, Connie Burwell, who impressed me very much, although I only talked with her for a short while. It seemed to me that this job might be of interest to her. It would take a year at least, probably two, and it would consist of correlating newspaper articles, Dad's daily notes and diary and actual events into a form somewhat similar, I imagine to the three volumes of Walter Hines Page.

I wanted to write to you first to check the matter before getting in touch with her. I thought you might have some ideas as to whether this would be in her line or whether you might have someone in mind who would fit better. Of course I haven't any idea what her plans are and she may not wish to start in on a job like this, but I wanted to get your re-action [sic] before doing anything about it.

My father will be up in New York at the Waldorf-Towers Friday, February 28th, for a few days and he would appreciate it very much if you would get in touch with him there. I was over in Nassau last weekend and saw Mr. and Mrs. Cannon, who looked very well but who seemed very regretful that you both were not there. I imagine you will agree with them.

Thanks very much for your help and I hope to see you again sometime soon. Please remember me to Frances Ann.

Sincerely,
JACK KENNEDY

We were curious about Jack's trip to Charlotte. Was he dating a new girl there? Connie Burwell, maybe? Connie Burwell was later a *Time* magazine researcher and had married a *Time* correspondent, William White. We talked with Connie Burwell White by telephone in Denver, where the Whites now live.

Frances Ann Cannon was a very close friend of mine. I was a bridesmaid in her wedding—the prettiest wedding I've ever seen in my life. The dogwood were blooming . . . tons of champagne . . . everybody in pink tulle dresses floating down a long marble hall in that beautiful house. Anyway, I got to know Jack when he came down to Charlotte to see Frances Ann. He didn't come often. I think Mama Cannon was trying to bust up the romance. She took Frances Ann on a round-the-world cruise on the *Kungsholm.*

I graduated from Sweet Briar in 1934 and got a Ph.D. from the University of North Carolina in 1937. I taught political science and history in a little college in Charlotte for several years. I spent a year in Germany and Europe before I started teaching. Jack was always interested in people who had done interesting things. So when Jack came to Charlotte he could relate to me. . . . I was of more interest to him than most people in Charlotte. We had a lot to talk about.

Q. Were you dating Jack in 1941?

A. Oh, no! I saw him entirely through Frances Ann. I don't know what he might have been doing in Charlotte for a weekend in February, 1941, but all of the Kennedys were always flying back and forth. I remember very well discussing the book with Jack. I expressed some reservations—his father had a reputation for being pro-German and I felt he ought to tell it like it was. After that I flew to Palm Beach and talked to his father. Jack wasn't there but I remember Mrs. Kennedy—very pretty—and Teddy and Bobby—little boys—playing under the piano. So I had an interview with Mr. Kennedy and decided to do the book. It was all set up and the papers were en route over from England when the ship they were on was sunk. I have a feeling the papers were later recovered but that ended that and the book was never done. And thanks to John Hersey I went to work for *Time-Life* the next year, 1942.

We are not certain what Jack was doing in March. Probably lying by the pool and on the beach, recovering his health and enjoying the social season in Palm Beach. Eunice was there, too. In our interview, she had said, "I had been a student at Sacred Heart College, Manhattanville, but in December, 1940, I had to drop out. I had stomach problems similar to Jack's. I went down to Palm Beach where I saw Jack."

Now that Jack himself had dropped out of school, he faced a certain draft call in the forthcoming month of July—not that there was any chance that he could pass the physical, which in this first draft of youngsters would be fairly tough. Perhaps to settle the matter in advance, Jack may have tried to enlist in the Army. Burns writes that this attempt was made "in the spring" but Jack was rejected "because of his old back condition." We asked the Kennedy Library archivists if there were any documents on file to verify this episode. They reported they could find none.

Jack now returned to the idea of going to Yale Law School. On March 31, 1941, he wrote the authorities at Harvard requesting, for the second time, that his transcript be sent to Yale. But there was no correspondence on file—such as an application—from Jack to Yale.

Then came a new adventure.

That spring Rose had decided to travel again. She and Eunice booked reservations on a cruise ship that would take them on a voyage through the Caribbean and down to Rio de Janeiro. Jack decided to fly down and join them in Rio and then go on to Buenos Aires, where the Kennedys had some good friends. On April 18 Jack was issued a new passport, with visas for Brazil, Argentina, and Chile.

In her book, Rose describes the voyage south. The ship stopped at Barbados May 14; Rio May 21. We think Jack left Miami by Pan Am Clipper and met them in Rio. Rose includes a photograph of Jack, herself, and Eunice, posed with Sugarloaf Mountain in the background. They are arm in arm, smiling the famous Kennedy smile, Jack in the middle. He is wearing white buckskin shoes, dark trousers, a plaid sports jacket, sweater, and bow tie. He lookes healthy and happy, very collegiate, very young.

Rose had an entry in her diary which mentioned Jack in Rio:

> Jack and Eunice and I invited by Ambassador Jefferson Caffery
> to dinner at the United States Embassy. The first dinner in an em-
> bassy I have attended since I left London. . . . I sat next to Señor
> Aranha, the Brazilian Foreign Minister, whose family has been in
> politics five generations. . . . It seems to me that the idea of a
> family serving in the government generation after generation, as is
> the case with so many English families as well, is one we might do
> well to think about and encourage in our own country. . . .

At Rio, Rose wrote, she and Eunice left the ship and continued the trip
by air. They flew to Buenos Aires then across the Andes to Santiago,
Chile. From there they turned north, stopping in Peru, Ecuador, Panama,
and Cuba. They arrived back in the States, Rose says, about June 20.

According to Jack's passport, he followed the same route but from the
date stamps—and since Rose does not mention Jack after Rio—it seems
that they split up and that Jack continued the trip alone. We could find no
entry stamp for Argentina, but Chuck Spalding had discussed this trip in
our interview, and he told us that Jack had stopped there. According to
our interpretation of the stamps, Jack arrived in Chile June 10 and departed June 14. By that time, we guessed, Rose and Eunice had gone on
ahead.

Spalding had told us that Jack's trip to South America had been a
"great success." By that he apparently meant that Jack had been royally
entertained by two very lovely girls in Buenos Aires. They were Stella
and Ana Carcano—better known as Bebe and Chiquita—daughters of the
distinguished diplomat Miguel Angel Carcano, who had been ambassador
to England while the Kennedys were there. According to *The Lost Prince*,
Joe Junior had dated the girls in London. According to Spalding, Jack saw
them on this trip. Jack was especially fond of Bebe. Afterward, Spalding
said, the girls came to New York "many times." He met them there
through Jack. Both girls later married Englishmen: Bebe, Lord Edmund;
Chiquita, Lady Astor's youngest son, "Jakey."

We wondered if Bebe had been a "serious" girlfriend. She was beautiful, intelligent, a world traveler and a Catholic. Today she might be described in the tabloids as one of the "Beautiful People." Her family tree
spread all through Argentine history; its branches were weighted with distinction. Her father was very rich—as rich, perhaps, as Joe Kennedy. It
would have been an interesting match.

While discussing the Carcano girls with Chuck Spalding, we broadened
the line of questioning somewhat, asking Spalding about Jack's attitude
toward women in general at that stage of his life. Why so many?

It seemed only natural to me that for someone as attractive as
Jack growing up, girls were a part of his life. . . . He was always
interested in seeing whether he had it or didn't have it. Can I do it
or can't I do it? To me, that always accounted for a lot of the *numbers*, if you will. And the other thing I think is having a very, very
strong father. All kids, I suppose, want to be better than their fathers. That's part of the game. Mr. Kennedy was a very strong and
also a very worldly fellow. And Jack had a short attention span,
which was kind of Byronic in a way. And Byron is somebody he
spent some time thinking about. . . .

In his oral history, when asked why Jack had married so late in life,
Spalding was reminded of Winston Churchill, the similarity of Churchill's
life and Jack's life—and of Jack's admiration for Churchill, who did not
marry until he was about thirty-six. Spalding went on: "I don't mean that
he decided he'd marry when Churchill did, but I know he had decided he
wasn't going to get married terribly early."

Jack probably celebrated his twenty-fourth birthday on May 29, in Buenos Aires with his mother and sister and the Carcanos. Rose and Eunice
then went on ahead. Thereafter, Jack continued his trip through Latin
America alone, we believe. He flew across the Andes to Santiago, Chile,
where he spent a few days. A passport stamp shows that on July 1, he
reentered the United States. He probably went to Hyannis Port.

During Jack's two-month absence from the United States, the country
had moved another notch toward war. On May 26 President Roosevelt
had declared a "state of national emergency." Many of Jack's good
friends were going into the military service. For example, Ben Smith, a
naval reservist, was called to active duty that month. According to *The
Lost Prince,* Joe Junior and Tom Killefer, facing the July draft call, had
joined the Navy's aviation cadet program. Joe Junior was already undergoing preliminary training at Squantum Naval Air Station near Boston.

Jack apparently now decided that he, too, would make another stab at
joining up. He told Burns how he finally managed it—by going through
"five months of strengthening exercises" for his back. Rose has a similar
story. But knowing that Jack had many other medical problems, we decided to look more closely at these accounts.

Captain Alan Goodrich Kirk was a brilliant naval officer who had been
the naval attaché in London when Kennedy was ambassador. In those
days, a naval attaché's prime function was intelligence-gathering. According to his official naval biography, upon his return from the London
Embassy in March, 1941, Captain Kirk was appointed director of the
Office of Naval Intelligence (ONI). He was a rising star in the Navy, al-

ready selected for promotion to rear admiral effective in late November, 1941. As the Navy's chief intelligence officer, he was in daily contact with the Secretary of the Navy, the Chief of Naval Operations, and others in the highest echelons of the Navy. In sum, a very important person.

For that reason, we consulted Kirk's papers, which are on file in the Navy's History Center in Washington, D.C. As we saw from his letters, Kirk helped both Joe Junior and Jack to get in the Navy.

In March, 1941, shortly after Kirk assumed his new post in Washington, Ambassador Kennedy wrote him regarding Joe Junior's plans to join the Navy. Apparently the ambassador was concerned that Joe Junior might have some problems with the physical examination. This was a surprise; we had always assumed Joe Junior was hale and hearty. On March 24 Kirk wrote a letter to Captain C. W. Carr, a Navy physician who was commanding officer of the Naval Hospital in Chelsea, a part of Boston:

> I am very much interested in trying to get the . . . son of Mr. J. P. Kennedy, our late Ambassador to England, into the Naval Academy Reserve Class. Not only am I doing this for my late chief in London but also for several other interested people. The boy has taken the attitude that he does not wish his father's position used in any way as a lever to secure him preferment. This is an excellent point of view, but, nevertheless, it has occured to me he might be helped in one way—viz., his physical condition.
>
> Therefore I am writing to ask you if it is possible to have him given a physical examination according to the requirements for entrance into the Naval Academy by these Reserve applicants.
>
> His other qualifications are not a matter of concern at this time, but I might say he is a very attractive young man, and if there is anything along this line that can be done, either officially or unofficially, I would be very glad to have your advice in the matter.
>
> I am writing to you chiefly because the boy is at the Harvard Law School and, therefore, is convenient to the Chelsea Hospital. I also felt you would not mind giving me quietly your reaction to such a proposition.

Captain Carr responded from the Naval Air Station in Quonset Point, Rhode Island, that he had been transferred from Chelsea February 28, having been relieved by Captain J. A. McMullin, Medical Corps, USN. On April 3 Kirk wrote Dr. McMullin a duplicate of the letter to Carr and then on April 8, a letter to young Joe Kennedy: "Arrangements have been made with Captain J. A. McMullin (MC), USN, Commanding Officer of the U.S. Naval Hospital at Chelsea, Massachusetts, for you to take a private preliminary physical examination prior to your possible entrance into the Naval Academy Reserve Class. . . . Hope you had a good vacation in Florida and found your family all well. . . ."

Captain Kirk evidently had in mind bringing Joe Junior into ONI in some capacity. Joe Junior went to Washington to discuss the job with Kirk, but must have found it unappealing. On May 6, he wrote Kirk, "I want to thank you very much for arranging for my physical examination at the Chelsea Navy Hospital. They took great care of me, and rushed me right through. I was delighted to see you again in Washington and was very glad to have spoken with you about the Intelligence Service. The way it looks now I think I shall go into the [naval] air corps. With many thanks for your interest. . . ."

There was, unfortunately, no such detailed correspondence regarding Jack's preliminary moves to enter the Navy. The first was from Ambassador Kennedy to Captain Kirk on August 4, written from Hyannis Port:

DEAR ALAN,

To write and tell you what a swell guy I think you are would be nothing new for you to hear because long before you were going out of your way for my two boys I knew what a real person you were.

This note is merely to tell you that I am most deeply grateful for your help and cooperation on the matters of Joe and Jack. Joe expects to solo on Wednesday and then go to Jacksonville. He seems very happy and is delighted to be with the Navy.

I am having Jack see a medical friend of yours in Boston tomorrow for physical examination and then I hope he'll become associated with you in Naval Intelligence.

It has been terribly nice of you to give them so much time and helpful suggestions and it furnishes me rather a new experience even after 25 years in business and seven in Government service. When I get out of a place or retire from a job I find that a surprisingly large number of people find it very difficult to do favors. It isn't an experience that I alone enjoy. I think it is human nature, but *you've* been most kind and I'm deeply grateful. Best to yourself and the family. Very sincerely yours. . . .

Four days later, August 8, Jack officially applied for a commission in the Navy, we saw by his records in the Kennedy Library. On that same day, Kirk replied to Joe Kennedy's letter:

DEAR MR. KENNEDY,

Thanks very much for your pleasant letter of the 4th. I am delighted to know you are enjoying cool weather on the Cape.

It was no trouble to me to be helpful with such fine young men as yours. We are delighted Joe is getting along so well and I think it is fine he is in the Navy air game. About Jack, I shall hope to hear that his plans are progressing favorably and I will see that he gets an interesting job. . . .

Hoping your family are all well and with my best to them all, I am sincerely yours . . .

Jack Kennedy was accepted into the Navy. He was not, as Rose wrote, sent to an officer's training program in early winter. According to his Navy records at the Kennedy Library, he was granted a commission— direct from civilian life without training—as an ensign in the Naval Reserve. Date of swearing in: September 25, 1941. Thus, a young man who could certainly not have qualified for the Sea Scouts on his physical condition, entered the U.S. Navy.

When Jack put on his Navy uniform and took the oath of office—the first of many he would take in his lifetime—we felt that one era had closed, another had begun. At the age of twenty-four he was for the first time (the brief tour at Stanford excepted) leaving home, the immediate and strong influence of his parents, especially his father, to strike out on his own. He was taking his first real job.

Part II

THE NAVY

9

A Dull Office Job

THERE are three books on Jack's naval service, all published in 1961 or 1962 while he was in the White House. All three were written with Jack's assistance or with the assistance of his aides and the Navy Department.

The most famous is *PT-109: John F. Kennedy in World War Two*, by Robert J. Donovan, a Washington journalist who was then chief of the *New York Herald Tribune*'s Washington Bureau, and a friend of Jack's. *PT-109* was excerpted at length in *The Saturday Evening Post*, republished in paperback, and made into a movie of the same title starring Cliff Robertson as Jack Kennedy. The Donovan book contains a brief foreword by Jack: "I have read this book with great interest. I find it to be a highly accurate account of the events of the war. . . ."

John F. Kennedy: War Hero, by Richard Tregaskis (the classmate at Harvard who beat Jack out for the swimming team), was originally a book for children, published under the title *John F. Kennedy and PT-109*. Tregaskis expanded that book by 20,000 words for publication under the new title in paperback as an adult book.

John F. Kennedy—Expendable! by Chandler Whipple, is, like the other two books, an account of *PT-109* set against the background of the South Pacific fighting. It contains a forward by Fleet Admiral Chester W. Nimitz, who says the book is "well written and detailed." (The title evokes *They Were Expendable*, a famous book about the PT boats by William L. White, later a movie.)

We studied these books closely. They are war journalism, not history, with war journalism's peculiar faults: chiefly hero worship, distortion, oversimplification, questions raised but left unanswered, judgments withheld. Each has a good account of the *PT-109* disaster—Donovan by far the best—but there is much that is vague. There are conflicting accounts of simple matters such as where Kennedy was at certain times. The same anecdotes recounted by shipmates occur at different points in the various narratives and sometimes with different sets of facts. The close friends Kennedy made during this crucial year—two would be ushers at his wedding—are mentioned, but little is said about any of them. And there are obvious gaps—large gaps—in the story.

So we started from scratch. We studied and indexed Jack's official naval records and other wartime documents that have been released at the
Kennedy Library. Under our telephoned guidance, our daughters, Marie
Louise Marvin and Sibyl Blair, carried out extensive research into officia
World War Two action reports, war diaries, logbooks, and other documents at the Naval History Center and the National Archives in Washington, and forwarded copies of pertinent documents to us. We reread widely through established authorities on the war in the Pacific and the Navy's
official PT-boat history, *At Close Quarters,* by Robert J. Bulkley, Jr. And
finally we tracked down and interviewed in depth some fifty people who
knew or served with Jack in the Navy.

In his first naval assignment, Jack was ordered to work for Captain
Kirk's ONI in Washington, an appropriate job for a man of his background as well as his physical condition. He arrived at ONI in early Octo
ber, 1941. Kirk, having been promoted to rear admiral, was detached
about the time Jack reported, going on to a succession of important com
mands at sea.

All the Kennedy Navy books pass over this assignment quickly or ex
clude it altogether. Burns, for example, gives it one line, which includes
an error: "For a time he worked in Intelligence on a news digest for the
Navy Chief of Staff in Washington." (The correct title of the top Navy
man is Chief of Naval Operations.) Tregaskis says it was a "dull" office
job "editing a news digest." Donovan places Jack "in the Pentagon"
(which had not yet been built), assigned to Naval Intelligence where he
"helped prepare a daily news digest." Whipple skips the Washington
duty altogether. And so does Jack's official Navy biography, which he
himself cleared for publication when he was president. This of a job at the
very highest level of Naval Intelligence at the time of Pearl Harbor.

With the help of Roger Pineau, the distinguished naval historian, we
identified Jack's boss at ONI: Captain Samuel A. Dulany Hunter. We
found Captain Hunter living in retirement in Fairfax, Virginia. We were
met by a slight man of seventy years, somewhat bent but extraordinarily
courteous and very chipper.

"I'm a historian by trade," he said, "and I'm glad somebody is going to
get this down before we're *all* gone."

Hunter invited us to examine a sheaf of papers he had gathered for our
meeting. They were official ONI documents describing the organization
of Jack's unit, personnel, and other matters. We saw the name of Ensign
J. F. Kennedy on one roster. Captain Hunter told us he had organized the
unit in prewar days. We asked him to tell us about his background and
how the unit was formed.

Hunter was born in Washington in 1904, son of a diplomat. He went to
Georgetown University where in 1936, he received a Ph.D. He then
taught history at Georgetown's School of Foreign Service. He said:

In 1935, after the Ethiopian War, a wonderful, resourceful man who was running ONI, Captain William D. Puleston, decided to drag ONI into the twentieth century. He recruited about six of us to serve as civilian analysts in foreign affairs. I didn't like being a civilian in the Navy, so I resigned. We compromised by my going into the Naval Reserve. So I remained at Georgetown, but for three years did a lot of active duty tours in ONI. Then on May 5, 1941—about the time Roosevelt declared a state of national emergency—I went on full-time active duty and set up the unit. Over the months and years, the unit changed, grew in size, got shifted around on the organizational charts, people came and went, but it was fundamentally the unit I set up. Its purpose was to collect foreign intelligence information from a variety of sources—attachés' reports, newspapers, wire services, codebreaking, State Department cables, and whatnot—and distill that information into daily intelligence summaries for the chief of naval operations and others. Later, we set up a kind of "situation room" patterned on the British model. Lieutenant H. Montgomery—Bob Montgomery, the movie star—came in right after Pearl Harbor to do that. He went over to London for a couple of weeks to see how they did it.

ONI was the Navy's chief intelligence arm, with many divisions, reporting to a director, who was, in Kennedy's day, Theodore Stark Wilkinson. His mother was a cousin of my father's. The assistant director was Howard Fithian Kingman. My unit—and Jack's unit—came under what was called the Foreign Intelligence Branch—we called it OP-16 Fi—which was then headed by William Augustin Heard. "Wild Bill" Heard. Heard's executive officer—or the man actually performing that job—was a cousin of mine, Harry W. Baltazzi. Our unit was known officially as the Daily Information Section. It ultimately divided—I'm not sure of the precise date but it doesn't matter—into two parts: daily reports and the so-called situation room that Montgomery helped us set up. Jack worked in both parts. I was in charge of all this most of the time he was here. Then I was sent to Guatemala and a man named Bailey—Vaughn Bailey—came in to run it. Of all the people I have named, only Bailey is still alive, but I don't think he can help because Kennedy was gone when he came. Come to think of it, I guess I am the only senior officer in the outfit, who is still living who had direct contact with Kennedy.

Captain Hunter then produced a roster of Kennedy's contemporaries in the unit. We recognized several of the names: Hedley Donovan, now editor-in-chief of Time, Inc., publishers of *Time, Fortune, Sports Illustrated,* etc., and Walter B. Mahoney, now executive editor of the *Reader's Di-gest*. Hunter read these names and others into the tape: Henry Mustin James Gledhill Simonds, Livingston Hartley, E. W. Jensen, E. McCollay III, J. G. Locke. Most were journalists or authors. Some had been naval reservists.

Later we made contact with several of these men. Hedley Donovan re-called meeting Kennedy in the hallway but had not had close contact with him. Mahoney wrote us a letter naming some of the people in the unit. He remembered Kennedy's being in the unit but could think of no special anecdotes. Simonds and others had died or could not be found.

One of Kennedy's contemporaries in the unit, who asked not to be identified by name, told us by telephone a little about how it worked:

> There were six of us in the room. It was a plain room with four metal desks and a little separate room where Bailey and Simonds sat. Our job was to prepare three intelligence bulletins: a daily bul-letin for the Secretary of the Navy and other top people, which was a summary of key developments; another daily bulletin—a four-page leaflet-type thing—which was less sensitive and more widely circulated to shore stations and ships at sea; and a weekly four-page bulletin. We never dealt in anything higher than "se-cret" and if we had codebreaking information, it came to us dis-guised so we didn't know its source. We all had typewriters at our desks and spent most of the day writing, condensing, editing. We ate lunch in the Navy cafeteria, or in the Department of Interior cafeteria nearby, or sometimes, when the weather was good, out on the Mall. There was not much socializing among the men and the families. I remember Kennedy quite well. He was a man of high intelligence, with a facile wit—a good writing hand. He also had a heavy social life. In those days he was still more or less in his playboy stage. . . .

Captain Hunter described his relationship with Kennedy:

> Just before the war there was a considerable increase in person-nel and the only reason that I really noticed him was that after I'd had him for some weeks, someone mentioned that he was the son of Ambassador Kennedy and I had read the book he had pub-lished . . . and, as it were, I took a second look at him. I saw him during the coffee breaks we would take when we were on duty at the same time. Both of us being interested in history and govern-ment, we talked at considerable length about those two subjects. I was a liberal and I soon found out that he was, too, and that sort of gave us a common bond in our discussions. There was nothing par-

ticularly noteworthy that I can think of in those conversations. Criticisms of certain policies, criticisms of certain individuals. . . .

In November, 1941, after Jack had been working for Hunter about a month, U. S. relations with the Japanese reached a crisis stage. While the Japanese Navy prepared to launch a sneak attack against the Pacific Fleet at Pearl Harbor, Japanese envoys came to Washington ostensibly in an eleventh-hour effort to avoid war. The U. S. was reading Japanese diplomatic codes. The intercepted dispatches were full of clues that the negotiations were phony and that war was imminent. Hunter told us there was no doubt in ONI that the Japanese were on the verge of attacking. The only question was where? Pearl Harbor, he said, was considered the least likely place.

All that month ONI was on full alert, trying to find a signal that would pinpoint where and when the Japanese would strike. Jack was part of that effort, Hunter said. Meanwhile, the section took on more chores:

> Each morning I went over to the Department of State with my yeoman, Glover. I was permitted to go through all the dispatches which State had received. I could not copy anything verbatim because of codebreaking security measures. I'd sit there and paraphrase to Glover and he'd take notes in shorthand. I probably read two or three hundred pages of material every morning. Then I'd go back to the office and boil this down into a summary of twelve or more pages. We then circulated that document—Summary of State Department Messages—to about forty select people in the Navy. It was classified secret.

The Japanese attack on Pearl Harbor demoralized ONI, Hunter said. It was, of course, one of the great intelligence failures in military history. He could still recall the end of the day: "That night, the Director of Naval Intelligence, Captain Wilkinson, and his principal subordinates sat in his darkened office trying to figure out whose head was going to fall. Who would be the fall guy—or guys—in the outfit. It's a picture I can never erase from my mind, seeing those men who were usually so self-confident broken by the news that was coming in."

Where was Jack Kennedy on that fateful afternoon? In *PT-109,* Donovan writes that on December 7, Jack had gone to a pro football game at Griffith Stadium with Lem Billings. On the way home in the car, Donovan says, they heard the news about the attack. But Billings told us a different story:

> I spent a lot of time in Washington trying to get into the military or something. Even trying working for the government. You just

can't believe how people of our age and era felt when they weren't doing anything. Meanwhile, Jack was stationed in Washington in Intelligence. . . . My mother lived in Baltimore so I was sort of operating out of Baltimore and was in Washington a lot with Jack. We used to play a lot of touch football down around the Washington Monument. One Sunday we'd gone down and were playing touch football with some strangers and after we'd finished and were riding home in the car we heard about Pearl Harbor.

Donovan goes on to say that "immediately" after Pearl Harbor, Jack applied for sea duty. We tried to verify that statement in Jack's naval records at the Kennedy Library. The records are not complete. They do not contain, for example, the most important documents: Jack's fitness reports, the periodic evaluations of his performance by his superiors. Nor do they contain his Navy medical records. We did find official requests for changes of assignment Jack had originated at various times, but none requesting sea duty in December, 1941.

Captain Hunter told us that on the day after Pearl Harbor, ONI went on full war footing. Wilkinson set up a twenty-four-hour watch, three shifts of eight hours each. Every available man was assigned a shift. He recalled that after Bob Montgomery established the situation room, Jack was shifted from report writing to that room, distilling information of Japanese force movements and putting symbols on the wall maps.

So in this "dull" assignment, Jack had had an inside view of the developing crisis between the United States and Japan. He had probably been one of the first to see the secret dispatches from Pearl Harbor (the full truth was withheld from the American public for years) and to realize the extent of the disaster. If he had not seen dispatches, he had certainly heard the talk within ONI. Then, in the following weeks, he was privy to the information on the Japanese military thrusts in the Far East—toward Hong Kong, Singapore, the Philippines, Java—information that was also held secret for a very long time.

There is, as we have said, a curious gap in the public accounts of Jack's naval career. Jack was transferred from ONI headquarters to what was essentially a public relations post in Charleston, South Carolina, in January of 1942—that is, after only about ninety days in ONI. With his background and education in foreign affairs, ONI would seem to have been the perfect slot for him. If heads were to roll, as Captain Hunter put it, because of ONI's failure to anticipate Pearl Harbor, would the scythe reach as low as this brand-new ensign? Perhaps. But a surprising episode in Jack's personal life during this time provides another explanation.

10

Inga-Binga

In the fall of 1941, about when Jack was assigned to Naval Intelligence, his sister Kathleen, then twenty-one, who had finished two years at Finch College, also moved to Washington. She took a job on the old Washington *Times-Herald*. The paper's owner and publisher, the celebrated (or notorious) Eleanor M. "Cissy" Patterson, had discovered, according to Alice Hoge, her grandniece and biographer, that "pretty finishing-school graduates with rich fathers were a particularly inexpensive source of labor." In several interviews, we had been told that Kathleen had many close friends on the paper and that her new friends became Jack's friends. In other words, Kathleen's professional and social circles in Washington became intertwined with Jack's.

Two people, we learned, helped Kathleen get the job: Arthur Krock, whose wife had worked on the paper; and another debutante coolie, Paige Huidekoper, daughter of a plastics manufacturer in Baltimore.

We found Paige, now Mrs. Thomas W. Wilson, Jr., a lovely, gentle woman living in Georgetown. She recalled:

> After getting out of secondary schools in Baltimore, I thought I might go into the Diplomatic Service, so I took a night course at Johns Hopkins. Then, through Jimmy Roosevelt, who was a good friend, I met Joe Kennedy, who was on the point of going to London to be ambassador. Thanks to Jimmy, Kennedy offered me a job in the London embassy. I first met Kathleen over there. When the Germans went into Paris, I came home and took a job on the *Times-Herald* as a special assistant to Frank J. Waldrop, who was called executive editor or something. About a year later, Kathleen called from the Cape. She said her father thought she ought to get a paying job and earn her own living and was there anything she could do on the paper? I was moving to the city desk then, so I talked to Frank without telling him who Kathleen was. I just described her as a friend of mine who was very bright without much experience. She came down and Frank hired her. . . . She was very natural, very outspoken, warm, full of vitality. She had a

strong face and very pretty coloring. She was not pretty in the classical sense, but she had much warmth and vitality. Very natural and seemingly very unspoiled by money. She had that same vein of strength that all the Kennedys have. She was also considerate and gentle. . . .

Frank J. Waldrop was a power at the *Times-Herald*, an archconservative and isolationist and one of those to whom Cissy willed the paper when she died in 1948. We found him living in Spring Valley, an affluent suburb of Washington. He was handsome, blue-eyed, forceful, somewhat military in bearing and manner. He told us how he had become involved with the Kennedys:

I met Joe Kennedy when he was at the Maritime Commission. He was extremely personable and intelligent, a man worth knowing. When he became ambassador, we had a common interest, which was foreign policy of the United States. What the president was going to do about it. It's interesting when you look back on it. The eggheads were isolationists then. They don't like to have that brought up—but I was there! A lot of people changed sides when the going got tough, but Joe Kennedy wasn't that kind of man. . . .

Waldrop had written a full-page rave review of Jack's book which was published in the *Times-Herald* in October, 1940. We asked why he had gone to so much trouble. He said, "That's because they were friends of ours." Then we asked if he remembered how Kathleen came to the paper. He said:

In the fall of 1941, I got a call from Arthur Krock who said Kathleen wanted to come down to work. Paige Wilson was involved somehow. . . . I talked to Mrs. Patterson. Then we hired her. Kathleen was a nice, sweet little girl, the daughter of a friend of ours, and it was fun to have youngsters like that around. It's been said, and it's true, that Kathleen would come in the office with her mink coat carefully wrapped inside a paper sack so she wasn't flashing improper evidence of being able to meet her bills. They had nice manners and they weren't ostentatiously slumming.

Waldrop told us that one of the Kennedy "gang" of those years had been John B. White, *Times-Herald* man who went into the Marine Corps in 1942. We found White in Cambridge, Massachusetts. He said:

Yes, you could say that I was part of Jack's and Kathleen's social set. I lived in Georgetown with my sister Placidia, who was a close friend of Kathleen's, and my brother-in-law, Dr. Henry Field, an anthropologist. When Kathleen came to the paper, I took her under my wing. Yes, I fell in love with her. After our first date she gave my name to her father and he had his men check me out. He told her, "eccentric, but OK to go out with" or something like that. We double-dated with Jack a lot. I never liked him that much, not as much as I liked Kathleen. He wasn't that likable. But he was a fast runner and an interesting operator, a typical Don Juan. You could almost imagine him checking off names in a book. He was a stereotyper. He liked to put things in order. The whole family was that way. The only thing that astonished me was when he said his favorite book was *Seven Pillars of Wisdom* by T. E. Lawrence. That was extraordinary good taste. Genuine taste. Other than that, he just didn't interest me a lot. He was so contrary to my nature. He was ambitious, actually good at most things. I guess I never interested him. He didn't favor me with any of those deep knowledges. . . .

At that point in his life, it seemed to me, he was very much under the influence of Kathleen. She had courage. She had broken with the family . . . I mean, she had defied the family so to speak, in matters of whom she was going to marry, how she would lead her life, and on religion. Jack had been following in her path, quite seriously questioning the Church. He tagged along behind Kathleen. She was his courage.

Jack's "old" friends and his sister Eunice, who was then twenty and becoming closer to Jack, had told us little about this period in Jack's life. The onset of the war was bringing momentous change into many lives; and Eunice was preparing to go to Stanford, and so was preoccupied with her own affairs.

Ben Smith had been little help:

After I was called up, Sis and I went to Point Pleasant, West Virginia, to commission a one-hundred-fifty-one-foot net-layer, the U.S.S. *Gum Tree.* So we were really out of touch with everybody. We were assigned to Newfoundland. On the way up—in December, just after Pearl Harbor—we stopped in Boston for final voyage repairs. In the Gloucester Navy Yard, my hometown. That was the only time I remember seeing Jack. He was up in Boston on leave. Torby Macdonald was getting ready to marry a Boston girl—a very lovely girl—Polly Cotter. The invitations had been sent out. Jack, who was going to be one of Torby's ushers, came down to the *Gum Tree* and had dinner with me in the wardroom. I remember Jack wanted to get Torby a wedding present, but as usual he didn't have any money. He never carried money. He borrowed money—I think it was twenty dollars—from me for the present and he never did pay me back.

Torby Macdonald:

I saw Jack around Boston in December, 1941, when he was on leave. I guess that was when Ben Smith was there with his ship. Yes, I was going to marry Polly Cotter. The announcements were out, the ushers notified—Jack was going to be an usher—but the war came along and screwed this up. I didn't want to get married if I was going off and maybe get killed. So I figured it would be better to wait. Polly agreed. I remember the present Jack gave us. It was a beautiful gold clock from Shreve, Crump and Low.

Rip Horton:

I got into America First and supported Wendell Willkie because I was very antiwar and anti-Roosevelt. But right after Pearl Harbor, I decided to join up. I had very bad eyes, twenty–two hundred like Billings, but I got some contact lenses, practiced with them, and got through the physical—as an Army private. They never knew. I was sent down to Camp Lee, Virginia, then went to officer candidate school. I had become engaged to a girl, Jane Mohan, the daughter of an English doctor from Garden City, New York. Jack knew her very well. We saw him in New York briefly—I can't remember where or when—and invited him to our engagement party in December, 1941. . . . We got married in July and then I went overseas to North Africa—a specialist in landing operations.

Horton had given the Kennedy Library a copy of a letter Jack wrote to Jane Mohan January 11, 1942, on official ONI stationery:

Dear Jane,
I was awfully sorry not to have been able to get up for your and Rip's engagement but I was glad, at least, to see you both for a few minutes in New York. Anyway, I just wanted to write a letter of congratulations.
First of all, I want to congratulate you. Rip, for various reasons which I imagine you now know considerably more about than I, is quite a fellow, contact lenses, Captain Sheridan and all.
Secondly, I'd like to congratulate Rip, which I'm going to do. He's exceptionally lucky which I think he knows.

Thirdly, I'd like to congratulate myself and quite heartily. I've known Rip for nearly ten years—and although I haven't seen him very much in the last two or three years, I've always counted him as one of my two or three close friends. As I hope to go on seeing him for quite a few years more whom he marries is of considerable importance. My limited experience has shown a wife can bollox things up quicker than most people. I am therefore very pleased that you are marrying Rip.

I hope to see you both again soon, and for a somewhat longer time.

Sincerely,
JACK

(We looked twice at the sentence: "My limited experience has shown a wife can bollox things up quicker than most people." What limited experience? Among his close friends, only Ben and Sis Smith—then in West Virginia—were married, and Jack had not seen much of them since Ben was called to active duty in May. They were very happy. Was it a young man's posture, or a genuine wariness about marriage that came from his father's attitude toward women in general and Rose in particular?)

Chuck Spalding, though, had at least been in Washington:

After I graduated from Yale in June, 1941, I went out to Hollywood to go into writing. . . . But on the day after Pearl Harbor, I went home to Chicago and tried to get into Naval Aviation. I wanted to be a pilot. But the quotas were filled or whatever, so I went to Washington. They said I was too tall, but one guy said, "Squat down a little when you take your physical." I hunkered down an inch or so and they said perfect and gave me a direct commission— but it was in Navy Public Relations! Later, I resigned my commission and got to be an aviation cadet. I was temporarily stationed at the Naval Air Station in Anacostia, just outside Washington. Jack was in Washington, living at the Dorchester. He had a Filipino who used to whip meals together.

By that time, George Mead and Paul Moore had been called up into the Marines and they were undergoing officer training at Quantico, Virginia. They'd come up for a Sunday and we'd have a party or dinner in the evening at the Dorchester—just a spontaneous thing. Another person I remember was an English girl, Lady Astor's niece I think, Dinah Brand, whose father was a member of the British Mission in Washington. She'd been a friend of Kathleen's in London. She later married a guy named Littleton Fox. The parties were fun. Between them Jack and Kathleen knew everybody in Washington. They'd talk about all these inside things—

important things—and what Arthur Krock said about this guy and
that. . . .

The girl Chuck Spalding would marry later in the war, Elizabeth Coxe,
was also in Washington during Jack's tour. We found Betty Spalding living in Greenwich, Connecticut. She and Chuck were divorced.
   She is a direct, forceful, intelligent woman. She said:

   I was brought up in Philadelphia, daughter of Eckley Coxe, a
stockbroker. I went to St. Timothy's, a very strict Episcopal
school, then Harkins Academy. I met Chuck at Jekyll Island,
Georgia, when I was sixteen. We were both on Easter vacation
with our families. I met all the Kennedys at the Cape—Jack in
about 1935 when we swam together on the Wianno Yacht Club relay team. After Chuck went to Yale, he used to come to the Cape
to visit George Mead on Great Island. George was then courting
Kathleen. So we were all very friendly. We visited back and forth
and played bridge and tennis. In October, 1941, I went to Washington to attend Walker Foreign Service School—a cram course. Jack
was down there in naval intelligence. Kathleen was working for the
paper.
   She and I shared an apartment at the Dorchester House out on
Sixteenth Street near Meridian Park. It was a fairly new building
and it was a very nice apartment. It had a bedroom, bath, kitchen,
and kind of living room-dining room. Kathleen was extremely ambitious and very personable, a great conversationalist and had a
kind of cheery way about her, plus a real talent for keeping conversation going. She hadn't any ambitions to work, but she wanted to
marry well—socially well. She was not a serious journalist. It was
a way to get jollies, a great way to get around and meet people in
Washington. She had several English beaus writing her. One was
Billy Hartington, another was Tony Rosslyn, and the third was
William Douglas Hume, a playwright. Another was Hugh Fraser,
who later married the woman who wrote the book about Mary
Queen of Scots—Antonia Fraser. But Kathleen was most interested in Hartington and Rosslyn. She couldn't make up her mind. She
would show me the letters and ask me who I thought was the most
attractive. All those vital things people talk about when they're
twenty! And, of course, John White was courting her. . . .

We asked Betty if she could recall anything about Jack leaving Nava
Intelligence. Why had he suddenly been transferred to the Siberia o
South Carolina after only ninety days in Washington? Her answe
stunned us: "He was shipped out of Washington because he had a lov

affair with a woman on the *Times-Herald* who had theoretically been the mistress of Axel Wenner-gren, the Swedish industrialist who had been put on the blacklist. Her name was Inga Arvad. She was a good friend of Kick's. Inga was somehow involved with Wenner-gren, Jack got involved with Inga, so they sent him off. At least, that is the story he told us. . . ."

Axel Wenner-gren first. From the January 26, 1942 issue of *Time* magazine:

Wealthiest Swede since Kreuger, Axel Wenner-gren is a mysterious globe-trotter, one of the last of the international capitalists. He built his fortune on wood pulp, aviation, munitions (Bofors), vacuum cleaners and refrigerators (Servel, Inc.). Since 1939 he has lived on Hog Island (near Nassau) on a magnificent estate called Shangri-La. He is an intimate of the Duke of Windsor. Two months ago he left Peru where he had sponsored an archaeological expedition, and arrived in Mexico, where he said he intended to "engage in economic activities." . . . The State Department black-listed him personally, but not his companies. . . .

Current Biography:

In February 1940 while he was yachting off Nassau, the newspapers reported that he had received a cable from Goering asking him to return to Sweden and attempt to negotiate the Russo-Finnish peace. Whether by coincidence or not, he sailed to Italy on the same boat with Sumner Wells and arrived in Berlin at about the same time. No more was heard of his role in the Finnish peace but on his way from Rome to Berlin he told the correspondent who accompanied Wells that he regarded Goering as the best hope for bringing Germany into mediation negotiations. . . .

Both sources had a lot of say about Wenner-gren's 320-foot yacht, the *Southern Cross*. At one time it carried a crew of 315 men. After Wenner-gren settled in Mexico, he kept his yacht in the port of Veracruz on the Gulf of Mexico. *Time* reported that Wenner-gren had given the yacht to the Mexican government, adding: "If he had not done so, the Mexican government might have taken it anyway. Quite clearly Mexico did not want Axel Wenner-gren to make personal use of the *Southern Cross*." Why? *Time* quoted Wenner-gren: "If I took it out, people would say I was fueling U-boats."

There is no mention in any of the stories about Inga Arvad or any other mistress. From all these accounts, Wenner-gren was happily married to a woman named Margaret Liggett from Kansas City, Missouri. Wenner-gren died in November of 1961, age eighty.

About Inga Arvad, there is nothing to be discovered in library reference sources. But we had learned a great deal through our interviews. Frank Waldrop:

Inga Arvad had come to us—again with some palaver from Krock. Krock was at that time on the board of trustees of the Co-lumbia School of Journalism. Inga was a student up there and she wanted to come to Washington. She asked him if he knew where she could get a job. So he called and said: "I've got another one for you." And I said as a joke: "What are you, our staff procurer?"

So he sent her down and she came in. She was beautiful and had a very appealing style of nonprofessional writing. There was a little feature called "Did You Happen to See?" that Mrs. Patterson saw in another paper on a trip somewhere. So she started one in the *Times-Herald*. At that time the war crowd was coming to Washing-ton, so this column, which was a brief profile, was a good way of introducing second- and third-echelon people. You wanted a rather artless, open way of looking at these people, which is what Inga had. So we put it on page two. Inga was very effective about it be-cause she didn't have the sense to be sophisticated. She was amazed to meet some klunk from Toledo who had been in the rub-ber business and who was now in Washington for a dollar a year to see what he could do to save the country. She did this thing very well. Then Jack began squiring her around. I don't know if she was concealing anything, but she was married all the time she was go-ing around. . . .

Q. Married to whom?

A. A Hungarian movie director named Fehost, I think it was. Inga was Danish. She went to the Olympic games in 1936 and Hit-ler saw her and said there was a perfect Nordic beauty. I have to give old Adolf something for having a pretty good eye. Then it seems that Goering, who had more sense than Hitler did about what to do when you run upon a perfect Nordic beauty, invited her for dinner—not alone, as I understand it. But that got a little boom-let for Inga going around Berlin. So then she got in Berlin movies. She met the Hungarian director Fehost, an archaeologist and docu-mentary moviemaker. They got married and went on a world tour and made a famous nature movie in Malaysia about a tiger fighting a boa constrictor. I think they met Wenner-gren in Singapore and Fehost persuaded Wenner-gren to put up some money to do a mov-ie on Machu Picchu, the famous ancient city of the Incas in the Pe-ruvian Andes. But then the war came. Inga went to Columbia, she

said, to learn English. Fehost was left in the Andes or whatever. . . .

We asked Waldrop if he could remember anything about Jack and Inga
getting into trouble. He reminded us that the Roosevelt Administration
viewed the *Times-Herald* as a Fascist mouthpiece because the paper had
furiously opposed entering the war and had, in concert with its sister
newspaper, the *Chicago Tribune*, publshed a secret American war plan
leaked to them by a conservative isolationist senator.

We were considered personally responsible for Pearl Harbor.
Don't forget I was the guy sitting there when the story about the
so-called Rainbow War Plan came in and made the decision to publish it on December 4. So three days later, when the Japs hit Pearl
Harbor, there wasn't any doubt about our treasonableness. You
have to go back to the times and the way people feel when something's happening . . . I do recall that Kennedy was [in Naval
Intelligence] I do know that he was taken off that assignment
abruptly and shipped out. . . . He was pretty insulted and indig-
nant at something. . . . Now, whether it was his old man med-
dling in his love life or the Navy raising the question of his capacity
to keep his love life separated from his business, who knows? But
it certainly is true that it was at that time that Inga was discovered
to be another one of those horrible operatives who headed up this
nest of vipers [at the *Times-Herald*]. Poor little ignorant girl. I'll
say this: I never thought Hitler had any too great organization
around here, but if he was depending on Inga he certainly didn't
seem to know his business.

Paige Wilson:

I knew Inga very well. I had been living in the house of some
good friends of mine and was looking for someone to live with. Arthur Krock asked me if I'd like to have Inga. I met her and she was
very attractive. So she came to stay with me until she found a place
of her own. She and Kathleen got to be great friends and she introduced Inga to Jack. Jack was very fond of Inga. She was extremely
pretty. She had a very good sense of humor. Very gay. Very mer-
ry. But not lacking in seriousness. She was one of those people
with a gift for happiness. And she was a good reporter. She wrote
those little profiles called "Did You Happen to See?" that Kathleen later wrote. She'd worked on a Danish newspaper, I think.
She didn't say much about her life in Europe. She was married, but
I gathered the marriage was dissipating. She was separating. I nev-

er laid eyes on her husband. He had some relationship with Axel
Wenner-gren. . . . She stayed with me a short time and then got
her own apartment. I don't remember where. . . .

We asked Paige if she could recall that Inga had got into some trouble.
She said, "There were rumors about a lot of people in Washington. I
think rumors like that are utterly unfounded. I don't think she was ever in
any trouble of any sort."

Inga's column was generally a feature article on second- and third-
echelon government officials, about equally divided between men and
women. On November 27, ten days before the Japanese attack on Pearl
Harbor, she devoted her column to Jack. A small photograph of Jack
accompanies Inga's piece. She wrote:

An old Scandinavian proverb says the apple doesn't fall far from
the tree. No better American proof can be found than John F. Kennedy. If former Ambassador Joe Kennedy has a brilliant mind (not
even his political enemies will deny the fact), charm galore, and a
certain way of walking into the hearts of people with wooden shoes
on, then son No. 2 has inherited more than his due. The 24 years of
Jack's existence on our planet have proved that here is really a boy
with a future.

Young Kennedy—don't call him that, he will resent it greatly—
did more than boot the football about at Harvard. He was extremely popular. Graduated cum laude, was a class officer, sailed on the
intercollegiate sailing team during his sophomore year, and most
important, wrote a thesis.

Arthur Krock from the *New York Times* read it and suggested it
be put in a book. Henry Luce of *Time, Fortune* and *Life,* must have
thought the same because he wrote the foreword, and by putting in
12 hours a day, cooled off with as many showers. Jack polished it
off during the summer and the much praised book, *Why England
Slept,* was the result. It sold like wildfire.

"Yes, I certainly have the same opinions as in the summer of
1940," says Jack Kennedy. "You must understand that the reason
I did not editorialize was because nobody is going to listen to a boy
of 23. Besides, it was not the idea to say I, I, I. The book is based
on facts, and I did a lot of studying in order to be able to write it. I
couldn't say if I am going to write another book. Now, I am in the
Navy, that is most important, but I have many plans for the future.
Some day, when I have time, I am going to study law."

Jack hates only one subject—himself. He is the best listener I
have come across between Haparanda and Yokohama. Elder men

like to hear his views, which are sound and astonishingly objective
for so young a man.

It was typical of all of Inga's columns: artless (as Frank Waldrop had
put it), to be sure. We wondered what Jack's cohorts in ONI had thought
when they read it. There must have been much good-natured kidding in
he office on the morning of November 27 and perhaps some unspoken
ealousy. If Inga had indeed been under close surveillance, then the inves-
igators must have read the column closely, too.

Arthur Krock:

What Jack didn't know and I didn't know was that Inga was under surveillance by the FBI. She had won a beauty contest in Berlin. She had been given the award in person by Hermann Goering,
who expressed great admiration for her, which, of course, made
her an object of surveillance by the FBI. So the FBI used to listen
to telephone conversations on her telephone and many of them
were with Kennedy. The extent of his infatuation I will not attempt
to describe, but certainly he was terribly attracted to her and they
kept very close company, let us say, over a period of time, until I
think he must have discovered this Goering thing and the fact that
she was under surveillance, though her claim always was that he
was inadequate. An inadequate suitor. At any rate, that was the
purport of a conversation overheard by the FBI one night—a conversation by Inga with a friend of hers from Denmark who was in
Washington, about Kennedy. He moved on to other things, so did
she, but he never forgot that I introduced Inga to him because
whenever I saw him as president, he would invariably say to me in
his Massachusetts accent: "How's Inga?" And I'd say, "You
know a damn sight more about that than I do." When he was grand
marshal of the Harvard commencement, as he walked up to the podium, Frederick Ayer, Jr., who had been at Harvard, and who had
also been assigned by the FBI to keep surveillance over Inga Arvad, said in a loud, audible stage whisper as Kennedy walked by in
his black silk hat: "How's Inga?" Whereupon Kennedy turned to
Ayer and hissed, "You son of a bitch!"

We were on the point of interrupting Krock to ask where we might find
Frederick Ayer when he said, to our astonishment, "Ayer died suddenly
1 Bermuda today. He was very wealthy, having inherited the patent me-
icine fortune of Ayer's Pectoral Compound, which every housewife in
New England used to drink, considering it nonalcoholic when it was, in
act, full of booze. He was a great sportsman and he had a very fine career

in government. He was a G-man in Greece at the time of the guerrilla uprising in 1948 and he was with the FBI for a good long time, doing important work.''

A few weeks after his funeral we telephoned Mrs. Ayer, offered condolences, then asked her if she remembered that her husband had operated a bug on one Inga Arvad that had caught Jack Kennedy. She said:

> Yes. Freddy told me about it. The reason they had a surveillance on her was that her loyalties were questionable. I think she was rushing in and out of the sack with somebody and they were worried about it. They did it with tape recorders in the room. As I remember this case, they had a microphone in her room. My husband and Jack weren't that close at this time. We'd just been married and come to Washington. It was Freddy's first big case at the FBI. I think. And, of course, he didn't know [in advance] that Jack was involved. And Jack wasn't the only one involved. He wasn't alone in her affections. . . .

John B. White:

> Inga was beautiful. Truly sexy. Blond, blue eyes, honey-colored hair. Luscious, really luscious, everything about her. Jack called her Inga-Binga. She rather liked Jack. Inga and I were quite close and she confided in me. She told me: "I have gooey eyes for him." She found him entertaining and probably pleasant in many ways. But he was infatuated quite quickly. She was amused by Jack mainly and sort of excited because he was such a wild new experience for her. She had never dealt with a naïve, spirited person like this. The four of us used to go out: Kick and me, Jack and Inga. We would hardly get around the corner before brother Jack had his shirttail out. He could hardly ever operate without his shirttail out. Kathleen and I would go off and leave those two alone. It couldn't have been better. The European style of the older woman was simply damned good. She was good-hearted, good everything. He should have stuck with her. But it would never have done.
>
> Q. What happened?
>
> A. She never really liked him all that much. She never said he was cold, but he was cool. We used to go out, the four of us, fairly regularly because it was such a good cover for everybody, so to speak. We'd part immediately and go about our business, then join again. Then Kathleen told me we might have to give up the idea of these foursomes because her father disapproved of Inga. Papa Joe didn't like Inga as anything except as an instructor. Kathleen said

that her father was getting ready to drag up the big guns. Because the thing was going too fast. Then there were rumors. . . . It was almost established that she was a spy, but not the usual kind. I just can't remember. . . . We had to sort of sneak around because Jack wasn't even supposed to be seen with her because her reputation was so dubious. The combination of possible marriage and dubious reputation frightened the old man.

Chuck Spalding:

Inga was a very attractive girl and I guess she was [for Jack] serious in the way people you care about suddenly—and for a while. She was on the paper, great fun, very enterprising, one of those active girls around Washington who was interested in that life. They went to a lot of things together and she went to a lot of things he probably arranged and at that point, I think he went to a lot of things because she was going. She was very attractive. Very animated and bright. She could take care of herself and she was sophisticated.

Q. Do you think Jack was serious about her?

A. He was interested in the sense that a young person is interested and you don't know who's coming by and she walked by and he was attracted to her. He liked her immensely. . . .

In our interview with Captain Hunter, we had approached the subject obliquely. We asked if he could recall a man named Axel Wenner-gren: whether there had been a belief in ONI that he was using his yacht in Mexico to refuel Nazi U-boats. We could not have asked a better source. He said:

Yes, and I'll tell you why. When I left ONI in the spring of 1942, I went to Guatemala. The American Navy was practically convinced that the yacht was being used for refueling U-boats. They couldn't understand how the subs could remain at sea as long as they did. I had a plane at my disposal and I spent all my time hunting down any trace along these lines. At the close of the war I was sent to Germany to interrogate high-level German POW's. One of these was Admiral Mueller, last director of German Naval Intelligence. So I asked him face to face. He laughed and said they never received any help from land. They *towed* fuel and food containers behind some of the subs. That delighted me because that was the conclusion I had reached after a year down there looking into it. . . .

We asked Hunter if he remembered that Jack Kennedy might have got into some trouble during his tour in ONI. He replied emphatically, "Oh yes!"

Q. How did it come to your attention?

A. When Captain Kingman called me in and said we have a very serious problem on our hands and we would have to get rid of Kennedy as soon as possible.

Q. And Kingman was assistant director of ONI under Wilkinson?

A. That's correct.

Q. And he said?

A. He wanted to get him out of the Navy as quickly as possible. Now I've always been very loyal to my juniors and I'm glad to say they've usually been most loyal to me, so I felt I had to do everything I properly could to protect him as one of my men. I pointed out that it was a delicate situation to begin with since his father had been ambassador to the Court of St. James's and stood in with President Roosevelt, and secondly, that I saw no reason for getting him out of the naval service because he did not have access to information that could be anything more than a bit embarrassing. . . . It seemed to me the best thing to do was transfer him to a seagoing unit. . . .

Well, Captain Wilkinson was so upset over this situation that you might say he was really frantic. For reasons I'm not fully aware of. Whether he would have been blamed . . . I don't know. But he wanted to get Kennedy out as quickly as possible. I realized, of course, that if Kennedy were cashiered . . . it would be damaging to him, never mind how prominent his father was nor how able he himself was. So I kept hammering away at transferring him to a seagoing unit. Captain Kingman, who I imagine talked things over with some of his cronies, saw that the sensible thing to do was move him out of Washington. I feel that if he had been cashiered, it is rather doubtful that he would ever have become President of the United States because the stain would have shown up.

Q. When Kingman called you in on this matter—

A. He did several times.

Q. Over a week or ten days?

A. Yes.

Q. Did he have a report on his desk or something like that?

A. No. Nothing that I saw.

Q. Did he explain the nature of the trouble?

A. His concern was that this woman was using him to find out all she could about what was going on in the Navy Department and ONI.

Q. A Mata Hari?

A. Right. Exactly.

Q. And the woman in question was Inga Arvad?

A. Yes.

Q. Was Kingman a martinet?

A. No. He was a very nice man. But a man who was very frightened at the time. Very upset over the whole situation.

Q. After you talked to Kingman did you go to Kennedy and tell him?

A. No. I never talked to him about this subject because I was forbidden to do so.

Q. So Kingman actually wanted to cashier Kennedy from the Navy? To withdraw his commission and send him back to civilian life?

A. Yes. And it gives you some idea of the terror and the mood of the times. But that terror must not be taken out of context. The whole naval establishment was in a state of terror from the moment they heard of the attack on Pearl Harbor.

11

Ronald

INGA Arvad moved to Hollywood and married the old Western movie star Tim McCoy. They lived on a ranch in southern Arizona near the border town of Nogales. She died in December of 1973. The obituary in the *Los Angeles Times*, under the headline WIFE OF ACTOR TIM MCCOY DIES OF CANCER, began: "Mrs. Tim McCoy, said to have been described by Adolf Hitler as the perfect Nordic beauty before she married the Western film star, died of cancer at her home near here Wednesday."

Tim McCoy, who was eighty-two, was not able to speak to us, but he referred us to his son, Ronald, age twenty-six.

Ronald McCoy, a tall, well-built blond young man, lived in a rustic home on a hillside in Carmel, California, overlooking the ocean. We talked with him for several hours. He said, "If my mother were still alive, I wouldn't talk to you about her. And I wouldn't talk about Kennedy to you either. But now she's gone and this is sort of a therapy trip for me."

His account of his mother's life and of her relationship with Jack Kennedy is odd and interesting in a number of ways, and it's difficult to know just how to evaluate it. It is amazingly detailed—few of us know so much about our parents' lives before our birth. It is impressively consistent in character with what we know of both Inga and Jack from other sources. It can scarcely be thought of as primary source material, of course; it is Ronald's three-year-old recollection of his mother's thirty-year-old recollection of events, documented only by some letters he showed us from Jack in the South Pacific to Inga. It is certainly true in its general outline, as we have already learned. It ends with a sensational revelation which cannot be proven but which we were also unable to disprove. Ronald McCoy has never told any of it before; and Inga, in thirty years at the fringes of celebrity life, never attempted to exploit it. It seemed at very least to be worthwhile to make it part of this book.

What is presented here is the segment of our interview that dealt with Inga's life and her relationship with Jack Kennedy in 1941–1942. We shall return to this interview later in the narrative.

Ronald's mother had raised him to think that he was an uncommon individual. In high school, he had played football. Then he took up debating. He won several American Legion debating contests, including Boys' Nation, which took him on a field trip to Washington to see the inner workings of the federal government. This activity inspired a strong interest in national politics.

Ronald went on to college at Arizona State. He majored in political science and Asian studies. He was elected president of the student body, but later he became "radicalized" and turned against the Establishment. Because of his past achievements in the American Legion contests, he was invited to work in Nixon's 1968 presidential campaign. McCoy said he would have preferred to work for Bobby Kennedy but Kennedy was shot and he thought the job with Nixon would be educational. In a sense it was, but he said he was completely "turned off" by most of the men in the Nixon campaign organization. He thought they were dishonest and that Nixon was a liar and a "shit." When he complained about Nixon to a fellow campaign worker, the worker said, "Sure he's a shit. But he's *our* shit."

After graduation from Arizona State, McCoy returned to the ranch for about a year. Then he went to Yucatan and studied Mayan ruins and the history of that civilization. From there he drifted to Carmel, where he tried writing. When that didn't work out, he took a job in a butcher shop, then another in an art gallery. The gallery owner fired him when he went to see his dying mother. Since the first of the year he had been "into" painting. He was "doing" Plains Indians in ink and watercolors. His younger brother Terrence, who had a store in Tucson, sold the paintings for him.

We asked about his mother. McCoy said:

> She used to be able to talk about Kennedy before he was killed but found it very difficult after he was dead. When he was killed, we were living down in Nogales. I'd come home from school for lunch. Mother picked me up. I said that somebody said that Jack Kennedy had been shot and I thought that was a terrible joke. She said be quiet, it's no joke. Of course, nobody went back to school.
>
> She sat for a long time in front of the TV and then somebody came on and said the president was dead. She just got up and left the room and went into her room and closed the door and was in there for a couple of hours. Finally my father went in to her and she was crying. She was really broken up. She always loved Kennedy, she told me that. . . .
>
> Up until the time she died—she was only sixty when she died—she was always very stimulating. She had a magnetic personality. She could walk into a room and everybody would know she was there. She was brilliant. Witty. A genius at getting to know people and getting them to talk. She could put people at ease—or

completely ill at ease—with a stare or a question. She was very curious, very empathetic. She could understand different points of
view. She loved to read. She loved art. She did some painting, but
most of her activities were people-orientated. In Nogales she was
president of the Library Board and the Speaker's Bureau. She associated with Mexicans, even though my father and brother
wouldn't. She was really interested in people. She'd go to the hospital to visit people she didn't even know. She had to have that human contact. . . .

She was born Inga Marie Arvad in Copenhagen, Denmark, October 6, 1913. She was the daughter of Olga Houman and Anton
Arvad-Peterson, an engineer-architect. The Peterson was dropped
later. Her father died when she was four years old. She spent her
childhood in Copenhagen and traveling around Europe with her
mother, living in Italy and the south of France, climbing in the
Alps, and so on. She went to a private school in Copenhagen and to
schools in Germany, France, and England and, later, the Sor-
bonne. She was raised a Lutheran, but had no real religion. When
she was sixteen or seventeen, there was a beauty contest—Miss
Europe, I think—in Paris. Maurice Chevalier was the master of
ceremonies. She won and became Miss Europe. She met a very
tall, dark Egyptian named Kemal Abdel Nabi who was studying in
Paris to become a member of the Egyptian Foreign Service. His
family was land-rich, with thousands of acres of cotton in Egypt,
but money-poor. They got married. She was always getting married, or about to get married. In order to get rid of someone, she'd
say yes, sure. They lived in Paris for a time off my grandmother's
money, with creditors banging on the door. Mother *made* him graduate, and years later he was Egyptian Ambassador to Paris during
the Suez crisis—or so she told me. Then they went to Egypt to live.
Mother found the situation extremely feudal. She left him and got
a divorce. She returned to Denmark, then went to Germany in the
1930s. She had a lot of friends there, including the daughter of a
World War One Admiral, von Leubetzow, who was chief of police
of Berlin. One day in 1935 she was having lunch at the Danish embassy. She heard that Hermann Goering was going to marry a German actress, Emmy Sonnemann. Mother—who could be very direct—called up Emmy, saying she was a Danish journalist—which
she wasn't—and asked if it were true. Emmy said yes and invited
mother for an interview that same day. Mother wrote it up and sent
it to the *Berlingske Tidende,* a Copenhagen newspaper, which not
only published it but hired her as Berlin correspondent. Emmy invited mother to the wedding—April 10, 1935. It was very small,
forty to fifty people. Adolf Hitler was best man. Joseph Paul Goeb-

bels, Minister of Propaganda, was there. He liked beautiful women and struck up a conversation. He asked if there were anything he could do for her and she said, yes, she'd like an exclusive interview with Hitler. He arranged it. They were entirely alone. Mother asked Hitler if he wore a bulletproof vest and he said, frisk me. She frisked him. (He wasn't wearing a vest.) Later, she had two more exclusive interviews with Hitler, including a Danish luncheon he had prepared in her behalf. She went to the 1936 Olympics with Hitler. She said he was furious that Jesse Owens—a black— won. That was when he said she was a perfect example of Nordic beauty, a great label to have in Germany, but bad to have in the U.S.

She got to know everybody of importance in Berlin. The foreign minister, Joachim von Ribbentrop, proposed that she go to Paris in their behalf. They'd pay all her expenses. All she had to do was go to parties and tell them what she heard. She realized she was being asked to be a spy, so she left Germany. After that she made a movie in Denmark. She hated the movie, but it was very successful. The director was Paul Fejos—F-E-J-O-S, a Hungarian who was an air ace in World War One. Then she and Fejos went to the Dutch East Indies to capture some Komodo dragons for a zoo, and make a movie, and test atabrine. She lived with Fejos in a hut in the jungle and later married him. Fejos hooked up with Wenner-gren, or was already hooked up with him, and went to Peru on a long archaeological dig. Mother wasn't interested in that, and for all practical purposes, the marriage sort of ended. Mother came to the U.S. to the Columbia School of Journalism and was admitted on the strength of her Berlin reporting. She spoke English, French, German, and Danish. Arthur Krock came up to Columbia to give a lecture. She told me Krock was a skirt-chaser. He made a point of seeing her afterwards and asked, "Who are you, young lady?" When she told him, Krock said that if she ever needed a job to call him in Washington. So she left school—without graduating—and Krock got her the job working for Cissy Patterson on the *Times-Herald*, writing "Did You Happen to See?" three times a week. Kathleen Kennedy was there. Somewhere along the line, she and Kathleen roomed together, I think after she met Jack. But Kathleen told her she wanted mother to meet her brother, that she'd really like him and he'd really like her. I imagine that when she was rooming with Kathleen, Jack was living with mother most of the time. He could always cover it by saying he was with his sister. He'd always be walking around with a towel around his waist. That's all he ever wore in the apartment—a towel. The minute he came in, he'd take off all his clothes and take a shower. He was always taking showers. She used to massage his back; he was always in bad shape because of his back. He ate steak, baked potatoes, and milk; gallons of milk and ice cream. She remembered him as very compassionate and somewhat insensitive. If he wanted to make love, you'd make love—now. They'd have fifteen minutes to get to a party and she'd say she didn't want to. He'd look at his watch and say we've got ten minutes, let's go. There was a certain amount of insensitiveness, an awful lot of self-centeredness. She remembered him as pretty much of a quiet person who'd never been healthy, had never had much stamina, and wanted a quiet life of writing, some research, and some teaching. American history. That was his dream at that point: to have a very quiet life, write, and live off his money.

She felt he was a humanist—he was interested in individual people as they related to the whole. He had a great disrespect for structures, probably because of his family structure. He had great respect for her brains. And she said he was very much aware of how he appeared to people. He knew how to make an impression and he knew what kind of impression he was making and he could make whatever kind of impression he wanted to make. They'd go to a party, she told me, and he'd say, "OK, now it's time to turn on the BP—Big Personality." And he'd come in with that great big grin and knock everybody out. When the party was over and they'd left, he'd say, "Jesus! What a drag, what a bore, Inga-Binga." That's what he called her. Inga-Binga.

We asked Ronald to give us his judgment as to how serious the affair had been. He said:

It got pretty heavy, awfully damned heavy. He wanted to marry her and she was still married. She loved him very much. Of the people she'd known, I think she liked him most of all. She wanted to marry him but there were practical matters that just wouldn't work. One was the old man—Joseph Kennedy. I guess that's what it all boiled down to. The family was just an extension of the old man's hard-line schizophrenic condition. She thought the Kennedy family was weird. The way she thought of it, the old man would push Joe, Joe would push Jack, Jack would push Bobby, Bobby would push Teddy, and Teddy would fall on his ass. Jack was going through a hell of a crisis about that. Mother liked Jack and Kathleen, but she couldn't figure out how two people who were that bright could stand for all that bullshit. She thought they had to want the money pretty badly.

She would have married him when he asked her to if it hadn't been for the old man and the family extension of the old man. She just didn't want to put up with that shit. He'd say, "Oh, we can move away." She'd say, "How can you?" He went to Palm Beach to talk to old Joe about marrying my mother. They went out to play golf. Joe didn't like the idea at all, but apparently went so far as to find out how much they would have to donate to the Church to get a papal annulment of her marriages. She said Joe told Jack he certainly hoped he'd reconsider and realize that that wasn't what he should do. But Jack apparently didn't realize because he kept talking marriage. She said that when the old man started to put on the arm, she didn't think Jack would be able to hold up under the pressure. She said that if they got married, she didn't want to spend any time with the Kennedy family.

She thought old Joe was awfully hard—a really mean man. He could be very charming when she and Jack were with him but if she left the room he'd come down on Jack about her and if Jack left the room, he'd try to hop in the sack with her. He did that one weekend at the Cape, she said. She thought it was a totally amoral situation, that there was something incestuous about the whole family.

We asked if Inga had told him anything about the trouble with the FBI.

Yes. Jack was furious. Through his father or through Arthur Krock he knew everybody, so he and mother went to see J. Edgar Hoover. Hoover told them his investigation showed that she was *not* a Nazi spy or had ever been employed by the Nazis or did anything for them. So Jack asked Hoover if he would give them a letter saying she wasn't a Nazi spy. Hoover said he couldn't because if he gave her a letter and then she went out and started working for them tomorrow, his ass was on the line.

We asked Ronald if he knew how long it had gone on? He said, "They were together constantly. When he was stationed in Charleston, South Carolina, she used to go down and visit him. And he would go AWOL and come up to Washington to visit her. Then Jack and his father had a 'final' talk about it. The old man said no. Jack said he didn't care what his father said, he was going to marry her."

Ronald told how his mother had left Washington and gone to Hollywood, and about correspondence and meetings with Kennedy later in the war—and after. We shall return to this interview, as we said, at the appropriate points in the narrative of Jack's life.

Our thoughts by now have been much on the FBI files on Inga Arvad.

They must have hung over Jack's public career like a dark cloud. Belief has long been widespread that J. Edgar Hoover held blackmail power over presidents. Is this file an example?

One source reports that Jack was concerned about it for years. He is Langdon Parker Marvin, Jr., a close social friend and a legislative aide to Jack in his early House days. Born into a prominent New York family— Franklin D. Roosevelt was his godfather—Marvin graduated *magna cum laude* from Harvard in 1941, entered the Navy and by age twenty-four was chairman of the War Production Board's Interdepartmental Air Cargo Priorities Committee. He had twice been featured in *Life* as a comer. He knew Joe Junior and Jack at Harvard, and, in Washington, Inga Arvad. She had profiled Marvin in the *Times-Herald before* she had profiled Jack.

We met him in New York, meaning to ask him about some details of Jack's congressional days, but he launched immediately and absolutely unprompted into a bitter attack on the Kennedys and Jack that began, "I'm going to blow the whole Jack Kennedy thing wide open. Have you ever heard of Inga-Binga?"

We had, in fact, learned all that we have recounted here, but he told us again anyway, substantially as we already knew it. He concluded with this on those FBI records: "When Jack came down to Congress, one of the things on his mind was the Inga-Binga tape in the FBI files—the tape *he* was on. He wanted to get the tape from the FBI. I told him not to ask for it, he'd never get it. Later when he got elected to the Senate, he said he was *really* going to get the tape now. I told him not to be stupid. . . ."

Why hadn't the story surfaced before now? If Krock and Waldrop and White knew about it, other journalists must have known. Had the Kennedy power been so threatening that no journalist dared raise the subject? Or had it not been told simply because of the Washington press corps' traditional taboo on the private lives of politicians?

In any case there was only one solid source remaining: the FBI files. If there had been an FBI investigation of Inga Arvad, and there is little doubt about that, the file might reveal much useful information. The transcripts of the tape recordings might indicate Kennedy's true frame of mind about Inga; possibly even a clue as to whether she was indeed a spy. They might also contain discussions between Inga and Jack about his father's position in the matter.

In July of 1973 Attorney General Elliot L. Richardson had issued a new policy directive to the FBI that "inactive" FBI files be made available to qualified historians and scholars. Among the first files to be released under this policy were those on Ezra Pound, Alger Hiss, Whittaker Chambers, and Ethel and Julius Rosenberg.

We were on the point of applying to the FBI for permission to examine this file when we read a column by Jack Anderson on February 25, 1974, which stated:

> Raw FBI files, containing sensitive information about Presidents and other prominent people were sneaked out of the FBI after the death of J. Edgar Hoover. . . . The missing files according to FBI sources included reports on the sex exploits of the late President John F. Kennedy. . . . One report, for example, claims that in late 1941 young John F. Kennedy romanced a woman suspected of espionage. His exploits with the lady occurred in Charleston, S.C., where he was working on a project for the Navy to protect defense factories against bombing. . . . The late FBI chief kept the files in his personal custody because he didn't want subordinates reading them and gossiping about their contents. Nevertheless our sources have seen the files which, they say, were removed by Hoover's faithful factotum, Clyde Tolson. . . . Footnote: Our sources say that Hoover's trusted secretary, Helen Gandy, handled the sensitive files for him. When we asked her about them, she stated firmly: "All official files were left there." Beyond that she had no comment. We couldn't reach Tolson, whose friends said he is in too poor health to respond to questions.

Clyde Tolson's name connected in our minds with Inga Arvad. We checked back through our notes on Inga's columns. On October 30, 1941, she had done a "Did You Happen to See?" on Tolson. Our disjointed notes: "No. 2 G-man in the U.S. Incredibly flattering column. 'Keenest most intelligent eyes, splendid physique,' etc., etc. Says she had long wanted to do a column on Tolson but 'He has been hiding from me for months.' "

If the FBI were conducting surveillance on Inga, Tolson probably *had* been ducking an interview with her. Why had Inga pursued the interview so relentlessly? Is that just cute hyperbole, or had she been attempting to form a friendship with Tolson by writing a flattering column? Was her real intent to penetrate the FBI through Tolson? Was her real intent to penetrate ONI through Jack Kennedy?

Jack Anderson told us, "The column's solid. I can't give you my source but he *saw* the documents in Tolson's possession. Tolson is a recluse, living in J. Edgar Hoover's house, which Hoover bequeathed to him. There's an old retired FBI agent out there acting as sort of a companion and guard. We've tried like hell to get to Tolson. They won't answer the door. They won't talk to *anyone*. You could try but I'd say your chances of seeing Tolson and getting to the documents were less than zero."

A year later, in 1975, two of Hoover's former assistants, Cartha D. De-

Loach and Louis B. Nichols, revealed to a *Washington Post* reporter that Hoover had kept such files on presidents and the "blackmail" gossip was, according to some, thereby confirmed. Attorney General Edward Levi told a Congressional committee Hoover had kept forty-eight files in his office—on presidents and on at least seventeen Congressmen. But no one said where the files were or much about what was in them. There was no specific reference to Jack Kennedy.

The whole subject had become so controversial and heated that we gave up hope of persuading either the FBI or Clyde Tolson to release these files to us. Perhaps in the future some historian will gain access to the FBI files.

12

Siberia

ON January 15, 1942, Jack left Washington and was, in effect, banished to Siberia: to a nonsensitive desk job at the Sixth Naval District Headquarters, Charleston, South Carolina. He had been transferred to an ONI field office. His job was to instruct workers in defense plants in how to defend the plants and themselves against an enemy bombing attack. Burns says that Jack found this job "dull and distasteful." Tregaskis calls it a "dreadfully dull assignment." Donovan says the assignment "bored him nearly to death." There's little reason to doubt their assessment. But he was still in the Navy; he had not been cashiered.

On the orders transferring him to Charleston, Kennedy gave his intended address in Charleston as "care of Mrs. G. A. Middleton, 48 Murray Road." Mrs. George Abbott Middleton still lives in Charleston. She remembered Kennedy clearly. She said:

> We had a big fifty-year-old home with white columns in a very nice section of town. There were six bedrooms. My son George was in the Navy; my daughters were married to men in the service and gone. There were a lot of naval officers pouring into Charleston so my husband and I decided to rent out four of the bedrooms to these officers. My husband, my mother, and I lived in the two bedrooms on the third floor. One of the officers brought Jack Kennedy by and he took the room right away. It had a good view overlooking the Ashly River. Kennedy was a nice-looking boy and just as polite as he could be. I remember there was something wrong with his back. We had to get a board to put under his mattress. He dated a pretty girl who lived on Tradd Street who was not from Charleston. He made a lot of long-distance calls. He paid for these, and he paid his rent on time. I remember that when the weather got better he rented a little house with some other officers out on Sullivan's Island, near the beach. I never saw him again until I was in Washington in 1960—eighteen years later. I was sitting in the lobby of the Mayflower Hotel and he came walking through it—it was during the presidential campaign—looked over, saw me and recognized me! I was astounded.

Mrs. Middleton could not remember much else. Not the names of the other naval officers who boarded at her home when Kennedy was there nor the name of the "pretty girl" who lived on Tradd Street. Ronald McCoy had said that Jack was still dating his mother when he was based in Charleston; had even gone AWOL to see her in Washington. If that were true, then who was the girl on Tradd Street? Could it have been Inga down on a visit to see Jack?

According to a document in Jack's naval records, he was back in Washington on Saturday, February 14, on weekend liberty, we guessed. On that date he put in a request for a transfer—to the Fourteenth Naval District in Honolulu, Hawaii. This was not a request for "sea duty"; merely a shift from intelligence duty in the Charleston branch office to the Honolulu branch office. However, it would have placed Jack closer to the fighting in the Pacific and into an intelligence branch office where more exciting things were going on. It was not granted.

Jack had not been in Charleston long when his old buddy Lem Billings came for a visit. During our interview Lem had told us:

My brother Frederic got married in Nashville, Tennessee, on February 21, 1942. I went down for the wedding and then on the way back to Baltimore I stopped off in Charleston to see Jack for about a week. He was *very* unhappy there in Charleston. It was a boring, lousy, stinking job. He just wasn't interested in U.S.-based intelligence at all. He hated it. He was the unhappiest man you ever knew in Charleston. While I was there, I saw Jack make his first public speech. He had to go to a factory and make a speech to the workers about incendiary bombs: the two kinds, what they were like and what to do and other technical things I don't think he knew very much about. But he was damned good. I remember I was terribly impressed. I never knew he could speak. When you see a friend speak in public for the first time you're always kind of nervous, thinking maybe he'll be awful. But he really impressed the hell out of me. And he was rather pleased with himself because it did go very well. But at the end he made the mistake of asking if there were any questions, which is stupid if you don't know your subject. Well, the first question was some highly technical question. God apparently gave Jack an ability to think quickly on his feet. He said: "I'm glad you asked that question. We're having a real specialist down here in several weeks and he wants to talk on that subject. . . ." And he got away with it!

Very soon after that visit, Billings finally found a niche for himself in a paramilitary outfit. He told us:

I finally settled on the American Field Service—the civilian-manned ambulance corps. I got into that despite my terrible eyes. Hell, they took the halt and blind, or even one-legged people. My outfit—the Sixteenth Unit, composed of about one hundred men—was on alert for about three months. Finally, in June, we sailed secretly from New York in a big convoy of about forty ships. We went to South Africa, then up through the Suez Canal to Cairo, then into the fighting in the desert in North Africa. . . .

In a letter following up our interview with Torby Macdonald, we asked for details of a visit he said he had made to Jack in Charleston. He declined to reply. Might that have been because Inga was there? We did not know. But, according to Ronald McCoy, Inga had met Torby. It is possible they met in Charleston, but they may have met in Boston when Inga spent a weekend in Hyannis Port. If Ronald's memory is accurate, Inga was not overly fond of Torby. But without Torby's cooperation we could not explore the matter further.

There was nothing in Jack's naval records to indicate what he was doing officially during the first part of March—presumably giving more lectures on incendiary bombs. On Sunday, March 23, we knew from our interview with Flip Price, he was in Palm Beach, probably for the weekend. That was when Henry "Hank the Tank" James showed up for a visit and wrote Flip the postcard which she produced for us.

James told us that he had been fifteen minutes late for lunch at the Kennedys'. When he got to the table, Joe Kennedy was in a towering rage. James said Kennedy gave him a "tongue-lashing" as though he had committed a grave sin." James added, "The other kids, including Jack, sat around the table, heads bowed, apparently frightened to death." James said he had never been treated that way in anybody's home before or since and it was the end of his friendship with Jack.

Shortly after the weekend in Palm Beach, Jack was a guest at a house party at the Meads' plantation in Aiken, South Carolina. Mrs. Mead told us that George and Paul Moore (who had not gone to the party) had been assigned to the Fifth Marine Regiment, which was then preparing to embark for the South Pacific. Kathleen and Chuck and Betty Spalding were among the guests. Betty recalled, "Mrs. Mead got us all to come down to Aiken on his last leave before he went overseas. Jack was down there and Chuck's cousin, John Coleman, who was a friend of Jack's. Chuck and I went down and stayed with the Meads. I remember the Meads had a record-making machine and we made a record down there for fun. Jack was playing the role of H. V. Kaltenborn and we were all being interviewed about this and that."

Chuck Spalding remembered another detail of the weekend:

> We had a recorder and we were doing these round-table discus-
> sions. One guy would be the farming senator from the Midwest,
> and one guy would be the garrulous senator, and Jack would be the
> coordinator, and Betty would be the women's vote, and we'd all sit
> down and make these recordings. Or you'd play different roles. It
> was really a constant game. The Meads had a couple of dogs
> around the house and right in the middle of one of those recording
> sessions, Jack got a very serious attack of asthma. He couldn't
> breathe.

We'd heard about Jack's allergy to dogs from Lem Billings. But w
wondered if he mightn't have had a serious illness. If so, it might explain
series of documents we had found in his naval records that indicate
another major breakdown in his health in Charleston.

These documents showed:

On Monday, March 24, the day after Jack returned from the weeken
in Palm Beach with Henry James, he requested ten days' leave in order t
consult with his private physician, Dr. Sara Jordan, at the Lahey Clinic i
Boston. The request was granted.

A couple of weeks later, on April 9, probably following the weekend i
Aiken at the Mead place, Jack requested six months' inactive duty on ac
count (he wrote) "of the necessity for an operation and the subsequer
period of convalescence." The operation, Jack wrote, would be pe
formed by the family surgeon at a private hospital "for a condition whic
existed prior to entrance in the Navy." There was a note on this doct
ment from a doctor attached to the Sixth Naval District stating that h
concurred that the operation was necessary. The request for six month
inactive duty was approved.

Two days later, on April 11, Jack was transferred from his duties in th
Sixth Naval District to the Charleston Naval Hospital "for the determin
tion of your physical condition."

About a month later, May 9, Jack was transferred to the Naval Hosp
tal, Chelsea (in Boston) "for further treatment."

We studied these documents. There had been nothing about all this
the Kennedy books, no hint that there had been a major illness or th
need for an operation, or a request for six months' inactive duty. Wh
kind of operation? The documents gave no clue. And the medical recor
were closed.

Torby was then stationed in Boston and certainly saw much of Ja
during his stay in hospital. We sent him extracts of the orders and ask
him if he could explain what happened. Again, no reply. This was wh

ll communications from Torby Macdonald ceased. Later, a government
source whose anonymity we have promised to protect told us:

> You asked about Jack's request for a transfer from Charleston
> to Chelsea? I have something for you. It was his back. When he en-
> tered the hospital in Charleston in April, the diagnosis was:
> "chronic and recurrent dislocation of the back." He asked for the
> transfer for his own convenience—I think that means the Navy
> didn't pay for it or anything—and said he wanted to be near his
> family. There is no indication he had an operation. It's not clear,
> but I believe he was ordered to do back-strengthening exercises.

So: Jack had probably come into the Navy on limited-duty status because of his physical condition. He fouled up in Washington and was
transferred to Charleston, where we know he was unhappy. He probably
wanted sea duty to get out of Charleston (and ONI). He may have been
advised to have an operation on his back in order to qualify for sea duty.
He went to Boston for this purpose, but then somebody—perhaps his
back doctor at the Lahey Clinic, Ned Haggart—advised against an operation, proposing instead a regimen of exercises.

And now we come to an important leap. Sometime during his two
months in the Boston hospitals, Jack was qualified for sea duty—apparently without having had an operation. Since his medical history indicated
he was a poor physical specimen even without taking his back into consideration, we assume that this could only have been managed with string
pulling, probably by his father.

Ronald McCoy had said:

> Suddenly, as if by magic, he got orders to the South Pacific. He
> wasn't at all interested in going to fight the war. He didn't like the
> war. He came up to Washington and said some son of a bitch had
> transferred me to sea duty and I'm going to find out who it was. He
> came back later and said his father had called up an old Wall Street
> friend, Undersecretary of the Navy James V. Forrestal, and asked
> him to transfer Jack to sea duty, to the Pacific. Apparently he was
> really pissed off at the old man. He asked Inga to wait for
> him. . . .

That was not exactly the way it happened, of course. Jack had not been
transferred directly from Charleston to the South Pacific. According to
our reconstruction, his duty status had been changed in Boston from limited duty to sea duty; but before he could go on a ship, he had first to go to
school to learn how to be a line officer. Still, it could well be that the gen-

eral thrust of Inga's recollection, as McCoy conveyed it, was correct: tha
Joseph P. Kennedy had used his influence with Forrestal to get Jack sea
duty status. Whatever the case, it was a very different story from the on
in the Kennedy books.

If Jack were, consciously or unconsciously, still competing with Joe Ju
nior, it must have been a trying time. In May, 1942, Joe was graduate
from flight training at Jacksonville, Florida, and received his wings and
commission as ensign in the Naval Reserve. He had been named "out
standing" cadet in his class. Ambassador Kennedy attended the gradua
tion ceremony and proudly pinned Joe's wings on his chest. By contras
Jack, so far, had made a mess of his naval service.

It was at this time that Joseph P. Kennedy, Sr., first established a polit
cal power base in Massachusetts. The aim was presumably twofold: firs
to begin the process of achieving for Joe Junior what he himself had bee
denied—the presidency—and, second, to gain a measure of reveng
against Franklin D. Roosevelt.

Ever since the 1940 elections, when the ambassador had reluctantly er
dorsed Roosevelt for a third term, the gulf between them had been grov
ing. As both Whalen and Koskoff report, the ambassador wired FDR in
mediately after Pearl Harbor: NAME THE BATTLEFRONT. I'M YOURS T
COMMAND. But Roosevelt had lost faith in Joe Kennedy's judgment, an
despite publicity from friends like Arthur Krock in the *Times*, pointin
out that Kennedy could be useful to the war effort, no job offer was fortl
coming. The ambassador remained sidelined for the duration and grew ir
creasingly bitter at Roosevelt.

During 1942 the ambassador's bitterness translated itself into politic
action in Massachusetts. In that state, that year, there was an importai
election: the Senate seat held by Republican Henry Cabot Lodge was u
Anticipating this election, and wishing to consolidate his strength in Ma
sachusetts, Roosevelt had hand-picked a Democratic candidate to ru
against Lodge: Congressman Joseph Casey.

The ambassador—who had long since left Boston—now injected hin
self into the campaign. He demothballed Honey Fitz, then approachir
eighty years of age, and put him into the primary race—backed,
course, by considerable Kennedy money—against Roosevelt's ma
Casey. Honey Fitz loved being back in the limelight after years awa
from it. He went after Casey hammer and tongs, creating a bitter split
the Democratic Party in Massachusetts. He denounced Roosevelt's co
duct of the war, forcing Casey to defend it. He lost in the primar
108,000 to 80,000 (a third candidate polled 17,000 votes), but Honey Fi
had so badly mauled Casey that he had no chance against Lodge.

Roosevelt had lost substantial political strength in the state. The amba sador had established himself as a local political power by reminding the voters that the Kennedy-Fitzgerald family was still alive and kicking. In addition, the exercise had provided an opportunity to survey the political scene in Massachusetts. The process of creating a President Kennedy had begun in earnest.

13

The Volunteer

JACK reported to Northwestern University in Chicago on July 27, 1942, for the officer training course. He was joining thousands of young men fresh from college who were getting their first taste of naval life and learning how to become seagoing officers—the so-called ninety-day wonders.

During our interview with him, Chuck Spalding had told us that while Jack was at Northwestern, "he saw a lot of my cousin, Johnny Coleman." From Coleman, now a stockbroker in Chicago, we learned something of what Jack's life had been like at Northwestern:

> There was no campus. It was a downtown university, about five blocks from the Drake Hotel. They had two converted office buildings about fourteen stories high—Tower Hall and Abbott Hall. There was also an armory and some other classrooms in other buildings. Jack lived in Abbott Hall, where I wound up. It faced right on Lake Michigan. They had rooms with four or five men in each one. You didn't live on the seventh *floor*—it was the seventh *"deck."* The walls were "bulkheads," the halls "passageways," and all that naval jargon. It was a crash course. They taught navigation, seamanship, gunnery, semaphore, naval etiquette and regulations. . . .

We told him that Chuck Spalding had said Jack had spent many weekends that summer at the Coleman house in Lake Forest. Coleman didn't remember much about it. "Yes. I don't think he knew anyone else in Chicago then. We didn't do much. We'd play golf and swim. We talked a lot. He was always a great reader and liked to write a lot of letters. And he had problems with his back. We used to kid each other about it because I had a bad back too."

We asked if Jack had ever mentioned a girl named Inga Arvad. The question seemed to make Coleman uneasy. He said, "No. He never mentioned an Inga. He didn't date any girls here that I am aware of. There was only one thing on his mind then—the war."

If that last statement were true, it bespoke a new seriousness in Jack.

154

While Jack was at Northwestern, the U.S. Marines stormed ashore on Guadalcanal, August 7. It was the first offensive move by U.S. forces in the Pacific since the Japanese struck Pearl Harbor. Lieutenant George Mead was killed in action on Guadalcanal on August 19. He was posthumously awarded a Navy Cross, the highest honor below the Congressional Medal of Honor, for "extraordinary heroism." On August 30 Richard Tregaskis made a note that would be published in his *Guadalcanal Diary:* "George Mead . . . had led the platoon brilliantly, disregarding Japanese fire until, finally, a bullet hit him in the face, killing him instantly. . . ."

Mr. and Mrs. Mead received the grim news from the Navy Department on September 22, while Jack was at Northwestern. The following day, Mrs. Mead wrote a long letter to dozens of George's friends telling about his death. She concluded her letter, "The love in our hearts for George certainly is there stronger, if possible, than ever before and always will be. What is death, then, but a physical change which does not interfere in any way with our power to love? With that power and love and George in our hearts, how can we be unhappy! We can't."

Kathleen Kennedy replied to Mrs. Mead's letter. Her response was printed in a commemorative book Mrs. Mead later had published.

> If I don't write you of what is in my heart I think I shall burst. . . . Your words to us meant more than all the things I have ever read, learned or been taught about death, war, courage, strength. You just seemed to hit the nail right on the head. You just said what was in your heart and I know that everyone who talks to you cannot help but know that what George did was just an act of obedience to you and Mr. Mead. You had always taught him love of duty and obedience to it. He was killed living up to that heritage.
>
> Future days may bring bad news to us all, but remembering your words, and the way you have acted, one cannot help but feel— Please God, let me act in a similar fashion. Mrs. Mead, you must know how we—and I mean Betty, Chuck . . . Jack and myself— admire you and Mr. Mead and now my heart is filled with gratefulness for knowing George and through him knowing you two.
>
> George was a reserved person and hard to fathom (remember when he wouldn't show he was pleased to see us in Aiken?) but he couldn't hide the fact that he was just one of the most perfect people any of us will ever meet. No matter what happens in the future there's a part of me that will always feel a very special love for George.

George Mead was the first of Jack's close friends to be killed in the war. Many months later, when Jack got to Guadalcanal, he would visit

George's grave and write the Meads a letter which left little doubt that he was as profoundly moved by the loss as Kathleen had been. For the first time, the war had become a grim reality for all of them. It may be that George's loss influenced Jack, giving him a new seriousness of purpose.

About the time George was killed, Jack put in a call to Torby Macdonald in Boston. Torby was still holding down an office job, he told us, and getting bored with it. He said:

> I suggested to Jack that maybe we ought to volunteer for the Marine Corps. He said he thought we couldn't do that but how about Motor Torpedo Boats? And I said yes. I put in a request through my immediate superior but he denied it. I then put it in a request in Washington—to the Navy Department—and it came back approved. I think Jack's father probably helped. There were people who wanted my job and I wanted out, so it worked out. There were many long, cold nights in New Guinea that I cursed the day he put in that call.

What had prompted Jack's interest in PT boats? From Robert Bulkley's official history of the U.S. PT boats, *At Close Quarters,* published in 1962 with an introduction by President John F. Kennedy, and from other sources we learned:

> When the Japanese attacked the Philippines in December, 1941, there was an incomplete squadron of PT boats based at Manila commanded by John D. Bulkeley, Naval Academy class of 1933 (not to be confused with Robert Bulkley). Bulkeley's squadron—Number Three—consisted of six boats manned by eighty-three officers and men. This little outfit fought bravely against the overwhelming Japanese forces and finally evacuated General Douglas MacArthur, his wife, son, and some high-level staffers from Corregidor. In the end, all six boats were wiped out by enemy action, grounding, or other causes.

> During those early days of the war in the Pacific, when all the news was gloomy, the exploits of the PT-boat skippers made uplifting copy for the war correspondents. Bulkeley and his skippers claimed the sinking of a heavy cruiser, a light cruiser, and several merchant ships. These claims were given widespread publicity in the press and later in the best-selling book, *They Were Expendable.*
> Professional naval officers from the first regarded all this publicity with wonderment. Could the PT's possibly have inflicted so much serious damage on the enemy? The frail little craft were always breaking down. Their torpedoes—like the submarine torpedoes at that time—were defective.

And in fact, when Navy investigators got a look at Japanese records after the war they discovered that the PT's at Manila had not sunk a single Japanese vessel. One cruiser, *Kuma*, had received a single torpedo hit, but the torpedo failed to explode.

The little squadron had certainly fought with awesome courage—but almost certainly futilely. Still, they had evacuated General MacArthur and his family. And MacArthur was, not unnaturally, kindly disposed toward the boats. When Bulkeley and the remnants of his tattered little band finally reached Australia, MacArthur sent Bulkeley back to the United States to propagandize for a larger PT force. MacArthur wanted one hundred PT boats, two hundred, if possible. Bulkeley did a superb selling job, within the Navy as well as with the public. The Navy Department set up a new school at Melville, Rhode Island, near the Navy's torpedo factory and school at Newport.

Bulkeley then faced a serious problem. Naval Academy graduates who knew better than to believe the publicity were not drawn to PT boats. They picked billets where their careers would profit more: aviation or submarines or big surface ships such as carriers, battleships, and cruisers. Of the 616 graduates of the Naval Academy in 1942, only twenty went to PT boats. In order to find men for PT's, Bulkeley was forced to turn to the reserve officers in the colleges and universities. To these amateurs—who included Jack Kennedy—Bulkeley was a glamorous figure with a glamorous product to sell. He promised "early command" and an exciting life in close contact with the enemy, in an outfit that did not know the meaning of spit and polish. He did not say much about the ceaseless dogged work required to keep the fragile little craft in operation, the indescribably primitive living accommodations and food, the defective torpedoes, the terrible physical hardship of manning these tiny boats with large engines in pounding seas, the long odds against inflicting any substantial damage on the enemy.

In the late summer of 1942, when Bulkeley's publicity drive reached its zenith, he stopped at the Northwestern campus for a recruiting speech. He had in tow another Naval Academy man from the class of 1934, John Harllee, who had been named executive officer of the PT boat school, to help him screen applicants. Their immediate goal was to pick about 120 men—enough for two classes at Melville. One of the officers who volunteered—and was accepted—was Jack Kennedy. John Harllee, now a retired admiral living in Front Royal, Virginia, told us in a letter:

> PT's were extremely popular with Ivy League graduates. The book *They Were Expendable* was serialized in the *Reader's Digest* in the summer of 1942. . . . Even before then PT's were popular with Ivy League graduates because many of them had had boating and yachting experience. . . . Also the background of many Ivy

League graduates was such that they preferred to be in command of their own boats and have the resulting independence rather than be under the hierarchy on a larger ship.

My recollection is that only a couple of hundred men had volunteered at Northwestern before John Bulkeley and I arrived. He was an excellent public speaker as well as a national hero and after a rousing speech which he made, my recollection is that about 700 volunteered [even though] Bulkeley told them that only 10% of his squadron came back alive. [Actually most of the rest had been taken prisoner.] The school authorities pared the list down to about 240, as it was utterly impractical for us to interview 700 men. . . . I recall the Kennedy interview specifically. He was selling himself hard and expressed a great desire to get in close combat with the enemy as soon as possible. This was one of the main reasons why both John Bulkeley and I voted to select him. The other reasons were that he was an intercollegiate sailing champion, had graduated from Harvard *cum laude* and made a favorable impression with relation to his appearance and personality. He did not have to take a physical for PT's. I did not know that he had a bad back until well after the *PT-109* event.

Why would a man who knew he was physically infirm volunteer for what he must have known, just from his knowledge of boats, would be physically punishing duty? First, Jack was undoubtedly influenced by Bulkeley's propaganda; the glamour, the informality, and the chance to command must all have appealed to him. And then, he may have set out to find the toughest physical challenge he could qualify for, just to prove that he could take it. It would be in character; as Rose wrote, Jack refused to concede he was infirm. Also, PT's were dangerous beyond the call of duty. Perhaps after his disastrous experience in ONI, Jack felt he needed to do more than the average sailor to offset the negatives in his record. Further, he may have been moved by George Mead's death to seek revenge in a close encounter with the enemy. Some men are motivated by such things in war, and not only in fiction and movies. Finally, Joe Junior had picked an elite corps, Naval Aviation. Could Jack do less?

Jack's official records show that on September 27, 1942, he completed his officer training at Northwestern University. Four days later, October 1, he reported to the PT training school in Melville, Rhode Island, only a stone's throw from the Kennedy home at Hyannis Port. The Massachusetts Senatorial primary voting had taken place only a couple of weeks before Jack reached Melville. No doubt Honey Fitz, a star in that show, had many new and amusing stories for Jack when Jack visited him.

About the time Jack arrived at Melville, he was automatically promoted to lieutenant, junior grade, having served a full year on active duty. The promotion meant that Jack arrived at the school senior to his fellow students, who were mostly boot ensigns fresh from universities. The extra half-stripe in rank set Jack apart. It gave him first choice over his more junior contemporaries; it may have excused him from some menial chores such as standing watch.

From *At Close Quarters*, we distilled some facts about the school. It had been founded about eight months earlier, in March of 1942. The commanding officer was a Naval Academy graduate, William C. Specht, who had commanded PT Squadron One at Pearl Harbor when the Japanese attacked. (Inevitably the school was called "Specht Tech.") John Harllee was second in command and senior instructor, the man who made most of the day-to-day decisions. The teaching staff was composed mostly of PT veterans from the Pacific. By October of 1942, when Jack arrived, Melville was growing like Topsy. There were almost one hundred Quonset huts in being or under construction. These were used for classrooms, living, dining, and recreational purposes and for housing technical shops. One PT squadron—Four—was permanently assigned to the school to provide boats for training men at sea. The school leaned on nearby naval installations for training in torpedoes, gunnery, fire-fighting, and so on.

In October, 1942, the standard training course at Melville was eight weeks. Specht and Harllee laid heavy emphasis on calisthenics to toughen the men for the rugged duty they faced. During the long hours in classrooms the men were presented facts and theory about PT construction, torpedo maintenance and firing (a very complex subject), and small-boat combat tactics. Manning the boats of Squadron Four, they went out into Narragansett Bay (north of Newport) to put theory into practice, simulating attacks on enemy vessels, learning to communicate with one another in rudimentary radio codes (and by semaphore and blinker-tube) and how to coax the utmost from the temperamental gasoline engines which powered the boats. All the while the students were being indoctrinated to believe that they were serving in the best damned outfit in the Navy.

Rhode Island was not the ideal place to locate a training school for men who would operate PT boats in the South Pacific. For much of the year, Melville is frigid, lashed by cold north winds. When Jack and his fellow students went out on Narragansett Bay in those little boats, it must have been so bitterly cold that concentration—and work with guns and torpedoes—was excruciatingly difficult. The climate in the South Pacific was the opposite of Melville's: tropically hot, humid, torpor-inducing.

Kennedy was evidently an industrious and conscientious student at Melville. Admiral Harllee recalled, in his oral history at the Kennedy Library and in his letter to us as well: "He was a sincere and hardworking student and showed particular aptitude in boat handling. During those days my wife Jo-Beth and I had dinner a few times with Kennedy . . . in the home of a mutual friend . . . Raymond C. Turnbull. . . . He impressed me as an eager, widely read young man of broad interests and tremendous dedication to his country and enthusiasm for the part he hoped to play in its great conflict. . . ."

Jack's best friend at Melville, of course, was Torby Macdonald, who arrived after Jack, having finally got out of the desk job in Boston with Ambassador Kennedy's help. The plan, Torby told us, was that when the two men had completed the school, they would ask to be assigned to the same PT boat in a new squadron—Twelve—that John Harllee was forming up to take to the Pacific. Jack would be commanding officer of the boat, Torby the executive officer, or second in command. Torby said, "I'd rather have been Jack's exec than have my own command." As we shall see, the plan went awry.

It was not all drudgery at Melville. On weekends the students were granted liberty. They went off to Boston and New York for dates and parties and nightclubbing. Jack may have still been seeing Inga Arvad. Torby was still dating Polly Cotter of Boston—the girl he almost married. But now both men were also dating new girls. Both girls were in show business, would-be starlets.

Jack's new girl was a stunning Irish-born blonde named Angela Greene With the help of two journalist friends, Colin and Kay Dangaard, we located Angela who, since 1946, has been married to a Los Angeles real estate investor named Stuart W. Martin. The Dangaards researched Angela's background in studio files, libraries, and columns. Then Colin interviewed Angela for us at her home in Beverly Hills.

Angela Greene was born in Dublin in 1921. Her father came to America and became a fireman in New York City. Angela studied dramatics at St Luke's Elementary School, St. Agnes', and the Bayside High School, all in New York. After graduating from high school, she took a job as a secretary, then became a model for the famous Powers Model Agency She told Colin Dangaard:

I met Jack in May or June of 1942. He was in the naval hospital in Boston. He was suffering from a bad back—this was long before the PT accident. I was then in a show playing at the Ritz Carlton Hotel in Boston. It was the Georgie Hale Review. We were Powers Models, dancing in the show. After the show, Jack's father and the singer Morton Downey, who was a close friend of the Ambassador, and Jack came backstage or whatever. I can't recall, but we all met that night, at the same time. Then Jack called and we dated. At the same time, I was dating my present husband, Stuart Martin, whose brother had gone to Choate with Jack. I didn't know that then—not until after I was married.

Q. What was your first impression of Jack?

A. I thought he was an absolutely madly attractive young man. I think I must have known something about him, I mean who he was. I do remember that when I was a young girl there were photographs of the Kennedys in the papers, when Mr. Kennedy was ambassador to the Court of St. James's. You remember that family picture? That was a pretty impressive picture.

Anyway, Jack was also a very interesting man. Extremely well read. . . . After that show in Boston, I went back to New York and I continued to date him.

Jack was stationed at the PT school in Rhode Island. He'd come down on leave for the weekend. I saw a great deal of him. I was sharing an apartment with some other girls—all young actresses. They were terribly excited when Jack came by. We used to double-date with Torby. We went to places like Sardi's, the Stork Club, and El Morocco. I remember one night at the Stork Club his older brother, Joe, was there, also in uniform. And I remember another thing. One night at the Stork Club a very young boy came over to our table and Jack said, "That's my kid brother, Bobby."

Q. What was his style when he took you out? Did he meet you at the door with flowers?

A. He was very casual. It was always, "Well, we're going to do this or we're going to do that." And very simple. Jack was not a big drinker, as I recall. He'd have *a* daiquiri. Later I heard such absolutely frightful stories that he was a big drinker or a big sex maniac, but then, in those days, this was the most simple, wonderful, beautiful man. Period. At least as far as I was concerned. What happened after he achieved that power and the White House is something else. When I knew him he was a marvelous date and a wonderful young man. He didn't drink—and he didn't dance, I remember. He had that bad back. I mean, he would dance, but he was always very careful not to put his back out. I remember only fun and games and happy times: going to nightclubs, being silly together, racing around. I remember we'd come home and he'd have milk and cookies. He was mad for chocolate. Those Hydrox cookies.

There was a lot of stuff in the columns about us. At that time I was very much publicized and so was he. I was in a show. I'd really had a tremendous success in New York. I only recently realized that when I put my scrapbooks together. I remember another strange thing. Jack never had any money with him. If you went to dinner, he could sign, but if you got into a taxi, you were always giving him a quarter tip or something. When we went to St. Patrick's, I think I put the money in the collection box. Money meant absolutely nothing to him.

I always had the feeling that Jack would have really loved to have been a teacher—a professor. He loved telling you things. You should do this and do that—read this or that. I think he would have been a marvelous teacher. I don't think he was really geared for the spotlight. I think he would have been quite happy in a more simple way. I think he was very dominated by his father, by both his parents as a matter of fact, and that he was pushed a great deal into politics—by his father, after Joe was killed. Jack was very easygoing. He liked everything. There was no pressure with Jack at all.

Q. Was he romantically pushy?

A. I don't think so. I never found him physically aggressive, if that's what you mean. Adorable and sweet.

Q. He settled for a handshake, then?

A. Well, I think he was like any normal red-blooded American . . .

Q. Do you think, in retrospect, that he was in love with you?

A. I would say no. I knew that if he were in town, I was the first one he called. That type of thing. I would say we had a tremendously wonderful relationship. I would say we liked each other a great deal. . . .

Torby's new girlfriend was Phyllis Brooks, a no less beautiful starlet who then had an important role in the smash musical comedy *Panama Hattie,* starring Ethel Merman. Torby had met her in Boston. Later in the war, he married her.

Angela Greene, we believe, was the first show-biz personality that Jack dated. There would be many others in the future. Like his father, he was strongly attracted to beautiful girls who were climbing the ladder in show business or Hollywood, more so than to the so-called socialites of New York and Boston whom he had met in his college days. This attraction for Hollywood women would continue throughout his lifetime.

As the days of October and November zipped by, Jack and Torby made new friends at Melville. Most were football players. Among all the new friends, there was one who would become Jack's lifelong buddy; Paul Burgess "Red" Fay, Jr., of San Francisco. He would be an usher at Jack's wedding. He worked in Jack's 1946 campaign for the House and in the 1960 campaign. He joined the New Frontier in a position of high responsibility, Undersecretary of the Navy. In 1966, after he left Washington, Fay published a book about his friendship with Jack, *The Pleasure of His Company,* one of the best and most candid of all the memoirs about Jack Kennedy. There is an honesty and freshness about the book found nowhere else in the Kennedy literature.

Red Fay, we knew, lived in San Francisco. He met us for an interview at the Pacific Union Club. We found the club in a formidable structure on one of the city's many hilltops. We were admitted by a doorman who carefully checked our credentials and purpose in being there. The club had no sign, but it might well have been labeled "Establishment." The men wandering about inside in conservative clothes were clearly lawyers, bankers, stockbrokers—San Francisco aristocracy. Red Fay appeared in a seersucker jacket, beaming boyishly. He is ruddy-faced, garrulous, charming.

He was born in San Francisco in 1918, one of six children of Paul Burgess Fay, who owned a heavy construction company, and Katherine Oliver Fay, daughter of a successful realtor of high social standing. He attended private schools, then Stanford, where he knew Flip Price and Nancy Burkett. He had not met Jack when he was there, but he had seen him in his Buick convertible and knew who he was. He told us:

Right after Pearl Harbor, I enlisted in the Navy's officer corps, but they didn't call me until June, 1942. While I was waiting, I worked as a welder in a shipyard. I went into V-7 at Notre Dame, then to Northwestern—Abbott Hall—in August, the same time Jack was there, but again we didn't meet. Commander Bulkeley came through on his recruiting tour. I volunteered and then had the most ridiculous interview I ever had in my life. They were looking for college athletes. Somebody told me ahead of time not to *downplay* my athletic achievements. When I got in there I found Bulkeley had me mixed up with a great Stanford football player, Peter Fay. Naturally I didn't go out of my way to unconfuse him so they picked me and I went on to Melville in October.

I first met Jack—he was a very skinny kid—in a touch football game with some other guys. I had a bad run-in with him at Melville a few weeks later—the one I tell about in my book—but I didn't really get to know him well until we all got out to the Solomons. . . .

We had a lot in common. We both came from big Irish families. We had both gone to non-Catholic schools, including Stanford. And we had friends—Flip and Nancy and some others—in common at Stanford. . .

We talked with Fay for several hours. It was a splendid and candid interview. Later, he invited us to his home for cocktails and we met his wife, Anita, who had known Jack as well, and who also had many interesting stories and observations about Jack. We will return to these interviews later.

Two other good friends that Jack and Torby made at Melville were

John L. Iles and Joe G. Atkinson, both Southerners, both college football stars. Through Peter Tare, Inc., of New York City, a PT officer veterans' organization, we found Iles and Atkinson—and many other officers who had known Jack—and talked with them by telephone.

Iles, who is a salesman living in Shreveport, Louisiana, told us:

> I was just a country boy from the sticks. By the time I got up to Melville, Jack was pretty senior. I was assigned to the hut, I think, because my last name began with *I* next to *K*. Jack and Torby were very close. As a matter of fact, Jack hero-worshiped Torby. Jack was very nice to me and invited me to go home with him, but I never did. Torby was nice, too.
>
> It was cold there, bitter cold. I mean, boy, it was *really* cold up there. Torby showed me how to put newspapers under my mattress to stop the freezing drafts.
>
> I remember Jack was dating Angela Greene. I don't know how serious this was, but he talked about her a lot.

Joe Atkinson, a plant manager who lives in Lebanon, Tennessee, told us:

> What I remember most about Melville was that it was cold. Real cold. Between classes, you'd hang out in these Quonset huts and that's where I met Jack and Torby and Johnny Iles. Jack was a fantastic guy, very interesting and very, very funny. He had a terrific sense of humor. He was a football nut, so he and Torby and I would talk football a lot. I remember Jack had had some plush desk job in ONI in Washington. He'd pulled strings to get out of it and into Melville. That impressed hell out of me because everybody else was pulling strings to get into the type of desk job he'd just left.

As the men were "graduated" from Melville, they were assigned to new squadrons then forming up in New York and elsewhere, Ten, Eleven, and Twelve, or were sent to the Pacific as individual replacements in the squadrons already there. According to Jack's naval records, he was graduated on December 2. Torby, who had arrived after Jack, was graduated a little later. As we said, both expected to be assigned to the same PT boat in John Harllee's Squadron Twelve. Harllee took Torby, but he did not take Jack. Jack was assigned to be an instructor at Melville.

In *As We Remember Him,* Torby indicates that the two of them were quite upset about Harllee's decision: "I couldn't understand it and I kept saying to Jack, 'God, Jack, they gave you a shafting!'—that being a Navy term of the time—and I repeated it a number of times. During part of his PT tour, if not all of it, when he was out in the Solomons, he was known as Shafty. So he always accused me of giving him the name Shafty, but I didn't do it on purpose, that's for sure. . . ."

In his oral history at the Kennedy Library, Harllee recalled:

> Kennedy was such an outstanding student that I selected him for the training squadron at Melville. This was in the days . . . before there were enough combat veterans to fill the ranks of the instructors . . . [and] a few of the best students were made instructors. Kennedy was extremely unhappy. . . . As a matter of fact, he and I had some pretty hard words about this assignment, and I thought I had made another enemy for life, but I insisted that he remain with us. It was not our intention to hold him as an instructor for the rest of the war but for six to twelve months . . . he saw me and insisted that he be sent overseas to one of the squadrons in combat. . . . He felt there was no reason why he should be kept in the United States . . . he was most insistent . . . I absolutely insisted that he remain, which made him extremely unhappy . . . .

Harllee had become a good friend of Jack's and Torby's. It seemed surprising that he would undercut their well-laid plans without a better reason. So we wrote him, asking for a fuller explanation. He repeated what he had said in his oral history, then added another reason: he had eighty applicants for only thirty billets in Squadron Twelve, and many men had applied ahead of Jack. But Torby, for example, who was behind Jack in school, had gone to one of the billets in Squadron Twelve.

Harllee is the only primary source—Specht is deceased—on this important point. From his oral history it is evident that he hero-worshiped Jack. He was closely associated with him in the postwar years. He had worked in Jack's behalf in the 1960 campaign and Jack, as president, had appointed him chairman of the Maritime Commission, one of the jobs Jack's father had had in the Roosevelt Administration.

A more likely explanation, it seems to us, would be that Harllee or Specht or both discovered at Melville that Jack's health—particularly his back—was not good. They would have judged him physically unfit for the terrible pounding of the PT boats and thus a possible liability in a combat situation as part of a small crew.

That, of course, would be contrary to what we have seen is the "Kennedy line" on Jack's health and on his naval career. Harllee, a friend and political associate who is indebted to Jack manyfold, cannot be counted a completely reliable witness.

The recollections of Johnny Iles and Joe Atkinson were consistent with our theory that Jack's health—probably his back—was the real reason for this noncombat assignment.

Iles:

Oh, yes. I remember distinctly that Jack had a problem at Melville. He had a bad back. Slept with a piece of plywood under his mattress. And because of the back, he had a hard time getting an assignment to a combat unit. What happened was they assigned him to the training squadron. And, I remember, he said to us, 'Boy, I got shafted'—he pronounced it sort of like sh*o*fted—and we all started calling him Shafty.

Atkinson:

I remember the Shafty nickname. Jack or somebody told Bob Donovan for the *PT-109* book I gave it to him, but it was Torby who kept saying, "Jack, you got the shaft." So really, it was Torby who was responsible for the nickname, not me.

It was because of the transfer to Squadron Four, the training squadron. Jack was really put out. Everybody was going overseas and that's where Jack wanted to be. He was very anxious about that. But the powers that be decided otherwise. I thought at the time it was because of his bad back. It was aggravated then, I think. Actually, to tell the truth, he had no business being in the military service at all.

They, of course, have only secondhand impressions. Atkinson, it will be recalled, had believed an inaccurate version of Jack's transfer from ONI. So the point must be considered unsettled.

Jack remained at Melville, an unhappy warrior. According to his naval records, on December 3, the day after he graduated from the school, he reported to a Squadron Four Boat, *PT-101*, a seventy-eight-foot Huckins-built boat. In her logbook at the National Archives, there is an entry on Decmeber 7, the first anniversary of Pearl Harbor, that stated Lt. (j.g.) J. F. Kennedy took command of *PT-101* at 1600 hours, relieving Lt. S. Hamilton.

Two days later, December 9, he was granted five days' leave. He went to Palm Beach. Joe Junior, who had been assigned to fly Navy patrol planes on antisubmarine missions from Puerto Rico, was also in Palm Beach. By our reckoning, it was the last time the two brothers met. They posed for a photograph, which was published in *As We Remember Him* Both are smiling handsomely, toothily, straight into the camera. Both are wearing Navy uniforms. Joe Junior, wearing a single gold ensign stripe is, for once, the junior man.

When he returned from Palm Beach, Jack got down to work training students. The *PT-101* log for December shows that the boat made a number of twelve-hour cruises at sea, between frequent trips to a drydock for repairs. Among the students who were scheduled to go out with Jack was Red Fay. But Fay had other ideas. They almost led to his undoing.

There are two published accounts of the confrontation he referred to in our interview, the one in Fay's book and one in *As We Remember Him*. We thought the *Remember* version was livelier:

> I was assigned to go on the 78-foot boat Lt. John F. Kennedy was in charge of. But the 78-footers were the old type boats, not the one we were going to receive when we joined our squadron. I wanted to go on one of the 80-footers, so I tried to semaphore down to the 78-footer that I wasn't going to ride with them. Which took an awful lot of guts for a young student at that time. My semaphore was so poor, nobody read me. Finally, after ten minutes, I got a signalman to signal down about 200-300 yards to this other boat to say that I wasn't coming. Well, when we got back after about an hour and a half I had orders to go right up to Lt. Kennedy's Quonset hut, that he wanted to see me.
>
> And that was when I really first met John Kennedy. He informed me that they had waited for ten or twelve minutes, with not only a full crew on the boat but also about fifteen students, so that I could make up my mind whether I wanted to go on his boat—the one I was assigned to. He said if this was a reflection of my sense of fitness as to what my role was as a naval officer, he had great misgivings as to whether I should stay in Motor Torpedo Boats, and was strongly thinking of recommending to the skipper of the base that I immediately be detached and sent to some other duty. I almost got on my knees to plead with him. He said, "Do you realize that if what you did was compounded by every single person in the United States going through training, the war would be won by the Japs inside of three months?" With some misgivings, he finally agreed that he'd give me another chance.

While Jack was thus unhappily occupied, Torby Macdonald and his other friends graduated and went off—as replacement officers for units already in combat or to new squadrons that would be commissioned and sent to combat. Johnny Iles and Joe Atkinson were assigned to Squadron Two in the Solomons, as replacements. Torby Macdonald went to Harllee's new Squadron Twelve. Red Fay went to Squadron Ten, which was to be commissioned at the Brooklyn Navy Yard.

After only four weeks at Melville as an instructor, Jack's boat was ordered transferred from Melville to the newly forming Squadron Fourteen, to be commissioned in Jacksonville, Florida, where *PT-101* was built. Squadron Fourteen would be permanently assigned to Panama.

Four other Huckins boats from Melville were also assigned to Squadron Fourteen. These were *98, 99, 100, 102.* Specht ordered them to proceed to Jacksonville under their own power, a long and tedious voyage in cold, uncertain winter weather. Kennedy's naval biographers, Donovan and Whipple, have two conflicting versions of Kennedy's role in the voyage south.

Donovan's account has Kennedy commanding *PT-101* on the trip from Melville to Jacksonville and includes a heroic little anecdote about Jack. "Passing North Carolina," he writes, "one of the boats went aground. Kennedy in *PT-101* went to her assistance and tossed a towline, which became fouled in *101*'s props. Seeing this, Kennedy dived into the icy waters and cleared the props. The water almost froze him. By the time the squadron reached Jacksonville he had a high fever and had to go to a hospital for several days."

By Whipple's account, Jack did not make the trip south in *PT-101*. He says that *PT-101* got under way from Melville on January 8, 1943, "but the commanding officer did not go with his craft." Jack, Whipple said "had wrenched his troublesome back in a rough sea and was briefly hospitalized." According to Whipple, Jack caught up with the boat in Jacksonville on January 25, where it was then undergoing repairs and alterations in advance of the squadron commissioning ceremony.

According to the logbooks of *PT-101*, the voyage south was made in six legs: Melville to (1) New York to (2) Cape May, New Jersey to (3) Norfolk to (4) Morehead City, North Carolina, to (5) Charleston to (6) Jacksonville. On the morning of January 8 the boat got under way with Kennedy commanding. On January 11, she left Norfolk for Morehead City North Carolina, not in the open ocean as Donovan implies but by way of the Intracoastal Waterway, no doubt to avoid the chronic stormy weather off Cape Hatteras.

According to the log, that afternoon *PT-99* went aground in the Waterway and Kennedy, attempting to give her a towline, put *PT-101* aground too. The log says *PT-101* backed off the bar under her own power and then got a line to *PT-99*. One of the men, Motor Machinist Mate First Class R. D. Tucker "suffered sprained ankle—necessitated release of towline." At 6:30 P.M. *PT-101* anchored in the Waterway. There was no mention of Kennedy going overboard to free the towline.

The next day, January 12, the boat reached Morehead City without further incident. That same day, there is an entry in the log that "Lt. (j.g.) J. F. Kennedy entered Section Base Hospital." That is, he left the boat in Morehead City for the hospital there and the executive officer, John Thompson, Jr., took temporary command. Thompson took her on to Jacksonville, Florida, arriving January 15. On January 25, Kennedy re joined the boat and Thompson noted in the log: "Lt. (j.g.) J. F. Kennedy returned from hospitalization and seven days leave."

There is no record available that indicates what affliction had hospitalized Jack on this occasion. In all, he was absent thirteen days.

The newly forming Squadron Fourteen, commanded by Lieutenant Richard E. Johnson, never got itself organized properly. Originally, according to *At Close Quarters*, it was to be equipped with twelve new Higgins-built boats (PT's *85-94* plus *197-8*) but those boats were siphoned off into Lend-Lease and sent to Britain and Russia. That left the Navy with a formal squadron designation and no PT boats on its roster. And that, apparently, was why *PT-101* and the other four were ordered down from Melville. Those five boats—PT's *98-102*— were all Squadron Fourteen ever got. After the commissioning ceremony on February 17, 1943, they were sent to Panama and never saw combat. In September, 1944, the outfit was disbanded and the five boats were returned to Squadron Four in Melville.

All this while, Jack was busy trying to find the right string to pull to get out of Squadron Fourteen and into combat. He finally found it. We found this statement in Tazewell Shepard's *Man and the Sea*:

> When the young officer heard rumors that the boats would be stationed in Panama for some time, he grew desperate for he feared that this would keep him out of the combat area, preventing his getting into action. Massachusetts Senator David I. Walsh was the Chairman of the Senate Naval Affairs Committee and easily the most powerful man in the Senate as far as the Navy was concerned. Through him Jack Kennedy achieved his goal. Senator Walsh wrote the Navy Department requesting that John F. Kennedy be assigned to a war zone. Shortly thereafter instead of going to Panama, he was . . . ordered to the Solomon Islands as an officer replacement.

Admiral Shepard could not find his notes and therefore could not tell us the source for his statement. We found confirmation in Admiral Harllee's oral history:

> Kennedy received orders to the war zone. I was somewhat surprised by the orders and suspected that some strings had been pulled. This suspicion was later confirmed when I had occasion to review his record in the Bureau of Naval Personnel in 1947. Tremendous effort had been brought to get him into the combat zone. . . . I saw a letter signed by Senator David I. Walsh. . . . He was known to be a friend of Ambassador Joseph P. Kennedy and there was no question that Joseph P. Kennedy (or perhaps

young Jack himself) had interceded with the Senator and the Navy Department had deferred to his wishes and sent Jack Kennedy out to the combat zone.

Jack Kennedy's pulling strings to get into combat, was, of course, one of the most vivid examples of his stubborn, indomitable courage. But the military's standards of physical fitness for men going into combat are set not so much for the sake of the man himself as for others who might depend on his physical capabilities in a tight situation. It could be said, then, that he was also reckless and irresponsible and somewhat selfish in this act. It must also be said that he was not alone in taking such an action, and that that sort of action was generally admired in that war.

Two days after Squadron Fourteen was commissioned, February 19, 1943, Jack was detached from it. His orders were to report to Squadron Two, then basing in the Solomons, as a replacement officer. He was granted a "Priority Three" travel status—routine for the time—and told to take the first available transportation from the West Coast. This turned out to be an old French liner, renamed U.S.S. *Rochambeau*. According to her logbook, she sailed from San Francisco at 1800 hours on March 6, stopped at San Diego to pick up men on March 8, then departed again at 0900 hours on March 10 for the South Pacific. It is not clear, nor does it seem important, where Jack boarded *Rochambeau*. Donovan says San Francisco, Tregaskis says San Diego.

14

South Pacific

ROCHAMBEAU'S destination was Espiritu Santo, a Navy staging base in the New Hebrides Islands, southeast of the Solomons. The ship was crowded with officer replacements, enlisted sailors, and Marines, and a varied war cargo of spare parts, rations, mail, and other essentials. She sailed alone, zigzagging at a fairly fast clip, blacked-out at night to avoid detection by Japanese submarines. At dawn and at dusk—the most likely times for submarine attack—the ship's crew went to general quarters. During daylight hours they held gunnery practice, firing away at imiginary targets, making a fearful racket.

The transient officers, crowded into *Rochambeau*'s once-luxurious staterooms, had little to do. They ate, slept, wrote letters, read, and gathered in bull sessions, speculating on what adventures lay before them. At some point in the voyage, *Rochambeau* crossed the equator. On naval vessels there is usually a madcap, day-long ceremony to celebrate this rite of passage; the neophytes are initiated into King Neptune's domains. But Kennedy's naval biographers say nothing about that.

During the voyage on *Rochambeau*. Jack met and became close friends with another young officer, Jim Reed. They would remain good friends for life. Reed was an usher in Jack's wedding, helped Jack in all his major political campaigns, then joined the New Frontier in an important job in the Department of the Treasury.

We found Jim Reed working in New York, the founder and boss of his own investment-banking company. We spoke with him in his handsome wood-paneled office overlooking Fifth Avenue.

Reed physically resembled Ben Smith, somewhat. He is tall and muscular and well-proportioned. He leaned far back in his chair, resting his head on the back, staring at the ceiling. We had never seen anyone in a Manhattan business office so thoroughly relaxed. Our interview with him was an excellent one.

He was born James Allen Reed in Pittsfield, Massachusetts in 1919. Reed attended Deerfield Academy, then Amherst (1941) where he played football, basketball, and baseball. He was captain of the basketball team. He majored in economics and American history. He said:

After graduation, I had offers to play pro sports—baseball with the Boston Red Sox or football with what are now the New York Giants. I was not interested. I tried to enlist in the Royal Canadian Air Force but I couldn't pass the eye test. So I went to work in the management training program of Armstrong Cork Company in Lancaster, Pennsylvania. By that time, I was engaged to a Pittsfield girl then at Smith College in Northhampton, Massachusetts, named Jewel Read. I sat next to her brother Richard Read in a class at Amherst (Read-Reed) and met her through him. We were married on December 20, 1941, a couple of weeks after Pearl Harbor. She wanted marriage and a career, so she went into the IBM training program in Endicott, New York, then worked for IBM in Hartford and Providence, Rhode Island. I went into the Navy in March, 1942, from Boston. They sent me to Harvard for a ninety-day officer training course. When I was commissioned ensign in June, I was sent to Newport, Rhode Island, attached to the small-boat facility and put in charge of getting food for the officers' mess. After about six months of that I got orders to go overseas—to the South Pacific. Being newly married, I was not particularly anxious to go. They assigned me to *Rochambeau*. We sailed from San Francisco March 6, then went down to San Diego where—I'm pretty sure—Jack Kennedy joined us. I was rooming with a guy named Paul G. Pennoyer, Jr., who was J. P. Morgan's grandson. On the trip over, old J. P. died of a stroke.

Jack and I became very close friends on the ship, almost overnight. There was a chemistry between us. We had much in common. We were both from Massachusetts. We were both deeply interested in history, economics, literature, politics. He loved football as did I. And there was something else: he didn't care for the service, the Navy. The discipline and all that. It was contrary to his nature. I remember he had a portable victrola. He was crazy about a particular record, "That Old Black Magic." Even today when I hear it, I remember Jack and *Rochambeau*.

Jack was an extraordinary fellow. He had amazingly broad interests. He'd been exposed to people in high places and had firsthand experience in foreign affairs, and was several steps ahead of all of us. He had a marvelous sense of humor; a light touch and then a serious side. There was an aura about him that I've never seen in anyone else. I wrote a friend of mine, Joe Kelly in Leominster, Massachusetts, telling him about Jack and saying that I thought Jack would one day be president of the United States. I remember after the election in 1960 Kelly called me and said, "Jim, you're quite a prognosticator!"

I remember his talking about his family and his father. He said to me, "Jamey"—he always called me Jamey—"you'd like my father. He thinks like this. . . ." Jack described how he thought, which was always directly to the point, clear and realistically, no fuzziness.

There was another guy in our crowd on the *Rochambeau* named Charles "Chick" Rowley who had been at Amherst with me. He told Jack he'd heard his father on the radio once and was surprised that he didn't speak like the rest of the Irish trash from Boston, or words to that effect. Chick really meant it as a compliment, but I could see Jack was furious. Jack was polite to Chick, but he told me later he wanted to punch him in the nose.

We spent a lot of time on the way over debating Britain. I was anti-Munich; Jack, of course, took the opposite view. I was then a transient officer, a replacement with no special skills. He said he hoped that when I got to my destination, which was Nouméa in New Caledonia, I would volunteer for PT boats. And I did. . . .

According to her logbook, the *Rochambeau* reached Espiritu Santo on March 28, after a voyage of eighteen days. The war in the Pacific had been in progress sixteen months. The Japanese dominated the Pacific. The war in Europe was still priority number one, and for that reason, the buildup of U.S. forces in the Pacific had been slow. Still, with its crippled fleet, the U.S. Navy (helped by codebreaking information) had won two substantial victories in the previous year, 1942, which had been severe setbacks to the Japanese: the Battle of the Coral Sea and the Battle of Midway.

In addition the U.S. Marines had landed on Guadalcanal in early August, 1942. This was intended as a defensive move, to prevent the capture of the island by the Japanese. The battle for Guadalcanal was a bitter, bloody engagement that had dragged on for about five months, and there were many American casualties (including as we have seen, George Mead). The Japanese poured reinforcements into the island from their main stronghold in the South Pacific, Rabaul, on New Britain. These reinforcements were funneled through a passage among islands which became known to U.S. forces as "the slot." Admiral Nimitz's colorful subcommander in the South Pacific, Admiral William "Bull" Halsey, labeled the Japanese reinforcing runs "the Tokyo Express."

Night after night the small U.S. naval force under Halsey put out to sea to intercept and destroy the Express, helped in part by the codebreakers. In most of these nighttime encounters, the U.S. Navy came off second-best. Japanese naval forces had far better torpedoes and they were superbly trained in night fighting. During the five-month period, the U.S. Navy lost many ships and a terrible toll of men to the Express.

As we saw from various sources including Bulkley's *At Close Quarters*,

PT boats had participated in the fight to stop the Express. In October, 1942, two months after U.S. troops first landed on Guadalcanal, the first new PT squadron—Three—reached the Solomons. A few weeks later, more boats arrived: Squadron Two and a portion of Squadron Six. Staging from Tulagi and Florida Islands, northeast of Guadalcanal, the boats buzzed into the Slot, bravely attacking Japanese cruisers, destroyers, and troopships.

Squadron Three, which had got there first, saw the most action. As in the Philippines in the early days of the war, correspondents, intrigued by the David-and-Goliath aspect of PT combat, wrote incessantly about the little boats, wildly exaggerating their achievements. The publicity for Squadron Three culminated in a long piece in *Life* on May 10, 1943, written by John Hersey. Three Squadron Three skippers, Leonard A. Nikoloric, Robert L. Searles, and Henry S. Taylor, appeared on *Life*'s cover. Hersey states that Squadron Three boats alone had sunk one Japanese cruiser, six destroyers, a patrol craft, and several other ships. In fact, Robert Bulkley reported in *At Close Quarters*, postwar Japanese records revealed that all the PT's during this four months of combat at Guadalcanal had positively sunk only one Japanese destroyer and one submarine.

We interviewed one of the Squadron Three skippers who appeared on *Life*'s cover, Leonard Nikoloric, now a lawyer in Washington. He told us, "Let me be honest. Motor torpedo boats were no good. You couldn't get close to anything without being spotted. I suppose we attacked capital ships maybe forty times. I think we hit a bunch of them, but whether we sank anything is questionable. I got credit for sinking a destroyer but I don't think she sank. The PT brass were the greatest con artists of all times. They got everything they wanted—the cream of everything, especially personnel. But the only thing PT's were really effective at was raising War Bonds."

Nikoloric told us that the PT boats had very serious defects as combat vessels. First and foremost, their torpedoes—World War One Mark VIII's—were slow (only 27 knots), short-ranged, erratic, and often failed to explode when they hit. In order to hit a fast-moving, zigzagging target in the darkness, PT's had to close to point-blank range before firing. The three powerful props kicked up a huge phosphorescent wake which was easily detected by Japanese lookouts. Thus most PT attacks were stillborn, frustrated by Japanese counterfire. Being frail craft made of plywood, the PT's had to turn tail and run when brought under fire or else face certain destruction. Each boat, when fully fueled, carried 3,000 gallons of 100-octane aviation gasoline for the three Packard-built engines. Thus, they were like floating firebombs. Besides all that, Nikoloric said, the engines proved to be high-strung. They required constant nursing and overhaul, creating a need for a long and complex pipeline of spare parts and legions of mechanics to do the work.

In January, 1943, the Japanese gave up trying to reinforce Guadalcanal. By that time, both sides were exhausted. Ships were in need of repair; aircraft squadrons had been depleted; and the men needed rest and recuperation. Soon, the growing U.S. forces would go on the offensive in the Solomons—an island-hopping campaign designed to end with the capture of Rabaul. (See Map No. 1) But in February a five-month lull in the Pacific was begun, when nothing of importance would happen. Jack arrived during the lull.

Jack left the *Rochambeau* at Espiritu Santo. PT Squadron Two, to which he was assigned, was then based on the small island of Tulagi, close by Guadalcanal. To get to that area, Jack boarded *LST-449*, an ungainly amphibious vessel crammed to the gunwales with Navy, Marine Corps, and Army replacements, and a large load of ammunition.

LST-449, according to her log, departed Espiritu Santo April 4; at about noon on April 7 she was approaching Guadalcanal. It was a day the Japanese had picked to launch one of the biggest air raids on the island since the lull began. About 177 Japanese planes came down from New Georgia and Bougainville. They attacked shipping at Guadalcanal and Tulagi, achieving some success.

The first official word *LST-449* received of the attack came from a destroyer and sub chaser that came barreling out of the bay at Guadalcanal. The destroyer *Aaron Ward* signaled that *LST-449* should withdraw the area at best speed, retreating toward Espiritu Santo. *LST-449* complied with this suggestion without hesitation, wheeling around, heading south.

She was not able to get beyond range of the Japanese planes. About three o'clock that afternoon, by Donovan's account, they caught her and began dropping bombs. The ship circled, attempting to throw off the aim of the Japanese bombardiers. The crew went to general quarters, firing at the attacking planes.

Luckily for Jack and his fellow passengers, *LST-449* escaped damage. Not so the *Aaron Ward*, which slowed down to serve as escort. A bomb fell in her engine room, inflicting mortal damage. A Navy minesweeper attempted to tow her to Tulagi but they didn't make it. Three miles short of the objective, the *Aaron Ward* sank to the bottom.

During the bombing, the *Aaron Ward* or some other vessel had shot down some Japanese planes. *LST-449* found one of the aviators bobbing in the sea in his lifejacket. Thinking to rescue and take him prisoner, the skipper of *LST-449* turned the ship toward him. When they were close alongside, the Japanese pilot raised a pistol from the water and fired two shots at the personnel lining the rails. Instantly a hail of machine gun bullets riddled the aviator. He sank from sight.

The ship continued southward, retreating toward Espiritu Santo at a leisurely pace. Donovan says that she "cruised about" for five days. After that she received an all-clear to reapproach Guadalcanal. According to the log, she docked in Lunga Roads, Guadalcanal, April 13.

This introduction to combat had not unnaturally made a vivid impression on Jack Kennedy. He wrote a letter to Torby Macdonald, who was still on the East Coast helping shake down the newly commissioned boats of John Harllee's Squadron Twelve. Torby recalled in *As We Remember Him*, "I got a letter from him which I still have at home written his second day out there. They had a big raid and he was saying watch out and really get trained because I didn't know as much about boats as he did and he said I should know what the hell I was doing because it's different out in the war zone."

The *LST-449* remained at Guadalcanal one day, then got under way on April 14 for the brief voyage to Tulagi. Although there is nothing in her log or Jack's naval records to indicate whether Jack was on board for the final leg, we assume he was since Tulagi was his destination. *LST-449* arrived at Tulagi April 14, and if our assumption is correct, Jack debarked with his gear (which, Donovan says, now included a Smith & Wesson .38 pistol and a sheath knife) and headed for PT headquarters at Sesapi. Rose writes that Jack wore a "sacred medal" which had been given him by Clare Boothe Luce, a close friend of the Kennedy family.

15

PT-109

J ACK's first sight of the PT headquarters must have been a jolt. Judging from an aerial photograph in Whipple's book, it was primitive: two or three Quonsets, a scattering of thatched-roof huts for living and dining, an officers' club (grandly called the Royal Palm), machine shops, and clusters of battered PT boats nested alongside makeshift docks. Other PT's were nested in the bushes along the shore. There was a PT tender, Tommy Manville's ex-yacht *Hi-Esmaro*, rechristened U.S.S. *Niagara*. The whole base would have a fit on the flight deck of the carrier *Enterprise*.

The Sesapi base was called "Calvertville" in honor of the man who then commanded all the PT squadrons in the South Pacific area, Allen Philip Calvert, Naval Academy class of 1924. There was a sign near the head of the dock designed to lift spirits:

CALVERTVILLE
Thru these Portals Pass
The Best M.T.B. Flotilla
in the World

Jack checked in with the commander of Squadron Two, Allen H. Harris, a reservist, one of the few to command a PT squadron in those days. We found Harris at his home in Quogue, Long Island, and talked with him by telephone. He told us:

> When Kennedy got out there, he was fairly senior, but fresh out of the training center. I assigned him to a boat to work with an experienced skipper. After a short time, we saw he was competent and qualified for his own command. He went to *PT-109*. About the time he arrived, Squadron Two was in great flux—a lot of the skippers had done their time and were being rotated back to the States or elsewhere—and we had, really, a shortage of skippers. He was made skipper of the *109* pretty quickly. And very shortly after that, I myself left the squadron. So I never really got to know Kennedy.

The interim boat Jack was assigned to was the *PT-47*, commanded by George S. Wright, who had seen plenty of action. We reached Wright, now an architect at the University of Texas in Arlington, by telephone. He told us, "When Jack got out there, Harris sent him to me. He was sort of an unofficial exec for a few training patrols. Maybe two or three. I can't remember. He was a fine lad, but we gave him the usual hazing we gave all the new officers. He took it quite well. Then he went to the *109*."

We obtained an official history of the *PT-109* at the Kennedy Library. It had been prepared by the Ships' Histories Section of the Navy. *PT-109* was an eighty-foot ELCO (Electric Boat Company), built in Bayonne, New Jersey. She had been delivered to the Navy July 10, 1942, while Jack was at Northwestern. Her first and only skipper until Jack took over had been Bryant L. Larson, a reservist. Originally assigned to Squadron Five, on September 22, 1942, *PT-109* was transferred to Squadron Two, arriving at Tulagi in late November during the thick of the fighting. The then-commander of Squadron Two, Lieutenant Rollin E. Westholm, had picked *PT-109* for his flagship. In December and January, she had seen much action.

We tracked down Larson at his home in Portland, Oregon, where he is a lawnmower distributor, and talked by telephone. He told us:

When Kennedy got out there, we were in a changeover phase. There was no permanent crew on the *109*. You see, what happened was this. On the night of January 10, we were supposed to go out. But the *109* had bad engines. In Panama, we'd got a bad load of fuel—fuel with water in it, I think—and ever since we'd had temperamental engines. That night the *109* wouldn't go. So the whole crew transferred en masse over to the *PT-112*. The squadron commander, Rollin E. Westholm, rode with us, leading a section composed of the *112*, the *40*, and *43*. We tangled with four Japanese destroyers. All three of us got off torpedoes, but the destroyers shot back, so badly damaging the *43* and *112* that both crews had to abandon ship. We were in the water a long time—until the next day when we were rescued by other PT's. Some of my men were injured, some were mentally shook up and no longer qualified for duty in the boats. So that's what happened to the original *109* crew—shipwrecked in the *112*! After that, we had a lot of coming and going in the crew. By the time Kennedy came along, most of the men had been transferred off for leave or rotation. So there was no crew, really.

Harris assigned Kennedy to me. I remember the day he arrived quite vividly. He was not the average guy. He was the millionaire son of Ambassador Kennedy—most of us knew that—and for that reason he had a mark on his forehead. It was a handicap, I thought. It meant he would be subjected to the most critical kind of review.

But he bore the handicap well. I found him to be not only personable, a really fine man, but thoroughly competent and sincere in what he was doing. I don't remember how long we overlapped on the *109*. Maybe two weeks.

The *109* wasn't operating then, not patrolling. In the movie, or someplace, they show her as war-weary, lost in the weeds. But that was an exaggeration. She was in combat status. But the lull was on and the changeover was going on. The crew was mostly gone—so she wasn't patrolling.

According to the *109* logbook, there were only two men assigned to her when Jack assumed command. They were Ensign Leonard Jay Thom, who had reported on board on March 30 as executive officer, and an enlisted radioman, C. B. Foster, who had been assigned to the boat on April 1.

For the next several months Lennie Thom would be an important man in Jack's life, and a close friend. We knew from Donovan's book that Thom had been killed in an automobile accident after the war. During the war, he had married Catherine Holway, nicknamed Kate, from Youngstown, Ohio. With the help of her mother in Youngstown, we found Kate living in Greensburg, Pennsylvania. She is a beautiful woman who has nine children—two by Lennie Thom, seven by her second husband, Dr. Hilary Kelley. She told us about Lennie Thom:

Lennie was born in Sandusky, Ohio, in 1918. He was one of eight kids—three boys, five girls. He was big and strong, a natural athlete. He was a star football player at Sandusky High School and for a year at Heidelberg College. The scouts from Ohio State saw him and he was invited to Ohio State, where he played guard and tackle for three years. He also played pro football with the Columbus Bulls at one hundred and forty dollars a game.

I met Lennie in Columbus when he was playing football for Ohio State. He was studying hard and in the summers he was a straw boss during the harvest on a big farm owned by a friend of his. When he graduated in 1942, he went into the Navy V-7 program. They sent him to Notre Dame for a while, then he volunteered for PT's. He went through Melville, then was sent to the South Pacific as a replacement.

We were writing constantly then and planning to be married. Lennie wrote me that he really liked Jack the minute they met. Their personalities meshed immediately. He would write me jokes about Jack's money. Jack *never* had any cash, it seemed. He was always borrowing money from Lennie at the PX. He told me about

Jack's bills arriving out there from the Waldorf-Astoria in New York! Lennie told Jack the money Jack sent the Waldorf alone would keep him for a year.

But the main thrust of Lennie's letters was that he was worried about Jack's health. He wrote me that Jack was ill—he didn't say what was the matter—but that a team of horses couldn't get him to report to sick bay. Lennie said Jack feigned being *well,* but that he knew he was always working under duress. I think Lennie actually admired Jack's courage for that, for not reporting sick. He and Lennie worked together very well.

We had several conversations with Kate, and with Lennie's brother and mother and his son, Leonard, Jr., who provided us with copies of a number of his father's official Navy papers. Kate and Lennie became quite close to Jack. Jack came to Lennie's funeral and in subsequent years kept in close contact with Kate.

Shortly after Jack reported for duty, Squadron Two got yet another commanding officer, Alvin Peyton Cluster, a graduate of the class of 1940 at the Naval Academy. Cluster was then twenty-four, very young for so responsible a job. (Jack was then nearly twenty-six.) Cluster now lives in Los Angeles. We had several long telephone conversations with him. From these, and from other interviews, we formed the impression that Cluster was not the usual Naval Academy graduate. He was not serious about his career. He hated spit and polish and was often in difficulty with his more straitlaced Naval Academy superiors. In 1947 he resigned from the Navy to embark on a business career.

When the war broke out, Cluster was in New York helping Specht organize Squadron Four and the Melville School. Later he took four boats from Pearl Harbor to Palmyra Island (a tiny island south of the Hawaiian Islands), then, in April, 1943, arrived at Tulagi to command Squadron Two. Like Jack, Cluster had not yet been in combat. In the coming weeks, he would play an important role in Jack's life. He told us:

> When I got out there—about the time Jack arrived—Squadron Two was pretty well beat up. It had been quite active in the Guadalcanal fighting for a couple of months. They had lost some boats and the others were badly in need of overhaul and repair. It was a kind of "McHale's Navy." ["McHale's Navy" was a television comedy series depicting the trials and tribulations of a fouled-up PT unit in the South Pacific.] I can't remember the exact composition of the squadron and, you have to remember, we shifted boats and crews back and forth between Squadrons Two and Three a lot, and a couple of the original boats had been sent to help out in New

Guinea. I do remember we were under strength and probably remained under strength all the time Jack was out there in the squadron.

I liked Jack right off. He was a fine young man and, of course, I knew his father had been ambassador to Britain. We used to argue—good-naturedly—about politics a lot. I was a Missouri Republican and he was, of course, a Massachusetts Democrat. . . .

Recalling Lennie Thom's concern about Jack's health as relayed to Kate by letter, we queried Cluster closely on this point. It would appear that Jack successfully concealed his infirmities—whatever they were at this time—from his commanding officer. Cluster told us, "As far as I can remember, his health was good. I don't remember any illnesses at that point. If there had been any serious problems I would certainly have relieved him of command of the *109*."

The logbook of *PT-109* for April 25, 1943 (local date—April 24 in the United States) contained these entries:

0830 Underway for Sesapi.

1100 Lt. (j.g.) J.F. Kennedy assumed command of the boat.

1145 Moored at usual berth in bushes.

On the following day there was a single entry, the first signed by the new commanding officer: "Moored in usual berth."

The first task Jack and Lennie Thom faced was to form a new crew for *PT-109* from the replacement pool. The official roster called for twelve men but the Tulagi boats usually made do with ten or eleven. Three new men reported the day Jack took command: Charles Albert Harris, twenty; Leon E. Drawdy, thirty; Edmund T. Drewitch, thirty. That brought the total to six. A few days later, May 1, two more reported: Maurice L. Kowal, twenty-one, and Andrew Jackson Kirksey, twenty-five. On May 5, they received another, Radioman John Edward Maguire, twenty-six, making nine men in all.

In time, we interviewed three of these crewmen: Harris, Kowal, and Maguire, by telephone. Again we closely explored the matter of Jack's health. None could recall any specific ailment other than Jack's chronic back problem. The radioman, Maguire, who now lives in Jacksonville Beach, recalled that Jack wore a "corset-type thing for his back." Both he and Kowal recalled that in addition, Jack had a plywood board placed under his mattress. But none of the three could recall Jack complaining about his back—or any other ailment.

Kennedy judged the *PT-109* needed sprucing up, Donovan writes. On April 27, he moved her to Sesapi for two days of engine and hull repairs. The boat was full of cockroaches and other insects. Below decks, there was a revolting odor, traced to a dead fish under a step. While the shipwrights and mechanics at Sesapi tended to the hull and engines, Kennedy and his new crew thoroughly cleaned and painted the boat. By April 2 PT-109 was shipshape and seaworthy.

According to the logbook, that night PT-109 went on a test run, a rou tine patrol in the safe waters between Guadalcanal and Savo Island, i company with PT-47. In the month of May, the 109 made ten more night time training patrols. The log shows that the boat usually got underway about 6 P.M. and returned to base about 8 A.M. On none of these patrol did anything noteworthy occur. Toward the end of the month, C. B. Fos ter left the boat and two new men reported aboard: A. Galewski and Ed mon Edgar Mauer, twenty-eight. That made ten all told. Mauer became the cook.

Like the other PT officers, Kennedy and Thom lived ashore in thatched-roof hut on Florida Island, "commuting" each day to the opera tions base on Tulagi by small boat. After they had got the hut cleaned u and livable, two other officers moved in. The first was Jack's roommat and friend from Melville, Johnny Iles. He told us:

> I went out, like Jack, as a replacement officer in Squadron Two. Actually, Lennie Thom, Joe Atkinson, and I went out on the same troopship. I was first assigned to the famous old PT-59, which was then commanded by David Levy. Lennie Thom and Jack were living in this hut, so they asked me to move in with them.
>
> We had this Melanesian houseboy named Lani, I remember. He could speak a little pidgin English. He told us he was a cannibal! He said he had eaten a missionary priest. He was always looking hungrily at Lennie Thom. He used to squeeze Thom's big forearms and say, "Best part to eat." We couldn't believe that. We used to discuss it. The forearm would be tough, we thought. Well, hell, we didn't take this seriously, but someone reported it to the New Zealand authorities there—the civil government people—and one day they came and took Lani away. We never saw him again.
>
> We all got to know each other pretty well then. Jack was a big letter-writer. He got a lot of mail from everybody in his family. We used to read our family letters aloud to each other. So I really got to know his whole family this way. I mean, you really get the feel for all of them.
>
> I do remember one thing very clearly. Jack was going through a troubled time with his religion. We were both Catholics and we talked about it a lot. I can clearly recall sitting in a jeep one night on Tulagi, having a long discussion. Jack had lost his religion. But you couldn't argue with him. He could beat you in any argument. He said he'd work it out someday. He told me he'd go see Fulton Sheen when he got home.

Iles told us that another officer moved in the hut with them. He was Eugene Foncannon, now a senior vice-president of the First National Bank in Kansas City, Missouri. We talked to Foncannon by telephone. He told us:

I was assigned as a replacement to Squadron Three. And yes, I was asked to live in the hut with Jack Kennedy. And I'll tell you an interesting thing. I was just a plain old Midwestern boy and I didn't even know who he was! I didn't know he was a celebrity, son of the ambassador and all that. In fact, I didn't know it until a couple of months later when the *PT-109* was lost. He just seemed like the ordinary young fellow—just like Lennie and Johnny.

I remember this, too. We had a wine mess—a bar. Everybody got three chits per night, for three drinks. Neither Jack nor I drank. We'd go to the mess for a while and spend our chits on other people, and sit around and chat. Then we'd go back to the hut.

Joe Atkinson hung around the hut. Atkinson and Thom had first met at Notre Dame and had then gone through Melville in the same class. They had become close friends and would remain so until Thom's death after the war. Atkinson told us:

I had been assigned as exec to a guy named Lemuel P. Skidmore—honestly, that was his name—on *PT-39*. Later I became her skipper. That's when I got to know Jack real well. We used to sit around that hut and talk a lot. He was very brilliant and had a way of really picking your brain if you knew something he didn't. He had everything going for him, personality, money, connections. I remember Lennie and Johnny Iles and I all thought he would be president someday. I remember, too, he had a picture of that starlet he was writing, Angela Greene. What a beautiful girl!

While Jack was training his crew, he consulted with some of the combat-wise skippers on Tulagi. One of these was Joseph Cawthorn Kernell, Irish Catholic, born in Brookline, Massachusetts in 1917. Kernell was a veteran of Squadron Three and had seen much combat. We interviewed him at his home in Palm Springs, California:

I think the PT publicity was drummed up mainly for American morale. Things were going badly in the Pacific. The idea of guys on a little PT boat attacking a Japanese battleship was attractive.

During the lull after Guadalcanal, I went down to New Zealand for R and R. When I got back, they gave me back *PT-61*.

About that time, Jack Kennedy got out there. We met on Tulagi.

I was the so-called blooded veteran coming back from leave. I think he cultivated me. He always seemed to seek out those he thought were the most proficient in any field. He wanted to talk about how to operate the boats. Always questions, questions—but never in an objectionable way. He had a great sense of humor. I liked him the minute I met him. Generally, he was very quiet. He read and wrote a lot of letters. I remember he had a little phonograph and was always playing a record, "My Ship." We played a lot of bridge for two cents a point. At the end, he owed me two hundred and fifty dollars. I remember he had a bad back before the accident and slept on a board—or a board under his mattress.

As Kernell (and Johnny Iles) said, Jack wrote a lot of letters while h was in the Solomons. At the Kennedy Library, we were given five letter Jack wrote to his father or family which have never before been pul lished. We believe that they were handwritten, then sent to the ambass dor, or his secretary, who retyped them and cleaned up the spelling. The they were distributed to the far-flung members of the family. Each of th five letters is well written. They reflect a coolly observant intellect a palled by the waste and inefficiency of war, a man (like the others in th Solomons) not happy with his lot, anxious to get home.

The text of a letter received by the ambassador on May 10, 1943:

DEAR MOTHER AND DAD:

Sorry that I haven't written sooner but have been unable. In addition am so bound by censorship that I can't say much now. Had some difficulty getting here—and frankly don't understand why Dad's stomach improved when he was in England.

I have learned, however, that what they say about the Japs is true—or at least in one case. The other day we went to pick up a Jap pilot that had parachuted into the water. We pulled along side of him to a distance of about 20 yards. He was young looking, powerfully built—short black hair. He suddenly threw aside the life belt he was wearing, pulled a pistol and started firing. We let go with everything but he didn't seem to get hit until finally an old soldier aimed with his rifle and took the top of his head off. He leaped forward and sank out of sight. That I understand is the usual story with the officers. With the men, however, there would seem to be no such desire for the glorious death.

Our life here isn't too bad. We live in tents—no hot water or anything, but the food is better than I ever had in Chicago, though there is still no sign of all those steaks that "the boys in the service" are getting.

Came out with a fellow called Pennoyer—whose grandfather is

J. P. Morgan. In addition to having a fine set of cigars with J.P.M. on the band—which would undoubtedly have pleased brother Joe—but which seemed to me inferior to my Robert Burns—he had lived a good bit of his life out at Wall Hall. Evidently the whole Morgan family has lived in some awe of Butler Bengley and he was extremely interested in Bengley's reaction to the nine Kennedys.

Roger Cutler, who used to be in charge of Joe's group, is out here, though I haven't had a chance to see him yet. I understand that he spoke out of turn down in Jax and that they sent him out with the Amphibian forces.

That's about all the news. Saw Harry Willis who is okay, but will give you more dope about him when next I write. Haven't heard from home as yet. How about someone writing. Suggest Mother read "Blind Date with Mars" by Alice Lone Moats. The part about Russia will interest her extremely.

Love to all,
JACK.

The ambassador added a postscript:

NOTE TO CHILDREN:
Please write to Jack as frequently as possible, using V-Mail stationery, a few sheets of which are enclosed. Write on one page only, but if it should be more than one page put each page in a separate envelope. Also send regular letters (not V-Mail) to Joe, who is in Norfolk as you know.

DAD

A letter dated May 14 reports on his health—and back—and adds a postscript touching on his religion:

DEAR DAD AND MOTHER:
Received your letter today and was glad to hear everyone was well. Things are still about the same here. We had a raid today but on the whole it's slacked up over the last weeks. I guess it will be more or less routine for another while. Going out every other night for patrol. On good nights it's beautiful—the water is amazingly phosphorescent—flying fishes which shine like lights are zooming around and you usually get two or three porpoises who lodge right under the bow and no matter how fast the boat goes keep just about six inches ahead of the boat. It's been good training. I have an entirely new crew and when the showdown comes I'd like to be confident they know the difference between firing a gun and winding their watch.

Have a lot of natives around and am getting hold of some grass skirts, war clubs, etc. We had one in today who told us about the last man he ate. "Him Jap him are good." All they seem to want is a pipe and will give you canes, pineapples, anything, including a wife. They're smartening up lately. When the British were here they had them working for 17 cents a day but we treat them a heck of a lot better. "English we no like" is their summating of the British Empire.

I was interested in what you said about MacArthur's popularity. Here he has none—is, in fact, very, very, very unpopular. His nick-name is "Dug-out-Doug" which seems to date back to the first invasion of Guadalcanal. The Army was supposed to come in and relieve the Marines after the beachhead had been established. In ninety-three days no Army. Rightly or wrongly (probably wrongly) MacArthur is blamed. He is said to have refused to send the Army in—"He sat down in his dug-out in Australia," (I am quoting all Navy and Marine personnel) and let the Marines take it.

What actually happened seems to have been that the Navy's hand was forced due to the speed with which the Japs were building Henderson Field so they just moved in ready or not. The Marines took a terrific beating but gave it back. At the end the Japs wouldn't ever surrender till they had found out whether the Americans were Marines or the Army, if Marines they didn't surrender as the Marines weren't taking prisoners. In regard to MacArthur, there is no doubt that as men start to come back that "Dug-out-Doug" will spread—and I think would probably kill him off. No one out here has the slightest interest in politics—they just want to get home—morning, noon and night. They wouldn't give a damn whether they could vote or not and would probably vote for Roosevelt just because they knew his name.

As far as the length of the war, I don't see how it can stop in less than three years, but I'm sure we can lick them eventually. Our stuff is better, our pilots and planes are—everything considered— way ahead of theirs and our resources inexhaustible though this island to island stuff isn't the answer. If they do that the motto out here "The Golden Gate by 48" won't even come true. A great hold-up seems to me to be the lackadaisical way they handle the unloading of ships. They sit in ports out here weeks at a time while they try to get enough Higgins boats to unload them. They ought to build their docks the first thing. They're losing ships, in effect, by what seems from the outside to be just inertia up high. Don't let any one sell the idea that everyone out here is hustling with the old American energy. They may be ready to give their blood but not their sweat, if they can help it, and usually they fix it so they can help it. They have brought back a lot of old Captains and Commanders from retirement and stuck them in as the heads of these ports and they give the impression of their brains being in their tails, as Honey Fitz would say. The ship I arrived on—no one in the port had the slightest idea it was coming. It had hundreds of men and it sat in the harbor for two weeks while signals were being exchanged. The one man, though, who has everyone's confidence is Halsey, he rates at the very top.

As far as Joe wanting to get out here, I know it is futile to say so, but if I were he I would take as much time about it as I could. He is coming out eventually and will be here for a sufficiency and he will want to be back the day after he arrives, if he runs true to the form of every one else.

As regards Bobby, he ought to do what he wants. You can't estimate risks, some cooks are in more danger out here than a lot of flyers.

Was very interested to hear what your plans were and the situation at home. Let me know the latest dope whenever you can. Whatever happened to Timulty? Jerry O'Leary is out here to the South of where I am, but I hope he will get here some one of these days. He has command of a 150 foot supply boat.

Feeling O.K. The back has really acted amazingly well and gives me scarcely no trouble and in general feel pretty good. Good bunch out here, so all in all it isn't too bad, but when I was speaking about the people who would just as soon be home I didn't mean to use "They"—I meant "*WE.*"

I figure should be back within a year though, but brother from then on its going to take an act of Congress to move me, but I guess that act has already been passed—if it hasn't it will be.

My love to every one,
Jack

P.S. Mother: Got to church Easter. They had it in a native hut and aside from having a condition read [Red] "Enemy aircraft in the vicinity" it went on as well as St. Pat's.
P.P.S. Air mail is better than V-Mail.

The ambassador's New York office aide, Paul Murphy, added a postscript:

DEAR EUNICE:
Please note that Jack says to send his mail regular airmail instead of V-Mail. In his last letter he also mentioned this and said the service was faster.

By the end of May the *PT-109* was fairly shipshape, except for her balky engines. Her ten-man crew was meshing into a fighting team. Jack and Lennie had taken the boat on a total of eleven night-training exercises, with old hands along to show them the ropes. Jack had talked at length with other old hands like Joe Kernell. He was thoroughly indoctrinated, as ready as a new officer ever is for combat.

June came. The long lull in the Solomons was drawing to a close. It was time to launch the drive against Rabaul. The major staging bases in the South Pacific—Espiritu Santo, Nouméa, Guadalcanal, Tulagi—throbbed with preparations for this, the first major Allied offensive move in the Pacific war. All eyes were turned toward New Georgia. The invasion days remained fixed: Segi, June 20; Rendova, June 30.

Tulagi was bursting at the seams with new PT boats. Remnants of Squadrons Two, Three, and Six were already there. That spring Squadron Five, commanded by Henry Farrow, arrived from Panama. Then came a brand-new squadron, Nine, commanded by a colorful officer, Robert B. Kelly, a hero of the PT fighting in the Philippines at the outbreak of the war. Finally, another new outfit, Squadron Ten, commanded by Thomas Glover Warfield, an older regular naval officer, Annapolis '32. In all, about fifty PT boats.

Within a few weeks the *109* would be closely involved with Squadron Ten and Warfield would play an important role in Jack's life. Warfield is now retired, living in San Francisco. We talked by telephone. He was crusty:

> When the war started, I was commanding a minesweeper in Manila. Then I took over a French merchant ship and escaped with her to Australia, then took her back to the States. I then received orders to go put PT Squadron Ten in commission. My exec, the squadron exec, was a man from the class of 1940 named Arthur Henry Berndtson. I was sort of upset at the way they ran those PT boats and the whole training situation there. I wasn't particularly happy about it. I made up my mind that Squadron Ten was going to have what it wanted and we were going to try to train them, but it was pretty hard.

As we said, Red Fay had been assigned to Warfield's Squadron Ten. He had felt the lash of Warfield's discipline. Red recalled:

> After we commissioned the squadron in Brooklyn, we went to Norfolk; Galveston, Texas; then down to Panama. We spent about two months in Panama shaking down and getting organized. One day I was reading *Time* magazine and my boat ran aground on a

sand spit. We got it off without damage, but I told our squadron commander, Thomas Warfield, about it. He relieved me of command! He was a shit.

In Panama they loaded our boats on a couple of tankers for shipment to the South Pacific. Then, just outside of Nouméa, on May 24, a Jap submarine torpedoed one of the tankers, *Stanvac Manila.* There were six boats—half our squadron—lashed down on her decks. She sank and we lost the *165* and *173*. They saved the other four boats, but some of them were damaged and had to be repaired. So we didn't arrive as a single contingent and we were short two boats. The first half of the squadron got up to Tulagi in May, the second four boats, later. I was assigned as exec of *PT-167*, commanded by Theodore Berlin. She was one of the boats on the *Stanvac Manila* that had been saved but damaged. Everything was all fouled up.

Jack's boss, Al Cluster, locked horns with Warfield the day Warfield arrived at Tulagi. He recalled:

He was a first-class SOB. A Captain Queeg. I'll never forget the day I met him. By chance I was sitting in Commander Calvert's office. Now Calvert was a very high-class naval officer. Not much of a combat record but an older, really nice gentleman. I was sort of close to him. I was not orthodox, I spoke my mind, and I think he was somewhat amused by me and probably liked me. Anyway, we were sitting there and in walks Warfield, very formal, and said, "Commander Warfield and Squadron Ten reporting in, sir" or something like that. Calvert said, "Hi" and "Welcome aboard." Then, to our astonishment, the next thing Warfield says was, "I want some lumber right away." Well, Calvert sort of smiled indulgently and said lumber was damned hard to come by, as it was, and what did he need it for? Warfield replied something like, "I want to build a brig. I want to build a brig right here on the end of the dock, and I want to put two men in it. I've had these two men in the forepeaks of the boats all the way from Nouméa." And he said he didn't care about air raids; the men could stay in the brig during them.

Well, you could have knocked us over with a feather. We had never had a need for a brig on Tulagi. Everything there was very informal. No court-martials or anything like that. No real problems. Calvert looked at Warfield and he said, "Warfield, get out of my office—and don't ever come back." So he walked out. And from then on, since I'd overheard that, we didn't get along.

I remember once we were talking about battle tactics. Some

PT's in New Guinea had been jumped by some destroyers with radar-guided searchlights and began bracketing them with very accurate fire. The PT's withdrew. Warfield said he thought they should have bored in. I said I thought they had been prudent. He looked at me scornfully and said, "You and your damned Stork Club PT boats." Well, there were some other people there then, so I didn't say anything. Later I met him in the privacy of his office and we had it out. I said, "Don't you ever say anything like that to me again in public." He said he was going to put me on report—give me a bad fitness report. I said, "I dare you." He didn't. But that's the kind of guy he was.

Another PT boat skipper in Squadron Ten, Philip A. Potter, now living in New Jersey, had a different view of Warfield—and Fay:

Warfield was a good man. A lot of the guys in the squadron didn't like him because he was all business. By-the-book. Part of the problem came when the *Stanvac Manila* was sunk. We lost two boats and saved four, including mine (*174*) but they were all damaged and had to be reparied at Nouméa. Warfield believed that those of us who had undergone this experience were probably all fired up to fight Japs, so he gave the survivors of the *Stanvac* command of the six boats that were already there and in good shape. We took these to the Solomons. The guys who had been commanding these six had to stay behind and fix up the other four damaged boats. This caused a lot of dissension. Some officers lost command and we found ourselves commanding other crews. The crews didn't like it. The teams were all broken up.

Red Fay? He was considered a joke. The squadron clown. Warfield was out there to fight a war. I'm sure he never even considered giving him command of a boat in combat. I can remember attending a PT reunion in 1960 or 1961. About that time, Jack appointed Red Fay Undersecretary of the Navy! Nobody could believe it. Of all the people in the world he was least likely. . . .

One point was clear, at least. Squadron Ten was an unhappy outfit, and seemingly plagued by bad luck. It would have more bad luck in the future and Jack would become involved in that.

By June, as U.S. forces prepared to move north, Admiral Halsey was commanding an impressive navy: two aircraft carriers, six battleships, nine cruisers, and sixteen or more destroyers. If and when the Japanese counterattacked to break up the forthcoming landings, this naval force would bear the brunt. The fifty-odd PT's under Calvert's command were relegated to a lesser status, befitting their size and vulnerability. They would assist with patrols and screening lines and night attacks against smaller Japanese barges and boats sneaking in reinforcements under cover of darkness. Few now believed that the PT's would ever again be used—as they were used during the battle for Guadalcanal—as weapons against enemy destroyers or other big surface ships.

In preparation for the invasion of New Georgia, on May 30, the day after Jack's twenty-sixth birthday, Calvert ordered a contingent of PT boats based at Tulagi to move north to the the Russell Islands. Robert Kelly and his Squadron Nine were already there. The old hand, John M. Searles, brother of Robert Searles, commanding the beat-up Squadron Three, moved up and took over the Russells base so Kelly could prepare to move on to New Georgia. Searles christened the Russells base "Searlesville," identified by a huge sign over the gate leading to his headquarters, an old plantation house. Al Cluster and portions of Squadrons Two and Six and Squadron Five from Panama also moved up. The *109* was part of this northward migration. By the *109* logbook, Jack got underway at 8:30 A.M., arriving in the Russells shortly after noon.

The Russells base was primitive. There were no mess halls, PX's, machine shops, or torpedo overhaul facilities. The boats were moored in the bushes on the banks of Sunlight Channel. Kennedy and some other officers found quarters in an old plantation house (perhaps the same old plantation house) but the crews slept on the boats. For recreation, they hunted crocodiles in the muddy back streams with rifles and hand grenades or gawked at the half-savage natives of the islands. To stave off malaria, rampant in those areas, they took atabrine pills.

Jack Searles, then the Russells Island PT commander, now lives in Davenport, Iowa. We talked with him by telephone. He recalled Jack Kennedy:

We were staged to the Russells to get the boats ready for the New Georgia invasion. We played a lot of cards. Jack never played cards. He spent most of his time looking for officers who weren't in any game, as he did with me. We'd sit in a corner and I'd recall all the political problems in New Jersey and Long Island where I come from. He did that with everybody—discussed politics. He was preparing himself for Congress—and eventually the White House. Jack would also ask questions about fighting PT boats. I guess I didn't get the message over to him in too good shape.

Jack's first skipper, George S. Wright, commanding the *PT-47* also moved up to the Russells. He told us:

The plantation house had a tin roof. We turned it into a sort of BOQ. One day most of us were sitting around playing poker. Jack was not a card player. He was lying in his bunk, reading, his favorite pastime. He had a mosquito netting rigged all around the bunk. Well, a Jap plane came out of nowhere—it was broad daylight—and started dropping bombs near us. Suddenly there was a terrifying rain of shrapnel on that tin roof. You've never seen a card game break up so fast in your life. We *raced* out of that house and dived into slit trenches. That was one race Jack lost. In his haste to get out of his bunk, he got all entangled in the mosquito netting. He had a hell of a time. Then he finally broke loose and dived in with us.

PT's based in the Russells made routine nighttime security patrols, pickets to attack undetected Japanese surface forces that might threaten the Russells-Guadalcanal-Tulagi area. But the chances of that happening were remote. The patrols were useful primarily as training exercises. Consulting the *109* log, we saw that in the first two weeks of June, she made five such patrols of twelve to thirteen hours' duration.

David Levy, commanding *PT-59*, and his exec, Johnny Iles, remembered an embarrassing incident that happened on the *59* at the tail end of *109's* second Russell patrol June 4-5. Levy, now an attorney in Rochester New York, told us by telephone:

While it was still dark, the *59* and *109* headed back for the Russells. There had been some destroyers basing there, getting ready for the New Georgia invasion. I came into the channel and I saw what I thought was one of the destroyers. I needed some fresh water so I decided to go alongside. Jack was following me. Well, it was not a destroyer. It was a little island. I crunched up on the coral reef surrounding it and stuck fast. The blow knocked a hole in the bottom. We took on a lot of water. To lighten ship, we dumped two torpedoes, as I recall. Jack came alongside to give us a hand. He was a strong swimmer. He dived into the water. I was walking the anchor out so I could use it to pull off the reef. I remember one thing clearly: I stepped right off into deep water carrying that anchor! Well, we got the *59* off, finally, with a lot of help from Jack and the *109*. We radioed Tulagi to give us priority on a dry dock and then we backed her all the way. Kennedy in *109* served as our escort over to Tulagi. I took one hell of a lot of kidding about that episode, I can tell you.

The Russells base had one advantage over Tualgi: it had a refueling dock where the boats could pull up and fill their tanks as easily as pulling into a gasoline station. Returning from patrol in the early morning hours, the PT skippers raced for the refueling dock. The boat that arrived first was serviced first and, consequently, its crew got to bed earlier.

Kennedy enjoyed the racing, Donovan wrote. He often won, tearing in toward the dock at high speed, reversing engines at the last second. His engine gang cautioned him against doing this. Someday the engines might conk out. And one day that happened—with near-disastrous results.

As Donovan tells the story, Kennedy bore down on the dock at tremendous speed. The refueling party, bossed by a warrant officer, was busy preparing lines and removing tools from a small shed on the end of the dock. At the last second, Kennedy reversed engines. All three conked out. *PT-109* smashed into the dock with a shattering noise. Some of the men inside the shed thought it was an air raid. Donovan writes:

> Tools flew in all directions. Wrenches, jacks, screwdrivers, and hammers plopped into the water. Some of the men who were still outside toppled off the dock. Those on the inside who weren't too terrified to move clawed their way out. When they burst through the door, however, they beheld not the expected formation of Japanese dive bombers overhead, but a single PT boat sliced into a corner of the dock, her skinny bronzed skipper standing in his motionless cockpit, ruefully surveying the scene. Some of his crew were motionless, too, having been knocked flat by the crash.
>
> The warrant officer howled at Lieutenant Kennedy, who was his senior. Shaken-up enlisted men stamped about on the dock, cussing out *109* and everyone aboard. A gale of indignation was blowing, and beyond uttering a word of quiet apology here and there, Kennedy could do little but wait for the storm to blow itself out. Unostentatiously he tried backing the boat out, but this only made matters worse as more tools fell onto his deck and into the water.
>
> The whole business might have had more serious consequences for Kennedy if Irish luck had not come to his rescue. At the height of the commotion two or three other PT boats were discovered to have been broken away from their moorings. The attention of everyone ashore shifted to this greater emergency and Kennedy idled *PT-109* away from the dock into a small stream where he moored out of sight until the trouble blew over.

After that, Donovan reports, Jack got a new (but temporary) nickname: "Crash" Kennedy. He was lucky his commanding officer was Al Cluster and not Tom Warfield. If Jack's boss had been Warfield, he might have been relieved of command like Red Fay, whose offense had been much less serious. But no such thought ever crossed Cluster's mind, he told us.

After the dock-crashing, Donovan writes, *PT-109* had to return to Tulagi for three rebuilt engines. This had been "contemplated" before *109* left for the Russells, he says. It was not a consequence of the accident.

According to the logbook, *109* left the Russells for Tulagi on June 13 at 10 A.M. and arrived at 2:30 P.M. At Tulagi the crew discovered there had been a lot of excitement three nights earlier, June 10. The Japanese had staged another air raid on Guadalacanal and Tulagi. Two ships had been badly damaged and beached at Guadalcanal. The PT's at Tulagi had got under way, gone to open water, and fired at the enemy planes. Since another raid could occur at any moment, Tulagi was on its toes. The replacement of *PT-109's* engines was carried out on June 15, according to the log.

By June 16 the *109* was back at the Russells, moored in the bushes. She made two more nighttime patrols, then, according to her log, remained in port for the following ten days, June 20 to June 30. There were a couple of changes in personnel in June. A. Galewski left the ship. A new man. J. B. Buckheit, reported for temporary duty. The total roster remained ten.

On June 30 U.S. forces invaded Rendova, a small island off New Georgia. (See Map No. 2.) According to the official Naval historian, Samuel Eliot Morison, there was little or no resistance (the Japanese had never really taken control of the island), but seas of mud nearly overwhelmed the invaders. Guns and supplies that were landed on the beaches had to be shifted to smaller outlying islands where the footing was firmer. Landing craft grounded before reaching the shore and their cargoes were swamped. Foul weather impeded the operation.

On the day of the invasion Calvert executed step two of the forward deployment of the PT's. Squadron Nine, commanded by the dashing Robert Kelly, moved up from the Russells to New Georgia. Kelly was supposed to establish a base at Viru Harbor on the West coast of South New Georgia, but the Marines ran into unexpected (if temporary) opposition at Viru, and besides that, Kelly judged the harbor was still too far away from the action. So he moved his boats northward to Rendova Island and made plans to establish the PT base on Lumbari Island, a small, flat atoll on the northeast tip of Rendova in the harbor.

On the night of the invasion, June 30, Kelly's boats went on patrol from Rendova. In the darkness they came across Admiral Turner's flagship, the 10,000-ton transport *McCawley*. She had been severely damaged by Jap planes and was being towed from the combat zone. Kelly had been assured there were no friendly ships in the area. His boats fired torpedoes at *McCawley*. The stricken ship went down. Fortunately no one was killed; the salvage party had already abandoned ship. But it could very well have been a disaster. Ironically, the *McCawley* was only the third confirmed sinking by all the PT's that had ever served in the Pacific—after the Japanese submarine and destroyer.

At Rabaul, the Japanese reacted vigorously to the invasion of New

Georgia. The naval commander took immediate steps to reinforce the garrisons at Munda airfield on New Georgia proper and a base at Vila Plantation on the south coast of Kolombangara. On the night of July 2-3, he mustered his available ships (a cruiser and nine destroyers) into an attack force, the first to sally forth in many months. The codebreakers gave the alert, but there were no big U.S. surface forces close enough to make the interception.

The honors went to Robert Kelly and three of his boats, the *156, 157* and *161*. It was a moment of high drama: the first time in five months or so that PT's had stood toe-to-toe with major enemy surface forces. The squadron did not distinguish itself. Kelly, whose information on friendly forces was still incomplete, cautiously closed the range before shooting to make positive identification—and lost any chance of surprise. The Japanese force detected the PT's and four destroyers peeled out of formation. They charged Kelly, firing heavy caliber shells. Kelly's skippers shot off six torpedoes, but all went wide of the mark and Kelly was forced to break off the attack and return to base. The attack force pounded Rendova, but most of the shells fell into the jungle.

Kelly had more bad luck. About this same time, two of his boats went aground on a reef and stuck fast. Other PT's took off the crews and on the following two nights they returned to the scene and destroyed the boats with gunfire to prevent their being captured. A few days later, three more ran aground, but they were salvaged. Kelly was relieved of command of PT boats at Lumbari and sent to command a small unit on the east coast of New Georgia. The man picked to replace Kelly was Tom Warfield, commander of Squadron Ten. He told us:

Kelly's boats got in some trouble. Some went aground on a reef at night; others sank the admiral's [Turner's] Flagship. That sort of stuff. So they put me in there to take charge. We went up on July 6 or 7 on an LST: Art Berndtson, an intelligence officer; William Devereaux, who was an ex-FBI agent who'd been in charge of the Chicago office about four years; another intelligence officer, Whizzer White; and my communications officer, a man named Woods. He put together the communication station—the radio—on Lumbari.

Woods was James Lafayette Woods, Jr., a native of New Orleans. We talked with him by telephone. He told us:

God, that Lumbari was an awful place! You'd dig down a few inches and hit water. We made a command bunker by filling a bunch of gasoline drums with sand and then reinforcing them with

coconut tree logs. We put the radio transmitter inside the bunker.
It was a fine Navy-issue Collins unit of about one hundred watts. I
made an aerial from an aluminum pole, using beer bottles for in-
sulators. We had very good communications, so good in fact, the
Army units fighting on New Georgia and Rendova used us for a relay station. We were in constant contact with Guadalcanal.

Warfield was a tough guy but a great man. Of course it was a
touchy situation between him and Bob Kelly, since Warfield had
got his job. They were constantly feuding. Did Warfield tell you
Bill Devereaux was his brother-in-law? Married to his sister? He
didn't tell anybody out there, either. That was a very sad story.
Just after we got up there, Devereaux was killed in a PBY. He was
a really fine man.

That left only Warfield, Berndtson, and me plus Whizzer White,
for the staff. White lived over on Rendova near the Army or Marines, I think, so he could get intelligence for us. He'd come over
once or twice a day and brief us. The rest of us lived on Lumbari in
tents with water-filled slit trenches just outside the door. It was a
lousy place.

Whizzer White, who would shortly play an important role in Jack's life,
was technically on Calvert's Flotilla One staff, detached for temporary
duty with the PT's at Lumbari. He and Jack had met and talked at Tulagi—their first meeting since Germany in the summer of 1939. When White
had returned from his Rhodes Scholar studies in Europe (Alfred Wright
reported in the *Sports Illustrated* interview with White), he had entered
Yale Law School, dropped out to play pro football (Detroit Lions), volunteered for the Marines but failed the physical (poor eyesight), was accepted by the Navy and assigned to ONI, then sent to the Solomons.

The Japanese kept trying to reinforce New Georgia and Kolombangara
with nighttime Tokyo Expresses. To interdict these, Halsey ordered up
cruisers and destroyers. Alerted by the codebreakers, they intercepted
another Express on the night of July 5-6 in what became known as the
Battle of Kula Gulf. The Japanese force had increased in strength. Firing
their superior "Long Lance" torpedoes, they hit the cruiser *Helena*. The
Helena went down. The U.S. forces sank the destroyers *Niizuki* and *Na-
gatsuki* .

The crew of *Helena* suffered severely. The ship, hit by three torpedoes,
jacknifed and went to the bottom. Scores were killed or drowned. Two
U.S. destroyers came to the rescue, taking men on board, but they were
soon called on to pursue the enemy. Then, as daylight approached, they
had to withdraw to Tulagi to escape Japanese air attack. They left small
boats and life rafts for nearly 300 *Helena* survivors still in the water.

The survivors split into two groups. About ninety of them made it to a nearby island where they were later rescued by two U.S. destroyers, *Woodworth* and *Gwin*. The other 200 drifted northward for several days, finally arriving at the unoccupied island of Vella Lavella. Some days later four U.S. destroyers rescued the remnants—165 men.

About a week after the Battle of Kula Gulf, the night of July 12-13, Halsey's surface forces met the Express a second time in what became known as the Battle of Kolombangara. Halsey lost the destroyer *Gwin*, and the cruisers *Honolulu* and *St. Louis* were badly damaged, but his ships sank an important Japanese vessel, the cruiser *Jintsu*, some of whose survivors also went ashore on Vella Lavella.

The two engagements—the largest naval actions in the Pacific in months—amounted to a standoff. The United States lost one cruiser and two destroyers (including *Strong*, sunk July 4 at Kula Gulf in a related action). The Japanese lost one cruiser and two destroyers. However, the interceptions had interrupted the primary job of the Express, which was to reinforce Japanese garrisons. This made the work of the U.S. ground forces a little easier.

It was a tough campaign. The ground forces suffered heavy casulties. It would take many days to close and overwhelm the primary objective on New Georgia: the airfield and strong Japanese force at Munda Point.

During all of this early July action in New Georgia, Jack Kennedy and the *109* remained in the Russells, waiting the call to action. The *109* logbook for July is missing—probably lost in the sinking—so her exact movements cannot be determined. The PT base commanders and squadron commanders did not file detailed war diaries on the movements of the boats, the way other naval authorities did on larger vessels. They filed "action reports," but only when the patrolling boats had contact with the enemy air or surface units. While in the Russells Jack Searles kept a personal dairy, but he told us he could find no specific reference to the *109*.

A thorough search at the National Archives of the logbooks of all the other PT boats basing at the Russells in July—boats of Squadrons Two, Three, Five, Six, and Ten—discovered only one reference to the *109*. This, plus the recollections of Al Cluster and Johnny Iles, provided the substance for two incidents involving the *109*.

The first took place on the night of July 2-3, when Robert Kelly sallied forth at Rendova. The Russells PT's must have been ordered to sea that night as a precaution, in the unlikely event the Express came farther south. By that time, John Iles was commanding the *48*. The *48*, like many of the older Squadron Two boats that had been through the heavy Guadalcanal fighting, was in terrible shape. On the night of July 2-3, she was back in the Russells patrolling in company with the *109*.

Al Cluster was riding the *48* with Iles. He told us what happened:

It was rough as hell that night. We hit a wave the wrong way and knocked a hole in the bottom of the *48*. Actually, there had been a hole there before, and we knocked the patch off. We started taking on water. The hole was above the waterline, so we tried to keep the boat up on the step, like a hydroplane, but I misjudged and we smacked a couple of waves and the boat began filling up again. I radioed Jack and he came tearing over. We could see some U.S. destroyers on the horizon, so I asked Jack to run over and see if he could borrow a pump—a hand billy. Meanwhile, to lighten ship, I fired all four of our torpedoes and dumped the two depth charges. On the way over, or back, Jack was bouncing pretty hard and one of his men got thrown and broke his knee and nose, I think. Anyway, the pump didn't work very well, so I thought we better try to beach her on the nearest land—a little island, Buraku, just north of the Russells. So, we *backed* the boat there and made it without sinking. We radioed for a repair ship and they came out and fixed her up.

I got on Jack's boat for a ride back to the Russells. I asked Jack if I could take the wheel. I got the *109* going pretty good and was sort of bouncing from wave top to wave top. Then I misjudged and we smacked into a wave so hard it started a "hot run" in one of the torpedoes—the props on the torpedo started turning. The damned thing broke loose and rammed into a depth charge, pushing the depth charge right through the deck, down into the crew's sleeping quarters. Fortunately, there was no one in the bunks.

The logbook of the *48* for the morning of July 3 confirms the substance of Cluster's account (though it does not mention the *109* coming to her aid). There are some minor differences. He reports "total damage to boat": two engines out of commission; three (not four) torpedoes expended to keep boat from sinking; severe damage to bow caused by heavy seas. He says that at 1 P.M. the *PT-36* came and towed the *48* back to the Russells and, on the following day, July 4, the *48* limped back to Tulagi on one engine.

After that, Iles told us, he left the *48* and was given "temporary" command of the *PT-125*, a Squadron Six boat. And not long after that he went up to Lumbari.

Donovan says that following this incident, the *109* had to be "laid up" briefly for repairs. The crewman who got banged up, Edmund Drewitch, was transferred off temporarily, to sick bay. About this same time J.B. Burkheit, who had been on board as temporary help for two weeks, left the boat and two other men reported aboard: William Johnston, thirty-three, and Patrick Henry McMahon. The roster remained ten.

Patrick McMahon would become a very special figure on the *109* and in

Jack's life. According to a speech of Jack's from the 1946 race for the House, on file at the Kennedy Library, McMahon was then forty-one years old. (Donovan said thirty-seven.) Before the war he had been a schoolteacher in a public school near Pasadena, California. He was married and had a son. (Donovan says a stepson.) After the Pearl Harbor attack, the son joined the Navy, volunteering for submarine service. McMahon, Jack said, "continued to teach for a few restless months," then he, too, joined the Navy. After boot camp, Jack said, the Navy "in one of those queer inexplicable acts" sent him to the PT School at Melville, "although he was well over the age limit set for these hard-riding boats." He specialized in PT engines—became a mechanic, or, as the Navy called them motor machinist mate—and wound up on the base at Tulagi. Due to the shortage of motor machinists, he had been assigned to the *109* . Because of his age and the fact that he was a father, he was called "Pappy."

The second *109* incident—of no consequence except that it firmly fixes a date that the *109* was still in the Russells—occured on July 10. On that date, the *PT-106*, Ensign R. W. Harris commanding, and the *109* made a brief trip from the Russells to Guadalcanal. Purpose of the trip: to transport Naval personnel. They left the the Russells at 9:30 A.M. and returned at 2:40 P.M.

A few days after that, the *109* was ordered forward to the advance base at Lumbari Island—into combat. Without the logbook, we can never know precisely what day she moved up. Donovan, who interviewed all the surviving crewmen in 1961, thinks "mid-July." That is certainly a reasonably accurate estimate.

There is one oddity about the movement. The *109* had been in the Solomons since the previous November, with the boats of Squadrons Two and Three. By this time, the boats of these squadrons were considered too beaten up for combat. Of the original boats of Squadrons Two and Three, the *109* was the only boat to be ordered into combat. All the others remained behind at Tulagi or the Russell Islands.

When Jacked moved the *PT-109* from the Russells to Lumbari, he was transferred, operationally, away from the jurisdiction of Jack Searles and Al Cluster. His new boss at the Lumbari Island base was Tom Warfield.

16

Combat

Now, three months after his arrival in the Solomons, Jack Kennedy had arrived at the front lines. Japanese aircraft from Rabaul, Bougainville, Vila, and elsewhere struck almost every day, trying to regain air superiority in New Georgia and destroy ships and bases. Big guns on Rendova and outlying islands were firing toward Munda Point, supporting ground operations. Whipple publishes a letter from William Barrett, Jr., skipper of the *PT-107*, to his family, describing the situation about the time Jack reached Lumbari:

> Up until a few hours ago some shore batteries (ours) have been going pretty regularly and they are located near us and fire over us so we get both the noise of the fire and the secondary racket as they go over. They're due to open up again soon so I gave up the idea of trying to snooze. Also, our dive bombers are pretty busy, and it's too good a show to watch to sleep through. Dogfights are also always an attraction and we've seen some dandies. Even better than the movies.
>
> The food situation is quite poor. We eat entirely out of cans—mostly corned willie, cheese and stew. We also eat Aircraft Emergency rations in between times—they are rich, but quite good. Coffee and cigarettes are the main staples (and our only luxuries). Aspirin gets quite a play, and we take vitamin A pills all the time, as they are supposed to improve our night vision, which latter is extremely important, in fact is almost everything.
>
> The territory we are operating in now is pretty, pretty hot, and I don't mean climatically. . . .We go way out past the so-called "front lines" in efforts to cut off the Japs. . . .

In our interview, Johnny Iles, then temporarily commanding the *125*, recalled nesting alongside the *109* about this same time. Jack had been in good spirits, he said:

> I remember when we were in port, we could pick up the baseball games on Armed Forces Radio Network or from somewhere. We

were following the White Sox because I had a cousin, Ted Lyons, who was pitching for them. They had another pitcher named Kennedy and Jack would joke that that was *his* cousin. When we came in from patrol we'd take the dinghies up the freshwater creeks. We'd jump in with a bar of soap and wash. That was how we cleaned up. Then, I remember, we'd go to the *109* for toasted cheese sandwiches. They were really good. Jack lived on those sandwiches.

July dispatches from Halsey to the PT commander at Lumbari, Tom Warfield, indicate that the twenty-five-odd Lumbari PT's had two primary missions: (1) To interdict the heavy nighttime Japanese naval traffic (mostly barges) plying between the islands to the north and Japanese-held positions on New Georgia and (2) to maintain a blockade (or picket line) to stop (or give warning of) an unknown Tokyo Express which might come down to assault U.S. forces in the New Georgia-Rendova area.

The "territory," as Barrett called it, where the patrolling PT's operated was to the northwest, in the waters near the islands of Kolombangara, Gizo, and Vella Lavella. They were restricted to the waters south of latitude 8° south, so that Allied aircraft operating to the north of that line could be free to bomb any naval craft on sight. The PT's left Lumbari after nightfall, traveled westward, then turned north. On the barge-hunting missions they penetrated Wilson and Gizo Straits into the lower Vella Gulf, along the south and east coast of Vella Lavella, and into Ferguson Strait and Blackett Strait, the waters flowing between Kolombangara and Gizo. (Kolombangara is a cone-shaped volcano rising dramatically almost 6,000 feet.) The blockade or picket boats patrolled south of Ferguson Passage. All the boats returned to base before daylight. Usually about eight boats went on patrol; eight were kept on full alert at Lumbari.

It was tough patrolling. The Japanese had developed a PT counter-weapon: float planes equipped with flares and bombs. The planes, based at Gizo, Vila, and elsewhere, watched for the phosphorescent wakes of the PT boats. Then they would pounce out of the dark sky, drop a flare, and make bombing and strafing runs. Some Japanese pilots even circled off Lumbari at dusk to watch the PT's go off on patrol, then followed.

To defend against discovery and attack by the float planes, the PT skippers evolved new operating procedures. To keep down the wakes, they patrolled at very low speed, five or six knots. Some skippers kept only one engine engaged—the center one whose prop was deepest and least likely to kick up the surface of the water. (The other two engines were kept running in neutral.) But this procedure was thought unwise by most of the experienced hands. Later it would be officially disapproved. Some skippers ran with their engines muffled—that is, certain valves were closed which resulted in the exhaust flow being directed beneath the water. This enabled the crews to hear the engines of an approaching float plane in time to take high-speed evasive action. Some even placed a special lookout on the bow, as far as possible from the engine noise.

The float planes were a serious impediment to PT operations. When they detected PT's and dropped flares, it was a signal to all Japanese naval traffic that a threat was in the area. On seeing the flares, the Japanese barges manned guns or scurried for cover close in to the dark shoreline of the islands. Some PT skippers believed the Japanese had PT lookout stations on the smaller islands near Gizo and Vella Lavella, which lit fires or flashed lights to alert the float planes. So, in the minds of the PT skippers, the Japanese had an efficient interlocking communications system (land and air) to thwart them and bring on the planes—and the inevitable bombs. All this made for much tension on patrol.

There was a division of opinion about what to do if a float plane detected a PT boat. Some bold skippers advocated shooting it out, firing the 20 mm cannon and machine guns at the planes, reasoning that the flares gave away the game and there was no longer a need for maintaining a blackout to find barges. They also advocated high-speed evasion—to hell with the phosphorescent wakes. But most advocated a more cautious approach, a slow-speed evasion (to keep down wakes), no return fire. Some even proposed immediately lying-to in order to eliminate any possibility of a wake. Others proposed laying smoke puffs to confuse the pilots.

Jack and the *109* began patrolling from Lumbari. Since the *109* log was evidently lost in the sinking, and Warfield did not keep a war diary and after July 15 submitted action reports only when his boats had contact with the enemy (except float planes) or engaged in a noteworthy special mission, it is not possible to describe precisely *109*'s combat missions from official Navy documents. Based on his interviews with the crew and with Jack, Donovan says, rather vaguely, that the *109* went on patrol "night after night." It may have seemed that way in retrospect to Jack and the crew, but the available documentation indicates a somewhat less intensive schedule than that.

A close analysis of action reports submitted by Warfield plus records of contacts between Lumbari PT boats and Japanese float planes, not usually covered in action reports, gives a general sense of Lumbari PT operations and turns up some specific mentions of *PT-109* on patrol.

On the night of July 15-16, the day *109* arrived in Lumbari by Donovan's estimate, six PT's went on patrol. The *109* was not among them. This force had no contact with the enemy. (After this, Warfield did not file an action report unless his boats made an enemy contact.) There is no action report for the night of July 16-17. The *109* could have gone out this night, but if she did, she had no contact with the enemy.

The night of July 17-18 was an exciting one; Warfield mounted a maximum effort. Instead of the usual eight, twelve PT's went on patrol in Blackett Strait—but *109* was not among them. At about 1:30 A.M., Oliver W. Hayes in the *159*, leading *157* and *160*, sighted what he believed to be six Japanese destroyers barreling in at 35 to 40 knots. Hayes alerted his two boats and the other nine lying to the south. The destroyers spotted the PT boats, Warfield reports, and two of them peeled out of formation to "box" Hayes and his group, firing Very pistol signals, flares, and then guns. Hayes in *159* bravely moved in and fired all four of his torpedoes from about 4,000 yards (two nautical miles) and retreated. The other two boats in his section, *157* and *160*, followed suit. Two of the torpedoes on *160* failed to fire. The skippers believed they got hits on two of the destroyers with the ten torpedoes they fired, but they were mistaken. The other nine boats lying to the south failed to make contact.

This stirring action was all a dreadful error. The destroyers were American—part of Halsey's forces. Hayes and his section of PT's had wandered too far north of the assigned patrol area. A U.S. Navy patrol plane sighted them and reported them as Japanese destroyers. Halsey had sent five (not six) U.S. destroyers to attack them. It is not clear exactly when the error was discovered. When it was, there must have been hell to pay; another PT foul-up. And no doubt Jack Kennedy was relieved to have missed the action this night.

The first official mention of *PT-109* on patrol occurs in a special study of Japanese float plane–PT boat contacts. According to this document, the *109* patrolled the night of July 19-20 with two other boats, the *105*, commanded by Richard E. Keresey, and the *163*, commanded by Edward H. Kruse, Jr., who, like Kennedy, would serve in the U.S. House of Representatives, a Democrat from Indiana. The section went up near Gizo to hunt barges.

Just before midnight the section, while lying-to off Gizo, heard a float plane. Adopting the bold approach, all three opened fire on the plane. It dropped no bombs. There were no casualties, no damage. The three boats resumed patrolling.

Then came thrilling—and chilling—news via the radio from Tom Warfield. About midnight, a Navy patrol bomber (according to a Halsey dispatch) picked up an Express in nearby Vella Gulf. It was reported to be three cruisers, six destroyers, and two transports. By radio, Warfield deployed his boats to try to find it. The hunters included *109*, *163*, and *105*. According to Kruse's *163* log, this section joined several other sections and "proceeded in search of enemy task force reported northwest of Vella Lavella." (That is, they crossed the 8° south latitude line.) No doubt the *109* crew was tense—and ready for this confrontation with enemy surface ships, the first for the PT's since Robert Kelly's encounter the night of

July 2-3. But none of the PT boats made contact with the force and, according to Kruse's log, about three hours after midnight they gave up the
chase.

About the time they were giving up, a second Japanese plane came over
and dropped a flare right over the group. The *109* was caught in its brilliant
light. Kennedy unmuffled engines and slowly pushed the throttles wide
open, zigzagging and laying smoke. Two big bombs straddled *109*. Donovan reports that two of Jack's men were hit by shrapnel. By his account,
Kennedy turned the helm over to Lennie Thom, grabbed a first aid kit,
and went to attend the wounded. These were Maurice L. Kowal and Leon
E. Drawdy. Kowal was hit in the leg; Drawdy in the arm. Neither wound
was serious enough to warrant terminating the patrol but when Jack got
back to Lumbari, he had to send Kowal and Drawdy to sick bay for treatment of their wounds, temporarily detached.

Jack later wrote his family that one of his men, Andrew Kirksey, twenty-five, was badly unnerved by the bombing. He had been with the *109*
since Jack took command, but this bombing was evidently a great shock.
From that time onward, he had a premonition that he was going to be
killed. He didn't ask to be transferred off the boat, but Jack had decided
that the next time they got back to Tulagi, he would replace him. Jack believed that men who thought they were going to die usually did. The transfer was never accomplished, however, and Kirksey would be killed soon.

At daylight on July 20, after Jack had returned to Lumbari, Admiral
Halsey sent a flock of Navy fighter planes and Army B-25 bombers to
look for the Express. They did not find it, but some of the B-25's found
three Squadron Ten boats, *164*, *166*, and *168*, in enemy waters, where
they were not supposed to be at that time of day. Four B-25's attacked
and strafed the PT formation. Trigger-happy gunners on the *164* and *166*,
thinking they were Japanese, opened fire without orders from their respective skippers. In the unfortunate foul-up that ensued, the PT gunners
shot down one B-25. The B-25's set the *166* on fire and it had to be abandoned. One officer and ten men in the PT's had been wounded—one man
lost his arm. Three men died in the B-25.

For Admiral Halsey, who'd seen one PT boat foul-up after another, this
must have been the final straw. He took immediate steps to gain absolute
control of PT boat operations. Until then, they had generally fallen under
command of the local senior naval officer. On July 21 Halsey ordered that
all PT's would report directly to his new amphibious force commander,
Rear Admiral Theodore S. Wilkinson (the boss at ONI when Jack was
nearly cashiered), basing on Guadalcanal. Two days later, July 23, Wilkinson appointed a subordinate on his staff to directly boss PT's: Captain
Edward Joseph "Iron Mike" Moran, ex-skipper of the *Boise*, and, as his
nickname implied, a tough commander.

About this same time—we do not know when exactly, but after Kowal and Drawdy were wounded the night of 19-20 July—four new men came on board the *109* as replacements. They were surplus personnel from Warfield's Squadron Ten, which had more crews than boats. The new men were: Ray Lee Starkey, twenty-nine; Gerald Emil Zinser, twenty-five, a regular who'd been in the the Navy since 1937; Harold William Marney, nineteen; and Raymond Albert, twenty. That put the official roster at twelve men. None of the new men, representing almost half of the enlisted crew, had had much combat experience. We imagine it took some little time to mesh with the six other enlisted hands and train them in *109* procedures. But there was not much time left in the life of *109*.

The *109* appears in the official records—the float-plane analysis—the second time on the night of July 23-24. She patrolled with four other boats: *103, 104, 117,* and *161.* They went to Gizo. A float plane attacked them, dropping three or four bombs, then strafed. The *117* returned the fire. The *109* evidently did not. There was no damage, no casualties.

The *109* officially appears for the third time in the float-plane analysis on the night of July 24-25. The *109* patrolled with five other boats: *105, 106, 117, 154,* and *161.* The section patrolled off Wana Wana and the float-planes were out in force. At 9:30 P.M. a Squadron Five boat, the *105,* received orders to return to base. Her skipper, Richard E. Keresey Jr., turned away and put on speed. Five minutes later a bomb hit, according to the log, "close aboard on the starboard quarter." Keresey's exec, Philip R. Hornbrook, Jr., was struck by shrapnel and one hour later he died, the first to be killed by a float plane.

Keresey now lives in New Jersey. We talked to him by telephone. He was bitter. He said, "One of the problems, at least with the Squadron Five boats, was that we had not had any realistic training. We had been assigned all that time in Panama. We didn't get out to the Solomons until after the heavy fighting at Guadalcanal was finished. By that time, most of the old hands had gone home. So we didn't have the advantage of learning from them. And besides that, if you can believe it, we had never trained at *night*. All our training was in the *daytime*. We were really completely green."

The float planes were persistent. Shortly after midnight, one dropped a bomb near the *106*, commanded by R.W. Harris. Keresey reported it a thousand yards astern of his boat. The *161*, commanded by John E. McElroy, logged two bombs dropped at 1 A.M., followed by a strafing attack. Then one more (at some distance) at 2:30. On the way into Lumbari, at 5 A.M., yet another float plane dropped a huge 500-pound bomb about 150 yards astern of the *161*. All boats, Warfield reported, evaded at high speed, but none returned fire. There was no specific mention of the *109* in any of these logs, but she must have been close by these attacks.

The *109* appears officially for the fourth time in an action report filed by Warfield for the night of July 27-28. This is the first time the *109* is mentioned in a Warfield action report, the fourth he had filed since July 15. The *109* patrolled with seven other boats. The *109* was assigned to section A, along with *157*, *159*, *162*, and *172*. The boats patrolled two miles north of Gizo Strait. They saw enemy aircraft, but nobody was bombed.

The second section, B, led by George C. Cookman in Bill Barrett's *107*, plus the *103* and *104*, split off from the first and had an interesting adventure. By that time, Halsey, believing the New Georgia campaign was coming to a successful conclusion, planned to bypass Kolombangara (with its 10,000 troops) and land on Vella Lavella August 15. The survivors of the *Helena* (rescued the night of July 15-16) had reported Vella Lavella unoccupied. To make sure, Halsey had ordered PT's to land a small party of spies there on the night of July 21-22. Now, after six days, Cookman was to recover them and drop two more spies.

At 2:10 A.M., Cookman and the *103* and *104* nuzzled close to the dark coast of Vella Lavella. The two new spies went ashore and the six old ones came aboard. They reported no Japanese except a few survivors of the Japanese ships sunk in the Battle of Kolombangara, July 12-13, confirming the report of the *Helena* survivors. The spies also had a surprise in tow: eleven survivors of a Navy patrol bomber which had been forced down at sea July 16 off the northwest coast of Vella Lavella.

We believe Jack must have been close by these operations, but there was no mention of the *109* in the other logbooks.

The *109* appears officially for the fifth time in a Warfield action report for the night of July 30-31. That night the *109* left on patrol in company with seven other boats, attached to section D, consisting of four boats: herself, *103*, *105*, and *106*. They were to scout in the lower reaches of Blackett Strait near Makuti Island. According to Keresey's *105* log, at 7:20 P.M., ten minutes before reaching patrol station, the *109*'s rudder failed and she returned to base. Section D had no action, but Section A (*117*, *157*, *169*, *170*) patrolling farther north in the strait, picked up a barge at 1:55 A.M. and poured a Niagara of small arms fire into it. They claimed it sank.

But had it?

Barge hunting, it turned out, was more difficult than anyone had anticipated. The barges, called *Daihatsus* by the Japanese, were like the U.S. amphibious craft, the LCVP. They could cruise at about 15 knots. They were heavily protected with armor plate. They had guns—larger guns, it was believed—than the PT's. To attack, PT's had to come close and fire hundreds of rounds of ammunition. In coming close, they exposed their crews to counterfire. Everybody lived in fear that a Japanese bullet would penetrate the thin plywood PT hull and set off the 100-octane aviation gasoline.

After a series of engagements with Japanese barges, Robert Kelly, commanding the small contingent of PT boats at Lever Harbor on the east coast of New Georgia, turned in a pessimistic report. He recommended that bigger ships, such as destroyers, take on the barges and that PT's be assigned to other tasks. Halsey shared Kelly's disappointment, reporting: "The use of PT boats as barge destroyers leaves much to be desired." But Halsey was not ready to give up entirely. He ordered Captain Moran to explore the idea of equipping PT boats with larger-caliber gun nests.

This idea was already being discussed at Lumbari. One enthusiastic proponent was Jack Kennedy. When the *109* returned prematurely from patrol on the evening of July 30 with a broken rudder, he knew he would have a day or two (while the rudder was being repaired) to install a larger gun.

The Army furnished the gun. It was an antique 37 mm, single-shot, breech-loading, antitank weapon mounted on a carriage with two steel wheels and bracing legs. In truth, it was not that much more powerful than the automatic 20 mm. It had the terrible disadvantage of being non-automatic. And there was no turret for it, no armor, no place to put it except on the bow, where the gunner would be fully exposed to enemy counterfire.

On July 31, a Saturday, Jack and Lennie Thom and some of the crew tried to devise a method for mounting this weapon. Basically, the plan was to bolt the steel-rimmed wheels to the bow planking and beams, then reinforce the two rear legs with large timbers to help absorb the recoil. Some of the men got an old coconut tree trunk to use for timber, but others found something better: a huge wooden timber, variously described to us as a four-by-four or four-by-six or six-by-six, ten or twelve feet long. The problem was, they needed a carpenter to cut it and bolt it properly behind the legs, and carpenters were hard to come by at Lumbari. They did not go out that night.

Summing up her action: between the time the *109* arrived at Lumbari about July 15, up to and including this day, July 31, there were sixteen patrol nights. From the action reports and the float-plane analysis we know positively that the *109* went out five nights, turning back the fifth night with a broken rudder, aborting the mission. In other words, from official sources we are positive of only four completed patrols. By the same action reports on these sixteen nights, we know positively that the *109* did *not* go out on five nights. That leaves six nights unaccounted for. If we concede (as Donovan wrote) she went out "night after night," then she could have gone out all six of these unverifiable nights, making no contact with the enemy. If so, that would be a total of ten completed patrols. But we seriously doubt she went out all six of these nights. It would mean that between July 18-19 and July 25-26, she went out eight nights in succession, a highly unlikely schedule, judging from the schedules of the other boats as we saw in an analysis of their logs. At most, we estimated, the

109 went out on 50 percent (or three) of the unverifiable nights, giving her a total of seven completed patrols through July 31.

In other words, a reasonable estimate would credit Jack and the *109* with seven completed patrols during the sixteen available nights. On four of these patrols, she had no enemy contact. On three, the section *109* was attached to was bombed by enemy float planes. One of the three attacks resulted in injuries or wounds to two *109* crewmen, Kowal and Drawdy; on the other two, the *109* escaped unscathed. On these patrols (in contrast to most other boats at Lumbari) the *109* had made no contact with, and consequently had not fired torpedoes or guns at, enemy surface vessels.

Four of the ten enlisted men were new to the boat and could not have made more than three of four patrols. The *109* was still pretty green to combat; her replacement crew was not yet fully integrated; her contribution in terms of damage to the enemy nil. And she had already suffered two casualties.

17

Meeting the Express

O<small>N</small> August 1, Warfield's communications officer, James Woods, took down an important encoded message from Admiral Wilkinson. We obtained the text of this message from the Naval Historical Center in Washington:

MOST SECRET

INDICATIONS EXPRESS MAY RUN TONIGHT ONE DASH TWO (1-2) AUGUST X ALSO HEAVY BARGE TRAFFIC TO BAIROKO OR SUNDAY INLET X WARFIELD OPERATE MAXIMUM NUMBER PETER TARES (PT) IN AREA BAKER (B) X KELLY OPERATE ALL AVAILABLE PETER TARES (PT) IN KULA GULF SOUTH OF LINE BAMBARI DASH RICE X BURKE WITH SIX (6) DESTROYERS GOES UP SLOT ARRIVING NORTH OF KOLOMBANGARA AT ZERO ZERO THIRTY LOVE (0030L) AUGUST SECOND (2ND) X IF KELLYS BOATS FORCED RETIRE TO LEVER DURING NIGHT ROUTE THEM CLOSE IN NEW GEORGIA SHORE X JAP AIR OUT TO GET PETER TARES (PT) X WARFIELD KELLY EACH ACKNOWLEDGE AND ADVISE NUMBER OF BOATS THEY WILL OPERATE TONIGHT X RICE ACKNOWLEDGE

It was the first big Express the Japanese had mounted in many days. Warfield assumed, correctly as it turned out, that its destination was Vila Plantation on southern Kolombangara. It could come down either the east or west side of Kolombangara. In Wilkinson's message, the main responsibility for stopping it was assigned to Captain Arleigh "31-Knot" Burke. He would meet it with six destroyers north of Kolombangara, taking station there at thirty minutes after midnight. In theory, whether it went east or west of Kolombangara, Burke would be in position to intercept it. The PT's, basing from Lumbari and Lever Harbor, would be backups in the event it got by Burke.

Shortly after the message arrived, Warfield told us, there was pandemonium at Lumbari Island. A flight of eighteen Japanese dive bombers attacked Rendova. Many of the PT's were then in the process of refueling. Most, including the *109*, got under way and fired at the planes. The Japanese bombs hit and demolished two PT's. Two torpedoes blew off the

deck of one of them and ran erratically around the harbor, finally ground-
ing on the beach without exploding.

To Warfield, the raid had special significance. If the Japanese had gone
to all that effort to knock out his PT boats in a dangerous daylight raid,
then it must mean the Express was coming down the west coast of Kolombangara. That is, through his baliwick, Blackett Strait. When the all-
clear sounded, he called a meeting of his skippers and staff at the bunker.
He told us, "We had a chart of the Blackett Strait area. I told them about
the Express and that I believed the air raid was a clear signal the Express
would come through our area. I showed them on the map exactly where I
thought it would come. And I stressed that it would not only *come down*
but *go back again*, so they would have two shots at it. Then we drew up
an action plan, dividing the boats into four divisions and gave each division leader his instructions."

The division leaders Warfield picked were the most senior PT officers at
Lumbari. Two of the four were Naval Academy graduates. They were (1)
Lieutenant Henry Joseph Brantingham, executive officer of Kelly's
Squadron Nine. "Hank" Brantingham, from the academy class of 1939,
had fought with Bulkeley and Kelly in the Philippines. He had more combat experience than any other PT skipper and was the second senior officer after Warfield; (2) Warfield's executive officer, Lieutenant Arthur
Henry Berndtson, from the class of 1940. He was then also acting as exec
for the Lumbari base; (3) Lieutenant George E. Cookman, a reservist
who had graduated from Yale in 1937 and who was then executive officer
of Farrow's Squadron Five; (4) Lieutenant Russel W. Rome, a senior reservist and Warfield favorite. Rome had come out on the *Stanvac Manila*
as a replacement officer. During the sinking, he had distinguished himself
by his coolness and courage and had helped save four of Warfield's PT
boats.

Warfield's deployment plan was that three of the four divisions would
be stationed inside Blackett Strait on a north-south line where the Express might be expected to pass if Arleigh Burke missed it. The fourth division would lie back in Ferguson Passage in reserve and pounce when or
if one of the divisions made contact, or in case the Express decided to go
through there to make an attack on the shipping at Rendova. Warfield
placed Hank Brantingham and his division at the northernmost point in
the strait. He, the most experienced officer, would make contact first. To
the south of him would be Art Berndtson's division. And to the south of
Berndtson, Rome's division, which would have last shot. Cookman would
command the backup division in Ferguson Passage. (See Map No. 3.)

There were fifteen PT's available for patrol that night. Four had primitive radar sets and these four boats were assigned as the four division
leaders. The boats were assigned as follows:

Division B (Brantingham)	*PT-159*	(Ron 9)	Radar
Lt. (j.g.) William F. Liebenow	*PT-157*	(Ron 9)	
Lt. (j.g.) John R. Lowrey	*PT-162*	(Ron 9)	
Lt. (j.g.) John F. Kennedy	*PT-109*	(Ron 2)	
Division A (Berndtson)	*PT-171*	(Ron 10)	Radar
Lt. (j.g.) Philip A. Potter	*PT-169*	(Ron 10)	
Lt. (j.g.) Stuart Hamilton	*PT-172*	(Ron 10)	
Ensign Edward H. Kruse	*PT-163*	(Ron 10)	
Division R (Rome)	*PT-174*	(Ron 10)	Radar
Lt. (j.g.) Richard E. Keresey	*PT-105*	(Ron 5)	
Lt. (j.g.) Joseph K. Roberts	*PT-103*	(Ron 5)	
Division C (Cookman)	*PT-107*	(Ron 5)	Radar
Lt. (j.g.) Robert D. Shearer	*PT-104*	(Ron 5)	
Lt. (j.g.) David M. Payne	*PT-106*	(Ron 5)	
Lt. (j.g.) Sidney D. Hix	*PT-108*	(Ron 5)	

When or if a division leader picked up a target on his radar, he would immediately flash a radio contact and begin closing to attack. The other boats of the division would "keep station" on the division leader—that is, they would follow the division leader to attack. The division leader would shoot first. The other boats would shoot as quickly afterward as possible along the bearing of his torpedo tracks. It was believed the destroyers would probably be moving at high speed so there would not be much time. After firing torpedoes, each skipper would turn his boat and get out of the strait and return to base to reduce confusion and congestion.

All fifteen boats were equipped with a standard PT boat radio. All skippers would keep their radios tuned to an assigned frequency. At Lumbari, Warfield would monitor the same frequency. Since the PT's had both transmitters and receivers, they could talk back and forth to either Warfield or any other PT boat. However, radio talk on this assigned frequency—other than contact or attack reports—was discouraged to reduce confusion and the chance of the Japanese picking it up. Warfield designated himself by the call sign "Oak." Each PT was given the call sign Oak plus a number. *PT-109* was Oak 14.

The PT radios—very high frequency (VHF) units—were not the best in the world. Originally they had been designed for aircraft, then adapted to the boats. They did not take the pounding well. They tended to drift off the assigned frequency. The Japanese used these same frequencies, cluttering up the air with unintelligible noise. Further, the radios were strongly affected by atmospheric conditions. Sometimes it was impossible to raise another PT boat one hundred yards away. However, an alert radioman could keep the set in tune and maintain communications with his base and the other PT's. The sets were located below decks in the "chart house." When the speaker was turned up full, it could be heard clearly in the cockpit. There was a mike in the cockpit for transmitting voice.

Some of the boats were assigned a second radio—portable short-range, ultra-high-frequency (UHF) units known as TBY, which Woods had managed to acquire from the Army at Munda. They were line-of-sight units that could not be heard beyond the horizon. The Japanese did not use UHF frequencies, so the PT skippers found these units useful as an additional means of boat-to-boat communications. Warfield encouraged their use since it helped the boats stay in touch without cluttering up the main communications frequency.

Some of the skippers going out that night were green. One was Philip Potter from Squadron Ten on the *169* in Berndtson's division. He was not only green, he had a problem with his boat. He told us:

> When Warfield went up to Lumbari, we followed him with about half of Squadron Ten. That is, about six boats. Most of them went out that night, as I recall. We had made some training patrols in the Russell Islands. But until that night I had never been on a combat patrol. And what they gave us to navigate by in Blackett Strait were some British Admiralty and captured Japanese charts and they were very old and inaccurate.
>
> Not only that, I was having trouble with my engines. Somewhere along the line somebody had failed to strain the gasoline through a chamois cloth when they filled the *169's* tanks. Some water got in the system. Ever since then, we'd had a problem with the engines. They'd conk out and you'd have a hell of a time getting them restarted. Or they ran rough. I had had trouble with them coming up to the Solomons and ever since I had been in the Solomons.

All that day, Kennedy had been trying to get the 37 mm properly mounted on the forward deck of the *109*. But there had been interruptions—first the air raid and then the briefing on the Express. He could not find a carpenter, Donovan reports. By nightfall, the job still had not been done. The big timber was still on the forward deck, not yet cut and bolted down. Not daring to leave either the gun or the timber ashore lest someone steal them, Kennedy had his men lash the gun and the timber to the deck with line.

Usually the PT's carried a life raft on the forward deck, but the *PT-109* raft had been put ashore to make room for the 37 mm. Nobody gave it much thought. PT's often went into combat without life rafts, technically a violation of Navy regulations. All the men on *PT-109* had big vest-type kapok life jackets which would keep them afloat until they could be rescued by other boats in the formation.

That evening, as Jack was preparing to leave for patrol, a Squadron Ten officer came down to the dock and asked if he could go along. He was George Henry Robertson Ross—"Barney" Ross—a good buddy of Red Fay's. Jack had met Ross at Melville, but he did not know him well; he may not even have recognized him. Jack invited him aboard and because of this impulsive, unofficial arrangement, Barney Ross would go down in the history books.

We found Ross working in Washington, D.C., in a program for the disadvantaged, the United Planning Organization. We met him at his office, located on the fringes of a black neighborhood. From all accounts, we had expected to find a big, burly, happy-go-lucky guy. His reputation was as a comic and good-hearted hell raiser. We met a somber-faced man who got about with the aid of double-jointed crutches. On November 5, 1965, while riding his motorcycle to work in Washington, he had collided with a car. He had been encased, immobile, in a body cast for two years. After that he had learned to walk again with the crutches.

During our interview, which went on for four or five hours, he seemed depressed and self-deprecating.

We began by asking about his background. He was born in Detroit in 1919, son of a Scottish-born certified public accountant and a British-born mother who was thirteen years older than his father. He grew up in comfortable—but not lavish—circumstances in Evanston, Illinois, a suburb of Chicago. He attended public and private secondary schools, then went on to Princeton. He told us:

I was always very big and very gentle, unaggressive as a kumquat. In the third grade I was taller than my teacher. I was not a great student. I flunked my college boards, spent a fifth year in high school, and somehow got into Princeton in the fall of 1937. I played football in high school and on the freshman team at Princeton, but I injured my right knee so I couldn't play varsity ball. I boxed— heavyweight. In the summer of 1938 I made a trip to Europe—my third—to see my many relatives. Then I traveled around by myself and had many adventures—some of them printable—but the next couple of summers I spent at Princeton making up failed credits. I finally got my degree in August, 1941, after yet another summer of making up credits. I messed around for the next eight or nine months hiking, riding bikes cross-country, going to house parties, canoeing, then in July, 1942, they called my number and I went into the Navy's V-7 program at Columbia University. I volunteered for PT's and went to Melville in October. I was in the class just behind Jack Kennedy. There were about fifty of us, including Red Fay, who became my big buddy in the Navy and after.

One day we were playing touch football at Melville and this little skinny kid with a funny accent comes up and asks in the game. I thought he was some high school kid or something, but we let him in. It was Jack Kennedy. He was senior to all of us ensigns in the game—a lieutenant junior grade!

I was assigned to that lousy Squadron Ten with Red Fay. The problem was the commander, Warfield. He was a real Naval Academy type and he didn't like us guys. We thought he was a real jerk. He wouldn't give me a command. He appointed me exec of *PT-166*, which was commanded by William Cullen Battle, who was later governor of Virginia and ambassador to Australia.

When the *Stanvac* got torpedoed, the squadron got all screwed up. We had to wait for the damaged boats to be repaired. Then we went on up to Tulagi in groups, then to Lumbari. Losing the two boats on the *Stanvac* left us with more crews than boats, so we had to shop around and bum rides. We'd lost another boat—the *164* —in the bombing raid August 1 and another, my boat, the *166*, in the B-25 fiasco on the morning of July 20. A guy named Carroll Donohue was skipper, replacing Bill Battle for that patrol. It was the *166* gunners who first opened up on the B-25's, and our boat that the B-25's set on fire, forcing us to abandon it. In other words, we'd lost four of our twelve boats. I had already been practically sunk once when I asked Jack if I could ride the *109* that night.

We talked for hours, covering much ground and painstakingly recon structing the *PT-109* disaster. During that intense and harrowing wee Barney and Jack had become, inevitably, close buddies. But after a week end at Hyannis Port the following year, when Ambassador Kenned showed strong disapproval of Ross, they separated. At Red Fay's insis tence, Jack mobilized Barney for the 1960 campaign and he later gave hir a minor job in the New Frontier, but Barney did not count himself a clos personal friend of Jack's.

So Barney Ross had come aboard "for the ride," bringing the tot complement to thirteen. Jack shoved off without adding Barney's name t the official sailing list. Later, this would cause some minor confusion. A they stood down the channel, Ross recalled, Jack told him jokingly tha his battle station would be the 37 mm gun.

The fifteen PT's set off in the darkness, keeping careful watch for Japa nese float planes. If the Express was headed for Blackett Strait, and th Japanese had gone to all the trouble of staging an air raid at Rendov surely the float planes would be out in force that night. The skippers tes ed radios. John Maguire told us, "The *109* VHF was in good working o der that night. As I recall, there was not much radio transmission. W were holding down the talk as much as possible." They eased throug Ferguson Passage into Blackett Strait. The night was pitch dark. Ther was an overcast.

Collectively, the fifteen boats constituted an impressive array of fire-power. Each had four torpedo tubes and four Mark VIII torpedoes, for a total of sixty torpedoes. It was by far the greatest lineup of firepower the PT force had ever deployed against an Express. If they made contact and fired, Warfield believed that despite their slow speed and history of erratic performance, at least some of the torpedoes would hit. If they managed to damage and thus slow down a destroyer, the others had a good chance of moving in and sinking it.

The boats patrolled slowly and quietly in the dark, keeping down wakes. Brantingham and his division (including *109*) cruised off Vanga Point to the north, Berndtson off Gatere, Rome between Makuti Island and the coast of Kolombangara. Cookman and his division lay back in Ferguson Passage. The radiomen on the four boats of the division leaders were glued to the primitive radar sets, watching the greenish horizontal and vertical displays for "pips" to show up. All boats had their radios tuned to the assigned frequency. Those with the portable UHF units, the TBY's, talked back and forth from time to time in subdued tones, making certain the units were working properly.

Back at Lumbari in the bunker, Warfield and Woods sat by their 100-watt VHF, listening and waiting. By now, Warfield told us, he was abso-lutely convinced his boats would meet the Express. From time to time, Woods remembered, Warfield spoke up on the main frequency to the boats, checking communications, trying to find out what was going on. Woods said, "A lot of the skippers out there that night later expressed re-sentment that Warfield was not with them, riding a boat. That he was sit-ting back at Lumbari, like a quarterback directing his team from the side-lines."

It was true that in the early days of PT fighting the squadron command-ers rode the boats and led them into battle. Bulkeley had done that in the Philippines. Others had done it during the intense phase of the Guadalca-nal fighting. Kelly had done it during the New Georgia invasion. But War-field was now much more than a mere squadron commander. He was commanding all the PT boats at Lumbari, which included elements of four squadrons—Two, Five, Nine, and Ten. He was almost certainly cor-rect in his belief that he could better control this disparate group from a base headquarters with superior communications than from the cockpit of a PT boat in Blackett Strait.

What happened in the next six hours is described by Robert Bulkley in *At Close Quarters* as "perhaps the most confused and least effectively ex-cuted action the PT's had been in." In fact, it was an utter fiasco and we suspect that many of the 150-odd PT officers and men who were a part of it, including Jack, felt a sense of shame and guilt for a long time after it.

It is difficult to reconstruct any naval action, and a night action involv-ing fifteen PT boats operating in strange and hostile waters can only be approximated. During PT actions, all hands were busy at several tasks. No one had time to keep a minute-by-minute log (as was done, for exam ple, on submarines and larger vessels). PT boats were constantly chang ing speed and course, with little idea of their exact position or the position of the enemy. Logs were made of the highlights. But these were prepared from memory, after the crew returned to base. Tom Warfield's action re ports were based on the logs, and on oral, or hastily drafted, action briefings by skippers who often had to guess what they might have been doing. In preparing official battle reports there is a normal tendency to or der events and place them in readable and logical sequence, whereas, the "real thing" is a great chaos.

A related point. The war correspondents who were to be the first to write about the battle and subsequent *109* events worked under strict cen sorship. They did not have access to the official, highly classified action reports or to intelligence reports. What they wrote was usually based on interviews with the men in combat or what they observed themselves. Ev ery word of it was then carefully gone over to make certain no operationa secrets leaked out to the Japanese. In practice, Navy censors were heavy handed. For these reasons, and others, the accounts of the battle an subsequent *109* events remained, for a period of eighteen years—unt Jack Kennedy reached the White House—terribly distorted and incom plete. The distortions and incompletness favored Kennedy, helping cre ate the image of a war hero. Moreover, even when the full facts wer known, and told, the judgments from these facts were drawn, for reason we will touch on, to favor Kennedy, further enhancing the superman role

In our reconstruction of the naval battle, the first full and objective ac count of it, we believe, we have made use of several official naval docu ments, the three Kennedy Navy books, and interviews of our own.

Thomas Warfield submitted an official action report on August 5, 1943 which was based on written and oral action reports given him by the skip pers on the morning after the battle. (These written reports cannot b found.) Warfield's report, declassified in 1959, is the most complete sun mary of the action extant, though it contains some errors and distortion In 1961–1962, Kennedy's three naval biographers relied on portions of i In using it, we bore in mind that Warfield, like any field commander, trie to put the best possible face on what was indisputably, for him, a persona and professional disaster.

An intelligence report prepared by Whizzer White and Lieutenant (j.g J. G. McClure is primarily an account of the survival of the *PT-109* crew men after the boat was rammed, but it begins with an account of the ba tle. In several important instances it differs from the Warfield report and also contains errors or distortions. The White report (as we called it) wa declassified in 1959. Portions of it were used by Kennedy's naval biogr phers and by Bulkley in *At Close Quarters*. In making use of it, we bore in mind that White was Kennedy's friend.

The available logbooks of the surviving fourteen PT boats for that night were not very helpful. In most of them the battle is covered in four or five one-sentence entries. As we have seen, PT logbooks were hasty and incomplete reconstructions made after the battle. Some skippers may have canted them to put the best possible face on their own actions. When we consulted them, we did so with extreme care.

Of the three Kennedy Navy books, Donovan's is by far the most complete account. In addition to utilizing portions of the declassified Warfield and White reports, Donovan traveled to the Solomons and Blackett Strait, interviewed six of the skippers in the action that night, all the living survivors of *PT-109*, plus Warfield, Woods, and others. In some minor respects, the Donovan account differs from the Warfield and White reports, and contains some obvious errors and distortions. In every respect, by his stated judgments (and withheld judgments) Donovan put Jack in the most favorable light. In making use of the Donovan version, we bore in mind that Donovan was also Kennedy's friend, that his manuscript was gone over and cleared by Kennedy and his White House aides, that as the Washington bureau chief of an important newspaper, Donovan was in no position to write anything severely displeasing the president—such as by raising questions about his courage or leadership.

For our interviews we went back over much of the ground Donovan had covered, perhaps with a different set of questions. We interviewed Warfield and Woods, two of the division commanders in Blackett Strait that night—Brantingham and Berndtson—and three of the skippers—Liebenow, Keresey, and Potter. (At least five of the fifteen skippers are deceased.) In addition, we interviewed four of the six living survivors of the *109*'s thirteen crewmen that night: Barney Ross; the radioman, John Maguire; Charles A. Harris; and Gerard Zinser. We also talked with George Wright, Jack's first skipper at Tulagi, who by chance was in Warfield's bunker on Lumbari that night.

There was a special problem in interviewing the *PT-109* crew. Most of them would, in time, benefit enormously by their association with Kennedy in the *PT-109* adventure. As Kennedy rose to fame, they were hauled from obscurity and thrust into the local and national limelight. Some of them—Ross and Maguire, for example—actively worked for Kennedy's election in 1960, appearing on television, and were rewarded with federal jobs after he won. They were made into heroes in Donovan's book and the movie version of the book. Thus, the *109* crewmen have a vested interest in putting Kennedy (and themselves) in the most favorable light. Moreover, we discovered that they were so accustomed to being interviewed and telling the story in the usual heroic way, that an unexpected question seemed to confuse them. The radioman Maguire, for example, could not positively describe the radio equipment on *PT-109*. And, under close interrogation, some would admit they were not sure whether they remembered a fact independently or had read it in a book or magazine article or had seen it in the movie. So do myths grow.

Jack Kennedy, because of who he was then (a minicelebrity) and what he became later (a popular president) is usually portrayed in accounts of the battle, and the subsequent survival episode of the *109* crew, as a superman. It would be well to remember that that night, as he conned *109* toward Blackett Strait, he was actually a relatively green skipper, and a human being—undoubtedly tense, presumably fearful. Men in such circumstances commonly wonder about themselves: will I have the courage to charge?

The Express barreled southward from Rabaul. According to Donovan (and official sources), it was composed of four first-line destroyers: *Amagiri, Hagikaze, Arashi,* and *Shigure.* It carried 900 Japanese troops. But it ran ahead of the schedule picked up by the codebreakers. It passed north of Kolombangara at about 11:30, where Arleigh Burke hoped to meet it at thirty minutes after midnight. It veered to the southwest and headed for Blackett Strait, just as Warfield had predicted it would. Minute by minute it closed the gap with the fifteen PT boats lying in wait. And here a point should be emphasized once again: the skippers had been briefed to expect destroyers, which might arrive about midnight. That was why this unusually large formation was there. It is not true, as Donovan and others report, that Kennedy and the other skippers did not know destroyers were in the vicinity.

By the Warfield account, at midnight Brantingham and his Division B, which included Jack Kennedy in the *109,* were patrolling off Vanga Point. This is an area north of the center line of Kolombangara, more or less on the northwestern corner of the island. Based on our interviews with the participants, we judged this to be correct. The White report makes an important error here. It has this division patrolling "five miles west" of Berndtson's division, and has Berndtson's division farther south in the strait. For this to be true, Brantingham's division would have to have been near Gizo Island or Ferguson Passage. This was simply not true. The effect of the error was to place Jack far from the scene of action that soon developed.

Three of the four boats of this division were from Squadron Nine. This was Robert Kelly's squadron, which had been based in Panama, then sent to the Solomons in May, then to Rendova on June 30. The Squadron Nine boats had been in almost continuous combat action for thirty days. As we have seen, these boats accidentally sank the *McCawley* and fired at a formation of Japanese destroyers in a confused action. But, in addition, the squadron had aggressively patrolled in Blackett Strait, chasing barges and dodging float planes. Of the fifteen boats out that night, the Squadron Nine boats were the most experienced and the most familiar with the waters.

Two of the three boats in Jack's formation were considered the most aggressive and skilled in combat of the squadron. These were Hank Brantingham's *159* (the skipper of the boat was Michael Richard Pessolano, later killed in the war) and "Lieb" Liebenow's *157*. Brantingham, as we have said, was regular Navy, a veteran of the PT fighting in the Philippines in the early days of the war, and one of the heroes of the book, *They Were Expendable*.

Liebenow, a Virginian who'd joined the Navy after Pearl Harbor, then went to the PT school at Melville, was considered to be a skilled PT boat operator. For example, when the squadron was in Panama, it was alerted for a visit by President Roosevelt, who wanted to go on a PT boat. Liebenow in *157* was chosen to be Roosevelt's host skipper. (The visit was canceled.) In the July operations of Squadron Nine, Liebenow had distinguished himself. He was so dependable and cool in combat that when Kelly and Brantingham were operating, they always chose Liebenow to ride wing on their lead boats. In the July action, Liebenow had fired torpedoes at enemy destroyers. He would emerge from the war with a Silver Star and a Bronze Star for valor.

The third Squadron Nine skipper, Lowrey in *162* (now deceased), was well liked, Liebenow recalled. But for one reason or another, he had missed the action against enemy destroyers. Liebenow thought he had been fired on by a float plane (or barge) but, as Liebenow remembered it, Lowrey had not fired torpedoes at the enemy. In sum: less experienced, probably less aggressive than Brantingham or Liebenow.

Squadron Nine was one outfit that did not subscribe to the controversial technique of running at slow speed with only one engine in gear to keep down phosphorescent wakes as a defense against float planes. Liebenow was emphatic on that point: "We *always* ran with all three engines in gear. We *never* took them out of gear. Kelly and Brantingham were experienced in combat. They knew all the tricks. If Kelly or Brantingham came on your boat and saw you didn't have three engines in gear, they would kill you. Well, anyway, they'd let you know about it in no uncertain terms."

The territory in which Brantingham's division patrolled was well known to him and the other Squadron Nine skippers. "That was our regular patrol area," Liebenow recalled. "We'd been up there plenty of times."

At midnight, Warfield reports, Brantingham picked up five pips on his radar. He believed in the first seconds they might be "large landing craft" (barges). Warfield says that Brantingham ordered Lowrey and Kennedy to "lay to" and moved in, with Liebenow following, to make a "strafing attack." About that time the enemy opened fire "with many large-caliber guns," indicating that Brantingham had found not landing craft but the Express and that all were firing at him. Brantingham, who now saw "four ships," fired four torpedoes at the targets. Liebenow, who reported seeing only two ships, fired two torpedoes. The torpedo tubes on Brantingham's boat "flashed" and "one caught fire," giving the Japanese a fine point of aim. The men on both boats saw a "large explosion" at the target.

Liebenow recalled:

I stuck close to Brantingham, as was the procedure. So close you could have stepped from one boat to the other. When I saw the destroyers, I got ready to fire all four of my torpedoes. The proper procedure was, you fired your two aft tubes first, then the two forward tubes. But my port aft tube misfired—it didn't go out with the starboard aft tube. Then I fired the starboard forward tube. I couldn't fire the port forward tube because by then I was swinging away from the destroyers and couldn't aim properly.

By then the destroyers were firing shells all around us. Brantingham's tube was on fire and it was like a beacon. I swung between him and the destroyer to lay a smoke screen so they couldn't see the fire and use it as a point of aim. Then we both got out of there, zigzagging and laying smoke.

According to the Warfield report, Brantingham and Liebenow retired to the northwest, ultimately reaching Gizo Strait. Liebenow told us, "Well, maybe so. As I recall, we zigzagged for ten or fifteen miles. I have no idea what direction we went. We were just going." Finally they hove to, Warfield reported, and held a megaphone pow-wow. Brantingham, out of torpedoes, would return to Lumbari. He ordered Liebenow, who still had two torpedoes (the cause of the misfire was corrected) to return to Blackett Strait, link up with Lowrey and Kennedy, and lie in wait for the destroyers when they withdrew from Vila.

In Squadron Nine, Kelly and Brantingham had a policy of always maintaining strict radio silence. The enemy could pick up radio transmissions and, with electronic gear, pinpoint their location. In addition, experience had shown that a lot of radio transmissions during combat usually tended to confuse the situation. For this reason, they did not broadcast a "contact" report. In his report, Warfield (by implication) was critical of them for not doing so, and declared that henceforth all Lumbari boats under his command would make such reports "immediately in plain language."

Now, let us return to the other two boats of Brantingham's division Lowrey's *PT-162* and Jack's *PT-109*. They did not attack. As will be recalled, Warfield wrote in his report that Brantingham had ordered them to "lay to" while he investigated the pips on his radar.

This seemed a strange order to us, a wrong note, contrary to PT-boat doctrine. As we were told in our interviews with various PT-boat officers, the standard doctrine was for all the boats of a single division to attack the enemy en masse, as a unified element, bringing maximum firepower to bear within the few seconds of surprise available to all the boats. If only two boats attacked, the other two had little or no chance. By the time they got ready and moved in, the enemy would be mounting counterfire dangerous to a frail PT boat.

Brantingham, who retired from the Navy in 1964, now lives in Southern California, where he is a college teacher. We reached him by telephone and in a long and detailed discussion of the action, we asked if he had given Lowrey and Kennedy orders to "lay to." He said, without equivocation:

No. And I don't think anybody else did either. Kennedy's boat was not in my regular squadron, but had been loaned to us for that night. We were the northernmost boats in Blackett Strait. As I recall, of the four boats, mine was first to the north and Kennedy was with me. All the boats were enjoined to radio silence. In our squadron we had a firm commitment to radio silence, even to attacking without talking on the radio. When the leading boat saw something and attacked, the other boats were to follow right along without further ado and no further conversation. That was the practice in our squadron. I don't think any written orders were actually issued that night but in the briefing before we went out we discussed it.

Our first thought on seeing the pips on radar was that they were barges. As we got closer and they started shooting at us, it became obvious they weren't barges. They were the destroyers we were more or less expecting. We could not see them clearly. We must have picked them up at a couple of miles because we ran toward them for a couple of minutes, trying to intercept. When I fired my torpedoes at them, the range was less than one mile—less than two thousand yards.

Q. At the time you fired your torpedoes, do you know how far away Kennedy was?

A. No. But he could have been as close as one thousand or two thousand yards from me. (See Map No. 4.)

Q. Then how come Kennedy didn't follow you in the attack?

A. I never asked him. He was in my command temporarily and one night only. By the time we went out and picked him up one week later, the action reports had already been filed by Warfield. The question never came up as to what his boat did or did not do about following the rest of us into attack. It could well be that his squadron did not do things that way. When he saw me take off toward the enemy, he lagged a little too far behind to see what was going on.

What Brantingham had said in effect was that the Warfield report was in error. Brantingham had *not* given Lowrey and Kennedy orders to "lay to." Their orders were to follow him into the attack, in accordance with standard PT procedures. But for some reason they had not done so.

To get another opinion on that doctrine, we telephoned another division commander who was out that night, Art Berndtson of Squadron Ten. Now also retired from the Navy, he lives in Washington, D.C. He told us, "The basic PT indoctrination, beginning at Melville, was, 'When in doubt, you always follow the lead boat.' Even if you're not sure what he's doing. Follow that lead boat and if you don't recognize the situation right now, eventually you'll recognize it."

We closely queried Liebenow about the orders to lay to. He told us, "No. I don't think Hank Brantingham told them to lay to. We always maintained strict radio silence at sea. I was right alongside Brantingham the whole time, guarding the VHF frequency. I didn't hear anything like that. The procedure was, they were supposed to keep station on Brantingham and me—stay very close. Then when Brantingham and I attacked, they were to follow the leader and fire about the same time."

In addition, we queried a *PT-109* crew member on the point, Charles Harris, who now lives in Waltham, Massachusetts. His memory confirmed Brantingham's and Liebenow's—that Brantingham had not ordered the *PT-109* to lay to. On the contrary, Harris said, there had been no word from Brantingham at all on the radio. Harris was still a bit miffed about that: "Our lead boat, the radar boat, picked something up but they didn't tell us anything about it. They took off after it and left us sitting there. When we got back, we were really going to look up that skipper and give him the business for leaving us high and dry like that. We were kind of mad. He had the 'eyes' and we didn't."

We asked Liebenow these questions: If Brantingham did not, as Warfield reported, order Lowrey and Jack to lay to, what was the explanation? Where were they? Why didn't they follow and attack? He said:

I think they simply got lost. It was a very dark night. They stayed too far back and Lowrey lost contact with me. Maybe they were running with only one engine in gear to hold down speed and the wake. If so, that was a mistake.

Q. But Brantingham told us they were only two thousand yards or so away from him.

A. Well, Brantingham had radar, remember. He could see them on radar, so he would know. I couldn't see them.

When Brantingham fired and I fired, and the destroyers started firing at us, and Brantingham's tube caught fire, they should have seen us by then. But they didn't come in.

In his report, Whizzer White introduces an entirely new, and somewhat complex, element in the problem, one that would tend to place the responsibility for whatever happened to the *109* and *162* on Lowrey. He writes, "Lt. Brantingham's boats were further subdivided into two sections: *PT-159*, radar equipped, operating with *PT-157*, while *PT-162*, under the command of Lt. (jg) J. R. Lowrey, was the lead boat of the second section with *PT-109* following. PT's *159* and *162* both carried TBY's for interboat communications. Instructions were issued to Lt. (jg) Jack Kennedy, captain of *PT-109*, to follow closely on *PT-162*'s starboard quarter, which would keep in touch with the radar equipped *PT-159* by TBY."

In other words, Jack was to take orders not from Brantingham but from Lowrey. In our interviews both Brantingham and Liebenow dismissed White's subcommand setup as nonsense. It was contrary to PT doctrine; contrary to Squadron Nine tactics. The setup is not mentioned in the Warfield report, which is a much more detailed tactical analysis of the battle.

For whatever reason, it seems reasonably clear that Jack had failed to follow his leader during this, his first exposure to enemy surface vessels and his first opportunity to attack them. We examined his movements in the next few minutes with extreme care.

The Warfield report: "PT's *162* and *109* lay to as directed. When the firing began there was so much and over such a long stretch of the coast, they thought shore batteries had opened up and retired to the northwest. . . ."

White, having established the dubious subcommand setup of Lowrey and Jack's two boats, says nothing about laying to. The group "patrolled without incident," he writes, ". . . until gunfire and a searchlight were seen in the direction of the southern shore of Kolombangara. No radio or other warning had been received of enemy activity in the area. It was impossible to ascertain whether the searchlight came from shore or from a ship close to the shore. Presumably it was not a ship as *PT-162* retired on westerly course toward Gizo Strait. *PT-109* followed and inquired as to the source of the firing. *PT-162* replied that it was believed to be from a shore battery. . . ."

Leaving aside the question of Lowrey's being in command of Kennedy, in the first place the gunfire was not first detected in the direction of the southern shore of Kolombangara. The opposite was true. The destroyers opened up when they were off the northern coast of Kolombangara. It is demonstrably untrue that the boats had not received warning of enemy activity in the area. They had been fully briefed on the incoming Express; in fact, as we said, they were there specifically to intercept it and every skipper was expecting it.

White writes that it was impossible to ascertain whether the search-lights came from the shore or from ships close to the shore. But so far as we were able to discover, there had never been a report of shore batteries or searchlights from this deserted end of Kolombangara. The lights were close aboard, strong and moving. Since Lowrey and Jack were expecting big ships—the Express—why wouldn't the first logical assumption have been that the lights and guns came from the destroyers?

Brantingham and Liebenow, who were not far removed from Lowrey and Jack (one nautical mile?), had not mistaken the gunfire and search lights for shore installations. They had logically and instantly recognized the threat for what it was: the Express. In our interview with Brantingham, we put this question to him:

Q. How could Kennedy have mistaken this gunfire for anything other than a destroyer?
A. I wouldn't pretend to know what went on in his mind. The point of it all was that we were told to go out after destroyers. They told us the destroyers were coming; we saw something at the spot where we expected to see destroyers. When the destroyers fired, we could see the shell splashes and knew it wasn't coming from barges. We were too far off the beach to think they were shore batteries. They couldn't have seen anything to shoot at from the shore.

Liebenow said, "We'd been close to that island a lot. We'd never been fired on by shore batteries or seen searchlights. Expecially on that end of the island. I don't think there were any shore batteries on that end, then or later. No. I certainly did not think they were shore batteries."

We turned to the Kennedy literature to see how the various author handled this sticky point. Donovan follows White, writing that the "instructions" were for Jack to "stay close" to Lowrey, so that when Lowrey received orders from Brantingham on the TBY, he could relay them by voice to Jack. Neither Lowrey nor Jack knew that Brantingham "had charged off on an attack." Donovan goes on:

They and their crews knew that something was happening because in toward Kolombangara they could see flashes and star shells. Not realizing that enemy destroyers were passing, they guessed that Japanese shore batteries might be firing on the PT boats. When the beam of a searchlight from one of the destroyers

THE MAPS ON THE FOLLOWING PAGES CLARIFY THE ACTION IN THE SOUTH PACIFIC DESCRIBED IN PART II

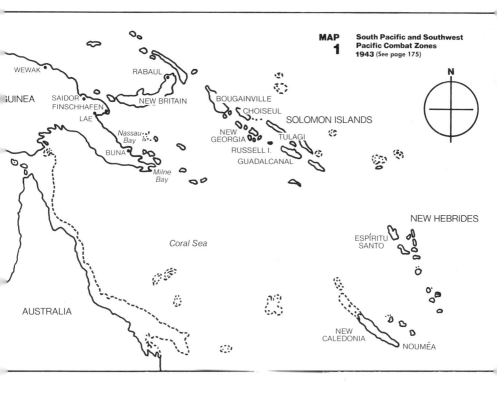

MAP 1 South Pacific and Southwest Pacific Combat Zones 1943 (See page 175)

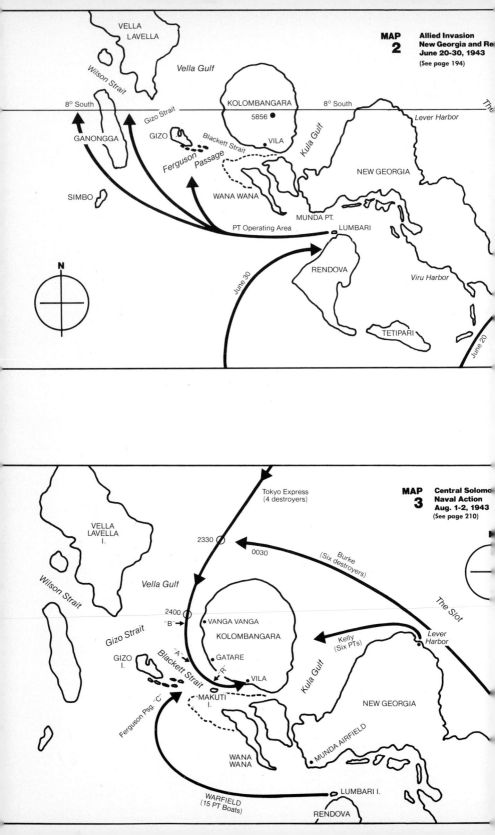

MAP 2 — Allied Invasion New Georgia and Re... June 20-30, 1943 (See page 194)

- VELLA LAVELLA
- Wilson Strait
- Vella Gulf
- KOLOMBANGARA
- 5856
- 8° South
- 8° South
- The
- Lever Harbor
- Gizo Strait
- GANONGGA
- GIZO
- Blackett Strait
- VILA
- Kula Gulf
- Ferguson Passage
- WANA WANA
- NEW GEORGIA
- SIMBO
- MUNDA PT.
- PT Operating Area
- LUMBARI
- N
- RENDOVA
- Viru Harbor
- June 30
- TETIPARI
- June 20

MAP 3 — Central Solomo... Naval Action Aug. 1-2, 1943 (See page 210)

- Tokyo Express (4 destroyers)
- VELLA LAVELLA I.
- 2330
- 0030
- Burke (Six destroyers)
- Wilson Strait
- Vella Gulf
- The Slot
- 2400
- "B"
- VANGA VANGA
- KOLOMBANGARA
- Lever Harbor
- Gizo Strait
- "A"
- GATARE
- Kelly (Six PTs)
- GIZO I.
- Blackett Strait
- "R"
- Kula Gulf
- VILA
- Ferguson Psg. "C"
- MAKUTI I.
- NEW GEORGIA
- WANA WANA
- MUNDA AIRFIELD
- WARFIELD (15 PT Boats)
- LUMBARI I.
- RENDOVA

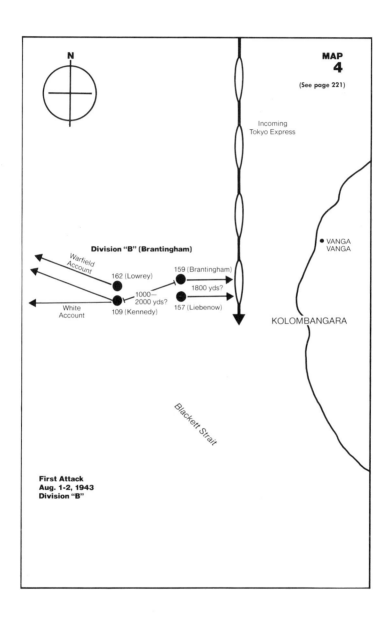

N

MAP
4

(See page 221)

Incoming
Tokyo Express

Division "B" (Brantingham)

Warfield
Account

162 (Lowrey)

159 (Brantingham)

● VANGA
VANGA

1800 yds?

1000—
2000 yds?

157 (Liebenow)

White
Account

109 (Kennedy)

KOLOMBANGARA

Blackett Strait

First Attack
Aug. 1-2, 1943
Division "B"

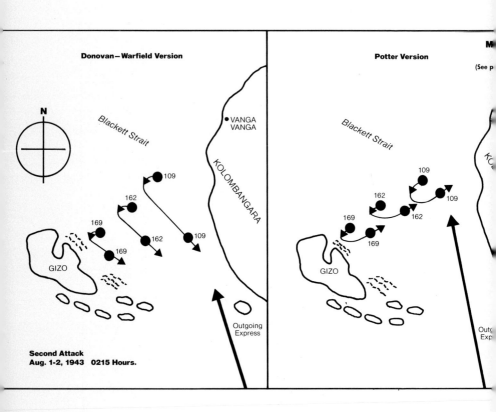

Donovan—Warfield Version

N

Blackett Strait

•VANGA VANGA

KOLOMBANGARA

109

162

169

162

169

109

109

GIZO

Outgoing Express

Second Attack
Aug. 1-2, 1943   0215 Hours.

Potter Version

(See p

Blackett Strait

KO

109

162

109

169

162

169

GIZO

Out
Exp

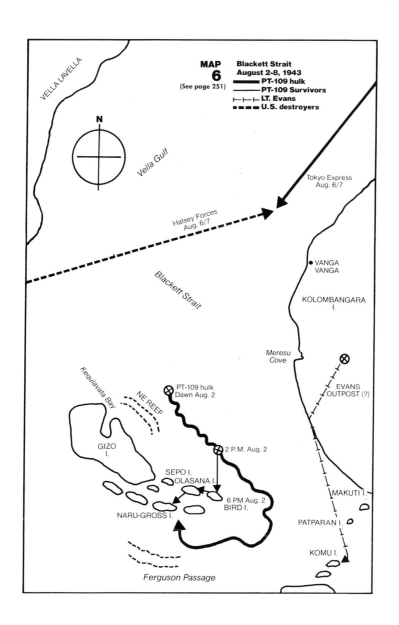

MAP 6
(See page 251)

Blackett Strait
August 2-8, 1943
▬▬▬ PT-109 hulk
▬▬ PT-109 Survivors
├─┤─┤─ LT. Evans
■■■■ U.S. destroyers

N

VELLA LAVELLA

Vella Gulf

Tokyo Express
Aug. 6/7

Halsey Forces
Aug. 6/7

Blackett Strait

VANGA
VANGA

KOLOMBANGARA
I.

Meresu
Cove

Kequlavata Bay

NE REEF

PT-109 hulk
Dawn Aug. 2

EVANS
OUTPOST (?)

GIZO
I.

2 P.M. Aug. 2

SEPO I.
OLASANA I.

MAKUTI I.

6 PM Aug. 2
BIRD I.

NARU-GROSS I.

PATPARAN I.

KOMU I.

Ferguson Passage

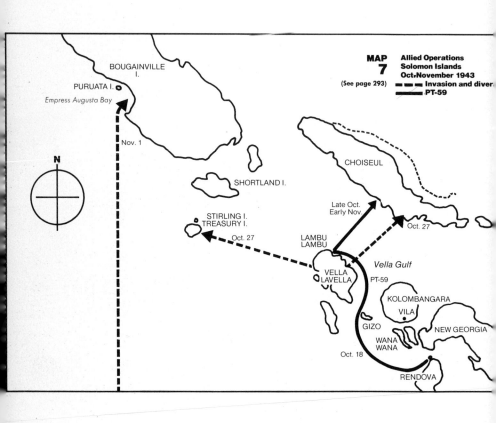

MAP
7
(See page 293)

**Allied Operations
Solomon Islands
Oct.–November 1943**
▬ ▬ ▬ **Invasion and diver**
▬▬▬ **PT-59**

BOUGAINVILLE
I.

PURUATA I.

Empress Augusta Bay

Nov. 1

N

CHOISEUL

SHORTLAND I.

Late Oct.
Early Nov.

Oct. 27

STIRLING I.
TREASURY I.

Oct. 27

LAMBU
LAMBU

Vella Gulf

VELLA
LAVELLA

PT-59

KOLOMBANGARA
VILA

GIZO

NEW GEORGIA

WANA
WANA

Oct. 18

RENDOVA

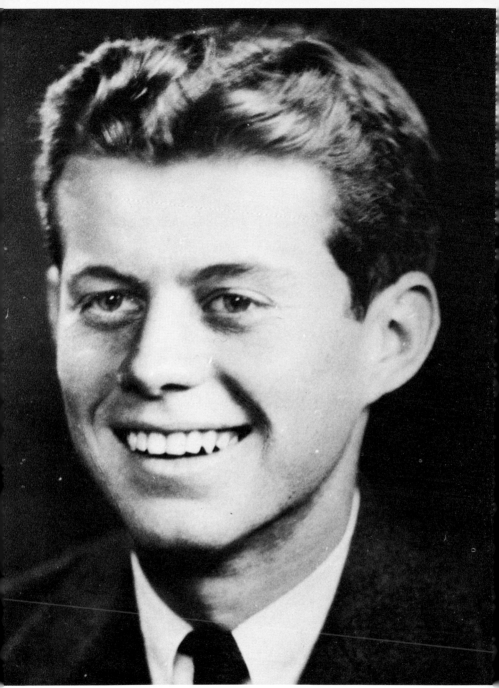

Student at The Choate School, circa 1934–35. *(Courtesy John F. Kennedy Library)*

A Christmas card from Rip Horton, Lem Billings and Jack Kennedy.
(Courtesy John F. Kennedy Library)

We're puttin' on our top hat,

Tyin' up our white tie,

Brushin' off our tails,

In order to
Wish you

A Merry Christmas

Rip.   Leem.   Ken.

Jack poses for his Choate graduation picture, May 1935.
(Courtesy of John F. Kennedy Library)

Joseph P. and Rose Kennedy sail for Europe in September 1935, taking Kathleen and Jack. Front row left to right: Jean, Edward, Robert, Patricia. Eunice stands to her father's right. *(United Press International Photo)*

Jack and Lem Billings traveling
in Europe, summer 1937.
(Courtesy John F. Kennedy Library)

Jack collapsed ill in London hotel at conclusion of summer 1937 trip.
(Courtesy John F. Kennedy Library)

Ambassador Kennedy in a shipboard pose with Joe Jr. (left) and Jack.
(Courtesy John F. Kennedy Library)

Jack, in white tie and tails, dances with unidentified woman at U.S. Embassy party in London, circa July 1938.
(© Erich Salomon, distributed by Magnum Photos, Inc.)

Joe Jr., Kathleen and Jack on a
London street, 1939.
(Courtesy John F. Kennedy Library)

Jack, on his 1939 travels to the Mideast, poses astride camel
with unidentified woman on adjacent camel.
(Courtesy John F. Kennedy Library)

Jack, following outbreak of war, arrives from Europe aboard Pan Am Clipper, September 21, 1939. *((ACME) 9-21-39 (CT) United Press International Photo)*

February 1940: Jack (extreme right) at the wedding of Harvard roommate, Benjamin Smith, to Barbara Mechem in Chicago. Left to right: Torby Macdonald, Ben Smith, Barbara Mechem, Charles Houghton. *(Wide World Photos)*

Summer 1940: Jack poses at a typewriter to promote his book, *England Slept*. *(Pictorial Parade)*

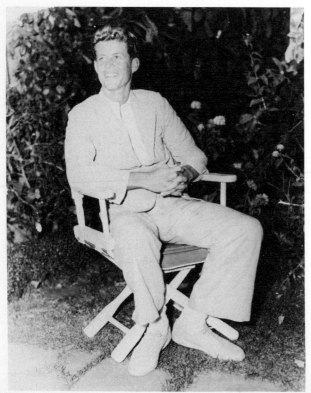

Jack, at Stanford University, in the fall of 1940.
(Courtesy Virginia Sisk Prejean)

Nancy Burkett.

Jack and Flip Price, fall 1940.

Jack, at Stanford University, registers for draft with Stanford students. *(Courtesy Stanford News Bureau)*

Rose, Eunice and Jack in Rio de Janeiro, May 1941. Sugarloaf in background.
(Courtesy John F. Kennedy Library)

swept close to *109* and a couple of shells burst nearby, the men feared that the coastal guns were getting range of them. Kennedy called "general quarters," and the crew went to battle stations.

Under the circumstances Lowrey swung away from Kolombangara and slipped up Blackett Strait toward Vella Lavella. Following his section leader, Kennedy pulled close enough to ask Lowrey if he had any word on what was going on. Lowrey replied that he had not. Shore batteries were probably firing, he said. Nevertheless on *109*'s radio the men could hear occasional exchanges like, "I am being chased through Ferguson Passage. Have fired fish." "Well, get the hell out of there." Obviously, some of the boats were engaged at sea somewhere.

Donovan (like White) gives the impression that Lowrey and Jack are miles and miles from the action, that they knew only that some PT action was going on "at sea somewhere." (In a very brief account of this phase, Tregaskis does the same, writing that Lowrey and Kennedy "were far removed from Brantingham in the dark and lost radio contact.") But, as we have seen, the PT boats were all tightly packed within the small confines of Blackett Strait, a point that Donovan stresses earlier in his narrative. If Brantingham's memory is correct, Lowrey and Jack were actually only a mile or less from him when he first attacked. In any case, within minutes—four or five—two other PT divisions also attacked the Express. All hell was breaking loose in the narrow strait. The destroyers were firing guns and star shells continuously and probing with searchlights. The PT's were charging around firing torpedoes. There was much more radio talk than Donovan relates and it quite specifically indicated, time and again, the presence of the Express they had been waiting for. Lowrey and Kennedy had to know within a very few minutes that the Express had arrived on schedule—and that because of their hasty withdrawal they had missed a golden opportunity to engage the enemy.

Finally, we asked Barney Ross what he thought about the withdrawal. He thought it had been a mistake. But he did not blame Lowrey. He blamed it on lack of training: "A lot of very strong searchlights came on. What we did was, when the searchlights came on, we did evasive action to get out of the light so we wouldn't get shot. If we'd been better trained we might have realized that they didn't have that many searchlights on shore and because they *were* strong they had to be from ships. We probably should have trailed the thing and attacked."

So ended Jack's first opportunity to attack the enemy. He and Lowrey lost contact with their division leader and trailed behind. When Brantingham and Liebenow attacked, they failed to follow up or to come to Brantingham's assistance. When the destroyers began firing, they quickly left the scene.

In the conclusion to his report, Warfield reemphasized PT attack doctrine: "PT's should stay together in 'V' formation and follow their division leader. All boats should fire their torpedoes when their section leader fires without deployment. They should spread torpedoes about the base torpedo course of the leader."

The Express continued south, undamaged but alerted. By Warfield's account, only four minutes after Brantingham made contact and attacked, Art Berndtson, leading the A division off Gatere, also made contact on radar. This was at four minutes past midnight, when Jack and Lowrey must have been highballing westward, away from the Express and Kolombangara, toward Gizo or Gizo Strait. Berndtson instantly recognized the pips as the Express. He told us:

> We saw pips on the radar screen, in line and moving fast. This indicated to me: here they come! I tried to make a quick approximation of the scene—the relative movement. I saw they were going to pass at long range from me, so the name of the game was to move over toward their track for a better shot. I called the other boats in my division, which were lying to, and gave them a "Delta" or whatever the signal was to "deploy on me." Nothing happened. I called a second time. Again nothing happened. Then I told the signalman to give it to them with a blinker tube. Still nothing happened, so I told Bill [William C. Battle, who was commanding the *171* on which Berndtson was embarked] to get moving anyway. We could clearly see the big phosphorescent bow wakes of the destroyers. When we got set, the first ship had already passed. So we lined up on the second ship and let fly four torpedoes at about fifteen to eighteen hundred yards. Our tubes flashed and we had a nice bright fire. That alerted them. One of the destroyers turned toward us to comb our torpedoes [parallel their tracks, to reduce the target area]. They turned on searchlights and started firing big guns at us. Well, we put on power, zigzagged, and laid smoke. There was shrapnel raining on deck. It looked like a junkyard.
>
> I tried two or three times to call Bill Rome, leading the division south of me, on the radio, to let him know they were coming. But I never did get in touch with Rome. Either he wasn't on the right frequency or we hit a blank spot. We headed for Ferguson Passage. I got on the radio and told Warfield there were four destroyers heading for Ferguson Passage [as it appeared to Berndtson at that moment], that I had fired four torpedoes, and I was pulling out of the area. That was standard procedure, to reduce confusion.

Warfield reports that the other three boats in this division "did not receive the contact report or any message to deploy for attack." He writes that after firing his torpedoes, Berndtson swung south across the bows of these three boats which, by now, saw the destroyers. However, they could not fire because Berndtson was in the way. Berndtson, he says, headed for Ferguson Passage, then "feeling that the first destroyer might be blocking Ferguson Passage," turned north, ran along the reefs of Gizo Island, and exited through Gizo Strait.

Phil Potter in the *169* was one of Berndtson's skippers. He told us:

> We knew there were Japanese destroyers coming. That was why we were there. Then, as I recall, Hank Brantingham had passed the word by radio that they were coming our way. I don't remember his exact words, but we definitely got a radio report on the contact. Our division leader, Berndtson, had radar. He was supposed to relay information to us on the radio in plain language. We never heard anything from Berndtson. Then the darn five-inch shells started bursting over us. We'd just been lying to, more or less in a picket line, mufflers in, barely underway.
>
> I tried to put on speed, but the old bugaboo on the *169* got us: all three engines went dead. So we were just lying there, sitting ducks, for eight or ten minutes—the longest minutes you'll ever realize. Then the good motor machinists I had got the engines going. The other two boats tried to follow Berndtson out of the strait, I think. We couldn't go because we had no engines. So we were left there, all alone.

The other two boats in Division A were the *172*, commanded by S. Hamilton, and the *163*, commanded by Edward Kruse. Having been denied an opportunity to shoot torpedoes because the *171* was in the way, they began zigzagging, looking for an escape hatch. The destroyer straddled them with gunfire. They laid smoke puffs and zigzagged toward Ferguson Passage. Going through, Warfield reports, they were attacked by four float planes which dropped three flares and two bombs, which missed the boats. They then ran out to safety in the open sea. In our view, these two skippers had performed remarkably like Lowrey and Kennedy.

Division C, the group of four boats deployed in Ferguson Passage to block a run on Rendova, made contact next, Warfield reports. The commander, George Cookman, riding Bill Barrett's radar-equipped *107*, first saw gun flashes and a searchlight to the north. That was probably Brantingham, making initial contact and coming under fire. Then, at 0005, one minute after Berndtson made radar contact, Cookman saw two pips on his radar, indicating (to him) two enemy ships. Cookman raced through Ferguson Passage at "high speed," making a big phosphorescent wake (which probably alerted the float planes) and leaving his other three boats behind. While still in Ferguson Passage, Warfield said, Cookman fired a spread of four torpedoes at one of the radar pips from what must have been very long range. What his target was remains a mystery. The destroyers were then close to the coast of Kolombangara, at least five or six miles away. Perhaps he had heard Berndtson's incorrect radio message that the four destroyers were headed for Ferguson Passage and shot on general principles. Or perhaps the destroyer that turned west to comb Berndtson's torpedoes appeared to Cookman, at least momentarily, to be heading for Ferguson Passage. He may even have shot at PT boats headed for the passage.

The other three boats of this division now speeded up to follow their leader. As they passed through Ferguson Passage they were attacked by the Japanese float planes. While they were under attack, Cookman passed back through the strait, southbound. Having fired all torpedoes, he was heading for Lumbari. His other three boats proceeded into Blackett Strait, heading for the area near Makuti Island, but they came too late to do any damage.

The Express, moving southward at high speed, now approached the last group of PT's, far south in the strait, Bill Rome's Division R, composed of three boats. Warfield reports that this unit saw the gunfire and searchlights moving their way for ten minutes, from 0010 to 0020. Then they were attacked by a float plane. At twenty-five minutes after midnight, Rome "made out the shape of a ship." He closed to 1,000 yards, fired four torpedoes, turned away, and ran for Ferguson Passage and home. The destroyers fired at him and a float plane made a strafing attack. Another of his boats, the *103*, (J. K. Roberts), saw the destroyers and futilely fired four torpedoes from very long range—4,000 yards. The destroyers fired back as the *103* retired for home.

The third boat of this group, *105*, was commanded by Richard Keresey, who told us:

I could see a line of gunfire coming right down the coast. I realized from the flashes that it was the group of destroyers that we had been briefed to intercept. I heard nothing on radio. Maybe I was off frequency. I wasn't even in proper contact with Rome. I saw him begin to increase speed slightly and I followed, in accordance with our standard tactics. Then, a little later, I saw him turn around and slowly pass me, going in the opposite direction. I didn't know if he had fired or not. I got on the radio and called him, "Where is the target?" And at about that moment, a Japanese float plane dropped a bomb near Rome, about a half mile behind me. Now Rome, frankly, didn't have a lot of experience. He got on the radio and said, "I am under fire from a Japanese destroyer and running." Well, I knew they were definitely aerial bombs. He had the radar so I came on the radio and said, "*Where* is the destroyer?"

About then he realized I wasn't with him and he came back and said, "Oak Seven (my call sign), get out of there! You're in a trap!" But I said, "Is the target behind me?" And then Warfield came on the radio, thinking I couldn't hear Rome, and said, "Oak Seven, get out of there. You're in a trap." This rattled me no end.

If you think these things are conducted with great skill and aplomb, forget it. I decided none of them knew what they were talking about. I was convinced there was a destroyer ahead of me so I kept on going. Then—by God—my gunner's mate in the forward turret, a seventeen-year-old named Paul Winners, spotted a destroyer. So we crept up—it wasn't a good angle to shoot—and I fired two torpedoes, hoping to get a better shot with the other two. [Warfield fails to mention these shots in his report. We believe it was an editing error.] But he got away and started firing at me and a float plane dropped some bombs near us. We broke off, retreated very slowly out into the open water of the strait. I tried to find Rome but he was gone. So we hung around, knowing the destroyers were unloading and that we'd get another shot at them when they came out.

Back at Lumbari, Warfield tried to follow this confused action by radio. Woods said, "They were all excited and talking on the radio. All hell broke loose. You'd think the damn war was starting all over again. Pandemonium. Warfield said to them, 'What the hell is the matter with you fellows? Get in there and fight!' That made them mad. And from then on they were mad at Warfield."

Warfield told us:

I had direct communication from the base. I could get them on the transmitter. I didn't want to interfere too much with the guys on the spot. But once in a while I'd ask them where they were and what was cooking. They were so damned busy—and I guess scared too, you can't blame them—that they couldn't reply.

There wasn't much discipline in those boats. There really wasn't any way to control them very well. I just had to leave them pretty much up to their own judgment. Some of them stayed in position. Some of them got bugged and didn't fire when they should have. One turned around and ran all the way out of the strait. The best— the ideal spot—was covered by Bill Rome. They were stuck in between Makuti Island and the coast—like being in the mouth of a funnel. I thought I could rely on them. They had some almost ideal shots but they didn't hit anything. I think Bill Rome was very depressed afterwards because he felt he'd fallen down on the job.

The southbound Express had run the blockade. In all, the fifteen PT boats had fired twenty-four torpedoes at it. Sixteen of these had been fired by the four division commanders with radar-equipped boats—Brantingham, Berndtson, Cookman, and Rome—all of whom returned to base. They claimed some hits and probable damage but, according to postwar Japanese accounts, it was not so.

At the Vila anchorage, the Express unloaded in feverish haste. Within about an hour and fifteen minutes the 900 soldiers and seventy tons of cargo were ashore or in lighters. The four destroyers got under way again at about 1:45 A.M.—the exact time is unknown.The Japanese skippers had a choice of return routes: east or west of Kolombangara. Perhaps suspecting that they would meet Arleigh Burke and his destroyers if they went east, they chose to return through Blackett Strait and once more face the PT "blockade."

In all, five PT's had returned to Lumbari; ten remained in the combat zone. About the time the Express was getting under way, they were scattered all over: five in the strait, five outside. Two of Berndtson's Division A skippers who had not fired torpedoes, Hamilton (*172*) and Kruse (*163*), were south of Ferguson Passage in open ocean. The three boats of Division C (less Cookman) that had not fired, the *104*, *106*, and *108*, were milling around inside the south end of the strait. At 1:37 A.M. Warfield ordered these three to resume station at Ferguson Passage (to stop a possible attack on Rendova) and they moved there. Keresey (*105*) was in the lower end of Blackett Strait. Liebenow (*157*) had returned to the area north of Vanga Point looking for Kennedy (*109*) and Lowrey (*162*), but they never did make contact. Kennedy and Lowrey, still glued together, were patrolling somewhere in the strait beneath Vanga Point and Gizo Island. Potter (*169*) had got his balky engines fixed and, looking for someone to join up with, moved northward. At about 2 A.M., according to his log, he found Kennedy and Lowrey. These three boats formed a new patrol section in the north end of the strait. None of the three had radar, but all had four torpedoes.

And now we arrive at another sticky point in the narrative. In a few moments Kennedy in the *109* would be run down by one of the destroyers, *Amagiri*, which had unloaded at Vila and was now getting under way for Rabaul. In the hours and days following, PT men (and others, as the story spread) would wonder how this could have happened. That is, how could a nimble PT boat be rammed by a big Japanese destroyer? It had never happened before; it would never happen again. Was Kennedy properly alert? Did he do something wrong?

In the Kennedy literature, we noted, most authors deal with these questions by evading them. Burns, as we said, skips the battle and simply begins the saga of *PT-109* with the ramming, no questions raised. The few authors who do deal with them—notably Donovan—have adopted the incredible position that Kennedy and *109* were properly alert but the big problem was that *he did not know* there were Japanese destroyers already in the area. Hence, in this second encounter, Jack was caught off guard. Donovan writes, "This new group (Kennedy, Potter, Lowrey) began patrolling to and fro on station, rumbling along on one engine. As a result of their briefing the skippers knew that Japanese ships were expected but not a man aboard any of these three boats knew that four enemy destroyers had passed through and would soon be returning on their way back to Rabaul."

The radioman on *PT-109*, John Maguire, and another crewman, Harris, stand on the Donovan version.

Maguire: "We never got any word that there were destroyers in our area. There were no instructions at all. Once we got out there we never heard from anybody. I remember hearing that somebody was shooting or firing and somebody said, 'Let's get the hell out of here.' I assumed it was one of our other patrols. There were four or five out that night."

Harris: "We had no idea there were ships out there that night. We didn't know the Express had gone down to Vila."

When the Express came down Blackett Strait, there was pandemonium for a period of about thirty or forty minutes. The destroyers were firing almost without interruption for all that time. They were turning on searchlights, firing star shells. Float planes were dropping flares and bombs, making strafing runs. The PT boats were tearing all over the place, firing twenty-four torpedoes. Some skippers had reported explosions on the target.

By all accounts, the VHF radio during that period carried an almost continuous (if confused) load of messages relating to the destroyers. There were many contact reports, movement reports, queries, and exhortations from Warfield, and reports from some of the skippers who had fired torpedoes. In the hour or so following, Warfield was busy relaying information to the boats remaining on station, redeploying them on picket lines to intercept the destroyers when they withdrew from Vila.

Are we to believe that Kennedy heard none of this? That his VHF was off frequency or otherwise malfunctioning? Donovan reports that Kennedy heard messages on the VHF at least twice: "I am being chased through Ferguson Passage . . . have fired fish." "Well, get the hell out of there." Surely those galvanizing messages were enough to tell him the Express had gone through—and would be coming back. And surely he maintained a close radio watch after that. And when the three boats (Kennedy, Lowrey, Potter) formed the new picket line, Donovan writes, Kennedy radioed Lumbari for instructions. "An order came back," Donovan writes, "to resume patrol."

We asked several of the skippers if it was possible Kennedy did not know the destroyers had come through. Berndtson said, "I find it very difficult to believe from my experience that night, with all the shooting and everything else that took place, and all the messages that were sent back to the base. If it were true, everybody had to have his mind in neutral and be half-asleep. I find it very difficult to understand."

Potter, who joined Kennedy and Lowrey, says it simply wasn't true. He told us:

I had talked to Warfield on the VHF. He told me to stay in the area. I found Lowrey and Kennedy. We talked back and forth on the VHF. We all knew then that four or five destroyers had gotten through to Vila. We *definitely* knew they had gotten through; there was no doubt in my mind. We'd called Warfield and he'd said stay there in the area and try to intercept them on the way back. We knew they had to get out of there before daylight. American scouting planes would fly over Vila at daylight and they wouldn't want to be there. They'd get hit by our bombers and fighters.

We decided to form a three-boat picket line. Since I was the senior officer, I led it. Lowrey was on my port quarter and Kennedy was on *his* port quarter. We started out near the coast of Kolombangara probably somewhere near Vanga Point and went in a southwest direction toward Gizo Island. The plan was that when we got near the Gizo reefs, we'd pivot around and patrol northeasterly. Back and forth across the strait on a diagonal. We patrolled at slow speed, with mufflers in, with about one mile between each of us. On the southwest leg, Lowrey came behind me, then Kennedy.

When the northbound Express emerged from the funnel between Makuti Island and Kolombangara, Richard Keresey, patrolling alone in the *105* with only two torpedoes remaining, was waiting. He was the first to see it. He told us:

Paul Winners with his wonderful night vision spotted this guy sneaking out of Vila. After about thirty seconds I managed to get the glasses on him and sure enough there was this destroyer, northbound. He couldn't have been going more than eight or ten knots. I no sooner figured what the right lead [to shoot] was than he spotted me. I saw his wake boil up. He knew I was a torpedo boat and what I was about to do. I was not in a good position but I fired my last two torpedoes anyway. Those torpedoes! I once looked on a manufacturer's plate and saw they were built before I was born! They must have missed. They were too old and slow. He opened fire on me, lobbing shells. I got on the radio and I said to the world in general, "Destroyers coming up through the passage. Have fired fish and am withdrawing through Ferguson Passage," or something like that. But by then it was obvious they were coming out. They were firing at me and I don't see how anybody in the strait could have missed seeing it.

The four destroyers came through the funnel, picking up speed. Keresey, now out of torpedoes, got out of the way. The destroyers continued northward, moving out into the deep water of the strait, heading toward the new formation of Kennedy-Lowrey-Potter. By Donovan's account, the group, at Kennedy's suggestion, was now on a southeasterly heading with Kennedy leading, Lowrey coming next on Kennedy's starboard quarter, and Potter bringing up the rear on Lowrey's starboard quarter. Warfield says the group was "headed south," which more or less is in agreement with Donovan. But Potter said in our interview that both Donovan and Warfield were mistaken. They were on a northeasterly heading, he says, with Kennedy leading, Lowrey next on Kennedy's *port* quarter and Potter last on Lowrey's port quarter. (See Map No. 5.)

It was now between 2 and 2:30 a.m.—the accounts differ as to the exact time. According to the Warfield report, the men on the middle boat, Lowrey's *162* , saw a ship due south about 700 yards away. The ship was northbound, making high speed, throwing up a big phosphorescent bow wave. Lowrey saw immediately that it was an enemy destroyer and turned to fire his torpedoes. But for reasons not stated in the report, "they did not fire."

Potter told us:

We picked up the destroyer bow wake at about two miles. It was black that night. On a real dark night like that those waters are highly phosphorescent. A lot of times we saw porpoises coming at us at a good clip and thought they were torpedoes! It's amazing. You can see it at great distances. We saw that it was more or less headed right at the *109* . We radioed Kennedy to look on his starboard bow. There was a bow wake coming directly toward him. No response. Nothing. And I think Lowrey warned Kennedy. But what amazed us was that we got no response from either of the boats. We saw the destroyer ram the *109* and it blew up. [In his log, he put the time at 2:12 a.m.] Just shot into flames. The destroyer turned toward Gizo—and us—and I had to begin thinking what I was going to do. We had our torpedoes armed and ready to go. I decided I would fire two of them after it cleared Lowrey. He had to pass in front of Lowrey before I could get a clean shot at him. Once he cleared Lowrey, I fired two torpedoes. [At 2:15 by his log.] But by then he was so damned close, our torpedoes didn't have time to dive and stabilize and run out four hundred yards to arm. Then he began firing at us. Knowing there were some more coming up, we turned to port, picked up speed, laid smoke, and headed for the Gizo reefs. Then I ran out through Gizo Passage evading and, I think, circled Gizo and came back into the strait again.

We tried to find the *109* and any survivors. We went back to that general area and lay to. We cut our engines, trying to listen for them. But we didn't hear a thing. Then I told Warfield the *109* had been hit and we patrolled around, very slowly, stopping and listening. Then we saw another destroyer. He was coming up from the south. I swung to port and fired my last two torpedoes from about two thousand yards. [At 2:45 by his log.] I thought I saw a hit in his starboard bow. Then, again, we evaded, zigzagging and laying smoke puffs and went on back to Lumbari. We never did see Lowrey again that night.

To the north of all this action, Liebenow in the *157* patrolled alone. He had two torpedoes remaining. By then, he had run in close to the shore of Kolombangara, probably slightly to the north of Vanga Point. He saw a dark shape against the shoreline. He turned, set up, and fired both torpedoes, the eighth and last in this second encounter. There was no explosion. The destroyer continued northward, apparently unaware Liebenow had fired at it. Following procedure, Liebenow, now out of torpedoes, returned to Lumbari.

There were still five PT's outside the strait, south of Ferguson Passage. These were the three boats of Cookman's Division C (*104, 106, 108*) and the two boats of Berndtson's Division A (*163, 172*). When the three boats of Division C saw the gunfire (and the explosion of *109*) they ran into the strait, but Warfield reports they were "unable to find anything." At 2:55, Warfield reports, the other two boats (*163, 172*) also went into the strait, but they were "too late to make contact." These five remaining boats were in the strait until 4 A.M., when Warfield ordered them to come home.

And so ended the Battle of Blackett Strait, August 1/2, 1943. The Express moved northeasterly into Vella Gulf, heading for Rabaul. In the two engagements, the PT's had shot a total of thirty-two torpedoes at the Express, but except for slight damage to *Amagiri* in the collision, the Express was not harmed. (Bulkley in *At Close Quarters* reports thirty torpedoes fired, but we believe he overlooked two that Keresey had fired.) North of Kolombangara, Arleigh Burke and his six destroyers just missed it. At 3 A.M., according to the destroyer division war diary, they had left the area so they could reach territory safe from Japanese air attack before daylight. The Express went on to Rabaul without further incident, its mission accomplished.

To review, briefly, Jack's action that night: The *109* had had two separate contacts with the Express, about two and a quarter hours apart. In the first, when the Express was southbound, the *109* failed to follow its leader to attack, and "bugged out" toward Gizo Strait. In the second, when it was northbound, the *109* was rammed and sunk. On the basis of this performance—Jack's first contact with enemy surface ships—we had to agree with Warfield, who told us, "He wasn't a particularly good boat commander."

It would be easy enough to conclude from this evidence that, so far from being a hero, Jack Kennedy had been a fool and/or a coward. But we're not interested in helping to create a new, reverse myth, either, so perhaps the reader will allow us a bit of reflection.

There aren't so many heroes as war fiction and movies and wartime propaganda—and campaign biographies—would have us believe. At least three other skippers in this same engagement behaved as Kennedy did, and the extent to which most of the others behaved differently can be put down to differences in their positions, the battle experience of their captains and crews, the condition of their boats, and such factors, as easily as to differences in their moral fiber or in their courage. We have ample evidence that Jack Kennedy was a brave man; to a fault, it may be; as overcompensation for his physical frailty and in competition with his brother, a psychoanalyst might choose to theorize; but characteristically, stubbornly courageous nevertheless.

He did not distinguish himself; he did encourage the general belief that he had, for as long as he lived; but then he wanted to be president of a people who wanted a hero, and who generally choose to understand their leaders in simple terms.

18

Destroyed

What happened on the *PT-109* when it was hit and what happened to Kennedy and the crew in the following six days is as well known as the story of George Washington chopping down the cherry tree. The *Amagiri* rammed the *109*, splitting it in half. Two men were killed and several were badly burned and injured. Kennedy, though he had badly bruised his back (aggravating the old Harvard football injury), saved the men who were thrown into the water, which was covered with gasoline flames. Jack swallowed a lot of gasoline, which thereafter gave him serious stomach problems. Other illnesses arose from the disaster.

No PT's came to rescue them. Having been left for dead in Blackett Strait, the survivors, encouraged by Kennedy, reached a small island behind Japanese lines. They hid from swarms of Japanese soldiers and subsisted on coconuts. Kennedy, who never gave up hope, drove himself to the point of collapse keeping up the spirits of his men, tirelessly devising and executing escape plans. Finally he made contact with some friendly natives. He carved a message for help on a coconut shell and persuaded the natives to smuggle it to friendly forces. The next day a war canoe arrived and sneaked Kennedy off the island. That same night he returned, leading a flotilla of PT boats, and rescued the other ten men.

The legend would become possibly Jack's greatest single political asset. It was a main theme of his early campaign literature, proof of his courage, resourcefulness, and coolness under stress. The ordeal of survival was used to explain (and, by implication, glorify) most of his many illnesses. Throughout his public career, there were ever-present visual reminders: the coconut shell on Kennedy's various desks; his PT buddies campaigning in his behalf in the streets and on television; *PT-109* tie clasps for male campaign workers.

The account that follows is, we believe, a more realistic analysis of the experience than we have seen. In preparing it, we made use of six principal sources: the White report, the Donovan book, a Warfield action report, our own interviews, a *New Yorker* article by John Hersey, and some documents uncovered at the Navy Historical Center in Washington.

236

The Whizzer White intelligence report suffers because White, we believe, drew almost all of his material from Jack. As far as we were able to ascertain, he did not interview Barney Ross or Lennie Thom or the enlisted men in the crew. As an inevitable result, Jack is the focus.

It will be recalled that John Hersey had previously written the long *Life* article in May, 1943, glorifying PT Squadron Three during its action in the Battle of Guadalcanal. Thus Hersey had a special interest in PT boats and, of course, he was a friend of Jack's. Hersey was still a *Life* correspondent when he wrote the *PT-109* article in 1944, but *Life* rejected the article, probably because of its length, and Hersey placed it in *The New Yorker*. The article is valuable. Hersey interviewed several (though not all) of the *PT-109* survivors while memories were fresh, including Jack, his main source. However, since it was written in wartime, the censors deleted, or disguised, certain vital elements of the true story. The Hersey article was republished in condensed form in the August, 1944, issue of the *Reader's Digest*. The manner in which the *Digest* editors cut the Hersey article and played the headlines and subtitles, tended to focus even greater attention on Jack, to the exclusion of others. The *Digest* article made Jack a national hero.

Since the White report and other official Navy documents remained classified until 1959, the Hersey *New Yorker* article (or the *Digest* version) was the principal source for feature writers and authors seeking information on the survival experience. Burns, for example, relies almost entirely on it for his account of Jack's *PT-109* survival experience. As far as we were able to tell, before Jack was elected to the White House, no writer went beyond the Hersey article.

Donovan relies heavily on the Hersey article, but he was the first investigator to go beyond Hersey. He reinterviewed the survivors of *PT-109*, the natives in the Solomon Islands involved in the rescue, and others we shall mention as we follow the story. The great value of the Donovan book is that for the first time he supplied the vital parts of the story that the Navy censors had removed. In our view, these new disclosures downgraded Jack's heroic role in the adventure, but Donovan seems to miss his own point. The movie *PT-109* continues the glorification in the same vein. In its final form, the Donovan version differs in some minor details from the White and Hersey versions, and on one occasion, perhaps due to haste, he makes a large error.

Our interviews included Warfield, Cluster, Woods, various PT skippers and friends of Jack's in the Solomons, the Thom family, and four of the six living survivors of *PT-109*: Barney Ross, Harris, Maguire, and Zinser. These interviews were conducted primarily to help us reconcile conflicts in the White-Hersey-Donovan accounts.

Warfield's action report was dated August 8, 1943. It describes the final rescue and includes the log of the rescue boat. Two war correspondents went along on the rescue. We tracked them down, interviewed them, and obtained copies of their heavily censored dispatches.

First Day (August 2-3)

Turning back to that fatal moment (0212 hours?) when the *Amagiri* was bearing down on the *109*, we asked Barney Ross if he could recollect what happened. He told us:

It was so dark the three boats in the formation had trouble staying together. We were supposed to stay in visual contact. That was part of the problem, part of the reason we got hit. When we first saw that wake——the bow wave of the *Amagiri*—we thought it was one of our boats from the formation. He was doing about thirty-five to forty knots and we didn't see him until he was right on us, about a block away. We were all night-adapted. The lookouts were out. I was on the bow serving as extra lookout. We weren't *all* sleeping. But our fatal flaw was probably that we were trying to keep station rather than worrying about Japs. We were all pretty green at this. It was the first time I'd ever seen an enemy ship. The next thing I knew he was turning into us. We all shouted at once. Kennedy started turning the boat. It happened fast—very fast—like an automobile accident.

Did Kennedy have his crew properly alert? There is evidence to suggest he did not. They were not at general quarters, Donovan reports. Thom was "lying on the deck." One man we interviewed, Harris, said he was off-duty and asleep. Hersey writes that Johnston was asleep. Donovan reports that Kirksey was lying down on the starboard side. Why, we wondered? They were used to fourteen-hour patrols. They had been out only seven hours. It seemed incomprehensible that at a tense moment like this, two of the thirteen men who could have served as lookouts were asleep and that Thom and Kirksey were lying down. (Four out of thirteen unalert.) The radioman, Maguire, was in the cockpit with Kennedy, Donovan reports. Why didn't Kennedy have him in the chart house monitoring the radio? If he had been perhaps he would have picked up Keresey's report "to the world in general" that destroyers were heading north, or Potter's last-minute warning to Kennedy that a destroyer was about to hit him.

None of the PT men we talked to could understand why no one on the *109* had seen the *Amagiri*'s wake until the last seconds. Potter had seen wakes from an estimated two miles. Lowrey had seen them from about a half mile. Art Berndtson told us, "When I made my attack on the incoming Express, I could see the bow wakes at fifteen to eighteen hundred yards [almost a mile]. When I heard the *109* was hit, I asked myself, 'If I could see at fifteen to eighteen hundred yards, why couldn't other people?' I never got an answer. It could have been they were doping off.''

It was the new crewman, Harold Marney, who was near the cockpit in the forward turret, who saw *Amagiri* first.

"Ship at two o'clock!" he cried.

Ross, who was on the forward deck by the 37 mm, probably saw it next.

White, Hersey, and Donovan imply that Kennedy was alert. White wrote that upon sighting the destroyer, Kennedy, standing at the wheel, "started to turn to starboard preparatory to firing torpedoes." Hersey wrote, "Kennedy saw a shape and spun the wheel for an attack but the *109* answered sluggishly. . . . Kennedy whirled the wheel to the left, but again the *109* did not respond."

White says that they sighted the *Amagiri* at "200–300" yards, moving at an estimated 40 knots, or about 22 yards per second. She hit the *109* within ten seconds, he reported.

If Kennedy did, in fact, have time to turn the wheel, it may have been a mistake. The turning would have retarded *109*'s forward progress, reported as about 6 knots, or 3 yards per second. Had Jack not turned the wheel, in ten seconds *109* would have advanced another 30 yards or 90 feet during the interval between sighting and collision. If this had occurred—if Jack had maintained a steady course—*Amagiri* would most likely have missed astern. If he turned the wheel, it helped *Amagiri* score an almost perfect bull's-eye: a smashing hit on the starboard side opposite the cockpit.

Some of the PT men we talked with, including Warfield, laid the blame for the collision on the fact that Jack was running with his engines muffled. They think that when he saw *Amagiri* he instinctively rammed on full power and the engine (or engines) either coughed severely from exhaust backup or conked out. They believed that since the *109* was out in the middle of Blackett Strait and expecting enemy destroyers, he should have been unmuffled, as ready as possible to put on full power. Warfield told us:

> The nearest thing I can figure out is they got kind of sleepy and weren't too alert and Kennedy was idling with his mufflers closed. He shouldn't have been muffled. He knew the destroyers were coming out. He saw this thing coming at him and got bugged a little bit and shoved his throttles forward. And I think he killed his engines. Actually, it doesn't matter if he had the engines muffled or not; if he shoved the throttles forward too fast, it would still have killed the engines. And that's what I think he did.

But others, including Art Berndtson, disagree. Earlier that night, they point out, float planes had attacked PT's (Rome, Cookman, etc.) and while there were apparently none in the vicinity at this time, they could reappear at any time. It would have been logical for Kennedy to believe they would return to support the departure of the destroyers. Therefore, Kennedy (who had already incurred two casualties to a float-plane bomb) was justified in doing everything possible to hear the float planes, including muffling his engine.

But Liebenow, who talked to Jack immediately after his rescue, had another theory:

My general impression had always been that the problem was Jack was running with only one engine engaged, a bad thing to do, and as I said, strictly against policy in Squadron Nine. It was a hot night, maybe the motor machinist down below was goofing off— had his head stuck out the rear opening to get some fresh air. I remember this: when we picked him up a week later, I was kidding him and I said, "Jack, how in the world could a Jap destroyer run you down?" Jack told me, "Lieb, I actually do not know. It all happened so quickly."

I think that when he made the move with the throttles—if he made a move—they didn't respond. Nothing happened.

At the Navy Historical Center we found Jack's own statement in the official Flotilla One newsletter, *Mosquito Bites*, dated September 15, 1943, classified Secret and not declassified until January 1, 1963. The item, published here for the first time: "ENGINES. Lt. (j.g.) Jack Kennedy believes that the reason that he was unable to get out of the way of the Jap destroyer which rammed him was because only one of his engines was in gear. He strongly advises that, whenever enemy destroyers are known to be in a patrol area, all engines should be in gear."

The *Amagiri* crashed through (or rode over) *PT-109* from starboard to port at an angle. The impact was horrifying. Maguire, who was in the cockpit with Kennedy, remembered the terrible noise and the towering gray side of the destroyer passing two or three feet away. He remembered he could even hear the Japanese on *Amagiri*'s deck talking excitedly. He and Kennedy were thrown against bulkheads in the cockpit. Hersey says that Kennedy thought: "This is how it feels to be killed." Ross, who was on the bow, had one overriding fear: that he would become entangled in the ropes lashing down the 37 mm. He jumped over the side. So did Zinser, Thom, Starkey, Albert, and others. Harold Marney and Andrew Kirksey were swept away, never to be seen again. "Pappy" McMahon was down in the engine room, but by some miracle he survived and popped to the surface. All hands in the water were supported by life jackets, which they routinely wore while aboard the boat. Most accounts say she was "split in half" but Ross and Zinser told us she was not: the rear section, containing the three heavy engines, was badly mangled and sank below the water and the bow lifted to an angle of perhaps 30 to 40 degrees. All four survivors we consulted remember the steep angle of the bow, which would indicate that Ross and Zinser are probably right. If the boat had been literally split in half, the bow section would have remained more or less level, since its watertight doors were shut and the bow section was fairly airtight.

Many authors write that it was at this point that Jack reinjured his old football back injury. In our interviews we pressed that point carefully. If he did injure his back then, he gave no sign of it. Both Ross and Maguire (who was standing next to Kennedy) were quite specific. Both said they did not recall Jack complaining about a back injury that night or later. Throughout the survival experience, he gave no sign that his back pained him.

The impact ruptured the gasoline tanks and the gasoline caught fire. McMahon and Johnston were badly burned, McMahon more severely. Kennedy, thinking *PT-109* would explode, ordered Maguire (and all hands) to abandon ship. They did. But the gasoline fires were mainly on the water. When Kennedy saw the hulk was not on fire, he shouted for all hands to get back aboard. This took some doing. By then—fifteen to thirty minutes later—the men had drifted away from the hulk. Some were a hundred yards or more away. Many had fainted from shock or perhaps were overcome by gasoline fumes, or the lack of oxygen when the gasoline had burned.

Then began the rescue operation to get the men back on the hulk. Here White is generous to Kennedy. He writes that Kennedy struck off in the dark and rescued Pappy McMahon, who had been badly burned. Since "a strong current impeded progress," this took about an hour. After this, Kennedy swam back and helped Charles Harris. "He traded his life belt to Harris, who was uninjured, in return for Harris's waterlogged kapok life jacket, which was impeding the latter's swimming." Then, White adds, "together they towed Starkey to the PT." Later, this action on Kennedy's part would become, in one official account, "personally" rescuing "three" men, and it helped earn him a medal.

The Hersey and Donovan accounts are more restrained. Hersey credits Kennedy with bringing McMahon to the boat and reports it took forty-five minutes. He gives Kennedy credit for an assist to Harris, but says nothing about exchanging life jackets. There is no mention of Kennedy saving Starkey. Donovan, who interviewed Harris and Starkey, writes that Harris was burdened by a heavy jacket and sweater under his life jacket and that Kennedy held his arm while Harris took off his life jacket so he could peel out of the jacket and sweater. Starkey, Donovan reports, was in an entirely different area and made it to the boat under his own steam.

Harris told us:

> I was a good swimmer—I had been on a Navy swim team. But I had two problems: my jacket and sweater and my knee. I hit my knee on something when I went over the side and I thought it was broken. Kennedy helped me get out of my jacket and sweater, but after that, I made it to the boat on my own. I was slow because of my knee. Kennedy egged me on with a wisecrack: "For a guy from Boston, you're certainly putting up a great exhibition." I told him to go to hell.

In sum, Jack rescued Pappy McMahon. Had he not, we believe, the badly injured McMahon would surely have been lost. He did not rescue Harris though he gave him valuable assistance and motivation. He did not, with or without the help of Harris, rescue Starkey.

Meanwhile, there were other rescue operations in progress. Donovan reports that two enlisted men, John Maguire and Edgar Mauer, mounted one from the hulk. While Mauer, a nonswimmer, swept the water with a battle lantern, Maguire tied a rope to the hulk and himself and swam to a group of three: Ross, Thom, and Zinser. Maguire, Donovan wrote, led the three men back to the hulk, Ross helping Zinser. When he caught his breath, Donovan says, Thom swam out and found William Johnston and brought him back. The eleventh man, Raymond Albert, made it to the hulk by himself.

In our interview Maguire said:

> That was more or less correct. It's hard to remember. I went up in the forward locker and got about two hundred feet of one-inch line. I tied that to the hulk and to myself. I could hear Zinser yelling that Mr. Thom was in trouble. Drowning. Mauer held the lantern on them. I swam out to the end of the line. I read in Donovan that Mr. Ross was helping Mr. Thom and Zinser. That may be true, I don't know. The way I remember it, I led Ross, Thom, and Zinser—and I think we picked up Albert along the way—back to the hulk.
>
> Q: You did all this on your own initiative?
> A: Yes, of course. They needed help.
> Q: Where was Kennedy?
> A: Out in the water getting Pappy McMahon and helping Harris.
> Q: Did you receive any award—any medal—for that rescue?

A: No. They just gave the three officers—Kennedy, Thom, and Ross—medals.

Thom received a Navy and Marine Corps Medal, the standard "lifesaving" award for rescuing Johnston, who was injured. The citation, provided us by his son, read in part, "Voluntarily leaving the wreckage to which he clung . . . Thom gallantly swam to the rescue of a seriously injured companion, towing the unconscious seaman for three hours against a strong current before he succeeded in reaching a piece of the wrecked boat to which other survivors were clinging. . . . "

We puzzled over this citation, trying to reconcile it with the Maguire account. If, as he said, Thom had been drowning and Maguire had helped him back to the boat with the rope, how did Thom then have strength to go after Johnston? Perhaps Thom had been stunned, then quickly recovered. He was a very strong man and, Kate told us, a good swimmer. Until we saw the citation, we had not been been told, by Donovan, Hersey, or any other source, that Thom had towed an unconscious and seriously injured Johnston for *three hours*. That, if it happened, was a much larger contribution to this phase of the rescue than Jack had made and worthy of special note.

The men climbed up on the sharply tilted bow and lay down, clinging to handrails and ventilators, bracing their feet so they wouldn't slip. McMahon and Johnston, the most badly injured, were made as comfortable as possible at a place just forward of the cockpit where they did not have to hang on. After this, some men passed out or dozed.

The men naturally expected to be rescued by the other PT boats in their formation—Potter and Lowrey. As Potter told us, he returned to the area and spent "thirty to forty-five" minutes looking for the *109* survivors and "found nothing." It is not known if Lowrey made a search, and Lowrey is deceased and cannot speak for himself. Based on our many interviews, we doubt that he did.

Among the items that survived the crash, White reports, was a Very pistol—a device for firing a distress flare. Had Jack shot it off in the first hour after the collision, it would have been seen by Potter, Liebenow, and Lowrey, and probably by the other five skippers in the area. It would have been a positive sign that there were survivors. Some—or all—of the boats may have come to investigate. But, White reports, *PT-109* did not fire it "for fear of giving away its position to the enemy. . . . "

This was surely a foolish decison. The enemy in this case was not the Express. Jack knew, surely, that it was highballing for Rabaul as fast as it could go and was no longer a threat. "Enemy" meant the Japanese troops on the nearby island, and float planes.

The *PT-109* literature is vague as to the extent of that threat. To define it more precisely, we searched a number of military histories dealing with the campaign in the Central Solomons. The best, we felt, was a volume of the U. S. Army's official history of World War Two, entitled *Cartwheel: The Reduction of Rabaul*, by John Miller, Jr. Miller reports that at about that time (August 1) intelligence accurately guessed there were 10,000 troops on Kolombangara. These were concentrated on the southern end of the island, near Vila Plantation, poised to go to the defense of New Georgia and to repel an expected invasion of Kolombangara. There were far fewer on the outlying westerly islands forming Blackett Strait: a dozen-odd marooned sailors on Vella Lavella and a military garrison of about 250 on Gizo. With the coming of daylight—three hours away—the floating hulk of *PT-109* would be clearly visible to Japanese lookouts on Kolombangara and the game would be up anyway. It would probably have been wiser to run the risk of firing the Very pistol, taking advantage of the hours of darkness remaining to maximize rescue efforts. It was unlikely, we thought, that with all the action in Blackett Strait that night, the Japanese would go out into the inky blackness in a boat or barge to investigate a shot from a Very pistol.

Jack and the men of *PT-109* must have known of the case of the *Helena*. She had been sunk ten miles off the north coast of Kolombangara early on the morning of July 6. Two hundred of her survivors, clinging to a bow section that floated for a while and some lifeboats left behind by destroyers, had drifted westward through Vella Gulf to Vella Lavella. No Japanese barges or aircraft from Kolombangara or Gizo had gone out in daytime (or nighttime) to investigate or harass them. They had made it to Vella Lavella, and those who survived the ordeal were rescued. All this had happened not more than fifteen miles north of the *PT-109* hulk, only three weeks earlier.

In any case, when no PT boats came, the men on the hulk thought that soon after daylight Rendova would send an escorted PBY (an amphibious patrol bomber) to rescue them. When the sun rose behind the volcanic cone on Kolombangara, all hands who were able kept a sharp watch on the southern skies. But they saw no PBY. By that time, Rendova knew positively that *PT-109* had not returned. The survivors were already bitter because they had been abandoned by *PT-162* and *169*. When there was no sign of a PBY, the bitterness intensified.

And they were scared. Now, in full daylight, they felt that they stuck out "like a sore thumb," as Ross put it to us. Surely the enemy on Kolombangara could see them. The hulk was well within range of shore batteries on Kolombangara—if there were shore batteries in that vicinity. Although the Japanese did not often risk boats and barges in the strait in daylight (for fear of Allied aircraft), they might send one at it any time. The men hugged the deck, fearing to move lest they attract attention.

The mounted machine guns had been wrecked beyond salvage, and the

37 mm was dangling over the side in the water, but they had mustered some small arms. Maguire found a Thompson submachine gun below. They had several .45 pistols and Kennedy had his Smith & Wesson .38. They talked bravely about putting up a fight if the Japanese came, but luckily they were never put to this test.

Kennedy, who knew the waters fairly well, made an estimate of their position, probably using the volcano and the rising sun for bearings. He calculated, according to White, that the hulk was about four miles north and slightly east of Gizo and about three miles from the reef off northeast Gizo. In a sense, they were lucky. They were nearer the lesser concentration of Japanese on Gizo than to the swarms on Kolombangara. Moreover, Gizo was a flat atoll. Unless the Japanese had a tall lookout tower, it was not likely they could see the hulk. Unless some efficient lookout on a high perch on Kolombangara alerted Gizo, they were safe for a while.

The problem now was drift. The hulk was sloshing slowly southward toward the eastern tip of Gizo and the string of smaller islands extending east and southeast from it. Were these little islands occupied? As they came closer, would the Japanese see them? Would they, after all, wash ashore into the hands of a trigger-happy Japanese contingent, to be summarily shot or brutally tortured?

Then, a new problem arose. The hulk had been taking on water slowly and they worried that it might sink beneath them. Hersey (and Donovan, perhaps relying on Hersey) reports that at 10 A.M., the hulk turned turtle. We thought that must have been a terrifying moment, but White had nothing about it, merely stating that about that time it became obvious "that the *PT-109* would sink. . . . " In our interviews, Harris and Maguire remembered clearly that the boat turned turtle, Ross could not remember if it had or if he had read it somewhere, but Zinser was positive it had *not* turned turtle.

In any case, they all began talking about abandoning the hulk and swimming to one of the little islands south and east of Gizo. They had been taught that chances of rescue were better if they stayed with wreckage, which could be seen from the air, but there were many other considerations to be taken into account. The hulk might sink and leave them worse off, or it might drift into the hands of Japanese. A Japanese boat might come out to investigate. A Japanese plane (or shore battery) might attack them. They would soon need water and food, which they might find on land. The underbrush on the island offered better concealment and a more stable platform from which to launch a do-it-yourself rescue effort. The badly injured McMahon and Johnston could be made more comfortable on dry land.

The four survivors we talked to all agreed it had been best to leave the hulk. Ross said, "The boat didn't look like it would make it through another night. That land over there looked pretty good and reasonably attainable. I think we did the right thing. If I had to do it again, I wouldn't stay with the boat."

And so, after midday, they made plans to leave the hulk. There was an island estimated by White to be two and a half miles away, but it was judged to be too close to Gizo, and probably occupied by Japanese. Instead of that, they chose as their target a small and remote-looking atoll estimated to be three and a half to four miles distant—more or less southeast from Gizo and south from the hulk.

One of the key points in Hersey's account of the experience is that Rendova had quickly given up all hope that there were any survivors of *PT-109*. To support this thesis, he includes two pieces of evidence: (1) the fact that the base "held services for the souls of the thirteen men," and (2) a portion of a letter from Red Fay to his mother (actually it was written to one of his sisters, Fay told us) indicating they believed all hands were dead.

The excerpt from the Fay letter was as follows: "George Ross lost his life for a cause that he believed in stronger than any one of us, because he was an idealist in the purest sense. Jack Kennedy, the Ambassador's son, was on the same boat and also lost his life. The man that said the cream of a nation is lost in war can never be accused of overstatement of a very cruel fact. . . . "

In the *Reader's Digest* condensation of the Hersey article, Fay's letter, set off in italics, was made the "lead." Placed thus, it heightened the impression that Rendova had given up hope and that nothing further was done for them. Thus the impression was created—and left standing until the Donovan book was published—that thereafter the men were on their own. Zinser told us that not even *he* knew the details until then!

Donovan revealed what Hersey could not print during the war. There was an Australian coast watcher on Kolombangara, Arthur Reginald Evans, a naval lieutenant, stationed high on the side of the volcano. In the weeks that he had been manning this secret outpost, Evans had organized a spy network made up of natives. Besides reporting what he could see from his perch in Blackett Strait, he passed along by radio the information his native spy network brought him.

Donovan interviewed Evans in Australia where Evans gave him access to the file of radio dispatches that he exchanged that week with his superiors on New Georgia and elsewhere. These show that on the first day after the crash, August 2, Evans and his superiors (for simplicity, we will call them Rendova) exchanged six messages, many involving *PT-109*.

The first was an early-morning report from Evans to Rendova, giving a brief rundown on the night action in Blackett Strait, concluding "small vessel possibly barge afire off Gatere and still visible." At 9:30 A.M. Rendova reported to Evans the loss of *PT-109* "two miles SW of Merest

Cove'' with a crew of twelve (it was not known, at first, that Barney Ross had gone on the *109*) and requested "any information." At 11:15 Evans responded, saying he had no information on *PT-109* survivors, adding, however, that there was an "object still floating between Meresu and Giao." This was, beyond doubt, the hulk of *PT-109* and Evans had it in sight. At 1:12 P.M. Rendova repeated the notice of loss of *PT-109* "between Vanga Vanga and group of islands SE of Gizo," and advised Evans survivors might be found on Kolombangara or the outer islands. At 4:45 P.M., Evans reported his apparatus was searching the Kolombangara coast and that his "Gizo scouts" would pick up survivors if any landed on the outer islands. He added, "object now drifting toward Nusatupi Is." Later, toward dusk, Rendova sent a flight of P-40 fighter planes over Blackett Strait and Gizo searching for *PT-109*. Evans saw them and requested information on what they had found. The following morning Rendova replied the results of the search had been "negative."

The air search mounted by Rendova would become a controversial subject. Some would claim there had not been one; others would say Warfield did all he could. We inquired about this point in our interviews.

Warfield: "I'm sure we had an air search, some kind of reconnaissance looking for them. I couldn't *tell* the fliers what to do. I couldn't even get them to send night fighters up against the float planes, but I'm sure I told [Admiral] Wilkinson's staff to get some kind of reconnaissance up there after them."

Woods: "That very morning we had them send up some air search. They looked around up there but they didn't see anything. Then, in the ensuing days, we got dispatches from Halsey and—well, everybody but the president—telling us to find Kennedy. And we sent more aircraft the next day and the day after. We were in daily contact with the coast watcher, Evans."

Others supported Warfield and Woods. Berndtson recalled vividly that an air search was mounted that morning. "They flew up over Blackett Strait, saw the bow section floating toward Kolombangara, but said there was nobody on it. It was depressing news. But they followed up with PBY's." Potter said, "They sent planes up that day and, as I recall, they covered the area pretty well."

Some of the PT skippers wanted to mount a daylight sweep up in the strait to look for them. Bill Battle, commanding the *171*, was one, Donovan reported. Another was Keresey. He told us:

There was a whole *group* of us who wanted to do this. We figured that if we didn't take torpedoes, we'd be pretty light and we could really travel fast. We could run in there at high speed before the Japs woke up to what we were doing and run back and forth and find them. But the base commander [Warfield] was not too impressed with this idea. It was extremely dangerous. It exposed a lot of people. I certainly don't fault him for saying it would be hopeless. Then Lowrey, who was pretty close to the *109* when she was hit, said, "There's no chance they're alive. The boat went up in a ball of fire."

What was most important, it seemed to us, was the early contact with the coast watcher. By this, Rendova had rather forcefully brought to his attention the loss of *PT-109* with an extremely accurate estimate of its probable position. Rendova had asked Evans to look for survivors and he had alerted his network.

There is another point not made in any of the accounts of *PT-109*. The activities of the coast watchers were well known to Kennedy, Thom, and other PT officers. They also knew there were friendly natives who served as scouts for the coast watchers. Later, in another context, Donovan points out that Thom had actually met one of these natives, John Kari, the chief scout on Wana Wana, who had visited Lumbari.

About 2 P.M., according to the White report, the survivors left the hulk. Lacking the life raft, they improvised a float from the big timber that was to have been used to mount the 37 mm gun. The nonswimmers, Mauer and Johnston, would hang on; the others would push and pull it toward the island. They took the lantern, the submachine gun, and the pistols.

Kennedy personally took charge of McMahon, whose hand burns and exhaustion made him unable to hold on to the timber. Separating from the group at the float, he put McMahon on his back, and towed him to shore doing the breaststroke. All the way, they were back to back, with Kennedy struggling and swallowing vast amounts of sea water. It must have been an extremely rough and painful ride for McMahon. It was a strain on Jack, who must have been weak from lack of sleep and tension. It is not clear why McMahon wasn't simply lashed to the timber and towed behind it. Perhaps because it would have made the float more cumbersome to move; or perhaps Jack thought he could go faster than the group pushing the cumbersome timber, thus reducing the time McMahon would be exposed to the salt water, which was painful to his burns. (But he got to the island only minutes ahead of the others.) Whatever the reason, it was an extremely gutsy performance by Kennedy. It is clear that Jack felt great compassion for this older man and was deeply concerned about his condition. McMahon was intensely grateful. For the rest of his life, he felt a deep love for Jack and would give him full credit for saving his life.

By White's account, the swim took about four hours. At 6 P.M. Kennedy and McMahon staggered ashore first. Kennedy, completely exhausted, vomiting, and still burdened with McMahon, was in a bad way. The atoll, about 100 yards in diameter, was deserted. According to our interviews with Ross and Harris, it had good cover: lots of low, thick foliage

They pulled the timber ashore and crawled into the foliage and collapsed. Along the way, they had lost their most important weapon, the Thompson submachine gun.

At this point, Hersey and Donovan introduce a melodramatic element into the story. They write that as soon as the men reached the island, they spotted a motorized Japanese barge chugging up Blackett Strait on patrol. Donovan says it was "only a couple of hundred yards away." The men lay flat, frozen and tense. Then it went away, but they worried that they had been seen.

It seems surprising that a Japanese barge would be chugging along in daylight in the south end of Blackett Strait, for one thing; and then, the White report had no mention of a barge. It seemed to us that had there been a barge, it would have been included in an intelligence report—intelligence officers dote on such details of enemy movements. When we asked Barney Ross about it, he seemed to dismiss it. "I know some of the guys told Hersey and Donovan they saw a barge. I went to sleep when we hit the island. I never saw any Jap barge. I couldn't say in a court of law if there was or wasn't a Jap barge. I just don't remember anything about it."

About the time they reached the island, the flight of P-40's that was out looking for them arrived in the area. The survivors saw them, Ross remembers. They had "white tails," he told us, identifying them as New Zealander planes. They came low and fast and were gone in a flash. The survivors had lain flat in the bushes, fearing at first the planes might be Japanese. "We were paranoid about being seen by Japanese," Ross recalled to us. "So in a sense, we were almost fighting rescue."

Maguire told us, "We didn't do anything to try to signal them. We should have, but we blew it." A brief report on the *PT-109* filed in 1943 by the coast watcher Evans in the Naval Historical Center says that when he met Kennedy, "I asked him how it was that he and his crew were not seen by U.S. planes. He replied that on the approach of any aircraft he made his crew hide themselves. . . . "

What if they had not left the hulk? Evans reported later that the P-40's flew low over the hulk. With Allied planes overhead, maybe Kennedy would not have feared using the Very pistol. The planes could have circled the hulk for a time, providing protection, and radioed for a PBY. Evans was watching the strait at dusk and saw the flight of P-40's. Even if they missed seeing the Very pistol flare, Evans would have seen it and, having been alerted by Rendova, he would have known it meant survivors. By dark, he could have had native canoes en route to the hulk. With luck, the survivors could have been rescued that night by one means or another.

Kennedy very quickly decided to take the lantern and a pistol, make his way over the reefs to the edge of Ferguson Passage, and swim out that night in his life jacket and try to flag a passing PT boat. The men objected and tried to dissuade him, Donovan writes. He was too tired. There were unknown currents and probably sharks. Donovan quotes Ross as saying the scheme was "absurd."

It was, and for another reason. The PT's entered Ferguson Passage on full alert. The men manning the guns were, to put it mildly, trigger-happy—as who wouldn't be in enemy waters at night? Suppose Kennedy had seen or heard them, shined his lantern on them, and fired his pistol? The reaction might well have been a reflexive hail of small arms fire in Kennedy's direction.

Kennedy dismissed the objections. Within thirty minutes after they arrived on the atoll, he was gone. He made his way along the reefs, swam to an island closer to the passage, then plunged in. By 8 P.M., White reports, Kennedy was in the passage, supported by his kapok life jacket.

That night, as Jack swam out, only six boats patrolled from Lumbari, we saw from an action report. They did not enter Ferguson Passage. They went barge hunting near Vella Lavella, attempting to force Wilson Strait. They were attacked by float planes, which delivered twenty-seven strafing attacks on the *104* and *108*. Three boats got through—*170*, *108*, *172*—and attacked light barges. The barges shot back and the PT's were unable to inflict any damage. According to the White report, Jack saw the flares of the float planes up north of Gizo.

As Kennedy was making his way back to shore, he was caught in a strong current which (apparently) swept him into Blackett Strait, then back into Ferguson Passage. He lost the lantern.

Hersey, who interviewed Kennedy, writes:

> He thought he had never known such deep trouble. . . . He stopped trying to swim. He seemed to stop caring. His body drifted through the wet hours and he was very cold. His mind was a jumble. A few hours before he had wanted desperately to get to the base at Rendova. Now he only wanted to get back to the little island he had left that night, but he didn't try to get there; he just wanted. His mind seemed to float away from his body. Darkness and time took the place of a mind in his skull. For a long time he slept, or was crazy, or floated in a chill trance.

Much has been made in the Kennedy literature of this swim into Ferguson Passage that night. It was considered by many writers to be another heroic act. Even crusty old Tom Warfield, who did not have a high opinion of Jack as a PT skipper, told us, "You have to give him a hell of a lot of credit for getting out there and swimming, whether it was the most intelligent thing to do or not. He was trying to take some kind of action. It's better than sitting there and starving to death."

Perhaps. It can also be seen as impulsive and reckless. It did not accomplish anything at all. And Jack could have been killed. The crew was at a point when reflection might have been called for, "estimating the situation," as military men say; calmly conceiving an escape plan or signaling devices; or reconnoitering. But reflection and careful planning were not Jack Kennedy's strong suits. He was an "action" man.

In Jack's absence, Lennie Thom was the senior man (Barney Ross was only a "visitor" in this situation). The crewmen we talked to thought Thom was a tower of strength and an inspiration, that he pulled the men together and did all the sensible things. This was noteworthy, we thought, but scarcely mentioned in the *PT-109* literature. Harris told us, "When Kennedy left, Thom organized us. He used to tell us stories about the farm and college days and all his women and the things he was going to do. He was *great*. He kept everybody's spirits up. He had no fear, no worry in the world. He could rule anybody. You'd just look at him and do what he told you. He was that big and awful nice."

Few slept soundly that night, Ross told us. They posted watches to warn of Japanese who might approach from the blind (western) side of the island. They were beginning to suffer from thirst. They dug in the sand trying to find fresh water. Some split open coconuts to drink the milk, but the coconuts were green. Harris found a set of Japanese blueprints, interesting but useless for survivial.

Where were they? Donovan ascertained on his trip to the Solomons that their little atoll was Kasolo, or Plum Pudding Island. That night the men discovered it was inhabited after all—by thousands of birds. They came in after dark, making a fearful racket. After that, a light rain fell. Some of the men lay on their backs with their mouths open, catching a few drops. Others licked leaves of the foliage, but this was distasteful. The leaves were covered with bird droppings. The survivors called their home Bird Island. (See Map No. 6.)

Second Day (August 3-4)

About dawn Kennedy bumped up on a reef, crawled ashore on a sand spit, and passed out. Later he awoke and made his way back to Bird Island, arriving about noon. The other survivors, who had given him up for dead, were overjoyed to see him. Kennedy could do nothing for their welfare. He was feverish, exhausted, nauseated. He collapsed again, passing out. Later in the afternoon he awoke briefly with his mind still fixed on the single rescue plan. He said to Ross, "Barney, you try it tonight." Then Kennedy passed out again and, presumably (the accounts are not clear) slept the night through.

By now, some of the men were suffering badly from thirst. It had been two days since anyone had had a good drink of water. It might be thought that it was long past time to carry out reconnaissance of the larger islands and to find a water source. But with Kennedy out of action, and his orders to Ross standing, nothing was done that night except to send Ross to Ferguson Passage.

Ross was less than enthusiastic about his orders. Yet he made a half-hearted attempt to carry them out. In the late afternoon, he made his way to the edge of the passage. He had no lantern, only Kennedy's pistol, so his chances of being killed by a PT boat were less and he evidently took precautions to make them even smaller. Hersey says he did not go into the water. Donovan says he went in the water but stayed only twenty minutes. According to Donovan, he fired his pistol three times as a test. To Ross, the noise on the water seemed "flat"—not loud enough to do any good.

Again no PT's came through Ferguson Passage. That night, according to Warfield's action reports, five of them went up to Vella Lavella. The skippers included George Cookman on *107* and Richard Keresey on *105*. Off the southeast coast of Vella Lavella, Cookman spotted a column of large and fast-moving barges. The five PT's attacked, following the leader. During the attack, the barges fired back and Cookman was instantly killed. Two other men were wounded. The PT's inflicted little or no damage on the barges.

After sitting on the reef for some hours, no doubt wondering what good he could do if he did see a PT boat, Ross found a place to sleep and turned in.

All during that day—August 3—the coast watcher, Lieutenant Evans, had been busy trying to find out what he could about *PT-109* survivors. His apparatus on Kolombangara reported no sign of survivors. Donovan says that that evening two of Evans's "Gizo Scouts," Biuku Gasa and Eroni Kumana, who lived on the island of Sepo, located between Gizo and Bird Island, arrived on Kolombangara to report new Japanese reinforcements at Kequlavata Bay, on the northern coast of Gizo. Evans asked if they had seen any *PT-109* survivors; they said no. On the following morning, Evans radioed Rendova "No survivors found at Gizo." He sent Biuku and Eroni back to Sepo with instructions to be on the alert for *PT-109* survivors. This was a key order in the drama—the one that probably had more to do with the rescue than anything else.

About that same time, Al Cluster, who was in the Russell Islands, got word that *PT-109* was missing. It was the first time any boat from Squadron Two had been lost since he assumed command. He went immediately to Lumbari and checked in at Warfield's command post. He told us he thought Rendova was doing all it could. "They had sent up some PBY's to look for them," he said, "but the PBY's reported no trace of anything."

The survivors we talked to also recalled seeing a PBY. They couldn't remember if it was one or more than one or when it (or they) came over.

Charles Harris said, "A PBY went over at a distance but it didn't spot us." And, if Ross's memory is correct, in their paranoia about being seen, nothing was done to try to signal the PBY.

Third Day (August 4-5)

When he awoke, Ross made his way back to Bird Island. Hersey says that Kennedy "felt a little better now." But spirits were flagging. Their only rescue plan had failed two nights in a row. They were all suffering acutely from thirst. Zinser told us: "Hunger didn't seem to bother me too much. Thirst was our main discomfort." It was now Wednesday. They had not had a good drink of water since Sunday.

It was thirst more than anything else, Ross told us, that dictated the next step. They decided to move from Bird Island to a larger island, later identified by Donovan as Olasana. It appeared to have many more coconut trees; some thought it might even have water. About midday, by White's account, they set off "using the same arrangement as before"— that is, Kennedy towing McMahon, the others using the timber for a float. This movement took three hours. Olasana had more cover and far more coconuts. They split open the coconuts and drank, trying to assuage their thirst.

Was Olasana occupied? There is some ambiguity in the accounts. White writes, "Their new home was slightly larger than their former. . . . and had no Jap tenants." But Donovan wrote that they did not explore the island. "None of them," he said, "ever saw more than a corner of the island, about fifty yards square." Zinser recalled they had not explored it. He told us, "The second island was much bigger. We were really concerned that there might be some Japs on it. We kept a watch all the time." Ross, Harris, and Maguire could not remember.

The weight of testimony indicates they did not explore Olasana. They did not know if it was occupied or not. Now, if they had been camped within a few hundred yards of a small Japanese outpost it would certainly have been prudent to know about it. If there was no outpost, there might have been other things on the island to aid survival. At least they could have walked about without fear of being ambushed at any moment. Cringing in a fifty-square-yard corner of the island can scarcely be seen as a rational policy. Possibly it is an indication that hunger, thirst, and exhaustion had reduced the men to a demoralized and confused state.

That day Rendova and Evans exchanged further messages regarding *PT-109*. Rendova was apparently concerned that the Japanese might obtain codebooks or secret electronics gear from the hulk or that the hulk was a dangerous obstacle to nighttime navigation in Blackett Strait. At 11:30 A.M. Rendova asked Evans where the hulk was and if he had seen any Japanese near it, and requested "complete destruction." Late that afternoon, Evans reported he no longer had the hulk in sight, could not positively confirm that it was a PT hulk. He gave its last position as two miles northeast of Bambanga Island, drifting south. His Gizo scouts had not seen it nor had they any knowledge of it. He added that there were no Japanese in its vicinity.

The request for complete destruction of the hulk presented Evans no small problem. It meant, apparently, that he had to shift his base of operations nearer to Ferguson Passage and the hulk. Perhaps (Donovan is not clear) he intended to carry out the destruction himself. In any case, that night he began making preparations to move.

Later that afternoon Kennedy fixed his eyes on yet another island, not far from their home. As Donovan explains, it was known by several names: Naru (sometimes spelled Nauru), Gross Island, and Cross Island. Kennedy knew it as Naru. Lieutenant Evans knew it as Gross Island. We shall call it Naru-Gross. It lay immediately alongside Ferguson Passage. Kennedy thought he and Ross should explore it and try to find food and water or whatever else might be useful.

That night, White reported, it was "wet and cold." In other words, it rained. Again the men lay on their backs, mouths open, to catch raindrops, and later licked leaves. No one went into Ferguson Passage.

According to Warfield's action report, six boats went on patrol that night. Some remained south of Ferguson Passage, maintaining a "radar watch"—a screen to detect Japanese destroyers should they try to make a run at Rendova. But most, we think—the report is not clear—went north to Gizo Island. The weather was miserable: "Frequent squalls, heavy overcast, visibility very poor."

Fourth Day (August 5-6)

That next morning Rendova and Evans again exchanged messages about the hulk. At 9:40 Evans reported it was in Ferguson Passage, one-half mile southeast of Naru-Gross Island. He said it could not be investigated by him for another twenty-four hours. Two hours later he told Rendova that he was now "certain" the object he saw was the bow of a small vessel. He reported it had washed up on the reef south of Naru-Gross Island. Still later, he reported he thought it would move off with the tide that night and that it was unlikely he could carry out its destruction. Rendova sent a plane up that morning. The pilot, Rendova told Evans, reported the hulk was so badly damaged it was not worth wasting ammunition on. Even so, Evans went forward with his plan to move closer to the hulk.

The *PT-109* had not sunk as the crew believed it might. Apparently it had not been seen—or explored—by the Japanese and, after a slow, winding journey, it had drifted into Ferguson Passage the night before and had finally washed up on the reefs of the very island Kennedy and Ross intended to explore that day. A P-40 had flown low over it again.

The survivors were still huddled in a corner of Olasana, keeping under cover. That afternoon, Kennedy went ahead with his plan to explore Naru-Gross. Leaving Lennie Thom in charge of the men, he and Ross swam the quarter mile or so, arriving, according to White, about 3:30 P.M. They saw the P-40 flying low over the island. White reports that it strafed, leading Kennedy and Ross to believe it was shooting at something Japanese. An outpost perhaps? In all probability, the P-40 pilot was strafing the hulk of *PT-109* on the reef.

They explored cautiously. Ross recalled that Naru-Gross was about a half mile wide and maybe two and a half miles long. At the center, he said, it had an elevation of perhaps fifty feet. This gave them a good view of the reef, Ferguson Passage, and the surrounding area. They found no Japanese. The island, it appeared, was deserted.

During this exploration they turned up some useful items. Near the center of the island, at the highest elevation, Ross recalled, they came upon a native lean-to. Near it they found a one-man dugout canoe and—most important of all—a fifty-five-gallon drum full of fresh water. Not far away they came upon a wooden crate with Japanese lettering on it. They broke it open and found some crackers and hard candy. They ate and drank greedily.

During this period the two Gizo scouts, Biuku and Eroni, had been making their way from Kolombangara back to their home on Sepo. According to Donovan they stopped for a time at the village of Raramana, on Wana Wana Island, south of Ferguson Passage, then continued northward. That day they crossed Ferguson Passage and, about the time Kenneday and Ross made their finds on Naru-Gross, Biuku and Eroni reached the south reef of Naru-Gross.

Now we come to a minor mystery. There are three different accounts of what happened next.

White reports that Kennedy and Ross saw the two men in their canoe and immediately recognized them as natives. White says that Kennedy and Ross tried to attract their attention, but "despite all efforts . . . they paddled swiftly off to the northwest."

Hersey introduces a new element: a Japanese barge grounded on the reef. He wrote, "There were two men by the barge—possibly Japs. They apparently spotted Kennedy and Ross, for they got into a dugout canoe and hurriedly paddled to the other side of the island. Kennedy and Ross moved up the beach."

Donovan reports the Japanese barge but the detail is different. He says the natives explored the barge and scavenged two rifles from it. About that time the two pairs of men saw each other. Both were startled, each thinking the other pair might be Japanese. Kennedy and Ross, Donovan wrote, "dived into the bushes." The two natives jumped into their canoe and paddled furiously away.

In our interview with Ross, we queried him about the barge, wondering why he and Kennedy had not scavenged it themselves. He could not recall seeing a barge. We also asked about the bow of the *109*, which Evans reported washing ashore on Naru-Gross. Ross could not remember seeing that either. In all probability, they did not, we thought. Surely Ross would have remembered that.

By Donovan's account, the natives left Naru-Gross and paddled over to Olasana. They must have been searching each island carefully; there was no other reason for them to pause at Olasana. The *PT-109* lookout watch spotted them and the group emerged from the foliage and went down to the beach.

The natives approached cautiously. Donovan says that they worried at first that the survivors might be Japanese. But it seems to us that they must have realized at once by the size, coloring, and clothes of the men that they were American. Their real reason for caution, we felt, must have been: how would the American survivors receive them? With pistol shots? The Americans had no way of knowing they were friendly.

Donovan and others say the survivors shouted at the natives, trying to entice them ashore: "Come. Come. Navy. Navy. Americans. Americans." Still, he writes, the natives would not come. They got nowhere, Zinser and Harris recalled, until they shoved Thom forward. He was big and had a blond beard, and could not have been Japanese. Seeing him, they say, the natives finally came ashore.

The natives were probably as excited and thrilled as the survivors. They had made the big find Evans had alerted them to. No doubt there would be a reward. They gave the men water, cigarettes, and C-rations, and built a fire by rubbing two sticks together. The fire was an indication that there were no Japanese on Olasana or nearby and that must have been a relief to the survivors. There was still no sign of Kennedy or Ross. They had missed the big moment.

Thom, the senior man present, had no way of knowing when, or if, Kennedy would return or what he and Ross were up to. Thus, after he established rapport with the natives, who spoke pidgin English, he conceived a rescue plan. He asked the natives to paddle him straight to Rendova—right then. The natives protested that the water was too rough. But Thom got in the canoe and, reluctantly, the natives set off with him. They were back in half an hour. Thom was too big for the craft. It had swamped as soon as they hit open water.

Thom then made an alternate plan. He would give the natives a note and they could take it to Rendova. He had a piece of paper and the stub of a pencil. Including radio callsigns as a signal, to show the message was authentic and not a Japanese trick, he wrote:

To: Commanding Officer—Oak 0
From: Crew P.T. 109 (Oak 14)
Subject: Rescue of 11 (eleven) men lost since Sunday, Aug 1st in enemy action. Native knows our position & will bring P.T. boat back to small islands of Ferguson Passage off Naru IS.
    A small boat (outboard or oars) is needed to take men off as some are seriously burned.
    Signal at night—three dashes(– – –)
    Password—Roger—Answer—Wilco
    If attempted at day time—advise air coverage or a PBY could set down. Please work out suitable plan & act immediately. Help is urgent & in sore need.
    Rely on native boys to any extent
L J Thom
Ens. U. S. N. R.
Exec 109

Over on Naru-Gross Kennedy and Ross were devising their own rescue plan utilizing the one-man dugout canoe they had found. That night they dragged it down to the water's edge. By the White-Hersey accounts, Kennedy took some of the water, candy, and crackers, and paddled out into Ferguson Passage, again hoping to hail a PT boat. He waited until 9 P.M. When none came, he gave it up and paddled around Naru-Gross to Olasana to rejoin the other survivors, arriving about 11:30 P.M. (Unaccountably, and lamentably, Donovan mixes up the events of this night with those of the following night.) Because there was no room in the dugout, Ross slept that night alone on Naru-Gross.

No doubt Jack Kennedy was astonished to find a fire going and two natives snuggled in for the night, helping the survivors and feeding them C-rations—astonished, and relieved beyond measure. These natives were obviously friendly and in contact with U.S. forces. Even if he did not learn about Evans (as Donovan says) and the rescue apparatus, Kennedy realized, as Thom had realized, that they could be employed as messengers.

That same night Evans, apparently still determined to do what he could about the destruction of the *PT-109* hulk, shifted his base of operations. He left Kolombangara and headed by canoe for the island of Komu, a small atoll in lower Blackett Strait, east and north of Wana Wana. It brought him closer to the hulk and, as it turned out, to the survivors and the rescue that was now about to unfold. From Komu, he would direct it.

Fifth Day (August 6-7)

The accounts of what happened on this day are a little confusing. The Hersey version is vague or was deliberately disguised by Navy censors. As we said, Donovan has his days mixed up. Thus, we were forced to rely entirely on the White account, which seems accurate enough on movements but short, or ambiguous, on the reasons for the movements.

Early that morning Kennedy got in the canoe with the natives to go back to Naru-Gross. White and Donovan wrote that the natives believed there were Japanese on Naru-Gross and wanted to prove this to Kennedy because it might complicate the rescue. (Donovan says that when the natives saw Kennedy and Ross the day before they thought they were Japanese.) But Kennedy and Ross had thoroughly reconnoitered Naru-Gross and Kennedy must have been certain there were no Japanese there. Perhaps he went along merely to convince the natives so they would not take erroneous and confusing information back to Rendova. Whatever the case, on the way over, they intercepted Ross, who was swimming the quarter mile from Naru-Gross to Olasana. He turned about, hung onto the canoe, and went back to Naru-Gross with Kennedy and the natives.

For the next several hours, they crept all over the island with the natives, proving to them there were no Japanese there. During this exploration, the natives showed Kennedy and Ross another secret cache. It contained a two-man canoe. There is no mention in any of the accounts of the Japanese barge or the hulk of *PT-109*. Had the *109* hulk drifted off with the tide? Perhaps so. There were no further reports about it from Evans.

Now—midday?—it was time for Biuku and Eroni to go to Rendova for help. According to Donovan, Kennedy now carved the famous message in the coconut:

NAURO ISL
NATIVE KNOWS POSIT
HE CAN PILOT
11 ALIVE
NEED SMALL BOAT
KENNEDY

The natives already had Thom's note. Why a second one from Kennedy, a brief and almost unreadable scrawl on a coconut? There may have been several reasons. Simply as a precaution—two notes are better than one; Thom's note might get wet on the voyage and be rendered unreadable. Perhaps the natives encouraged it—one note for each of them so they might each receive a reward for their rescue. Or it may have been vanity or competitiveness on Kennedy's part. It might seem odd if the only note from the survivors came from Lennie Thom. Where was the commanding officer of *PT-109*?

Jack sent the natives to Rendova, but they knew what to do first: report to Evans and the apparatus. They paddled directly to Wana Wana. They landed at Raramana. By Donovan's account, they made contact with one of Evans's English-speaking scouts, Benjamin Kevu, and briefed him on their discovery. Kevu dispatched a messenger to Evans, who was then on Komu. Biuku and Eroni then walked to the village of Madou. There they picked up a third native, John Kari, got a larger canoe, and set off for Rendova with Thom's note and Kennedy's coconut.

Kennedy and Ross remained on Naru-Gross that night. They could not be certain when the natives would bring rescue, so they kept on trying to rescue themselves. By White's account, after nightfall they hauled the two-man canoe from the cache and paddled out into Ferguson Passage, intending to try to flag a passing PT boat. A squall came up and swamped the canoe. They flailed back to Naru-Gross in heavy seas and were brutally cast up on the coral reef. Ross was painfully bruised and cut. They crawled to the beach and collapsed in deep, exhausted sleep.

Later, Ross (like Thom) was awarded the "lifesaving" Navy and Marine Corps Medal. It was not given for rescues on the night of the collision (as was Thom's), but for follow-up activity, including his forays into Ferguson Passage. The citation, in part: ". . . . forced to abandon the sinking boat . . . Ross swam to a small island, courageously towing two injured comrades and assisted them over the reefs to safety. Despite painful burns which he received during the engagement, he twice swam out from the island into Ferguson Passage in an attempt to intercept our boats on nightly patrol and effect a rescue. . . ."

The other nine survivors spent that night in more comfortable circumstances on Olasana.

That night, August 6-7, the survivors must have seen flashes of light to the north, from a big naval engagement, the Battle of Vella Gulf. The codebreakers had picked up word that Rabaul would send four destroyers—another Express—down Blackett Strait to Vila Plantation on Kolombangara. The Express carried 900 soldiers and fifty tons of supplies, virtually a repeat of the trip on the night of August 1-2. Halsey held the Lumbari PT's in port and again sent six destoryers to intercept. They went into Vella Gulf via Gizo Strait and met the Express at 11:45 P.M., on the 6th, about five miles northwest of Vanga Point. In a classic destroyer action—one of the few of the war—Halsey's destroyers did what the PT's failed to do a week before. They scored a smashing victory, sinking three of the four destroyers, *Kawakaze*, *Arashi*, and *Hagikaze*. The fourth, *Shigure*, turned tail and fled. The naval historian Samuel Eliot Morison wrote: "Awed PT sailors in Kula Gulf 28 miles away sighted the loom of flame and thought the volcano on Kolombangara must have blown its top." Over 1,500 Japanese soldiers and sailors perished in the water that night. About 250 reached Vella Lavella. They were captured there a week or so later when the Allies invaded.

Sixth Day (August 7-8)

When Evans reached Komu Island and received the oral report on the survivors, he promptly set rescue operations in motion. He recruited a big war canoe, manned by seven natives, and sent them to Naru-Gross with a note which Donovan published:

> To Senior Officer, Naru Is.
> Friday 11 p.m. Have just learnt of your presence on Naru Is. & also that two natives have taken news to Rendova. I strongly advise you return immediately to here in this canoe & by the time you arrive here I will be in Radio communication with authorities at Rendova & we can finalise plans to collect balance of party.
> A.R. Evans Lt
> R A N V R
>   Will warn aviation of your crossing Ferguson Passage.

At 9:20 A.M. that same morning Evans radioed his superiors a message for relay to Rendova:

> Eleven survivors PT boat on Gross Island X Have sent food and letter advising senior come here without delay X Warn aviation of canoes crossing Ferguson

That same morning, by Donovan's account, Biuku, Eroni, and John Kari arrived at Rendova in their canoe. They gave Thom's message and Jack's coconut to authorities. At 11:30 Rendova jubilantly informed Evans that the natives had arrived and thanked him profusely for his previous message and assistance. During the afternoon Evans and Rendova finalized a joint rescue plan. It was decided that if Kennedy arrived at Komu as planned, Evans would send him to Rendova via war canoe. PT boats from Lumbari, equipped with rubber rafts, would go directly to Naru-Gross and Olasana and pick up the remaining ten men.

The war canoe arrived at Naru-Gross early in the morning. A native delivered Evans's note to Kennedy. Kennedy and Ross then got in the canoe and went over to Olasana to join the other survivors. The natives had brought food, water, and a cookstove. They fed the survivors, White wrote, "and were extremely kind at all times." Then, as per the plan, Kennedy left in the war canoe for the trip to Evans's headquarters on Komu Island. He lay down in the canoe; the natives covered him with ferns. Hersey wrote that "thirty" Japanese aircraft buzzed the canoe on the way. Donovan says three. White mentions none. At 4 P.M. the canoe arrived at Komu and Evans politely offered Kennedy a cup of tea.

Kennedy did not think much of the rescue plan. He understandably wanted to have a hand in directing the rescuers to the place he now knew so well. Accordingly, the plan was modified. The PT's would first pick up Kennedy at Patparan Island in Blackett Strait, then go in for others. Some of the men involved in the rescue thought this was an unnecessary complication and added risk, but it was done Jack's way.

There was intense excitement at Lumbari and a great deal of careful planning to effect the rescue. Warfield named Hank Brantingham, under whose command Kennedy had been lost, to head up the operation. Brantingham picked a skilled skipper for the mission: Liebenow in *157*. Another boat, the *171*, commanded by Art Berndtson, which had radar and was going on regular patrol, would serve as a temporary backup during the rescue.

Then, the senior officers at Rendova realized that with a newsworthy person like Jack Kennedy, son of the former ambassador to the Court of St. James's, involved, the survival and rescue would be a good story for the press. It had upbeat elements, good for the folks back home. Survival experiences of this kind were common in the Pacific war—witness the far more dramatic and complex survival and rescue of the *Helena*'s crew only three weeks before—but they usually didn't have a celebrity to focus on, so most went unreported. Anyway, God knows the bedraggled PT group at Lumbari needed some positive publicity to offset its long string of fiascos.

That day, two war correspondents traveling in company on Rendova got the word about the rescue. These were Leif Erickson of the Associated Press (who had come from AP's Denver Bureau) and Frank Hewlett of United Press (who had been in UP's Manila Bureau when the war began). Hewlett, now a Washington journalist, told us by phone:

> I'd known Hank Brantingham from Manila days. I dropped by to see him that day. He said he was going out that night and asked if I wanted to go. I said hell no! I knew the PT's. You went out for about fourteen hours, all night, and maybe shot a few rounds at barges. Never much of a story. Then he told me they were going out to rescue Ambassador Kennedy's son. That was a horse of a different color. I said hell yes! Then I tried my damnedest to ditch Leif Erickson—told him I was going to play poker with Hank or some ruse like that—but he wasn't fooled. So, in the end, we both made the trip.

Erickson, now working in the San Francisco Bureau of AP, told us by phone, "I don't remember Frank trying to ditch me, but it wouldn't have worked. I had a tip from a naval officer on Rendova, whom I do not want to identify. I very definitely knew when we left we were going out to rescue Kennedy, and that it would be a good story."

After dusk that night, seven of the eight boats going on regular patrol departed Lumbari. They went into the lower Vella Gulf, off the east coast of Vella Lavella. Berndtson, in *171*, who would join them later, remained in port with Liebenow's *157*. The men collected rescue gear, including rubber rafts and walkie-talkies for communicating between the two boats. The two war correspondents, Erickson and Hewlett, the two natives, Biuku and Eroni, and Jack's squadron commander, Al Cluster, joined the regular crew of the *157*. At about 8:30 (according to Liebenow's log) the two boats got under way.

At about the same time, Kennedy set off for Patparan Island for the rendezvous in a native canoe. It was, according to Warfield's report, another dark night, much like the night of August 1/2. There were occasional showers. Visibility was poor to fair. Kennedy was cold. He wore a pair of coveralls Evans had given him, Donovan wrote.

There was a problem at the rendezvous, not fully explained in any of the accounts. Kennedy was supposed to meet the PT's at 10. But it was not until about 11:15 that they all found one another. Luckily, no float planes attacked the PT's. According to a prearranged recognition signal, someone on the *157* fired four pistol shots. Kennedy, replying, fired the last three shots from his .38 pistol, then one from a Japanese rifle Evans had given him.

When the craft were within hailing distance, Kennedy shouted, "Where the hell have you been?"

Berndtson told us, "It was an unfortunate thing to say, I thought. I know it irked a lot of people on the two PT's. There was a war on. The guys were going out every night, getting killed and wounded. We were busy as hell. I had a patrol to lead that night and I was taking time from it. And then he hit us with that comment, like he was the only guy around!"

Berndtson's feelings seem understandable, but then so, in the circumstances, do Jack's. After Kennedy had climbed aboard the *157*, the two boats swung toward Ferguson Passage and Naru-Gross, moving slowly, engines muffled, doing everything possible to keep down wakes and noise. Berndtson, on the *171*, watched his radar and relayed information to Brantingham on *157* by the walkie-talkie. When they approached the reef, Berndtson laid back in Ferguson Passage and Brantingham took the *157* in. Berndtson said, "I coached him through. Left. Right. Left. Right. Like that."

All that time, the war correspondents Erickson and Hewlett were interviewing Kennedy. He told them how the accident had happened—and that he had turned to make a torpedo run—and a little of what had transpired afterward. He praised Pappy McMahon's courage.

When he had passed through the main group of islands, Brantingham ordered a rubber raft over the side at 12:30 A.M., according to his log. Biuku and Eroni got in it and paddled ahead, guiding the *157* through the reef toward Olasana. White does not mention this in his report, stating that Kennedy "directed" the PT boat to the rest of the survivors. Donovan also gives Kennedy the major share of credit for guiding *157* through the reef. Hersey says more accurately, "with the help of the natives, the PT made its way" to the rescue.

When the *157* approached Olasana, Jack stood on the bow and shouted, "Lennie! Hey, Lennie!" Thom and the nine survivors rushed to the water's edge. They were brought on board in the rafts, two or three at a time. By 2:15, according to the log, all ten had been rescued. With the help of Berndtson, still lying off in *171*, the *157* withdrew through the reef without incident, mission accomplished. Berndtson then went on to Vella Lavella to make a regular patrol with the other boats. The *157* headed for Lumbari.

On the way home, a medical corpsman distributed rations of brandy. Hersey reported that Johnston, Biuku, and Eroni sang, "Jesus loves me, this I know, for the Bible tells me so. . . ."

Donovan wrote that Biuku and Eroni playfully chided Kennedy for losing his boat. And, as he told us, so did Liebenow. Erickson and Hewlett were busy interviewing the crewmen, getting their stories. Hewlett told us, "As I recall, Kennedy went down below, probably to lie down, and we didn't talk to him much on the way home. My main source was Lennie Thom and Pappy McMahon. Lennie was a really striking guy. Big. He had a blond beard and looked like a Viking. He was very, very colorful."

In these interviews, Hewlett and Erickson told us, the *PT-109* enlisted men all praised Kennedy to high heaven. They recalled his swimming into Ferguson Passage (three nights, they said) and his help to Pappy McMahon. Erickson told us, "There was no question in my mind that Jack Kennedy was a legitimate hero." Curiously, Hewlett said, he had been more impressed with Thom. "I almost blew it," he told us. "I damned near put him in my lead instead of Kennedy."

On the way back to Lumbari, Al Cluster went below to talk with Jack. He was lying in a bunk. Cluster told us, "He was very tired. There were tears streaming down his face. He was bitter about the skippers who had left them behind. If they had come to look for them, he thought, maybe the other two men lost on *PT-109*, Marney and Kirksey, could have been saved."

The *157* arrived back at the Lumbari base at 5:15 by the logbook. In a final (minor) error, White reports it had been "seven days" since the *PT-109* was rammed. Actually, it had been six days.

Hewlett and Erickson immediately sat down to write their stories. Because their stories (and the follow-up magazine article by John Hersey) were so crucial to Jack's political future, we dug them out for inspection, and then talked to Hewlett and Erickson about their impressions at the time, and their general approach to the story.

Hewlett told us that after a mental struggle, he abandoned the idea of using Thom in his lead and shifted to Kennedy, the "less colorful" but the more newsworthy name. He kindly sent us a Xerox of the carbon of that story with a note saying that it was "widely used." Text, typos, and all:

SOMEWHERE IN NEW GEORGIA, Aug. 8 (1943) (delayed by censor) (UP)—The luck of the Irish and some first class skill brought lanky Lt. JG. John F. Kennedy, son of former Ambassador Joseph Kennedy, and 10 of his torpedo boat mates back from a brush with the Japanese and death today.

A week after they had been lost and practically given up, another PT boat went through hostile waters to rescue them in response to an SOS scrawled on a coconut and carried through enemy lines by a native boy.

Three men, including Machinist Mate (2nd class) Patrick H. McMahon, 39, of Los Angeles, who has a son in the navy, credited the 27-year-old Kennedy with saving their lives.

Their extraordinary adventure began the night of Aug. 1, in Blackett Strait, just west of Kolombangara island, north of New Georgia. A Japanese destroyer bore down on the lead PT boat commanded by Kennedy and manned by a crew of 12 and cut the boat in two.

"I'm certain that destroyer was going 40 knots," said Kennedy. "I summoned the crew to general quarters and then tried to get into position for a shot with the torpedoes. But we were too close."

The crewmen were flung in the water. Some were painfully injured. The gasoline went up in flames. One section of the boat didn't burn.

"We clung to the unburned bow of the boat for nearly 12 hours," said Kennedy, "and we left it only when it was just a foot above water."

They had drifted near a Japanese island that had a big garrison but a sudden shift in the current saved them and they finally reached a tiny, unoccupied island. They were still surrounded by Japanese, however.

Kennedy particularly lauded the work of Gunnersmate Second Class Charles Harris, of Boston, Mass., who he said was invaluable throughout the ordeal, and McMahon, who remained cheerful and never complained though badly burned on the face, hands and legs.

Big Blond Ensign Leonard Thom, Sandusky, Ohio, and a former Ohio State football player, recalled how Kennedy swam three times out to Ferguson Passage in hopes of intercepting a PT boat on patrol. He said the distance was several miles.

Ensign George "Barney" Ross said Kennedy not only helped the injured by towing them through the water to their first island but also moved them again to another island after the coconut supply, their only source of food and water, became exhausted. It was on this latter island that they found friendly natives.

There Kennedy scratched an appeal for aid on a coconut husk. A native carried it through the enemy lines to this base.

Last night in a PT-boat under the command of Lt. Henry J. (Hank) Brantingham of Fayettesville, Ark. we went into Japanese-controlled waters to pick them up. Brantingham was a member of the famed squadron in the Philippines at the outbreak of the war which prompted the best seller book *"They Were Expendable."* There his boat evacuated Philippines President Emanuel Quezon from Corregidor. He is now back in the fray with his own squadron.

Kennedy rowed out in a native canoe to meet us and guided our boat through a narrow reef to within a few hundred feet of the island. Rubber boats made two trips ashore and brought back the 10 other survivors, including the trio who needed prompt hospitalization.

The injured are in the hospital and Kennedy is now resting his weary body in his long vacant bunk which his mates never expected him to occupy again.

HEWLETT

Erickson filed a more conventional account of the episode. He misspelled Mauer's first and last names and got Starkey and Zinser's first names wrong, but his account was far more thorough. The text:

A United States Torpedo Boat Base, New Georgia, Aug. 8 (Delayed).—Out of the darkness, a Japanese destroyer appeared suddenly. It sliced diagonally in two the PT boat skippered by Lieut. (j.g.) John F. Kennedy, son of the former American Ambassador in London, Joseph P. Kennedy.

Crews of two other PT boats, patrolling close by, saw flaming high octane gasoline spread over the water. They gave up "Skipper" Kennedy and all his crew as lost that morning of Aug. 2.

But Lieutenant Kennedy, 26, and ten of his men were rescued today from a small coral island deep inside Japanese-controlled Solomons Islands territory and within range of enemy shore guns.

The PT boat making the rescue performed a daring and skillful bit of navigation through reef-choked waters off Ferguson Passage. (Ferguson Passage is between Gizo and Wana Wana Islands in the New Georgia group.)

Two men of Lieutenant Kennedy's crew were lost when the enemy destroyer rammed the boat at a speed estimated by the skipper at forty knots.

Those who were rescued with Lieutenant Kennedy were:

Ensign Leonard Thom of Sandusky, Ohio, executive officer and former Ohio State tackle; Ensign George Henry Robertson (Barney) Ross of Highland Park, Ill.; Machinist's Mate Patrick H. McMahon, 39, of Los Angeles; Machinist's Mate Gerald E. Zinser of Belleville, Ill.; Gunner's Mate Charles Harris of Boston; Radioman John Maguire of Hastings-on-Hudson, N.Y.; Machinist's Mate William Johnston of Dorchester, Mass.; Ordnanceman Edmond Mowrer of St. Louis; Torpedoman Roy L. Starkey of Garden Grove, Calif., and Seaman First Class Raymond Albert of Cleveland.

McMahon was burned badly on his face, hands and arms. Although the burns were infected by salt water and exposure, he did not once utter a word of complaint.

"McMahon's a terrific guy," Lieutenant Kennedy said. "It was something which really got you seeing old Mac lie there."

"You could see he was suffering such pain that his lips twitched and his hands trembled," Ensign Thom added. "You'd watch him and think if you were in his place you'd probably be yelling, 'Why doesn't somebody do something?' But every time you asked Mac how he was doing, he'd wrinkle his face and give you a grin."

Zinser suffered burns on both arms. Johnston, a tough little fellow called "Jockey," was sickened by fumes he had inhaled. Ensign Ross was unhurt, but suffered an arm infection from coral cuts. All the others came through their experience without injury.

On three nights Lieutenant Kennedy, once a backstroke man on the Harvard swimming team, swam out into Ferguson Passage hoping to flag down PT boats going through on patrol. Ensign Ross did the same one other night. But they made no contacts.

On the afternoon of the fourth day two natives found the survivors and carried to the PT boat base a message Lieutenant Kennedy crudely cut on a green coconut husk.

Chronologically, Lieutenant Kennedy, Ensign Thom, and the crewmen told the story this way:

Four Japanese destroyers came down Blackett Strait around the south coast of Kolombangara Island about 2:30 A.M. on Aug. 2. In two phases of a confused engagement the PT's claimed three hits and three probable hits on one of the enemy ships.

It was while the destroyers were returning, probably after delivering supplies and reinforcements near Japan's base at Vila, on Kolombangara, that the enemy ship rammed the Kennedy boat. Ross and Kennedy saw the destroyer coming.

"At first I thought it was a PT," Kennedy said. "I think it was going at least forty knots. As soon as I decided it was a destroyer, I turned to make a torpedo run."

But Kennedy, nicknamed "Shafty" by his mates, quickly realized the range was too short for the torpedo to charge and explode.

"The destroyer then turned straight for us," he said.

"It all happened so fast there wasn't a chance to do a thing. The destroyer hit our starboard forward gun station and sliced right through. I was in the cockpit. I look up and saw a red glow and streamlined stacks. Our tanks were ripped open and gas was flaming on the water about twenty yards away.

Kennedy went out to get McMahon who had been at the engine station and was knocked into the water in the midst of flaming gasoline.

"McMahon and I were about an hour getting back to the boat," Kennedy said. Watertight bulkheads had kept the bow afloat, the skipper explained. "There was a very strong current."

After getting McMahon aboard, Kennedy swam out again to get Harris.

The skipper and his men shouted and called for the two missing men but could get no response.

"We seemed to be drifting toward Kolombangara," Kennedy said. "We figured the Japs would be sure to get us in the morning, but everybody was tired and we slept."

Just before dawn the current changed to carry the survivors away from the Japanese-held coast. About 2 P.M. Kennedy decided to abandon the bow section and try to reach a small island.

Kennedy swam to the island, towing McMahon. The others clung to a plank and swam in a group. It took about three hours to make it. The men stayed on this island until Wednesday, when all coconuts on the island's two trees had been eaten.

Late that afternoon they swam to a larger island, where there were plenty of coconuts.

At night, Kennedy put on a lifebelt and swam into Ferguson Passage to try to signal an expected PT boat. The two natives found the survivor group Thursday afternoon. On Saturday morning a large canoe loaded with natives brought food and a small kerosene stove and gave the men a real feed and hot coffee. That night, a little after midnight, a PT rescue boat, guided by a native pilot, went in the twisting passages to make contact with Kennedy on an outer island.

As can be seen, these stories, while fair approximations of what happened, leave out crucial facts and distort others. Erickson plants the idea—carried forth in the Hersey article—that all hope was abandoned for the crew on the morning of August 2, when in fact, an air search was being improvised and the coast watcher Evans had been alerted. There is no mention of Evans or his behind-the-lines rescue apparatus, merely a reference to "two natives" who seemed to happen along. All that, of course, would certainly have been stopped by the Navy censors, as Hewlett and Erickson knew. Both stories ignore Thom's written message, mentioning only Jack's more memorable carved coconut. Both stories quote Jack as saying he turned the *109* and tried to attack the destroyer. Hewlett writes that three men "credited" Kennedy with saving their lives, but names only McMahon. Erickson reports that Kennedy saved two: McMahon and Harris. Both stories say Jack swam into Ferguson Passage three times to try to flag help from PT boats—when in fact he had swum out only once. (The second try was in the dugout, the third in the two-man canoe.)
Hewlett explained:

As I recall, we probably sent them from New Georgia to Guadalcanal. Everything had to go through Navy channels—the censors. So they were probably couriered down to Guadalcanal to Admiral Wilkinson's headquarters and then to Halsey's headquarters in Nouméa, and then to Nimitz's headquarters in Pearl Harbor. From there, they went to the Navy Department in Washington, where they were finally cleared and then released from there. Some kind of problem developed along the way. I think it was an administrative snafu: I don't think there had been an official communiqué from Wilkinson's headquarters announcing the loss of the *PT-109*, so they couldn't clear a story right off that the crew had been found! Anyway, I know there was a long delay for some reason.

By our reckoning, the story was cleared by the Navy Department on the afternoon of August 19. On the following morning, August 20, the Leif Erickson AP version appeared on the front page of the *New York Times* (circulation 400,000) in the lower right-hand corner. In the early edition, as we saw from a reprint of the *Times* story in the *Choate Alumni Bulletin* of November, the headline was:

KENNEDY'S SON SAVES 10 IN PACIFIC
AS DESTROYER SPLITS HIS PT BOAT

We wondered at the headline. It does not accurately reflect Erickson's story. Was it a deliberate misrepresentation, or was there something mystical about this story that *unconsciously* led people to conclude Jack saved the crew? Whatever the case, in later editions of the *Times*, including the final edition now preserved in libraries on microfilm, the headline was changed by someone to this judgement:

KENNEDY'S SON IS HERO IN PACIFIC

AS DESTROYER SPLITS HIS PT BOAT

Lennie Thom's fiancée, Kate Holway, then in school in Columbus, Ohio, first learned about the *109* calamity in the newspapers. She told us, "I hadn't heard from Lennie for about a week. That was very unusual. His mother called to say she hadn't heard from him either. We were sort of uneasy. Then it hit the papers. There was an awful lot of publicity. The Ohio papers focused on Lennie. It was all about them being saved."

The *New York Times* issue of August 20 featuring Erickson's story had a brief shirttail story by AP which would lead the reader to believe the Kennedys found out in the same way. Datelined Hyannis, Massachusetts, August 19, it said, "Former Ambassador and Mrs. Kennedy today shouted in joy when informed of the exploit of their son. Mrs. Kennedy, first to hear the news by telephone at their summer home, expressed 'deep sorrow' for the two crewmen who lost their lives. 'That's wonderful,' Mrs. Kennedy said when told her son was safe. The former Ambassador then exclaimed: 'Phew. I think Mrs. Kennedy has said enough for both of us.'"

But, in all probability, the Kennedys already knew that Jack had been saved. There is a Kennedy family belief—the story appears in different forms in various Kennedy books—that when the *109* was first lost, the ambassador heard about it, unofficially, from some source. He did not tell Rose, the story goes, and when she first heard about his being saved on a "radio broadcast" she was mystified. The first part of the story seems credible—that the ambassador was told Jack was missing and that he did not tell Rose then. But surely, when Jack was rescued, the ambassador was again told unofficially; and surely at this point he would have told Rose all about it. If the Kennedys gave the AP reporter the impression they were learning he was saved for the first time, it was probably either to be polite or to conceal the fact that they had inside government sources who had technically violated censorship rules to keep them informed.

If Hewlett and Erickson recall correctly, the stories did in fact receive wide press coverage. Leo Damore, in his book *The Cape Cod Years of John Fitzgerald Kennedy*, reports that the *Boston Herald* carried it on the front page with four drawings depicting "the ramming and the crew's deliverance." We could not confirm this in the Kennedy Library newspaper clips, but we found no reason to doubt it. Though they were now official residents of Florida and New York, the Kennedys were still big news in Boston.

John Hersey did not begin his research for another six months. He, too, skips the battle and begins with the collision. Because of censorship, he could not write about Evans and the rescue operation, and the crucial role it played in saving the men. The rescue, Hersey writes, was effected by a

New Zealand infantry unit on New Georgia to whom the two natives took the coconut. Nor did he mention Lennie Thom's note; only the coconut. He carries forth the idea—giving far more detail—that Lumbari quickly gave up hope for the men. He has Jack turning to attack the destroyers. The impression created is that Jack "saved his crew," and that Jack was the sole hero.

This story was one of hundreds of such incidents in the Pacific war. *Time* magazine said in its July 11, 1960, issue four months before election day, that Jack's "gallant and harrowing role" in "rescuing the crew" during this episode was "one of the great tales of heroism in the South Pacific." It was certainly not. To his credit, Jack was trying all the time, just as Thom and Ross were trying. But his efforts came to naught. He did not rescue his crew. Evans, with the help of the Lumbari base and many other people, rescued the castaways.

19

A New Command

THE *PT–109* survivors traveled from Rendova to Tulagi by slow-moving amphibious vessel. By August 9, probably, they had been checked into a medical facility on Florida Island for more thorough physical examinations. A Navy doctor who had recently arrived at that facility examined the men. He was Joseph B. Wharton, Jr. In 1961 he wrote Jack a letter at the White House recalling this moment in history. Through this letter, now on file at the Kennedy Library, we were able to find Wharton, living in El Dorado, Arkansas, where he has been practicing medicine since World War Two. He told us:

> The crew of *PT–109* was brought in from Rendova. None of them was seriously hurt. They were in pretty good shape—not starving or anything. A lot of them, including Kennedy, had bad coral cuts that were infected. And fungus, which we then called "jungle rot," ear infections, and so on. We sent the more seriously injured over to a hospital on Blue Beach, Tulagi, or to a larger unit on Guadalcanal. I remember we had to get them out of the sick bay pretty quick because we had a crew coming in that all had infectious hepatitis.
>
> I remember Jack Kennedy at that time quite clearly. He was one of the finest and most brilliant men I had ever met. Very strong and mature for his age. His knowledge was very versatile—everything from poker to philosophy. . . .

Wharton's memory of Jack's precise physical condition is hazy but we judge from his recollections that, contrary to some accounts, Jack did not spend the month of August in a hospital on Florida Island or Tulagi or elsewhere but that, by and large, Jack emerged from the survival ordeal in fair shape. Somewhere, in some government archives, there must be records of Wharton's unit—Mobile Hospital Number Four—containing precise descriptions of Jack and his crew. But until these medical records are released, we cannot know his condition with any precision.

271

While Jack was in sick bay, he had many visitors. One was the old Squadron Three hand, Joe Kernell. He told us:

He was in this hospital—not a real hospital, a tent affair—and wearing only skivvies. He didn't look any worse than the rest of us. He was skinny, but we were *all* skinny because the food was lousy. When *109* was lost, we were all depressed. Kennedy was such a sweet guy. When I saw him in sick bay, I said, "Jack, what went through your mind when you saw that destroyer coming and you thought you might be killed?" He looked real serious and asked, "You really want to know?" I said, rather seriously myself, "Yes." Then he said, "I thought, my God, I owe Joe Kernell two hundred fifty dollars in bridge debts and I haven't paid him!" So, right there, he whipped out a check and paid me. Then, in that funny way of his, he made me feel terrible: that the only reason I'd come to the sick bay was to get my money.

I was on my way home then. Many weeks later—in October—I wound up in New York, by chance visiting with a friend of the ambassador's. He said the ambassador was then at the Waldorf and would probably want to talk to me. So that was arranged and by that odd coincidence, I was the first one from out there to see his father. I talked to him for about an hour in his suite. He was very nice. He was very interested in how Jack had been doing before the accident and in Jack's physical condition. I filled him in and he thanked me and I left.

Another visitor was Johnny Iles. He told us:

I was back on Tulagi then, I can't remember why. I remember when I heard the *109* was lost, I was very upset. I went to the Catholic chaplain, Father McCarthy, and I asked him to say a mass for Jack. Then Jack and the *109* crew arrived on Tulagi. I didn't think Jack looked too good. He was *really* skinny, and limping—from the coral cuts, I guess. I gave him a big hello. Then I happened to mention about the mass. He was furious! He read the riot act to me. He said he wasn't ready to die just yet and why the hell had I given up hope? I couldn't understand it.

Following his medical treatment, we assumed, Jack was assigned to light duty for a while. During this time he was probably busy helping Whizzer White prepare his intelligence report, dated August 22. There was probably much other paperwork to be done concerning the loss of PT-109 and the lives of Marney and Kirksey. However, none of this has come to light.

There was another piece of official paperwork in progress. Al Cluster recalled that he decided Jack deserved some kind of award. He put him in for the Silver Star, the Navy's third-highest award after the Medal of Honor and Navy Cross, a coveted decoration, not freely bestowed in the Navy and Marine Corps, and usually awarded only for exceptional heroism in combat. As was the practice, Cluster drew up the citation and sent it up through channels. "The medal was for the survival phase," Cluster told us. "Not the preceding battle."

At the same time, Jack put in a recommendation that Ross and Thom be given awards. We think he recommended them for a Silver Star, too. Our basis for this is a letter in *As We Remember Him* which Jack wrote to Barney Ross' father, dated January 23, 1944. Jack says (in part) that Barney ". . . saved one man's life—and contributed to a great degree to the rescue of the entire group. For his actions through that week he was recommended for the Silver Star—(which) he richly deserves. . . ."

If the recommended awards followed the usual course, they went up through the local chain of command—to Iron Mike Moran, Rear Admiral Wilkinson, and Halsey—and then on to the Navy Department in Washington. At each step along the way, the recommendation was carefully studied by staff officers. At any of these levels, an award could be (and often was) reduced, or denied altogether. The Awards Board in Washington usually had the final say. Somewhere along the chain of command, a downgrading occurred. The three Silver Stars were reduced to the "life-saving" Navy and Marine Corps medals.

In researching the award of Jack's Navy and Marine Corps Medal, we turned up another mystery. Two significantly different citations for Jack's medal have been published. One is reproduced in full in the photographic section of Donovan's book. The other is contained in Kennedy's official Navy biography, the official Navy history of *PT-109*, and elsewhere.

The citation in the Donovan book is signed by the commander, South Pacific, Admiral Halsey, but not dated. Cluster could not recall details, but we assume that it was the citation he composed for Jack's Silver Star. The full text:

> For heroism in the rescue of three men following the ramming and sinking of his motor torpedo boat while attempting a torpedo attack on a Japanese destroyer in the Solomons Islands area on the night of August 1-2, 1943. Lieutenant Kennedy, Captain of the boat directed the rescue of the crew and personally rescued three men, one of whom was seriously injured. During the following six days, he succeeded in getting his crew ashore, and after swimming many hours attempting to secure aid and food, finally effected the rescue of his men. His courage, endurance and excellent leader-

ship contributed to the saving of several lives and was in keeping with the highest traditions of the United States Naval Service.

The other citation is on the letterhead of the secretary of the navy. It is signed by James V. Forrestal and is dated May 19, 1944. We assumed it was composed at a later date than the Halsey citation and probably reflected the work of the Awards Board in the Navy Department. Text:

> For extremely heroic conduct as Commanding Officer of Motor Torpedo Boat 109 following the collision and sinking of that vessel in the Pacific War Theater on August 1–2, 1943. Unmindful of personal danger, Lieutenant (then Lieutenant, Junior Grade) Kennedy unhesitatingly braved the difficulties and hazards of darkness to direct rescue operations, swimming many hours to secure aid and food after he had succeeded in getting his crew ashore. His outstanding courage, endurance and leadership contributed to the saving of several lives and were in keeping with the highest traditions of the United States Naval Service.

The differences are not minor. In the second citation the assertions that he was attempting a torpedo attack, "personally" saved the lives of three men, and "finally effected the rescue of his men" are deleted. Instead, and more generally, he "braved the difficulties and hazards of darkness to direct rescue operations," got his crew ashore, swam "many hours to secure aid and food," and "contributed" to the "saving of several lives." On the other hand, the adjectives in the second are heightened somewhat. Halsey's "heroism" is elevated to "extremely heroic conduct," and the adjective "outstanding" is inserted to modify Jack's courage, endurance and leadership.

Why?

We could only speculate. Perhaps at some step along the way, someone (the Awards Board?) checked the facts, realized that Jack could not have attempted a torpedo attack, that he did not personally save three men, but only one, McMahon, along with assisting a second, Harris, and that Evans and his apparatus, not Jack, effected the rescue of the crew. Whatever the case, the second citation is more in accord with the facts than the first one.

This second version of the citation, we assume, was the final version since it came from an authority higher than Halsey and appears in Jack's official Navy biography. If that is so, we wondered, then where did Jack obtain a copy of the first citation that is reproduced in Donovan's book and signed by Halsey? Was the Navy and Marine Corps Medal authorized by Halsey based on Cluster's original citation for the Silver Star, then later modified by the Awards Board in the Navy Department? If so, then why did Jack or his aides make available to Donovan the first citation rather than the version finally approved by the Awards Board? How many other journalists and authors had been given this original citation over the years? (James MacGregor Burns, for one.) And, finally, why didn't Donovan point out that there were two citations? Surely he must have found the other version in the course of his research.

When the paperwork had been completed, Kennedy called a meeting of his crew. McMahon and Johnston were absent. They had been transferred to other hospitals.

In that 1946 campaign speech, Jack says that McMahon was ordered back to the States to be discharged from service " because of his badly scarred hands." But there was then a great shortage of motor machinists on Tulagi, and when he recovered, McMahon requested duty there. Jack says "he was allowed to stay nearly six months more." Then, we think, he was sent home and honorably discharged—with a Purple Heart for his injuries. We do not know what finally happened to Johnston.

All the others came to the meeting, including Edmund Drewitch, Maurice Kowal, and Leon Drawdy, who had now recovered from their injuries and wounds and were happy to be reunited with their old shipmates. We talked by telephone to Kowal, now living in a suburb of Boston. He said:

> Of course when we heard the *109* was lost we were shocked. Then they came back to Tulagi, where we were. Kennedy called everybody together to explain they had a choice. They could either go to New Zealand for leave—rest and recuperation—for about a month or they could stay in the outfit and get home sooner, back to the States. In other words, you had to put in so much time in the Solomons. They could go to New Zealand if they wanted to, but they'd have to spend that much more time in the Solomons before they became eligible to go home. Kennedy said he'd decided he was going to ask for command of another boat and do his time as fast as possible. Everybody else there decided to do the same. The New Zealand leave didn't apply to me or Drawdy or Drewitch. That was something special for the survivors. We just went to the meeting to see what everybody was going to do.

When the meeting was over, the survivors began to scatter. Ray Lee Starkey was lost track of: nobody could remember where he went. Barney Ross, Zinser, and Albert returned to their old outfit, Squadron Ten, on Lumbari. The others—Kennedy, Thom, Harris, Maguire, Mauer, Drewitch, Drawdy, and Kowal—remained at Tulagi awaiting reassignment.

All the while, the war in the central Solomons was picking up steam. On August 15 Halsey landed a strong force on unoccupied Vella Lavella. He expected a counterattack but it was not forthcoming. By then, Tokyo had decided to write off the central Solomons. The Japanese would hold a line farther north and closer to Rabaul: the islands of Bougainville and Choiseul. That meant the 10,000 troops on Kolombangara had to be evacuated, at night, by barge. To assist in this undertaking, the Japanese established a small barge staging base on northeast Vella Lavella, manned by a few hundred men. The Japanese troops on Kolombangara were evacuated through that base or directly to Choiseul, thence to Bougainville.

The Solomons PT force was steadily growing. The new Squadron Eleven, under LeRoy T. Taylor, entered combat in August, basing from Lumbari, adding twelve new boats to the roster. But the sixty-odd PTs and the 600-odd men manning them (plus base personnel) were not achieving much. As the August 1-2 battle in Blackett Strait had demonstrated, they were little more than a nuisance to enemy destroyers. Nor had they had much success against the armed barges. The PT's were simply undergunned and too vulnerable to enemy counterfire. In their efforts to increase firepower, the PT's had tried, unsuccessfully, to use the 37 mm Army gun (such as Jack had) and even Army bazookas and mortars.

In searching for new ways to get at the barges—and create a new mission for the PT's—a staff planner came up with an astonishing and dismaying new idea. How about a daylight raid on known enemy positions in southern Kolombangara? The Allies had now gained air superiority in Blackett Strait. With an air escort, perhaps some of the PT's could slip into coves along the shore, board the holed-up Japanese barges, and blow them up with dynamite charges. Just like in the movies!

An attempt was actually made to implement this scheme. On August 22, two weeks after Jack was rescued, one week after the Vella Lavella invasion, a force of eight PT boats, supported by aircraft, set off in broad daylight for Kolombangara. Johnny Iles, serving as exec to Richard Keresey in *PT-105*, was on the raid. He said they had no illusions. All thought it was a suicide mission.

When the eight boats approached the coast near Vila Plantation, they broke into two groups. Douglas Kennedy in *169* led *104* inside a cove. They found four barges concealed in the bushes. As they were preparing to board them, the Japanese opened up with a hurricane of small-arms fire from the shore. The PT's withdrew hastily. Keresey and Iles in *105* laid smoke to help the retreat. The second group tried another cove. Sidney D. Hix in *PT-108* led the *125* inside. They also encountered instant and withering small-arms fire. Hix was killed; most of the men on his boat were badly wounded. All eight boats withdrew in a hurry and raced for Ferguson Passage.

Al Cluster, an innovative as well as a free spirit, conceived a radical new idea: a PT gunboat. In our interview, he explained the concept rather proudly:

I guess you could say we were in a kind of miniature arms race with the Japs. They armed the barges with big guns and protected them with armor. Then we responded by creating what we called a gunboat, a radical departure for the PT force. We took three old seventy-seven-footers, *PT–59, 60* and *61,* and completely revamped them. We removed the four torpedo tubes and the two depth charges. In place of this armament we put relatively big guns on them: forty-millimeters and extra fifty-caliber machine guns mounted along the starboard and port sides. We reinforced the decks with armorplate. They were really very heavily armed little boats.

Not everybody shared Cluster's enthusiasm for the gunboat idea. The PT men had been trained, since Melville, to be torpedo shooters. Their dreams of glory, in spite of all the setbacks, still centered on going up against the Express at night and sinking destroyers with torpedoes. The gunboat would have no torpedoes. It would not go on the glamorous missions. It was an offbeat, oddball concept, untried and possibly dangerous. Few skippers wanted anything to do with it.

The exception was Jack Kennedy. Why the concept appealed to him is a matter of conjecture. Perhaps because it was new and different, a challenge. Or perhaps because he perceived that his boss, Al Cluster, wanted it to succeed very badly. By that time, Jack and Cluster were very good pals. Or there may have been another reason. The *59* represented about the only opportunity within the framework of Squadron Two to see combat again. The remaining Squadron Two boats (*36, 40, 47,* and so on) were, by this time, a ragtag lot, unfit for the forward area. They were then engaged in routine chores at Tulagi and the Russells. With the shortage of boats in Squadrons Five, Six, Nine, and Ten in the forward areas, and the surplus of officers who had helped commission the squadrons, it would probably have been impossible at that time for Jack to transfer to another squadron and get command of a newer boat.

Whatever the reasons, Cluster offered and Jack accepted command of *PT–59,* scheduled to be converted to gunboat status. The preliminary work had begun under its original commander, David Levy. But Levy had been in the Solomons through most of the heavy fighting at Guadalcanal, and it was time for him to be rotated home. On September 1 Jack relieved Levy and took command. The other two gunboats went to friends of Jack's in Squadron Two. Lennie Thom took command of *PT–60* and Joe Atkinson took command of *PT–61.*

Jack's first task was to assemble a new crew. There were only two enlisted holdovers on the *59*: Homer Facto, a first-class motor machinist then in his mid-forties (and therefore called "Pappy") and Edward Seratius. Five enlisted men from the *109* followed Jack to the *59*: Edgar

Mauer, the radioman John Maguire, Maurice Kowal, Edmund Drewitch, and Leon Drawdy. (Charles Harris, who had become close to Lennie Thom during the survival experience, went to the *PT-60* with Thom.) Of the five, two, Mauer and Maguire, had been on the *109* when she was sunk.

Al Cluster provided the next bloc of men, former shipmates from Pearl Harbor and Palmyra, when he commanded the old *PT-21*. These men had recently brought the *21* (in company with the *23*, *25*, and *26*) from Funa Futi to Espiritu Santo for duty in the Solomons. But on the voyage south, the keel of the *21* broke and she was "surveyed"—put out of commission and cannibilized for parts at Espiritu Santo. Thus the *21* crew became "surplus," reporting to Al Cluster on Tulagi. Cluster sent many of the *21* crew to the *59*.

These included the ex-skipper of the *21*, Isaac John Mitchell. He replaced Albert Hamn, who had been assigned to the *59*, but who came down with ulcers and was shipped back to the United States. For some reason, Donovan does not include Mitchell in the *59* crew. We found him living in Tulsa, Oklahoma, and talked to him by telephone.

Mitchell was not overjoyed at being assigned to the *59*. He told us, "Kennedy was a fine young man, an excellent gentleman. Very gracious, very considerate. We got to be really close friends; we got along great with no problems. But I didn't think much of the *59*. It was not what I was trained for. I wanted a torpedo boat. I was very surprised that they put Jack on the *59*. But he was an excellent guy, and they thought it would take somebody like that to put this sort of thing over. But I really didn't like it too well."

Among the enlisted men from the *PT-21* were first class gunnersmate W. Glen "Chris" Christiansen; second class gunnersmate Shirley Nolan King, a "hillbilly" from Kentucky; an older (thirty-two years) Texan, and the radioman, Vivian Francis Scribner, also called "Pappy." Chris Christiansen and Pappy Scribner had joined the Navy before the war. They were both serving on the *West Virginia* when she was sunk at Pearl Harbor, after which they volunteered for PT's and wound up on Cluster's *21*.

Chris Christiansen was only twenty-one years old, but because he was the senior topside man in rating, he automatically became the *59*'s boat chief. We found him living in Atlanta, Georgia, where he is a home builder, and talked by telephone. He told us:

> My initial impression of Jack Kennedy was that he was a fine man. I liked him very much. He was real skinny, and very young-looking. He always had a good rapport with the crew. He kept to himself, mostly to keep from getting too involved with us, I suppose. But he'd come down to the crew's quarters every night and sit around and have a cup of coffee, then go back to his stateroom

and write letters. He was easy to be with. A good officer in that he knew how to handle men. Very tactful with discipline, never brutal or difficult. We'd have our run-ins once in a while, but he was always a hell of a man about it. He had lost the *109* and he was very gung ho. I think he felt compelled to get in there and knock hell out of the Japs as bad as he could. It was like a vendetta or a revenge thing.

Since the *59* would have a larger crew than normal—to man her many guns—Al Cluster decided she should also have a third officer. The man he picked was Robert Lee "Dusty" Rhoads, a newcomer to PT boats and Squadron Two who had survived the sinking of his ship, the U.S.S. *Aludra* in the Solomons. Rhoads is now the captain of a merchant marine ship. We wrote him and the next time his ship called in the States, he telephoned. He said, "What impressed me most about Jack then was that so many of the men that had been on the *109* had followed him to the *59*. It spoke well of him as a leader, I thought."

The assignment of both Mitchell and Rhoads to the *59* caused an administrative problem. Rhoads was senior to Mitchell by date of rank. Yet Mitchell, a graduate of Melville, who had commanded the old *PT–21*, deserved, on account of his training and his experience, to be exec. This set up a strained relationship between Rhoads and Mitchell. In the logbooks, both men are listed as exec. What happened, in fact, was that Kennedy considered Mitchell his exec. Rhoads remained more or less in limbo. When we asked Mitchell about Rhoads and Rhoads about Mitchell, both men fell silent, as though unwilling to discuss their relationship. Mitchell actually said, "Mr. Rhoads? I never did get to know the gentleman."

From our interviews with seven of the men who served on the *59*, we gained the impression that the final crew was composed of three blocs: the two *59* holdovers; the four or five so-called "battleship sailors" from the *PT–21*; and the five *109* men. The blocs never really meshed as a social group, as the crews of other PT boats did.

There was an odd belief about—and among—the *59* crew. At first it was considered a joke, but later, in combat, it preyed on the minds of the superstitious. The story was that "all but one" (as Jack would put it in a letter home) of the crew had been previously "sunk" on other vessels. The story was not true: Mitchell had not been sunk, nor had Kowal, Drewitch, or Drawdy—who were not on *109* when it was lost—and the holdovers, Homer Facto and Ed Servatius, had not been sunk. But a large percentage of the crew *had* been sunk: Jack, Mauer, and Maguire from the *109,* Rhoads from the *Aludra*, Christiansen and Scribner and other battleship sailors from the *West Virginia* and other vessels at Pearl Harbor.

The logbook of the *59* for September is missing, so her precise movements for that month cannot be charted. However, the boat chief, Christiansen, recalled that soon after September 1, they took her over to Guadalcanal for the major conversion work to gunboat. They moored her alongside a repair ship. Kennedy and the crew commuted each day from Tulagi (Florida Island) to Guadalcanal to carry out the conversion work. Some nights they slept on the repair ship.

It was hot work. First they stripped away the *59*'s four torpedo tubes and the torpedo firing gear. Then they installed an Army semi and full-automatic 40 mm cannon on the bow and another on the stern. Next came batteries of twin .50 caliber machine guns—three mounts on the port side, three on the starboard side. In addition, two more twin .50 calibers were installed in mounts up behind the cockpit. Finally, they mounted two twin .30 caliber machine guns at the forward end of the cockpit, port and starboard. In all, twelve mounts.

If the *59* was to approach and engage enemy barges at close quarters, there was an obvious need to provide protection—or shields—for the gunners. This became a problem because armor plate is heavy. They had got rid of 9,000 pounds by discarding the four torpedo tubes and the torpedoes, but the installation of twelve guns had offset much of that loss, and the result was there wasn't much weight allowance for armor plate. So they chose a lightweight plate for the guns. Rhoads told us, "One day Jack and Lennie Thom and I went out to test the armor plate. We set a sheet of it in a remote area, then we fired fifty-caliber machine gun bullets at it. Well, it was too thin. Shooting dead on, we riddled it like Swiss cheese. I mean, it wasn't worth a damn. But we went ahead with the shields anyway. They could ward off a glancing shot and they were good for morale."

But the crew wasn't fooled. They knew the armor plate was virtually useless. Said Scribner, "There was a big gap in the shields where the twin fifties stuck through. Hell, anything could have come through the gap and blown you in half." And more: within the weight allowance, there was no room to put armor plate around the gasoline tanks and engine rooms. Thus, the *59* (and her sister ships, the *60* and *61*) were as vulnerable to enemy fire as any ordinary PT boat. Nonetheless, the conversion work continued.

During September, while the *59* was undergoing conversion, Jack spent his nights in his hut on Florida Island or on the repair ship writing many letters—to his family, to girlfriends, and to old and close friends who were scattered all over the world and who wrote to him when they read about *PT–109* in the newspapers. We found three hitherto unpublished letters from Jack to his family at the Kennedy Library. From interviews and other sources we collected several others. These letters give a good feeling for Jack's post-*109* mood.

We gather from Rose's book that Jack kept up a more-or-less steady correspondence with his favorite sister, Kick. In June of that year (1943), Kick and her roommate, Betty Coxe, had given up the Washington apartment and joined the Red Cross. Kathleen had gone to London, Betty told us, to pursue Billy Hartington. Betty had gone to the 34th Infantry Division and would soon be serving in the front lines (and mud) in Italy. Rose published several of Kathleen's letters, but not Jack's to Kathleen. On July 29, Kathleen wrote Jack:

> Billy is just the same, a bit older, a bit more ducal, but we get on as well as ever. It is queer as he is so unlike anyone I have ever known at home or anyplace really. Of course I know he would never give in about the religion, and he knows I never would. It's all rather difficult as he is very, very fond of me and as long as I am about he'll never marry. However much he loved me I can easily understand his position. It's really too bad because I'm sure I would be a most efficient Duchess of Devonshire in the postwar world, and as I'd have a castle in Ireland, one in Scotland, one in Yorkshire, and one in Sussex I could keep my old nautical brothers in their old age. But that's the way it goes . . . I really can't understand why I like Englishmen so much, as they treat one in quite an offhand manner and aren't really as nice to their women as Americans, but I suppose it's just that sort of treatment that women really like. That's your technique, isn't it?

Kick, Rose writes, found out about the *109* disaster—and the rescue—from the London newspapers. On August 24 she wrote her mother, giving her reaction. "Of course the news about Jack is the most exciting I've ever heard. There wasn't a very big piece in the English newspapers but quite enough for me to gather that he really did big stuff. I rang up Mr. Raymond Daniell at the New York *Times* (London Bureau) and he told me where I could read all about it in last week's *Times*. . . ."

About that time Jack was writing the third of the five letters to his family that we saw at the Kennedy Library. His parents received it on September 12. It was retyped (we think) and distributed to the other children. It is the only letter we have ever seen giving Jack's reaction to the *PT–109* incident—"a completely black time." The "show" Jack refers to in the third paragraph was one the ambassador was then backing on Broadway, *Another Love Story*. Text:

DEAR MOTHER & DAD:

Something has happened to Squadron Air Mail—none has come in for the last two weeks. Some chowder-head sent it to the wrong island. As a matter of fact, the papers you have been sending out have kept me up to date. For an old paper, the *New York Daily News* is by far the most interesting.

I saw where . . . Chuck Spaulding [sic], who roomed with George Mead, has published his book "Love at First Flight." It's dedicated to George and is the story of his (Chuck's) pre-flight training. It's supposed to be excellent. Would you send it out?

I see where the show is going to be produced. I'm sorry it isn't going to be a musical. I'm just about ready to come back and laugh for a week with a lot of chorus girls. I also saw where Bunny Waters had received a diamond bracelet from an unknown admirer—who one week later in the same column, turned out to be Pal Jolsie. I guess her heart still belongs to Mammie. Bunny sent me her picture with a loving inscription and she is now my No. 1 pin-up, now that Miss Angela Green's picture is buried deep in the heart of Ferguson Passage.

In regard to things here—they have been doing some alterations on my boat and have been living on a repair ship. Never before realized how badly we have been doing on our end although I always had my suspicions. First time I've seen an egg since I left the States.

As I told you, Lennie Thom, who used to ride with me, has now got a boat of his own and the fellow who was going to ride with me has just come down with ulcers. (He's going to the States and will call you and give you all the news. Al Hamn.) We certainly would have made a red-hot combination. Got most of my old crew except for a couple who are being sent home, and am extremely glad of that. On the bright side of an otherwise completely black time was the way that everyone stood up to it. Previous to that I had become somewhat cynical about the American as a fighting man. I had seen too much bellyaching and laying off. But with the chips down—that all faded away. I can now believe—which I never would have before—the stories of Bataan and Wake. For an American it's got to be awfully easy or awfully tough. When it's in the middle, then there's trouble. It was a terrible thing though, losing those two men. One had ridden with me for as long as I had been out here. He had been somewhat shocked by a bomb that had landed near the boat about two weeks before. He never really got over it; he always seemed to have the feeling that something was going to happen to him. He never said anything about being put ashore—he didn't want to go—but the next time we came down the line I was going to let him work on the base force. When a fellow gets the feeling that he's in for it, the only thing to do is to let him get off the boat because strangely enough, they always seem to be the ones that do get it. I don't know whether it's just coincidence or what.

He had a wife and three kids. The other fellow had just come aboard. He was only a kid himself.

It certainly brought home how real the war is—and when I read the papers from home and how superficial is most of the talking and thinking about it. When I read that we will fight the Japs for years if necessary and will sacrifice hundreds of thousands if we must—I always like to check from where he is talking—it's seldom out here. People get so used to talking about billions of dollars and millions of soldiers that thousands of dead sounds like drops in the bucket. But if those thousands want to live as much as the ten I saw—they should measure their words with great, great care. Perhaps all of that won't be necessary—and it can all be done by bombing.

Has Joe left yet—I hope he's still around when I get back. Saw Jack Pierrepont the other day who had received a letter from Marion Kingsland (of Palm Beach) who reported Joe in New York with two of "the most beautiful English girls she had ever seen." I hope, if Joe is planning to leave, he will leave a complete program with the names and numbers of the leading players.

We have a new Commodore here—Mike Moran—former captain of the *Boise*—and a big harp if there ever was one. He's fresh out from six months in the States and full of smoke and vinegar and statements like—it's a privilege to be here and we would be ashamed to be back in the States—and we'll stay here ten years if necessary. That all went over like a lead balloon. However, the doc told us yesterday that Iron Mike was complaining of headaches and diarrhea—so we look for a different tune to be thrummed on that harp of his before many months.

Love,
JACK

P.S. Got camera and Reading glasses. Thanks. Summer beginning and it's getting hot as the devil hence letter blurred. If you should see Mrs. Luce would you tell her that her lucky piece came through for me. I understand she has five of them herself. At their present rate of luck production, there is no telling where it will all end.

About this time, September 10, Kick wrote Jack a letter from London. It is included in Rose's book. Excerpt: "Goodness I was pleased with your letter. Ever since reading the news in all the newspapers over here I have been worried to death about you. All sorts of people have rung up about it and sent congratulations. I read the clipping in the *New York Times* but long to hear the whole story. Am sure Mrs. Luce is blaming your survival on her medal. . . ."

During that summer, the ambassador had met, through Arthur Krock, a *Reader's Digest* editor named Paul Palmer. Palmer's papers are now on file at the Yale Library. Through the kindness of the chief research archivist, Judith A. Schiff, we obtained copies of correspondence between the ambassador and Palmer. It indicated that the ambassador was then trying to write an article on "economics"—something about the world economy, we think. But neither the ambassador nor Palmer could ever get the article in shape, the correspondence indicated. During this work in New York the ambassador also met the *Digest's* editors, DeWitt and Lila Wallace.

We believe that following the episode, Jack wrote his father a very long letter describing most of what had happened. This letter has never been released. The ambassador, in turn, we believe, sent Jack's letter to Paul Palmer at the *Digest*, with the idea of promoting a story in the *Digest* on Jack and the *PT-109*. This is indicated by a letter dated September 10 from the ambassador to Palmer in Palmer's correspondence at the Yale Library. Text:

MY DEAR MR. PALMER:

Thank you for your note in which you returned the copy of Jack's letter. I'm sure he'll be delighted to talk with you when he gets back. If the Navy would let him tell the complete story, he should have a good one then.

I expect to be in New York, at the Waldorf Towers, around the 21st, and will be between there and Washington for the next two and one-half weeks. Let's get together then!

Sincerely yours,
JOE KENNEDY

This was the first important step of many that the ambassador would take to get the *109* story into the mass-circulation *Digest*. As we shall show later, this effort finally paid off. But it wasn't easy, and a less persistent man might have given up.

In his letter to the family, Jack had alluded to his friend Chuck Spalding and his book. We had discussed this with Chuck in our interview. He told us:

After joining the Naval Air Arm in Anacostia, outside Washington, I was sent to the Naval Air Training Center in Corpus Christi, Texas. I was a terrible pilot, or, I should say, a terrible student, and had a terrible time getting through.

While I was at Corpus Christi, a fellow from Lake Forest I knew named Otis Carney and I went to see one of those terrible war movies. Otis was having problems, too. He'd been kicked out of training. So we decided to write a funny book about it—just for fun. It was a joint thing but I did all the writing. We were sent to separate bases, and I'd call Otis on the telephone. It took me about six months. My father suggested I send the book to a friend of his, Hardwick Moseley at Houghton-Mifflin Company. He published it in the fall of 1943. It sold about one hundred thousand copies. It was the biggest seller of its kind until that really fine book, *Mr. Roberts,* came out.

I exchanged a lot of letters with Jack in the Pacific—lighthearted, kidding letters—but unfortunately, I didn't keep his.

Later we checked the Spalding-Carney book, *Love at First Flight,* from the library and read it. The dedication to the dead George Mead concludes: ". . . who might have laughed some himself." He certainly would have, we thought. The book is a deft, funny account of an inept student undergoing Naval Aviation training—from enlistment to final graduation. Carney, Spalding told us, went on to publish many more things. Spalding, who had actually done all the writing on this book, did not.

While Jack was working at Guadalcanal on the conversion of the 59, he sought out and found George Mead's grave. Then he wrote George's mother a letter she included in the commemorative book to her son. Text:

I think you all know how we felt about George. He inspired a tremendous respect that was unusual in as young a fellow as he was. Though I know that it was a terrible thing for him to die—yet I think it can be truthfully said that George had a fuller life in his relatively short one than most people have in a much longer time.

That last weekend down at Aiken when he came home he seemed really happy in what he was doing—and he took a tremendous pride in his job. He was doing a job which he really believed in and wanted to do—and he did it with the same sincerity that characterized everything he said or did.

Went over the other day and visited George's grave—he is buried in the very first row—down near the beach where they landed. On his grave carved into an aluminum plate is "Lt. George Mead—August 20, 1942. A great leader of men—God Bless him." It was really moving to see his grave there when the last time I saw him was down in Aiken.

Jack also exchanged several letters with Inga Arvad who was in Hollywood about this time. Her son Ronald McCoy showed us three letters during our interview, and read portions of one of them into the tape. One was similar to the letter to Mrs. Mead—all about visiting George's grave.

Inga had much exciting personal news to report. Sheilah Graham, the famous Hollywood gossip columnist (and later author of a book about her relationship with F. Scott Fitzgerald) had married, had a baby, and wanted to spend some time in England. John Wheeler, her boss at North American Newspaper Alliance, which syndicated her column, had offered Inga the job in Hollywood as Sheilah's replacement.

Jack wrote her on September 26. It was a portion of this letter which Ronald McCoy read into the tape recorder during our interview. Jack seemed in a lugubrious mood:

Inga Binga. I'll be glad to see you again. I'm tired now because we are riding every night and sleeping is tough in the daytime but I've been told they are sending some of us home to form a new squadron in a couple of months. I've had a great time here, everything considered, but I'll be just as glad to get away for a little while. I used to have a feeling that no matter what happened I'd live through. It's a funny thing that as long as you have that feeling you seem to get through. I've lost that feeling lately. As a matter of fact, I don't feel badly about it. If anything happens to me I have this knowledge that if I live to be 100 I could only improve the quantity of my life, not the quality. This sounds gloomy as hell but you are the only person I'd say it to anyway. As a matter of fact, knowing you has been the brightest part of an extremely bright 26 years. . . .

He was also writing other girlfriends. During our interview, Charlotte McDonnell told us, "I got a letter from Jack from the South Pacific. When I opened it up, I saw it wasn't meant for me. He had written two letters and got the envelopes mixed up. The salutation was 'Dearest ————.' She must have been some starlet."

He wrote to Angela Greene, but she has none of the letters.

According to Hank Searls's book, *The Lost Prince*, about this time Joe Junior was en route to England. He had been assigned to U.S. Fairwing 7, the first U.S. outfit to be attached to the Royal Air Force Coastal Command. He would fly radar-equipped patrol bombers at night on antisubmarine missions. Kathleen was looking forward to his arrival.

On the way over, Joe Junior stopped at Hyannis Port to say good-bye and to join in the celebration of his father's fifty-fifth birthday on September 6. He found a big crowd down from Boston, including a judge and the former Boston police commissioner, Joseph Francis Timilty, who was a close pal of the ambassador's. Searls writes that during the dinner, the judge raised a glass and proposed a toast: "To Ambassador Joe Kennedy, father of our hero, our *own* hero, Lieutenant John F. Kennedy of the United States Navy."

Searls goes on to say that Joe Junior, on the point of going overseas to risk his own neck, was put out that he had not been included in the toast. Later that night, Timilty, who shared the bedroom with him, could hear him "crying in the other bed."

We thought this might have been overdrawn, but Timilty, now living in retirement in Miami, not only confirmed the story, but strengthened it. He said the toast had put Joe Junior in a perfect rage. He sat on the bed clenching and unclenching his fists and said, "By God, *I'll* show them." Timilty believed that Jack's new-won fame—and the snub during the toast—led to Joe Junior's tragic end a year later, when he volunteered for the flight that killed him.

Jack must have written Joe a letter bringing him up to date. That letter has not been published, but portions of a letter from Joe to Jack, written from England, appear in *The Lost Prince:*

> I understand that anyone who was sunk got thirty days' survivor leave. How about it? Pappy was rather indignant that they just didn't send you back right away. . . . Delighted to find you in such good health and such anticipation of the pleasures which await you in the Big City [New York]. I know that you will be disappointed to hear that before leaving I succeeded in dispersing my first team in such various points that it will be impossible to cover all the territory. If you give me a rough idea of your itinerary I will try to fit in a few enjoyable evenings for you en-route. If you ever get around Norfolk, you will get quite a welcome if you mention the magic name of Kennedy, so I advise you to go incognito.

Searls says that Joe talks of a girlfriend of Jack's he had met: ". . . just after your burst into the front pages. She doesn't think you will even speak to her now. She was looking extremely well, having taken off about 15 pounds. I was tempted to take her out myself but knowing how you feel about that sort of thing and knowing what a swell job you are doing in winning the war I decided to lay off."

20

Gunboat #1

THE conversion of the *59* (or *Gunboat #1* as she was sometimes grandly called) and her sister ships proceeded very slowly. One reason, Cluster recalled, was that the approval for the armor plate got bogged down in red tape at Halsey's headquarters. Another was that the repair ship had higher-priority work: battle-damaged destroyers and cruisers. Then there were other refinements that caused some delay: installation of a radar set and a smoke generator.

Meanwhile, the Allied drive northward through the Solomons toward Rabaul continued unabated. Vella Lavella, invaded on August 15, was an easy landing, but the leapfrogging of Kolombangara and its 10,000 Japanese troops created a special problem. The Japanese were now withdrawing those forces at night by barges. They had even, rather boldly, set up a barge-staging base on northeast Vella Lavella, which made securing Vella Lavella more difficult.

During the month of September, Warfield's Lumbari-based PT force, swelled by the arrival of Squadron Eleven, went out night after night to break up the barge traffic. Bulkley reports in *At Close Quarters,* that the Lumbari boats found and attacked twenty-eight barges. Two PT's, *118* and *172,* grounded on Vella Lavella on September 6 and had to be destroyed to prevent capture. The crews were saved. The skippers claimed some sinkings, but these were doubtful. The majority of the barges got through. Halsey sent in Arleigh Burke's destroyers to help. They, too, claimed many doubtful sinkings. In the end, historian Samuel Eliot Morison estimated, about 9,000 of the 10,000 Japanese troops on Kolombangara got through to Choiseul and Bougainville to fight again.

All the while, ground forces were closing in on the barge-staging base on Vella Lavella. In support of this drive, on September 15, the PT's staged another harrowing daylight raid on the north coast of Vella Lavella. Surprisingly, they met no opposition and managed to set afire five barges. It was one of the most significant contribution PT's had made to the war effort since Guadalcanal. On September 25 LeRoy Taylor, commanding Squadron Eleven, set up an advanced PT base at Lambu Lambu Cove on the northeast coast of Vella Lavella. On September 26 *PT–156* finally shot down the first Japanese float plane. This feat led Halsey to comment in a dispatch, "Hydrant sprinkles dog."

The Japanese made one last effort to reinforce the barge-staging base on Vella Lavella. On the night of October 6-7 they sent a big Express from Rabaul: ten destroyers transporting about 700 soldiers. Halsey dispatched six destroyers to intercept it. Three of these came too late, but the other three attacked, in what came to be called the Battle of Vella Lavella. U.S. forces sank one destroyer, *Yugumo,* but they lost the battle. One of the U.S. destroyers, *Chevalier,* was sunk; the other two, *Selfridge* and *O'Bannon,* were severely damaged and nearly sunk.

On the morning after this battle, October 7, some PT's cruised into the waters north of Vella Lavella, looking for survivors. One of these was the *163,* commanded by Edward Kruse. One of the survivors of *PT-109,* Raymond Albert, was now serving on the *163.* The PT's picked up seventy-eight survivors of the *Yugumo;* Kruse alone got thirty-six. Albert was assigned to help guard them. One of the Japanese grabbed Albert's machine gun and shot him in the head, killing him instantly and wounding another sailor. Albert was the third of the thirteen *PT-109* crewmen to die by accident or violence—after Kirksey and Marney. Several more would (Kennedy, Thom, Drewitch—the last-mentioned killed by a falling tree) leading to a superstition that they would all die that way. When Ross suffered his motorcycle accident in November, 1965, it was believed for a time that he, too, would die. John Maguire told us, "But he lived, thank God. Then, a little later, Johnston died by natural causes, breaking the damned cycle."

The *59* logbooks for October and November are preserved in the National Archives. They reveal that by about October 1, most of the conversion work was finished. From October 2 to October 8, she was in Tulagi. On the 2nd and 3rd, Jack took her out for a trial run off Savo Island. On the 5th, 6th, and 7th she was in drydock. On the 8th, Jack got under way for publicity photos.

During these long weeks on Guadalcanal and Tulagi, Jack's friends, new and old, dropped by to visit: Red Fay, Barney Ross, Johnny Iles, Joe Atkinson, Whizzer White, Lennie Thom. Red Fay wrote in his book:

His tent was set up in the back of the base, almost in the jungle. There he would conduct informal seminars, which resembled radio discussion shows. We talked about foreign policy, politics, military strategy, military leadership, education and—infrequently, because we tried to keep them out of the discussions—girls. Jack always emphasized that we had no right to complain about political decisions unless we exercised some leadership in local or national politics. . . . Barney and I made book in 1943 that someday Jack

Kennedy would be President of the United States. We set the odds at ten thousand to one, because he was still out in the war zone, his health was poor, he was young, and unforeseen circumstances could make it impossible for him to reach the white House.

The football player from Amherst, Jim Reed, whom Jack had met and become friends with during the voyage to the South Pacific on the troopship *Rochambeau*, had taken Jack's advice and volunteered for PT boats. He wound up in one of the zaniest projects in the area. This duty removed him from the mainstream of PT activity and he saw Jack only occasionally. He told us:

> That fall I was assigned to an unusual Marine outfit called the Beach Jumper. What we did was this: we put some broadcasting gear—some loudspeakers and amplifiers—on a PT boat. Then we had some records that sounded just like an invasion. We'd creep up to a Jap coast in the PT boat in the dark, then turn on the electronic gear. The idea was to make the Japs think this was an invasion and draw them there. Then, of course, the real invasion would go in elsewhere. I stayed with that outfit until the middle of 1944— then I got malaria and I went home.

By October 9 apparently, the *59* was judged ready for combat. On that day she left Tulagi with Jack at the helm and headed for the forward area. She stopped at Guadalcanal and the Russells, remaining overnight. On October 10 she reached Lumbari. She stayed there for the next eight days, making more trial runs and conducting gun tests. During these, she developed a bad center shaft—it needed new bearings—and the prop kept falling off, Homer Facto recalled.

By now the new advance base at Lambu Lambu Cove on Vella Lavella had been operational for about three weeks. According to the *59* logbook, on October 18 Jack departed Lumbari for Lambu Lambu. The logbook does not describe the route, but we guessed that Kennedy probably went up through Ferguson Passage, into Blackett Strait. If so, he left Gizo (now occupied by U.S. troops) on his port hand. Traveling these familiar waters in broad daylight no doubt brought back memories of Bird Island, Olasana, and Naru-Gross to Jack and the other *109* survivors. By 4:30 P.M. the gunboat was moored at the new base, ready for combat.

The Lambu Lambu base, established by LeRoy Taylor, commanding Squadron Eleven three weeks before, was then commanded by a reservist, Craig C. "Snuffy" Smith, commander of Squadron Six. PT's from Squadrons Eleven, Ten, Six, and others were basing there. And now, once again, there was a lone representative of Squadron Two—the *59*.

By all odds, the Lambu Lambu base was the most primitive of all the PT forward bases. There was a dock and a few tents (one with a radio headquarters) and not much else. Refueling had to be done by hand from fifty-five-gallon drums. The place was hot and humid, infested with flies, lizards, and rats. The men slept topside on the boats or in tents along the edge of the water. Mitchell slung a hammock topside—the envy of all, Rhoads remembers. Everyone was on the alert for Japanese stragglers from the now-defunct barge-staging base. Scribner recalled that the Kentucky hillbilly, Shirley Nolan King, set up a sophisticated still in the jungle to distill the torpedo alcohol for drinking purposes. "That was one place we had a social meshing of the crew," he said.

About this time, Jack wrote the fourth of the letters to his family that we saw. It was received by them on November 1. Text:

DEAR FAMILY:

Will send this to New York as I imagine you will have left the Cape by the time this gets to you. Not much news to report but doing business in the same old stand.

Tough accident happened the other day. One of the boys who had ridden with me got killed. They picked up some Jap prisoners and he went forward to the part of the boat to give one of them a drink of water—as they had been floating around all night. He reached out his canteen—the Jap sprang forward—grabbed a tommy gun he held in the other hand, and in spite of the fact that he had four slugs poured into him, shot the boy. It is tough to go through what he went through and then get it that way—but you just can't fool around with these babies. They're murderous.

Got a real good boat now and a top crew—all very experienced men—and it helps a lot.

Can't tell now when I shall get back—will probably be here till they clean up this area—but I imagine Dad heard that from Wilson. Feeling O.K. though.

Got promoted on the last [list?]—purely routine—and am now a full Lieutenant. (Mother, you can look that up on your little chart—it's the same as a Captain in the Army.)

Tell all the kids that I enjoy all their letters and while I don't answer them sometimes individually, as there is so little news that I'm allowed to write, all of the letters are tremendously appreciated.

How's the show? If it stays on till I get back it should have a great run.

Love,
JACK

According to the *59* logbooks, Jack retained command of the boat for the next month, October 18 to November 18. In that month they made thirteen patrols from Lambu Lambu, all to the bypassed island of Choiseul close by. Their primary mission was to interdict Japanese barges. These patrols are carelessly documented in all three Kennedy Navy books. For example, Tregaskis includes some log excerpts, but dates them incorrectly. To reconstruct the patrols and other events of the month, we relied on the logbooks and action reports from the National Archives, and on interviews with the seven members of the *59* crew and several other officers who were associated with Kennedy at Lambu Lambu during this month.

The *59* went on her first war patrol as a gunboat on the very night she arrived at Lambu Lambu, October 18/19. She was part of a six-boat unit, composed of two boats from Squadron Ten (Bill Battle's *171* and Phil Potter's *169*) and three from Squadron Eleven (*177, 180, 183*), divided into two sections.

Kennedy's section, "George," which included the *59, 169,* and *183,* was commanded by the exec of Squadron Eleven, Jack E. Gibson, a Naval Academy graduate. He told us that one of the first things he observed that night about the *59* was the lack of cohesion in the crew:

> I went out that night just to see how Kennedy would do. I noticed that there was something different about his boat. There was a definite *rank* structure. The captain, the other officers, and then the rest of the men. You didn't find the bond that you saw on the rest of the boats. Kennedy sort of separated himself from the others, like the captain of a cruiser or a destroyer might. If you told the captain of a destroyer to put a crew aboard a motor torpedo boat and start operating, that's the way they operated.

The patrol got under way well after dark at 9 P.M. On the way over, the *59* developed engine trouble and she had to lay to while repairs were made. By 11 the boats were on station off Redman Island, off the southern coast of Choiseul. It was a bright moonlight night. Jack's radioman, Scribner, watched the green screen of the radar set, keeping a sharp watch for float planes. The *183* cruised on the starboard quarter of the *59,* the *169* on the port quarter.

At about thirty minutes after midnight, the formation was attacked by a Japanese float plane, undetected on the primitive radar set. It came out of nowhere and dropped two bombs. They fell about three hundred yards astern of the formation. No damage. No injuries.

The three boats responded aggressively; they opened fire. Kennedy's senior gunnersmate, Christiansen, got in a few rounds from his station at the bow 40 mm. But none of the boats hit the plane. It went away.

The formation cruised close to the coast of Choiseul. They saw no barges or other targets. Then, while returning to base at high speed, at 3:40 A.M., another float plane, also undetected by radar, dropped several bombs into the formation. Two of these landed only fifteen feet off the bow of *183*. The shrapnel ripped holes in her hull, but fortunately there were no injuries. All three boats fired back. The *59* responded with a deafening fusillade: both bow and stern 40 mm cannons, and several of the .50 caliber machine guns. "Apparently no hits," Jack wrote in his log. After that, the group returned to Lambu Lambu, arriving at 5:40 A.M.

It was a disappointing first patrol, engine failure and two attacks by float planes, undetected by radar. (It was probably a mistake to run home at high speed, kicking up a phosphorescent wake.) No enemy barges. In all, a night of frustration. It would go on like that the whole month.

Essentially, the problem was there were so few barges on Choiseul. During daylight hours, Halsey's fighters raked the island in air strikes. They shot up villages and whatever they could see floating in the coves and rivers. We could find no accurate intelligence figures, but our guess, based on our interviews, was there were only a handful of barges left. At night, they operated with extreme care. Rhoads told us, "The *59* experiment was a failure. The theory was to provide one gunboat with each section of PT's. The gunboats, screened by the PT's, would move in and attack the barges. Unfortunately, by the time we got the three boats converted, the barge threat was gone. We never fought anymore. We only - *certainly* saw barges on one night. They were coming out of Choiseul and they went right back in. So everything we were built for—barge fighting— we never did."

The logbook shows that in the following week, the *59* made three more patrols to Choiseul in company with other boats. Nothing noteworthy occurred on the first two. On the third, October 25-26 (in bad weather), the formation was attacked by a float plane at about 3 A.M. It dropped a parachute flare, then two bombs which, the *59* log reported, "missed the boat by 150 yards." Fortunately, there were no casualties, no damage to the boat. Because of the poor weather they could not see the plane and *59* did not try to fire at it.

Meanwhile, the Allied drive on Rabaul moved onward. The next target: Bougainville. D-day: November 1. (See Map No. 7.)

In preparation for the invasion, Halsey's planners ordered up heavy air strikes on Rabaul. Most of these were carried out by MacArthur's air general, George C. Kenney. On October 12 he launched a massive raid of 349 bombers and followed up with daily air strikes. Later, Halsey gave a hand with carrier-based aircraft. These air attacks did much damage at Rabaul, and to the aircraft and ships which had been sent there to help stop the northward Allied march.

The invasion of Empress Augusta Bay, Bougainville, was preceded by two diversionary attacks, launched October 27. A force of 725 Marines, led by Lieutenant Colonel Victor H. "Brute" Krulak, landed on Choiseul. His mission was to make noise and convince the Japanese that Choiseul was the prime objective. A second force landed on the Treasury Islands, which were defended by only about 225 Japanese. Its mission was to seize those islands, establish an airfield and staging base, and make the Japanese think the next step would be Shortland Island. Both diversions achieved their aims.

When Krulak's diversionary force landed on Choiseul on the night of October 27-28, the PT's at Lambu Lambu, of course, had to suspend barge-hunting operations against that part of Choiseul to avoid becoming entangled with friendly forces. PT's went over, taking station north of Krulak to act as a screen, but not the 59. She remained in port from October 26 to October 30, on standby or alert status in case Krulak needed her support.

This must have been frustrating and discouraging for Jack. They were really not accomplishing anything. In four patrols, two weeks' operations, they had not found a target worthy of one bullet, other than the float plane on the first patrol. On October 30 Jack wrote his family the fifth of the letters that we saw at the Kennedy Library. Text:

DEAR DAD:

How is everything? Did the show go over?

It looks now as though—unless it has a considerable run—I won't get a chance to see it. They will not send anyone back while there is fighting in this area. When it's over I'll get back. As a matter of fact, I am in a bad spot for getting out as I am now Captain of a gun-boat. It's the first one they've ever had of its type. It's a former P.T. and is very interesting. It fights all small Jap auxiliaries—which the Japs are using now instead of bigger stuff. Have a picked crew—all volunteers—and all very experienced. Every man but one has been sunk at least once, and they have all been in the boats for a long time. It was sort of a dubious honor to be given the first, so I will have to stick around and try to make a go of it.

Feeling fine, but after this present fighting is over will be glad to get home. When I do get out of here you'll find that you have a new permanent fixture around that Florida pool. I'll just move from it to get into my sack. Don't worry at all about me—I've learned to duck—and have learned the wisdom of the old naval doctrine of keeping your bowels (open)—your mouth shut—and never volunteering.

Love to all,
JACK

On the day Jack wrote that letter, Halsey's huge invasion forces were bearing down on Empress Augusta Bay, Bougainville. The PT's at Lambu Lambu put to sea on security patrols (to detect and attack Expresses) and to hunt barges. During this phase the *59* made two patrols at Choiseul the nights of October 30-31 and October 31-November 1—D-Day. The first night she saw nothing worthy of noting in the log. The second night, at 11, she saw a "barge or ramp lighter." But Jack withheld fire, thinking they might be part of Krulak's diversionary forces.

When Jack returned to port on the morning of November 1, he took on fresh water but did not refuel. He last refueled at 9 A.M., October 31, taking on 1,530 gallons, filling the tanks, which held 2,000 gallons. The fact that he did not refuel the morning of November 1 would cause a minor controversy.

Homer Facto told us:

> It was a slow process to get gassed up at Lambu Lambu. There was a little YP—a barge or lighter—we called the Yippie, that brought the barrels of gas to us. It had some winches to raise the barrels and tip them so the gas would run out. Well, we couldn't get the Yippie to gas us up. I complained to Kennedy. We were on alert, to backstop the Marines on Choiseul. I said, "Mr. Kennedy, we're supposed to be able to operate at any time." He went to the office, but they told him we would *not* go out that night, so he came back and told me that. I said, "But what if we *have* to operate?" He went back again and they said no, the *59* wouldn't have to operate. So he took their word for it. And we didn't gas up; that was all.

Meanwhile, the Marines landed at Bougainville. The Japanese resisted furiously. The fighting on the beaches was bloody. Late on the afternoon of D-Day, November 1, Rabaul sent the biggest Express anyone could remember: four cruisers and six destroyers. Its aim was to destroy the landing ships. Halsey met it with a slightly larger force—four cruisers and eight destroyers. The two forces joined battle in the early hours of November 2 in what was called the Battle of Empress Augusta Bay. Halsey won. His force sank the cruiser *Sandai* and a destroyer, *Hatsukaze*. No Allied ships were lost.

That night, November 1-2, the *59* remained in port.

When Halsey's forces met the Express, no doubt Kennedy and the other officers at Lambu Lambu listened to the headquarters radio, trying to find out what was going on. The group now included Art Berndtson, exec of Squadron Ten, who had come up temporarily to run operations at Lambu Lambu.

Over on Choiseul that night, "Brute" Krulak's diversionary force made plans to withdraw. But a problem arose. One of his units, an eighty-man patrol commanded by Warner T. Bigger, which Krulak had sent north from the main base, got into trouble. The native guides had led Bigger into a swamp. They became lost. Some Japanese soldiers discovered the patrol and moved in to close off their escape route to the coast. Bigger sent a call for help to Krulak.

Krulak had, as part of his force, a "navy" consisting of four LCPL's (Landing Craft, Personnel, Large). These were steel amphibious craft, designed to deliver men to beachheads. Krulak decided that Bigger should fight his way to the coast and after dusk the following evening, November 2, he would send three of the LCPL's north to pick up Bigger's men at the edge of the Warrior River.

Richard Keresey (ex-*PT-105*) had gone along on the Krulak expedition. His mission was to scout a suitable location for a PT base on the south shore of Choiseul, in case Halsey decided, after all, to invade it, or in case the Japanese withdrew. He told us that Krulak asked if PT's at Lambu Lambu could provide firepower at the Warrior River—if needed. Keresey called PT headquarters on the radio and ordered up help.

The following afternoon, Keresey's call for help reached Art Berndtson at Lambu Lambu. It seemed a situation made to order for the *59*—a gunboat. Berndtson rushed down to the dock. He said he found Jack, who had now been in port for almost a day and a half, finally refueling. Berndtson told us, "It was a hell of a place to try to refuel. All by hand. Jack had about seven hundred gallons. That was not enough to get over and back. He needed at least one thousand gallons. I asked him if he would go anyway. I was sending two other PT boats along. If Jack ran out of fuel, one of the other boats could tow him home. He was disconcerted, but he agreed to go."

The three-boat expedition set off in broad daylight. At 4:35 P.M. they left Lambu Lambu and raced toward Choiseul. Fortunately, the weather was foul: overcast and squally. No Japanese float planes attacked the formation. It arrived off Krulak's main base, Voza, at 6:15 P.M. in a rain squall. By that time, Krulak had sent three of his LCPL's north to the Warrior River, retaining one.

Keresey told us, "I went out from Voza on the LCPL and met the three PT's. Jack was absolutely astonished to see me. He said, "What the hell are *you* doing here?" A Marine officer and I got on the *59* and we headed north to the Warrior River, about fifteen miles north of us. We briefed Jack on the evacuation plan and helped show him where to go."

When this little formation reached the mouth of the Warrior River, it was dark. Bigger and his men were up to their necks in trouble. They were retreating toward the water, but the Japanese were closing in, firing from every direction. Several Americans had been killed; three were seriously wounded. The three LCPL's had gone in under heavy fire and picked up the men. When Jack arrived, they were just putting out to sea. The three PT's lay to, but they did not fire for fear of hitting friendly forces.

Going out, one of the LCPL's hit a coral head and holed her bottom. She began to sink about 250 yards offshore. Another LCPL took her in tow, but she was clearly doomed. The Marines scrambled into the other two LCPL's and scuttled the disabled craft. Kennedy then brought the 59 alongside the two overcrowded LCPL's and took aboard about ten men, including three who were seriously wounded. The little flotilla then proceeded slowly southward to Voza.

When they reached that place, the Marines on the 59, with the exception of the three badly wounded, debarked and joined Krulak. The three PT's waited around for several hours to provide assistance. The 59 was burning her precious supply of gasoline at an alarming rate. Finally, after midnight, the PT's set off for Lambu Lambu. On the way, one of the wounded, Corporal Edward James Schnell, died in Kennedy's bunk.

At 3 A.M., while en route home, according to the logbook, the 59 "exhausted gas supply." She lay to while the other two PT's threw her towing lines. Slowly—very slowly—the procession continued on to Lambu Lambu. The dead Marine was laid out on the fantail. At 8 A.M. they reached the base. The two wounded and the body were turned over to "doctor's care." That afternoon, the 59 took aboard 2,000 gallons of fuel and Kennedy apologized to Homer Facto. The boat chief, Glen Christiansen, recalled, "I remember one thing about the night we ran out of gas. We called for air cover. We were sitting out there vulnerable as hell, out of gas. As I remember, they sent us a bunch of Australian P-40's. Either four or six of them. Well, none of them came back. They all got shot down. It wasn't our fault—we'd been ordered out and they knew we'd run out of gas—but there was a big stink about it."

That same night, November 3-4, the 59 was called to action again. Krulak was ready to evacuate his main base. The Navy would take him off with three LCI's (Landing Craft, Infantry) staging from Vella Lavella. Berndtson sent seven PT's, including the 59, to escort the LCI's over and back. This operation was carried out without a hitch. Jack arrived back at base at 5:55 A.M. and promptly took on 900 gallons of fuel, topping off his tanks.

The 59 was under way for another patrol on the night of November 5-6. Whizzer White may have made this patrol. In a brief reference to this period, he told Alfred Wright of *Sports Illustrated*, "I remember riding on his boat a couple of times—that is the boat they gave him after he had lost his first boat. As a result of these encounters . . . I began to get a strong feeling about what kind of fellow he was. He proved himself to be very intelligent in the way he ran his boat, as well as cool and courageous under fire. I concluded he was a pretty solid sort of person."

In a thin biography of the late Senator Joseph R. McCarthy, Roy Cohn

writes that McCarthy, then a Marine attached to the First Marine Air
Wing on New Georgia, made two nighttime patrols from Vella Lavella
with Jack on the *59* and "got to shoot the machine guns." His source for
this statement was given as Penn T. Kimball, also a Marine on New Georgia. Kimball is now a professor of journalism at Columbia University. We
called him to check the story. He insisted it was true. Checking further,
we contacted McCarthy's Marine boss, (now) Colonel Glenn L. Todd,
USMC (Ret.). He replied:

> I have checked my flight logbook, which is one hundred percent
> accurate, and Joe McCarthy and I were in the rear area at the island of Etate from 18 October to 18 November, 1943. . . . [He]
> was a good Marine Officer and made many combat flights that he
> did not have to. He was far from a coward; in fact, he was a brave
> man. I believe that he would have gone for a ride on a PT boat if he
> had the chance, but never without telling us. . . . [And] I doubt
> that Joe met Kennedy in the South Pacific. . . .

We asked the seven men on the *59* we interviewed if they could recall
Joe McCarthy coming aboard. None did—and all said they thought they
would remember if he had. However, the query reminded Vivian Scribner
of one of the most famous incidents on *59* while Jack was her skipper. He
told us:

> One day we put out to sea with some Marine officers on board.
> That day Shirley Nolan King, the hillbilly from Kentucky, was
> really looped. I think he'd been in the boondocks at his still. He
> was standing up on the bow—or rather weaving around up there—
> holding an air-cooled Lewis machine gun. A sea gull took station
> forward of the bow at quite some distance. Jokingly, we all hollered at King—we called him Donald Duck because he could do a
> fair imitation of him—to shoot the sea gull. Still weaving, so
> looped he could hardly stand up, King raised up the Lewis and
> fired a single shot. Damned if he didn't kill that bird. Those Marines were really impressed. They said; "Man, that's some shooting!"

That night, November 5-6, the *59* patrolled in company with R. M
North on the Squadron Six boat *187,* which had an old 37 mm. They left a
7 P.M. and went to the northwest coast of Choiseul where, finally, Kennedy found action. At about 11 P.M., off Moli Island, south of Choiseu
Bay, they picked up what were believed to be three barges hugging th
coast. The two PT's converged on the targets, guns manned. When the
had them in range, they opened fire. Christiansen got off three round

from the bow 40 mm. On the *187,* North let go a couple of rounds of 37 mm. But then the barges disappeared into the darkness.

They broke off the attack, swung around, and reconnoitered Choiseul Bay. No targets. At 3 A.M. Kennedy ordered another look at Moli Island. It was now very late, ordinarily time to be heading for Lambu Lambu. But Kennedy, probably thinking of the barges that had eluded them earlier, refused to go home. They were still off Moli Island at 5:30. By then it was light.

Suddenly a lookout shouted. There were six barges along the shore! Kennedy, followed by North, swung in to attack. As they got closer, Kennedy saw that three of the barges were wrecked, but, as he wrote in his log, three were "possibly serviceable." They were evidently not manned. He gave orders to fire. The bow gunner, Christiansen, and the rear 40 mm gunner opened fire. Twenty-five rounds hit the first barge, "destroying its portside" and causing a fire. Fifteen rounds hit the second barge, destroying the bow. The third barge—400 yards away—got sixteen rounds plus twenty rounds of 37 mm from North in the *187.* It was "crippled." None of the three barges returned fire, nor was there Japanese fire from the beach.

After that, Kennedy broke off the attack and headed home, arriving at 8:30 A.M. He must have been exhilarated. It was the first time—and it would be the last time—that he had ever fired at an enemy surface craft. True, the barges were beached. They were empty. No Japanese had been killed or forced into the water. There had been no counterfire. But three "possibly serviceable" barges had been damaged.

The *59* went out again the following night, November 6-7, in company with two sections of two boats each. North, in the *187,* was assigned to Jack's two-boat section. For unexplained reasons the *59* did not leave until very late—midnight. The *187* lost touch with the *59,* became separated, and returned alone to base. Jack joined the other two boats.

They heard a plane, but fortunately it did not attack them. Finally they were all ordered home after a fruitless night of fouled-up communications and thrashing about. The *59* docked at 7 A.M. She remained in port the next four nights.

If Jack had been depressed on October 30, as the letter home indicated, we thought that by now, November 10, or thereabouts, he must have really been in the dumps. The *59* had been operational for a month now. She had made ten patrols to Choiseul, including the Krulak rescue mission. In all that time, she had seen only six barges, three wrecked, three "possibly serviceable." They had not seen a living enemy nor shot at one.

In truth, Jack was caught in a backwater. The main PT force had moved forward with the invasion of Bougainville. Robert Kelly had set up a base on Stirling Island in the Treasuries. Two days after the invasion forces landed on Bougainville, Henry Farrow, commanding Squadron Five, had

established a PT base on Puruata Island, right inside Empress Augusta
Bay. From those two places, dozens of conventional PT's were fanning
out along the coast of Bougainville, intercepting barges bringing in reinforcements. That was where the real action was. By now, most of the Japanese troops on Choiseul had slipped through to Bougainville. For all
Jack knew, Choiseul might have been completely evacuated.

Now Jack began to talk boldly to his crew about taking the 59 on a daylight raid against Choiseul. They could penetrate the coves and river
mouths, searching for barges. One of the men, Vivian Scribner, thought
that was not a bad scheme. All things considered, he did not think the risk
was too great. But others, perhaps recalling the "suicide mission" daylight raid on Kolombangara in August, which caused many PT casualties,
were less than pleased. Homer Facto told us; "If you ask me, it was stupid. You'd take the chance of losing the boat and crew. You'd have Japs
on both sides of you. You wouldn't have a chance of getting in—or out—
of that river. But I think this wild talk was mostly just that—talk, to build
their morale up and impress the higher officers. I don't think they would
have let anybody do it."

The boat chief, Glen Christiansen, recalled:

> Mr. Kennedy was very gung ho. As I said, he had this vendetta
> or revenge thing on his mind. I was concerned. Kennedy wanted to
> go up the Warrior River in daylight. We had terrific firepower, and
> could have raised hell in the river, but I had read a report on the
> Kolombangara raid where all those people got killed. The problem
> was, they got inside the river and couldn't turn around. It was real
> hairy. I couldn't see risking our lives. I felt we ought to try to do
> something to get at them, bomb them with aircraft or something,
> but let's not go up the river ourselves.

Jack's squadron commander, Al Cluster, normally at Tulagi, came by
Lambu Lambu for a visit. Christiansen, who had served under Cluster at
Pearl Harbor, went to see him—to complain about Jack's plan for a daylight raid. Cluster recalled that episode. He told us, "Jack got very wild.
Some of my old guys—Christiansen among them—said he was crazy and
would get them killed." The outcome was, Christiansen recalled, Cluster
scotched the plan. "He didn't think it was advisable to risk the men and
the boat," Christiansen told us.

So Gunboat #1 went on patrolling her backwater routinely. Between
November 11 and 16 she made three more runs to Choiseul in company
with other PT's. On the first they saw three barges standing out to sea, but
before they could get close enough to shoot, the barges ran back up the
river. On the second they saw no barges, but they concluded the patrol by
bombarding Guppy Island at the mouth of Choiseul Bay. (59 expended

seventy-five rounds of 40 mm ammo; results undetermined.) On the third they saw nothing, fired no guns.

On November 14, Jack got off a letter to his younger brother, Robert, which is reproduced in Donovan's book. According to a biography of Bobby by Margaret Laing, which contains an extract from his official naval record, Bobby, now age eighteen and in his final months at Milton Academy, joined the Naval Reserve in Boston on October 5. He would not be called up for about five more months (to a V-12 unit at Harvard) but it was the swearing-in, publicized in the Boston papers, that prompted Jack's letter—joking advice from an old salt to the new boot. Text:

Nov. 14

DEAR ROBERT,

The folks sent me a clipping of you taking the oath. The sight of you up there, just as a boy, was really moving particularly as a close examination showed that you had my checked London coat on. I'd like to know what the hell I'm doing out here, while you go stroking around in my drape coat, but I suppose that what we are out here for, or so they tell us, is so that our sisters and younger brothers will be safe and secure—frankly I don't see it quite that way—at least if you're going to be safe and secure, that's fine with me, but not in my coat brother, not in my coat. In that picture you looked as if you were going to step outside the room, grab your gun, and knock off several of the house-boys before lunch. After reading Dad's letter, I gathered that cold vicious look in your eye was due to the thought of that big blocking back from Groton. I understand that you are going to be there till Feb. 1, which is very nice because it is on the playing fields of Milton and Groton, and maybe Choate, that the seeds will be sown that in later years, and on other fields, will cause you to turn in to sick bay with a bad back or a football knee.

Well, black Robert, give those Grotties hell and keep in contact with your old broken down brother. I just took the physical examination for promotion to full Looie. I coughed hollowly, rolled my eyes, croaked a couple of times, but all to no avail. Out here, if you can breathe, you're one A. and "good for active duty anywhere" and by anywhere, they don't mean the El Morocco or the Bath and Tennis Club, they mean right where you are. See you soon, I hope.

JACK

By mid-November, the beachhead at Empress Augusta Bay was secured. In a remarkable military operation, Halsey put 35,000 men ashore and they stayed. They set up a perimeter defense and Seabees began construction of airfields for fighters and bombers. The Japanse were never able to mount an effective counterattack. Choiseul, Shortland Island, and southern Bougainville had been bypassed. Rabaul itself was now close at hand. In the coming weeks, aircraft basing from Bougainville (assisted by Halsey's carriers) would begin a systematic bombing of the base, inflicting so much damage to ships and military installations that, in the end, the decision was made to bypass Rabaul.

On the 59, some of the men, long in overseas service, began to leave her, relieved by fresh replacements. First to go were three of the "battleship" sailors who had been at Pearl Harbor nearly two years before: the boat chief, Chris Christiansen; Shirley King; and another. They were all gone by November 15, and happy to leave godforsaken Lambu Lambu. They went to Tulagi to look for transportation back to the States.

The next to leave was Jack Kennedy himself. In the 59 logbooks for November 18, there is this entry: "1430: Lt. J. Kennedy left the boat as directed by the Dr. at Lambu Lambu."

What had happened? In his October 30 letter to his father, and in the November 14 letter to Bobby, Jack had indicated that he had passed his routine physical for promotion to lieutenant and expected to remain in command of the 59 at least until all the fighting in the area was completed—that is, for many months. Four days later he was relieved of command on orders of a doctor.

Tregaskis says that by now, Jack was suffering from a variety of crippling ailments: a bad back, malaria, severe undernourishment (weight down twenty-five pounds), mental and physical "exhaustion." Whipple reports that he had a "splitting headache" and malaria. Donovan says he had malaria, his back "pained him," 'and he had "spells of feeling poorly." The disk between his fifth vertebra and his sacrum was "ruptured." Furthermore, he reports, "the abnormal strains of the crash [of *PT-109*] and the swimming had done certain lasting damage to his adrenal glands."

Were these statements true? We closely queried the seven men who served on the 59 with Jack about the state of his health at this point. None could remember that he had "malaria" or "severe undernourishment." (He was skinny, but, as we have seen, all PT men lost weight. Mitchell, for example, told us he dropped from his usual 180 to 145.) They could not recall his "exhaustion," or "splitting headache," or anything like that. On the contrary, Mitchell remembered Jack being "in excellent spirits," and Facto recollected that "he looked real good." But Mitchell, Homer Facto, Vivian Scribner, and Chris Christiansen remembered that it was a "back problem." They could not recall a specific trauma, merely, as Christiansen put it, that "it had to do with his back."

If there had been no specific trauma, no crippling incident, why, we wondered, had Jack's bad back suddenly surfaced? Had it come to light in the physical for promotion to lieutenant? If so, how? Or did Jack himself—bored with the *59* and the backwater—deliberately call attention to it to get a transfer home, as he had apparently used it to get out of Charleston, South Carolina?

In our talk with Dr. Wharton, the doctor who had examined the *109* - crew at Tulagi in August—he recalled that at about this time he was visiting Vella Lavella. (He traveled to advance bases often, he said.) He recalled seeing Jack at that place, and might well have been the doctor who performed the physical and the "Dr." alluded to in the log. He remembered that Jack had a dog named Savo and he, Wharton, had a cat named Greer Garson. Another man snapped a photograph of Wharton and Jack holding the animals.

We asked Wharton what he could recall about Jack's physical condition at the time Jack left the *59*. He could not recall malaria or the other maladies mentioned by Tregaskis, Donovan, and Whipple, but he definitely recalled a "back" problem. A "chronic" back problem. He told us:

> The X-ray machines picked up a problem with Jack's back. He had an injured intervertebral disk in the lumbar region. Not a fracture. It was what we call a chronic disk disease of the lower back. . . .
>
> Q: Chronic?
>
> A: He told us that he had had a problem with the back *before* he came to the Pacific. It was not a disabling disease, but something that, at times, could be quite painful.

When Jack left the *59*, there was a bit of a problem about just who should relieve him—Mitchell or Rhoads—since Jack had never clearly established the seniority between the two. Jack decided on Mitchell. Rhoads told us, "Jack said he had information that I would be going home soon—where he got it I don't know—and that pleased me. So I was happy to serve as exec to Mitchell temporarily." If Jack had such information, it turned out to be wrong. Rhoads would stay in the Pacific several more months, though not on the *59*. A couple of weeks after Jack left her, the *59* returned to Tulagi for upkeep. By the end of the year, Mitchell, Rhoads, and most of the original crew went to other duty—or home—and she sailed into the new year with a new crew.

When Jack officially departed the boat that day, November 18, there was no "change of command" ceremony—no official reading of orders, Mitchell recalled. Maurice Kowal (ex-*109*) remembered that Jack jotted down the names and addresses of the families of the crew and promised to telephone them with a word of cheer when he got to the States. And,

Kowal remembered, Jack made good on the promise. Vivian Scribner remembered that when Jack left, he was "weeping."

In his book, Donovan quotes a letter that gives the impression that Jack got home for Christmas with the family at Palm Beach. Not so. He went from Vella Lavella to Tulagi and remained there for several more weeks, trying to get transportation home. His naval records show that he was not officially detached until December 21. Two of his best friends, Red Fay and Johnny Iles, remembered seeing him then; Iles (and Dr. Wharton) clearly recalled he was still there at Christmas.

Wharton: "I can't remember exactly the day he left, but he was still there at Christmas. He gave me a camera his family had sent him as a Christmas present. It was a very fine camera, an Argus—or Argoflex or something—but of course we couldn't get film for it. I gave it away later."

Johnny Iles: "I had taken command of the 105 by then. For some reason, I was back at Tulagi at Christmas. I remember—and the memory is vivid—that Jack and I went to midnight mass together on the base, there in Tulagi. And it's strange, I don't remember another thing except that. What I do know, absolutely, is that we went to that mass together."

While Jack was on Tulagi, Admiral Richard S. Edwards, right-hand man to the Chief of Naval Operations, Admiral King, sent a naval speed-letter to Halsey inquiring further into the 109 loss. We obtained a copy of this letter from the Naval Historical Center. It is dated December 16. Text:

SOME QUESTIONS HAVE COME UP WHICH MAKE IT DESIRABLE THAT THE DEPARTMENT HAVE DETAILED INFORMATION CONCERNING THE LOSS OF PT-109 WHICH OCCURRED DURING THE NIGHT OF 1-2 AUGUST, 1943. THE ONLY INFORMATION NOW AT HAND IS A VERY BRIEF SUMMARY OF CERTAIN NIGHT ACTIONS ON THAT DATE. IF THERE IS ANY DETAILED ACCOUNT OF THE LOSS OF PT-109 AVAILABLE, PLEASE SEND IT TO COMMANDER IN CHIEF, UNITED STATES FLEET.

We do not know why Edwards made this request. We speculated that perhaps the recommendation for Jack's Silver Star had reached the Navy Department's Awards Board and they wanted more detailed information before proceeding. On December 30, Halsey forwarded the request to Iron Mike Moran. On January 13, William Specht, now working for Moran, forwarded a copy of the White report and two of Warfield's action reports, dealing with the night of August 1/2 when the 109 was lost, and August 7/8, when the crew was rescued.

It seems likely that a few days after Christmas, Jack found transportation back to the United States. Homer Facto, then detached from the 59, recalls "absolutely" that the last time he saw Kennedy on Tulagi, he was "determined to get air transportation." We believe that although air transportation was difficult for a lieutenant to obtain, Jack got it—perhaps with the help of Dr. Wharton or some other medical officer who could have given him some kind of air travel priority. The official naval records are mute. They show only that Kennedy was ordered to report to Portsmouth, Rhode Island, for duty at the PT school in Melville.

And so, after nine months in the South Pacific, the war service of John F. Kennedy, which would become so famous with the passing of time, drew to a close. Most of Jack's friends—Red Fay, Barney Ross, Lennie Thom, Joe Atkinson, Johnny Iles, and Jim Reed—went to New Guinea and served on for another six months. But the main war effort now focused on the Central Pacific—the invasion of Tarawa and the Marshall Islands—and the PT's sank from the news.

For the rest of his life, Jack Kennedy would be inordinately proud of, and would capitalize politically on, his war record. In the postwar years, he would hold offices in veterans' organizations and maintain close contact with many PT buddies from the Solomons, especially Red Fay and Jim Reed. In private, he would be scornful of other politicians who did not serve in the war, and encouraged reporters to look into their "war records." For example, the *Washington Post* executive editor, Ben Bradlee, recounts in his recent book *Conversations With Kennedy* (during Jack's presidency) a telephone conversation during which Jack asked if the *Post* was going to look into Nelson Rockefeller's war record. Jack said, "Where was old Nels when you and I were dodging bullets in the Solomon Islands?"

Part III
TRANSITION

21
Coming Home

MOST of the Kennedy books give the next two years of Jack's life short shrift. They say that in 1944 he returned to the States, underwent a "disk" operation, and by the end of the year had been released by the Navy because of his physical disabilities. In 1945 he undertook a career in journalism, covering the United Nations Organization opening meeting in San Francisco and the British elections, during which he cannily predicted the defeat of Winston Churchill. But journalism was too "passive" for Jack. He gave it up, wrote a brief memorial book about Joe Junior, killed on a flying mission in England, then (the legend goes), at his father's demand, he reluctantly stepped into Joe Junior's shoes and entered politics in Boston in early 1946.

That account raises interesting questions. After leaving the Navy, he had first to decide on a career. What happened to his prewar ideas for being a teacher or a specialist in international law? Was the fling at journalism a serious one or merely a lark? Did his father really demand he go into politics to fill Joe Junior's role? Or did politics naturally appeal to Jack? Most of his friends married and settled down to raise families. Why didn't Jack? To what extent did his poor health influence his decisions?

There is little at the Kennedy Library bearing on these questions and the little information in the Kennedy books is often contradictory. It is difficult merely to plot out Jack's physical whereabouts during this period. Our reading of these years is based largely on extensive interviews with dozens of people.

We do not know when Jack arrived in the United States from the Solomons. Our best guess is about January 10, 1944, and probably by air. In a letter to Red Fay written later (and reproduced in Fay's book), he says he landed in San Francisco, but remained only a few hours, heading immediately for Los Angeles by train. He did not even take time to telephone Red's father as he had promised.

Why? He had no Navy business in Los Angeles. We could find no evidence that he sought medical attention in Los Angeles. None of his close buddies were then in Los Angeles. His family were in Palm Beach for the post-Christmas season, or in schools in the East. Eunice had left Stanford. Kathleen and Joe Junior were in London.

Inga Arvad was in Los Angeles. Jack saw her as soon as he arrived, or perhaps the following day. Her son, Ronald McCoy, told us:

> She was doing the Sheilah Graham column then. She may have gone up to San Francisco to meet him. He came down and stayed several days with her. She told me that Jack looked like hell. He was so thin and drawn and out of it. He joked about the *PT–109* thing. He told her it was a question of whether they were going to give him a medal or throw him out. That was the only thing he joked about. His sense of humor was gone.
>
> The romance was over by now. He'd been out there in the war and she'd been back doing her thing in Hollywood: going to parties, meeting Hollywood people. There wasn't a hell of a lot for her and Jack to talk about. She'd been through the thing about the old man's violent objections and she just didn't want to go through it again. Her life was fine; she was having a good time. Also she could see that Jack was in no condition to make any decisions about anything. He was just worn out. So that was the end of what had happened before. . . .

In the letter to Red Fay, Jack said he was in Los Angeles "four days." Donovan writes that he "spent a couple of days with friends in Beverly Hills." While there, Donovan says, he telephoned Pappy McMahon's wife, who lived in the Los Angeles area. Jack "did not feel up to going into the city," so Mrs. McMahon drove out and spent the afternoon with Jack. She thought he looked "pale and weak." McMahon, now recovered from his burns, was still on Tulagi repairing PT engines.

While Jack was in Los Angeles, he evidently held a press conference to talk about the *PT–109* experience. Just who arranged the conference and cleared it with the Navy (if it was cleared) we were not able to determine. Nor, with one exception, were we able to track down any printed newspaper article deriving from the conference. However, in the photographic libraries of both AP and UPI, we turned up two pictures of Jack (in Navy khakis, looking thin and wan) at this conference. The AP photo was dated January 10, the UPI photo January 12.

The one newspaper story we found was a column by Inga Arvad, dated January 13. We found a reprint of it in the April, 1944, issue of the *Choate Alumni Bulletin*. We assumed—but could not confirm—that it received fairly wide distribution by Inga's syndicate, North American Newspaper Alliance. Excerpts:

LT. KENNEDY SAVES HIS MEN AS
JAPS CUT PT BOAT IN HALF.

This is the story of the 13 American men on PT Boat 109, who got closer than any others to a Japanese destroyer and of the 11 men who lived to tell about it. It is about the skipper-hero, 26-year old Lt. John F. Kennedy, son of Joseph P. Kennedy, former U.S. Ambassador to Great Britain, now on home leave, who though he saved three lives, and swam long hours through shark-infested waters to rescue his men, today says:

"None of that hero stuff about me. The real heros are not the men who return, but those who stay out there, like plenty of them do, two of my men included. . . .

"We were patrolling at low speed on one engine when a dark shape suddenly loomed up on our starboard bow about 250 yards away. I turned into him to fire my fish, hoping that I could get on him before he saw us. I guess he saw us a couple of seconds later because he turned into us, going like hell, with a speed of more than 40 knots. By the time we were bow on to him for the shot, he was bow on to us, 40 yards away and getting closer. There was no point in letting the fish go, because they have to travel a certain distance before they explode on contact. . . . I can best compare it to the onrushing trains in the old-time movies. They seemed to come right over you. Well, the feeling was the same, only the destroyer didn't come over us, it went right through us. . . ."

[After Inga described the rescue, she went on:] "Then you are a hero," I said and Lt. Kennedy looked reproachfully at me as he answered. "The job of a PT boat officer is to take the men out there—and just as important—to bring them back. We took them out . . . we just had to get them back."

Not long after Inga wrote this column, she was dismissed. Sheilah Graham missed her column and returned to Los Angeles to take it back.

After the four days in Hollywood, Jack went East. There is evidence in a letter written by his father a few weeks later that he stopped off at the Mayo Clinic in Rochester, Minnesota.

Although we could find no record of it, he must have been granted a thirty-day leave en route to his new post at Melville. He apparently went from the Mayo Clinic to Palm Beach to visit his parents. Chuck Spalding met Jack at the Palm Beach airport. He told us:

When I was in Palm Beach his family got the word Jack was coming in. They asked me to meet him at the airport. I did. He looked very thin. After I drove him home to see the family, he wanted to go out—to his favorite haunts. There was this place in

Palm Beach where everybody went, the Everglades Club, a supper club and nightclub that had a roof that pulled back. It was great. But it was really tough that first night. He was very sensitive in a way that didn't show, but this night it was a great shock having gotten back from this thing he'd been through and going to this place where he used to dance all the time and seeing everybody and trying to fit in. You know, the difference between being at war and being at home. The tensions of war and the pleasures of Palm Beach. He could usually make those transfers kind of easily, but that night it was tough. . . . I remember he talked about my book and he was very pleased I'd done it. He loved the idea. He liked anything that was doing and succeeding and happening. We talked about writing. He thought he might write. Writing was more on his mind than it was on mine. My mind was on the war. Jack was back— finished. But my outfit was preparing to leave. I remember I got a copy of Hemingway's *Men at War* and I remember a phrase from that book. Something like war wasn't any good, but you could do it because other people had done it before.

When Jack arrived in Palm Beach, he must have found his mother and father in a state. Kathleen, who had been seriously dating Billy Hartington since the previous July, had announced that they wanted to marry. At that time, Billy, who had been a captain in the British Army—the Coldstream Guards—had temporarily resigned his commission so he could run as a Churchill Conservative for a seat in the House of Commons. Kathleen was helping Billy in his campaign, mailing out brochures and leaflets, answering telephones.

As Rose explains at some detail in her book, the Kathleen-Billy romance had put everybody in an "impossible dilemma." Billy's parents, the Duke and Duchess of Devonshire, were among the most conservative of Britain's ruling class. Billy's ancestors had been, traditionally, the British rulers of Ireland. For decades they had suppressed and persecuted the Irish who espoused independence from Britain. They were pillars of the Church of England. Billy's father, the tenth Duke of Devonshire, was the head of the Freemasons, and the Freemasons had been "condemned" by the Pope. Rose writes:

During the winter and spring of 1944, all of us—Joe and I, the duke and duchess, and of course Kick and Billy—tried to find some way by which, through some stretch of the rules, the marriage could be sanctioned or at least tolerated by both the Roman Catholic and Anglican Churches. One of our closest friends among the Catholic clergy in America was Francis Spellman, once bishop of the Boston archdiocese . . . and by then himself a cardinal and archbishop of the New York archdiocese. We enlisted him as our adviser and also as our friend at court, so to speak, with Pope Pius XII. . . . But, finally, it couldn't be worked out. The only way for Kick to marry Billy within the Sacraments of the Catholic Church—and even this would be a civil ceremony—would be for Billy to agree that their children would be raised as Catholics; and, of course, he could not agree to do that. . . .

Jack arrived home in the middle of this flap. A reasonable guess would be that the debate divided the older children: Joe Junior, then in England flying anti-U-boat patrols, with Kathleen; Eunice and Robert, both fiercely devout, probably opposed the union. Since Kathleen was Jack's favorite sister, and since his own faith (as John Iles told us) was none too strong at this stage, Jack was probably sympathetic to Kathleen's position. This stand—if he took it—would have put him at odds with his parents. We could find no evidence, however, to support or refute this.

Jack spent about two weeks in Palm Beach, resting in the sun, telephoning and writing the families and sweethearts of his PT buddies still in the Solomons. Lennie Thom's fiancée of that time, Kate, told us:

> One day, right after Jack came home, the telephone rang. I answered and a voice said, "Kate? This is Jack Kennedy." It was just like we had known each other. We talked for quite a while and he told me everything that had been going on out there, how he had left Lennie. Everything was fine. Lennie had developed an ear infection, a fungus from being in the water so long, but there was nothing else physically wrong with him. And then Jack said he was going to be in Palm Beach at his parents' home for a while and why didn't I come down? But I did not go to Palm Beach.

On January 23, from Palm Beach, Jack wrote to Barney Ross's father. The full text, from *As We Remember Him:*

> DEAR MR. ROSS,
> I had the pleasure of serving with your son George in the Solomons for the last seven months—and as I saw him at Tulagi slightly more than a month ago—I just wanted to write and let you know that he is well—looks fine—and is as usual in good spirits.
> I am enclosing some pictures that were taken just before I left that he asked me to send to you to be kept for him.
> Barney has done a good job out there—and everyone—particularly the enlisted men—are devoted to him. He rode on my boat during a particularly difficult time—and I have been thankful he was with us ever since. He saved one man' s life—and contributed

to a great degree to the rescue of the entire group. For his actions through that week he was recommended for the Silver Star—and he richly deserves [sic]

If there is any further information I can give you please let me know.

Sincerely,
JACK KENNEDY

Miami—then about a three-hour drive from Palm Beach—was the scene of much PT-boat activity. In April, 1943, the Navy had established a small shakedown unit there, a subsidiary of the Navy's Submarine Chaser Training Center (SCTC). It was located at a waterfront park in downtown Miami, an idyllic setting for fun and games. Many of the older hands from Squadrons Two and Three at Tulagi—Joe Kernell, John Kearney, Nick Nikoloric, Jack and Bob Searles, and Clark Faulkner—were stationed there, either permanently or with new squadrons preparing for deployment to the Pacific or European war zones.

Joe Kernell recalled:

> I was stationed down in Miami at the shakedown unit and running around with a girl named Lili Damita, who had been married to Errol Flynn. She lived in Palm Beach. One night I went up to see her. I believe we'd gone to a movie and when we came out, we ran into Jack. I knew he was back in the States but I didn't know he was in Palm Beach. He came up and said, "My God! What are you doing with that French movie actress?" And I said, "Oh, you know, Jack, we have a lot of laughs."
>
> Jack came down to Miami. I had a little apartment with John Kearney, who knew Jack from the Solomons. Jack came by the apartment. I had some rum. I should say we *all* had some rum. Lots of rum. The Coast Guard had nailed a rumrunner from Cuba and captured a fifty-five-gallon barrel of it. One of the guys in the shakedown unit, a mustang lieutenant, had stolen it from the Coast Guard and divided it up with us. Hell of a story in itself. Anyway, I asked Jack if he wanted a rum and Coke and he said, "Haven't you got anything else?" I said no, it was tough to get booze. Didn't he know there was a war on? The next thing I know, his old man called me from Palm Beach and asked me if I wanted a *case* of Haig & Haig pinch-bottle scotch. I said yes. He told me a place to go on Miami Beach. I had to pay for it, but it was very nice of him.

The shakedown unit, Nikoloric recalled, was like being assigned to a country club. "The typical routine was eighteen to thirty-six holes of golf, then some swimming at The Bath Club, an exclusive place on the Beach, which had extended us courtesy military memberships, some drinking and chasing around at night. I think we had the duty about twice a week and we didn't work very hard."

The duty, the sun, or the free spirit of wartime Miami must have held strong appeal for Jack. It would be his next official duty station.

Jack left Palm Beach on Saturday, February 5, northbound. A day or so later, a letter arrived from Al Cluster forwarding Jack's Purple Heart, which had been sent to Squadron Two in the Solomons. Ambassador Kennedy responded for Jack. Al Cluster saved his letter of February 7, 1944 and very kindly made it available to us:

North Ocean Boulevard
Palm Beach, Florida

MY DEAR LIEUTENANT:

I speak for the entire family when I tell you that we were very much touched with your letter of January 9 enclosing the Purple Heart Award for Jack.

Jack had already told us what a great boss you were and how you had the happy faculty of getting your men to be willing to do anything for you, and I can assure you that this from Jack meant a great deal to us.

We found him in reasonably good shape when he returned, but the doctors at Mayo's don't entirely agree with me on this diagnosis. However, Jack is insistent that he wants to get going again, so he left here on Saturday to go and see his brothers and sisters and then report for duty on the 15th.

It is very difficult to give a proper expression of a parent's gratitude for the kindness of others to his children, but let me assure you that your kindness and interest in Jack will always be deeply appreciated by the entire Kennedy family.

My best to you and your boys—and with our grateful thanks, I remain

Very sincerely yours,
JOSEPH P. KENNEDY

We have no evidence that Jack actually saw his brothers and sisters. They were all in various schools in the East—Bobby preparing to enter the Navy V-12 unit at Harvard, the younger girls in various private schools. Perhaps they all met on weekends. The moment is left unrecorded, but we seriously doubted that if Jack was ailing he would travel about from school to school on uncertain, crowded wartime trains and airplanes.

By February 9 he was in New York City, going to the theater and nightclubbing. He saw John Hersey and his wife, Frances Ann, and had a date with a girl named Florence Pritchett, whom he met about this time and who would become a very, very close friend. "Flo" was then fashion editor of Hearst's *New York Journal American*, an ardent member of what was then called "café society." Later she would marry Earl Edward Tailor Smith, a millionaire (and a much older man), who was President Eisenhower's ambassador to Cuba during the rise of Castro and who wrote a book, *The Fourth Floor*, in 1962. Today, Smith is unofficial "mayor" of Palm Beach.

Flo Pritchett died of leukemia in 1965 at age forty-five. To fill in her background, we interviewed "Mayor" Smith in Palm Beach and Flo's sister, Dancy Pritchett Foster, now living in Ridgewood, New Jersey. Smith professed to know little of Jack's early relationship with Flo, but Dancy did, and she spoke freely during our interview:

She was terribly good-looking. Five seven. Brown eyes, brown hair. Lots of girls were prettier, but she had so much personality. In her next to last year in high school, she went to see John Robert Powers and got a job as a Powers model. The minute school was over, she got on the bus and went to New York to pose. Her first photograph was a shaving ad in *Life*—the second issue, I think. I had a dull little job in New York by then and I married a magazine writer, Robert Leary.

Flo wanted to be part of the scene, to be somebody, do interesting things, meet interesting people. The modeling was the first step toward being somebody. Then she met Richard Canning, son of the bubble gum king. He was a Catholic, part of the McDonnell-Murray group in New York and Southhampton. Prep schools, Georgetown University, all that. He was not enormously wealthy, but he could afford to drift in and out of the Stork Club every day, when he wanted to. She converted to Catholicism, and in 1940 they were married in Ridgewood. He went into the Air Force in Texas. By then Powers had started his modeling school and he put Flo in charge of fashion. She told the girls what "type" they were and what kind of clothes they should wear. She'd gotten to know Lorelle Hearst—wife of William Randolph Hearst, Jr.—and she spent many weekends at the Hearst place in Manhassett—great estates, twisty roads, big stone gates. She knew everybody: Brenda Frazier, who married the famous football player Shipwreck Kelly, and got to be very close with Robin Chandler Duke—Angier Duke's wife, who was then married to the movie actor Jeffrey Lynn. And she got to know Lorelle Hearst very well. Lorelle was woman's editor of the Hearst paper, the *New York Journal American*. She offered Flo a job as fashion editor.

Flo had outgrown her husband (still in Texas), so they decided to part. They were divorced around 1943 in Las Vegas. She did not let her religion handicap her. I'm not exactly certain when Jack and Flo first met, but I have a picture of them both, sitting at a table in the Stork Club, right after he got back from the South Pacific. . . . From then on, they were good friends. I remember after she died, Lem Billings or Chuck Spalding said she was the one person who could always be guaranteed to make Jack Kennedy laugh.

Dancy sent us a copy of the photograph. It was dated February 9, 1944. Jack is smiling. His hair is short and curly. He looks thin but otherwise hale. Flo's vivacious personality leaps from the picture. Checking the picture portfolios of the Kennedy books, we found the photograph is often used—but invariably with Flo cropped out.

Flo Pritchett, Inga Arvad, and Angela Greene are the three women who, up to now, were most frequently mentioned in our interviews with Jack's friends. There were similarities. All three were, first and foremost, beautiful women. Inga and Angela were stunning, Flo Pritchett less so, but what she lacked in classic beauty, she made up in taste in makeup and dress. All three were, or had been, models—Angela and Flo had been Powers models. Inga and Angela had been (or would be) in films. None had earned any formal college degrees and none was, in the strictest sense, intellectually inclined. None had "social standing" by the criteria of those times. Inga was a Danish immigrant; Angela was an Irish immigrant. Two of the three, Inga and Flo, were associated with journalism or parajournalism; Inga as a Washington and Hollywood columnist, Flo as fashion editor for a Hearst paper. All three were "sharp"—witty and "with it," regulars in café society. All three were ambitious, career-oriented. All three would eventually marry well.

Is there a pattern here?

At least on the surface Jack was following a pattern established by his father and older brother. There is ample evidence that the ambassador was drawn to the Hollywood star or starlet, or the femme fatale of the café society set. From *The Lost Prince* and other sources, we gained the impression that Joe Junior was attracted to the same type.

To Ambassador Kennedy, life was a game to be won, whatever the cost. Perhaps this view extended to women as well: they were to be "won" against other male competitors; and displayed. As trophies, the women had to be glossy.

We asked Betty Spalding, the most introspective and brightest of Jack's female friends, what she thought about Jack's relationship with women. She considered the question for a long time, then said:

Jack and I had a warm brother-sister relationship. A very long association that way. He would say personal things to me. I mean, ask me personal questions about women and marriage—and later he talked to me about his sex life with Jackie. This was a rare relationship, I think. He was not the kind of person to have self-revealing conversations. Jack had a total lack of ability to relate, emotionally, to anyone. Everything was so surface with him in his relationships with people. All of the Kennedys were blocked, totally blocked, emotionally. Eunice survived best. I don't know how or why. Knowing the old man and Mrs. Kennedy, spending so much time in the house, I can readily see the limitations.

Mrs. Kennedy, for all her kids, was not a mother, not a homebody, but a driving, dominating force. And the old man—having his mistresses there at the house for lunch and supper! I couldn't understand it! It was unheard of.

Betty Spalding would not be the only Kennedy friend to tell us the ambassador brought his mistresses into the Kennedy home. In fact, it became a routine "revelation" as the friends attempted to explain the ambassador's character and his relationship with Rose.

Betty Spalding went on:

I think that was one of the things that was so difficult for Jack when he finally married Jackie. Both of them were blocked emotionally. She had the same emotional blocks and panics that Jack had. And their relationship was extremely stormy at the beginning. But it was getting better. They were both growing up emotionally. You see, there's something about the emotional imprinting of people. If they don't go through their proper psychosexual emotional development corresponding to their chronological age, they're going to go through those developments sometime, as late bloomers.

The first I ever saw Jack able to relate was when he had Caroline. That was a marvelous relationship. He was able to release some of his emotions to her and it freed him from the fear of it and he was able to exchange better with Jackie and she with him. Until he had Caroline, he never really learned how to deal with people. It was the first time he ever revealed any kind of emotion. It was fascinating to watch him grow in this capacity.

But, as I said, in the earlier years, he was not able to emotionally relate to anyone. His friends—the people around him—were followers and worshipers—Lem Billings, Torby Macdonald. They were his satellites, living in a lot of reflected glory. They were all servile and subservient. He compartmented his friends. And I think that is part and parcel of his inability to relate to people.

Nobody gets involved with that many girls on anything but a superficial basis. Flo Pritchett was a rather serious girl of his. She was a great *friend.* He may have talked closely with her. Over a long period of time, it was probably the closest relationship (with a woman) I know of. She was very bright, very amusing, and by far the most intelligent, competent girl I ever saw him with. But it could never have resulted in marriage because she didn't have what he would need, politically.

This interesting portrait of Jack and his family is clearly very thoughtful, and we find it illuminating. Betty Spalding is unquestionably intelligent, and she impressed us powerfully as fair-minded and kindly disposed toward Jack.

We asked Eunice Kennedy Shriver if she remembered Flo Pritchett. She told us, "Oh, yes. I knew Flo Pritchett very well. Jack liked her a lot. He always liked her. She was great. Bright, very bright, good-looking, great fun, and *au courant* with the news that was going on. She loved life. She had a good time. She knew everything. She wasn't an athletic type but she was a great dancer and loved to talk. She laughed all the time. I think he really enjoyed her company."

22

Shaking Down

On the same night that Jack and Flo posed for the photo in the Stork Club, he went to the theater with John and Frances Ann Hersey, according to a note in Hersey's appointment book.

Hersey was still a war correspondent with *Time-Life*, His first book, *Man on Bataan*, had been published in July, 1942. His second, published in 1943, was *Into the Valley*, the story of a Marine battle on Guadalcanal October 8–9, 1942, which Hersey witnessed firsthand. The third, *A Bell for Adano*, had been published that very week in February, 1944. It is a novel based on a *Life* article Hersey had published in August, 1943, about a day in the life of an American military governor in a seaport on the southern coast of Italy and it became a very celebrated book. It was awarded the Pulitzer Prize for fiction for 1944.

Hersey told us:

> We met in a nightclub. Something Uptown and something Downtown. Zero Mostel was playing there. We sat at a bar for a while and he began to give an account of this adventure he'd had. Right away I said I'd like to do a piece on it, if he'd be willing. He said he'd think about it. Then we met again and by then he'd talked himself into letting me do it. But he said he wanted me to see his crew first. So I set it up with *Life* to do the piece for them. Then I made arrangements to see some of the crew who were then up at the PT base in Melville, Rhode Island. I think there were four of them there and I talked to them at length, getting the story from each one and then collectively.

In the meantime, we believe, Jack must have reported either to Portsmouth, Rhode Island, or to Melville, on or about February 15, as the ambassador told Cluster he would. We could find no official document in his naval records to confirm this nor any that told what happened immediately thereafter. We assumed that Jack made known his desire to be stationed at the shakedown base in Miami. However, he next appears in our documentation in a hospital.

What had happened? After interviewing the *109* crew members at Melville, John Hersey then talked to Jack. In a brief statement in *As We Remember Him* he said, "I visited him in the New England Baptist Hospital in Boston where the disk between his fifth lumbar vertebra and his sacrum, ruptured in his [*109*] crash in the Solomons had been operated upon."

But, as we shall see, this was not correct. Jack may have been in the New England Baptist Hospital, his back was undeniably giving him trouble, but it had not yet been operated upon; that operation would come later in the year. Perhaps the Mayo Clinic had urged an operation and the visit to the hospital was a preliminary examination of some kind. Or perhaps he had gone in for an operation and the Lahey Clinic doctors had recommended against it.

We asked Hersey to elaborate on his meeting with Kennedy in the hospital. He told us:

> I have a picture of a rather small hospital room. There was nothing splendid about it. He was in the room alone, as I remember. And, by my appointment calendar, I visited him on February 23. He was in bed and was about to be operated on for his back. I don't believe the operation had taken place when I saw him. He must have explained about the operation to me that day, what it was going to be technically. He gave a full account of the fall on the PT boat that he felt was responsible for his back problem.
>
> He asked if the crew had given a decent account of him and I assured him they had. His insistence that I see the crew first struck me very favorably. It didn't seem to me to be self-serving. There was a real kind of officer modesty about it. He said all along that some of his crew members were the ones who really ran the boat, although I don't think that was true. He had a kind of diffidence about himself that seemed to be genuine at that time. So in a joking way he wondered how he looked to them. They were wildly devoted to him, all of them. Absolutely clear devotion to him by the crew. No reservation about it. They really did like him.
>
> I had pieced together from the men a kind of chronology of everything that had happened. I went over that with him, step by step. He drew me a map of the area particularly to illustrate the night he got off the reef and was in the water all night long and was carried out by the current. And also to illustrate the actual collision that took place. Sketched it on the back of a piece of paper. I don't remember how long I was with him, but it was certainly a long time for him at that point. I would think all afternoon and part of the evening too. It was a good long time because I had the whole story in hand after these two sessions. . . . What appealed to me about

the Kennedy story was the night in the water, his account of floating in the current, being brought back to the same point from which
he'd drifted off. It was the kind of theme that has fascinated me always about human survival, as manifested in the title of the piece.
It was really that aspect of it that interested me, rather than his heroics. The aspect of fate that threw him into a current and brought
him back again. And that sort of dreamlike quality. His account of
it is very strange. A nightmarish thing altogether. I was then interested in using novelistic techniques in journalism. I went back to
New York and wrote the piece fairly soon after that.

So far as we were able to determine, John Hersey was the first reporter
to hear Jack assert that his back problems stemmed directly from the
PT-109 incident. Hersey did not know, and Jack did not tell him, that he
(Jack) had been born with an "unstable" back and had always had problems with it, had applied for a six months' leave of absence from the
Navy in the spring of 1942 for a "back operation," had probably pulled
strings to pass a physical for sea duty, had probably been assigned to Melville as an instructor because of his bad back, had again pulled strings to
get to the Solomons, and had finally been sent home (as Dr. Wharton told
us) from the Solomons because of a "chronic" back condition.

Should Jack have revealed these facts to Hersey? Was it deceptive or
wrong, per se, to directly relate his back problems to the *109*? Frankly, we
did not know what to think. It was a troublesome point for us. There is no
reason to doubt that Jack's PT service had exacerbated his chronic back
condition. As many PT boat skippers told us, the pounding of PT hulls de-
stabilized many completely healthy backs. He may well have injured it on
the *109* or the *59*, although as we have seen, no one recalled a specific
trauma on either boat. If he had revealed the history of his unstable back
before the *109*, it would have raised questions about his health in general
and how he managed to get in the Navy—and PT's—in the first place. No
doubt Jack was reluctant to get into that area—to reveal that he got in the
Navy in the first place with his father's help, and overseas with the help of
Senator Walsh. In any event, ironically enough, John Hersey did not
mention the back injury in the final draft of his story.

Jack remained at the hospital a few more days, perhaps a week. Jack's
old pal Lem Billings was in Boston at the same time, a boot ensign stationed at Babson College. He told us how this came about:

I was in North Africa for about two months, driving an ambulance for the American Field Service, attached to a New Zealand
division, picking up wounded on the battlefields. We went across
North Africa to Tunisia. I wasn't too happy. I was neither fish nor
fowl—not really in the service, not really a civilian. I came home to

Baltimore in November on leave of absence, trying to get in the Navy. A friend of the family, a Naval Academy graduate pulled from retirement to be captain of the Port of Baltimore, helped. It turned out he knew not only my grandfather but also my father. . . . He sent me to a medical examiner. I rushed out and got some contact lenses and passed the eye test. I received a commission as ensign and was assigned to the Navy Supply Corps. In about February, 1944, I was sent to Babson, to a supply corps officer training school. And that was when I saw Jack again. He was back in the country after that terrible experience and, I think, on survival leave. I would have seen more of him except that I came down with scarlet fever and was quarantined in a hospital myself. But Jack left me his Buick convertible to use. . . .

While he was in the hospital at this time, Jack wrote Red Fay a letter which Fay included in his book. Text:

(Written on my back so writing will be one by one)
DEAR RED:
Glad to hear from you and get the news both late and strate. I regret that I did not get a chance to look over the establishment of the Fay Construction Company—sell a few bonds—and talk with the impresario himself but due to what is known in train circles as "an extremely close connection," I had time for only a short pilgrimage up Nob Hill on my knees to light a candle—and then I executed Tare 90° & headed southward where I spent my next four days . . . in lower California. I did have the pleasure of communicating with the young Fay girl & sending her the pictures to be forwarded to the great industrialist. I also put in a few plugs for you which I hope they will take seriously but which I trust you won't—as we both know how consistently you've been dropping the ball out there. The picture of Ross Park—somewhere in the Solomons—is a moving one—wherever that mighty man moves he leaves his mark. Time will never erase from my mind the picture of that tall gaunt figure stopping me at a touch ball game at Melville. Hey, Bub, where did you get that sweater with the H, huh? When he thought he was going to die one night on the island, he confessed to me he thought that I was an enlisted man and had stolen it—and it took quite a bit of juice power for me to keep from pushing his head under water for a period.

Haven't been down to Melville as yet—but did get to the base at Miami, where it looks like no strain. The squadrons are piling up there—they are turning them out faster than they can get them out there. I was extremely glad to hear that the relief situation was finally worked out and that you and Ted had your prospects for getting out this spring.

Tell Moriarity I talked with his folks and they sounded fine. Spent the weekend up in Boston where I gave an exhibition of talking where I should have been listening.

The States is just about what you would think. Everyone very optimistic and it's very true that "hell hath no fury like a civilian"—and when I read the papers I think the war will be over tomorrow—but I know it won't. You don't have any chance to tell any war stories as everyone is too busy telling you one. . . . The bull some guys are handing out here is unbelievable. The favorite question they ask you is "How many destroyers did you get?" If you didn't get at least five, which they think makes you an ace and is par for the course, there is no sense coming home. There is no sense in handing out any bull though—it's *nice* to be home—and I sincerely hope to see you boys soon back here or back here soon (which is better English? Ever since I went to Stanford I've had trouble with my English).

I'm in the hospital for another couple of weeks on my back—& then down to report at Melville—& then in a month or so later I'm afraid I'm going to have to have an operation on it—but perhaps it will all work out.

Best to Ted and Barney and all the boys. Tell Barney that there has been a slight case of mislaying of addresses re B. T. Sweetie, but when I get out of here—I will make my Pilgrimage to the shrine. I talked with Jude the Obscure—the beloved of James Reed—she sounded extremely nice. Will call Burkett. Drop me a line.

                                                    Best,
                                                    JACK

As Fay explains in his book, "Ted" is Theodore Berlin, skipper of *PT-167,* on which Red was exec; "Moriarity" was the cook on the *167*—a Boston Irishman; "Jude the Obscure" is Jewel Reed, Jim Reed's wife; and "Burkett," of course, was Nancy Burkett, whom both Jack and Red knew from Stanford days. Barney Ross' "B.T. Sweetie" was Barbara Taylor of Rye, New York, Ross told us. They had been engaged since New Year's Eve, 1943, when Ross was stationed in New York, commissioning Squadron Ten.

In late February or early March, Jack was transferred to the PT shakedown unit in Miami. We could not determine from his naval records in the Kennedy Library if he went directly from the hospital or via Melville—or even if he ever got to Melville at all. No matter. He was once more southbound—toward the sun and tropical breezes. Perhaps the idea was that if he recovered sufficiently he would not have to have the operation.

He passed through New York City and saw Hersey. Hersey had finished his article but *Life* had turned it down. Hersey could not remember why exactly. It was a very long article for *Life*, and it dealt with a relatively minor incident which had occurred in the past. The magazine was trying to cover war around the entire globe, and this piece would have occupied most of the text space in an issue of *Life*. So its length may have been a factor. Hersey told us, "When *Life* turned it down, I took it to Harold Ross at *The New Yorker*. He took it. This was the first time I sold anything outside of *Life*. About that time I saw Kennedy in a nightclub in New York again. I told him *The New Yorker* was going to publish the piece. I daresay he was a little disappointed at that news. *Life* would have been a better vehicle for him."

Ross scheduled the article to run in the June 17, 1944, issue under the title "Survival." Ambassador Kennedy was already making plans to see that it got larger circulation through his friend Paul Palmer at the *Reader's Digest*. Hersey said:

> At some stage of getting ready for publication, Joseph Kennedy suggested the *Reader's Digest* might run it. Joe Kennedy raised the question with *The New Yorker*, but *The New Yorker* and the *Digest* were at loggerheads. Ross hated the *Reader's Digest*; he hated the whole principle involved in condensation. He thought it should be condensed before it got into the first magazine and shouldn't be tampered with after that. So Ross first said no. Then there was a negotiation to which I was not admitted. It got quite strenuous, I gathered, indirectly. I don't know what kind of pressures Joe Kennedy brought to bear, but he somehow persuaded Ross to allow the *Reader's Digest* to run it on a one-shot-only basis. The *Digest* always buys rights in perpetuity for anything they get so they can run it over and over again if they want to or resell it. This is one of the things Ross objected to. He allowed them to print it once and once only.

We wrote *The New Yorker* to see if they could find anything in their records to shed further light. We received a reply from Milton Greenstein, a vice-president:

> *The New Yorker* had terminated its reprint arrangement with the *Reader's Digest*. When the *Digest* asked for reprint permission on the Hersey piece, the automatic answer was no. The *Digest* persisted, and when we learned that Hersey had no objection, that John Kennedy—to whom we were grateful for having made the piece

possible—was for the reprint and, finally, that all commercial taint
had been removed by the *Digest* promise to make a substantial contribution to philanthropy benefiting the widows and orphans of naval personnel, Ross and his associate editors relented. Permission
was granted as an exception to the policy that had been laid down
regarding *New Yorker* material in the *Digest*. It seems to me I recall
hearing at one time, that Joseph Kennedy was the one who thought
up the idea of the charitable donation to combat Ross's initial turn-
down. That may have been the "strenuous" negotiation Hersey referred to. . . .

Jack checked in at the Miami shakedown unit in March, 1944, according to an extract of his naval records. The unit was commanded by Alan
Robert Montgomery (Naval Academy, 1927), now deceased. Montgomery had led Squadron Three (immortalized by John Hersey in *Life)* into
battle at Guadalcanal. His exec in Miami was Clark Faulkner, who had
won a Navy Cross for fearlessly attacking destroyers off Guadalcanal.
We talked by phone with Faulkner, who now lives in Lincoln, Nebraska.
He said:

> Jack came down to the shakedown unit to work for me. He was
> officially on "limited duty" as far as the PT's were concerned. He
> spent very little time at the base because he was on limited duty.
> He was seldom around the base and he didn't go out on the boats
> on training missions. To be honest about it, I don't recall seeing
> *anybody* around the base very much. Miami was not a serious time
> for any of us. We were having a ball. I remember my fiancée and I
> spent an evening with Jack up in Palm Beach. We went to a place
> called Colonel Bradley's. We had dinner. There was a gambling ca-
> sino there. We couldn't gamble in uniform and I remember some-
> one loaned us sports jackets to wear. Jack was a very friendly,
> very affable, but *shy* kind of guy.

The PT officers maintained an apartment on Miami Beach at 91st Street
and Harding Avenue. It was passed on, like a legacy, as the various
squadrons came through Miami for shakedown. Nick Nikoloric and Bob
Searles, who had been roommates through four years at Princeton, lived
there until they both got married. Then John Kearney, Joe Kernell, Robert Wark and others. These and Faulkner believe Jack lived there, too, at
least some of the time. But it was an informal, revolving door arrangement and nobody could remember for sure.

Robert Searles told us, "The Bath Club was where everybody met.
They let naval officers have a military membership. That's where the ac-

tion took place. We thought it was a terrific break for us at five dollars a month, but what you'd do was go run up a huge bill and at the end of the month, you'd say, My God, can I afford this five-dollar membership? But you'd keep going back anyway."

Both Robert and Jack Searles married Miami girls who moved in the Bath Club set. Jack's wife, Barbara, was best friends of another Miami girl named Barbara—Barbara Cox, daughter of James Middleton Cox, former Governor of Ohio who, in 1920, was the lackluster Democratic presidential candidate against Warren G. Harding. (Franklin Delano Roosevelt was Cox's vice presidential running mate.) Cox owned a string of newspapers, including the *Miami Daily News*.

Jack Kennedy met Barbara Cox at the Bath Club, Barbara Searles recalled. She told us:

> Barbie Cox and I grew up together in Florida. Our families were friends. We went to the same school down there in the winter— Miss Harris's. At the time Jack Kennedy was in the Miami shakedown unit, my family had gone north and I was living at the Cox home. Barbie had married Brad Ripley, Princeton, 1938, but he had been killed in a fighter plane crash. Barbie was just beginning to go out with people again. She and Jack dated some, not a great deal. Jack was there quite often for dinner. He and Governor Cox were good friends and shared somewhat similar political views. The conversations that usually took place were along those lines. It certainly was not a hot or heavy romance between Barbie and Jack—more or less a good friend type of thing. Jack was down there recuperating from his back problem.

While Jack was in Miami, stunning news came from London. Kathleen and Billy Hartington would be married, after all. The ceremony, a civil one, was performed at the Chelsea Registry Office on Saturday, May 6. We found a long story about it in the *New York Times* on the following day, May 7, dominating other marriage notices. Excerpts:

> The wedding was a simple civil ceremony, but the bareness of the office was relieved by vases of pink carnations. A distinguished group of guests attended, including the Duke and Duchess of Devonshire, the Duke's sister, Lady Elizabeth Cavendish, the Marchioness of Salisbury and Lady Astor. The bridegroom, whose age is 26, was the first to arrive at the register office. He was accompanied by his sister Lady Anne Cavendish. Lord Hartington is a captain in the Coldstream Guards and attending him as best man was a fellow officer, the Duke of Rutland. The bride, who is 24 years old,

arrived with her brother, Lieut. Joseph P. Kennedy, Jr. USN. The bride wore a frock of pink suede beneath a short jacket of brown mink and a small hat of blue and pink feathers. . . . Flower petals were tossed over the couple as they left the register office, and afterward there was a reception. . . . The wedding cake had no icing in conformity with the wartime "austerity" but there was champagne. The Marquess and Marchioness went by train afterward to Bournemouth and walked from the station a half mile to Compton Place, one of the Duke of Devonshire's several estates, where they will spend two or three weeks. Within the next day or so it was learned tonight from acquaintances of the Marquess, a private religious ceremony will be held in the drawing room of Compton Place. The family has not yet confirmed this report. The nature of the ceremony could not be learned but it was assumed that it would be Protestant. . . .

A friend of Kathleen's, Marie Bruce, who attended the wedding and reception, wrote Rose a letter for her book, correcting an error and adding a new tidbit. She said the wedding dress was pale pink crepe, not suede. The cake came from Claridge's and to get around the rationing regulations she gave the headwaiter a £5 bribe.

Everybody knew what this marriage meant: Kathleen had parted with her religion. Knowing this must have been a severe shock to her parents. U.S. reporters fanned out to elicit reaction. On the afternoon following the ceremony, a *Times* reporter found Rose at New York's La Guardia airport. She had been confined for the two previous weeks at New England Baptist Hospital, the story said. She was en route to Hot Springs, Virginia, for a "much-needed rest." When the reporter asked her about the wedding, she replied tartly: "I am not making any statements." There was no comment at all from the ambassador.

Later Kathleen wrote:

Never did anyone have such a pillar of strength as I had in Joe [Junior] in those difficult days before my marriage. From the beginning, he gave me wise, helpful advice. When he felt that I had made up my mind, he stood by me always. He constantly reassured me and gave me renewed confidence in my decision. Moral courage he had in abundance and once he felt that a step was right for me, he never faltered, although he might be held largely responsible for my decision. He could not have been more helpful and in every way he was the perfect brother doing, according to his own light, the best for his sister with the hope that in the end it would be the best for the family.

We could find no hint in any of the Kennedy books as to how Jack received the news or his reaction to it. Our guess is that Jack, like Joe, approved. And he must have written Kathleen, sending his best wishes, but no such letter has ever been released. For Jack personally, it must have been pleasing in another sense. His first brother-in-law was one of the richest and most promising young heroes of that British ruling class that Jack had met and liked so much in London.

What stands out most clearly about Jack in the memories of the PT men—and their women—who were associated with him at the Miami shakedown unit is his ardent pursuit of a model named Bab Beckwith. Nick Nikoloric said:

> Girls were almost an obsession with him. We liked them too, but we didn't make a career of it the way he did. There was a perfectly gorgeous girl down there, Bab Beckwith, a very well-known New York model. You should have seen Jack going after her. A continuing campaign with flowers, candy, dinner. She told me a very strange thing, too. One night she invited him to her place. She was feeling dreamy and romantically inclined. There was champagne, the radio was turned low. Then, just at the crucial moment, Jack jumped up, ran for the radio and turned up the volume. There was a news bulletin. Jack said to Bab, "Wait a minute, baby. My father says I have to keep up with current events." So Bab kicked him out of the apartment.

That last may be assumed to be apocryphal. In any case, though, we felt certain that Jack's pursuit of Bab Beckwith was no serious matter, out of curiosity we telephoned her. She lives in Coral Gables and works as an interior decorator. She seemed surprised—and somewhat apprehensive—that anyone would recall her fleeting moments with Kennedy in Miami, but agreed to meet us for lunch. She arrived an hour and fifteen minutes late, coming into the restaurant in a rush, apologetic, wearing enormous sunglasses and jangling bracelets. She was very tall, brown-eyed and dieting fiercely. Clearly she had once been gorgeous.

Before World War Two, when she was still at Finch College, she began modeling through the John Robert Powers Agency in New York. She posed for illustrators Bradshaw Crandell and McClelland Barkley, who were doing covers for *Redbook* and *Cosmopolitan* magazines, among others. She was also on the cover of *Vogue*. She worked up to $75 an hour, top scale for those days. She married a New Yorker, Winthrop Gardiner, a wealthy, well-known socialite. This marriage, the first of three, ended in divorce. The modeling led to an invitation for a screen test in Hollywood at MGM Studios. Nothing ever came of it.

Her meeting with Jack Kennedy came about after this. She told it this way:

I had learned to fly in Florida. About the time of the screen test, the war broke out. I returned to Florida and got my commercial license, with an instructor's rating. I used to fly wearing pigtails poking from my helmet. I joined the CPTC—Civilian Pilot Training Course—and taught young American and British boys the fundamentals of flying at Chapman Field near Miami. Randy Hearst [Randolph Hearst, now Patty's father] was then in the Air Force, flying for the Air Transport Command, based in Memphis. He was ferrying planes to Europe. I knew Randy. One day in the spring of 1944, he brought Jack Kennedy by. I called Kennedy "Jackson." The three of us went to the Bath Club and had a ball. Jack was very cute, really a darling. He had bristly, wavy, reddish hair. Very coarse. He laughed a great deal. He was very easygoing, happy-go-lucky. I remember one day we had a cold bottle of champagne and went swimming in the ocean and drank it.

At that time, he was having a very bad time with his back. He wore a baby blue belt—for back support. At the time we dated—and I saw Jack a lot while he was here—I was going with a boy overseas: a six-foot-five inch pilot named George Raymond Gibson, who was later killed. I remember Jack telling me about the *109* thing. He joked about it. He said when he swam out that night to try to signal the other PT boats, he was nude, and always thinking about sharks biting off his . . . sharks taking a bite out of him. "I swam a lot of backstroke," he joked. And he said, seriously, "I never prayed so much in my life."

After he left Miami, we didn't keep in touch. In 1945 I married a naval aviator named Dana Gibson Noble, divorced him, and in 1951, Alfred Corning Clark of New York. We were divorced too. I didn't see Jack again until he was a Senator. We met one night in El Morocco. He was married to Jackie then. He said, "Well, look who's here." He gave me a kiss on the cheek and introduced me to Jackie. I whispered to him, "How's the blue belt?"

And, with that, we concluded our research into Jack's brief tour at the Miami PT shakedown unit. Since he was seldom at the base, and no one could remember where he lived, we concluded that Jack had probably spent most of his time at Palm Beach at his parents' home, coming to Miami occasionally to date Barbara Cox and Bab Beckwith.

One fact came through loud and clear in our interviews. In Miami, among the old PT hands—his peers—Jack was not a war hero. Nobody ever mentioned the *109* incident. Nikoloric told us, "There was a lot of criticism in the Navy about the loss of the *109*. MacArthur is supposed to have said that Jack should have been court-martialed, but I think he denied it. Jack was actually in a lot of trouble over that, so we never said a word about it."

23

Surgery

TWO days before Jack's twenty-seventh birthday, May 27, 1944, he was transferred from the Miami shakedown unit to the Chelsea Naval Hospital in Boston. The orders, on file in the Kennedy Library, state that "an operation is to be performed and as this officer's family lives in Boston . . . he wishes to be near them." The sunshine therapy had failed, apparently; now at last, the oft-postponed back operation was to be carried out.

Of course, Jack's family did not live in Boston. Their residences were in Palm Beach and Hyannis Port. His grandparents lived in Boston. He probably chose Boston for the operation so that the Lahey Clinic know-how and facilities could be brought into play, and possibly the staff of the New England Baptist Hospital, where Jack had already spent so many months of his life.

All this time, for almost nine months, Jack's medal had been in the works. It seemed to us an inordinately long time. But since the records of the Navy Awards Board have not been opened to researchers, we could find out no specific details about what had happened. Our guess was that for some reason it had been held up. Perhaps because it had been downgraded; perhaps because the wording of the citation was changed.

This much we know. On May 10, 1944, Ambassador Kennedy's old Wall Street pal, Undersecretary of the Navy James V. Forrestal, was nominated to replace Navy secretary Frank Knox, who had died of a heart attack. On May 19 Forrestal was sworn into office. On that very day, May 19, he signed the citation for Jack's medal. Perhaps it was mere coincidence. But it seemed more likely to us that it took Forrestal, and the power of his office, finally to resolve the matter of the medal.

According to some documents on file in the Kennedy Library, Forrestal's office forwarded the medal to the Miami shakedown unit on May 30. The forwarding letter requested that the medal be presented to Kennedy in a fitting ceremony. But by the time the medal reached Miami, Jack had gone. It was reforwarded to Chelsea Naval Hospital and a simple ceremony was organized for the morning of June 12.

On June 11, the Navy Department put out a press release in Washington containing the text of the "second" citation. We found two newspaper stories based on the release. The first was in the *New York Times* on the morning of June 12. It appeared on page 7, beneath the headline:

LIEUT. KENNEDY CITED AS HERO BY THE NAVY
FOR SAVING MEN OF PT CREW IN SOLOMONS

It was accompanied by an Associated Press photograph, Jack's half of the joint Jack-Joe photograph made in December, 1942 in Palm Beach. Jack is smiling handsomely.

The other story we found was from the *Boston Globe* of the same date, June 12, with the headline:

LT JOHN FITZGERALD KENNEDY
GETS MEDAL TODAY FOR HEROISM

The story said that Jack had been staying at Hyannis Port and that he had gone from there to Chelsea Naval Hospital, where the medal would be presented that morning. "Lt. Kennedy," the *Globe* said, "entered the hospital last evening for an operation to cure back injuries sustained in the Pacific war area last August."

The ceremony was held at the Chelsea Hospital that morning, June 12. There are at least two published photographs of it, one in Rose's book, one in *As We Remember Him*. The medal was presented by the commanding officer of Chelsea, a doctor, Captain Frederic L. Conklin. Both photographs were taken outside the hospital, with the red-brick walls for a backdrop. Jack is wearing a dress blue uniform. In the full-length photograph in Rose's book he looks very sickly. In the head shot photograph in *As We Remember Him*, he is smiling wanly. In both, the medal has been pinned beneath his modest row of fruit salad: the Purple Heart, the American Theater Ribbon, and the Asiatic Pacific Theater Ribbon, with what appears to be two battle stars, probably for the invasions of New Georgia and Bougainville.

There is no evidence in either photograph that any members of the Kennedy family attended the ceremony. The *Globe* story said that Ambassador Kennedy had an important speaking engagement in Chicago and could not attend. Damore, in *The Cape Cod Years*, includes a newspaper quotation from the ambassador in Chicago: "Jack's a pretty good lad. Naturally I'm proud of him. I only wish I could have been with him." In the photo caption in *As We Remember Him*, it is stated that Jack always thought it ironic that his medal had been presented by a Navy doctor.

This same week—on June 17, 1944—the long John Hersey article on Jack and the *109* episode finally appeared in *The New Yorker*. We could find nothing to indicate Jack's reaction to its publication. But when Barney Ross finally saw a copy of it, he was astonished. He told us:

Our reaction to the *109* thing had always been that we were kind of ashamed of our performance. I guess you always like to see your name in print and that Hersey article made us think maybe we weren't so bad after all. We'd never gone around saying, hey, did you hear about us? But suddenly your name's in print and Hersey made you sound like some kind of hero because you saved your own life. So I suppose my reaction to the article was to be pleased with myself. I had always thought it was a disaster, but he made it sound pretty heroic, like Dunkirk.

Meanwhile, thanks to the ambassador and his friend at the *Reader's Digest*, the condensed version was now about ready to go to press for the August, 1944, issue. On his way through New York, Jack had met Palmer to arrange for the author's (that is, Hersey's) payment to go to Kirksey's widow through a naval relief fund, and, to confer on certain editorial points. Concerning the latter, Jack was insistent that Hersey's statement that "Kennedy saw a shape and spun the wheel to turn for an attack" be kept intact, even though any suggestion Jack had been making an attack had been deleted from the medal citation. On June 16, probably from the hospital, he wrote Palmer a letter regarding these matters, which is on file in the Palmer Papers at the Yale Library:

DEAR MR. PALMER:
    Referring to our talk of yesterday, the money should be sent to:
    Massachusetts Auxiliary of Naval Relief
    Bank Building
    Thompson Square
    Charlestown, Mass.
    Attention of: Chaplain Applehoff
    As Chaplain Applehoff has discussed the whole matter with Washington, the money can be administered under his guidance most satisfactorily, and I can also keep an eye on it and look after the widow Kirksey's interests.
    Regarding cutting the article itself, I was referring to the paragraph at the beginning which starts "Kennedy saw a shape—" and ends with "avoid detection from the air." The paragraph has only two sentences, but I hoped that they would both be left intact as they are significant from a tactical point of view.
    I enjoyed meeting you in New York and I appreciate very much your cooperation in the above matters.

                                        Very sincerely,
                                        /s/ JOHN F. KENNEDY

Both matters were handled as Jack requested. In the *Digest* story, the text is, "Kennedy saw a shape and spun the wheel to turn for an attack. . . .'' There is a notation that the article was printed ''by special agreement with *The New Yorker* and the Navy Bureau of Public Relations'' and that the author ''has donated his fee for this condensation to the Navy Relief Fund.''

When the article was finally set for publication, the ambassador wrote a letter to Palmer, dated June 20. Full text:

DEAR PAUL,

I have already thanked you about the Hersey piece, and you have demonstrated very clearly to me why it is that people really want to do things for you. It is because you always are gracious enough to make them think that they are doing you a favor. It's an art which has been lost by almost everybody whom I have ever met. You are a great fellow to work with!

If the gift of writing came to me at all easily, I wouldn't have to wait for the revolution or the days when business opportunities are thin. I would accept your editorial job on the *Reader's Digest* right now because I think it is an institution that America can feel very proud of. It really teaches a great lesson in publishing in this country in that the people who own it, and make it successful, always hide their talents behind the words *Reader's Digest*. I think I could really do a better job writing about what the *Reader's Digest* means to America and what the people who have owned it have done than I could about any other article.

That is a feeling I have had for a great many years and that was the feeling I had when representatives of the *Digest* came to me in London to ask for some support in launching some work. As they made a report of my statements to them then, that would serve as the subject for the article. Thanks again and my best to the nice people who own the *Digest* and insist on nobody finding out very much about them.

With warmest regards, I am
/s/ JOE KENNEDY

The *Digest* condensation of the John Hersey article would become a valuable political tool for Jack Kennedy. In his two important early political campaigns, 1946 and 1952, hundreds of thousands of reprints of it would be distributed in Massachusetts. In 1959 the conservative news magazine *U.S. News and World Report* republished extensive excerpts from the piece in the issue of December 21, to prove that Jack was qualified to handle the job of president. After Jack became president, the *Digest* published the story again—in its issue of February, 1961.

John Hersey and the Kennedys saw little of one another after writing this article. In fact, Hersey supported Stevenson for the Democratic nomination in 1960.

We now come to another medical mystery. Beyond question Jack now had the operation on his back. But there are no details about it in any of the Kennedy books or magazine articles, beyond the fact that it occurred. No mention of what was done, who did it, or where it was done.

We visited Chelsea Naval Hospital (soon to be abolished) but they no longer had records on file. We combed the Kennedy Library. Nothing. We tried to find Dr. Conklin and others of the Chelsea staff in 1944 (doctors who might have performed the operation) but Conklin is deceased and nobody could supply us with the names of the other staff physicians.

Something seems to have gone wrong during the operation, judging from a portion of a letter from Jack to "an inquiring friend," reproduced in Sorensen's book, *Kennedy*: "In regard to the fascinating subject of my operation, I should naturally like to go on for several pages . . . but will confine myself to saying that I think the doc should have read just one more book before picking up the saw . . . "

We wrote Sorensen to ask if he could provide us the name of the inquiring friend. Three months later he responded, giving her name as Mrs. Florence Mahoney, now living in Washington, D.C. We telephoned Mrs. Mahoney. It turned out she was, in those days, the wife of the publisher of the *Miami Daily News*, a Cox paper. She had met Jack when he was at the Miami PT base. She claimed that she introduced Jack to Barbara Cox. She had kept the full letter from Jack, plus another. She promised to send Xeroxes of both. But she never did.

Our speculations about the operation, supported by our interviews, as we shall see, are as follows:

Jack was attached to Chelsea Naval Hospital at this stage merely for administrative purposes.

The operation was probably performed in mid-June by a civilian doctor, or team of doctors, working under direction of Dr. Gilbert Edmund Haggart, Jack's "back doctor" at the Lahey Clinic for many years. It seems inconceivable that Jack would have entrusted his back to any but the finest doctors available, and doctors who had knowledge of his care in depth.

The operation was probably performed at the New England Baptist Hospital, rather than Chelsea. From other sources (see below) we know that he was in the Baptist Hospital at this time.

On the basis of Jack's comment to Florence Mahoney, the operation, like most disk operations of those days, was less than successful.

There followed many long weeks of postoperative convalescence.

There was no end of visitors. Lem Billings was still at Babson College—delayed in his training by his bout of scarlet fever. Bobby was now at the Navy V-12 unit at Harvard. Jack's sisters—Eunice, Jean, and Pat— were out of school for the summer. Ambassador and Mrs. Kennedy had opened the house at Hyannis Port and (we assume) were in Boston frequently to see Jack.

And then, one by one, Jack's old and new friends in the PT force returned from the Pacific, reporting to Melville for further assignment. One of the first of these was Torby Macdonald. What war stories he had to tell! He had fought his boat, the *194*, from eastern New Guinea across the north coast of that huge island to Biak, invaded in May, 1944. He had been in countless barge-destroying actions and had earned a Silver Star. He had recently injured an ankle during an air raid and had been sent home.

Torby described Jack at this time for the authors of the 1961 *Coronet* article:

> He was lying in bed all strapped up as part of the treatment to mend his back. He was suffering from a recurrence of malaria, and his skin had turned yellow. His weight had dropped from 160 to 125 pounds. When I came into his room, he raised a bony wrist and gave me a shaky wave. I asked him how he felt. He tried to lift his head. I had to lean over to hear him.
> "I feel great," he said.
> "Great?" I echoed. "Well," He smiled, "Great considering the shape I'm in."

Torby is quoted as saying, "I visited him in Chelsea Naval Hospital in Boston . . . " but all others remember that it was New England Baptist.

We wondered what these two old and close friends had talked about after that? Or how Jack felt about Torby now. As at Harvard, Torby had done it all the way it should have been done. He was a supremely well organized and successful PT boat skipper. He had inflicted damage on the enemy. He had won a Silver Star. But being the son of a former ambassador and a man well connected in publishing had some advantages. Hersey's long article on the *109* had now appeared in *The New Yorker* and the condensation was to appear in the August issue of the *Reader's Digest*. Publicly, Jack Kennedy had a far more distinguished war record than Torby. Did they joke about that?

Others returned. Lennie Thom got back in May. On June 1 he married Kate Holway in Youngstown, Ohio. Lennie was then assigned as an instructor at Melville. They moved into Mrs. O'Brien's boardinghouse, Kate recalled. Joe Atkinson, Johnny Iles, and Bill Battle got back from the Pacific. Iles and Atkinson had been reassigned to new squadrons going to Europe. One day Lennie, Kate, Johnny, and Joe Atkinson went up to see Jack in the hospital. Iles, a Catholic, who worried about Jack's religion, told us: "We borrowed a car or got somebody to drive us. When we got to the New England Baptist Hospital, his mother was there, just leaving. We met her, but she didn't stay. He was lying in bed. The first thing I noticed was a rosary hanging on the bedpost. And I said, 'Well, boy, it looks like you got back into favor.' And he just looked at me and grinned and didn't make any comment at all."

Kate remembered: "He was in the New England Baptist Hospital, not the Naval Hospital. That was my first meeting with Jack. He had private nurses. We didn't realize he was as sick as he was. He was just lying there in bed, lying flat. He looked awfully frail and sick, but delighted to see the guys. I remember the nurse came in very soon after we went in, and she said we'd have to leave. Jack didn't say oh, no, or anything like that. You could tell he was tired."

Joe Atkinson said, "It was definitely not a Navy hospital. He had just had an operation. At least that was our understanding. His back or a disk or something. It was something that was overdue. He had strained it again. It was some small operation on his back. We were quite concerned about him. But, as I recall, he was not in pain. He seemed to be just like he always was. In real good spirits."

The enlisted men who idolized Jack visited, too. Among them were Mauer, Kowal, Maguire, Johnston, Christiansen, and Scribner. Christiansen told us:

Scribner and I were sent back to Melville as instructors. On July 8, when I was twenty-one—going on twenty-two—I got married. Right after that, we borrowed a four-door Lincoln convertible and we drove up to New England Baptist Hospital to see Kennedy. He had just had his back operated on —the first back operation. He looked thin, but otherwise fine. He was very jovial. An artist had done a sketch of the Jap destroyer hitting the *109* and Jack had had some copies made. He gave us both a copy, and I still have mine. When we got ready to go, he asked me to stay back. When the rest of them were all out of the room, he said, and he wasn't joking, "Man, you're too young to be getting married."

By August 1 Jack was probably feeling somewhat better and perhaps a little stronger. He also had access to a typewriter. On that day, he pecked out a long letter to Al Cluster, who had returned from the South Pacific, left PT boats, married, and was stationed in Washington. Cluster kindly gave us a copy of the letter. We include it here, with Jack's atrocious spelling and typographical errors and with an occasional bracket insert to correct errors and identify the people he refers to:

New England Baptist Hosp.
Parker Hill Ave.
Boston, Mass.

DEAR AL:

Been wanting to write you for some time and to-day Bart Connolly was up and gave me your address. Want to thank you for writing my folks that time- it was much appreciated by them, also for getting married- congratulations.

I am putting in my eigth week at the hospital where things are fairly grim. Have an advanced case of bed-sores and a slight touch of scurvy- due to our inability to get any limes to mix with the mediacl alcohol. Should be leaving here in a few days for the Old Sailors Home, where I go before a survey board-probably to be issued a rocking chair, a sunny place on the lawn- with the thanks of a grateful Republic wringing in my ears.

Some of the boys have been up. Iles, Webb [Albert Webb, a PT friend] and Atkinson have left for the Mediterranean—Iles, Joe, Lennie and his wife, Hurley and Fanniman were up one evening. Joe was rather gross, taking numerous sips out of my rubbing alcohol. Scrib. and Chris were up and their wives—Chris had just been married a few days before. Chris said something about having a possivility of getting an Ensigns commission which had been killed by Rice. I don't think he may have enough formal education for it, but I wrote Keresey, who has taken Rice's price [place] and will see what the story is. Have also seen Mauer, who went from quarter-master to cook and now seems to be a quartermaster again- with ambitions to be an ekectrician- he's going to end the war up as a seaman. Koval, maguire and Johnston were also around and all have seemed to dig in in excellent fashion, they figure to be there through this summer. You certainly did a good job getting everyone out, and they all think you are red-hot. Incidentally, have received several letters from Mrs. Kirsey who I investgated by the Red Cross- and she is making out OK. We got $2,ooo for a saga on the io9 disaster which has been turned over to her-so she should make OK.

They say it's murderous down at Melville-with the knives and shivs flying. They say that if an officer happens to make a remark like "this place is horse-shit" or "I wouldn't mind getting out of here" that this name rank and serial number with his fleet preference (this so they can send him the other way) are on Walsh's desk in an hour, initialed by every officer who heard him make it. If he was in his rack when he said it, he leaves that after-noon-if not, the next morning. Rome seems to be Gaulieter and Comm Rons Gestapo down there.

Heard from J.B. Green yester-day from England. He says the weather has tied them up over there for the last three weeks—also that the Manilla Gorilla [Robert Kelly], the man from Batann- J. Dog B. [John D. Bulkeley] had left the boats with little Al and was now numero uno driver of a new tin can.

Thats about all the news. I will be leaving here for the Naval Hosp. and then will probably be sent home to the Cape for awhile. If you should be up this way, it would be fine if you and wife could come down to the Cape for a weekend or any convenient time. Just drop me a line and let me know when you might be up at Hyannis-port, Cape Cod, Mass. It would be a broadening experience for you to meet some Democrats.

Best,
SHAFTIE

24

Tragedy

IN early August, Kathleen—the Marchioness of Hartington—suddenly returned from London. Billy Hartington, now back in the uniform of the Coldstream Guards, had returned to his regiment, which was deployed into the fighting in France. Kathleen would remain with her parents until Billy returned to England—until the war against Hitler had been won. It must have been a dramatic homecoming, but it is not described anywhere in the Kennedy literature. No doubt there was a joyous meeting between Jack and Kathleen—they had not seen each other since early 1943—but this moment is also left unrecorded.

She brought Jack and the family firsthand news of Joe Junior. He had now been in England eight months, flying Navy patrol bombers on antisubmarine missions. It was miserable, dangerous duty. The overwater patrols were often fourteen hours long. The planes were cold. They flew over wavetops. The flying weather in England was almost perpetually bad—fog or rain. Many of Joe's squadron mates had died in accidents. Joe had not yet spotted a submarine, had never attacked the enemy.

Hank Searls, in *The Lost Prince*, has more. He writes that Joe Junior was terribly frustrated by all this. He wanted desperately to sink a submarine, earn a medal, and receive some recognition. Two forces seemed to be motivating him: (1) rumors and whispers in England dating from the Kennedy family's departure in 1940 that the Kennedys were "yellow" and (2) jealousy of his brother, whose PT heroics had been so widely celebrated. Joe had volunteered for a second tour of patrol missions.

He had another reason for extending his tour, Searls writes. Joe had fallen in love (or was having a wartime affair). Searls does not name the woman, but writes that she was the wife of a British Army artillery officer based in North Africa. She had once been a countess, Searls reports, and her husband was an extremely wealthy peer.

In time, Joe Junior's crew was rotated home. But not Joe. In his desperation, Searls reports, he volunteered for even more dangerous duty. It was so far beyond good sense that we had to believe Commissioner Joe Timilty's theory—that Joe was determined, at any cost, to show the family and outdo Jack.

For months Allied leaders in Europe had been concerned about a new Nazi superweapon: the V-1 buzzbomb. They had first learned about it from intelligence sources. Then they spotted the telltale "ski ramp" launching pads going up in occupied France. In the six months prior to D-day, Allied air forces had mounted an enormous effort to destroy these launchers and the plants where the bombs were made: 25,000 sorties, on which 771 airmen and 154 planes had been lost.

After D-day, the Nazis had begun launching the buzzbombs against London. They were not efficient weapons, but they struck terror into the hearts of Londoners. The high command became determined to do everything in its power to demolish the launching ramps. The best bet seemed to be what now looks like a lunatic scheme. They would send radio-controlled, pilotless bombers with huge bomb loads against the target.

Both the U.S. Air Force and the U.S. Navy sent radio-controlled planes to England. The Navy model was a PB4Y, the same type Joe had been flying for eight months. On takeoff, it would carry only sufficient fuel to reach the target on a one-way flight. Thus lightened, it could carry 25,000 pounds of explosives—by far the heaviest payload ever put into the air. It would be guided to the target by two "mother planes" flying not far from it.

There was one considerable problem. The crude electronic guidance system (which was based on a tiny, primitive TV set) was not sophisticated enough to take the plane off. Thus it was necessary to have a couple of pilots on board for takeoff and until the drone had climbed and smoothed out in flight. After the stable point had been reached, the pilots would bail out and the mother planes would take the drone on to the target.

Joe Junior volunteered to be the senior pilot for the drone takeoff.

In the early days of August—about the time Kathleen returned to the States—Joe Junior began making practice hops in the drone. By Saturday, August 12, the outfit was ready and the weather was good. At 5:52 P.M. Joe and his copilot, Wilford "Bud" Willy, took the drone off with its twelve tons of explosives. They climbed to altitude. Then, twenty-eight minutes after takeoff—before the bail-out point—the drone blew up in midair with an awesome explosion. Joe Junior and Willy were instantly killed, of course; and of course their bodies were never found.

That same night, by Searls's account, the Navy sent word to Secretary of the Navy James Forrestal. The next day, Sunday, August 13, two Navy chaplains left Boston to deliver the sad news to Ambassador and Rose Kennedy at Hyannis Port. Rose tells how the family received the news:

I remember that it was Sunday afternoon and we all had lunched outside, picnic style, on our big porch at Hyannis Port. It was about two in the afternoon, and Joe Sr. had gone upstairs for a nap.

The younger children were in the living room chatting quietly so as not to disturb their father; I sat reading the Sunday paper. There was a knock at the front door. When I opened the door two priests introduced themselves and said they would like to speak with Mr. Kennedy.

This was not unusual: Priests and nuns fairly often came to call, wanting to talk with Joe about some charity or other matter of the Church in which he might help. So I invited them to come into the living room and join us comfortably until Joe finished his nap. One of the priests said no, that the reason for calling was urgent. That there was a message both Joe and I must hear. Our son was missing in action and presumed lost.

I ran upstairs and awakened Joe. I stood for a few mements with my mind half paralyzed. I tried to speak but stumbled over the words. Then I managed to blurt out that priests were here with that message. He leaped from the bed and hurried downstairs, I following him. We sat with the priests in a smaller room off the living room, and from what they told us we realized there could be no hope, and that our son was dead.

Joe went out on the porch and told the children. They were stunned. He said they must be brave: that's what their brother would want from them. He urged them to go ahead with their plans to race that day and most of them obediently did so. But Jack could not. Instead, for a long time he walked on the beach in front of our house.

There were no tears from Joe and me, not then. We sat awhile, holding each other close, and wept inwardly, silently.

The impact on the ambassador was almost indescribable. Joe had been his favorite. In his *Memoirs*, Arthur Krock wrote, "The death of Joe, Jr., was the first break in this circle of nine children nearly all extraordinary in some way: handsome, intelligent, with a father and mother to whom they were devoted and who were devoted to them. It was one of the most severe shocks to the father that I've ever seen registered on a human being. . . ."

More than a dozen years later the ambassador still found it impossible to talk about Joe Junior. In May, 1957, Bob Considine, preparing a five-part series on the Kennedys for distribution by International News Service, obtained an interview with him at Palm Beach. Considine asked the ambassador to sum up each of his nine children. Considine wrote:

He named and characterized eight, paused, and went on to another subject. After a long detour, I asked discreetly, if he wanted to speak in any way of Joe, Jr.

One of the top financiers of the age, a man known in many fields as cool beyond calculation under fire, suddenly and terribly burst into tears at the luncheon table and for five full minutes was racked with grief that cannot be described.

"No," he finally was able to say. "No. Mrs. Kennedy can, but I'll never be able to."

Joe Junior's death was announced by the Navy a few days later. On Tuesday, August 15, page 8, the *New York Times* carried a heavily censored story, merely stating that he was flying a special mission. Joe was recommended for the Congressional Medal of Honor, Searls reports, but this was downgraded by the Awards Board to a Navy Cross, presented six months later. Still later, the Navy, perhaps at Forrestal's urging, named a new destroyer for Joe Junior.

Life at Hyannis Port went on. Sometime after this terrible news had arrived—we do not know when—Jack was permanently discharged from the New England Baptist Hospital, sporting a thin walking cane, as we saw from photographs of this period. He went to Hyannis Port to join his family and to recuperate. By that time still more of his PT buddies had returned to the Boston area—Red Fay, Jim Reed, Barney Ross.

Red Fay and Barney Ross had come home by way of Australia and Hollywood. Ross told us:

Red and I and about six or eight others went to Sidney, Melbourne, having a ball and supposedly looking for "first available" transportation. Our theory was that if we took long enough to get back to the States, the war would be over. We finally gave it up and came home on a transport, landing at Long Beach, California. One of the guys' father was Cecil B. DeMille's lawyer, so we went to Hollywood and met him and had another ball. One of the guys got engaged to a starlet, but that didn't last too long. Then we all went home for thirty days' leave and reported to Melville.

That year Labor Day fell on September 4. Although the family was still in mourning for Joe, Jack decided to have a weekend house party, inviting Jim and Jewel Reed, Lennie and Kate Thom, and the two bachelors, Red Fay and Barney Ross. It was the first time any of them had ever been to the Kennedy home and none of them ever forgot the visit. The two ladies remembered the details best, so we give them the floor.

First, Jewel Reed. When we interviewed her in 1974 in Longmeadow, Massachusetts, outside Springfield, she had long been divorced from Jim. It had been a sad, bitter affair. When Jack invited Jim into the high Treasury post in the New Frontier, she had come to Washington full of excitement. Then, the glitter and glamour had wrecked their marriage. Jim's social life had become entangled with Jack's, and Jewel was increasingly left out. Then she went home to despair and divorce. That is all a much later story with no bearing here, except that the experience had possibly tinted her views about certain people. She told us:

I was still working for IBM when Jim got back to Boston about August of 1944. I transferred to the Boston offices of IBM. Jim was assigned to take an advanced Navy course at the Harvard School of Business. We took a little apartment on Boylston Street. We saw quite a bit of Jack, who was an outpatient then.

That famous weekend, Barney came up and spent the night with us. The next day the three of us drove down to Hyannis Port. The others came over from Newport. Red Fay, a bachelor then, didn't care for Lennie's wife and made it quite clear. Just the way he did later in Washington about Barney Ross's wife.

We were organized from the moment we arrived. The Kennedys organized everybody. I hated playing tennis, so Eunice invited me to play golf. The next day we played touch football, which was hideous. But we *had* to play and it was relentless. At the dinner table at night, Mr. Kennedy went around the table checking on what you'd done that day. His approval was almost automatic if you'd scored first or second. If somebody came in fifth there was a lot of ribbing and disapproval. Rose was in mourning for Joe Junior. Kathleen was home from England. She was very much of a live wire. Red and Kathleen got along famously. The Kennedys played the word game Categories endlessly, and they were terribly sharp at it. The whole weekend we were always competing with somebody over something.

Kate Thom told us:

So many things happened that weekend! I remember Eunice was in a sailing race and didn't have a crew. I'd never been a boat in my life and I was made her crew. They were in everything to win, not just to participate. I remember how cruel I thought she was because she kept barking orders at me and if I did something wrong, she'd scream. But she knew what she was doing and what she had to do to win. And we won the race.

Joe had just been killed. Kathleen was home. I spent a lot of time with Kathleen. She was more or less the quiet one. We had a lot in common. And I was pregnant at the time and wasn't doing as much as everyone else. I remember vividly my conversations with her. We talked a lot about the war and religion and Joe. She'd been the last one to see Joe. I was also married to a non-Catholic and we talked about that.

Did anybody tell you about sneaking into the kitchen to get the scotch? They only served one cocktail before dinner. But these were a bunch of Navy men. So when the cooks left, we'd sneak into kitchen and get the scotch. Bobby came home from Harvard. He was a scrawny little guy in a white sailor suit. He was very upset that we were sneaking booze in the kitchen. He was afraid his father might catch us and he knew his father's wrath. But Kathleen handled him. She told him to get lost.

In the evenings, the Kennedys would retire early and we'd sit on the lawn. I remember that Red and Barney were clowning around and we were all singing and clapping our hands and Mr. Kennedy leaned out the window and said, "Jack, don't you and your friends have any respect for your dead brother?" Which shut us up.

That harsh cry from the ambassador's window put a damper on the rest of the weekend. It also ended whatever friendship there had been between Jack and Barney Ross. Jewel told us she saw Barney approach the ambassador the following morning to apologize, but that the ambassador "coldly cut him off." Ross told us that, following that weekend, he did not see Jack again for sixteen years—until in 1960 when Jack, urged by Red Fay, mobilized him to help in the presidential campaign.

There was still more tragic news for the Kennedy family. On the Saturday following Labor Day, September 10, less than a month after Joe Junior's death, Billy Hartington was killed in France. We could find nothing in the Kennedy books describing how this news arrived—or Jack's or the family's reaction to it. Only that, as Rose writes, the British Government sent a plane for Kathleen so that she could return to England. There, she buried her new husband and collected Joe Junior's personal effects to ship home.

Kathleen did not go back to the Church, according to those who knew her. Nor did she come home. From that point onward, she made her life in Europe, returning to the United States only to visit her friends and family. Billy had left her more than enough to live comfortably for the rest of her life.

We suspect that Jack did not disapprove of her leaving. But, of course, there is no hint of his feelings on the record. Only the insistence of all his friends that Kathleen was, to the end, his favorite sister.

25

Father and Son

W E believe that for the next three months Jack was an outpatient at the Chelsea Naval Hospital.

We visited Chelsea, an old, decrepit structure soon to be closed. The duty officer told us there had once been a photograph of Kennedy in his room at the hospital, surrounded by nurses and family, but that it had disappeared. In those days, he said, Chelsea had a good physical therapy section for rehabilitating the wounded—paraplegics and the like. He surmised, as we did, that following the operation at the New England Baptist Hospital, Jack reported to Chelsea in outpatient status to receive treatment designed to strengthen his back.

He was in Hyannis Port on September 14 to witness an amazing and awesome sight. That night, according to Damore in *The Cape Cod Years,* the "worst hurricane in Hyannis Port's history" struck. *Life,* October 2, 1944, said the huge storm, which reached from New Jersey to New England, caused twenty-seven deaths and $50 million in damage. *Survey Graphic* for October, 1944, reported that on Cape Cod all the trees were uprooted and telephone and electrical lines down, the boatyards and harbors were a shambles of smashed boats, and that the waterfront homes were "badly mauled" along the south shore of the Cape.

Damore writes that Jack, "on leave from Chelsea Naval Hospital," was at home that night. He saved the family sailboat *Victura,* then drove his Buick convertible into Hyannis, where he was stranded by high water. In the days following, Jack joined a *Life* photographer-reporter team who came to cover the storm damage. The reporter and Jack, Damore writes, picked up a couple of young girls. Jack's was named Ann—an eighteen-year-old telephone company employee with sparkling blue-green eyes. They went dancing at the Panama Club in Hyannis and later to a movie at the Center Theater. While they were dancing, Ann, Damore reports, asked Jack how his back was and Jack replied, "Right now it's not very good."

Jack's pals were once again on the move. Lem Billings, having graduated from the Supply Corps School at Babson College, told us he "used drag" to get sea duty—the new U.S.S. *Cecil (APA-96),* an attack transport—then fitting out in Portland, Oregon. Torby, declared physically unfit for further sea duty because of his ankle wound, he told us, was sent from Melville to Fort Schuyler, Long Island, as an instructor for midshipmen. Red Fay and Barney Ross left PT boats for another duty.

Lennie and Kate Thom were still at Melville. Lennie had been assigned to a newly forming squadron that would go back to the Pacific. Kate recalled:

> Lennie played football that fall on the Melville PT team. Jack came down for several games and sat on the bench with him. I remember the Melville-Harvard game. Lennie was there in his football uniform smoking this big cigar and little Jack was sitting next to him on the bench in street clothes smoking this big stogy. I was sitting up in the stands giggling—they looked so funny. Melville beat Harvard. And after the game we all went to a little pub. Jack had rooted for Harvard, but he wasn't disappointed. He seemed delighted that Melville won. He'd lost his summer tan and he still looked kind of fagged out.

Jim and Jewel Reed were living in the apartment on Boylston Street in Boston. Jim was in the Navy course at Harvard Business School; Jewel at IBM. Jack called on them frequently, and this led to a problem in their marriage that would go on for years. She recalled:

> Jack would frequently ask Jim to parties—but not me! It was a male prowling thing and Jack couldn't understand why Jim couldn't leave me behind and prowl with him. Maybe this is acceptable in the "upper classes." I think Jack felt this was being manly. But, it seemed to me, he had a contempt for women, possibly because of his father's attitude toward women.
>
> I remember when he was an outpatient at Chelsea, he came by with this scrumptious-looking nurse in uniform. He left her sitting with me in the living room and took Jim off to talk in another room. I don't know what they were talking about. The girl was beautiful, stunning. She was beautifully made up and coiffed, but she didn't know how to talk. I had absolutely nothing in common with a Navy nurse at that time.
>
> Well, as it turned out, Jack invited Jim to go with him to the theater and to a party afterwards. I wasn't invited! I told Jim I thought that was rotten. So he didn't go.

Jim Reed gave us his impressions of Jack's attitude toward women then, and later. Like Kathleen, he thought Jack had the "English attitude" toward women.

I think he looked on women in a different way than I do. I think he thought they were there for a purpose. I think the conventional way we Americans look upon women—you know, romantically— escaped him. They were sort of chattel. He treated them that way. In a casual, amiable way. Maybe defensively is a good way of describing it. I think it was more of a cat-and-dog sort of thing. I think he had the feeling it was a war between the sexes, in a sense. A man would always try to conquer a woman. And she was there to sort of be conquered. Sort of a game. It was hard for him to wrap around a woman the American concept of furniture, motherhood, and all that type of thing. I'm sure it must have flowed from his father's attitude about women. I think this is an English attitude toward women. And sometimes I think they're right.

From several of Jack's friends (who asked not to be identified) we learned that Jack dated two nurses at Chelsea Naval Hospital during this period: Elinor Dooley and Anna Marie McGillicuddy, called Ann by everyone. Lieutenant Commander Janice A. Emal of the Navy's Bureau of Medicine and Surgery provided us the official, releasable information on their naval service. From other sources, we added a bit more.

Elinor Mae Dooley now lives in Bethesda, Maryland, with her husband of nearly thirty years, Dr. Clyde Johnson Dawe. She was reluctant to talk with us about her relationship with Jack Kennedy. She said, "He had had his back operation. I don't remember when or where or who did it. I remember his brother had just died. There were many, many doctors involved, civilian and Navy. Consultants and so on. His family was in and out—and he had many, many visitors. And yes, I remember Ann McGillicuddy. Jack dated her. She could tell you a lot. I'm sorry I can't help you further. It seems to me you could easily find out who operated on Jack by getting his official medical records. . . ."

Ann McGillicuddy was difficult to find, and totally unwilling to discuss her relationship with Jack when we did find her. So much so that we suspected that a relationship of some significance and duration had existed. Her Navy record provided clues. Some of her shifts in duty stations, and her resignations from the Navy and returning to active duty, seemed to coincide with major shifts in Jack's life. We were to discover that there was a relationship of some duration, though we were never able to learn very much of interest about it. What little we did discover will be dealt with at the appropriate place in the narrative.

As to this period in Jack's life, Ann McGillicuddy did confirm our theory about the operation. She said, "Jack was operated on in the New England Baptist Hospital by civilians, not at Chelsea by Navy doctors. The civilians were connected with the Lahey Clinic. Afterwards, in the fall, he was attached to Chelsea. That's where I first met him."

That fall Jack was preoccupied with two other matters besides his health. The first was the national election, the second was a book that he decided to write, a tribute to his brother Joe.

By now, Ambassador Kennedy, still embittered because he had not been drafted for a wartime job in Washington, hated Roosevelt. But he supported the vice presidential nominee Harry Truman—at least financially. According to an oral history we found in the Kennedy Library given by one of his old pals, Edward M. Gallagher, when Truman came to Boston during the campaign, the ambassador gave him $5,000.

In *Plain Speaking,* by Merle Miller, Truman gives his version of that visit:

> Old man Kennedy started throwing rocks at Roosevelt, saying he'd caused the war and so on. And then he said, "Harry, what the hell are you doing campaigning for that crippled son of a bitch that killed my son Joe?" I'd stood it just as long as I could, and I said, "If you say another word about Roosevelt, I'm going to throw you out the window." And Bob [Hannegan] grabbed me by the arm and said, "Come out here. I'm gonna get ten thousand dollars out of the old son of a bitch for the Democratic Party." And he did. . . .
> Old Joe Kennedy is as big a crook as we've got anywhere in this country. . . .

The Kennedy family friend, Clare Boothe Luce, standing for reelection to a second term in the House of Representatives from Connecticut, attacked Truman unmercifully. Worse, she went after Truman's wife, Bess, exposing the fact that Bess was on Harry's Senate office payroll. Truman was furious. "The way she talked about my wife," he told a newspaper reporter, "Well, if she were a man, I would have done something about it." Margaret Truman, in her book *Harry S. Truman,* reports that her father never forgave Mrs. Luce those "snide remarks" and for the seven and three-quarters years the Trumans were in the White House, never invited her to a social function there.

By this time the Kennedys and the Luces had become fast friends, socially and politically. Henry Luce was, like Joe Kennedy, an avowed Roosevelt-hater and fully supported Dewey. In truth, Joe Kennedy was ideologically more Republican than Democrat. In time, they would also all become Truman-haters.

How did Jack register and vote in 1944? We searched the Kennedy Library high and low for some official documents. There are none; nor do any of the Kennedy books have anything to say about it. Later, we saw in Boston papers of 1948, that Jack claimed he had registered in 1944 as a Democrat in Massachusetts.

The second preoccupation—the book on Joe Junior, which finally emerged under the title *As We Remember Joe*—was launched while Jack was an outpatient at Chelsea Naval Hospital. Red Fay says in his book that Jack conceived it as a Christmas present for his mother and father. But it was delayed and not presented until later—in 1945. Privately printed by the Harvard University Press, the slim little hardbound book is now a collector's item, worth perhaps $2,000 a copy. The Kennedy Library has a Xerox on file for researchers.

It is not really a book in the strictest sense. It is a collection of twenty letters from relatives and friends of Joe's (Tom Killefer, Ted Reardon, and so on) with a biographical introduction by Jack Kennedy. It is dedicated to George Mead, Cyrus Taylor, William Coleman, and other friends of Jack's and Joe's who were killed in the war.

Excerpts from Jack's introduction:

> Joe did many things well, as his record illustrates, but I have always felt that Joe achieved his greatest success as the oldest brother. Very early in life he acquired a sense of responsibility towards his brothers and sisters, and I do not think that he ever forgot it. Towards me who was nearly his own age, this responsibility consisted in setting a standard that was uniformly high. For example, I never heard him utter a foul word or, until the last two or three years, ever swear. I suppose I knew Joe as well as anyone and yet, I sometimes wonder whether I ever really knew him. He had always a slight detachment from things around him—a wall of reserve which few people ever succeeded in penetrating. I do not mean by this that Joe was ponderous and heavy in his attitude. Far from it—I do not know anyone with whom I would rather have spent an evening or played golf or, in fact, done anything. He had a keen wit and saw the humorous side of people and situations quicker than anyone I have ever known.
>
> He would spend long hours throwing a football with Bobby, swimming with Teddy, and teaching the younger girls how to sail. He was always close to Kick and was particularly close to her during some difficult times. I think that if the Kennedy children amount to anything now or ever amount to anything, it will be due more to Joe's behavior and his constant example than to any other factor. He made the task of bringing up a large family immeasurably easier for my father and mother for what they taught him, he

passed on to us, and their teachings were not diluted through him, but rather strengthened. . . .

It is the realization that the future held the promise of great accomplishments for Joe that has made his death so particularly hard for those who knew him. His worldly success was so assured and inevitable that his death seems to have cut into the natural order of things. But at the same time, there is a completeness to Joe's life, and that is the completeness of perfection. His life as he lived and finally, as he died, could hardly have been improved upon. . . .

That fall Jack drew closer to a PT buddy he had met in the Solomons, another from Warfield's ill-starred Squadron Ten. He was a big, happy-go-lucky, red-haired Boston Irishman, Edward F. McLaughlin, Jr., son of a famous old Boston pol who knew both of Jack's politician grandfathers. Eddie, the Squadron Ten paymaster, had become good friends with Red Fay and Barney Ross and through them, Jack. He was a graduate of Dartmouth College (1942).

Eddie was never as intimate a friend as Torby or Lem Billings or Jim Reed or Chuck Spalding, but he was a good friend of Jack's and one who helped him from the first in his political campaign. That fall when Eddie came home from the South Pacific, he was assigned to a Navy unit in South Boston and he was then one of Jack's few personal friends in the city.

We interviewed Eddie McLaughlin, now a Boston lawyer and a former lieutenant governor of Massachusetts, at some length in his office and later in his vacation home on Cape Cod. At their home, we also talked with his wife Elizabeth or "Cis." These interviews were extremely valuable for shedding light on this little-known period of Jack's life. We will return to them as appropriate. For now, what interested us most was Cis's recollection of her first meeting with Jack that fall, and the rather strange way that both Jack and his father pursued her.

Cis was then Elizabeth Drake of New York, Eddie's fiancée. Eddie invited her up for a Boston weekend, including a football game at Fenway Park. Afterwards they went to a party at Jim and Jewel Reed's apartment, around the corner from the stadium. It was that evening that Cis first met Jack and Torby, who was up from New York also. She recalled:

Jack came up to me in the kitchen at the Reed's and said, "You must be Cis. I recognize you from your pictures." I thought he was charming—a nice guy. He looked better than I expected he would. He said next time he was in New York, he'd call me. And he did—some weeks later.

We went out. We met at 21 for dinner. We went from there to the theater to see *Brigadoon*. We took a cab. I had to pay for it because he didn't have any money—no cash. He was OK at places like 21 where he could sign the check, but he never had any cash. He wasn't chintzy at all, he just didn't think about money. At the theater, we had seats next to Joan Bennett and her husband. Jack knew them—he knew everybody in New York, far more people than he knew in Boston because New York had really been his home—and introduced me. Afterwards we went to the Starlight Room of the Waldorf Astoria Hotel and danced. He was a terrible dancer—all over my feet. I had a great time. Every time he came to New York he called. It wasn't a romance, we were just good friends. He was a ladies' man, the women loved him, but he didn't have much security in those days. He was very shy, and not sure of himself at all. He said he never knew if a girl liked him for himself or for his money. He said he had a feeling that every time they looked at his face they saw dollar signs. He had a very famous father and I think he felt he shone by reflection. He didn't know what he wanted to do with his life. He wanted to write. . . . I think I saw him as often as I did because he was shy and he was not sure of those girls who were always chasing him. He felt more comfortable with me. He wasn't really, basically, a party boy anyway. He really didn't like nightclubs. It was just a place to go, a place to have company.

He was always asking me if I thought I really wanted to get married [to Eddie] because there were so many unhappy marriages. At that time we [Eddie and I] weren't as much aware of so many unhappy marriages as we are at this time. I now think Jack was looking back in his own head to his own mother and father. But he never said that.

After the Jim and Jewel Reed party, Cis recalled, Jack had invited her and Eddie down to the Kennedy house in Hyannis Port. She met the ambassador there. And then she told us a story that brought to mind the experiences that Charlotte McDonnell and Inga Arvad had with the ambassador, who was then fifty-six years old:

One day in New York when I was at home, Mr. Kennedy called and invited me to lunch at the Waldorf. My mother was plenty impressed. Mr. Kennedy said Mrs. Kennedy would be there, but she wasn't. When I walked in he said to me, "You should consider yourself a very lucky young lady. I just canceled a luncheon date with Herbert Hoover to have lunch with you. There are not many young ladies I would do this for. I'm very selective. But you have so much maturity. I was very impressed with you at the Cape."

I was flattered. We talked and he asked if I wanted a drink. I didn't drink, and neither did he, so I had a Coke and he had a Horse's Neck—ginger ale and lemon. Then he said, "Why don't we have lunch here?" When the room service man came, I ordered a sliced chicken sandwich. Mr. Kennedy took two eggs out of his pocket—he'd brought them from the Cape, I think—wrote his name on them with a pen, and sent them to the kitchen with orders they should be boiled two and a half to three minutes and no more. Well, I could hardly believe all this, but the eggs came back with his name still on them. And then he laid out about seven pills on the table. He ate the eggs and then he took the pills. He must have had loads of things wrong with him.

He asked me how much I thought Eddie would make when he [returned to civilian life and] started working. I said I didn't know but that he hoped to be a lawyer. Mr. Kennedy said he paid his butler more than Ed would ever make. He said I was wasting my time with Ed. I was a nice-looking girl and I could do better than that.

I couldn't even eat I was so nervous. And I began to see the handwriting on the wall. I got out of there as fast as I could. I didn't think I'd ever hear from him again, but I did. He called again. And I—foolish me—went again twice more, I think. It was a challenge in a way. I thought I could handle this guy. Nothing was going to happen to me. But each time he got tougher to fend off. The third time, I really had a rough time getting out of his apartment. I literally ran out. And then I'd see him down at the Cape and he'd be perfectly charming.

I've had other girls tell me almost identical stories. He was just that kind of guy. He liked younger women. So I believe all the stories I've heard about him and Gloria Swanson. . . .

Jack's days in the Navy were drawing to a close. The back operation had not been a success to the extent that would make him capable of returning to active duty, even on a limited basis. As a couple of letters of the period show, he was told that he would soon come before a medical survey board and be discharged, formally, from the Navy.

In November, 1944, he wrote a letter to Red Fay, then in Hollywood, Florida, from the Chelsea Naval Hospital. It appears in Fay's book.

DEAR RED:

Needless to say, the old eyes filled a bit when I got your dispatch from your beach-head in Hollywood. I appreciated your offer to share your foxhole and I have delayed answering until I have a definite idea of what's going to be done. Unfortunately or fortunately, depending on how you look at it, and I won't ask for a statement—sometime in the next month I'm going to be paying full price at the local Loew's. I will no longer [be] getting the forty-per-cent off for servicemen—for the simple reason that I'm going to be in mufti. This I learned yesterday—as they have given up on fixing me up O.K. From here I'm going to go home for Christmas, then go to Arizona for about a year, and try to get back in shape again.

In any case, I'll be in Palm Beach fairly soon—so you'll have to come up for a few weekends as the facilities are ample for even a guy who throws his weight around like you. Pappy is going down with Commissioner Timilley [Timilty] the 29th of November. Any-way I hope for a guest-star spot from you for Christmas. At the Kennedies' own Christmas, the wassail flows like molasses, but the chow is excellent.

Drop me a line up here if you get the chance, as I am based here now.

Best,
JACK

About this same time, Jack wrote a letter to one of the *PT-109* crew-men, John E. Maguire. Maguire, Charles Harris, William Johnston, and Maguire's brother, William J. (who had also been in PT's in the Solo-mons), had joined Lennie Thom on his new boat, *PT-587* (nicknamed the *Thomcat)* in Squadron Thirty-nine which was being commissioned at the Brooklyn Navy Yard. A partial text of this letter is included in Donovan's book and, as we said, Donovan mistakenly implies the letter was written in 1943, not 1944. "Went up before the Survey Board the other day—and I'm on the way out. It's going to seem peculiar paying full prices at those movie theaters again. It won't seem quite right until everyone is out, I don't think. Going to spend Christmas with the folks . . . "

Some time after this, probably in the first or second week of December, Jack went to Palm Beach for Christmas—presumably to await the final paperwork on his discharge. Red Fay, close by in Hollywood, was a constant visitor at Palm Beach. Another visitor was Jack's old friend and Harvard roommate, Ben Smith, who was now stationed in Miami.

Since Ben and Jack last met in Boston in December, 1941, Ben had a lively time captaining Navy net tenders and net layers in both the Atlantic and the Pacific. He was in Miami for instruction in destroyers. He told us:

> I saw Jack up at Palm Beach when we were in Miami. But by that time, we had three children and I was a lot more domesticated than Jack and Torby. Jack had had his operation by then. His spir-its were great, but his back really bothered him. I remember he did a lot of swimming and that he rested a lot. I met Red Fay up there. I didn't particularly care for Fay. He was too loud.

Rose invited Red Fay to Palm Beach for Christmas. Since he was far from home, he wrote in his book, he readily accepted the invitation. He arrived with dozens of small trinkets wrapped in gay Christmas paper. On Christmas Eve, he wrote, they all decorated the tree. "Jack kept joking with me and the others, trying to keep his father's and mother's minds off Joe. This was the first Christmas since Joe's death." Fay did not say so, but Kathleen was not there either, and that, too, must have been cause for sadness.

Behind all the joking and Christmas gaiety, Fay reported, there was a very serious discussion going on between Jack and his father regarding Jack's future course. Now that his military service was drawing to a close, what would he do in life?

The Boston legend, as James MacGregor Burns describes it, goes as follows: A few weeks after Joe Junior's death, the ambassador summons Jack to his presence. In a dramatic scene the ambassador tells Jack that now that Joe Junior is gone, Jack must carry on the family tradition of public service. Jack, there and then, answers the call.

In the early days of Jack's presidential campaign, the ambassador and Jack both gave interviews containing statements that tend to support the legend.

The ambassador, to writer Eleanor Harris, who published an article on the Kennedys in the August, 1957, *McCall's* magazine: "I got Jack into politics. I was the one. I told him Joe was dead and that it was therefore his responsiblility to run for Congress. He didn't want to. He felt he didn't have the ability and he still feels that way. But I told him he had to. . . ."

The ambassador to reporter Joseph McCarthy, quoted in his book of 1959, *The Remarkable Kennedys* : "I thought everyone knows about that. Jack went into politics because young Joe died. Young Joe was going to be the politician in the family. When he died, Jack took his place. . . ."

Jack, in the Bob Considine series written for INS in May, 1957: "It was like being drafted. My father wanted his eldest son in politics. 'Wanted' isn't the right word. He *demanded* it. You know my father. . . ."

Jack to Eleanor Harris, in *McCall's* : "My brother Joe was the logical one in the family to be in politics and if he had lived, I'd have kept on being a writer. . . . If I died, my brother Bob would want to be Senator and if anything happened to him, my brother Teddy would run for us. . . ."

Later, when Jack became a serious and avowed candidate for the presidency in 1959–1960, everybody apparently had second thoughts about leaving those (and many similar) statements on the record. They seemed to confirm a view held by Jack's critics that Jack was a mere puppet, dancing to his father's string-pulls; that he was wishy-washy with no strong life goals or character; that a vote for Jack was, in effect, a vote for his father. Nor was it good politics to imply that the Massachusetts Senate seat had been given the Kennedys by divine right, and they could pass it on from brother to brother. Thus Jack and others began then, and continued after his death, to soften the ambassador's role in Jack's decision to go into politics.

Ted Sorensen, in his book, *Kennedy:* "Early in our acquaintance he told me that he . . . entered the political arena *not* to take Joe's place, as is often alleged, not to compete subconsciously with him, but as an expression of his own ideals and interests in an arena thereby opened to him. His entry was neither involuntary nor illogical. . . ."

Schlesinger, in *A Thousand Days* : "Though Ambassador Kennedy did not, as myth later had it, automatically promote his second son into the slot now so sadly vacant, Jack, like many young veterans, felt the need of doing something to help the world for which so many friends had died. . . ."

In *Candidates, 1960*, Fletcher Knebel recalled the legend, then made it appear that Jack had wanted to be in politics all his life: "Jack Kennedy does not remember it that way. 'It was the other way around,' he says. 'We all like politics, but Joe seemed a natural to run for office. Obviously, you can't have a whole mess of Kennedys asking for votes. So when Joe was denied his chance, I wanted to run and was glad I could.' "

But much, much later, in 1968, Arthur Krock, in his *Memoirs* , wrote: ". . . Ambassador Kennedy began definitely to plan for Jack the political career he had designed for Joe Junior. Until then, I think, he shared a belief which was mine that Jack was suited to a career in journalism, in literature or in teaching . . . ."

In our interview with Krock, we explored the question further:

Q: Do you fully subscribe to the theory that when Jack entered politics he was filling Joe's shoes?

A: Yes. In fact, I knew it. It was almost a physical event: now it's *your* turn.

Q: Did you have the impression that Jack wasn't too happy about that?

A: He wasn't very happy. It was not his preference. But his father gave all the arguments: I'll make you the first Roman Catholic president of the United States. And you be a good boy and take up the burden that has fallen from your brother's hand. Joe Junior— who volunteered for his final mission to prove the Kennedys were not yellow. . . .

Another very close friend of the Kennedy family, Edward M. Gallagher, had a recollection similar to Krock's. In 1965, while giving his oral history for the Kennedy Library, he was asked about the legend and he replied:

> The father may have firmly impressed upon Jack that the mantle was his to carry on when young Joe was killed over the English Channel.
>
> Q: Was there any occasion when there was some conversation about that?
>
> A: I believe there was. I was not present, but I have heard and I recall strong discussion to that effect took place in the home, at Hyannis Port, that Jack made up his mind that day, that that's what his father wanted, and I think he set out to do it.

Later, we conducted a telephone interview with Gallagher. He told us, "The ambassador didn't have the personality for politics. He accomplished through his own children what his personality denied him. Jack definitely did not want to be a candidate for public office. Joe Junior was the one. He was personable as hell and the old man had been grooming him—probably to run as governor when he came back from the war. But when he was killed, Jack had to step in, against his will at first, and do the job."

In our interview with Joseph Timilty, the onetime Boston police commissioner who held the belief that Joe Junor was killed trying to outdo Jack, we asked about the legend. Timilty, who was almost a member of the Kennedy family, told us, "The ambassador had a great hold on that family and steered them all—including Jack. I had thought of Jack as anything *but* a politician. A writer maybe, but *not* a politician. I'm sure Jack never would have entered politics except for the urging of his dad. There's no question in my mind about that."

Red Fay's book quotes Jack at Christmastime, 1944, as saying, "I can feel Pappy's eyes on the back of my neck," and then adds a significant quotation that sounds like something Jack wrote him in a letter, rather than something he would have spoken: "When the war is over and you are out there in sunny California [working for the Fay Construction Company] giving them a good solid five and a half inches for a six-inch pavement, I'll be back here with Dad trying to parlay a lost PT boat and a bad back into a political advantage. I tell you, Dad is ready right now and can't understand why Johnny boy isn't 'all engines ahead full. . . .'"

We can understand Jack's cautious approach to the decision. For one thing, he surely knew that politics is a strenuous profession, physically. Jack knew, as did his father, that his health was uncertain. The back operation had not helped; in political contests—parades, door-to-door campaigning, handshaking—he was bound to overtax his back and bring on the excruciating pain again. For another, Jack had not mentally prepared himself for the role. He was not naturally a glad-hander or a backslapper. On the contrary, as Cis McLaughlin and others told us, he was basically shy and a little unsure of himself. To be anything else, he would have to work at it—to *act*. He would have to play a public role that was not himself.

He had many political assets, to be sure: good looks, a famous family, millions of dollars. But, like every other human being, he also had some liabilities. One was the Inga Arvad relationship. Although politicians did not ordinarily introduce sexual history into a political campaign, the Inga affair had the "Nazi spy" angle. There was the fact that Jack had almost been cashiered from the Navy. It would be a tough charge to answer. There was was the *PT-109* sinking. Thanks to the ambassador, the publicity had been enormous—and favorable. But Jack must have known there were many who had a different view of the incident. At any time, he could face a charge from a political opponent that he had been less than heroic. It might not succeed, but again, it would be difficult to combat. Another was his health—and not just the back, which had now been successfully transmogrified into a "Navy injury," but his generally frail constitution which, as we have seen, had put him in and out of hospitals for months at a stretch during his life. He *looked* bad—skinny and sickly. If an opponent called attention to physical condition, Jack might have been hard-pressed to argue that his health was good and sufficient.

There was the question of a political base. Jack Kennedy had no roots. He had been born in Boston, into a well-known political family—two families, really—but he had not lived there since he was a small child. Still, Massachusetts offered the most advantages. Jack's grandfather, Honey Fitz, was still a fixture around the State House and City Hall. Jack had gone to Harvard, he had dozens of cousins, aunts, and uncles in Boston, a well-known, if not magical, name politically, and at least a tenuous residency at Hyannis Port. Most of the Boston papers had been favorably disposed to the Kennedys.

If it were to be Massachusetts—and there was really no alternative—there was finally the question of when and how and for what office. Massachusetts, politically, has always been a maze. There were no simple, monolithic political machines, Democrat or Republican, but rather a series of complicated, interlocking, or warring, political fiefdoms built around personalities. It would take time to court the personalities in the Democratic Party, find a suitable slot for Jack, then organize the campaign to best advantage.

But 1944, an election year, was just over. The next Massachusetts elections, primaries, would not take place until early summer of 1946—eighteen months off. That was time enough for Jack to go to Arizona and regain his strength, and time enough for the ambassador to thoroughly scout the political scene in Massachusetts.

And so it was decided. There is no document or letter extant, to our knowledge, pinpointing when the decision was reached. Our best guess is that the discussions began in the fall at Hyannis Port, continued in Palm Beach in December and, that about Christmastime, 1944, when Red Fay was there, Jack gave his father a tenuous and not very enthusiastic OK.

On the day after Christmas, December 26, 1944, Jack received official naval orders to appear the following day before a Naval Retirement Board in Washington, D. C., according to a set of papers we found at the Kennedy Library. While examining these orders, we noted with surprise that the authority was given as "telephone orders from Lt. Comdr. Charles Houghton, Jr.," in the Navy Bureau of Personnel. Was this the same Charlie Houghton who had been Jack's roommate at Harvard?

Yes, it turned out. Houghton explained how, after three years of duty on patrol craft (PC's) and destroyer escorts (DE's),

> I was transferred to the Bureau of Personnel in Washington and made detail officer for PC's and DE's. That is, I was in charge of assigning officers to, and transferring them from, these classes of ships to other duty stations. The PT detail officer was a friend of mine—a guy named Hall—in an office down the corridor. Every now and then we exchanged favors on assignments for friends and VIP's. Maybe Jack called him for orders to get to Washington for the Survey Board and he turned it over to me because I knew Jack. Frankly, I don't remember a thing about it. It was certainly no big deal—just a routine thing we did a dozen times or more a day.
>
> I do remember that when Jack came to Washington then, Stella and I asked him to dinner at our house in Arlington, Virginia. What a night! Charles, Jr., was just a baby—about four months old—and we had a Great Dane. As soon as Jack walked in, the dog jumped all over him. Jack had asthma and if he got within five feet of a dog he couldn't breathe. Stella wasn't much of a cook, and she was trying to get some dinner ready. I'd mixed up some kind of milk punch and had it in a pitcher on top of the icebox. Jack opened the icebox door and the pitcher of milk punch fell down all over the stove. And then the stove blew up. Jack, surveying the scene and sick with asthma, said, "Charlie, I've got to go." And he left.

Presumably on December 27, 1944, Jack appeared before the Retirement Board in Washington, D.C. We could find no record of the appearance in his naval files, nor any other notice until March 16, 1945—his final orders. He was then transferred to the retired list in the rank of full lieutenant "by reason of physical disability." The orders stated that "your incapacity is permanent, is the result of an incident of the service, and was suffered in the line of duty. . . . '' The order was signed by James V. Forrestal. A final note. Jack took no retirement or disability pay or pension (which he surely would have been entitled to) but he did keep his $10,000 GI insurance policy in force. So far as we know, this is the only life insurance he ever held.

26

Rebuilding

J ACK'S primary goal now was to rebuild his health. In January, 1945, while Roosevelt and Truman were being inaugurated, Jack made arrangements to go to Arizona where, in the spring of 1936, he had successfully bounced back from the illness that struck him at The London School of Econonics. He chose the Castle Hot Springs Hotel, a resort about thirty miles northwest of Phoenix, in the 5000-foot-high Bradshaw Mountains. He evidently planned to stay a long time—a year, he told Red Fay. In the Kennedy Library we found a letter from Jack to the *Boston Post*, dated February 7, ordering a mail subscription to the hotel for the next six months.

Soon after he arrived he wrote Red Fay, among others. Fay published the text of the letter in his book (incorrectly dating it a year earlier):

DEAR RED:

I'm sorry I haven't come through with a report on how the Irishman is doing. Frankly, Red, it's a bit slow. Either they haven't read the August issue of the *Reader's Digest* or something, for every time I introduce Kula Gulf into the circle (in itself no mean feat), the conversation just seems to pick itself up and walk into a corner and die. In all fairness to myself I've got to admit it's a tough audience—former Presidents of the local Kiwanis, who have put in their three score and ten and are half way round again. When you fire a fast one at them—that's high and just hitting the corner of the plate, they make no attempt to go for it; they just *know* that they have one that is going to knock you right off that easy chair. I don't mean that in a derogatory sense—but you wouldn't get a ripple out here with the Sarge—unless the tousle-headed lieutenant saved you as he has so often in the past. I'm not knocking the Sarge—it's just that Castle Hot Springs is where self-panickers come to die.

Nevertheless, the facilities are excellent—good swimming pool and hot baths, and a rubber in charge who is a poor man's Sergeant Casey—being an ex-marine and now a rubber and combining the loquacious characteristics of both professions.

The food is just fair—but you can have all you want for thirty

362

bucks a day. If I stay here very long, I'm going to end up my life scratching a beggar's ———. What are your plans? . . . Are you coming out here? I hope so because I'd like to get started socially in Burlingham—but I suppose we would hang around the house all the time waiting for your old man to put out a fire. . . .

I don't believe I told you about my meeting with Robert Kelley—the Manilla Gorilla. When he asked me where I was going I told him Arizona and I took the better part of a morning to explain the difference between the U.S.S. *Arizona* [and] Arizona USA.

The news about the post-war drive of Red Fay's straight-men was good news but while I agree that the Coot Kid and the Big George and the Rod and Shafty boy etc. will all end up as buddies, what do you think about Mrs. Coot Kid and Mrs. Rod and Mrs. Barney Boy and Mrs. K. (money on both sides)? Is there any possibility that they will take a dim view of the old Redhead? Please answer this question in your next.

Best,
SHAFTY

Red Fay explains the references:

"Sarge" is Sergeant Tom Casey, one of the great figures of the Stanford-Palo Alto area. "Burlingham" is a reference to Burlingame, which I had described as the social apex of the San Francisco Bay Area. The reference to my father and putting out fires is a result of his being also the fire commissioner in Woodside. Robert Kelley is the Kelley [Fay means Kelly] of PT boat fame, who along with John Bulkeley brought General MacArthur out of the Philippines. "Coot Kid" is Quentin "Cootie" Thompson, an insurance executive. "Big George" and "Barney Boy" is Barney Ross. "Rod" is John C. Warnecke, former Stanford all-American tackle in the Rose Bowl, now a distinguished architect for the president's grave.

What interested us in the letter is the question Jack poses at the end. He could foresee that the men would all be buddies after the war, but how would the wives fit in? By now, he had encountered the wives of many of his friends. In at least one case, Jewel Reed, there had been a problem. There may have been a similar problem with Sis Smith, since she and Ben now had children, and Ben emphasized to us that he had become more "domesticated" than Jack. Perhaps Jack had met the same situation at the Houghtons' and elsewhere. In sum, all his friendships were now entering a more complex phase.

Reading these lines, we were reminded of the interviews with Cis McLaughlin and Betty Spalding. It seemed to us that Jack was unconsciously expressing to Red Fay what they had stated bluntly. Jack, perhaps based on his own family experience, had developed a chariness, or fear, of marriage. He did not want—or could not have—a deep emotional relationship with a woman. Whether he knew it or not, while his buddies and pals all around him were getting married, or preparing to marry, Jack was now embarked on a course of prolonged bachelorhood.

During his early days at the mountain resort, Jack turned his efforts to writing a magazine piece. What inspired this, we do not know. Perhaps sheer boredom, or perhaps it was a plan devised by Joe Kennedy to keep Jack's name before the public—anticipating political developments in Massachusetts. We are certain that his father encouraged it—and tried to get it into the *Digest* through his friend Paul Palmer.

There is a typescript of the article (never published) on file in the Kennedy Library. The topic was one that was on everybody's mind: how to keep the peace once it had been won. Jack argued against the idea of the United States maintaining a large army and navy on the grounds that this burden would mean crippling taxes and a stifling of private enterprise. Instead, he proposed a strict agreement between the United States, Britain, and the USSR for limiting postwar armaments.

In truth, it isn't much of an article. The writing is pedestrian. Jack's proposed plan for arms control—the heart of the piece—is lamely and vaguely argued. It winds up with several hundred words of exhortation about the Four Freedoms.

He forwarded it to his father who, on February 15, sent it straightaway to Paul Palmer at the *Digest*. The forwarding letter is on file with the Palmer Papers at Yale. Full text:

DEAR PAUL:

I have asked Mr. Murphy in my office to send this manuscript of Jack's to you and to sign this letter.

Jack felt so strongly about the question of rearmament that I suggested he put his feelings on paper. I think he was worked out a rather publishable article, which subject to revision that news developments might call for, is about in final shape.

Would you be good enough to let me know if you could use it in the Digest or any other publication.

With kindest regards, I am

Sincerely,
/s/ JOE KENNEDY

But Palmer did not think the article suitable for the *Digest* . On February 21 he wrote the ambassador, whom he now addressed as "Joe," a gentle rejection. Full text:

Thanks for letting me see the article by your son Jack. It is an intelligently-reasoned and well-written piece. Unfortunately, it is not definite and exact enough for *The Reader's Digest*—we do not use the exhortative and editorial type of article very often. I wish I could give you a different answer on it, but I can't.

As to publication elsewhere, I think the best plan would be to put the article in the hands of a good agent. I can recommend Carl Brandt, of Brandt and Brandt, 101 Park Avenue, New York City; George T. Bye, 535 Fifth Avenue, New York City; or Ann Watkins, 77 Park Avenue, New York City. I would suggest sending the article to one of them and leaving the matter of its publication to him. If you do this, please say that I suggested it.

I hope I will have the pleasure of seeing anything else Jack writes in the future. Perhaps he will drop in at the office and talk to me about his future writing plans when he gets back to New York.

With best regards,

Correspondence at the Kennedy Library shows that Jack or his father sent the piece to Edward Weeks, editor of *Atlantic* . A letter from Weeks to Jack, written some time later, indicates that Weeks turned it down.

Jack made a new friend at the Castle Hot Springs Hotel, a Chicago-based entrepreneur named Joseph Patrick Lannan, who called himself J. Patrick, or Pat. He was a tall, well-built man with blue eyes, thirty-nine years old then, married and the father of six children. Like Jack, he was recuperating from an illness: serious bronchiectasis, which had brought on a major hemorrhage. The doctors at the Mayo Clinic, where he had gone for a diagnosis, had recommended Arizona. For the next several years Jack and Pat Lannan were close, and often in touch. Today J. Patrick Lannan is a man of immense wealth and power. He is a top executive of ITT and controls the Macmillan Publishing Company and several other large corporations. We visited him at his home in Palm Beach.

Lannan's house is one of the most awesome establishments we have ever seen. Called Four Winds, it is enormous, and crammed with paintings and sculpture including work of Jackson Pollock, Alexander Calder, Salvador Dali, Morris Louis, Sam Francis, and Kenneth Noland. A critic in *Art News* has judged this to be "one of the country's most impressive private collections," valued in the millions. He wrote, "The character of Lannan's acquisitions is the character of Lannan himself: daring, pas-

sionately individualistic, totally nonconformist, with a great streak of un-
predictable enthusiasm.''

Lannan—tall, portly, silver-haired and tanned—spoke with us for several hours. He was, he said (referring us to a long article about him in the
August, 1956, issue of *Fortune*) a self-made man, son of a casketmaker.
Born in June, 1905, he grew up in Duluth, Minnesota, where he attended
parochial and public schools. After a succession of menial jobs (bottle
washer, electrician, real estate salesman) he began selling bonds for a
Chicago house, weathered the Depression, then went on to make a small
fortune in various business enterprises in Chicago and the Midwest. He
was a patron of *Poetry* magazine, published by the University of Chicago.
When the war came, he signed on as a dollar-a-year man for the War Production Board in Chicago, touring production plants, prodding managers,
conferring with generals and admirals. Reading the piece in *Fortune*, and
in talking with him, we began to think of Pat Lannan as a kind of Midwestern Joe Kennedy, though the appreciation of the arts had no counter-
part with Kennedy.

He told us about his meeting with Jack and how their friendship developed :

> The place in Arizona was a semiprivate club, established by
> some Eastern people. It had been an Air Force installation and was
> in process of being converted. I had a room with no bathroom. You
> shared the hall bath. There was a pay telephone outside the bath on
> the wall. I used this rather than walking up to the main club, which
> was a long way off. This guy—yellow as saffron and thin as a rail—
> kept stumbling in all the time to use the same phone. He'd just
> been mustered out of the Navy and he wasn't feeling well. This
> was Jack Kennedy and, of course, I knew who he was. He had a
> room near mine in this old building. We got to talking about our ac-
> comodations and decided that if we joined forces, we could do bet-
> ter. So we arranged to get a little cottage together—living room
> with a nice fireplace, two bedrooms, and a bath and our own tele-
> phone.
>
> We were there together, in the cottage, for several weeks. It was
> a wonderful place to ride horses, and we did that every day. He
> was a wild rider. He would charge his horse down a mountainside.
> He loved speed. He was a very daring fellow, but not that good a
> horseman. He was always taking chances. He always wanted to
> race—he was very competitive, but in a nice way.
>
> Twice a day, no matter what the weather was, we'd walk down
> the hill and swim in the pool, usually before lunch and dinner. And
> we read and talked. Jack didn't drink, but I'd have a cocktail be-

fore dinner. We had a table for two in the dining room. Then we'd sit up to one or two in the morning, talking.

One thing I remember distinctly. Every evening at five his father, Joe Kennedy, would telephone him. You could set your clock by it. It was a wonderful relationship, I thought. He was always asking if there was anything he could do for Jack. Once, I remember, he asked his father to send us some meat. Not long after, some frozen steaks and lamb chops arrived. They were wonderful. We actually felt sort of guilty about having them, which was sort of silly, but we did.

He was working on this book about his brother Joe—later he sent me a copy of it. He had a lot of notes and letters and material. He told me all about Joe, how he'd been killed and that was why he was putting this book together.

I asked him what he was going to do now that he was out of the Navy. He said his father had set up a trust for him and he, Jack, didn't see any point in making any more money, or going into business, so he said he thought he'd go into "public service." It was the first time I'd ever heard that term. I said, "You mean politics?" He wouldn't say "politics" to save his life. It was "public service."

We talked about politics. I told him that after the war, labor was going to be a very important force in the country and, it seemed to me, that any aspiring politician ought to understand this force as fully as possible. I said, "Jack, you don't know the difference between an automatic screw machine and a lathe and a punch press and you ought to!" Well, he took that very seriously, and talked to his father on the phone about it. The next thing I knew, a whole crateful of books on labor and labor law arrived at the cottage. Jack sat up to one or two in the morning reading those books until he'd finished the whole crate. He earned my respect for doing that. I had all those books until not long ago.

Most of the people in that place—wealthy people from the East and Midwest—knew of the Kennedys or had read about Jack in the newspapers or *Reader's Digest* or someplace. He was a hero to them and they were sort of enchanted by him and were always trying to get him aside and visit with him. He was always trying to politely avoid them. I don't think he liked the role. He preferred to be left alone. So we had a nice quiet visit.

Actually, it got pretty dull for both of us. We decided we had to get out of there and have a vacation. As I recall, we gave that place up and went down to Phoenix to the Biltmore Hotel, a very fancy place. Jack was wearing his old fatigues from the Navy, and he was, by Biltmore dress standards, out of place. I could just sense all those people looking at him. He was, in that way, very irreverent. We didn't stay there long. Jack didn't like it. It was too dressy.

So then we moved over to the Camelback Inn for a couple of weeks. It was an expensive place, so we shared a double room—didn't even have a sitting room. His father shipped us another box of steaks and chops and we gave them to the chef. Jack was then having a considerable amount of trouble with his stomach—chronic indigestion—and was very uptight about his inability to digest food properly. I persuaded him to drink a little red wine with his dinner.

The Camelback Inn was a small, but very nice place. We rode here every day also. I remember we'd ride out into the desert to an area they called Sun Valley, where Frank Lloyd Wright had his place. We would wile away the hours talking about buying the whole valley and developing it. We actually talked to a couple of real estate men about it, but we lost interest. There was no water; nothing but wild, uncultivated, barren land.

Jack's father telephoned one night and told Jack he should look up a certain Phoenix family: the Goldwaters. Jack called one of them up. I think it was Barry Goldwater's sister. So the Goldwaters came down and had lunch with us at the hotel one day. Then we went to a party at a Goldwater home. I'm not sure which one.

Then, I remember, John Hersey and his wife, Frances Ann, arrived. Jack told me he used to date Frances Ann in college. It seemed to me that John Hersey really and truly liked Jack. You could see there was a very warm feeling. And Jimmy Stewart, who'd just been mustered out of the service, was there. . . .

In our extremely brief chat with Frances Ann Cannon, she had told us that she and John had seen Jack at the Camelback Inn in the spring of 1945. She remembered the occasion: April 12, the day Roosevelt died and Harry S. Truman became president of the United States. Jack had been in Arizona about two months.

By then Jack was evidently feeling much better and anxious to taste the sweets of Hollywood again. Sometime shortly after Roosevelt's death—we could find no record of the exact date—Jack and Pat Lannan took a plane to Los Angeles and checked into a suite at the Beverly Hills Hotel, Lannan recalled. The day they arrived, whom should they meet in the lobby but Jack's pal Chuck Spalding, back from a long tour on an aircraft carrier in the Pacific. Spalding told us, "By that time, I'd sold my book, *Love at First Flight*, to Gary Cooper for a movie. Like every other actor in Hollywood in those days, Cooper, who was married to the daughter of a banker, Paul Shields, hoped to do a thing they called a collapsible corporation and make a lot of money. So I was there in Hollywood, talking to Cooper about the book and the movie and then I saw Jack and Pat Lannan in the Beverly Hills Hotel.'' Pat Lannan told us:

I had met Walter Huston, the actor, someplace before. He was doing a movie and living in a cottage on the grounds of the Beverly Hills Hotel. I called him and he invited us for lunch the day we got there. He was involved with Sam Spiegel, the producer. Spiegel gave a party one night and invited Jack and me. There were four or five very attractive girls there, one really pouring on the charm.

We went to a party at Gary Cooper's. We met Sonja Henie, who was then married to Dan Topping, who owned the New York Yankees. I knew Topping. He was still in the Marine Corps in the Pacific. Sonja said she wanted us to see her house. So we drove up to these huge wrought-iron gates that opened by electric eye. Then all the lights on the grounds and by the pool and house went on. It was one or two in the morning but there was a butler in uniform. We looked at all her ice skating trophies—hundreds or thousands of them in a special room in glass cases.

Then one afternoon, the three of us—Jack, Chuck Spalding, and I—went for cocktails at the home of Olivia DeHavilland. She had just broken up with Walter Huston's son, John. I think she rented a butler for the day. He was all dressed up in formal day clothes at five in the afternoon.

Jack and Chuck did not drink, but I asked for a scotch and soda. He brought me a scotch and water. I sent him back, asking for soda. He came back with a big silver tray. On it was a beat-up box of Arm and Hammer baking soda! Chuck and I broke up and Jack started laughing. It was one of those days.

Chuck Spalding recalled that visit:

Jack was just fascinated with Oliva DeHavilland. He put himself out to be attractive as he could be. He leaned toward her and fixed her with a stare and he was working just as hard as he could, really boring in. And Lannan and I might as well not have been there, we were talking, wondering what we were doing there. So finally we got up to leave and he is still working on her to come out to dinner. But she had another date and wouldn't break it. Then, taking his leave, Jack, unable to take his eyes off Olivia, put his hand on the doorknob and walked straight into the hall closet! Tennis rackets and tennis balls and everything came down on top of his head. We broke up again.

Later that night we went to dinner at a restaurant and Olivia was there with the writer Ludwig Bemelmans. Jack said, "I can't understand it. Just look at that guy! I know he's talented, I know he's got great ability, but really! Do you think it was me walking into the closet? Do you think that's what really did it?" He could make fun of himself. He was really a priceless fellow. . . .

Jack saw other old friends that week in Southern California: Angela Greene and Inga Arvad, who was then an aspiring screenwriter for MGM. By then, too, one of his nurse friends from Chelsea, Ann McGillicuddy, was stationed at the Naval Hospital in Long Beach. Jack may have seen her, too.

After that, Lannan recalled, he and Jack flew to the Mayo Clinic for another checkup. The clinic would not release Jack's records to us, but Lannan obtained the dates he was there with Jack: April 23-25. Chuck Spalding went on to Philadelphia to marry Betty Coxe, who had returned from her tour of Red Cross duty in Italy.

27

The Journalist

W E do not believe that in 1945 Jack Kennedy seriously considered journalism as a career—though that is often given as a fact in the Kennedy books. Before the war, when *Why England Slept* reached the best-seller list, he probably considered writing (or writing and teaching) as a career, but by 1945 the decision had been made that he would enter politics. The journalism of 1945, which began with the lackluster piece for the *Digest* (subsequently sent to *Atlantic*) was very likely meant to keep his name in the public eye, in preparation for his entry into Massachusetts politics.

If Jack had seriously entertained the idea of going into journalism in 1945, his most logical move would have been to see Henry Luce. Luce, who had praised Jack in the preface of *Why England Slept,* would have been delighted, we feel sure, to take Jack on the staff of *Time* or *Life* or bring him into his publishing enterprises in some other capacity. In 1945 Time, Inc., was on verge of a vast postwar expansion. Orders had gone out to hire as many new journalists and writers as possible. Young Jack Kennedy, with his background and social and business connections, would have been as asset to the corporation.

The journalism Jack elected to perform was of a very different character. During May, June, and July he served as a special correspondent for the Hearst newspapers, covering the first United Nations meeting in San Francisco and then, cursorily, the British elections.

We believe the idea for this originated with Ambassador Kennedy. Our surmise is based on a copy of a telegram at the Kennedy Library from Louis Rupper, executive editor of the Hearst *Chicago Herald-American,* to Dr. Paul O'Leary, a dermatologist at the Mayo Clinic, with a message for Jack. Jack was there with Pat Lannan. Rupper asked Dr. O'Leary to have Jack telephone him. His telegram concluded: . . . VISITED WITH HIS FATHER SATURDAY AND ANXIOUS TO FIND OUT IF YOUNG JACK WILL COVER AN ASSIGNMENT. We could find no further correspondence bearing on the matter, but a day or so later, the *Herald-American* ran a brief item under the headline, HERO COVERS PARLEY FOR H-A.

The story, accompanied by a photograph of Jack in Navy uniform, said

371

that Jack, "a PT-boat hero of the South Pacific," and son of former Ambassador Joseph P. Kennedy, would cover the U.N. conference in San Francisco "from a GI viewpoint." It mentioned his book, *Why England Slept* and, in addition, gave *Herald-American* readers the usual version of his war record: "Rejected for Army enlistment early in 1941 because of a back injury suffered in a football scrimmage of Harvard University's junior varsity team, Kennedy underwent five months of almost tortuous, exercises and manipulation to strengthen his back so that he was fit for acceptance in the Navy. On August 2, 1943, he swam to the rescue of two of his crew who had been hurled overboard in the midst of flaming gasoline when their PT-boat was sliced in two by a Jap destroyer in the Solomons." If, as we believe, this assignment was the idea of Joseph P. Kennedy, it was another good example of his shrewd grasp of press agentry. It would keep Jack's name—and the positive reading of his war record—before the public eye, day after day. It would place Jack at the epicenter of an important international conference, which would occupy his mind and talent and bring him into close contact with movers and shakers in the government and the policymakers.

In addition to all that, it would be fun. Jack had had a marvelous time in Southern California with Pat Lannan and Chuck Spalding. An assignment to San Francisco would place him within easy reach of Southern California by plane, and press credentials would give him a high air-travel priority. He had told Red Fay in the February letter from Arizona that he was anxious to get started socially in San Francisco. The U.N. conference would advance that objective, too.

One of Jack's first moves, in fact, was to contact Red Fay, who was languishing at the Navy base in Hollywood, Florida. Somehow Jack managed to spring Red loose so that he could come to San Francisco and pal around with him.

Fay told us, "The base in Florida was closing down so I asked the skipper if I could go out to help Jack at the U.N. He let me!"

Chuck Spalding and his new wife, Betty, were there too. After his wedding in Philadelphia, Chuck, who told us he was at that time trying to get an assignment to the OSS, had been assigned to another aircraft carrier, the *Cabot,* which was then being overhauled in San Francisco, and would soon return to the Pacific. He said:

> Everybody was there. And it was San Francisco on top of everything else! It was a wonderful time. Betty and I couldn't find a room, so we moved into the cellar of somebody's house. Jack was staying at the Palace Hotel, a correspondent for Hearst. He somehow managed to get us a room at the Palace, which was tremendous.
>
> By then, Jack had made up his mind to go into politics. I remem-

ber we were sitting in Union Square waiting for somebody to pick us up to go play golf or tennis and he said to me, "You know, as soon as I can, I'm going to run for office." I said that was just perfect for him, that there was no end of what could happen because nobody was better suited for it. I told him it was the best decision he could have made.

It was there that I met Red Fay, too. We became good friends. He took us to play golf and he got us a couple of cars to help load things on the *Cabot*.

The U.N. conference was surrounded by a great social swirl. Receptions, teas, cocktail parties and grand parties hosted by the various delegations and the elite of San Francisco society. During one of these parties, Jack met a gorgeous girl who caught his fancy. She was Anita Marcus, daughter of a San Francisco banker, William Marcus, great-granddaughter of a Peruvian poet, José Arnaldo Marquez.

In time, Anita would become Red Fay's wife. When Fay invited us to his home to meet her, we found a slim and beautiful woman. She described her first meeting with Jack:

> I was working in a hospital in San Francisco at the time of the U.N. They had a big party at what was called the Legion of Honor Museum at the Presidio. A boy named Jack Bates, who claimed he knew Jack, took me and we were looking for Jack. I went to the powder room. All the girls there were talking about Jack Kennedy. When I came out, I couldn't find Jack Bates. I sat down at a table. The first person who came up was Jack Kennedy. He sat down to talk.
>
> I thought he was extremely attractive. I fell madly in love with him. No, I didn't. I think the main thing was that when he talked to you, he looked you straight in the eye and his attention never wandered. He was interested in finding out what I was doing there— why I was there. It was a drawing-me-out thing. It was undivided attention. I was the most envied girl in the room. He had a way with women. There's no question about it.
>
> We were talking about silly things, what he was doing. I kidded him about the ink under his fingernails. I think it came from his typewriter or the carbon or whatever. Then Jack Bates returned. I had to refresh Jack's memory about who he was. After that, Jack took us with him for the rest of the evening and we met everybody there. Later, we took him back to the Palace Hotel.

Anita saw Jack several more times during the U.N. meeting, she thought. And he had other dates. Nancy Burkett, the beauty he met at

Stanford, was back. She recalled seeing Jack at the Legion of Honor party.

He went to Los Angeles and saw Angela Greene again. She recalled:

> I was then under contract to Warner Brothers, making a film. I remember that at that time I was interested in the work of a very liberal writer and I talked to Jack about him. Jack said, "Now, you've got to stop reading that kind of thing. You've got to read these other things." And then he started me reading. He gave me a copy of his own book, *Why England Slept.* It's inscribed May 10, 1945: "For Angela, who gave me most of my information." It was during this visit that I first realized he was seriously interested in politics.
>
> I remember he took me out, here and there. We went to Sonja Henie's house and—oh, yes!—to Gary Cooper's. Being a very young starlet, I thought that was smashing. I think at the time I was more impressed with Mr. Cooper than I was with Mr. Kennedy. It sounds crazy in retrospect to say a thing like that. . . .

Life reported (May 14, 1945) there were 1,200 accredited journalists at the conference—six for every delegate. There were lightweights such as Earl Wilson, Walter Winchell, and Hedda Hopper, and heavyweights such as Walter Lippmann, James Reston, and Arthur Krock. Krock recalled Jack in his *Memoirs:*

> I saw much of him in the off-hours devoted to social activities. But I shall always regret that I was not one of those in his bedroom at the Palace Hotel one evening, where according to a friend— John Andrews King, and in King's words—this delightful incident occurred:
>
> "Jack, dressed for a black-tie evening, with the exception of his pumps and dinner coat, was lying on the bed, propped up by three pillows, a highball in one hand and the telephone receiver in the other. To the operator he said, 'I want to speak to the Managing Editor of the *Chicago Herald-Examiner.*' (After a long pause) 'Not in? Well, put somebody on to take a message.' (Another pause) 'Good. Will you see that the boss gets this message as soon as you can reach him? Thank you. Here's the message: "Kennedy will not be filing tonight."
>
> I think this was the same evening I saw him cutting in on Anthony Eden, the British Foreign Secretary, who was dancing with the beautiful lady who became the Viscountess Harcourt—and getting promptly cut in on again by Eden himself.

Cissy Patterson, of the *Washington Times-Herald*, sent a task force, including one of her beautiful columnists, Bootsie Cassini (later Mrs. William Randolph Hearst, Jr.). Jack and Bootsie became friends in San Francisco. We interviewed Bootsie in her New York apartment, where she told us about her background and her meeting with Jack. She was born Austine McDonnell in Warrenton, Virginia. In 1942 she married Igor Cassini, who was then putting out Cissy's most famous gossip column, "These Charming People." When Igor went into Army Intelligence, Bootsie took over the column. She told us:

> I made a success of the column. I got more fan mail than anyone else on the paper. Cissy sent me to San Francisco. I stayed at the Palace Hotel. I remember I was waiting for the elevator and there was this very attractive young man standing there. And that was one of the most appealing things about Jack Kennedy—that he looked awfully boyish and helpless, like a kid.
>
> Arthur Krock came up and introduced me to him. I already knew Eunice—I was in her wedding years later—and I said, "I've heard your sisters talk about you." I thought he was attractive, with a good sense of humor. And I'm sure he thought I was attractive.
>
> I knew a lot more people than he did in San Francisco. So we went to some of the press conferences and parties together. Jack was awfully bright—brighter than I was. He knew more about the guts of the U.N. I was much more interested in the frivolous and surface things, like what people were wearing and saying.

We had heard from various sources that Jack and Bootsie may have been closer than just friends. She was certainly his type: beautiful, bright, fashionable, etc. But after interviewing Bootsie—who is still fabulously beautiful and charming—we concluded it probably wasn't so. Their paths crossed many times in later years and they had many close friends in common, such as Flo Pritchett, but there seems to have been no intimate relationship. At San Francisco, Bootsie told us, she had met Will Hearst, Jr. The following year, 1946, she said, she and Igor Cassini were divorced. In 1948 she married Hearst.

Another journalist Jack met in San Francisco was Robert Norton, an influential reporter on the *Boston Post*. Jack may have committed an indiscretion and hinted to Norton about his political plans in Massachusetts. Certainly he turned his great charm on Norton. In *Front Runner, Dark Horse,* a 1960 campaign biography by Ralph G. Martin and Ed Plaut, the authors interviewed Norton (who is now dead) and wrote that in San Francisco, "Norton started out skeptical of Kennedy, but ended up liking him so much that he wrote a story about Jack Kennedy for the *Post* that was never printed. It was a story saying that Kennedy would be the next mayor of Boston and forecasting a tremendous political future for him."

It was probably just as well the story was not printed at that early stage. Had it been it could well have caused Jack a mountain of needless trouble. But credit Norton for smelling out a good local story.

The origins of the U.N. conference are to be found in an earlier conference held in Washington, D.C., in the fall of 1944. It was known as Dumbarton Oaks (named for an estate is Washington where the conference was held). Representatives of the Big Three (the United States, the USSR, and the United Kingdom) met to create the rough outlines of an international organization to maintain world peace and security—in effect, something to replace the League of Nations. What emerged was a crude plan for a United Nations Organization with a General Assembly and its most important working body, the Security Council. The Russians made several controversial demands that would give them a dominant position in the organization. They wanted to seat delegates from all sixteen of their republics, or states, and insisted on a veto system in the Security Council weighted in their favor. In addition, there was considerable disagreement about which nations were entitled to seats in the body.

The discussions were continued at a highter level when Roosevelt, Churchill, and Stalin met at Yalta in early February, 1945. The Big Three resolved some of the major impasses. Stalin withdrew his demand that all sixteen Russian states be given a seat and then agreed on a compromise veto plan for the Security Council. In addition, they agreed that the first U.N.O. meeting would be convened in San Francisco on April 25, 1945. At that time, some of the smaller problems would be worked out and the U.N.O. charter ratified.

All this was well and good—or appeared to be—but the more important work of shaping the postwar world, the spheres of influence, and a lasting, stable peace, was carried out in secret at Yalta.

As the war raced to a climax in Europe in March and April, the United States and the United Kingdom stuck by their Yalta agreements. But wherever the Russians penetrated, they began setting up puppet governments and taking a tough line toward the United States and the United Kingdom. By March 13 Churchill was complaining to Roosevelt of the "utter breakdown of what we settled at Yalta" and urging a blunt stand against Stalin. In a cable dated April 6, recently unearthed and published in Margaret Truman's book on her father, *Harry S. Truman,* Roosevelt agreed, writing: "We must not permit anybody to entertain a false impression that we are afraid. Our Armies will in a very few days be in a position that will permit us to become 'tougher'. . ." The so-called Cold War had begun.

In the face of this deteriorating situation, there was a division of opinion in the U.S. Government about what to do. The policymakers divided into what would now be called hawks and doves. James Forrestal, ambassador to Moscow Averell Harriman, the Russian expert George Kennan, diplomat Charles "Chip" Bohlen and others took a hawkish position. When he ascended to the presidency on April 12, Truman tried to steer a compromise course between the extreme views.

Against this background, the U.N.O. meeting convened in San Francisco on April 25. Harry Truman launched the conference (by long-distance telephone, piped into the meeting hall) on a hopeful note, then went on to other business.

At the Kennedy Library, we found two sets of clippings of the stories Jack filed for Hearst from San Francisco. One set is from the *Chicago Herald-American*, the other from Hearst's *New York Journal-American* (indicating that Jack's copy might have been used by many Hearst papers, but how many we could not determine). Neither set is complete. But by combining the two, we believed we had made a complete set. In all, during a thirty-day period, he filed sixteen stories of about 300 words each: more or less 5,000 words, or about the length of one magazine article.

A letter at the Kennedy Library shows that Hearst paid Jack $750 for his work. Each clip carried a small photograph of Jack, and his by-line "Lt. John F. Kennedy," although he had been retired in March. Each clip was preceded by this statement: "Lt. John F. Kennedy recently retired PT boat hero of the South Pacific and son of former Ambassador Joseph P. Kennedy is covering the San Francisco conference from a serviceman's point of view. . . . Before the war he wrote the best seller, *Why England Slept*."

Jack filed his first story on April 28—he must have arrived late and missed the opening. He complained that the U.N. conference had been given too much of a buildup and that it wasn't going to bring peace to the world. He went on to say that there was not much news to report—except that the Russians were trying to get their way about everything. He said the average GI on the streets of San Francisco did not have a clear-cut idea of what the conference was all about. At the end of the story, he quoted a bemedaled Marine: "I don't know much about what's going on—but if they just fix it so that we don't have to fight anymore—they can count me in." Jack concluded, "Me, too, Sarge."

As the days passed, Jack's stories became more pessimistic. They reflected the "shock" and frustration the United States and United Kingdom delegates were feeling as a result of the tough, demanding attitude of Russian Foreign Minister Vasily Molotov. But Jack counseled patience, writing, "There is a heritage of 25 years of distrust between Russia and the rest of the world that cannot be overcome completely for a good many more years. . . . Before becoming too discouraged with the shape of things here it is well to remember that by the very fact of coming to this conference—the Russians have admitted a necessity for building some type of world organization."

In the midst of the conference, May 8, the Germans officially surrendered. It was, in a term of the time, VE Day (Victory in Europe Day). Jack reported that San Francisco took the celebration in stride and reminded his readers that in San Francisco "war" had always meant the war with Japan. He wrote, "When you have just come home from long months of fighting and are returning to the war zones in a few days, it is difficult to become excited about 'the end of the war.' V-Day for them is a long way off."

Jack's copy was sprinkled with sporting metaphors and similes: "This conference from a distance may have appeared so far like an international football game with Molotov carrying the ball while Stettinius, Eden and the delegates tried to tackle him all over the field." And in another piece, speaking of Molotov as the "key man" at the conference, he wrote, "This would have been true even if he had thrown the ball straight—it was particularly true when he started throwing curves." And: "We juggled the ball and then came forward in favor of 'self-government' for dependent people." And: "The word is out more or less officially that Molotov is about to pick up his marbles and go home. . . . His record as far as what he got was .500."

Almost every story reflects disillusionment. He does not say so outright, but implies that the conference had been torpedoed by the Russians. In plain English: the Russians were bastards; peace would be difficult to achieve; there might even be war with Russia in the future. There was doubt if the U.N. Organization could be effective.

In his book *A Thousand Days,* Arthur M. Schlesinger, Jr. quotes a letter Jack wrote to a "PT-boat friend" who had asked for Jack's opinion of the conference. Jack's response is more eloquent than his newspaper stories. Partial text:

> It would be very easy to write a letter to you that was angry. When I think of how much this war has cost us, of the deaths of Cy and Peter and Orv and Gil and Demi and Joe and Billy and all those thousands and millions who have died with them—when I think of all those gallant acts that I have seen or anyone has seen who has been to war—it would be a very easy thing for me to feel disappointed and somewhat betrayed. . . .
>
> You have seen battlefields where sacrifice was the order of the day and to compare that sacrifice to the timidity and selfishness of the nations gathered at San Francisco must inevitably be disillusioning. . . .
>
> Things cannot be forced from the top. The international relinquishing of sovereignty would have to spring from the people—it

would have to be so strong that the elected delegates would be turned out of office if they failed to do it. . . . We must face the truth that the people have not been horrified by war to a sufficient extent to force them to go to any extent rather than have another war. . . . War will exist until that distant day when the conscientious objector enjoys the same reputation and prestige that the warrior does today.

During Jack's final days in San Francisco, Edward Weeks, editor of *Atlantic*, wrote him proposing a revision of the piece Jack had earlier written on a postwar peace-keeping plan. We could find no reply, or any evidence that Jack attempted a revision. His exposure at San Francisco possibly showed him how shallow his original article had been and perhaps led him to think the subject was too complex to handle in a brief magazine article. Nothing further came of it.

Sometime during the waning days of the San Francisco conference, Jack decided to go to England. Ostensibly, he was going to cover the British elections (which would culminate on July 5) for the Hearst papers. But he may have had more reasons than just that; Jack had, of course, as many reasons as anyone to want to visit Europe, and then some. He had friends there—and he must have looked forward eagerly to seeing his sister Kathleen.

Military regulations were still in effect throughout Europe; nobody could get around without some sort of official status. A press pass from Hearst would get him to England and anywhere else in the European Theater of Operations.

On the way to England, Jack spent a few days on the East Coast, in New York and Boston, visiting friends and family. On May 29 he celebrated his twenty-eighth birthday—where or how we do not know. He probably saw Torby, who was still at the Navy Midshipman School, Fort Schuyler, in the Bronx. Torby had some surprising news: he was going to marry Phyllis Brooks soon. According to New York State marriage records, they were married on June 23, at Tarrytown, New York, when Jack was in England. It was a small wartime ceremony with no fanfare. After that, Torby told us, he finished out his Navy tour at the Virginia Military Institute, then made plans to reenter Harvard Law School that fall.

From New York, Jack went up to Boston and Hyannis Port. He saw Jim and Jewel Reed and the newlyweds (April, 1945) Cis and Eddie McLaughlin. Jim and Eddie were both now assigned to routine Navy jobs in Boston and both were attending law school at night—at Northeastern University. Both would soon be discharged from the Navy. Jim Reed could not make up his mind whether to go to Harvard Law or to the Harvard Business School. Eddie planned to continue going to Northeastern Law at night and to work in the daytime.

Ambassador Kennedy was already advancing Jack's political plans in Massachusetts. As a first stop, in April, he had Governor Maurice Tobin appoint him—the ambassador—head of an "economic survey" of the state. This position gave Joseph P. Kennedy semi-official political status in Massachusetts. It also placed him in an ideal position to "scout" the state, politically, for Jack.

Jim Reed told us that at this time Jack fully confided his plans for entering politics in Massachusetts. He recalled being down at Hyannis Port: "Present were Ambassador Kennedy, Arthur Krock, Honey Fitz, and some others. As a joke, someone said to me, 'Jim, you're going to be president of the United States someday.' Jack piped up and said, 'After me!' Whereupon Honey Fitz stood up very seriously and proposed a toast: 'To the future president of the United States, my grandson, John Fitzgerald Kennedy.' "

The Kennedys at this time were engaged in a family social-political event of great importance. A big (2,500-ton) new Navy destroyer, Number 850, named for Joe Junior, was to be launched on July 26, at the Bethlehem Steel Company building yards in Quincy, Massachusetts. Massachusetts Governor Maurice Tobin would make the principal address; Jean Kennedy would be the sponsor and swing the bottle of champagne to christen the ship.

In June the Kennedys were busy drawing up an invitation list and making other arrangements. We found a copy of the list on file in the Kennedy Library—a valuable index of relatives and close personal friends at this time. Among the bigwigs, the list included: Justices Felix Frankfurter, William Douglas, and Frank Murphy; Senators Burton K. Wheeler and David I. Walsh (but, interestingly, not the Republican Senator from Massachusetts, Leverett Saltonstall); U. S. House majority leader John W. McCormack (Democrat of Massachusetts); the new secretary of state, James F. Byrnes; diplomat Robert Murphy; and a scattered assortment of judges and politicians in Massachusetts. From the press: Cissy Patterson and Frank Waldrop, of the *Times-Herald*; Arthur Krock, William Randolph Hearst, Jr., Henry and Clare Luce; Joseph Patterson, of the *New York Daily News*; and William Mullins, a political columnist on the *Boston Herald*. From the Church: Archbishops Francis J. Spellman of New York and Richard Cushing of Boston.

Among Jack's friends we noted: Torby, Lem Billings, Charlie Houghton, Jim and Jewel Reed, John and Frances Ann Hersey, Charlotte McDonnell Harris, Eddie and Cis McLaughlin, Chuck Spalding (and his parents), Red Fay, Johnny Coleman (and his parents), and Pat Lannan. Ben and Sis Smith are not on the list, an oversight, we felt sure.

There was a surprising number of doctors on the list—five—perhaps an indication of how frequently Jack and his father made use of them. They included: Sara Jordan; Paul O'Leary, the dermatologist at Mayo Clinic (and brother of one of the ambassador's partners in the liquor business); Thomas Cloney of New York City; Frederick L. Good; and John H. Foley of Boston.

The launching went off on schedule and without Jack, who had gone on to England to cover the elections. The Kennedys who attended were: the ambassador, Rose, Pat, Jean, Eunice, and Teddy. Honey Fitz and his wife were there. Jewel Reed recalled, "Governor Tobin came late with a police escort, a tasteless arrival that did not appeal to the Kennedys at all."

There was a big turnout of Boston and New York press for the launching. We found a *New York Times* story reproduced in the *Choate Bulletin* of December, 1945, describing the ceremony. Evidently few dignitaries showed up. The *Times* listed only Governor Tobin and House majority leader McCormack. Monsignor John J. Wright from Archbisop Cushing's office gave the benediction. The *Times* reporter wrote, "As Jean christened the ship, tears welled in the eyes of Kennedy, who stood at rigid attention while 'The Star-Spangled Banner' sounded across the yard where workmen on other warships paused to watch the big destroyer slip into the water. . . ."

And so to England.

Before setting off, Jack had called his new friend from Chicago, Pat Lannan, to invite him along. Lannan must not have been very busy then, or else he had in mind scouting Britain for investment opportunities, because he readily agreed to go, he told us in our interview. The travel restrictions caused a problem. Lannan solved it, he told us, by getting press credentials from a friend on the *Chicago Journal of Commerce*.

We could find nothing in the Kennedy Library to indicate exactly when Jack got there—we assume he left in mid-June. Lannan told us:

Jack flew over and I went over on the *Queen Mary* because I wanted to carry a lot of recording equipment, which in those days was very heavy and bulky. I was bringing this for both of us to use. He met me at the boat. It wasn't easy to get accommodations in London, but the London bureau chief of the *Chicago Tribune*, who was a friend of mine, got us into Grosvenor House: two rooms and a parlor.

I met Kathleen for the first time. She was very industrious, very British. She had really melded herself into the City of London— and England. She loaned us a little car to get around in. It was very small and the windshield wipers didn't work, but we were very glad to have it.

Churchill was campaigning. He'd speak at stadiums and race-tracks and dog tracks and what have you. But we'd drive out in Kathleen's little car. I was a great admirer of Churchill's and I couldn't believe how the people were reacting to him. They just didn't want to make any more sacrifices and they were just booing the hell out of Churchill. I've never heard a politician in America booed like he was. Jack damned well thought Churchill was going to win, but I was certain he wasn't. We'd sit up all hours—with me saying Churchill was going to be defeated, and him saying the opposite. He said I just didn't understand politics. . . .

At the Kennedy Library we found four articles filed by Jack from England to the Hearst papers. They were signed John F. Kennedy, and each was preceded by a synopsis of his war service. The first was dated June 23, the headline: CHURCHILL MAY LOSE ELECTION.

Jack wrote that Churchill was "fighting a tide that is surging through Europe, washing away monarchies and conservative governments everywhere" and that Churchill and the Conservative Party "may" lose. He said Britishers were tired of ten years of government and wanted change. He foresaw socialism—state ownership and control of industry and land. "By watching England," he concluded, "we have much to learn."

In his oral history at the Kennedy Library, Arthur Krock said that Jack had written him two letters from England and that, "They gave me the only intimation I got from anyone that Churchill would be defeated. . . . I made up my mind that this boy had the makings of a very good political observer. . . ."

In his *Memoirs,* Krock expanded: "He was the only source of my expectation that Churchill would be turned out of office. This he strongly indicated in his dispatches, and more definitely in a private letter to me." Getting his timetable mixed, Krock goes on to say that, "In recognition of his reportorial prescience" in predicting the British election, "he was assigned to report on the organization meeting of the United Nations at San Francisco. . . ."

Returning to Pat Lannan: "Every afternoon, about five, we'd have from two to six young Englishmen about Jack's age in for refreshments. They'd all just returned from the war. They'd all sit and talk about politics, and I made these recordings. They were all very literate and bright—and fascinated by my equipment. These were all people Jack had known before the war."

One of them, Lannan recalled, was Hugh Fraser, one of Kathleen's earlier boyfriends and a close friend of the Kennedys'. Fraser was standing for election to the House of Commons. In his oral history at the Kennedy Library, Fraser said that Jack came out to watch him campaign for two days: "It was my first shot at politics and I must have been pretty peculiar. Certainly Jack thought it was peculiar. . . . . Jack was a great listener—and a great questioner. He wanted to know the root cause of things. He was much more serious than he gave on. . . ."

Jack also met the British writer Barbara Ward (Lady Jackson), who was a friend of Kathleen's. According to an article by Selig S. Harrison in the June 27, 1960, issue of *The New Republic*, Barbara Ward took him around to Labor Party political rallies. Harrison says that when Kennedy asked her where the United States should concentrate in postwar Asia, she said, "India first, India second, India last." This importuning made a lasting impression on Jack, Harrison wrote.

Lannan recalled other activities:

> I remember we took a train trip out in the country. We stayed at the home of Douglas Fairbanks's ex-wife. And, I think, that was the night the lights were turned on for the first time since the war ended—the blackout ended. Every house was lighted up and there was a fantastic celebration. On the third floor, some upperclass young men got in the most dramatic poker game you have ever seen in your life—a wild, tough game. Everybody drinking. One of the young men lost a huge amount—one or two hundred thousand pounds! The people—the other guests—weren't very proud of this game, what with all that was going on in the world. They sort of urged us to forget about it.
>
> The races at Ascot were running. But neither I nor Jack was interested in going. We stayed home and spent most of the day in the lovely gardens. It was a beautiful summer day. We were served a nice lunch. We talked about politics—and economics. I was intensely interested in how Europe would recover, economically. Jack was too. He was always asking me questions about the balance of payments and things like that.

The next story we found at the Kennedy Library is dated July 6—the day after the election. In keeping with British tradition, the returns would not be officially published until July 26. Until then it was anybody's guess as to who won.

In his dispatch of June 23, Jack had written that Churchill and the Conservatives "may" lose the election; but contrary to what Krock (and others) have remembered, Jack's final pronouncement, in his dispatch of July 6, was not "prescient": "This election has been bitterly fought, and although . . . the voting will be close . . . the Conservatives should win this time. . . ."

In fact, the voting was not close at all. The Labourites buried the Tories in a landslide, turning Churchill out of office.

In London, Jack had a heavy social schedule. One source, who asked not to be identified, told us that he squired around a beautiful young widow, Patricia Wilson, a friend of Kathleen's and probably the girl Joe Junior had been dating when he was killed. Patricia had been married to the Earl of Jersey, divorced him and married Robin Wilson, who was killed in the war.

He also began a long, lasting friendship with a beautiful and famous English tennis star, Katharine Stammers, who was married to an officer in the British Army, Michael Menzies. We discovered that the Menzieses now live in Oyster Bay, Long Island. We went there for tea with Kay. Like all of Jack's female friends, she is beautiful and charming.

Kay told us that she had been born in St. Albans (north of London) in 1914 (making her three years older than Jack), the only child of an insurance agent. Her mother and father were keen on tennis and encouraged her to take up the game. She became one of the most famous women tennis players in the world, bursting onto the scene in 1935 at the age of twenty-one. She reached her zenith in 1939—before tennis matches were curtailed for the duration. That year she reached the women's single finals at Wimbledon but lost the match to Alice Marble. During the war she married Michael Menzies and in 1943 she had a child.

Kay told us:

Actually, I met Jack's father, Joe, first, through an English friend of mine, Sir William Wiseman. I went to the embassy in London with Willy in—oh, 1938 or 1939—and we had dinner with Joe Kennedy. He had great charm. He was very nice looking—that same smile all the Kennedys have. And I went with Willy to Joe's place in the country—outside London. Then, in the summer of 1945, I was in a nightclub in London and Jack came in with Pat Wilson, who knew everybody in London.

I found Jack terribly attractive. Wonderful sense of humor. From then on, until 1950, when I went to live in South Africa, every time he'd come to London he'd let me know and we'd do things together. And I'd see him when I came to the States to play tennis.

British men treat women differently from the way American men do. American men idolize women, but to an Englishman, his clubs and sports are likely to come before his women. They are much more realistic. Jack had much more of an Englishman's attitude toward women. He really didn't give a damn. He liked to have them around and he liked to enjoy himself but he was quite unreliable. He did as he pleased. I think he was probably spoiled by women. I think he could snap his fingers and they'd come running. And, of course, he was terribly attractive and rich and unmarried—a terrific catch, really.

Did I love him? I thought he was divine, yes. I wouldn't say that

as an Ensign at Chelsea Naval Hospital in Boston, circa 1942. *(Courtesy John F. Kennedy Library)*

Joe Jr., in training as a Naval aviator, circa June 1942. *(Courtesy John F. Kennedy Library)*

Jack (left) and Joe Jr. pose in Palm Beach, circa December 1942.
(Pictorial Parade)

nga Arvad with Tim McCoy in 1947, at the time of her marriage to the cowboy novie star. *(Wide World Photos)* ·

Angela Greene.
(Courtesy Angela Greene)

Phyllis Brooks

The crew of *PT-109*, posed on deck, June–July 1942. Jack (extreme right) wearing sheath knife on belt and baseball cap.
(Courtesy John F. Kennedy Library)

Jack, posed in the cockpit of *PT-109*. The religious medal on the chain around his neck was given him by Clare Booth Luce.
(Courtesy John F. Kennedy Library)

Jack and the second-in-command of *PT-109*, Leonard Thom. *(Courtesy John F. Kennedy Library)*

Jack and his PT buddies in the Solomons: Barney Ross, Red Fay and Jim Reed. *(Courtesy John F. Kennedy Library)*

Jack, back home in Palm Beach, poses with Lem Billings.
(Courtesy John F. Kennedy Library)

Relaxing at Palm Beach,
February 1944.
(Courtesy John F. Kennedy Library)

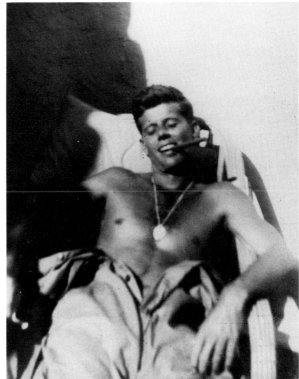

And in New York, at the Stork Club, with Flo Pritchett, Februa 1944. *(Courtesy Dancy Foster)*

Wedding of Kathleen Kennedy and William Hartington, May 1944, London. Joe Jr. behind Kick.

(Courtesy John F. Kennedy Library)

Bab Beckwith

In June 1944, at the Chelsea
Naval Hospital prior to back
operation, Jack receives Navy and
Marine Corps Medal from
Captain F. L. Conklin.
(Courtesy John F. Kennedy Library)

In the fall of 1945, before declaring for office, Jack addresses a veterans' group in Boston. *(Courtesy John F. Kennedy Library)*

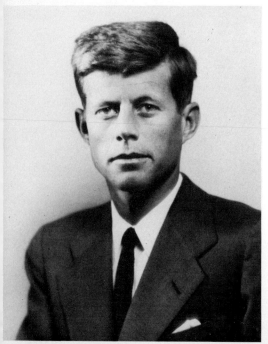

Official 1946 campaign photo.
(Courtesy John F. Kennedy Library)

Principal opponent in 1946
House race: Mike Neville, mayor
of Cambridge.
(Courtesy John F. Kennedy Library)

Campaigning, 1946, finds Jack
(extreme right) in rare pose:
holding goat, wearing a hat.
(Courtesy John F. Kennedy Library)

Jack, surrounded by political co-workers in Boston, celebrates his 29th birthday. Left to right: Frank Morrissey (seated), Mrs. Fitzgerald (seated), Lem Billings (standing, in glasses), Paul Mackin (behind Lem) Peter Cloherty (in vest, shirt sleeves), Eunice (seated), Eddie McLaughlin (between Cloherty and Eunice), Jack, Honey Fitz (seated), Joe Timilty (seated, extreme right), James F. Kelley and Cis McLaughlin standing behind Jack. *(Courtesy John F. Kennedy Library)*

Windup of the 1946 campaign: Bunker Hill Day parade, June 17. Here posed with Charlestown secretary, Dave Powers.
(Courtesy John F. Kennedy Library)

Marching in the parade. Note Jack is carrying, not wearing, his hat.
After parade, he collapses. *(Courtesy John F. Kennedy Library)*

Casting ballot, June 18, with his grandfather Honey Fitz and his grandmother, Mrs. Fitzgerald. *(Courtesy John F. Kennedy Library)*

Posing for a victory picture: Jack with his mother, Rose, Mrs. Fitzgerald, Honey Fitz and Ambassador Kennedy. *(Courtesy John F. Kennedy Library)*

June 23, 1946, five days after the voting, Jack relaxes at Hyannis Port with Kennedy dog "Mo." *(Courtesy John F. Kennedy Library)*

September 1946: the VFW encampment, Boston. Left to right, Mayor James M. Curley, Governor Maurice Tobin, Jack Kennedy. *(Courtesy Boston Public Library, Print Department)*

Freshman Congressman Jack Kennedy poses with sisters, Eunice and Jean, in Georgetown home. *(United Press International Photo)*

This political pose, February 10, 1948, shows a sickly-looking Jack five months after the onset of Addison's disease. *(Courtesy John F. Kennedy Library)*

I was in love with him but I was terribly attracted to him. We got on terribly well together. We had great fun when we saw one another. . . . It was a nice, lasting friendship, not just a flash in the pan. . . .

While Jack was in England the Big Three had yet another summit conference—in Potsdam, Germany. This was a final attempt on Harry Truman's part to reach a reasonable accord with Stalin. The meeting convened on July 17. Churchill came from London. On July 26, while he was attending the conference, the British election results were announced. He was turned out of office in mid-conference, and replaced there by the new Labourite prime minister, Clement Attlee.

The delegates at Potsdam made further concessions to the Russians which tended to strengthen Stalin's hold on Eastern Europe. They divided Germany down the middle, giving the eastern half to Russia. Immediately thereafter, Stalin stripped that zone of its industry, shipping it to Russia, and installed a Communist government. (The United States, the United Kingdom, and France occupied the other half of Germany.) Berlin and Vienna were divided into four occupation zones—one each for the United States, the United Kingdom, France, and Russia. Truman, still hoping that Stalin would be reasonable, emerged from one meeting and made the famous (or infamous) comment, "I like Uncle Joe."

Jack got involved in the Potsdam conference in a minor way, but we are not certain of the details. So far as we were able to determine, he did not file any dispatches to Hearst about it, but we know from two sources that he went to Potsdam. We found a letter in the Kennedy Library postmarked Dublin, Ireland, July 25, and signed by the U.S. minister to Ireland, David Gray. It stated that Jack had been given a "special mission" to carry a diplomatic pouch from Ireland to the Honorable James M. Byrnes, secretary of state, in care of the presidential party, Potsdam, Germany. Jack had gone to Ireland to do a story for Hearst on the controversy over Irish independence. He filed it from London July 26, on his way to Potsdam.

While Jack was in London, the official British election results were released. He paused long enough to file his fourth and last story for Hearst—and the last piece of journalism he ever did. For it, he interviewed the old family friend Harold J. Laski at The London School of Economics. Text:

LONDON, July 27—England has been hit by some blockbusters in the last five years but none of them ever shook her like today's election results.

As the Labour majority piles up, even the most optimistic Labourites were stunned by the extent of their victory.

For the first time in Labour's history Labour holds a clear majority in the House of Commons.

Explanations for the crushing Tory defeat are already forthcoming and they will be pouring in for the next few weeks.

People are already saying "I told you so," which they may have done, but if they did I do not remember it.

Professor Laski himself told me he had only anticipated a Labour majority of 50 seats.

Looking back over the campaign, I think the Socialist victory is due chiefly to two factors.

First, the general feeling that after 10 years of Conservative government, it was "time for a change."

That was a good slogan of Gov. Dewey when he ran for President against the late President Roosevelt. He was just in the wrong country.

Second and most important is the fact that living conditions in England have always been difficult for the working man.

Long ago, Disraeli wrote of two nations in England, rich and poor, and in the last five years things have been particularly difficult.

Enemy bombings, high prices, and being forced to stand in long queues have taken their toll of the people's tempers and patience.

The Socialist Party took full advantage of this opportunity and their party literature accentuated the class struggle.

They pulled out the stops on the "campaign oratory" and it was "happy days are here again for everyone."

The Socialists promised that "things will be better for the workingman" and to the Socialist Party, just everyone is a working man.

Churchill, on the other hand, took the same line in this campaign that had been so successful in 1940.

He offered them nothing but "toil and sweat" and said the Conservative Party would make no glib promises it could not keep.

Unfortunately, for the Conservatives, the people of this island have been on a diet of toil and sweat for the past five years.

The British people will take that diet in an emergency but they feel the emergency has passed.

About this time, Secretary of the Navy James V. Forrestal arrived in Europe in his private plane. He was, according to his *Diaries*, making an "uninvited" visit to the Potsdam conference. We believe that Jack met Forrestal in London or Paris and flew on to Germany in Forrestal's plane.

There is a photograph, published in *As We Remember Him* and elsewhere, showing Forrestal's arrival at the airport in Frankfurt. He is being greeted by General Eisenhower. In the background, barely visible, is Jack, walking with a Navy lieutenant identified as Seymour St. John, son of the Choate headmaster and later headmaster himself. The caption states that on this occasion, Jack first met Eisenhower.

We called St. John to see if he could shed any light on the event. He told us:

> Yes, I remember. Jack came in on the plane with Forrestal. I was aide to the head Navy admiral there and we had a big parade formation at the airport—for Forrestal. The plane doors opened up, and out came Forrestal. Then, to my amazement, Jack Kennedy. Ike was meeting Forrestal, so Jack met Ike in the crowd.
>
> After the inspection of the troops and the ceremony, I took Jack to lunch at the officers' mess in the I. G. Farben Building in Frankfurt. We talked about what he was doing and where he was going and the war situation. Then he went off—where, I have forgotten. Potsdam, I assume.

According to Forrestal's *Diaries*, he left Potsdam and flew to London on August 2. We believe that Jack probably returned to London on the same plane and then he came down with a desperate illness.

Pat Lannan told us:

> He came back to Grosvenor House. Then he got very sick. I've never seen anyone so sick in my life. He had a hell of a high temperature. It scared hell out of me. I thought he was going to die. He told me it was a recurrence of malaria. I'd never seen anyone go through the throes of fever before. Yet Jack was uncomplaining, not a moan.
>
> I got hold of a naval officer who was attached to Forrestal's party. Then some Navy doctors came and they confirmed it was malarial fever. Then, late one night, Forrestal came by to see Jack. He—Forrestal—was very tender to Jack. He was really worried about him.
>
> This went on for several days, then Jack got better. I went over to Paris for a few days by myself. I'm pretty sure Jack went back to the States on Forrestal's plane. I didn't see him again until I got back to the States—a week or so later.

The U.S. Air Force dropped the first atomic bomb on Hiroshima August 6. That same day, according to the Forrestal *Diaries*, Forrestal left London. He arrived back in the United States at 2:30 P.M. on August 7. We assume Jack was on the plane and he probably went immediately to Hyannis Port or into some hospital. On August 8 Russia entered the war against Japan. On August 9 the Air Force dropped the second atomic bomb, on Nagasaki. Five days later, August 14, Japan surrendered. At 7 P.M., at the White House, President Truman made it official with a statement: "I deem . . . full acceptance of . . . unconditional surrender. . . ."

We could find nothing to indicate where Jack was that day. Nor could we find out where he was on September 2, when the Japanese signed the surrender papers on the deck of the USS *Missouri* in Tokyo Bay. Our guess was that he was either at New England Baptist Hospital or at Hyannis Port.

Sometime in early September, Jack sent Forrestal a box of cigars—perhaps a token of appreciation. We found a letter from Forrestal at the Kennedy Library, dated September 8, 1945, thanking Jack for the cigars and offering him a job. Forrestal added, "What are your plans? Do you want to do any work here—if so why don't you come down and see what there is in hand? I can put you up. Regards to your father. Let me know how he comes through his operation. . . . ."

We could find no response to this letter from Jack. But, of course, he had no desire to work for the secretary of the Navy. It was time now to begin his political career—the first step into the maze of Boston and Massachusetts politics.

Part IV

BOSTON

28

The Bay State

THE impression is given in many Kennedy books that when Jack entered politics in Boston, he ran for office independent of the old and corrupt Boston pols and their machines; that Jack's principal managers and supporters were idealistic amateurs. James MacGregor Burns, for example, describes Jack's organization as consisting of "political neophytes . . . a motley group of former Navy officers, self-appointed political advisors, veterans still in uniform, old school chums and family friends."

After an extensive study of Jack's 1945–1946 race for the House, we came to a rather different conclusion. To be sure, there were amateurs out front, highly visible. But the real managers of Jack's campaign were in fact seasoned old Boston pols. In this most crucial of Joe Kennedy's political moves, nothing was left to chance—or to amateurs. And, as we saw, it was a much chancier, more difficult race than the impression given in the standard Kennedy literature.

Approaching the subject, we consulted Kennedy books with our now ingrained caution. We were surprised to find how little has been published about the race. Burns gives it about ten pages—valuable mostly for setting the big picture. The longest account, twenty-six pages, appears in the book *Johnny, We Hardly Knew Ye* by two of Jack's political aides, David F. Powers and Kenneth P. O'Donnell. It is valuable because Powers was a direct participant, but is flawed by hero worship, omissions, and distortions.

The best account appears in the sixteen pages of the Martin and Plaut book, *Front Runner, Dark Horse*. They interviewed several key participants, now deceased, and generally wrote with more objectivity than the other Kennedy biographers. The other accounts are too thin or unreliable to bother citing.

The Kennedy Library, we felt sure, would be bulging with documentatin on the election: speaking schedules, appointment books, position papers, and so on. No such luck. The material available—and we believe that very little has been withheld—is astonishingly skimpy. Less than a dozen letters, three or four drafts of speeches, a few undated newspaper clippings, no record books of any kind. The best the library had to offer was about a dozen oral histories from men and women who participated in the campaign, but most of these are amateurish.

To reconstruct the campaign, we had to again resort to pure legwork. From books, magazine and newspaper articles, and other works, we compiled lists of people who worked in the campaign. Then, in Boston, we tracked down those who were still living for taped interviews. During these interviews, we asked for names of key people who might have been overlooked. In this way, little by little, the campaign—and the people who worked in it—came into focus. In the end, we interviewed two dozen men and women.

Massachusetts is about fifty miles deep, from north to south, and about 150 miles wide, not counting the Cape Cod appendage. In 1945 it had only one metropolitan area, Boston. The population of the state was 4.5. million—2.7 million in greater Boston—and static. Many of that number were first- and second-generation Americans of Irish, Italian, and Canadian descent. Most of the major industry was located in Boston or its environs, together with the state and Boston city governments, the major universities and colleges, medical and cultural centers, the principal newspapers, radio stations, and book and magazine publishers.

Massachusetts had once looked to the sea for its economic well-being. Boston, with its fine harbor, had once been a major seaport, home port of the great clipper ships that plied the Far East and elsewhere. This trading had built huge fortunes for the old Yankee families—the so-called Boston Brahmins. The smaller coastal towns such as Gloucester and New Bedford had been centers for the sizable fishing and whaling industries. But New York, Philadelphia, and Baltimore, which were closer to rail centers, had displaced Boston as a major seaport. The clipper trade disappeared into the mists of history and the whaling and fishing industries dwindled in importance. The industrial base gradually shifted to milling and manufacturing: textiles, leather products, furniture, electrical appliance, and whatnot. There was no single dominating industry, such as Michigan's automobiles or Texas's oil. Unlike most states, farming played only a minor role in the economy. As the Pilgrims discovered, the land and weather were too harsh for agriculture on any substantial scale.

During World War Two the economy of Massachusetts had boomed. Much of the industry had been converted to war production. The Boston Navy Yard, a huge installation, worked three shifts a day building and repairing naval vessels. But now, as the war was winding down, defense contracts were being canceled. Worse, many of the Massachusetts textile mills were moving south to be closer to the cotton fields and cheaper labor. Massachusetts was falling on hard times.

In 1945 there were 2.3 million registered voters in Massachusetts, about evenly divided among Democrats, Republicans, and Independents (most

Independents voted Democratic). In its early history, Massachusetts had been a Republican state, but with the onset of the Depression, it swung to the Democratic side, going for Roosevelt, and for a time, sending two Democratic Senators to the Senator: David I. Walsh and Marcus A. Coolidge. The governorship swung back and forth between Democrats and Republicans during the 1930s and 1940s. The large blocs of Catholic Irish and Italian votes had much to do with the swing to the Democratic side. Boston had been a Democratic stronghold since the great Irish and Italian immigrations at the turn of the century.

There were no strong statewide political machines, either Republican or Democrat. Both parties were, it seemed, constantly in a state of civil war, tearing themselves apart from year to year. And the voters did not hesitate to cross party lines to vote for an opposition candidate. What machines did exist were built around personalities. Hence, in both parties, the political mosaic was composed of a series of individual fiefdoms, which might be allies in one election, enemies in the next.

In 1945 the key political personalities controlling fiefdoms in the state were two Senators, a Democrat and a Republican; the governor, a Democrat; Henry Cabot Lodge, a Republican; and James Michael Curley, a legend. Democratic Senator David I. Walsh, a Roman Catholic, a bachelor, was the first Democrat elected to the U.S. Senate in modern Massachusetts history. He took his seat in 1919 and had served almost continuously since then. He was by all accounts a distinguished Senator, but in 1945, Walsh had a problem. His name had been associated with a homosexual scandal three years earlier. Whether Walsh, who had never married, was a homosexual or not, the brand was on him. He faced a certain end to his long political career when he came up for reelection in 1946. Under the circumstances, Walsh, who had pulled the right strings to get Jack to the South Pacific, could now be only a liability to the Kennedys.

Former Republican Senator Henry Cabot Lodge, Jr., took his Senate seat in 1936. What was remarkable about his victory was that he was only thirty-four years old, and he had won in 1936, the great Roosevelt landslide year, when Roosevelt carried almost every Democratic politician in Massachusetts and the nation into office with him. Lodge, who had served a couple of terms in the State Legislature, went to Washington a liberal on domestic matters but a committed isolationist. When war broke out, however, he changed to a progressive internationalist and supported Roosevelt on most of his preparedness measures. He was on better terms with Roosevelt than Walsh was. As we have noted, in 1942 Lodge easily beat off a challenge for reelection by Joe Casey.

From his earliest years, Lodge had been a strong advocate of the military. He had joined the U.S. Army Reserves. Year after year, including his years in the Senate, he had gone off on Army maneuvers. He had become close friends with the Army's great tank general, George S. Patton. After the Pearl Harbor attack, Lodge had gone on full-time active duty—the first Senator to do this since the Civil War. He fought in North Africa until Roosevelt declared that Congressmen could not serve on active duty. Thereafter he spent most of his time as a Senator touring battlefronts.

Then, in early 1944, Lodge had thrown his fiefdom—and Massachusetts politics in general—into a tizzy. He resigned from the Senate and went on full-time duty in the Army in Europe, where he served with distinction, winning a Bronze Star and other decorations. In the opinion of many Boston pols, this gesture was enormously helpful to Lodge politically. In 1945 the talk was that when he returned from the war to a hero's welcome, he would be a dominant political force in Massachusetts. He would most likely run against Walsh in 1946 and win hands down.

Republican Senator Leverett Saltonstall, a wealthy blueblood Republican, had easily won the seat vacated by Lodge in a special election. Like Lodge, Saltonstall (who had been governor from 1939 to 1945) was a liberal and one of the most popular politicians in the history of Massachusetts. He supported welfare for the aged, labor reform, and other measures that must have set his conservative forebears spinning in their graves. He was also one of the least prepossessing. He was plain-spoken and plain-looking, without a shred of charisma. Saltonstall had taken office on January 3, 1945. His special term would run through 1948, when there would be a regular election. He would certainly be a candidate to succeed himself.

Democratic Governor Maurice J. Tobin was a young "reform" Democrat, remarkably handsome, remarkably charismatic, and at first very popular in Massachusetts. A son of Irish immigrants in South Boston, he had never gone to college. He zoomed up through the political ranks and in 1937, at age thirty-six, ran for mayor of Boston and won. He was reelected mayor in 1940. In 1944, when "Salty" Saltonstall stood for Lodge's Senate seat, leaving the governorship open, Tobin declared for it and won. He took office in January, 1945, for a two-year term. He would be up for reelection in the fall of 1946.

Though Tobin was a proven vote-getter, the voters were beginning to blame him for the postwar economic problems in the state. He was already being helpful to the Kennedys—by appointing the ambassador to conduct the economic survey, by making a public appearance at the launching of the destroyer *Joseph P. Kennedy*, and so on. But how much help he could be in the future was uncertain.

James Michael Curley had come along on the heels of Honey Fitz in 1914 as a major force in Boston politics. He was then, at age forty, a charming, hardworking, innately shrewd pol. He had served in the U.S.

House from 1911 to 1914. At that time, there was only one blemish on his public record. Earlier, as a ward-level pol, he had tried to help an illiterate campaign worker obtain a federal job as a mailman by posing as the man and taking his Civil Service exam. Curley was caught and was sentenced to ninety days in jail. This incident did not hurt him politically; on the contrary, among the poor Irish of Boston, it made him a folk hero.

In 1914 Curley was well enough known to challenge Honey Fitz for mayor. As Joseph Dinneen points out in his biography of Curley, *The Purple Shamrock*, Curley did not go the usual route of getting the support of the ward bosses. Rather, he first ignored them, then scared them all to death by attacking them. Honey Fitz, Dinneen points out, made the decision not to stand for reelection. Dinneen wrote, "His decision was unpopular throughout the city and particularly in his own ward, where it shook the confidence of his loyal followers. They felt that John F. was unwilling to defend his title against the new champion."

Curley won easily and served four years in City Hall. When he came up for reelection in 1917, the ward bosses went after him with everything they had, accusing him of graft and corruption on a huge scale. In the summer of that year, Honey Fitz was a possible challenger. Curley scared him out of the running by threatening to expose Honey Fitz's personal life in a series of three speeches. The proposed titles: (1) Graft, Ancient and Modern; (2) Great Lovers: From Cleopatra to Toodles; and (3) Libertines: From Henry VIII to the Present Day. In his book, Richard Whalen says, "Fitzgerald, alarmed at the prospect of plain speaking on the subject of Miss 'Toodles' Ryan, discreetly withdrew from the race."

In even raising the possibility of using his opponent's private life in the campaign, Curley committed a political mortal sin. That was not the way the game was played by Boston politicians. It turned Honey Fitz and his family into implacable enemies of Curley for life. Curley was defeated for reelection.

He was soon back in the political arena, an indefatigable campaigner and often a winner. He served again as Boston's mayor from 1922 to 1926 and yet again from 1930 to 1934. He was governor from 1935 to 1937. In 1936 he had sought the Senate seat vacated by Marcus Coolidge, but lost it to Henry Cabot Lodge, Jr. In 1937 he tried again for the Boston mayoralty, but that was the year Maurice J. Tobin (who had been a Curley protégé) won the job.

By the late 1930s Curley had become involved in several serious political scandals.

In 1942, Curley, down on his luck and out of a job, turned his eyes toward the U. S. Congress. He ran in the 11th Congressional District—the same that Honey Fitz (and Curley) had held decades earlier. It had been gerrymandered to favor a candidate like Curley. Curley was so certain of winning that even before the election he went to Washington to look for a house. His confidence was well-placed. In spite of the scandals hanging over his name, he won overwhelmingly.

In 1945 he still held that seat, having been reelected even though under indictment for yet another misadventure, this one in Washington.

In May of 1945 Curley returned to Boston and stood the city on its ear by announcing he would once again run for mayor. The elections would be held that fall. His opponent would be the acting mayor, John Kerrigan former president of the City Council, who had taken over City Hall when Mayor Tobin won the governor's race. Tobin, of course, would back Kerrigan.

If Curley won, he would have to resign his U.S. House seat in the 11th Congressional District. This district was heavy with Irish voters. Jack's grandfather, Honey Fitz, had launched his political career there. Both the Fitzgeralds and the Kennedys had roots—and relatives—in the district. The name John Fitzgerald Kennedy would automatically assure many votes.

Based on this assessment of the situation, the Kennedys made a tentative decision. If Curley won the mayoralty race, Jack would enter Massachusetts politics by declaring for Curley's 11th Congressional District in early 1946, and face election that year. But, we imagined, before declaring, or even hinting at their purpose, they must first see if Curley won and then resigned his House seat. Above all, they must not give the impression that a deal had been made with Curley, clearing the way for Jack.

The Kennedys had now to hope that their archenemy, James Michael Curley, then being vilified in the national media as one of the most notorious political crooks in history, would win his fourth separate term as mayor.

29

Old Pols

As we have seen, Joe Kennedy was not without savvy in Massachusetts politics. His father was a Boston ward politician. Rose's father, Honey Fitz, was a renowned Boston politician. In 1942, he had involved himself in the Democratic Senatorial primary running Honey Fitz against Joe Casey. In April, 1945, Joe Kennedy had accepted an assignment with Governor Maurice Tobin to conduct an "economic" survey of the state—primarily to scout the political scene for Jack. By the fall of 1945 he had traveled to every corner of the Commonwealth and had met everybody of consequence in politics, the government, and media. By now Joe Kennedy himself could be considered a powerful Massachusetts pol.

As fall came, Ambassador Kennedy, who had set up headquarters in Boston's Ritz Carlton Hotel, devoted more and more of his time to Jack's political debut, less to the economic survey of Massachusetts. He had decided that he, personally, would manage the coming campaign, but behind the scenes, never out front in any capacity. During these days, he relied politically on seven men as a sort of private brain trust. They were not a formal body; they never met as one. But the ambassador had almost daily contact with all, either in person or by telephone. He sought their advice, used their talents or contacts, tested ideas on them. The seven can be described as the founding planks of the vaunted Jack Kennedy political organization. They were Joe Timilty, Eddie Gallagher, Joe Kane, Frank Morrissey, Jim Landis, Jack Dowd, and Arthur Krock.

Joseph Francis Timilty was then forty-nine, a bachelor, long one of the ambassador's closest personal friends—a sidekick, golfing partner, and reputed to be, in the words of a Massachusetts pol, Kennedy's "beard." ("Beard" is a term that may have originated in Hollywood. It means a disguise, a cover, specifically for illicit romances. When the ambassador took a girl out on the town, he brought along bachelor Joe Timilty. If they were seen, the assumption was supposed to be that the girl was with Timilty.)

Timilty was born in 1896, the second of seven sons of a locally famous Boston pol, James P. "Diamond Jim" Timilty. The senior Timilty, a paving contractor and a pal of Curley's, wore two large diamond rings and a diamond stud. Son Joe was graduated from Boston English High School in 1913, became a page in the U.S. House of Representatives for three years, then returned to Boston where he served in various political jobs. In 1935 he was appointed police commissioner of Boston and served in that largely ceremonial post until 1943. In 1944 he toyed with the idea of running for governor but, as he told us, "Tobin wanted the job, so I acquiesced." For a number of years Timilty helped groom Joe Junior for his political debut in Massachusetts. They had been extremely close. Timilty had been devastated by Joe's death. For years, Timilty had been a household fixture at the Kennedy homes in Hyannis Port and Palm Beach; a sort of aide to the ambassador.

We asked Timilty to recall the ambassador's role in Jack's political debut and his own role in the planning. He told us,

> Joe Kennedy was *the* mastermind of all Jack's campaigns, including his presidential campaign. When Jack started running for Congress, he truthfully didn't know ten people in Boston. Of course, he had great family background—Honey Fitz and the ambassador's father, who'd been a politician in East Boston, and the ambassador himself, who had hundreds of friends in Boston. When Jack started out, he was extremely shy. He didn't have much to say; he certainly wasn't a backslapper.
>
> The ambassador was the mastermind of everything. I was very much involved in that campaign. I'd arrange meetings with some of the political leaders, take Jack to luncheons and political rallies. But I was just carrying out the ambassador's orders. And I was never out front. Then, I'd report to the ambassador. I was his closest friend—but never his confidant. He never confided in anybody. And he was completely in charge of everything, every detail.

Edward M. Gallagher, then thirty-six, a close Kennedy friend and a folk hero in Boston, now an insurance executive, was the son of a Boston politician allied with Honey Fitz. He had been president of the Boston City Council, a powerful political post. Eddie was graduated from Boston College in 1932, an outstanding baseball player—a left-handed pitcher. He was elected lifetime president of his class—a singular honor.

Upon graduation, Eddie was immediately signed by the Boston Red Sox major league team and was soon pitching in Boston's Fenway Park. But during spring practice the following year, he was hit by a hard line drive which nearly killed him. For the next dozen years, he told us, he had to have "one or two operations a year"—in all, about twenty. "I was a guinea pig for penicillin," he said. In 1943 he was finally cured and married Priscila Phelan, daughter of a very wealthy Boston banker, James J. Phelan, one of the few Irish ever to be accepted socially in Boston.

During these years, Gallagher had opened an insurance firm in Boston. Being the son of an old pol, he knew everybody and was a natural, though cautious, politician; a behind-the-scenes kingmaker rather than a front man. He drew James Roosevelt into his Boston insurance firm, forming a strong link with the Roosevelt family. Since James Roosevelt was also involved in the liquor business with Ambassador Kennedy, Eddie and the ambassador soon became friends. Eddie got to know Joe Junior and most of the Kennedys (and Joe Timilty, of course). He was a very good golfer—as was Ambassador Kennedy—and soon the two men, despite the age gap (twenty year) were close friends. He told us:

> I had a lot of older friends like that. I drew from them. By the 1940s, I had daily contact with Mr. Kennedy. He was a marvelous, well-organized person. I was with the family when they got the news about Jack and the *PT-109*. I was with them when they got the news about Joe Junior being killed, the first of many shocks for him. We were on the Cape. I remember I said to Mr. Kennedy, "Well Joe, why don't we go over to the club? There won't be anybody there. We might play four or five holes of golf." And we did that. I could imitate Honey Fitz fairly accurately. I think he enjoyed that.
>
> When he took the economic survey job for Tobin—we later called it the "Baby Hoover Commission"—it was to scout the state politically for Jack. He met a lot of people who were helpful. Then when Jack got ready to run, it was natural that the ambassador would turn to me. I was in touch with him every day—in person or on the phone. He was all over the phone. Always calling. He'd bounce ideas or ask about people—who was linked with whom—and so on. He was, without question, the manager of that political campaign in every sense of the word. The mastermind.

Joseph L. Kane was a cousin of Ambassador Kennedy's. When we commenced our research Joe Kane was dead and he left no widow or children. Like Joe Timilty, he was a bachelor.

Kane's obituary ran in the *Boston Globe* of March 21, 1967. He had died the day before, at age eighty-seven. (In 1946, when he worked in Jack's campaign, he was sixty-six years old.) The obituary said that Kane was "one of Boston's most colorful political figures," that Kane considered himself a "political engineer" who "attributed his political skill to an endowment" from Honey Fitz and Kane's uncle, Patrick J. Kennedy, the ambassador's father, described as an East Boston banker and State Senator. Kane, the obituary said, was "a familiar figure in the cafeterias around City Hall."

Another politician told us:

Joe was a very colorful fellow, a sort of mystery man. He was about five foot nine, white hair, ruddy complexion, rather large nose and some false teeth that used to get in the way of his being able to talk as fast as he thought. He was an old-school politician, familiar with every facet of the trade. He always wore his hat—a Collins and Fairbanks fedora—with one side of the brim turned down and the other side up, like Edward G. Robinson. [Hats were important pieces of equipment for Massachusetts politicians. Wearing one proved a pol supported the large hat industry in the state. Talk of hats—style, size, and so on—cropped up all through our political interviews.]

He smoked a cigar and wore a vest. He was cute, smart, clever, and cunning, the Connie Mack of politics. His mother and the ambassador's mother had been sisters, which made them first cousins.

Joe Kane was an *old* old pol. In 1918 he was secretary to a man named Peter Tague, who ran against Honey Fitz for the U.S. House seat in the 11th District. Honey Fitz won by 238 votes, but Tague claimed voting irregularities. A U.S. Congressional committee investigated and found in favor of Tague, who got the seat and held it for years. After that, Honey Fitz and Joe Kane were political enemies. Kane continued to be Tague's secretary, and knew the 11th District and its families as well as his own. In 1937 Kane managed Tobin's campaign for mayor (against Curley). In 1942 the ambassador recruited Kane to manage Honey Fitz's primary battle against Joe Casey. In her book, Rose says:

Joe [Kennedy, Sr.] was wise in the fields of national and international political affairs, but his interest dwindled as the political unit grew smaller. Events at the level of district, city, town and ward left him progressively bored. Particularly in Boston. . . . Yet he was keenly aware of the importance of the organization, strategy and people in Jack's campaign. To this end he asked his favorite, experienced realist, Cousin Joe Kane, to be Jack's advisor.

Cousin Joe was quite a rough diamond, with an abrasive style of thought and speech. My husband wasn't at all sure how he and Jack would get along, but they hit it off quite well. Jack was surprised, entertained and informed. . . . Cousin Joe could tell him about the winds and tides, the shoals and channels in this particular form of navigation. . . .

Francis Xavier Morrissey, then thirty-five years old, had been a right-hand man for Governor Tobin. In time, Morrissey would become head of Jack's Boston congressional office. He was a key man in the original Kennedy political machine, a close friend of the ambassador's and, finally, a controversial character whom Jack grew to distrust and dislike as a "spy" for his father.

In 1973, when we were in Boston, Morrissey was a Municipal Court Judge, involved in a front-page political scandal. He was accused of accepting $4,000 from a man who was under stock fraud investigation by the SEC and whose case was mysteriously dropped. In 1974, the State Supreme Judicial Court "censured" Morrissey for accepting the money, but found no evidence that Morrissey had played any role whatsoever in having the case dropped. The high court found Morrissey guilty of "careless disregard" of his obligation as a judge to avoid "even the appearance of impropriety" but did not think the matter grave enough to warrant his removal from the bench. But it had been a near thing.

We repeatedly sought an interview with Morrissey during this tense time, but he would not grant it. No doubt he was not at that point kindly disposed to journalists and writers.

Morrissey first received national attention in 1962-1963 when Jack, then President, sought to promote him from the workaday Boston Municipal Court to the U.S. District Court in Massachusetts. Many in the Massachusetts legal profession did not think Morrissey was qualified for the job and rose up to oppose the appointment. Senator Edward Kennedy tried to ram the appointment through again in 1965, and again there was strong opposition to the appointment, leading to a stormy hearing before the U.S. Senate Judiciary Committee on October 12, 1965. Later Teddy withdrew the appointment. In Washington we obtained a transcript of these hearings which, among other items, had some valuable and little-known biographical material on which the following is based.

Frank Morrissey was born in Boston, May 21, 1910, the second of twelve children of a very poor Irish family. He was short: five feet two inches. At age seventeen he set out to be a banker, eventually landing a job as a clerk-teller in the Atlantic National Bank. On the side, Morrissey attended law school, thinking law would be helpful in his banking career. From 1927 to 1930 he attended Suffolk Law School, Boston (not an accredited law school until 1953) but he failed four key courses and was not awarded a degree. In spite of this, he took the Massachusetts bar exams, and failed.

Morrissey then resorted to what many would come to view as a slippery course of action. In those days, the State of Georgia had no bar examinations. There were two or three "diploma mills" in the state. With a degree from one, a prospective lawyer could gain admission to the Georgia bar "on motion." Massachusetts had a reciprocal agreement with Georgia: if you were a member of the Georgia bar, and could prove you'd practiced law in Georgia a reasonable length of time, the Massachusetts bar would license you.

In June, 1933, Morrissey went to Georgia for "review" at the Southern Law School in Athens. Within three months, he testified, he obtained a diploma and was admitted to the Georgia bar and also to the U.S. District Court in Georgia. But Georgia was in the grip of the Depression. Morrissey testified he could get no law business and was forced to resort to sales jobs. After six or seven months he returned to Massachusetts. However, since he could not show any evidence of having practiced law in Georgia, he could not gain admittance to the Massachusetts bar. Morrissey testified that he was young and naïve in those days and never tried to use the Georgia bar credentials to his advantage.

He gave up trying to be a banker. In 1935 he took a Civil Service examination in Boston and won a job as a social worker for the city. In 1938 he shifted to the state payroll as a social worker in reform schools. But he was still intent on practicing law. In 1942 and 1943 he returned to Suffolk Law School, obtained his law degree, and again failed the bar exams. On a third try, in 1944, he passed. The next year, 1945, Governor Tobin (for whom he had worked politically) appointed him deputy commissioner of corrections and personal secretary. He was serving in those jobs when Ambassador Kennedy emerged from retirement to conduct the economic survey for Tobin and met Morrissey.

In 1945, Morrissey, perhaps stung by his earlier academic failures, was still pursuing studies. He was working, part time, at Suffolk for a masters degree in law. He was also working toward a doctors degree in oratory (!) at Staley College in Brookline. He had married and had several children—ultimately he would have seven. He had not done any military service.

As we shall see, Frank Morrissey was not universally loved. However, Joseph P. Kennedy liked him, trusted him, and drew him into his personal orbit. He would become the ambassador's personal "eyes and ears" within Jack's fledgling political organization. Jack didn't like this, but Joe Kennedy stood by Morrissey through thick and thin. In Boston, it is said that Morrissey was on the Kennedy payroll, in one way or another, for twenty-five years—and may still be. The ambassador is said to have paid for the college education of some of his children. It was probably at the insistence of the ambassador that first Jack then Teddy risked political storms by proposing Morrissey for the federal bench. Morrissey in turn has remained steadfastly loyal to the Kennedys.

James McCauley Landis, then forty-six and dean of the Harvard Law School, was a close personal associate of Joseph P. Kennedy's. He played important roles in Jack's political campaigns, and for years would be one of Jack's key advisers. In 1964 he committed suicide. For our information about Landis, we relied mainly on Koskoff, who had the last interview with him.

From all accounts, Landis, born in 1899, was an egocentric, unstable character with a brilliant mind. In 1933 he and Benjamin V. Cohen (both protégés of Justice Felix Frankfurter) drafted the Securities Act, designed to combat fradulent stock exchange operations. The next year Cohen and others drafted the legislation which created the SEC. Landis was then serving as a member of the Federal Trade Commission. When Roosevelt appointed Joe Kennedy to head the SEC, Jim Landis came over to help him. When Kennedy moved over to become chairman of the Maritime Commission, Landis replaced him as chairman of the SEC for a couple of years. Leaving that post in 1937, he became dean of the Harvard Law School. During the war he served (1942-1943) as director of the Office of Civilian Defense, and in 1943-1945, as special minister to the Middle East in charge of economic operations.

All those years, Landis and Kennedy kept in close touch. When Connie Burwell, the Charlotte, North Carolina, writer, went to *Time*, Landis took over the job of writing and preparing Kennedy's diplomatic memoirs for publication. They were never published, Landis told Koskoff, because "he concluded that publication of the memoirs would cause embarrassment to John Kennedy."

In 1945 Landis returned from the Middle East and resumed his duties as dean of Harvard Law School. Though he was not a politician in the strictest sense, he was an important figure on the faculty of Harvard, which was located in the 11th Congressional District, and he had more than a little influence in that community. He was also a fair writer and a voluble—if erratic—idea man. We searched the Landis papers at the Library of Congress for documents relating to this campaign, but found none.

John C. Dowd owned an advertising agency in Boston—John C. Dowd, Inc. Dowd, too, was dead in 1973 and the Kennedy Library had no oral history or other data from or about him. He is mentioned in some of the Kennedy books, notably in Martin and Plaut and in Whalen (who interviewed him in 1962). From these sources and from an obituary in the *Boston Globe*, July 13, 1971, kindly forwarded by a Kennedy Library archivist, and from our interviews with a Boston politician and one of Dowd's ad agency employees, we pieced together the following brief profile.

Dowd was born in Lowell, Massachusetts, in 1901. He was a child prodigy, the youngest student ever to be graduated from Lowell High School. He was admitted to Harvard at age fifteen, and was graduated in 1920, age nineteen. He enlisted in the Marine Corps and was later a reporter for the *Lowell Sunday Telegram,* the *Manchester Union-Leader,* the *Boston Herald,* the *Worcester Post,* and the *Washington Post.* The former employee told us he was a man of tremendous drive and imagination and, in the early years, a two-fisted drinker. He married Marguerite McCann and had five children, one daughter and four sons.

In 1927, Dowd, then age twenty-six, founded an advertising agency in

Lowell. Shortly afterward, he moved it to Boston and in 1938 he merged it with another firm operated by Edward D. Parent. In the 1930s, when Joe Kennedy founded his liquor importing company in New York—Somerset Importers—he gave Dowd the Boston advertising account for one of his smaller operations—Riondo Rum. It was not a big account like Haig & Haig, for example, but it featured full-page color ads in *Esquire* and other magazines and was considered, for Boston, "a pretty good account." Dowd, then, was in effect a Kennedy PR man in Boston. He was, of course, widely acquainted in Boston business circles.

By 1945, Jack Dowd, age forty-four, was a pal of Governor Tobin's and heavily involved in city and state politics. He then had a small state government account—the Greater Boston Development Committee—whose aim was to stop the drain of industry from Massachusetts and attract new industry to the state. Here, his interests overlapped with those of Ambassador Kennedy, who was making his economic survey and reaching gloomy conclusions. Ambassador Kennedy retained Dowd as a kind of personal PR adviser as well, probably paying for this service through the Somerset advertising account.

The seventh was Arthur Krock, still Joe Kennedy's very close friend. As Koskoff and Whalen write, Kennedy seldom made an important public move or statement without consulting Krock, at least using him as a sounding board.

That, then, was the ambassador's behind-the-scenes "brain trust." Joe Kennedy called the shots but he relied heavily on these men for advice. Five of the seven—Kane, Gallagher, Morrissey, Timilty, and Dowd— were old Boston pols. If Joe Kennedy himself is counted (as we counted him) then six of the eight-man strategy group were old pols. And Landis, a veteran of the SEC wars, and Krock were not exactly idealistic political amateurs.

Nowhere in the Kennedy Library or literature could we find a document remotely resembling a "strategy" paper for Jack's campaign. Since the ambassador worked so much on the telephone, there may not be one. But the ambassador, with the help of his brain trust did arrive at a strategy. Judging by the events to unfold, and from our interviews, a brief distillation of the strategy might run as follows.

First, bring Joseph P. Kennedy out of retirement. Restore him to the status of a prominent national personage, beginning in Massachusetts, then spreading nationwide. Have him speak out on important national and international issues, perhaps take a Cabinet-level post in Washington. A viable, committed Joseph P. Kennedy (as opposed to a reclusive, embittered Joseph P. Kennedy) would help Jack politically. The Kennedy name would be kept before the public. Especially emphasize his Boston background.

Second, keep the name of Joseph P. Kennedy, Jr., alive. Joe Junior had won a Navy Cross posthumously and a destroyer had been named for him. He had been an outstanding athlete and student. Keeping all this in the press would enhance the Kennedy name. The destroyer would be a handy PR tool if properly exploited. They would found—and fund—a new VFW post in Joe's honor and invite his veteran friends around Boston to join. Properly managed, the Joseph P. Kennedy, Jr., VFW Post could get in the news from time to time. They could start a Joseph P. Kennedy Foundation to make charitable gifts in Boston, timed to best political advantage. Finally, Jack had written his memorial to Joe—and it had been given away to many influential persons—but the ambassador asked, why not a real book on Joe Junior?

Third, Jack would not declare for a specific office or become involved immediately in Boston politics. (For one thing, they had to await the outcome of Curley's race for mayor in November.) Jack would first be exposed in an apolitical fashion, as a luncheon and dinner speaker, at VFW and American Legion Posts, community fund-raising events, Red Cross, Lions and Rotary Club meetings, and the like. He would appear as a veteran who was also an author, returned from the wars, concerned about the community, state, national, and international affairs: the economy, the postwar geopolitical world, the atomic bomb, and other lofty (and not locally controversial) issues. A young statesman, so to speak, and spokesman for the new generation of veterans. He would write magazine articles or book reviews or whatever would keep his name in the public eye.

And so the strategy was, from the beginning, to mount a family effort. That is, not a lone Jack Kennedy in frail health and without glittering qualifications for office, but the Kennedy men: the ambassador, Joe Junior, and Jack. Each reputation would complement the others, so to speak, and become merged in the public consciousness. It was, we thought, a brilliant strategy.

The ambassador and Jack launched a simultaneous blitz in Massachusetts in September. Joe Kennedy used his economic survey as a vehicle. In a period of ten days, he made thirty speeches in Massachusetts, tearing around in a midnight-blue Chrysler. His message was bound to make Bay Staters sit up and take notice: the economy of Massachusetts was dying. In a *Time* story of September 24, 1945, his emergence from obscurity was noted. *Time* gave the thrust of his talks:

> I'm willing to come back [to Massachusetts] to live because this
> is where my heart is. But I don't expect to come back to stay until I

think there has been a change for the better. For the past 24 years, Massachusetts has been consistantly losing business—in that time 2,300 industries have left the State. . . . We haven't done a blessed thing to find out why they are leaving or to keep them here. During the next five years Massachusetts will have its last chance to keep itself out of the grave. . . .

Time reported that some Bostonians were angered by Kennedy's sudden onslaught and asked why, if he was so interested in Massachusetts' future, had he recently bought the Merchandise Mart in Chicago? Kennedy was ready with an answer: "Because the condition of real estate in Boston is scandalous and that of politics is worse. The only property offered to me in Boston was a building in bad condition that was 20% vacant. . . ."

Time seemed puzzled by Joe Kennedy's sudden emergence into the limelight and sought to explain it: "Joe Kennedy was not embittered; he is not a bitter man. . . . He says he has no political ambitions, that he is too old to return to public life. But he and Secretary of State Jimmy Byrnes are close friends and he and Harry Truman have high regard for each other. Joe Kennedy might still wind up in Washington."

The *Time* story was followed by an extensive picture story in *Life*, on October 1. There are photographs of the ambassador addressing a luncheon meeting in Lowell, posing with Tobin, setting up a scholarship in honor of Joe Junior, and talking to a woman working as a riveter on the destroyer *Joseph P. Kennedy*. One *Life* picture, posed at Boston Harbor, emphasized the ambassador's Boston connections. The caption said Kennedy was "near his boyhood home. . . . The millionaire businessman began his career by delivering newspapers to ships at the nearby Cunard pier. . . ."

The articles in *Time* and *Life* were perfectly executed public relations, and there were many similar articles in local Massachusetts newspapers at this time. The ambassador was on his way to being rehabilitated. *Time* was mentioning him for a prominent job in the Truman Administration. The *Life* article had depicted him as a concerned citizen of Massachusetts—with deep roots there. Both the *Time* and *Life* articles had prominently plugged Joe Junior.

Jack was launched at a lower level. According to Leo Damore, in *The Cape Cod Years*, he began with a speech to the Rotary Club in Hyannis in September. Damore, who was either there or found a newsclip about it, writes:

> Taking as his subject "England and Germany; Victor and Vanquished" Jack Kennedy . . . more closely resembled a highschool senior chosen as Boys' State representative . . . than a

young man on the threshold of a political career. His loss of weight made the collar of his white shirt gape at the neck above the conservative, uncertainly knotted, blue-patterned tie. His suit of gray cheviot hung slackly from his wide, but frail-seeming, shoulders and gave him the look, a Rotarian recalled, "of a little boy dressed up in his father's clothes."

The speech was not a memorable one. . . . In a voice somewhat scratchy and tensely high-pitched, Jack Kennedy projected a quality of grave seriousness that masked his discomfiture. No trace of humor leavened his talk. Hardly diverging from his prepared text, he stood as if before a blackboard, addressing a classroom full of pupils who could be expected at any moment to become unruly. Although he was not a natural speaker, some of his own personality irrepressibly shown through. Stumbling over a word, he flashed a quick self-deprecating grin that, a member of his audience remembered, "could light up the room." An appealing waif-like quality showed through, and above all a winning sincerity. . . .

After that, Jack went on to a very important speaking date in Boston, September 11. That day he addressed the Crosscup-Pishon Post of the American Legion in the Statler Hotel ballroom. It was evidently the same speech. Joseph F. Dinneen, political reporter on the *Boston Globe* and an old friend of the ambassador's, wrote a story about it in the *Globe* September 12. Extract:

JOHN KENNEDY TELLS LEGIONNAIRES
HOW LABOR WON BRITAIN

Jack (John F.) Kennedy, hero of a Pacific naval action, who saved the lives of three of his crew when the PT boat he commanded was rammed . . . gave his views on foreign policy for kinds of government that are now taking over Europe, with particular reference to England the victor, Ireland the neutral and Germany the vanquished. . . .

Dinneen goes on to give Kennedy's views on what had happened to Churchill and the Conservative Party in England. It appears to be a rehash of the ideas Jack filed in his last piece to Hearst, analyzing the elections. Dinneen did not comment on Jack's speaking style, or speculate on why he might be speaking to the American Legion. That is, no mention that Jack might be a political candidate in Massachusetts.

Over the next eight weeks or so, Jack gave this speech—or variations of it—many times. These appearances were arranged by the John C. Dowd ad agency. In October and November he spoke before the Kiwanis Club of Worcester, the Erie Society in Boston, the Boston Association of

Geography Teachers, the Lions Club in Attleboro, and the Aristos Club in Boston. In October, according to one letter we found, he was speaking in behalf of the Greater Boston United War Fund, which was headed by a Boston pol, Michael T. Kelleher, and supported by the Dowd Agency. Jack donated $1,000 to the fund.

What was Jack's personal reaction to all this? We do not know; we could find nothing on the record. He was probably uncomfortable. It was not a role he had chosen. He was a stranger in Boston. And he was involved in what was surely one of the most audacious ploys in the audacious history of Boston politics. His father had arrived on the scene to grab, with his shrewdness and his money, an important political post for him—a job usually awarded by the old machines only after a man had spent years grubbing at the precinct and ward levels. Jack had few apparent qualifications for national office, and only the slimmest qualifications to represent a constituency. He would present himself as a representative of the working man—he who had never held or needed a regular job.

It reminded us a bit of British politics. Many of Jack's aristocratic friends went out to working-class districts to stand for seats in the House of Commons, as though they were entitled to them by a sort of divine right, and feeling at the same time a sense of noblesse oblige.

30

Old Pals

THAT fall, as Jack dipped his toe into Boston political waters, he had little help from his old school chums, Navy buddies, and close friends, we discovered from our research and interviews. They were mostly scattered. Chuck Spalding left the carrier *Cabot* at Okinawa and made his way back to Philadelphia where Betty was living. Following his discharge, they made plans to go to Hollywood where Chuck would work for Gary Cooper. Red Fay volunteered for the Navy's aviation program and reported for primary flight training in Dallas, Texas. Fay said, "Jack thought I was crazy." Lem Billings, who had entered the Navy late, continued to serve on the attack transport *Cecil*, bringing sailors and soldiers home from the Pacific. Rip Horton, who had been in the Army in Europe and the Far East, came for a visit to the Cape with his wife, Jane, following his discharge. He recalled Jack was practicing his speeches on a tape recorder, the first one Horton had ever seen. But something in this friendship went awry. Whereas in 1942 Jack had counted Horton as one of his "two or three" closest friends, it was no longer so. Horton returned to New York and went into the dry cleaning business.

There were four good friends—old and new—living in the Boston area: Torby Macdonald, Ben Smith, Jim Reed, and Eddie McLaughlin. Ben and Sis Smith, who now had three children, settled in Gloucester and Ben reentered the family fish business. Ben was now thoroughly domesticated and his life in Gloucester was exactly what he wanted: serene, uncomplicated. He and Sis saw Jack infrequently, usually at football games. He did not participate at all in the campaign, he told us. But Jack saw Torby, Reed, and McLaughlin and their wives. As part of the "amateur" image-building, they were described in a national magazine—*Look*—as Jack's "junior brain trust."

But how accurate was this chacterization? Torby, for one, dismissed it as more or less nonsense. At that time, Torby had reentered Harvard Law School. His wife, Phyllis, was now pregnant. He indicated to us in our interview that he played little or no role in Jack's 1946 campaign. "I think he was his own brain trust," Torby said, alluding to the magazine article. "You know, as time goes by, people enlarge on their importance in Jack's life, in my judgment. Jack was his own man. He'd ask for advice but he didn't necessarily follow what people told him."

On January 4 Boston newspapers reported the Macdonalds had had a baby—Torbert Hart, Jr. (Torby told us Jack was the godfather at the christening.) The arrival of the baby further complicated a complicated relationship. A contemporary explained:

> I think Phyllis, who was well-launched on a movie career, intended to marry money and her marriage to Torby was a comedown. Torby was a great guy—man-about-town, football and war hero, really handsome and very likable, Jack's best friend. But he had no money. I don't think he was really ready for marriage yet. So it was not by any means the ideal marriage. The baby coming along so soon didn't help. Jack would naturally side with Torby in the domestic disputes and was forever asking Torby to go with him here and there. Naturally Phyllis began to resent Jack. In fact, it went beyond resentment. They had almost no relationship at all. For these reasons, Torby played almost no role in Jack's campaign and Phyllis never came around.

Jim Reed, who was discharged from the Navy about this time, was not much help at this stage either. At first he was involved in a heavy personal decision: whether to go to the Harvard Business School or to Harvard Law School. Jewel told us:

> I remember about that time Jack told us he had been down someplace and had taken a series of aptitude tests. On one of the tests, they flashed six-digit numbers on a screen and you had to try to remember them. So we played around at home doing that—Jack would write the numbers on a shirt cardboard, hold them up, and then we'd try to remember the digits.
> Anyway, Jack suggested that Jim should go down and take these aptitude tests. He did. The upshot was they told him he should go into selling because he was essentially a persuader. He had a lot of creative imagination. They told him he shouldn't go into law because he didn't have the right kind of personality.

Jim Reed told us he was invited to work for the Kennedys full time, but he declined:

> I couldn't make up my mind whether to go to law school or business school. Jack came by one day and said his father would like me to come into his organization as a salaried employee. I said no. If you worked for the Kennedys, your relationship and position

was transformed into something that wasn't quite the way I wanted it. I wanted to keep my independence. So Jack said he was going into politics and he really wanted me to study up on economics, to become his economic adviser, so to speak. I asked him if I should become a Democrat—I'd be perfectly happy to be a Democrat. But he said, "No, Jamey. I'd rather have you stay a Republican. You can do more good for me as a Republican in the years ahead. I already have Democratic friends. I need Republican friends."

So Jack said he would write a letter of recommendation for me to the dean of the Harvard Business School. I thought this was a little arrogant of Jack. What business did he have in writing to the dean? But he *did* write to the dean.

Later, Reed sent us a copy of the letter Jack wrote. Dated October 2, 1945, it said:

DEAR SIR,
Lieutenant Reed served under my command in Motor Torpedo Boat Squadron Two during the Solomon Islands campaign. He showed great courage on a number of occasions, an extraordinary zest for work and fine ability which made him one of the outstanding officers in the area.

Now he has returned and has applied for admission to the Harvard Business School. He has many fine qualities and should be a credit to the School.

> Very truly yours,
> JOHN F. KENNEDY
> Lieutenant, USNR, retired,
> Former Executive Officer,
> Motor Torpedo Boat
> Squadron Two

There were, of course, two small fibs in this letter. Reed never served under Jack in Squadron Two, and Jack was never the executive officer of Squadron Two. In any event, at the last minute Reed changed his mind. He entered Harvard Law School. A few weeks later, Jewel, who was still working in the Boston office of IBM, became pregnant.

About this same time Jack, Jim Reed, and another Navy veteran entered into a business deal—one of the few business deals Jack ever became involved in. We thought it might be related in some way to the political campaign, but it turned out not to be. Jim Reed, Jack, and Fred Wilson, a friend of Reed's, bought a newspaper, the Narragansett *Times*, in Wakefield, Rhode Island. Reed told us, "It was Wilson's idea. He wanted to buy the paper. He felt the area it served was growing and it would be a good investment. Jack and I thought it would be a good idea—maybe a good base for politics or pressing your own ideas. His father was not involved at all. I think it was the *only* time Jack ever got into a business deal on his own. And he said it was the first time he'd ever put money into something and got it all back—plus a profit.''

Fred Wilson and his wife, Susan, still own the paper. We talked to Wilson by telephone. While in the Navy, he had attended a special Navy course at the Harvard Business School, where he and Susan met Jim and Jewel Reed. He said:

> Then I met Jack Kennedy. He was just back from Berlin. I remember he said it had been a grave mistake—one of the greatest mistakes in history—to stop Eisenhower and let the Russians take East Germany and Berlin. He told us how the Russians had raped and looted. . . . He said we should have "gone all the way to the Pacific."
>
> I was about to get out of the Navy. The paper was up for sale. I wanted to buy it and live in that area. I formed a small corporation. Jack and Jim Reed—the nicest guy I ever met—each put up two thousand dollars. That was for twenty shares at one hundred dollars a share. We three were the sole stockholders. Officially, I took over the paper February 1, 1946. I then had three kids, ran the paper, and taught school. Later we merged the Narragansett *Times* - with another paper, the North Kingston *Standard*, which last year [1973] won an award for excellence.
>
> Jack was never involved with the newspaper, editorially or otherwise. It was all a very casual thing for him. He liked newspaper work. He certainly didn't need the paper for a political base. Rhode Island was already a Democratic, Catholic state. On July 21, 1947, I bought Jack out, by mail. Jim Reed—the corporate secretary—was involved longer—to 1949. Then I bought him out.

But a serious hitch was developing in Jack's friendship with Jim Reed, one he had expressed fear of in his letter to Red Fay when he wondered how everybody would get along with the wives. Like Torby, Jim was soon studying hard at Harvard Law School. Jewel, still working at the Boston office of IBM, had become pregnant. Like Phyllis Macdonald, she resented her husband's relationship with Jack—Jack asking Jim to go out with him, leaving Jewel at home alone. For these reasons, neither Jim nor Jewel were able, or in Jewel's case, willing, to help out much.

Nor did Jack's new friend Pat Lannan help. Several letters in the Kennedy Library indicate that they were in close touch, but from a distance. One letter, dated November 7, 1945, contained this cryptic note: "Glad to hear that you're enjoying good health and that you apparently are avoiding an operation." We suppose that is a reference to Jack's chronic back problems, in the absence of any other evidence of a new affliction at this time.

The letters indicate that Lannan had talked Jack into investing with him in at least three different companies: American Window Glass, Interstate Power, and the New York publishing firm of Henry Holt and Company. Holt was then barely struggling along with a textbook line. Lannan correctly foresaw a huge postwar baby crop and a concurrent need for huge numbers of textbooks. Lannan had already bought some shares and had gained a seat on the Holt board of directors. His aim was to bring in more capital and gear up for big profits. He told us, "As I recall, the plan was for Jack and Chuck Spalding to put up a certain amount of money. Then Jack, or maybe Chuck, or both, would run the company. Jack bought some shares, but he had no interest in running the company and Chuck wanted to go back to Hollywood and work with Gary Cooper."

Of all Jack's Boston friends, new and old, the only ones we could discover who helped him in any extent that fall were Cis and Eddie McLaughlin, son of the old Boston fire commissioner. It appeared to us that Jack cultivated the McLaughlins. As an ex-member of PT Squadron Ten, McLaughlin was a visible link to Jack's war record. He was also a conduit into an important old Boston political fiefdom. Inasmuch as Eddie had political aspirations of his own, no doubt he welcomed the association with Jack.

But Eddie McLaughlin was still in the Navy—he would not get out until December. That fall he continued going to Northeastern Law School at night. Cis—not yet pregnant—took a job in the Boston bureau of *Newsweek*. Jack often came by their apartment on Boylston Street to discuss politics and to eat. His eating habits had not changed—in fact, they may have become worse, perhaps due to an onset of the old prewar stomach problems. Cis McLaughlin recalled:

He was a very finicky eater. I remember one night he came by and, out of deference to his stomach, I had some chicken à la king. What a fiasco! I put too much milk in it and it turned to soup. So I strained the bits of chicken out and put them on Jack's plate—over toast. There was nothing left, so Ed and I had the soup on our toast. And Jack wouldn't eat his food. He just pushed it around on his plate.

Another night, I remember, we took Jack to Ed's father's house for dinner so he could talk politics. My mother-in-law was a marvelous cook. She put out a great dinner: oyster stew, a beautiful steak, Delmonico potatoes, everything just wonderful. But Jack did the same thing he did at my house: just pushed the food back and forth on his plate. Then he whispered to me that I was a better cook than my mother-in-law! Thank God she didn't hear him. Afterwards she felt bad he hadn't eaten anything but I said, "Don't worry, that's the way he eats."

He never did really like to eat a meal. He liked ice cream with chocolate sauce. He ate that by the gallon, at home and when he was out in Boston.

When Ed got out of the Navy in December, 1945, we noted with interest, it was one of Joe Kennedy's brain trusters, the ad man Jack Dowd, who got him a civilian job—with the Snyder Fuel Company. He continued going to Northeastern Law School at night. Cis left her job at *Newsweek* for one in a Boston ad agency. Shortly after this she would become a full-time Kennedy-for-Congress worker.

What was clear from this research was that in the fall, 1945, stages of the campaign, Jack did not have extensive help from his school chums and Navy buddies; not from Torby nor Jim Reed nor Ben Smith nor the others. The only substantial help came from his newfound PT friend Eddie McLaughlin, who had both roots and ambitions in Boston politics. But because of a full-time job in the Navy, and later with the Snyder Fuel Company, and going to law school at night, even Eddie's contribution to the campaign—other than introducing Jack to his father and his political cronies—was not major.

31

Palm Beach Interlude

IN early November, while Jack was going around giving his Britain-victor, Germany-vanquished speech to various groups, the citizens of Boston were hypnotized by the goings-on in the mayoralty race. Here was that seventy-one-year-old anachronism, James Michael Curley, under federal indictment, running against a big field of candidates. His opponents included the Tobin-backed incumbent acting mayor, John Kerrigan; William Arthur Reilly, a music publisher and former fire commissioner; Michael P. Feeney, described by Curley as a "fuzzy-minded liberal"; and two Yankees—John Sawtelle and Joseph Lee.

Curley wrote in his autobiography *I'd Do It Again*:

> During this campaign I jolted the complacent by warning that Boston would become a ghost town after the war unless I was elected. . . . The Fall River shipyard closed, and the cancellation of war contracts threw thousands of persons out of work in the textile, leather, machinery and tooling industries. Inflation was rampant and the housing shortage was serious. Meanwhile such municipal facilities as parks, beaches and roads were in a sad state of disrepair. Boston was in the throes of another depression. . . . There was less levity than usual in this contest. . . .

The Boston voters cast their ballots on November 7. The anachronism swamped his opponents. With 111,799 votes, Curley grabbed 45 percent of the total. John Kerrigan, the runner-up, polled only about half Curley's vote. And now, incredibly, for the fourth time in the twentieth century, Curley would be Boston's mayor.

Less than two weeks later, Curley's trial in Washington began. It ran through November, December, and into early January. On January 17, 1946, a couple of weeks after Curley had been sworn in as mayor of Boston, the jury, after twenty-two hours of deliberation, found Curley guilty. His lawyers immediately appealed, and by means of various legalisms, managed to delay sentencing for another eighteen months. Curley wrote that in January, 1946, he "relinquished" his seat in Congress, donating his $10,000 salary for the year to the Boston City Hospital. With Curley's election to mayor, the way was now open for Jack to declare for his vacated seat in the 11th Congressional District. But, as we shall see, Kennedy did not do so immediately.

For the Kennedys, this off-year election must have provided some valuable intelligence. It showed, generally, that the voters were in a rebellious mood. Like the British, they were tired of wartime controls and sacrifice. The election of Curley was less a display of affection for him, although there was a great deal of that, than a repudiation of the established order, including the once popular Governor Tobin. To some, the trend presaged a Republican sweep in the general elections in November, 1946.

The 11th Congressional District was a safe Democratic seat, no matter whether there was a Republican sweep or not. Yet it was a time to take care. After his repudiation in Boston, Tobin might be a political liability. And Curley mustn't be offended. If he got his dander up and put a candidate in the race against Jack—and supported him vigorously—it might be fatal. So stretched the tightrope.

The strategy of keeping the Kennedy name before the public proceeded through these events. On October 25 there was a very long story about Joe Junior in the *New York Times* by Anthony Leviero, explaining for the first time in detail how he had been killed. This story was reprinted in *The Choate Bulletin* and, we presume, in Boston newspapers.

On December 15, at the Navy Yard in Charlestown (the largest single employer in the 11th Congressional District), the destroyer *Joseph P. Kennedy, Jr.*, was commissioned. By that time, the ship's skipper had been chosen. He was Commander Harry Grimshaw Moore, a Naval Academy graduate from the class of 1932. He is now retired from the Navy and living in Gainesville, Georgia. He very kindly sent us his personal scrapbook which contains many photographs, newspaper clippings, and personal letters from the Kennedys.

The commissioning received major coverage in the Boston papers. Sample headlines:

HERO FLIER KENNEDY HONORED
AS NEW DESTROYER JOINS FLEET

HERO'S MEMORY HONORED
U.S.S. KENNEDY COMMISSIONED

From the clips (which were in conflict) we judged the following members of the Kennedy family were present: Rose, Jean (the ship's sponsor), Robert, Teddy, and Honey Fitz and his wife. Definitely absent: the ambassador, Jack, and Kathleen, who (we think) was then in the United States for a Christmas visit. One story said Kathleen "remained in New York with her father."

Actually, the ambassador was in Palm Beach. He sent a telegram from there which is in Moore's scrapbook: VERY SORRY NOT TO BE WITH YOU AT THE COMMISSIONING OF THE DESTROYER KENNEDY. MY HEART IS WITH IT AND WILL STAY ABOARD AS LONG AS I LIVE. MY VERY BEST TO YOU THE OFFICERS AND CREW. PLEASE TELL THEM THE DESTROYER WAS NAMED AFTER A GREAT BOY AND GREAT AMERICAN.

During the ceremony, which was presided over by Rear Admiral Felix X. Gygax (commandant of the First Naval District), the citation of Joe Junior's Navy Cross was read to the crew. They were dressed in blue uniforms, standing at attention on the afterdeck. It was again a difficult moment for Rose. One newspaper story said, "Overcome by emotion at the Admiral's reading of her son's citation, she [Rose] sank down in the seat on the stand. Because of a request from Mrs. Kennedy, who wished the ceremonies to be quiet and simple, the Admiral cancelled a public broadcast of the commissioning ceremonies. . . ."

Four days later, from Palm Beach, Rose wrote Commander Moore a letter of thanks in firm, elegant script:

DEAR COMMANDER MOORE,

Mr. Kennedy and I and the children want to extend to you, the officers and crew of the U.S.S. Joseph P. Kennedy, Jr. our heartfelt thanks and deepest appreciation for your invitation to us to witness the interesting and moving ceremonies connected with the commissioning of the ship named for our beloved son. As we stood on the deck, all of us felt that you and the other officers appreciated our feelings of pride as well as our sadness, and that you used every facility at your command to make us comfortable.

You may be assured, dear Commander Moore, that we Kennedys are proud and delighted to have you in command and please remember that our hearts and our prayers will be with you and your valiant men always.

Very sincerely,
ROSE KENNEDY

Robert was still in the Navy V-12 program. He had now been going to college, in the Navy, for twenty-two months, at Bates College, Lewiston, Maine, and Harvard. After Christmas it was arranged that Bobby enter active service as a seaman, second class, on the *Joseph P. Kennedy, Jr.* He reported to the ship on February 1, 1946.

We could find nothing in the records to pin down Jack's movements in the month of December. His absence at the commissioning of the *Joseph P. Kennedy, Jr.*, probably indicated one of two things: either he was back in the hospital in Boston or he was in Palm Beach with his father. We leaned to the second alternative.

He was there at Christmas, in good spirits and strong enough physically to spend a lot of time nightclubbing. During this period he met a man who would become one of his closest friends, Charles Leffingwell Bartlett. Some years later, Bartlett introduced Jack to Jacqueline Bouvier and would be an usher in their wedding.

Charles Bartlett is now a Washington-based newspaper columnist. We met him at his home for an interview.

He gave us his background. He was the son of a Chicago stockbroker, educated at private schools and at Yale—he was the sixth generation on his father's side to attend Yale.

At Yale, he worked on the campus newspaper, the *Daily News*, majored in English, and was the president of his fraternity, Fence Club. When he was graduated in December, 1942 (with the class of 1943), he was commissioned an ensign in the Navy and assigned to Communications Intelligence. He spent eight months in Washington learning the ropes, then six months in Honolulu. His specialty was radio eavesdropping—monitoring Japanese military traffic, analyzing "callsigns," and sending the stuff on to the codebreakers. Later in the war he helped set up advance monitoring stations on Kwajalein, Guam, and Okinawa.

Bartlett "loved" this hush-hush work. The men in his outfit were "a pretty erudite group": former journalists, college professors, and so on. They passed their off hours discussing literature, politics, and philosophy. It was very stimulating, he said. "I was brought up a Republican, but during the war I started forming my own opinions."

After the shooting stopped, Bartlett returned to the United States. That Christmas, 1945, he went to his parents' winter home in Hobe Sound, a lush watering hole north of Palm Beach. He told us:

> There were a lot of people in Florida then, sort of resting up. There was a very attractive girl there, Dodo Potter, whose brother, Robert, had been with me at St. Mark's and was a good friend. Dodo was from Boston and had married Alfred Clark, whom she was then divorcing. Dodo was a good friend of Kathleen Kennedy's. Anyway, I went down to a nightclub in Palm Beach with Dodo, The Patio. That night Dodo, who knew Jack, introduced us.
>
> We liked each other very much. We were very simpatico. We liked to laugh about the same things. We talked about the newspaper business. Arthur Sulzberger of the *New York Times* was a great friend of my father's. I'd decided that when I had enough points to get out of the Navy, I'd go into the newspaper business.

Mr. Sulzberger had offered me a job on the *Chattanooga Times*, which the *New York Times* owned. Jack told me he'd tried the newspaper business—nothing specific—and now he was getting ready to run for public office in Boston.

After that we saw each other several times over the holidays. There was a golf course—Seminole—where we'd meet. . . . Then I didn't see him again for several years—when I moved to Washington and he was a congressman.

It was not all play. Jack, no doubt, was busy working on speeches for his coming political campaign. He advanced his image as a spokesman for the veterans by reviewing a couple of books by veterans for the *Boston Globe*: *The New Veteran*, by Charles G. Bolte, and *More Lives Than One*, by Hobert Douglas Skidmore. The reviews were published in December.

Bolte, who lost a leg at El Alamein fighting with the British, was head of a new veterans group, the American Veterans Committee (AVC), which he had founded because he believed the American Legion and VFW were obsolete and reactionary, the members "red-faced and paunchy." His book was his rationale for founding the AVC and a denunciation of the existing organizations. In his review, Jack declared he could not agree with Bolte. Better, he wrote, for the veterans to join the old organizations and infuse them with progressive ideas.

There was good reason for his position. By some means—there was nothing at the Kennedy Library to explain it—Jack or his father had pulled off another publicity coup: Jack had just been elected chairman of the VFW national convention which would be held in Boston the following September.

32

The Eleventh

J ACK'S victory is given in the Kennedy books as an easy one. It was a safe Democratic district with no Republican opposition. He had merely to bump off a few old hacks who might challenge him in the primary, then he was home free.

That's an easy conclusion in hindsight; he did win by a good margin. But in fact Jack's 1946 political campaign was a long, tough, mental and physical struggle against one very strong candidate and two others less strong, but still troublesome. Had Jack not worked so hard, had his father not had so much money to spend (and his opponents so little), had he made just one mistake along the way, he might have lost. It was certainly not taken for granted as a pushover in advance, either by Kennedy's people or by his opposition.

The times were freighted with uncertainty. The war was over, but now Russia was being tough—the Cold War had begun—and people worried there would be yet another holocaust. The United States was undergoing the difficult transition from a strictly controlled wartime economy to a laissez-faire peacetime economy. There was a critical shortage of meat, tires, and other items that had created long waiting lines, a flourishing black market, and rampant inflation. Labor was flexing its muscles with strong new demands for shorter hours, higher pay, and improved fringe benefits. President Truman had precipitously demobilized the 15,000,000-man military establishment. Veterans were returning home—or to what had been home—by the millions, creating an overwhelming housing shortage.

In times of such uncertainty, no one could predict how voters would react to a Jack Kennedy. He was immensely rich: Choate and Harvard, Stork Club and Palm Beach. Would the voters of this district accept such a young man with no political experience to uphold their interests in Washington?

It was not a solid, homogenous district, but a crazy quilt of six disparate towns or neighborhoods with 328,000 constituents in all. In 1946 each had its own distinct flavor, its economic and political power structure and, in several, Jack's potential opponents held sway.

Here, reconstructed from our interviews with various people who worked in the Kennedy campaign, is a word map of the way Jack most likely saw the district in 1946:

Cambridge

Cambridge was the largest single piece of real estate in the district. In 1946 it had a population of 110,000, of which half were registered voters, organized into eleven wards. These 55,000 voters represented about 30 percent of the total vote in the entire district, so Cambridge was a vital area politically, a crucial battleground.

Jack—and the Kennedys—were no strangers to Cambridge. It was, of course, the home of Harvard (and Radcliffe and MIT). The ambassador, Joe Junior, Jack, and Bobby had all attended Harvard. Jim Landis was then Dean Landis of the Harvard Law School. This was some strength in the academic community (the old school tie) but there would also be opposition. Young Harvard students and teachers in the liberal camp such as Arthur M. Schlesinger, Jr., and John Kenneth Galbraith considered Ambassador Kennedy a reactionary and many disliked him personally. Would they support Jack? No one knew.

There was much more to Cambridge than academe. The tree-lined streets around Harvard, with row after row of beautiful old houses, were impressive, and formed the basic image of Cambridge. But in East Cambridge there was also a large, low-income enclave of Italian-Americans who were not so visible. There were thousands of these people, closely enmeshed in the local political machinery. On election day they supported the candidate who offered them the most help economically. It is not likely that Jack had ever set foot in the slums of East Cambridge. In that area his name would have meant nothing.

Cambridge put forth the strongest opponent Jack would have to face in the primary. He was the very popular mayor of Cambridge, Michael Neville. Neville was a criminal lawyer with a thriving practice. He had come up the convential political ladder, serving in the state legislature. Mayor of Cambridge was primarily an honorary job—the city manager did most of the executive work—and it was not an elective position. The nine-man City Council chose the mayor from among its ranks. But Neville had proven his vote-getting power in his election to the legislature and to the Cambridge City Council. He was popular and he had political connections all over Boston. Thus, on this most crucial of political battlegrounds, Jack faced his strongest opposition. The feeling among the pols was that Neville would "murder" Jack in Cambridge.

Brighton

The 11th Congressional District included the northern tip of the suburb of Brighton, Ward 22, just across the Charles River from Harvard. The ward had an unusually large number of registered voters—22,000. The area was mixed Irish and Italian. In 1946 it did not propose a candidate. By a happy coincidence, Jack had been born and spent his early childhood in the adjacent town, Brookline. The Beals Street house was only six or seven blocks from the eastern border of Ward 22. Eddie Gallagher was very well known in Brighton. Barring some unforeseen disaster, and with proper organization, Jack could run strong in Brighton.

Somerville

Lying to the north of Cambridge, Somerville was a town far different in character. In its heart lay a massive rail and freight center. Around the center were warehouses and factories, and at the extreme north end, the Mystic River. For the most part, Somerville in 1946 was a lower-class neighborhood, a mixed population of Irish- and Italian-Americans. Three wards, numbers 1, 2 and 3, of Somerville were assigned to the 11th District.

Somerville had put forth a candidate: astonishingly enough, a woman. She was Catherine E. Falvey, a lawyer and more recently a major in the WAC—and now, of course, a veteran like Jack. But this was Boston, 1946. The conservative Irish- and Italian-Americans were not ready to catapult a woman from her traditional place in the kitchen to the U. S. Congress. The pols figured she might get a thousand or two thousand votes in Somerville, but she would have no strength outside of Somerville. At most, she was a nuisance to contend with.

Charlestown

Lying to the east of Somerville, toward downtown Boston, was the solid Irish-Catholic enclave of Charlestown, Ward 3, in every respect a fascinating, intensely political neighborhood. Some of the great moments in the early phases of the Revolutionary War took place in Charlestown. Paul Revere set off from there on his famous midnight ride, April 18, 1775. A couple of months later, June 17, the Battle of Bunker Hill was fought in Charlestown. The most prominent landmark in the city today is a massive (and ugly) monument to that skirmish and one of the big political events of the year is the Bunker Hill Day parade which, in 1946, would be held on Monday, June 17, the day before the primary. Describing the clannish, Irish-Catholic, solidly Democratic people of Charlestown in his book, *The Kennedy Family*, Joe Dinneen wrote, "It is probable that there is not a single Republican anywhere in Charlestown."

Charlestown was oriented to the sea. For well over two hundred years, the Boston Navy Yard had been located there. Along its northern boundry, on the Mystic River, were docks for oceangoing vessels. Rail lines came over from the yards in Somerville and ran out on the docks. The Navy Yard and the docks, plus a few surrounding factories, provided the principal place of employment for Charlestown for decades. In 1946 it was a low-income area, a tough neighborhood of stevedores.

The Irish settled Charlestown in the nineteenth century. They jammed "three-decker" houses—three-story apartments—together along Charlestown's hills. One family usually owned the house, the other two (one per floor) rented. In 1946 there were 30,000 people (15,000 registered voters) crowded into Charlestown's small area, and most knew one another; many were related. Most of them worked at the Navy Yard or on the docks, but some worked in downtown Boston, only a short distance away via the Charlestown Bridge. Except for his Irish heritage, Jack had little in common with the "townies" of Charlestown.

Charlestown had put up a candidate, a strong one, an old pol named John F. Cotter, who had deep roots in the 11th Congressional District. In 1934, when a distinguished lawyer named John P. Higgins unseated the longtime (five-term) incumbent in the 11th, John J. Douglas, one of his chief campaign lieutenants had been Cotter. Higgins took Cotter to Washington to serve as his secretary. In September, 1937, Higgins was appointed chief justice of the Massachusetts Supreme Court. In the interim, between the appointment and a special election to fill the seat, Cotter had carried on the job, a sort of unofficial "acting congressman." In the special election in late 1937, Cotter stood as a candidate, but he was defeated by Thomas A. Flaherty, who held the seat until 1942 when the district was gerrymandered and won by Curley. Cotter had also served as secretary to Curley.

During his twelve-year service in the district, Cotter had dispensed countless favors to constituents, not only in Charlestown, but all over. He was well known to many, many families in the district. His weakness was that he lacked outstanding credits and polish. He had held no major elective jobs (such as the state legislature), he was not a charismatic personality. Yet, because of the clannish loyalty of the voters in Charlestown, Cotter was certain to give Jack a hard time there.

Boston

Sprawling southeastward across the Mystic River basin from Charlestown, the 11th Congressional District also included a large chunk of downtown Boston, known as the North End and the West End. Much of this area was occupied by business offices, hotels, docks, and railroad stations, but in the North End, there was a large enclave of residents, jammed together in red-brick tenements. The North End, site of the famous and historical Old North Church, was once Yankee territory. But the Yankees had been displaced by the Irish, who referred to themselves proudly as "dereos"—Dear Old North Enders. When the Irish moved on to greener pastures such as Charlestown, Somerville, Brighton, and Cambridge the Italian immigrants took over the North End. In 1946 it was heavily Italian. Like Charlestown, it was a tough neighborhood.

This territory, no less political and clannish than Charlestown, was known politically as Ward 3. The ward had put up a candidate, Joseph Russo, who had lived there and been involved in politics there for twenty years. In 1946 Russo held a seat on the powerful Boston City Council. He had been elected to that post for four consecutive two-year terms, and had served on the City Council for seven years. He had also served on many city committees, handing out countless favors. He was considered the third-strongest of the candidates Jack faced, so strong that he might conceivably defeat Jack in Ward 3 and carry Italian-American neighborhoods.

But Jack had a lot going for him in the North End, too. Honey Fitz had been born there, and so had Rose. Honey Fitz was now in his eighties, but he had represented this territory, not only as mayor, but also as U.S. Congressman. He was still fondly remembered, as was Rose, who also had many friends (and relatives) still living in the ward.

East Boston

Lying to the northeast of downtown Boston, across the interior harbor was another very rough area, a slum of red-brick tenements, Ward 1. Today this area is dominated by Boston's huge Logan International Airport and its satellite businesses. But in 1946, the airport was not so large and overwhelming. On the southwest end of East Boston, the densest population area, were more docks and related facilities and solid blocks of tenements. On the northeast end of the area, near Suffolk Downs racetrack, a hilly area known as Orient Heights, there were many three-deckers. The ward was mostly Italian, with about 20,000 registered voters.

Jack had roots in East Boston. Years before, when the area was teeming with starving Irish immigrants who had fled the potato famines, his paternal grandfather, Patrick Joseph Kennedy, ran a saloon in East Boston and had been a major political power in the area. The ambassador had been born in East Boston and still owned a bank there, the Columbia Trust Company. But how much this would mean to the Italian population was anybody's guess. It was expected that Joseph Russo would run strong in the area—as strong or stronger than in the North End and West End.

To recapitulate:

Cambridge. Thirty percent of the registered voters. Eleven wards. Mixed liberal academic population, Italian slums. Experienced, well-entrenched opponent, Mike Neville. Murder for Jack.

Brighton. One ward. Mixed Irish-Italian. No candidate. Jack probably be home free.

Somerville. Three wards. Mixed Italian and Irish population. Lower middle class. Opponent ex-WAC, Catherine Falvey, would run weak. A coin toss.

Charlestown. One ward. All Irish. Clannishly behind local pol, John Cotter. Trouble for Jack.

Boston. One ward. Possibly strong candidate, Joseph Russo, possible trouble for Jack.

East Boston. One ward. Predominately Italian. Russo territory. Trouble for Jack.

Thus, in each of the three key areas of the district—Cambridge, Charlestown, and Boston/East Boston—there were strong politicians who stood a good chance of winning on their own turf. The real question was: How would each of these candidates do outside his own enclave? The early guessing was, not very well. In other words, it would probably be a close enough race to require a second, runoff election.

Granted that neither Neville nor Cotter nor Russo had sufficient strength outside his own area to win, then a broad-appeal outsider winning second place in all three areas might muster enough total votes in the district to win. This became the Kennedy strategy.

This particular election was complicated by one other factor. Usually primaries in Massachusetts (and other states) are held in late September. The candidates spend the summer months resting up and preparing for the battle, which traditionally begins on Labor Day weekend. The weather is pleasant; crowds gather in ball parks and plazas in shirtsleeves. But because there were many tens of thousands of Massachusetts voters still in the military service who would have to cast an absentee ballot by mail, it was necessary to stretch out the time between the primaries and general elections in November so the mail could get back and forth. Thus the primaries—all primaries, Democrat and Republican alike—were set for Tuesday, June 18.

This meant that the hard campaigning would have to be done between April and June, rather than in the fall. If Jack (or anyone else) wanted to get a head start, it meant launching a campaign in the dead of winter, when the daylight hours were shortest, the temperatures lowest, the snow and ice heaviest, the winds most biting; a time when people were, for the most part, either inside their places of employment or holed up at home. It meant that people would be harder to reach.

33

Tactics

JACK arrived in Boston to begin his political campaign sometime in early January—we could find no precise date. It was bitterly cold, a stark contrast to the languid climate of Palm Beach. He took a suite of rooms at the Bellevue Hotel on Beacon Street, an old political hangout near the State House, where his grandfather Honey Fitz and his grandmother had had a suite for years. Jack's rooms were plain, with dingy old furniture—nothing pretentious—but it was a legal residence within the district, as required by Massachusetts law.

No doubt Honey Fitz was in his element, the old fire horse responding to the bells of a new campaign, ready to pitch in with all his effusive energy. If so, he shortly came in for a disappointment. Martin and Plaut tell this anecdote:

> Joe Kane [they write] was tutoring Jack in the fundamentals of politics. ("In politics, you have no friends, only co-conspirators," and so on.) Honey Fitz strolled down the hall and came into Jack's suite. Kane took one look at Honey Fitz and yelled, "Get that son-ofabitch out of here!"
>
> Jack looked at Kane incredulously. *"Who?* GRANDPA?"
>
> The colorful old relic was disposed of. Thereafter Honey Fitz was used only as a prop: for photographs with Jack, or for limited, special appearances. He was the link to the past, proof of Jack's Boston roots, the political tradition of the Kennedy family. He played no other role in the campaign.

By the time Jack arrived in Boston, five key decisions had been made about the tactics of the campaign, each very important.

First, Jack would run as a young, Catholic, Democratic war veteran with an outstanding combat record. He would not associate himself publicly with any established political group. His initial power base would be the Joseph P. Kennedy, Jr., VFW Post, which Jack would organize immediately and command. Joe Kane coined a campaign slogan designed to set Jack apart from the old order: "The New Generation Offers a Leader." The visible campaign staff would be composed strictly of youthful World War Two veterans from Boston. The ambassador and his brain trust—Timilty, Dowd, Landis, Gallagher, Morrissey, and Kane—would stay out of sight. Thus, in effect, they would operate two teams: an outside, highly visible, idealistic group of amateurs led by an Irish-Catholic war hero, and an inside, invisible group of old pols.

The decision to project Jack mainly as a war hero looks obvious now, but it must have seemed chancy then. It immediately and rather decisively identified Jack with one single population element, a move that can be fatal in politics. There were many, many voters in the 11th Congressional District who were not veterans: defense workers who had spent the war in the Navy Yard or in other arsenals, the aged and, of course, most of the female population. The returning veterans were yet to be reintegrated into the community. Many of them were not even registered voters; when they went off to war, they had been too young to register. There was no guarantee that they could be quickly organized into an effective political power, or that many of them would even give a damn about politics after what they had been through.

And there was a larger point. By what logic did war hero equal effective politician and legislator? Because Jack commanded a PT boat and rescued his crew when the boat was rammed (as the story went), did it follow that he was qualified for the give-and-take of politics, the art of leadership and compromise, the knack of wheedling from a large and experienced U.S. Congress the greatest good for the greatest number in the 11th Congressional District? In truth, there was no logic; it did not follow. Many so-called war heros discovered the hard way that voters who admired their courage still voted their own pocketbooks.

However, there was no alternative. What else had Jack done? Written a book at Harvard. But it would not do to stress his Harvard background in the slums of Charlestown and the North End. Besides, the book could be attacked as a whitewash of Munich or a defense of the upper classes at the expense of common people. He had never even held a job, let alone a political job.

Second, Jack would not declare for a specific office until the very last minute. If he failed to make inroads in the 11th Congressional District, he could shift to some other goal. It would keep his opponents guessing. It would postpone the solidification of the opposition. It would create speculation and therefore publicity in the newspapers. It would postpone the day that the inevitable hordes of political parasites would flock to Jack, deflecting his concentration.

Third, Jack must make an enormous effort to meet everybody possible in the district. This would mean an early start and very hard physical work right up to the day the votes were cast. Jack would have to tramp from door to door in the tenement districts, climb the three flights of stairs in the three-deckers in Charlestown, meet stevedores on the docks, give four or five speeches a day, march in parades, attend banquets, breakfasts, luncheons. All this in bitterly cold weather. And so one of the frailest men ever to enter Boston politics would conduct the most physically punishing campaign anybody could remember.

Fourth, there would be no financial limitations. The sky was the limit. Kane told Martin and Plaut, "Politics is like war. It takes three things to win. The first is money and the second is money and the third is money. They spent a staggering sum. . . ." Just how much, and for what, no one has ever revealed. But the ambassador and Kane put one important stipulation on the spending. It was to be as unobtrusive as possible, to minimize the inevitable charges that Jack—or his father—was buying the election. Jack, for example, should not be seen throwing money around. (Not a difficult restriction since Jack never carried money anyway.) Although a "staggering sum" would be spent on big items (advertising, etc.), the campaign comptroller was chintzy in small matters such as secretarial salaries and expense accounts. This tightfistedness would lead to a great deal of friction—and some outright bitterness—in the campaign headquarters.

Fifth, there would be a heavy emphasis on local public relations, utilizing the Dowd ad agency. Today, politicians routinely employ ad agencies in campaigns. In 1946 it was not unknown, but it was uncommon. (Many ad agencies refused politicians as clients because they would not—or could not—pay their bills whether they won or lost.) Dowd would help Jack with Boston's fiercely competitive "newspaper row" composed of four morning papers (*Globe, Herald, Post,* and *Daily Record*), three afternoon papers (*Globe, Traveler, American*) and four Sunday papers (*Globe, Herald, Post,* and *Sunday Advertiser*) with press releases and interviews with key political writers and columnists. The idea was not so much to aim for editorial endorsement (of dubious value in a local election among Democrats) but simply to get the Kennedy name in the paper day after day.

Early in the campaign, a vexing tactical complication intruded itself, brought on by the personal plans of a man named Paul Andrew Dever. In the coming years, Dever would become the most prominent of Massachusetts politicians, rising, so to speak, side by side with Jack. He would be governor and, in 1952, the keynote speaker at the Democratic National Convention.

Dever, born of poor Irish-American parents in 1903, was a gifted politician. After graduation from Boston Latin School in 1919, he put himself through college and then Boston University Law School, working nights. He was a brilliant student: two years editor of the *Law Review*, recipient of the highest honors in his class. Two years after graduation, he was elected to the General Court from the Cambridge district. He was reelected in 1930 and again in 1932.

During the 1930s, Paul Dever had a dazzling political career. In 1934, not quite thirty-one years old, he ran for attorney general of Massachusetts and won, thereby becoming the youngest man in the history of the Commonwealth to hold that post. He was a clean, crusading attorney general who took out after James M. Curley (then governor) and launched a succession of attacks against loan sharks, fraudulent stock promotors, and other swindlers, sending many to jail. He was reelected in 1936 and in 1938. In 1940 he bucked the Democratic Party machinery, declared for governor, and won his party's nomination in a bitter, divisive battle. But in the general election, he lost to Leverett Saltonstall—by 5,588 votes.

In May, 1942, Dever, a resolute bachelor, then thirty-nine years old, received a commission in the Navy. In the summer of 1945 he was released from active service. He returned to Boston and resumed his law practice. Maurice Tobin, friend, contemporary, and then governor, had assumed that Dever would reenter politics immediately and hoped he would run for lieutenant governor on Tobin's slate in November, 1946.

Thomas P. "Tip" O'Neill, in 1974 Congressman from the 11th Congressional District and majority leader in the U.S. House of Representatives, was an insider to what happened in those days. In an interview in his Boston Office, O'Neill, a huge, engaging politician with a shock of unruly white hair told us:

> Paul Dever was a rising star in the Democratic party in Massachusetts. A tremendous vote-getter. Tobin extracted a promise from Dever that he'd go on the ticket. It would be David I. Walsh for Senator, Tobin for governor, Paul Dever for lieutenant governor.
>
> Then, suddenly, Dever changed his mind. He'd been away in the Navy and wanted to practice law for a while and make some money. And also, he was a close personal friend of Mike Neville's, who had his eyes—and heart—set on being Congressman. Dever was the only one of us who anticipated what a force Kennedy would be in that race. The rest of us were pooh-poohing Kennedy because he was a young, skinny, frail-looking kid, a carpetbagger whose father lived in Palm Beach.
>
> But because Dever wanted to make some money and help out his friend Mike Neville, he told Tobin he wanted off the ticket and suggested that in his place they pick Jack Kennedy. Tobin was not averse to this because the Kennedy name was big in Massachusetts and Jack might have helped the ticket. So Dever went to work on

the ambassador, trying to convince him that Jack should let Neville have the 11th Congressional District and go on the ticket with Tobin.

From our various interviews with Kennedy's associates, it was apparent that, for a while at least, Jack seriously considered this switch in plans. Eddie McLaughlin recalled:

> I remember one night I was up in the Bellevue suite. Tobin's secretary, Frank Morrissey, was there, trying to talk Jack into going on the ticket with Tobin. Jack was in the tub—he took these hot baths to rest his back—and Frank and I were standing in the bathroom. Later, Jack and Cis and I went out to dinner. I said to Jack. "My God! We've got enough gall running you for Congress, let alone lieutenant governor!" In those days we all thought the lieutenant governorship was an exalted job. Well, we discussed it for a long time—the pros and cons.

The pros: Tobin was a good man, a clean governor, in the reform tradition, one of the new generation in Massachusetts politics. It would not harm Jack to be associated with him. He was a good vote-getter. With Jack on the ticket (and the ambassador's money behind them) there was a good chance of winning. In his first shot out of the box, Jack would be lieutenant governor of Massachusetts, a heartbeat away from the governor's chair. It would be an ideal position from which to begin molding a statewide political machine. He would control some state patronage. It would be a good experience for Jack. In 1948 he could run for governor.

The cons: If there was a widespread rebellious mood among voters, as many believed, incumbents were in trouble, and so might Tobin be. Jack had seen it happen in England. (Dever, one of the shrewdest politicians in Massachusetts, may have sensed this and decided to withdraw because of it.) Some counseled Jack that the lieutenant governorship was a thankless job. He would be besieged day and night by countless thousands looking for a handout, a job, or a personal loan. Inevitably, he would become enmeshed in the grubby, tedious interplay of state politics, including the dirty deals.

Ambassador Kennedy, O'Neill told us, was sorely tempted. In those days, it was not yet the established tradition that U. S. presidents came from the Congress. So far in the twentieth century, four presidents (Theodore Roosevelt, Woodrow Wilson, Calvin Coolidge, and FDR) had come from state houses, two (William Howard Taft and Herbert Hoover) from the presidential Cabinet and two (Warren Harding, Harry Truman) from the legislative branch.

In the end it was decided that Jack would not run on the ticket with Tobin. Tip O'Neill thought it was Joe Kane whose influence ultimately prevailed. In spite of all, Kane believed Jack could be elected to Congress, and that the state ticket was still more chancy. The offer was rejected. But not right away. In keeping with Kane's strategy of not declaring until the last minute, it was left up in the air for weeks and weeks.

Not all of Jack's advisers and helpers would be pleased by this decision. A congressman, especially a junior congressman, has limited patronage compared to a lieutenant governor. For the helpers, there would not be many job openings or opportunities to take advantage of the patronage system. The decision would also cause some bitterness in Tobin's camp and within the state party generally. This, in turn, would further limit opportunities for Kennedy men to get on the public payroll.

34

Young Pols

CIS McLaughlin was one of the first to sign on as a volunteer worker for Jack. She told us:

> At that point, Jack had no personal staff at all. After work I and another working girl, Rita Dunlap, would go over to the Bellevue suite to do what we could. It was a dingy bedroom, living room, bath. The living room had a couple of desks and an overstuffed chair and, I think, one typewriter. Typewriters were very hard to get in those days.
>
> I remember when we first started there was an absolute mountain of unanswered mail. People who'd seen his name in the paper and wrote in, unopened Christmas cards, invitations to speak before this or that society, and so on. So we tackled that mess and began making card files and lists of names—all the drudgery work that goes on in the beginning of a political campaign. Jack would be in and out—he was making talks here and there—and would go in the bedroom and lie down for a nap. Later in the evening we'd all go down to the Bellevue dining room, which had pretty good food, and eat dinner. Then, about ten-thirty, Eddie'd get out of school, swing by, and pick me up.

But Joe Kennedy and Joe Kane were not leaving the campaign organization in the hands of amateur volunteers. Soon after Jack arrived in Boston, Joe Kane began putting together Jack's visible, working campaign staff—a hard core of hired hands or volunteers who would count on a payoff job if Jack won. He chose not ex-Navy officers or political amateurs, as the legend has it, but men of a different stripe—former enlisted men from the working classes of the district. These men, who would take Jack around on his speaking engagements and run his inside office, were by no means political amateurs. They were young, but every one of them had had experience working for one old Boston machine politician or another. In short: young pols, not yet tarnished by overlong exposure to Boston politics, but with experience and instincts for practical politics.

432

The first of these men was William Joseph "Billy" Sutton, recruited on January 13, 1946. For the next five years, until he and Jack had a dispute and a parting, Billy Sutton was almost constantly at Jack's side. He served four years in Jack's congressional office in Washington and during most of that period lived in Jack's house in Georgetown.

Today, Billy Sutton lives in Boston and works in a modest political job. After a great deal of parrying—he seemed reluctant to talk about his days with Jack—he agreed to see us. In the end, we conducted two extensive taped interviews which were extremely valuable.

When we first saw Billy Sutton, we mistook him for a young lawyer. He dressed in Brooks Brothers clothes: trim, single-breasted suit with thin lapels, striped tie, buttondown shirt. He was small and trim, with brown hair slightly graying. He appeared quite serious, and wary, but after a few minutes, he relaxed and became gregarious, immensely likable. He has a gift for mimicry. He can "do" Jack or Cardinal Cushing almost flawlessly. He bore the scars of his bitter parting with Jack well. No bitterness, no outward animosity. He told us he had once been a heavy drinker, but had not had a drop in ten years or more.

Billy was born in Charlestown September 25, 1913, one of five children of working parents. His father was a bridge tender, a political job which he got through then-Mayor Honey Fitz. His mother was a legal secretary. As a boy, he sold newspapers at the Navy Yard. In 1932 he was graduated from the Boston High School of Commerce (where he learned shorthand and typing) and after a couple of false starts, wound up in prewar days working for the Boston Consolidated Gas Company. He went from house to house delivering bills and reading meters. In 1943 he went into the Army.

During his gas company days, Billy was in and out of hundreds of Boston homes and "met everybody." In 1934 he became involved in 11th Congressional District politics. He worked for John F. Cotter, then secretary to John P. Higgins, who ran for the House seat and won. In 1937, when Cotter stood for the post in the special election, Billy worked for him again. He said that Joe Kane had worked for both Cotter and Higgins and that he had first met Kane then. It was Billy who described Kane as the "Connie Mack of politics."

He told us about his postwar meeting with Joe Kane and Jack Kennedy:

> I was still in uniform. I had my honorable discharge and a mustering-out check for three hundred dollars. I went to a bank on School Street to cash the check and then to Walton's Lunchroom, a hangout for pols, where Joe Kane used to hold forth at a table. We had some coffee and Joe told me what he was up to. Then we went up to the Bellevue Hotel to meet Jack. He reminded me of Charles Lindbergh. And I thought: a hundred and fifty pounds of

pure cash. I asked him if he thought he could win and he said yes.
He asked me if I thought he could win and I said, "I *think* you
can."

After they had talked awhile, Billy Sutton (who had been planning to
return to a job at the gas company) agreed to go to work for Jack in the
campaign. His official title was secretary. At the Kennedy Library, we
found a letter to Jack from Paul E. Murphy, boss of the ambassador's
"New York Office," where all the Kennedy financial dealings were handled, explaining why Billy should have that title:

> . . . if you put him on your payroll now as a secretary, we will
> have a good claim to deduct his salary and expenses from your tax-
> able income as an ordinary and necessary expense incurred by you
> for the production or collection of income, or for the management,
> conservation or maintenance of property held for the production
> of income, which if and when realized will be included in your tax-
> able income. Under this reasoning, you could claim that he is tak-
> ing care of your bank accounts, brokerage accounts, collecting div-
> idends, etc. I think if he is not too closely associated with your
> campaign publicity or literature, there should be no kick-back and
> you should be allowed to deduct the total amount paid to him from
> your gross income.

Billy was concerned about Jack's physical appearance. He was thin and
looked very young. His complexion was yellow—from the atabrine he
took for his malaria, Billy said. Billy advised Jack against wearing pink
shirts because the pink clashed with his yellow skin. Jack took off the
shirt and gave it to Billy, along with several others. "I wore those shirts
for three or four years," he recalled.

After that, Billy's first political move was to make a quick recruiting
drive among the veterans in his own turf, Charlestown. He got in touch
with a contemporary, Owen Brock, and then another, Dave Powers. Both
turned him down cold. They were committed to John F. Cotter. Billy
pressed Dave Powers, taking Jack to Charlestown to meet Powers face to
face at a tavern, Billy recalled. They found Dave drinking beer in his
leather Air Corps jacket. He was polite, but the answer was still no. The
recruiting drive was beginning badly. But not long afterward, Dave Powers changed his mind and came over to the Kennedy camp, playing a key
role in the 1946 campaign. He would remain one of Jack's closest com-
panions until the end of Jack's life.

Powers, who at this writing was director of the "museum" division of
the Kennedy Library, granted us two very long and valuable interviews.
He is balding, dapper, and spoke in a voice eerily like Jack Kennedy's.

We found him genial, comfortable to be with, and eager to help—to a point. He would not tolerate the faintest suggestion of criticism of Jack Kennedy or, as Powers refers to him always, "the president." He is without doubt the Chief Keeper of the Flame. His recollections of Jack are heroic and noncritical.

David Francis Powers, born in April 25, 1912, was first-generation American, son of John Powers and Catherine Green Lowney Powers, both born in County Cork. His father first worked in a mine in Butte, Montana, then on the docks in Boston. He married a young widow, Catherine Lowney, with six children. They had two children, Edward and Dave. In 1914, when Dave was two years old, his father died in an influenza epidemic, leaving his mother, now twice widowed, with eight children to raise. Dave went to parochial schools in Charlestown, and at age ten, he spent six hours a day selling newspapers at the Navy Yard gate and later inside the Yard. It became a very lucrative business: on Sundays he would sell one thousand newspapers. He gave much of his earnings to his mother to help run the Powers household, in a three-decker in Charlestown. In due course he hired Billy Sutton as a helper.

After graduation from Charlestown High School in 1930, Dave went to work for a publishing company, Sampson and Murdock, then engaged in preparing street directories of Boston for business concerns. Dave was an "enumerator" who went from house to house, checking the card file index to make sure it was up to date. This work, like Billy Sutton's, took him into thousands of homes, sometimes three hundred a day, he said, so that he, too, got to "know everybody." In his off hours he played amateur baseball, avidly followed the big leagues on radio, and developed an uncanny store of knowledge about teams, players, and their statistics.

All during the 1930s Dave was engaged in politics in a minor capacity. "To live in Charlestown is to be engaged in politics," he said jokingly. "There was always somebody asking you if you'd go around and put flyers under people's doors. You'd get paid for it. Or you'd hang banners on your house."

In 1942, a few months after his mother died, Dave joined the U.S. Air Corps, eventually winding up as a base intelligence specialist in China with Claire Chennault's Flying Tigers. He was discharged in early 1946. When he met Jack, he was living with his widowed half-sister, Nellie, on the top floor of a three-decker in Charleston, a member of the 52-20 Club. (While veterans were looking for jobs, the government supported them with $20 a week for a maximum of 52 weeks—hence 52-20.) Nellie had married a man named Robert Powers and had ten children. People often thought Dave was the oldest of Nellie's children.

A few nights after he had turned down Kennedy, Dave recalled, Jack arrived alone at the three-decker. Dave was at home, baby-sitting for his half-sister's children. They chatted for two hours. Jack was "aggressively shy," Dave said, "picking my brain about what *I'd* do if *I* were running in the district." Powers thought the situation was ludicrous: a millionaire's son from Harvard running in a district of longshoremen, truck drivers, and waitresses. He thought they would laugh him out of town. Yet he gave him a few names and suggested he get a good "waterfront man" like William McNamara. "And you know, McNamara became his man there?" Dave said. But when Jack left, Dave had to tell him again that he was with Cotter.

A few days after that, Jack made his political debut in Charlestown. He addressed a meeting of Gold Star Mothers (those who had lost sons in the war) at the Charlestown American Legion Hall. Dave had promised Jack that he'd go with him to the meeting. He recalled:

> He started to talk to all these wonderful ladies who'd all lost a son in World War Two, and he was not a great speaker at that time. I think at that time we used to compare public speakers to James Michael Curley, who was a great one. But he had an honest sincere manner of talking. But the most difficult thing for a beginner to do is bring a political talk to a suitable climax. He started to stutter a little bit and I was getting sort of nervous and then he looked out at all these wonderful ladies and said, "I think I know how you feel, because my mother is a Gold Star Mother too."
>
> And all the years I've been in politics, smoke-filled rooms and from Maine to Anchorage, Alaska, this reaction was unbelievable. He immediately was surrounded by all these Charlestown mothers and in the background I can hear them saying he reminds me of my own John or Joe or Pat, a loved one they had lost. Even I was overwhelmed.
>
> Then we decided to walk back to the Bellevue Hotel, where he lived. We started talking and he said, "How do you think I did?" And I said, "It was great." And then he reached out his hand and said, "Then you will be with me?" And I shook his hand and I was with him from that day to Dallas.

The next important recruit of this stripe was Peter Joseph Cloherty, an enlisted Army veteran who'd been mustered out early because of a chronic bad knee. Cloherty, born in 1923, was the son of a motorman on the old Boston elevated. When we interviewed him, he told us that when Jack first began appearing in Boston, he, Cloherty, was working for an electronics firm and was involved in organizing an alumni dinner for Brighton High School. Mike Ward, a notorious old Boston pol, then president of the Boston School Board and pal of Joe Kane's, got in touch with the principal of the school and suggested Jack be the speaker at the dinner. This sounded fine to Cloherty. He said, "The next thing I know, I received a letter from the John C. Dowd advertising agency with an eight-by-ten glossy photo of Jack and some background material for the local papers. So we had the dinner. Jack made a short speech and stayed around afterwards for the dancing. He told me he liked the way I handled the evening and asked me to come in to see him at the Bellevue.''

Cloherty had an important political friend in Brighton, Charles J. Artesani, then serving in the State Legislature. When Peter was a student in Brighton High School, he had worked voluntarily for Artesani and helped elect him. In 1946 Artesani was a strong political power in Brighton. "He was actually Spanish-Irish," Cloherty told us, "but, because of his name, the Itlos [Italians] thought he was Italian." Cloherty swung Artesani behind Jack.

Joe Kane brought Cloherty into the organization as an ''inside man,'' a sort of administrative assistant at the Bellevue Hotel to help keep things organized. Later, Jack and Cloherty had a falling out. But during the 1946 campaign he was a key man. He told us:

> I used to get to the Bellevue about eight or eight-thirty every morning. I'd get his schedule worked out for the day; then he'd leave with Billy Sutton. Then I spent the day making appointments for the days ahead and writing thank-you letters to people he'd already met or talked to. When he finished the last appointment of the day—about eleven-thirty or twelve at night—I'd take a folder full of letters for him to sign over to the Ritz second-floor lounge where he'd go for supper. He was a great one for tomato bisque and ice cream. He'd sit there, eating his bisque and ice cream, and go through the folder of correspondence, signing the letters, adding postscripts, and so on.
>
> As I saw it, his father was the number-one political expert around there. Very serious—the most serious of all. He'd come into town and put up at the Ritz and send for people individually—Joe Kane, Billy Sutton, me, and others—to get reports from us about the progress of the campaign. Then he'd compare the stories. You might spend only ten minutes with him—in his suite at the Ritz. He'd ask questions—three or four very pointed questions about areas or people—and then ask if you had any suggestions. He was all business. Not severe, but he didn't waste time on amenities.

Joe Timilty recruited yet another member for the team, James F. Kelley, a young enlisted Army veteran discharged in January. Kelley, whom we interviewed, would become a key figure in the 1946 campaign, but, like Cloherty, he would drop out of the Kennedy machine after the race, to engage in state politics. We interviewed Kelley at breakfast at the Ritz Carlton. We found him direct, tough-minded, and candid. He told us that he was born in Jamiaca Plain in 1918, son of a coal company employee. Like Sutton, he attended the High School of Commerce, graduating in 1936. He worked for Railway Express as a billing clerk, engaged in politics, met and became friends with Timilty when he was fire commissioner. (They shared, among other things, a fondness for dancing.) In 1942 he went into the Army. He wound up a first sergeant in an infantry division in England and landed in France three days after D·day. He was wounded by German machine-gun fire, spent seven months in a hospital. He told us:

> When I got out of the Army, I went back to Railway Express, but I planned to get in the wool business. Then one night I ran into Timilty—I called him Joe T—at the Copley Plaza Hotel. He said, "What are you going to do?" and I told him. Then he told me Jack was going to run for political office—lieutenant governor or Congress—and that I knew my way around Boston and that I should go see him. So the next day I went around to the Bellevue. . . .
>
> I liked Jack. He was a real charmer. He said he was considering politics but didn't know yet what office. He asked me to help. The whole idea appealed to me. He didn't offer to pay me but I thought if he won I'd get a job out of it. It was a gamble for me, but I'd saved some money in the Army, so I went to work for him. I knew how to move around and operate and protect him. To a lot of people, Jack was a rainbow in the sky, a pot of gold. And a lot of them were trying to con him. I kept him out of trouble. Sometimes he'd get mad at me—but when he did, I'd tell him to go to hell. . . . .

We gathered that Kelley—Jack called him Jamey—and Billy Sutton alternated in taking Jack around. Kelley recalled:

> He had this terrible back problem and was usually in the tub when I got there. Then we'd have breakfast in the Bellevue room. He was a picky eater—he'd leave half his bacon. Then we'd go out in these junky cars he used—so as not to call attention to his wealth. It really got to be an expensive thing for me. Jack never had any money. Everywhere we went I'd pick up the check. People, of course, thought I was carrying Kennedy money, but it was mine. When he made these speeches and talks, I noticed one thing: the girls were on the edge of their chairs. After a luncheon, we'd come back to the Bellevue and he'd take a nap. Then the tub again—with everyone going in and out of the bathroom, talking and making plans. Then he'd get a rubdown and off we'd go again until eleven or twelve at night, never wasting a minute. Finally we'd wind up here, at the Ritz lounge, for tomato soup and scrambled eggs.

And there was one more staffer, difficult to categorize, a curiosity named Patrick J. Mulkern, a paid worker brought in by Joe Kane. He was an old pol, dating back to nobody knew when, perhaps to the turn of the century. He was a "street man" with pipelines into every political fiefdom. Dave Powers told us:

> Patsy Mulkern was a Joe Kane type, hard to explain. Like someone out of Damon Runyon. Small, wiry, always wearing a hat. Talked a mile a minute, swore like a sailor. He talked politics twelve months a year. The night before Christmas, Christmas Day, Rose Bowl game, he'd have no other interest. You'd meet him in the middle of January and he'd have a pocketful of campaign buttons. Really, really, really strange. He'd say to me, "Powers, where you from?" And I'd say, "Patsy, I'm from Bunker Hill, I'm a Bunker Hill Boy," as Charlestownites were sometimes called. And then he'd say, "Good. Good. I thought you were one of those screwed-up college kids campaigning for Kennedy."
>
> He was well known in the South End, where some of the precincts in the Third Ward were. He came from there and was known around town as a character and the fact that a millionaire's son from Harvard would have someone like that working for him seemed helpful. It sort of brought Jack down to everybody's level.

Patsy was evidently an endless source of amusement for Jack, a sort of court jester. One of Jack's workers told us of an incident that concerned him and Patsy:

> One day I came to the Bellevue suite. Patsy, ever watchful, ever suspicious, said to Jack, "Who's this guy?"
> "He's all right," Jack said.
> "Who *is* he?" Patsy insisted.
> "He's a friend of mine."
> Patsy shook a warning finger in Jack's face. "I'll tell ya da troot. Every guy tells ya dere witcha. Well, I'll tell ya da troot. I don't know if *I'd* be witcha if ya wasn't a millionaire."
> Jack broke up.

Patsy, now dead, left a colorful oral history at the Kennedy Library. He described taking Jack around in the Third Ward:

> The first day I met Kennedy he had sneakers on. I said, "For the love of Christ, take the sneakers off, Jack. You think you're going to play golf?" It was tough to sell the guy. We had a hell of a job with him. We took him to taverns, hotel lobbies, club rooms, street

corners. Young Kennedy, young Kennedy, we kept saying. But they didn't want him in the district. The Curley mob wouldn't go for him right away. They called him the Miami candidate. "Take that guy and run him down in Miami. . . . (or) Palm Beach. . . . give him an address over in New York." We had a helluva fight. . . .

He was sick at the time, crippled and everything else. The guy was in agony. He had a bad back; wore a brace. Every afternoon he took a bath and got a rubdown. He told me he played football. I took a look at him and I said, "What were you—waterboy?" Play football! Christ! But I think that [being sick and crippled] helped him a little bit. Sympathy. The women. The women. You can't lick sympathy. Not sympathy and money with it!

We'd start out in the North End early in the morning. We'd go to Faneuil Hall, meet truck drivers, butchers, and so on. We'd sit in doorways and talk to people, doing it the hard way; which is the best way. Jack would say, "I don't know about the best but I know it's the hard way." He'd eat frappes [milk shakes]. I've never seen so many frappes. Frappes! Frappes! Frappes!

These, then, were the principal, hard-core, working hands: Billy Sutton, Dave Powers, Jamey Kelley, Peter Cloherty. All experienced, though untarnished, young pols. All from the working classes of the district. None had attended college. Most were recruited by Joe Kane and Joe Timilty.

35

The Visible Team

BY early February the undeclared candidate was working like a demon. The word went out through the Dowd ad agency that Jack was available as a speaker. The invitations flooded in. With each acceptance, the Dowd agency sent out a photograph and a background biographical sketch. Each appearance usually netted newspaper space—sometimes small, sometimes large.

Billy Sutton, who was now with Jack day and night, remembers that he accepted every single invitation: high schools, colleges, veterans groups (American Legion, VFW), Catholic societies, clubs and societies of every description, labor, Irish, and Italian groups. Jack was parading himself and looking for help, founding the Kennedy political machine. Sutton recalled:

> He wore me out. I slept at the Bellevue suite. We'd get up at six-fifteen A.M. Then from about eight to noon, we'd walk the streets in the district, going in stores, firehouses, tailor shops, factories, drugstores, post offices, anywhere we could find people. Anybody he'd meet, he'd say, "I'm glad to see you. How's it going? Have you got any suggestions?" Everybody he met, even the most ordinary people, seemed eager to help. Especially the women. All the girls wanted to marry him, and all the mothers wanted to mother him. At lunchtime, we'd go to some gathering and he'd make a speech. He was not a good speaker—too shy and he talked too fast. Then we'd go back to the hotel. He'd take a hot bath for his back—he was a great tub man—and then he had a rubber there, a guy we called Coogy McFarland (he was really an Italian named Bevilaqua) who had worked with prizefighters. Coogy would give him a rubdown.
>
> By then, we had a couple of drivers, Walter Power [no kin to Dave Powers] from Charlestown and a black named George Taylor, who had been Joe Junior's and Jack's valet when they were at Harvard. So in the afternoon, either Power or Taylor would drive us around. Then by about seven P.M. we'd be back at the hotel.

441

He'd lie down and take a good nap. I'd get on the telephone for a while, lining up engagements for the next day. Then we'd be off again for a dinner or a banquet speech. Then, even though it'd be late at night, he'd ask, "Is there anyplace else we have to go?" And I'd say, "Well, do you want to go to ———?" And he'd say, "Yes!" Then we'd go there (maybe a tavern or a legion hall or an Italian club or whatever) and then, finally, we'd get home about, maybe one forty-five and then we'd go to sleep. He got no more than four and a half hours' sleep every night for four months.

At first, as he went about, talking and meeting people, Jack did not take positions on political issues or personalities. The main object was to present himself as a war hero. Billy Sutton told us, "The *PT-109* was the great theme of the campaign. We did all we could to make sure every voter in the district knew that Jack had received the Navy and Marine Corps Medal as well as the Purple Heart for his service in the Solomons during World War Two. By the time the preliminary election day rolled around, 'Kennedy the war hero' and *'PT-109'* were household phrases in the Eleventh District."

Jack wrote a speech which he read at the big assemblies. A typescript is preserved at the Kennedy Library. It begins with a simplistic narrative account of the ramming of *PT-109,* putting Jack in the best possible light ("The commanding officer . . . turned the bow of his PT boat to make a torpedo attack. . . .") It then focused on Pappy McMahon's courage—and, of course, by association, Jack's courage. Then there is a transition ("We face critical times") followed by a long, exceedingly dull account of what happened to the British Conservative Party and why Americans should take a deeper interest in their government and politics. We had the feeling this ponderous effort must have put many people to sleep. But, overall, it probably gave the impression of an earnest young man who'd done his homework in international affairs, worrying out loud about the precarious state of the world.

Not everybody was eager to help. They ran into stiff opposition in Mike Neville's stronghold, Cambridge. One Neville man was Daniel F. O'Brien, a tough-minded undertaker in Cambridge who buried most of the Irish-Americans in that city and had vast local political influence. Billy set up an appointment with the help of Chief Justice John P. Higgins. Billy recalled:

It was a cold, snowy night in January when we entered his funeral parlor on Massachusetts Avenue. After explaining the situation to O'Brien and requesting his aid, we were lectured on how to get out of the race while the getting was good. O'Brien made his feelings clear by saying he thought Jack was a political interloper and carpetbagger who had no right to oppose Mike Neville. . . . He then promised Jack a job as secretary to Neville if he would withdraw. . . . As we were leaving, Jack indicated that he would rather not have O'Brien handle his funeral arrangements.

In an oral history at the Kennedy Library, O'Brien confirmed this confrontation. O'Brien went on to say he didn't think Jack even knew where the district was at that point, had to have a guide, and that he "looked to me like a boy just out of school." As a countermove, Neville and O'Brien went to see the ambassador to ask him to back Neville and "give Jack a shot later on." The ambassador "coldly sat back in his chair," O'Brien recalled, and said, "Why, you fellows are crazy. My son will be president in 1960."

So Joe Kane and Jack looked for other men to help them penetrate Cambridge. They put together a group of officer veterans from both the Army and Navy, most with a direct connection to Harvard. Some had had experience in Cambridge politics, others not. Some were old friends of Joe Junior's. Some were of Italian extraction, to appeal to Cambridge's numerous (though not very visible) Italian-American voters.

One of the first they recruited was Anthony Galluccio. Galluccio was an ex-officer just out of the Army. "Galooch," as Jack called him, had been a friend of Joe Junior's (and to a minor extent, Jack's) at Harvard before the war. Now he was returning to Harvard Law, living in Cambridge. He would play a key role in organizing Cambridge and much later—in 1951—he joined Kennedy's staff full time to help in the 1952 senatorial race.Then, like Billy Sutton, he had a falling out with Jack. We interviewed Galluccio in Cambridge, where he still lives and practices law.

He told us that he was born in 1917 in Italy, one of twin boys, the product of a wartime romance. His father had been an Italian soldier. Tony was sent to an Italian orphanage and then adopted by the Galluccios. His real father later married his real mother and then tracked down Tony and tried to get him back. However, Tony's adopted parents would not give him up. In 1922 the Galluccios emigrated to the United States, settled in Cambridge, and opened a grocery store. Tony grew up in Cambridge and got a scholarship to Harvard. He was an exceptional athlete who played football, basketball, and baseball and, later, semipro baseball. He was graduated from Harvard in 1939, a year ahead of Jack. In the fall of 1940 he entered Harvard Law (where Joe Junior was then enrolled) and in 1941, having failed the physical for the Naval Aviation cadet program because of poor eyesight, he was drafted. After officer training, he wound up an intelligence officer in the Air Corps and got married during the war. In January, 1946, when he bumped into Jack, he had just left the Army. He said:

I had no idea of going into politics until I met Jack. I had nothing to do with politics; my family wasn't interested in politics. I helped Jack because I liked him. We were friends. And all the guys in Cambridge I asked to help Kennedy were friends of mine and they did it on a friendship basis. They'd never been in politics. They were all guys I'd played baseball with, strictly political amateurs. It turned out to be the best type of operation for Jack, because Mike Neville, the mayor of Cambridge, was a hell of a guy, who'd done a lot of favors for people and was a good politician and had a lot of friends. So we were unknowingly reaching the people he didn't know. We were attracted to Kennedy because he was a young veteran coming back from the war, and had a hell of a name, a magic name. . . .

One of the big advantages Jack had in this campaign—often overlooked—was that he didn't have to work. I mean, he didn't have a job like Neville and Cotter and Russo and the others so he could devote full time to politics, whereas they could do it only part time. And that's a big, big advantage. He did work very hard. He was everywhere. He was a lousy speaker when he started. He wasn't forceful. It was pathetic. . . . The only thing, he was *quick*. And relaxed and smiling and informal.

I started recruiting people to our side. We got Benjamin Jacobson, a Jewish guy—a real character—who ran the Gold Coast Valeteria in Harvard Square. He'd known Jack and Joe when they were at Harvard. Benny was a good pal of Mike Neville's, but when Jack went to see him, he took down his Neville poster and put up Jack's. We had a lot of blacks in Cambridge—about three to five thousand. I got a black named Ted Williams, who'd gone to Harvard with me, to help down there. Then I went to see Arthur Schlesinger, who lived in the district. I knew him. I asked him to help. He was the only guy who turned me down. He gave me the intellectual stuff. He said Jack's father never did anything creative, he was only interested in making money, and this sort of stuff, so Arthur wasn't going to help Jack Kennedy.

One man Galluccio put the arm on turned into a tireless and effective worker. He was a Navy veteran, an ex-officer, John J. Droney. Today, John Droney is the district attorney for Middlesex County, in Cambridge. Tony told us that Jack Kennedy later gave Droney his job—"one of the few people Kennedy ever did anything for." Droney is apparently ultrasensitive about the Kennedys. He became the second man of Jack's 1946 campaign, after Morrissey, who would not see us, even to give us the basic facts of his life and military service. Later, we obtained a brief biography from Droney's office, which reads like a campaign handout.

The biography states that Droney was educated at St. Paul's Grammar School, Cambridge, and Cambridge Latin High School. In 1941 he was graduated from Suffolk Law School—the same nonaccredited school Frank Morrissey attended. After graduation, the biography goes on, Droney was "admitted to the Massachusetts Bar." Then he went into the Navy, "served on the U.S.S. *Alaska* and distinguished himself in service during the Okinawa and Iwo Jima campaigns." From Navy records we learned the *Alaska*, a cruiser, was commissioned in June, 1944, and joined the Pacific Fleet in January, 1945, so Droney must have put in a lot of Navy duty elsewhere before going to the *Alaska*. In 1946, the biography states, Droney did graduate work at Suffolk Law School and "was awarded an L.L.M. degree." From this, we assumed he was going to graduate school while he was working in Jack's behalf in Cambridge.

Galluccio told us:

> Before the war, Droney was a young guy who worked in a hardware store owned by a city councilman. He played baseball with me. We were pals. We called him "Cut" because he cut his hair so short. He was a great outfielder but a lousy hitter. Every time he came to bat, he'd kneel down and make the sign of the cross. It didn't help. . . . So I called up Droney and took him down to the Bellevue to meet Jack. Kennedy was very personable, very relaxed, casually dressed with his hair all tousled. He had a very easy manner. People liked to help him. He could win people over. So Droney said, "Yeah, I like the guy. I'll help him. . . ."

In 1959, Droney told Martin and Plaut in a rare interview:

> I had no intention of going into politics, but I went up to the Bellevue . . . and saw Jack talking to a lot of brass—commanders, Army officers—and I thought I'd had enough of that and started to leave. Jack followed me and we talked. I told him how I felt about politics and he said he had the same feeling, but that his brother Joe had been killed in the war, his family seemed to feel he was best fitted to carry on, and he said, "Sometimes we all have to do things we don't like to do."

Martin and Plaut added, "A day or two later, Kennedy's father made Droney official."

Galooch coralled another important Cambridge figure, Joseph Peter

Healey, a young lawyer with political ambitions, who had also known Joe Junior at Harvard. Joe Healey was an expert on economics who in the coming years would become one of Jack's inner circle, a principal adviser on labor and economics with a major role in the 1952 Senate race. He would become, with no help from the Kennedys, the most financially successful of all the men who helped Jack in 1946. In 1973 he was president of Boston's Middlesex Bank and a member of a dozen civic organizations in the city. We interviewed him in the posh top-floor executive suite of the bank headquarters in Burlington, a Boston suburb. He was modest, soft-spoken—so soft-spoken it was difficult to hear him on the tape later—extremely precise and very helpful.

Healey, born in Cambridge in 1915, was the second oldest of six sons of Hugh Henry Healey, who was born in England of Irish parents. His father had a gas station and was employed by the city of Cambridge as a sealer of weights and measures. Joe went to a Jesuit prep school, Boston College High School, played golf and tennis, and won prizes in debating. He started college at Holy Cross, but in his second year he got a scholarship to Harvard, which he believed to be "more on top of contemporary problems." He majored in economics, was an outstanding debator, and graduated in 1938 *magna cum laude,* making the main commencement address. He started Harvard Law School that fall, but because of money problems at home, had to drop out for a year to work (at odd jobs in Boston law firms). He reentered Harvard Law in 1939.

Then came the war. Healey joined the Army Quartermaster Corps and was sent to the Harvard Business School, where he was an honors student and obtained a masters degree. After that he was assigned to duty as an officer at Fort Lee, Virginia, but an old ankle injury he had suffered in high school playing sandlot baseball flared up and at the end of 1943, he was returned to civilian life. He married in October, 1943, reentered Harvard Law School, was graduated *cum laude* in March, 1945, and joined a Boston law firm. Then Galooch called. Healey told us:

Galluccio was looking up contemporaries of Joe Junior's to help Jack. It put me in a somewhat awkward position. One of my very good friends was Tip O'Neill, who was then minority leader in the Massachusetts House of Representatives. Tip was working very hard in Mike Neville's behalf. It was the only time in my life I voted differently from Tip. I met Jack and liked him and agreed to help organize the upper end of Cambridge, my home precinct, back-stopping John Droney, who was, as they say, a real political animal. I don't think Tip was too happy about it. I told him I'd carry my precinct for Jack. I mobilized my three brothers and we did. I didn't travel around with Jack at all. I did a little speech writing and helped on the advertising copy a little, but I didn't see too much of Jack in 1946.

The tough Italian ghetto of East Cambridge was a special problem, requiring a special personality. Joe Kane and Jack found him in the person of Joseph Austin deGuglielmo, who, in 1973, was a judge in the Boston Municipal Court, like Morrissey. "DeGug," as Jack and others called him (his car license plate is DE GUG), would play a key role in the 1946 campaign and in the 1952 campaign for the Senate. We interviewed him in the judges' library at Boston Municipal Court. We found him candid, casual, and often amusing.

He told us his father and mother were Italian immigrants who settled in East Cambridge and had ten children. He, the oldest, was born in 1907. His father was a barber, his mother had a "two-by-four" grocery store. His father was one of the few men in this area who could speak English, so "every poor slob in trouble with the law" came to him for help, inspiring in DeGug a desire to go into law. DeGug got through high school, then (feeling lucky his family could afford the $250 per year tuition) went to Harvard from 1925 to 1929. "I was a freak in East Cambridge," he said. "One of the few to go to college—let alone Harvard."

In 1930 he entered Harvard Law, "flunked out," then entered the Boston University Law School, graduating in 1933. During the 1930s he practiced law in Boston and East Cambridge and dabbled in Cambridge politics. In 1943 he served one year in the Army as an officer but was discharged because of poor eyesight.

After leaving the Army, he returned to Cambridge, opened a law office in Central Square (near Harvard Square), and plunged into politics in a serious way. In 1943 he was elected one of Cambridge's nine councilmen. He was reelected in 1945. When Jack first met him, he was serving his second term on the council. He was an archfoe of Mayor (and fellow councilman) Mike Neville's. DeGug told us:

I was hornswoggled into helping Jack. A cousin of mine, Walter W. Cennerazzo, president of a watchmakers' union in Waltham, dragged me from dinner at the Copley Plaza one night, out to Waltham, where Jack and another friend of mine, Anthony Di Cecca, city solicitor of Somerville, were waiting. Well, Jack looked like an underfed, scrawny baby. He started talking. He wasn't so suave in those days. Finally I got the idea: he was running for Congress. Well, Walter and Tony gave me a sales pitch. "He's going to win," they said. "He's old Joe Kennedy's son." Well, I didn't even know who old Joe Kennedy was, but I said if you're against Mike Neville, I'll help you. So I worked Cambridge and East Cambridge

with Galluccio and Droney. The hope was, we could hold the vote
down to five to one against Jack. We did a hell of a lot better than
that.

Joe Kane arranged for Jack to stick a toe into Somerville through the
old pol Joseph F. Leahy, who worked at the Navy Yard and was a member of the Somerville School Board. Leahy liked Kennedy, but was dis-
mayed by his speaking style. In an oral history at the Kennedy Library,
Leahy recalled that he told Jack, "You're a Harvard graduate but sometimes when you talk and speak you don't sound as though you're going to
say anything. You ought to go around to the Staley College of the Spoken
Word where Curley went. . . . He was nervous, but that three-inch
Kennedy smile won over many people. All the girls went for him a mile a
minute."

It fell to Leahy to take Billy Sutton and Jack to pay a call on John M.
"Pat" Lynch, mayor of Somerville, and a fiercely loyal Neville man.
Leahy recalled:

> Jack told us to wait outside. He went in and Lynch gave him
> hell. Jack said, "He called me a carpetbagger; that I shouldn't be
> running in the district, and that he was with Mike Neville." He
> [Lynch] thought I had a hell of a nerve taking Jack to see
> him. . . . I took Jack to the Olympic Club—the oldest social club
> in Somerville—and to the Cozy Grill, where Jack bought every-
> body a drink. He didn't have any money so he asked *me* to pay for
> the drinks. It was only a dollar sixty—they were all beer drinkers. I
> put him in touch with Anthony Lagone—the Lagone family was
> worth eighty votes alone. When Tony got married, Jack went to his
> bachelor dinner and made a speech. . . .

They had better luck in Brighton, Ward 22, the area south of the
Charles River adjacent to Brookline, where Jack had been born. Since
Brighton had no candidate, it was considered relatively friendly territory.
The ambassador's pal, Eddie Gallagher, who grew up in Brighton, helped
a great deal. In our interview he recalled, "I knew just about everybody
in Brighton. I took Jack out there and began introducing him around. He
was very shy. He didn't have a hat then. I remember I took him into a
store, Arthur Johnson's, and bought him a new hat for twenty dollars. I
said, 'If you're going to be a Congressman, you've got to wear a hat.' He
tried it on and looked in the mirror. Then, we left, with Jack *not* wearing
the hat, but rather, holding it in his hand. He said to me, 'Gee! I can't
wear a hat!' "

One of Gallagher's most important contributions was to put Jack in
touch with Mrs. J. Frank Broderick, president of the Brighton Women's

Club, where Jack made a speech. Thereafter, Agnes Broderick became a tireless worker and organizer in Jack's behalf. She recruited her brother-in-law, Thomas Broderick, a Navy veteran (enlisted man), who had been wounded in the South Pacific. Then about forty, Tom Broderick was tall, skinny and jumpy—too jumpy and restless for many. In this campaign, and in the coming years, Tom would work voluntarily in Jack's behalf, and Jack responded by getting him a job in the VA Hospital in Framingham. He died in 1968, but he left an oral history at the Kennedy Library giving some of his initial impressions of Jack:

> Jack was always giving people nicknames. He called me Tommie or the Thin Man. I remember he got on a double-decker trolley car in Brighton. It was jammed. He pushed through the people saying, "I'm Jack Kennedy." The people were amazed. They didn't know who he was or what he was doing. I came behind and explained. He looked like a juvenile . . . no hat . . . blue suit. . . . Then we took a subway to Harvard Square, and he did it all over.
>
> Then, going to church he'd say, "Do you have any change?" I had a little. I paid for the seat and then gave him a dime for the collection plate. Later I said, "I'm sick and tired of paying your church fare. If we have to do that to get you to church. . . ."
>
> He wanted direct answers, always. For example, there was a story going around that Jack was "using" religious groups to further his politics. He said to me, "Have you heard it?" I turned to someone and said, "What do you think?" Jack got mad and said to me, "Tommie, when I ask *you* a question, *you* answer the question."

In East Boston, the rough Italian-Irish area near the airport and Suffolk Downs racetrack, Jack turned to another old pol for help. He was William F. Kelly, a contemporary of Joe Kane's, who had worked in all of Honey Fitz's campaigns since the turn of the century. By the time we came on the scene, Bill Kelly had died. But he left a brief oral history at the Kennedy Library. He remembered Jack this way:

> I was handling East Boston for Jack. When I first met him, when he announced his candidacy, I didn't think he had much on the ball at all. He was very retiring. You had to lead him by the hand. You had to push him into the poolrooms, taverns, clubs, and organizations. He didn't like it at first. He wanted no part of it, and he just went along with it and finally he could see it. . . .
>
> Cotter was strong in Charlestown, Neville was strong in Cambridge, and Jack was fearful that Joe Russo would carry East Boston, which was mostly Italian. We enlisted some older Italians—

people who *knew* Joseph P. Kennedy. And we also registered Italians in the lower end of East Boston. My wife, Mary, formed a woman's committee for Jack.

One of the men Bill Kelly recruited to help Jack in East Boston was Joseph Rosetti, a young Marine Corps veteran (enlisted) just returned from overseas. Like Billy Sutton, Joe Rosetti would remain on Jack's office staff after the election—until 1951. He worked in Jack's Boston office with Frank Morrissey and in Washington, directly under Jack. In 1973 he was an employee of the Department of State in Washington. We interviewed him there. He was pleasant, dapper, concise.

He told us that he had been born in 1921, in the Orient Heights section of East Boston, son of an American-born lithograph operator. He went to Boston English High School, then to Kent Hills Prep in Maine for one year on a scholarship, graduating in 1941. He worked one year at Sears, Roebuck to get money for college, but when the war came, he volunteered for the Naval Aviation cadet program. He was turned down because he walked in his sleep. He then went into the Marines, was assigned to the Third Division, which wound up on Okinawa in 1945. He was discharged in October, 1945. He told us:

I was planning to enter a hotel management school in Ithaca, New York. But there was a waiting list to 1947, so in 1946 I was unemployed, waiting. My father was a friend of Bill Kelly's so that's how I got involved. Bill Kelly had some job in City Hall, exactly what, I'm not sure. He was a lot older than I was. He was active in many, many organizations and married to an Italian, so he was perfect for the job. He asked me if I'd be interested in helping Jack. I knew nothing about Jack Kennedy then—only that he had a great war record. I wasn't highly motivated in politics. I just felt it was time for a change. It was hard to find jobs. . . .

The North and West Ends—in downtown Boston, close by the Bellevue and solidly Italian—were also special situations. Billy Sutton, well known in the West End, helped organize that area. Everybody worked on the North End. But to organize the person-to-person drive there, Jack picked a young veteran, William "Yammy" DeMarco.

DeMarco left an oral history at the Kennedy Library, describing his first impressions of Jack:

Billy Sutton brought Jack around. He was very, very thin, sort of shy, but easy to meet. He couldn't get around too well—because of his back. I took him to my club, Club 28 on Hanover Street in the Testa Building. There were about sixty-five guys there—veterans—celebrating, playing [cards] for a glass of beer or a bottle of wine. I called them to order—said there was an important man here—and that his mother had lived around the corner. He asked me to take care of the North End. Later, I'd take him along the street, into the stores and places. Honey Fitz was well known in the area. He had worshiped at St. Stephen's Church on Hanover Street. They remembered Jack's mother living on Garden Court Street, so they took a liking to him.

There were so many engagements to attend per day that they often fell far behind in the schedule. Jack's staffwork left much to be desired. Dave Powers, who was now Jack's "secretary" in Charlestown, recalled in Rose's book:

> Jack had a funny sense of time and distance. He'd get interested in these people and he'd forget about time, and it was hard to disengage him and drag him away. And, anyway, he'd have the feel-, ing that everyplace else was only fifteen minutes away. I've been with him in . . . the middle of Boston and he's soaking in the tub at quarter of eight, and we're due in Worcester at eight and he'd say, "Dave, how far is it to Worcester?" And I'd say, "Well, if we're driving, we're late already." It would go like that. . . .

Meanwhile, the Joseph P. Kennedy, Jr., VFW Post was organized. Jack was commander, Eddie McLaughlin was named vice-commander. He did most of the work. He recalled that the post had been founded early in the year at a meeting in the Boston Room of the Parker House Hotel. From the outset it was more or less an elitist group. In time it became a very popular post. Eddie recalled that many young men who would later become prominent lawyers, politicians, and businessmen, joined the post, which grew to four or five hundred dues-paying members who convened once a month. There was only one flaw: the post had no permanent home or meeting place. They met first at the Vendome Hotel, then at the Puritan Hotel, but never did build a hall or club.

Eddie McLaughlin recruited an important member for the VFW post. He was John I. Fitzgerald, Jr., a returning Marine Corps officer, who was then sick with what was thought to be malaria (actually, it was a kidney infection) and was an outpatient at the Chelsea Naval Hospital. Fitzgerald's father (no kin to the Honey Fitz family) was a contractor and insurance broker and an old Boston pol then serving a one-year term as fire commissioner. In the old days, he had been leader of Ward 3, served in the State Legislature with Eddie's father, was president of the Boston City Council (1935–1937), and chairman of the Democratic City Committee.

John I. Fitzgerald, Jr., had grown up in a political environment. He went to Boston Latin and Dartmouth (with Eddie). In his Dartmouth days he had dated Ann McGillicuddy. Then, long before Pearl Harbor, he went into the Marine Corps. He fought in the Pacific for two years and came home a much-decorated major. In January, 1946, while home on leave, he was stricken with what was thought to be malaria.

Today, Jack Fitzgerald is a city planner in Boston. From 1946 onward, he was involved in Massachusetts politics and often worked in Jack's behalf. We interviewed him at his office in the swank new City Hall in Government Center. We found him youthful and trim; handsome, soft-spoken, and modest. He told us:

Eddie called me up one day and asked me if I'd join their new Joseph P. Kennedy VFW post. By then, several people had asked *me* to consider running for the Eleventh Congressional District—Curley's seat. But I didn't know what I was going to do. I told Eddie this—that I might wind up as a candidate—but he said he wanted me to meet Jack anyway. So I went to the organizational meeting one rainy night in February and met Jack. As it turned out, I was too sick to run—I didn't recover as fast as I'd hoped—so I threw in with Jack and served as a sort of friendly adviser. I was attached to Chelsea all that spring and had a lot of time on my hands. I got my wife, who was pregnant, and my sister and my father behind Jack. My father sent a personal letter in Jack's behalf to every person he knew in the district.

36

Rehabilitating the Ambassador

As we saw, Ambassador Joseph P. Kennedy had emerged in rather spectacular fashion in the fall, with coverage in *Time, Life,* and the Boston newspapers. The campaign to rehabilitate him was now proceeding apace. During the first week of January, 1946, Governor Maurice Tobin announced to the press that Ambassador Kennedy would invest half a million dollars in "small Massachusetts industries." This startling announcement was designed, apparently, to create investor confidence in Massachusetts, to reverse the drain of capital and industry from the state; thus to create more jobs for the unemployed and for returning veterans.

We found a story about the plan in the *New York Times* of January 8. It said that the ambassador would raise the half million by disposing of his holdings in the Columbia Trust Company in East Boston. It would be sold to the National Shawmut Bank of Boston, provided the stockholders of Columbia approved the deal at a special meeting on January 14.

We could find nothing further in the *Times* about the deal. We assume it went through. By shifting half a million from one Massachusetts investment to another, the ambassador had generated favorable publicity for himself, for Tobin, for the State of Massachusetts—and, indirectly, for Jack.

The ambassador next began to speak out on two national issues that were preoccupying the nation: "big labor" and what appeared to be the increasing threat to America posed by the Soviet Union. Organized labor was now seen by most Americans as out of control, demanding the moon. In January there was a crippling strike of steelworkers. In March Walter P. Reuther led the United Automobile Workers on strike against General Motors. In April John L. Lewis led his 400,000 coal miners on strike. In May railroad workers threatened a strike that would have immobilized the nation. (It was averted when Truman threatened to take over the railroads.)

By now, Ambassador Kennedy, who had surveyed labor-management problems in Massachusetts for Tobin, considered himself an expert in the field. So did Arthur Krock. In a column in the January 8 issue of the *Times,* Krock approvingly told the story of how a small Detroit manufac-

453

turer of auto components, failing financially because of unionization, had decreased production, saved itself by revealing candidly its state of affairs to the employees, who then voted to return to an "incentive" production system to save their jobs. Krock added at the end of his column, "This Detroit company's approach to its problem is in line with what Joseph P. Kennedy has been preaching to management and labor throughout Massachusetts—that it localize its issues as much as possible and settle them, plant by plant, company by company, in this concentrated way. . . ."

Translated into simple terms, what Krock and Kennedy were saying was: Keep big labor out, and each plant could solve its own problems. Throughout the winter and spring, Ambassador Kennedy stumped the country fighting big labor. At every turn, Koskoff reports, the ambassador urged businessmen to be politically active to combat the increasing power of big labor; otherwise it would dominate everybody's life. Kennedy saw the country drifting toward welfare-statism or "creeping socialism." He deplored the growth of the federal government and taxes which were destroying the incentive of businessmen.

He kept holding Britain up as an object lesson, using Harold J. Laski as a whipping boy. On May 18 (as reported in the *New York Times*), he told the Illinois Junior Association of Commerce in Chicago, where his recent acquisition the Merchandise Mart was booming to success, "I know Laski, and I have, before this, referred to his habitual attacks upon what he calls our 'rotten, decadent, capitalistic system' despite the fact that the same decadent, capitalistic nation has twice saved the British Empire from defeat. . . ."

Britain, in fact, was nearly bankrupt. In January and February, 1946, Washington had decided to advance her $3.75 billion to stave off disaster. Some wanted to charge her a minimum interest of about 2 percent, others wanted to make it an outright gift. The ambassador, usually considered hostile to the British Government, startled everybody by pronouncing that he favored the "outright gift."

This apparent turnabout landed him on page one of the *New York Times* on March 4, in a story by John H. Crider. Kennedy's reasoning: Britain was a good customer for U.S. trade goods and a bulwark against Communism. The United States had spent $200 billion on the war. It was worth another $4 billion to save Britain.

The second big issue troubling the nation was what to do about an increasingly hostile Soviet Union. Some, such as Secretary of Commerce Henry Wallace, advocated a soft approach. Others, notably Harry Truman and Navy Secretary James V. Forrestal, had become hard-liners and were moving toward a "containment policy" advocated by the Soviet specialist George Kennan. (If "contained," he argued in a long and historic cable from Moscow, the Soviet Government would ultimately suffer an internal collapse.) On March 5, the day after Kennedy's views on the British "loan" appeared in the *Times*, Winston Churchill delivered his famous "Iron Curtain" speech in Fulton, Missouri, bringing the matter to the forefront.

Ambassador Kennedy had been slowly formulating his views on postwar American foreign policy in his speeches. In February he crystallized them into an article. He sent the article to Henry Luce for publication in *Life*. Luce decided to give the ambassador the space, but thought the article needed work. *Life* articles editor Robert Coughlan (who later worked with Rose on her book), then in Cuba recuperating from pneumonia, was sent to work with Kennedy in Palm Beach. "The article had a middle," Coughlan told us in a phone interview, "but no beginning and end." Coughlan got it in shape in a day or so and it was published in the March 18 issue of *Life*.

The article as it finally appeared is long and complex, and so densely written it is difficult to sum up briefly. Kennedy examines the entire world, the national and international interests and aspirations of all major nations, the points of pressure and conflict, and outlines a program for the United States. As we read it, Kennedy seems to be advocating an isolationist position: be strong, be tough with Russia, support our Allies (such as Britain) but don't meddle in the affairs of other nations.

Kennedy does not mention Harry Truman explicitly, but throughout the article, he is critical of the U.S. Government's wishy-washy approach to Russia, and thus there is implied criticism of Truman. (By this time Henry Luce, too, was becoming impatient with Truman; shortly he would be hostile.) Kennedy writes of the "inability of our government to function effectively in either world or domestic affairs" and "the lack of strong leadership" and "a government ineffective at home and only somewhat less so abroad." He sees the "apparent" policy of the United States toward Russia as combining "appeasement, uncertainty and double talk."

Several months later, in the issue of June, 1946, the *Reader's Digest* published a condensed version of the ambassador's article. We could find nothing in the Paul Palmer papers at the Yale Library regarding this publishing coup, which greatly extended the readership of the piece. Perhaps by then, the *Digest* editors were also cooling toward Truman. But we take off our hats to the man or woman who condensed it. As it appeared in the *Digest*, the article is clearer and to the point. The ambassador must have been pleased to see it in the *Digest*. It was the only article he ever published in that magazine.

No doubt this article by Ambassador Kennedy made Truman angry. It may have decided Truman against bringing Kennedy into the federal government, if ever there was such a plan. About that time, the *New York Times* said there was. Here is the background:

James Forrestal had been thinking of resigning his post as secretary of the Navy. According to a note in his diary in January, 1946, there was some discussion that he might run for governor or senator from New York. But Forrestal, a temperamental, driven man, could not make up his mind whether to stay in the Navy job, go into politics, or retire quietly to private life.

Meanwhile, the job of Undersecretary of the Navy had opened up through the departure of Artemus L. Gates. Since it was believed that Forrestal might resign, the undersecretary's job was now being considered as an immediate stepping-stone to the top job. Truman had nominated Edwin W. Pauley, an oil man who had been treasurer of the Democratic National Committee in 1944. Almost immediately, strong opposition to his appointment arose, led by former Secretary of the Interior Harold L. Ickes, Massachusetts Senator David I. Walsh (still chairman of the Senate Naval Affairs Committee), and others, who remembering Teapot Dome, did not think an oil man should be secretary of the Navy.

Truman held firm—for a time. But then, on March 8, the *New York Times*, in a front-page story, reported Pauley was ready to withdraw his name. In the story, the *Times* reporter Thomas J. Hamilton wrote, "Former Governor Colgate Darden of Virginia and Joseph P. Kennedy, former Ambassador to London, are being mentioned for the nomination of undersecretary. . . . For some time the President and his advisers have been seeking to bring about the return of Mr. Kennedy to government service, and it was believed that he would accept if there was an understanding that he would succeed Mr. Forrestal as Secretary. . . ."

But a complication arose. For years there had been discussions in progress about "unifying" the War and Navy Departments into some form of single service. Harry Truman was a strong advocate of the plan, and on December 20, 1945, he had asked Congress to consider it. The Army (and the Air Corps, which wished to separate from the Army) favored the measure, but the Navy admirals bitterly opposed it on various grounds which usually boiled down to a matter of surrendering sovereignty in the bureaucracy. By the spring of 1946, the admirals were in open rebellion against the administration. They had many supporters in Congress.

Forrestal had approached unification cautiously. But after much study, he had come to the conclusion (as he says in his diary) that he favored it. About the time of the Pauley flap, he was very much involved in moving the plan forward and now hoped to see it through Congress, which would mean a tough fight. Perhaps for this reason (he does not say) he made up his mind that he would not resign immediately. Thus he could not assure his friend Joseph Kennedy that if he took the undersecretary job, he could move up in six months or so.

At about this point, the Kennedy article in *Life* was published, by design or coincidence. That, we believe, closed the matter as far as Truman was concerned. The job was filled by the simple expedient of promoting the Assistant Secretary of the Navy, John L. Sullivan, to undersecretary. Thereafter, we could find no evidence that Truman was "seeking to bring Kennedy into government service" (if in fact he ever really intended to do that; the speculation in the *Times* may have been Kennedy public relations). Henceforth, both the ambassador and Jack would become increasingly hostile to Truman.

The ambassador next appears in the news back in Massachusetts. After its commissioning in December, 1945, the USS *Joseph P. Kennedy, Jr.*, with Bobby embarked as a seaman second class, went on a long shakedown cruise to Latin America and the Caribbean. On March 3, 1946, her skipper, Commander Moore, wrote Jack, "We have had a rugged time with our engineering plants but I think the troubles are about squared away now. . . . Bobby seems to be getting along fine. I see him frequently on the bridge as he is standing helmsman watches. The ship will return to Boston about 1 April for a two weeks stay in Charlestown Navy Yard . . . be sure to visit us. . . ."

On April 11 Ambassador Kennedy, accompanied by his sidekick Joe Timilty, visited the destroyer. The following day the Boston press was full of stories and photographs of the visit, some of which are in Moore's personal scrapbook. It may have been another emotional trial for Joe Kennedy. In one story the ambassador is quoted as saying, "I wish all hands the very best of luck. This destroyer, named in honor of my son, is very dear to me. . . ."

Jack does not appear in the pictures or the news stories. But the visit must have had a considerable impact on the voters in the 11th Congressional District. Here was the ambassador, on board the *Joseph P. Kennedy, Jr.*, named for a war hero, shaking hands with Bobby (a seaman), in the Charlestown Navy Yard, the largest employer in Jack's would-be district. Could the most imaginative press agent in the world have staged a media event better calculated to convey the image of Kennedy family solidarity and devotion and service to country?

By April then, it seemed to us, the ambassador had been substantially rehabilitated. Instead of a character in gossip columns or a producer of Broadway shows, or a mysterious real estate operator, he had once again become a prominent national figure, speaking out on domestic and foreign policy matters—his old, feisty self. He was back on the front page of the *New York Times* (and Boston papers as well), and in *Life* and *Reader's Digest*. Beyond question, all this publicity was beneficial to Jack Kennedy.

37

High Gear

DURING the first week of April, the Kennedy political machine moved into high gear. It was drawing close to announcement time. His aides let it be known, privately, that Jack would run for the 11th Congressional District. With that, Tobin was forced to draft Paul Dever as a candidate for lieutenant governor. Dever went along with the deal, probably somewhat grudgingly. He had not been out of the Navy very long. He could not have made much money in his private law practice. And since it now appeared that Jack might beat his friend Mike Neville, and that Jack would make little or no effort to support the statewide ticket, Dever had more than sufficient reason to be irked with Jack Kennedy.

About that time an old friend showed up in Boston—Red Fay. His presence lent credence to the myth that Jack's old Navy buddies substantially helped him in the campaign. For example, coincident with Fay's arrival, the *Look* reporter-photographer team was on hand and counted Red (with Torby, Eddie, and Jim Reed) as part of Jack's "junior brain trust." Some accounts of the election state or imply that Red was working in Jack's behalf all during the key phase of the campaign. Dave Powers and Kenny O'Donnell, for example, write that Fay was present "two months." But by our reckoning, he was in Boston about two weeks. He was on vacation—a lark. His presence (a Republican college kid from San Francisco) was not welcomed by some of Jack's workers.

Fay told us:

> I got out of the Navy on March 1 in San Francisco. My father was expecting me to go to work in Fay Construction on or about May 1. I went East, first to Charlottesville, Virginia, where I visited Bill Battle who was in the University of Virginia Law School. Then I went up to Manhattan and dated Jack's sister, Jean, who was at Manhattanville College. Then, about April 1, I went up to Boston to see how Jack was getting on in his campaign.
>
> When I arrived, I met Jack in the lobby of the Bellevue. He was on the way to a meeting. He was pretty casual. He gave me the key to the room and said to go on up, he'd be back later. I felt I'd got-

458

ten a fast brush and I was plenty teed off. I went up to the room and stared at the four walls for a couple of hours. Then I saw his mail: piles of unpaid bills, unanswered invitations, and unopened letters. I sat down and made a list of the bills and wrote out checks for him to sign, then I drew up a list of invitations for him to go over. When he got back, I told him I was shoving off, but he ought at least to pay his bills. Seeing I was irritated, he said, "Red, you're staying right here and you're going to get this campaign on a businesslike basis." He knew how to handle me. I stayed.

I was with him and his touring guides day and night for the next couple of weeks. Slept in his room and went around with him to the meetings. I was a sort of expediter, or troubleshooter on the organizational side, jumping in where it looked like things were falling down. I remember one day we were walking down the street and some old pol stuck ten hundred-dollar bills in his coat pocket and said, "Jack, here's a contribution." He was a pal of the ambassador's, and Jack thanked him and said to me, "*That's* support."

Jack's grandfather, Honey Fitz, was always coming down to the suite to tell Jack dirty jokes. He took us down to City Hall one day so Jack would meet all the city employees. He got all excited, shouting greetings to old friends, like an old campaigner, and soon he was waving his arms and singing "Sweet Adeline." Then all the city employees started singing with him. What a scene! He got so carried away, Jack had to remind him why we'd come. After that, he introduced Jack around.

Jack's back was bothering him a lot. He spent a lot of time in the tub at the Bellevue. The inner sanctum was the bathroom. You had to segregate those who could go in and talk to the candidate while he was in the tub. At night we'd eat dinner on the mezzanine of the Ritz. Usually I ate filet of sole Florentine. One night, I remember, there was a really good-looking woman at the next table—about thirty-five. We had a contest to see whether she'd join us or we'd join her. Jack bet me ten dollars I couldn't get her to our table. I couldn't do it.

By this time, Red Fay had been dating Anita Marcus for several months and he planned to marry her in the fall—if she was willing. While he was in Boston, he wrote Anita and Anita wrote him. Jack adopted the role of provocateur. In his book Fay described how Jack would do it:

"By the way," he said, "did Anita ever tell you about the Air Force flier? The good-looking one that—" He broke off in the middle of the sentence with a guilty look, as if he had said something which shouldn't have been told. Although I knew just what was happening, I bit right in. Visions of some dashing, irresistible flier making mad love to my darling crept into my mind. Obviously my face had betrayed my thoughts, because Jack said with a tone of solace, "I'm sure it was just a passing fancy for both and meant nothing."

Fay recalled that Patsy Mulkern was one Kennedy worker who was particularly bitter about his presence and ranted, "Why the hell do we have to take orders from a goddamned redhead from San Francisco? . . . What the hell does (he) know about Boston politics?" Another was Torby, who came around occasionally. Red and Torby did not get along.

On the day Jack finally and officially announced his candidacy for office, April 23, two other men were drawn into the campaign. Both were Navy veterans (officers), both were brainy, both were Bostonians who would become key figures in Jack's political career over the next six years.

The first of these men was John Thomas Galvin, who was just back from the Pacific and who had just gone to work for the Dowd agency. On official announcement day Jack needed a press release and speech. Jack Dowd turned this chore over to Galvin, who in turn recruited the second man, Mark Dalton, also just back from the Pacific, who had just opened a law office in Boston. We interviewed both men in Boston, Galvin at his home, where he is semiretired and working on a book about Boston mayors, and Dalton at his office at the Massachusetts Employees Association, near the State House.

Galvin went to Boston College High School, then on to Boston College, working part time. He was graduated in 1937. After that he took a fling at politics, running for a seat on the Boston City Council against an incumbent. He lost. In subsequent years, he helped in other Boston political campaigns, then took a job as a PR man for the Community Fund. In 1940 he joined the Naval Reserve, received a commission, then served almost four years on various ships as a gunnery officer in the Pacific, from the Solomons to the surrender ceremonies in Tokyo Bay. When he got out of the Navy in December, 1945, he went to work as a PR man for the Red Cross campaign. At the final Red Cross dinner in late March, Jack Dowd hired him. He had been at Dowd's less than a month when he was asked to help Jack Kennedy prepare his announcement publicity.

Galvin told us:

Dowd came to me one day and he said, "What are you doing this afternoon?" I said, "What have you got in mind?" He said, "A young guy named Jack Kennedy is coming in. He's either going to announce for Congress or lieutenant governor, and I'd like you to hang around and write the announcement." And Jack came in, late as usual, very late in the afternoon, with Red Fay. He had part of an announcement speech that he was going to use on the radio that night, WNAC, which was called the Yankee Network. And so there were two things to do. One was to write a press release, the other was to fix up the speech. I got on the phone and called an old friend of mine, Mark Dalton, a very bright guy who'd been with me at Boston College. So he came up to doctor up the speech.

We had heard from others that Mark Dalton had later been treated shabbily by the Kennedys. He was not outwardly bitter. He is tall, thin, gentle, erudite—perhaps too intellectual and too sweet-natured for the rough and tumble of Boston politics.

He is also a Boston College man. He wrote for the campus paper, the monthly magazine, and the yearbook. After graduation he went to Harvard Law but kept a hand in the writing game by doing movie, play, and book reviews for the *Boston Herald*. He dabbled in Cambridge politics. In 1941 he was graduated from Harvard Law *cum laude*. He clerked for a judge in Providence, Rhode Island, then, after Pearl Harbor, went to Washington to work for the OPA. In December, 1942, he joined the Navy, was commissioned and assigned to Naval Intelligence. After a series of shore jobs he was attached to the U.S. Naval Staff planning the Normandy invasion, and went ashore on D-day in the sixth wave to send back firsthand intelligence reports. He transferred to the Pacific and performed staff intelligence work in preparation for the invasion of Okinawa. After the war, he spent eight months in China on various intelligence assignments. When he was discharged from the Navy in March, 1946, he opened a law office on State Street in downtown Boston. Then John Galvin called. Dalton told us:

At that point I didn't even know Jack Kennedy existed. I was very busy trying to find office space and start a law practice. I was sitting alone in my office when John Galvin called. I took a cab over to the Dowd agency and met Jack and Red Fay. I was as thin as I could be at that time, but Jack was even thinner. He was actually like a skeleton, thin and drawn. He did not seem . . . to be built for politics in the sense of being the easygoing, affable person. He was not much of an orator. He was shy but, deep down, aggressive. I went over the speech he had brought along. It was pretty much OK and I didn't do much to it. That night he gave it on WNAC.

Jack and I took an immediate liking to one another. He asked me to work on some more speeches and I did—four or five. It was a strictly volunteer basis. I remember the next time he went on radio, he asked me to give the introduction. Well, I'd done some speaking in high school and at BC and in Cambridge politics before the war and—if I do say so myself—I was fairly articulate. After the speech we went back to the Ritz—up to the ambassador's room. He was there with Joe Timilty and Timilty said to the ambassador, "These two men should never again go on the air at the same time." He meant that Jack suffered by comparison. And so I didn't.

After that, Jack asked me if I'd take over as his campaign manager. I said no. It was too much of a job. Too big. I didn't realize then that what he meant, really, was a figurehead campaign manager. The ambassador was the essential, real campaign manager. So then Jack asked me if I'd go over to Cambridge and set up and manage a headquarters in Cambridge. This was familiar ground to me—I was then living there—and our family was well known in Cambridge. So I said yes. Cambridge was a large part of his district and I thought if I came out for him, I'd carry some weight. And I think I did.

Jack soon had five campaign offices going in the district, each full of volunteer workers. The main one was in downtown Boston, a small suite on the second floor of a dingy old building at 18 Tremont Street. Joe Kane hired a full-time secretary, Grace Burke, an older woman, to oversee the volunteer workers. When Grace came, Cis McLaughlin worked less. The ambassador sent his chief business associate, Edward Moore, to supervise spending. Dave Powers, who had recruited a valuable Charlestown ally, Mary S. Colbert, opened a small office in a vacant store on Main Street in Charlestown. (Rent: $50 a month.) Bill Kelly and Joe Rosetti set up headquarters on Maverick Square in East Boston, on the second floor over Iver's Lunchroom. Every night anywhere from twenty-five to fifty volunteers showed up and they had another ten men and ten women working the area house-to-house. Mark Dalton, John Droney, and Tony Galluccio set up headquarters in Cambridge at 678 Massachusetts Avenue, on Central Square. But after two weeks or so, Dalton changed his mind and agreed to become the "figurehead" campaign manager, moving to the main headquarters downtown on Tremont Street. (Droney became a figurehead treasurer.) Joe DeGug opened a headquarters in East Cambridge—on the second floor at 801 Cambridge Street. There were, as yet, no formal offices in Somerville or Brighton.

Now that Jack was formally in the race, he began to take positions on the major political issues of the day. And here we come to an interesting question, raised, in part, by the peculiar nature of the constituency of the 11th Congressional District.

Most of the people in this district were Catholics with European family backgrounds, educated in parochial schools. In foreign affairs, they distrusted—or were hostile to—Godless Communism, Russia in particular. Most probably agreed with the ambassador's world view as expressed in the *Life* article: keep America strong, keep out of foreign entanglements. Not a few probably wanted to "stop" Communism at any cost. So, in this sense, the constituency was decidedly conservative.

Yet most of these same people were union members, and at a low income level. For this reason they favored liberal economic measures, such as public housing, rent controls, minimum wage laws, unemployment benefits, expanded Social Security, controls on inflation, federal aid to parochial schools and hospitals, and so on. In this sense, then, they were decidedly liberal.

Thus, in taking his public positions, Jack Kennedy had to appeal to the voters of the 11th District both as a conservative and as a liberal. He was opposed to Communism (and Fascism and Nazism and Socialism) and thought of himself in that sense as a conservative. At the same time, as we saw in four documents at the Kennedy Library (two speeches, one press release, a questionnaire turned in for the National League of Women Voters) he favored such measures as low-cost housing for veterans, a veteran's bonus, the GI Bill, price and rent controls (then still in effect through OPA) to avoid a disastrous rise in the cost of living, a national health program "immediately" (but one that would not enslave the medical profession), extension of Social Security benefits, enactment of a minimum wage law (minimum hourly wage: $.65), fair employment, the right to organize and strike, reasonable working hours, collective bargaining, a much stronger United Nations Organization, a strong U.S. military force, the "modernization" of Congress, and a busier, better Boston by building it as a seaport and international air hub.

Billy Sutton told us that deep down, Jack was "an ultraconservative" like his father and his friends, that he did not begin to "grow" liberal until much later—after he entered the Senate and developed presidential ambitions.

The militant liberals at the colleges in Cambridge distrusted him and did their utmost to nail him down ideologically, or to expose him as a conservative. For example, during a Liberal Union meeting, a Radcliffe student asked Thomas H. Eliot, distinguished Yankee and eminent New Dealer, whether Eliot thought Kennedy would make "the kind of progressive representative we're looking for." Eliot replied frostily, "I spoke with Jack for about three hours the other afternoon on many of the issues facing this country—and I don't really think I'm qualified to answer your question."

Selig S. Harrison, editor of the *Harvard Crimson*, tried to pin Jack down for an interview for the *Crimson*. In a 1960 article for *The New Republic*, Harrison remembered:

It would be difficult to forget the irritation which Kennedy displayed when this reporter . . . peppered him with questions in an interview during his 1946 campaign. Kennedy at 29 gave the same impression as he does today of an earnest and engaging personality. But he was clearly determined to avoid specific commitments. . . . Candidate Kennedy spoke in vague terms of "the struggle between capitalism and collectivism, internally and externally," adding, however, that he was not for *laissez-faire*—business did need regulation by the government "to eliminate the trends of overproduction and low purchasing power which periodically throw the economic structure out of kilter." If it was necessary to tag him, he asked, "Make it 'Massachusetts Democrat.' I'm not a doctrinaire. I'll vote them the way I see them." My conclusion in *The Crimson* was that "Kennedy seems to feel honestly that he is not hedging . . . by refusing to offer a positive specific platform. He feigns an ignorance of much in the affairs of government and tells you to look at his record in two years to see what he stands for."

Ten candidates filed for the 11th Congressional District—nine men and one woman. In addition to Jack, Mike Neville, John Cotter, Joseph Russo, and Catherine Falvey, there were Joseph Lee (a perennial candidate for Boston offices), Francis X. Rooney from Somerville, and three more Italians from Boston: Michael DeLuca, Robert B. DiFruscio, and a second Joseph Russo. The last-mentioned was placed in the race, the "real" Joseph Russo maintained in a brief oral history at the Kennedy Library, by Kennedy forces to "complicate the names." That is, to split Russo's vote in the Third Ward—not an uncommon practice in Boston politics.

We could find only two documents in the Kennedy Library that gave any hint of the political stands of Jack's opponents. These were two radio speeches, one by Cotter, one by the "real" Russo. Both thought the big issue was Communism. Cotter, sounding very much like Joseph McCarthy and Richard Nixon four years later, said, "Communists are illegally entering our country, spreading their doctrine of hate and destruction. . . . We have seen Spain thrown into revolution, fighting against the onrush of Communism. The press and radio would have you believe that justice is on the side of the Loyalists . . . names that are only synonyms for Communism. High-ranking officials of our State Department are today—as they have been for some time—conspiring to bring about the overthrow of the Spanish Government. They are trying to deliver this nation into the hands of the Communist plotters." Most of Russo's speech is given over to warning about the dangers of Soviet Russia "which would take away from us our most cherished and religious heritage."

Both men, in these speeches, attacked Jack Kennedy or his father (while avoiding naming them). Cotter raised the ambassador's approving position on the $4 billion gift to England, implying that the ambassador favored Laski and the British Socialists. He added darkly, "Harlod Laski [is] the man who told Americans in Madison Square Garden that the Roman Catholic Church was growing wealthy at the expense of the poverty-stricken people of Spain." He blasted Jack for "basking at Hialeah [the racetrack in Miami, in which the ambassador had an interest] and the sun-baked sands of Palm Beach," adding, "They came to Boston to buy another racetrack and they came to buy a seat in Congress."

Russo began his speech by saying, "I introduce myself to you as Boston City Councilor Joseph Russo because one of my major opponents has seen fit to buy out a man who has the same name as mine. . . so the voters of this district will be confused and deceived." In addition, he accused Jack of putting Neville, Cotter, Falvey, and Rooney into the race to split votes away from him. He went on:

> We have a very young boy, a college graduate, whose family boasts of great wealth. It is said they are worth thirty million dollars. This candidate has never held public office. He is registered at the Hotel Bellevue in Boston, and, I daresay, that he has never slept there. He comes from New York. His father is a resident of Florida and because of his money is favored by the newspapers of Boston, making it impossible for any other candidate to obtain news space to give their candidate publicity. . . . Insofar as certain responsibilities are concerned, this candidate does not live in the district . . . and knows nothing about the problems of its people. . . .

Russo had a point about the publicity. By now Jack (assisted by the efficient Jack Dowd agency) was dominating the Boston papers. For example, Martin and Plaut wrote, "A Boston *American* reporter was assigned to check into Kennedy campaign headquarters every day—but not into any of the others."

They added, "One evening, while strolling through the State House, candidate Mike Neville spotted a crap game and complained to a companion, 'The only way I'll break into the newspapers will be if I join that game and get pinched by the cops. . . .'"

In addition, the national media, encouraged by the ambassador, were taking an unusual interest in Jack's race. *Time*'s Boston reporter, Jeff Wylie, filed a long story, but it did not run until after the primary. *Life* sent a team, headed by *Life* photographer Yale Joel, but the *Life* story didn't run either. *Look* sent a writer, Henry Ehrlich, and a photographer, Hy Peskin. Their story (which called Jack a "fighting conservative" and covered five pages) was published in the *Look* issue of June 11, almost on the eve of the voting. The ambassador, we learned from letters at the Kennedy Library, also mobilized an old friend at RKO Pictures, Inc., who arranged for a Pathé News newsreel team to come to Boston and shoot some footage of Jack campaigning. These newsreel clips would be shown in first-run New England movie houses on the eve of the voting.

Nor was that all. Jack recruited an old schoolmate Thomas P. O'Hearn (whose older sister had married Rose's brother John F. Fitzgerald, Jr.) to become an outdoor advertising (billboard) specialist.

We interviewed O'Hearn in his office in downtown Boston. He told us:

I ran into Jack on Tremont Street. He asked if I would help him. He was not really satisfied with the Jack Dowd agency. He told me the agency's ideas lacked originality. And before I knew it, I was in charge of billboards. Dowd didn't like that—and we clashed frequently. But Jack didn't like the locations Dowd had picked. I had a kind of flair for this and took the lead—and Jack backed me up.

He had this fear of seeming to spend too much money, so I set out to get the best possible locations with the most economical expenditure of money. For example, I ruled out back streets completely. In the end we had only ninety billboards, but they were so strategically placed that people actually thought we'd bought all of Boston.

One billboard display ingeniously joined the old with the new. It depicted a young veteran with his father, both looking at a big facial close-up of Jack. The *father*, pointing to Jack says to the *son:* "There's our man, son."

Then Walter Cenerazzo, the Watchmakers Union chief in Waltham, came up with another idea. That was to get *other* people to sell Jack. So we brought in another ad agency [Irving Gold Associates] to handle this—and Dowd was very resentful. They'd take a picture of Jack somewhere talking to, say Mrs. Jones. Then they asked her why she liked Jack. Then they'd do an ad of Mrs. Jones giving her reasons. This was labeled "The People Speak for Kennedy." The ads were placed in some newspapers, but most importantly, in the subway trains. It was unique.

The opposition spent very little money for advertising. One newspaper ad that must have rankled Jack was placed by Boston City Councillor James S. Coffey, probably in the "real" Russo's behalf:

CONGRESS SEAT FOR SALE
No Experience Necessary.
Applicant must live in

New York or Florida.
Only Millionaires need apply.

Joe Kane ran scared and kept raising little things—the hat, for example. Billy Sutton recalled that Kane insisted that Jack wear his hat so he would not antagonize the hat makers and hat wearers, and so that he would "look older" and like a serious politician. Sutton said that Jack thought his shock of curly hair was a political asset (appealing to the women and the girls) and that a hat "took away half his personality." Jack conceded to the point of wearing his hat in the St. Patrick's Day Parade, but usually he just carried it. And, Sutton remembered, Jack was forever leaving the hat behind.

38

Landslide

ACCORDING to Whalen, as Jack's campaign was peaking in May, the *Boston Post* published a poll showing Jack running far ahead of all his opponents. The ambassador would not believe it. He telephoned his good friend Joseph Patterson at the *New York Daily News* and "borrowed" the team that conducted the *News'* famous "straw polls." The team scoured the 11th Congressional District, using its well-developed polling methods. It confirmed the *Boston Post* poll almost to the decimal point.

Yet the ambassador, Joe Kane, and the whole team continued to run scared. Polls or no polls, they would leave nothing to chance.

There was one element missing in the Kennedy campaign: a sense of family. Jack was a bachelor. Some of his advisers thought this was an advantage, because he had natural appeal for young, unmarried women. But there were far more married female voters than single, so steps were taken to fill the family gap by mobilizing the women in the Kennedy family. The main helpers were his mother and his sister Eunice, who quit her job at the State Department in Washington to come to Boston. In June, after Pat and Jean (then eighteen) got out of college for the summer, they came for the final days of the campaign.

The Kennedy women, Rose in particular, were celebrities in their own right. To many of the poor Irish women in the district, they were the culmination of the success dream: living examples of what could be done in this land of opportunity. They were eager to rub shoulders with Rose and Eunice, to examine them close up, and then, (perhaps) brag to their neighbors that they'd been with the Kennedys the night before. Thus the young Kennedy political machine had stumbled on yet another weapon, which Martin and Plaut call "snobbism" but which might better be labeled something like "applied charisma," or perhaps "star quality."

Rose, who in her youth had appeared with her father in political campaigns, and who was at ease with the press and was an articulate and interesting speaker, threw herself into the campaign heart and soul. Dave Powers reminisced for Rose in her book:

> She was important to Jack politically in 1946 because she made herself available for apperances anyplace, and because with

the double-barrelled name Fitzgerald and Kennedy she was better known than any in that Eleventh Congressional District. . . . They related to her. . . .

You have to grow up in politics to really know it. She wasn't "In" politics—she wasn't running or seeking—but she was looking and listening. I remember one rally where she spoke, she was appalled that there wasn't somebody taking the names of everyone who showed up—because that's what her father used to do. She was always writing notes to us about things like that. In 1946, she had a greater understanding of precinct politics than anyone in our organization.

Rose, Dave went on, had a very appealing routine. "She talked about raising the family, with the index cards and all that [listing the children's medical records] and about living in England, and told some interesting stories about the embassy. And that's one way I knew she was a real 'pro.' People want to hear about something different, and that's what she gave them. When she finished, she got a standing ovation."

One of the old traditions of Boston politics was the "house party." A campaign worker would invite the candidate to his or her home to meet twenty or thirty neighbors, serve coffee and sandwiches, cookies, cake, and ice cream. After meeting everyone informally, the candidate usually gave a little talk. Because Joe Kane thought Jack should meet everyone in the district, the Kennedy machine utilized the house party more intensely than any candidate in memory. Eunice (and later Pat and Jean) participated in these festivities.

According to an oral history at the Kennedy Library by Mary McNeely of Charlestown, who had been recruited to the Kennedy apparatus by Billy Sutton, the first house parties were held in Charlestown. She said that at first she was "skeptical" about Jack, didn't even know who he was. "He was very yellow and you could never imagine—he was so young-looking that he didn't look as if he was old enough to go to Congress." But when Jack told her his father had been ambassador to England, Mary's father (a political wheel in Charlestown's 7th Precinct) remembered he had known the ambassador "and that made the difference."

Mary McNeely gave a house party. About one hundred people came. Eunice appeared with Jack. Mary McNeely recalled, "As Jack gave his speech, Eunice stood there, saying every word along with him and it was very noticeable. After, Jack called her to the kitchen and said, 'Eunice, you made me very, very nervous. Don't ever do that to me again.' And Eunice said, 'Jack, I thought you were going to forget your speech.'"

Billy Sutton recruited another Charlestown man, Robert L. Lee (no kin to Jack's opponent Lee), then serving in the State Legislature. In an oral history at the Kennedy Library, Lee recalled:

Jack was very shy and almost afraid to talk. He didn't have the confidence that a man should have who was going to follow politics. My first impression was that he was a very sick boy. . . . I had tremendous respect for Mike Neville . . . but I got to like Jack, even though there was a great feeling against him in Charlestown because he was a carpetbagger, was not known in the community, had no experience, and was starting halfway up the ladder rather than from the bottom. . . . I arranged house parties. I'd get on the phone and invite twenty to thirty people. He was great for shaking hands, moving fast, and you could never find out too much from him.

During one of these Charlestown gatherings, Eddie McLaughlin went along. He recalled, "There we were in the heart of Cotter country. A woman whom I knew to be a Cotter supporter told me she was going to vote for Jack. I asked why. She said it was because Jack reminded her so much of her own boy. Well, we got a huge laugh out of that. Her own boy was the town drunk!"

After the initial house parties in Charlestown, Jack's staff began to organize them in other parts of the district. In his oral history, Bill Kelly told how they did it in East Boston, utilizing the Kennedy women:

We'd set up six to nine parties—or more—for a single evening with anywhere from twenty-five to seventy-five people at each. Jack, Pat, and Eunice would set out for party number one. They'd drop Pat or Eunice at number one. Then Jack'd go to number two and drop another sister. Then Jack would go alone to number three. The sisters would circulate, shake hands, and talk. Then we'd backtrack to number one, pick up the sister, and take her (and Jack) to number four and drop her and so on and on, carrying this on for hours.

Jack shrewdly assigned Eunice to work in his toughest battleground, Cambridge. And when Bobby left the destroyer *Kennedy* and was discharged from the Navy on May 30, he was assigned to Cambridge, too. In addition they recruited Jack's good friend Lem Billings for the last two weeks of the campaign. He told us:

I got out of the Navy in Washington, D.C., in March or April. I went home to see my mother in Baltimore, then had to decide what to do. I could have got my job back with Coca-Cola, but it didn't interest me at all. I decided to go back to school—to the Harvard Business School—and I enrolled for the June class. When I got up to Boston, Jack, of course, was running for Congress. I stayed with him at Bellevue, which was crowded with these strange individuals and he didn't know which would be helpful or whether they were trying to get some money out of a rich kid or what.

He had some trouble in the Cambridge office. There was an old lady there who claimed some guy in the office was stealing or making trouble. So he asked me if I'd go over and work there three or four days and see if it was true. So I did. And I got to know the lady, a really fine person, Rose Reynolds. She was a volunteer. And she was right; this guy was a mug. I had three or four weeks before Harvard began, so I stayed in the Cambridge office, working to three or four in the morning, then taking the subway back to the Bellevue. And I wound up postponing Harvard until the fall term. I worked with John Droney, who was absolutely superb. John and his sister Mary Droney worked their cans off. Joe De-Gug, the Cambridge councilman, was great too. And here I was, a Republican, a native of Pittsburgh, and an Episcopalian!

Bobby and Eunice spent much of their time in the tough area of East Cambridge, where Joe DeGug was political boss. Jean was there too, Billings recalled, bringing along her roommate from Manhattanville College, Ethel Skakel, from Greenwich, Connecticut. DeGug recalled, "When Bobby showed up in East Cambridge, I assigned my brother Lawrence to go around with him in the three wards we were supervising. What they did, they went around and met the kids, and played a lot of touch football with them. It had the effect of proving the Kennedy's weren't snobs—that Bobby was willing to pal around with them. And Bobby made a lot of friends in East Cambridge."

Bobby in turn drafted a friend of his from Harvard. This was Kenneth P. "Kenny" O'Donnell. In time, O'Donnell would become one of Jack's principal political aides and would go all the way to the White House, as appointments secretary. As we said, he was coauthor, with Dave Powers, of the book *Johnny, We Hardly Knew Ye.* While we were in Boston, we interviewed Kenny, who, after his White House days, in 1966 ran for governor of Massachusetts, received 46 percent of the vote, but lost to John A. Volpe. After that he helped Bobby in his 1968 race for the presidency, then returned to Boston as a "management consultant to private industry," according to a brief biography his secretary (and sister) provided us.

Kenny O'Donnell was a small, lithe, taciturn man, whose short-cropped dark hair was graying. He had recently had a stroke, but seemed to be recovering. His office was a bit seedy—and noisy. The waiting room was crowded with Boston pols having coffee and talking loudly. A constant fixture there, we learned, was Kenny's elder brother by two and a half years, Cleo, who was shot and paralyzed a few years ago trying to break up a holdup on the streets of Boston. He is confined to a wheelchair.

Amid all this clatter—and telephone interruptions—Kenny talked into our tape. We noticed a curious parallel between Jack's friendship for Torby and Bobby's friendship with Kenny. Kenny's father was a football coach around Boston, more famous than Torby's father. Kenny's older brother, Cleo, was captain of the Harvard team. Then, in his senior year, 1948, Kenny was captain of the Harvard team, too. Like Jack, Bobby wanted to be a football player.

Kenny, born in Worcester in 1924, was the second of three sons (there were also three daughters) of Cleo O'Donnell. His father had a very successful career as a college football coach. He was coach and athletic director at Holy Cross at this time. Kenny said, "Around Boston, he was more famous than Joseph P. Kennedy."

In the book he wrote with Dave Powers, Kenny says that Bobby asked him to work in Jack's behalf in Cambridge. (Probably East Cambridge.) Kenny recalled he said to Bobby, "I'll do it as a favor to you, but he'll never make it." But no one else we interviewed could remember Kenny working in that 1946 campaign. If he did, the work was brief and inconsequential—like Bobby's.

Even with all this family shoved into Cambridge, everybody worried about the vote there, DeGug especially. He told us he felt they were moving, but he was not satisfied with the rate of movement. He searched his mind for an "event" that would put the Kennedys on the front pages. Then one day it came to him: Why not a huge formal reception for the women voters of Cambridge, presided over by Ambassador and Mrs. Kennedy? He told us:

> The Irish are social climbers. I thought if we got a hotel, a ballroom, sent out engraved formal invitations to the women voters in the name of the ambassador and Rose, we'd be sure to draw a crowd. I mentioned it to Eunice and she said, "We'll do it." Just like that. I said it would cost a lot of money. She asked how much. I said, plenty. We had to invite every registered Democratic woman on the voting list. If you left anybody off, they'd be furious and you'd risk losing that vote and maybe others besides. There was some opposition. John Droney was against it—too effeminate. They argued that the people who'd come were people who had probably already made up their mind to vote for you, so you wouldn't be making any converts, and you'd be wasting time and effort. And the old pols would rather have spent the money on beer busts. But Eunice said "Let's go." And she got twenty-five volun-

teer secretaries and had the invitations engraved and they started addressing them.

This project, the culmination of the Kennedy family participation in Jack's campaign and the big, final push in Cambridge, was an enormous, backbreaking job. We were not able to ascertain exactly how many invitations were sent out, for nobody could remember. It had to be in the thousands, probably at least ten thousand. In addition to that, they had to rent the ballroom—they chose the Commander Hotel—and arrange for flowers, tea and coffee, sandwiches, and so on for an enormous number of guests.

The reception was held on Saturday, June 15, three days before the voting. The ambassador and Rose were host and hostess. Jack was in the receiving line. (Galluccio remembered that Eunice, Pat, and Jean were not there.) DeGug recalled it was a fantastic success. At least 1,500 women came, all dressed to the nines. "It created a gigantic traffic hazard," De-Gug recalled. "No one could get in Harvard Square." The reception line leading into the hotel was a block long, he recalled. This was the ambassador's one and only public appearance in Jack's behalf; he stayed in the background. Rose gave her little talk. The next day, Sunday, the Boston newspapers carried stories about it. It was on the front page of the Cambridge edition of the *American*.

Jack's staff was amazed and awed by it all. Patsy Mulkern told Martin and Plaut, "Every girl there was gonna be Mrs. Kennedy, for crissakes. There was a storekeeper tol' me, 'I let out more gowns this week than in a whole year before. I wish he'd run forever.'"

John Droney told Dave Powers, "I was dead wrong. . . . An old Cambridge politician who was with me looked at the turnout and said, 'This kid will walk in.'"

DeGug was proud as a peacock. The tea was the talk of Cambridge, and he claimed, probably accurately in this instance, that it was a big factor in chipping away at the Neville vote. In later years, the Kennedy "teas" would become a standard item in the Kennedy campaign style. Kennedy aides would still argue the pros and cons of spending money on votes that were probably already sure, but no one could deny that the teas had great publicity value.

For all the good work that Joe Leahy and his helpers were doing in Somerville, Jack still thought more ought to be done. Torby recalls that Jack asked him to work there in his behalf, but Torby was now busier than ever. His brother-in-law, John A. Prior (married to Torby's older sister, Margaret), was the head football coach at Medford High School, which Torby had attended for a while, and where he had played footall.

Prior had gotten Torby a part-time job at the school, coaching the back-field. The team was now in spring practice.

The problem was solved one day, May 18 to be exact, when Joe Junior's Harvard roommate and closest friend, Timothy James "Ted" Reardon, Jr., appeared in Air Force uniform at the Bellevue with his wife, Betty Jane, in tow. Reardon had been born and raised in Somerville. He was on the verge of leaving the Air Force. Jack asked if he would take over Somerville. And he did.

Ted Reardon not only took over Somerville for Jack, he later joined his Congressional staff, and remained with Jack all the way to the White House, a key insider, or so we thought at first. Later we were told that Ted had also been treated shabbily by Jack and that the road to the White House had been rocky, with many setbacks along the way. Today he is an executive at the Federal Deposit Insurance Corporation in Washington, D.C. He was reluctant to talk about his years with Kennedy, but he agreed to be interviewed about his background and his brief role in the 1946 campaign. When we saw him at his office, he was extremely pleasant, candid ("call me Ted"), and bouncy, even though he was at that time bedeviled by cataracts.

Ted was the ninth of ten children (six boys, four girls) of Timothy James Reardon, who was also born in Somerville. The senior Reardon owned a barrel-manufacturing business—"whisky barrels, I think," Ted told us. Ted went to parochial schools, Boston College High School, and then to Harvard.

Ted Reardon told us:

When I left the Air Force, I was planning to settle down in the Midwest and go to work for the Monarch Tool Company in Sidney, Ohio, as advertising manager. I had some terminal leave, so I went back to Boston and was showing my wife around town. We walked past the Bellevue Hotel and I thought I'd drop in and see Jack. Jack said he needed somebody in Somerville. I still had a couple of weeks—or a months'—leave, so I helped. I swept out a store, hired girls, got speakers and voting lists. . . . Betty Jane didn't work. She stayed home and looked after young Timothy the Third.

The big competition in Somerville was the WAC, Catherine Falvey. One day there was a meeting where they had all ten candidates on the stage, to answer questions from the audience. Falvey made a crude crack at Jack about money. But Jack didn't let it ruffle him. He handled her very well. And then, on the question and answer thing, I was *really* impressed. That was his forte. He was so *quick*. After that meeting I told him I was just helping because I was a pal, but now I was really going to vote for him. And that was how it began.

Mark Dalton, too, had an inspiration: Why not get tens of thousands of reprints of the *Reader's Digest* article on Jack and *PT-109* and send them to every registered voter in the district? The idea met instant approval in Kennedy headquarters, but then a hitch developed. "The *Reader's Digest* wouldn't allow it," Tom O'Hearn recalled in our interview. "That would seemingly have put the magazine in the position of endorsing a particular political candidate, and it was against their policy. However, the ambassador talked them into it in this instance."

How? we wondered. We wrote to authorties at the *Reader's Digest*, but we got a polite brush-off. They reported that "our files on reprints don't currently go back far enough to dredge up the detailed information you're after." We assumed the ambassador worked through his contact at the *Digest*, associate editor Paul Palmer, but there was nothing in the Palmer-Kennedy correspondence at the Yale Library concerning it.

At the Kennedy Library we found one letter bearing on the subject. It was dated May 16 (pretty late in the game, we thought) and signed by someone in the *Digest* reprint division. It said that, "In compliance with your telephone instructions, I have put through your order for 100,000 reprints of 'Survival'." The reprints should be there in "two weeks," the letter said, and the charge would be $794. Another item revealed that Jack ordered the envelopes from another source at $5.25 per thousand—or $525. So the total cost of this campaign tool—the only one we could document—was $1,319, plus postage and volunteer help to address and mail the envelopes.

These well-laid plans went awry. There must have been a delay in the printing schedule. Both Billy Sutton and Bill Kelly in their oral histories at the Kennedy Library recalled that the reprints did not arrive until the very last minute—a couple of days before the voting. Sutton recalled that they were printed in Philadelphia and shipped to Boston by train. They got hung up in the railroad station in New Haven, he said. One of Jack's drivers, Walter Power, went down to New Haven in the middle of the night and with the help of railroad officials searched through the locked cars until he found them. He came back with a "huge box" of them. The rest came the next day. They were apparently addressed over the weekend of June 15–16 (an enormous job) and mailed out on the day before the election, June 17. Kelly recalled that he had to put the arm on the Boston postmaster to get special mailing services for them because that Monday, June 17, Bunker Hill Day, was a holiday in Charlestown. But, said Kelly, "They delivered."

The last-minute distribution of these 100,000 reprints to every voter in the 11th Congressional District was the *coup de grace*, Tom O'Hearn thought. He told us, "It was the clincher, a knockout blow, the jig was up. A story went around that after one of the opposing candidate's wife had read the reprint, she said she'd have to vote for Jack."

The Kennedy forces mounted the last great effort of the 1946 campaign in Charlestown. The Bunker Hill Day holiday was celebrated by the Irish with zest and gusto and much politicking. Actually, the celebrating began "The Night Before" (as it's called) with parties and political gatherings all over Charlestown. Most of the big politicians running in the primaries (Henry Cabot Lodge, unopposed in the Republican Senatorial primary; David I. Walsh, unopposed in the Democratic Senatorial primary; Tobin; Paul Dever) crisscrossed the town, appearing at the Knights of Columbus Hall, American Legion Hall, and VFW posts. That night, Sunday, Dave Powers recalled, Jack spoke at five different gatherings, including the "free banquet" (paid for by the City of Boston) at the Armory. And then, Sutton recalled, they went to the Charlestown Stork Club and the Hen Club, staying until 2 A.M.

On Monday the climactic event was the Bunker Hill Day Parade. Here, for the first time, the Joseph P. Kennedy, Jr., VFW Post made a public political display, marching in the parade. Dave Powers recalled:

> We had about two hundred eighty members in the parade. First came three fellows—Billy Sutton, Frank Dobie, and another guy— carrying the banner: "Joseph P. Kennedy, Jr., VFW Post Number 5880." Then came Jack, the first commander of the post. Then we had the members walk three abreast behind him, spread out like that so that it looked like hundreds and hundreds of men. They were all dressed alike: dark trousers, white shirts, black ties. You could hear people in the crowd yelling, "Where did you get the shirt?" because white shirts were still hard to come by. By then, the crowd all knew Jack Kennedy (who *carried* a hat) and they cheered him. Then, the next day, primary day, the papers all had pictures on the front page of those crowds cheering Jack.

The parade was a five-mile walk. When it was finally finished, Jack, Powers said, was "exhausted." They stopped in the home of the state Senator, and Kennedy supporter, Bobby Lee. Lee recalled in his oral history, "Jack was ill. He turned yellow and blue and collapsed. He looked like he had had a heart attack. We took him up to the second floor, took off his underwear, and sponged him over. I called his father and I was instructed to wait until a doctor came. His father asked me if he had his pills. He did, and he took some pills. Then, after several hours, they took him from my residence."

That night, Mark Dalton recalled, there was a big radio show in Jack's behalf. It was broadcast from the Copley Plaza Hotel at 7:15 on WCOP. There were seven participants, each from a town or neighborhood, speaking in Jack's favor, while Dalton served as moderator. The speakers:

Edward Gallagher—Brighton
Peter DiSessay—East Boston
Dave Powers—Charlestown
Joe Healey—Cambridge
John Ryan—Somerville
Mrs. Edna Fitzgibbons—Boston

On that same day, Monday, June 17, the *New York Times* carried an unsigned story from Boston dated Sunday, June 16, which must have cheered Jack. Headline and partial text:

BAY STATE IS IN DOUBT ON PRIMARY TURNOUT;
RETURN OF VETERANS MAY SWELL THE VOTING

There are two schools of thought on the Massachusetts primary election Tuesday. One holds that with some 400,000 war veterans having returned to the Commonwealth, about 35 per cent of the voters will turn out to select the finalists for the November test. The other foresees considerable apathy, partly due to the prolonged session of the legislature, which finally was prorogued at 5:47 a.m. Saturday.

In the primaries two years ago, in mid-July, only about 20 per cent of the voting population bothered to vote. That was due partly to absence of voters with the armed forces, and partly because so many others were away on vacation. Massachusetts tradition calls for September primaries. . . .

Only a few real battles loom for Congress, with the principal one being for the Democratic nomination in the Eleventh Congressional District, where Mayor James M. Curley of Boston has dropped out to devote his time to City Hall. There are ten aspirants, the leading one apparently being John F. Kennedy, war hero son of Joseph P. Kennedy, former Ambassador to Great Britain. . . .

On Tuesday, June 18, the voters went to the polls. A story in the *New York Times* on June 19 reported, "It appeared that only about 30 per cent of the registered voters participated in the first June primary held in the state. The weather was rainy today."

The big push on voting day was to get out the vote. The Kennedy machine, Yammy deMarco recalled, did a "remarkable" job and "got a lot of votes out." He remembered sending six poll workers to Joe Kane, each of whom was paid $15, good money in those days. But there was a minor foul-up in the Cambridge office. Tom Broderick recalled in his oral history, "We had plenty of cars in Brighton to take voters to the polls. Then at about five P.M., twelve taxis showed up—from Cambridge. Someone had sent them to Brighton by mistake. I called Lem Billings. Billings was frantically looking for the cabs."

Jack went to vote with his grandparents, Honey Fitz, and his wife. Then he went from ward to ward, thanking his workers. That night, Broderick recalled, Jack, the ambassador, and Rose came to Brighton headquarters. Broderick said, "He thanked everybody, but then choked up, there were tears in his eyes, he broke off, got down and shook hands with everybody." Then, John Henry Cutler recalled in his book, *"Honey Fitz": Three Steps to the White House,* that Jack slipped off to the movies to see the Marx Brothers in *A Night in Casablanca.*

When the votes were counted—and the voting was light—there were no surprises on the statewide tickets. David I. Walsh would face Henry Cabot Lodge for the Senate seat in November. Governor Maurice Tobin beat off a Democratic challenger, Boston lawyer Francis D. Harrigan, carrying Boston by a two-to-one margin. His Republican opponent in November would be Robert F. Bradford, a Yankee Brahmin. Paul A. Dever won the nomination for lieutenant governor. His opponent would be Arthur W. Coolidge of Reading, president of the Republican-controlled State Senate.

If there was a surprise in this primary, Jack provided it—by the margin of his victory. He won by a landslide, polling 42 percent of the total vote in his district. According to an unofficial (and incomplete) ward-by-ward breakdown in the June 19 *Boston Globe,* accurate enough to show the voting pattern, Jack polled 21,322 votes, Neville 11,227, Cotter 6,087, and the "real Joe Russo" 5,294. The area breakdown:

Cambridge	Neville	7,606
	Kennedy	6,366
	All others	1,438
Brighton	Kennedy	4,005
	Neville	757
	All Others	1,285
Charlestown	Cotter	2,448
	Kennedy	2,157
	All others	1,092
Somerville	Kennedy	2,790
	Neville	1,329
	Falvey	1,273
	All others	926
Boston	Kennedy	2,757
	Russo #1	2,323

	Russo #2	236
	All others	2,465
East Boston	Kennedy	3,277
	Russo #1	2,230
	Cotter	1,351
	Russo #2	377
	All others	2,360

Thus, the Joe Kane strategy of trying to win second place in the various neighborhoods and a cumulative total to exceed all other candidates worked. Neville carried Cambridge, but by only about 1,300 votes. Cotter carried Charlestown, but only by 300-odd votes. Jack did better than expected in Boston and East Boston. He outran the "real" Joe Russo about 6,000 votes to 4,500. The "fake" Russo didn't fool many. He polled only 613 votes. Had these gone to the "real" Russo, it still would not have been enough to beat Jack in those wards. Brighton, as expected, delivered a handsome 4,000 votes to Jack, very few to his opponents. In Somerville, Jack beat both Falvey and Neville by better than two to one.

According to the book *Massachusetts Election Statistics*, the final official breakdown for all ten candidates was as follows:

Kennedy	22,183	Falvey	2,446	Rooney	521
Neville	11,341	Lee	1,848	DiFruscio	298
Cotter	6,677	Russo #2	799	Blanks	2,444
Russo #1	5,661	DeLuca	536	Total	54,754

In its story on June 19, the *New York Times* featured Kennedy over all other candidates in the Massachusetts primary. There was a picture of Jack with his grandmother—Mrs. Fitzgerald. The story was headlined KENNEDY MAKES POLITICAL BOW. A week later, Henry Luce gave Jack a leg up with a big story in *Time*'s National Affairs section, with a photograph of Jack (holding his hat) leading the VFW Post in the Charlestown Bunker Hill Day Parade.

Excerpts of the *Time* story:

> In his opening campaign speech young Jack Kennedy recalled a promise he had made when he was a PT-boat skipper in the Solomons. Said he: "When ships were sinking and young Americans were dying . . . I firmly resolved to serve my country in peace as honestly as I tried to serve it in war. . . ."
>
> A boyish-looking bachelor of 29, he worked hard to prove he was no snob. By campaign's end, he had made some 450 speeches before luncheon clubs, Catholic societies, the Camelia Lodge of

Sons of Italy. He ate spaghetti with Italians, drank tea with Chinese, sipped sirupy coffee with Syrians. He stuck to local topics: restoration of Boston's port, encouragement of New England industries, aid for veterans.

Jack still faced a Republican opponent in November. He was Lester W. Bowen, of Somerville, who beat out Edward J. Goodman, of Brookline, in the Republican primary. But no one gave this technicality much thought—except perhaps Bowen. In the safe Democratic 11th District, winning the primary meant winning the election. Jack was home free.

Looking back over this long and arduous campaign, we had to conclude that it was one of the most brilliantly executed political sallies ever staged. As we have seen, it was not the work of a "motley" group of amateurs, but rather the shrewd, exacting work of Joe Kennedy and his behind-the-scenes brain trusters, especially the old pol Joe Kane. True, a public veneer of amateur idealism had been projected by the brief presence of a few school chums (Lem Billings, Tom O'Hearn), one college chum (Torby), and three "Navy buddies" (Reed, Fay, McLaughlin), and some members of the family (Joe, Rose, Eunice, Bobby). That was part of the clever strategy of presenting a new leader for a new generation. As we have shown, their contributions (Eunice excepted) were either nil or extremely minor—mostly as window dressing; see, for example, the hoked-up "junior brain trust" picture in *Look*. The real hard-core work, leaving absolutely nothing to chance, not even the hat, was carried out by Jack and the old pols—or the young pols such as Billy Sutton and Dave Powers. And, as far as we could tell, no one made a single mistake, not even Jack. For that, he deserves much personal credit. This strategy of the so-called new politics, placing a veneer of idealistic volunteers out front while the old pols actually retained control behind the scenes, would characterize all of Jack's future political campaigns and take him to the White House.

Now it was time for Jack to play. But, in Boston, he was hard pressed for playmates. Lem Billings and Bobby set off on a long trip to Latin America—at the ambassador's expense. Torby was graduated from Harvard Law and took a job in New York, working for Eric Johnston at the Motion Picture Association, taking along Phyllis and their son Torbert Jr. Eddie McLaughlin and Jim Reed continued law school through the summer, Eddie keeping his job with the Snyder Fuel Company. Pat Lannan, who'd spent another three months in Arizona recuperating from his bronchiectasis, was back in Chicago working on his Henry Holt publishing deal and other ventures.

Jack was not, however, lacking in female companionship. Billy Sutton recalled that during the campaign, Jack had continued to date the two nurses from Chelsea Naval Hospital, Ann McGillicuddy and Elinor Dooley. Ann McGillicuddy, Sutton told us, had helped, briefly, in the campaign.

Cis McLaughlin recalled another girl. Her name was Pamela Farrington. At that time she was working as a model for Boston's famous department store, Filene's. Cis told us, "She was gorgeous. Black hair, beautiful sapphire eyes. Jack used to see her in Boston and would invite her to the Cape and to Florida."

Considerable investigation finally led us to the fact that Pamela had died of cancer in 1969. We learned, too, that she had a daughter living in the Boston suburbs, Mrs. D. Barr Clayson. We met Mrs. Clayson at her home. She is breathtakingly beautiful: petite, black hair, sapphire-blue eyes, about twenty-eight. From photographs she showed us, it was apparent that she was the image of her mother and about the same age her mother was when she met Jack. And her name was also Pamela!

Her mother was the daughter of a comfortably-off Massachusetts family. In 1935, at the age of twenty, she married Donald Farrington, son of Harry J. Farrington, who owned the Farrington Manufacturing Company. Young Pamela was born on July 23, 1936, and has always been called "Honey." A second child, Steven H., was born in 1940. On May 7, 1945, Pamela and Donald Farrington were divorced. Her daughter told us:

She worked—to have something to do. She liked to be involved with other people. She worked for a while at Filene's and then part time for a Boston modeling agency. She modeled shoes because she had a "sample-size" foot. It was about then she met Jack Kennedy. I was about nine years old and my brother was about five. At that time we lived in a house in Newton Center.

Their relationship? I don't think it was a serious thing. For one thing, he was Catholic and she was divorced. He had political aspirations and she wouldn't have been an asset. I think they were both aware of this. I think they were just very good friends. She went out with him, periodically, for dinner and to parties. They had a good time together. She had a good sense of humor. She enjoyed ribbing him. They joked a lot. I remember him—he was friendly and fun. I was a little in awe of him, too. He was becoming a public figure.

I remember one time they went out to dinner and they talked about food—what they each liked to eat. One thing Kennedy just loved was waffles. He told Mother nobody made good waffles. Mother said she did, so they came home and got me up and we all sat around and ate waffles and syrup. So, we've always saved that waffle recipe. We call them our "presidential waffles."

Another time, I remember Mother and I were in New York and we went out with him one evening. To the theater or something. I recall the three of us riding along in a taxi. He asked me what I wanted to do when I grew up. I don't remember what I said, but I said I was "gonna" do something. His answer was, "'Gonna'? How do you spell 'gonna'?" I was so embarrassed.

Pamela worked for Jack in the 1946 campaign. Her daughter remembered they had a "Kennedy for Congress" campaign button. And she worked for him again in the 1952 Senate race. But in 1954, after Jack's marriage, she moved to New York. The children went away to school— Honey to Vassar. In 1966 Pamela married a man from Bronxville, New York, George Stevens. Three years later, at age fifty-four, she died.

Pamela Farrington was clearly Jack's type: beautiful, bright, and interesting. And, like others, she was "safe." That is, there was no possibility that (given Jack's religion coupled with his political aspirations) he could seriously consider marrying her.

But, we gathered from our interviews, Jack was anxious to get out of Boston, away from the pols and the family. He went first to New York, to the Stork Club and other haunts. He saw the ambitious and engaging Flo Pritchett, among others. Her sister, Dancy Foster, told us that by then Flo was absorbed in some other exciting parajournalistic ventures. Through her friend Walter Winchell, she "got her toe" in radio. She was a panelist on a Saturday night talk show with Dorothy Kilgallen and others.

Inga Arvad was now living in New York. According to her son, Ronald McCoy, Jack started seeing her again in this period. He told us:

At that time Mother was seeing a doctor in New York and the author John Gunther, whom she had met during the war. It wasn't a great sexual thing, they were just awfully good friends. He was just a wonderful old gentleman, she said, and the greatest mistake she ever made was *not* to marry John Gunther. She was also seeing the Western movie actor Tim McCoy, who was then about fifty-five. He'd married during World War One and had three children, but now he was divorced. He'd given up making Westerns after Pearl Harbor and went into the Army, rising to the rank of colonel. And then she saw Jack in New York—in 1946 and into 1947.

From New York Jack flew out to Los Angeles for a long visit with Betty and Chuck Spalding, who was working for Gary Cooper.

Chuck Spalding told us:

Cooper was still involved in these collapsible, independent corporations. But not too much was happening, because he wasn't really interested in that sort of thing. So I'd see publishers and read scripts but nothing would ever happen. On my own, I took an option on a book—I think it was *The Big Sky*, by Alfred Bertram Guthrie, Jr., who later won a Pulitzer Prize. I thought it was a perfect property for Cooper, but nothing happened on it either. . . .

After his primary election to the House Jack came out for a visit. I remember Jack was very much concerned about image. It wasn't even called "image" then. The first person to understand about public relations in politics was the ambassador. I mean, he was the first person I ever knew who really understood that what you did was to merchandise a conception and he had enough experience in radio and motion pictures to grope around in that whole thing, which has now become a common practice.

In California, Jack was beginning to notice the parallels between people out there, like personalities drawing crowds. Why did Cooper draw a crowd? And the other people out there: Spencer Tracy and Clark Gable and others who were floating through that world. So even though he was terribly self-conscious about it, he was always interested in seeing whether he had it—the magnetism—or didn't have it. We'd spend hours talking about it.

Betty Spalding recalled:

We were living in Cheviot Hills in a rented house on the Hillcrest golf course. It was just before my first baby was born. Jack was quite thin and sickly at that time and he got out of Boston, deliberately, because he didn't want to be sucked into paying off a lot of election debts and be bound by it. So he ducked out there for his jollies and sun and rest.

He was very, very fussy about his food. He liked simple things: chops, baked potatoes. But he picked at it. I didn't know much about cooking. He taught me how to cook scrambled eggs in a double boiler. He would be sitting on the table next to the stove and he and Chuck would be talking and Jack would be fiddling with the eggs.

I enjoyed Jack a lot. He was amusing and bright and fascinating to listen to. Chuck was very much the same way, sort of slapdash, so it wasn't any different to me, one way or the other. I just enjoyed him. He was marvelous company. Chuck and I didn't drink at all either, so that worked out. We went to the movies a lot. That's what he liked best. And we walked, always, because he liked to get his exercise.

His clothes were always horrible until he got in the White House and got very fastidious. His manners were really terrible. He didn't have any manners, in the sense of letting women go through the door first or opening doors for them or standing up when older women came into the room. He was nice to people, but heedless of people, heedless about his clothes, and heedless about money.

He never had any money with him. And he was very tight with his money too. He was parsimonious. Just a funny habit he had. Kathleen was the same way. I have no idea why this was. I just think he never thought about it.

During this visit to California, we believe, Jack met and became friends with the Hollywood talent agent and lawyer, Charles Kenneth Feldman, originally a New Yorker. Feldman gave the best parties in Hollywood. In earlier days, he had known the ambassador and for the rest of Jack's life they would be close friends. Chuck Spalding worked for him briefly. Among Feldman's clients were Tyrone Power, William Holden, Edward G. Robinson, John Wayne, Randolph Scott, Charles Boyer, Ava Gardner, Irene Dunne, and later, Arlene Dahl, Marilyn Monroe, and scores of others.

In coming years (as we saw in correspondence at the Kennedy Library) when Jack visited Hollywood, he usually saw Feldman and sometimes stayed at his house in Beverly Hills. Later, Feldman's client Marilyn Monroe lived across the street. Through Feldman, Jack met many Hollywood stars, including Marilyn. Feldman died in 1968, but when we were in Los Angeles, we interviewed his ex-wife Jean Howard (they were divorced in December, 1946), who was a close friend of Flo Pritchett's; and Feldman's longtime secretary, Grace Dobish. They confirmed our assumption that Jack first met Feldman on this trip.

He also saw some other Hollywood friends: Sonja Henie and Angela Greene. Angela had just finished making a film, *The Time, the Place and the Girl* for Warner Brothers. She told us that she informed Jack on this trip that she planned to marry the Los Angeles real estate man Stuart Martin. In a Louella O. Parsons column, October 14, 1946, it was reported Angela was wearing "the largest square-cut diamond ring seen around Hollywood in a long time." On December 7, 1946, Angela married Martin in St. Patrick's Cathedral in New York City. Jack did not attend the wedding, Angela told us.

He also met and dated a Charles Feldman client, Peggy Cummins. In January the Hollywood columnists had Peggy cast in the coveted title role in *Forever Amber,* but the role went to Linda Darnell. In a column published on August 15, Sheilah Graham gushed: "News from the Hollywood love front. Peggy Cummins and Jack Kennedy are a surprise twosome around town during the 29-year old Congressman-from-Boston's visit here. . . ."

Betty Spalding confirmed the item. "Yes, he saw a girl named Peggy Cummins and brought her to the house. She was a nice girl—an English girl—better educated than most starlet types. It wasn't a serious thing; she was just a girl to date."

By now, Red Fay was back in San Francisco, working for his father's construction firm. He told us he was an outside man, a sort of working foreman, driving a pickup truck, the only means of transportation he had. Red invited Jack to San Francisco and Jack accepted. But Jack treated Red a bit highhandedly, which very nearly led to a serious break in their friendship. Fay recalled:

> My mother and father set up a big party for him at our place in Woodside, on the Monterey Peninsula. Anita and I were engaged by then, but she was up in the mountains so she didn't participate. But I invited all my friends in the San Francisco area, including Nancy Burkett.
>
> I really got annoyed at him because he almost didn't make the party. After we had everything laid on, he sent me a flip wire from Hollywood saying Lana Turner was insisting that he stay down there, or words to that effect. I sent him a wire back about Lana Turner, saying hell, we're having a big crowd just to meet you— you get up here. So he came up and I picked him up at the airport in the pickup truck. He was bragging about seeing Sonja Henie. I was a little edgy about the whole thing. I remember he didn't have any money. I loaned him twenty dollars—a lot of money to me in those days—and I had to write him a couple of letters to get it back. I was really irritated.

Nancy Burkett told us:

> Red Fay called me one day and said that Jack was coming through and he was going to have a party for him at Woodside, a luncheon, and could I come? I said yes. I'd never been to his parents' place before. There was a long walk up to the house. There were great banners made out of paper, great huge strips of paper that said KENNEDY FOR PRESIDENT. And I wondered what *that* was all about. . . . We had a chat there, and I didn't see him again until the 1960 presidential campaign, when he came to San Francisco.

Red Fay said:

> Jack didn't make too many friends with my father or mother or myself. We thought that after the party we'd all sit around and have dinner. But there was a guy there from PT's named John Gal-

vin—no kin to Jack's public relations guy in Boston. We called him "Dirty John" Galvin. Anyway, Jack and Dirty John just up and left and went to the movies! Then, I think, he went back to Boston that night or the next day.

According to a newsclip we found in the scrapbooks, Jack must have arrived back in Boston in early August. On August 9, the *Boston Globe* reported Jack was back "after several weeks rest at Santa Barbara, California." The *Globe* reporter said he looked "tanned and had gained a little weight."

All this time, Jack's political apparatus had been idling along at the Tremont Street headquarters. The inside administrator, Peter Cloherty, recalled:

> There was a lot of correspondence to be attended to—thank-you letters to campaign workers and all that and a lot of stuff for the upcoming VFW National Encampment, which Jack was to chair. He didn't like to send out form letters, so we'd type up all these letters and send them out to him in Los Angeles, where he was vacationing.
>
> He must have been having a good time, because when he got back from the Coast, there in his luggage were all the letters we'd sent out to him to sign and mail. They were all so messy by then we had to do them all over again.

Jack now had to make some important decisions about his political team: Who would go with him to Washington? Who would man the Boston office? His father, we believe, had a large voice in these decisions.

Ted Reardon, who had arrived late in the political campaign to give a shove in Somerville, became Jack's first and most important choice. He would go to Washington as Jack's right-hand man. A close associate of Jack's and Ted's in this period, who asked not to be quoted by name, had this explanation: "Ted went to Washington because he was a friend of Joe Junior's. He'd been Joe's roommate at Harvard and Joe had promised Ted that they would stick together and he would take Ted wherever he went in life. Joe had told this to Jack at some point and now Jack was making good on Joe's promise."

Reardon told us:

> After we won, I was thinking of going back to Ohio. Then before Jack went out to California, he had a final talk with his "field commanders," thanking us. He wasn't looking too good at that time— he was thin and he had that malaria thing, but we were all telling

him how wonderful and how handsome he was. Then I left and
walked down the hall and he came after me and said, "How about
staying with me?" I said I had to talk to Betty Jane and think about
it a little bit. When I saw him again, I asked him if he was sure
about this because I knew nothing about this business. He said,
"Neither do I. Let's go!" Well, that was it. I guess the reason Jack
asked me was that he knew Joe Junior and I had got along great and
he trusted me. And, he'd known me longer than any of his other
field commanders.

And so, Ted Reardon gave up his plans to go to work for the Monarch
Tool Company in Ohio. He signed on full time on the Kennedy payroll.
He vacated his apartment in Ohio and returned to Boston about August 1,
to operate from the Tremont Street headquarters until they went to Washington in January.

Jack's next pick for the Washington staff was Billy Sutton, already on
his payroll for tax purposes as a "secretary." Reardon said, "I sort of
picked out Billy Sutton to stay on. I thought he was a guy who would get
off his duff and try to help somebody. He was a decent fellow, who had a
nice way with people, and a great natural wit. By then, Jack called him
'Golden Boy.'"

No one else was picked to go to Washington. Jack, Ted Reardon, and
Billy Sutton made up that team.

Probably at the urging of the ambassador, Frank Morrissey was chosen
to head up Jack's Boston office, a controversial appointment for a number
of reasons. For one, Morrissey did not live in the district, a fact that
caused embarrassing newspaper publicity when the appointment was announced. (Morrissey lived in Jamaica Plain.) For another, he was not well
liked by many in Jack's embryonic political machine. Many considered
him "the eyes and ears" of the ambassador; that is, a spy. For another,
Morrissey had a small law practice by then. Many felt that the practice
took up too much of Morrissey's time, and that he sluffed off a lot of the
Boston office work.

There was a slot in the Boston office staff for an assistant. Because
there were so many Italian-Americans in the district, it was decided it
should be offered to Galluccio, who'd done such good work in Cambridge. Galluccio told us:

He asked me to be a secretary in the Boston office, working with
Frank Morrissey. He wanted an Italian. I was still going to Harvard Law School and I couldn't see it. I mean, it would interfere.
We continued to see one another and all that, but when I graduated
in 1948, I went to work in New York for a guy Jack and I both

knew, Mike Grace, whose father was Grace Steamship Lines. Then, after a couple of years, in 1950, I came back to work in Boston—for Jack.

Frank Morrissey had been impressed when he met Bill Kelly's assistant in East Boston, Joe Rosetti, the young Marine veteran waiting for the hotel management school to find a place for him. Rosetti was still unemployed, still waiting. He told us:

> I got a call to go down and see Frank Morrissey. He interviewed me and told me what the job would entail. He said I'd be the Italian representative in Jack's Boston office. Even though I had no political background, I had no reservations about saying I'd be delighted. One learns very quickly. I had no direct contact with Jack. Later I got a letter from him, thanking me for accepting the position. After I went to work, I went to Northeastern University at night, studying labor-management and business administration.

The final recruit for the Boston office was Joe Kane's friend, Grace Burke, who had been working as a secretary in the Tremont Street headquarters. Rosetti told us:

> Grace Burke was a tremendous lady. She was about fifty, not married, though she did have a companion, a guy called Doc Winneck, a bail bondsman, or something. She didn't live with him, just saw a lot of him. Grace was Irish, round-faced, five two, about one hundred fifty pounds. Big boned. She had a young niece who died very suddenly and I think she'd been hurt by that, severely hurt. She was very dedicated. She would not allow anything to take place in that office that was going to be detrimental to Jack. She kept her three-by-five cards, her filing system, had her own personal contacts at City Hall and the State House. She was on top of everything. And, of course, Joe Kane was always dropping by to see her and give us some sage advice.

In time, although Jack had little or no patronage, he got two more of his field commanders, Dave Powers and Tom Broderick, jobs on the public payroll. Dave Powers went with the Boston Housing Authority as director of recreation in South Boston. Tom Broderick, who had had training in pharmacy in prewar years, went to the Veterans' Administration Hospital in Framingham. Through the years, both men would continue to serve Jack loyally in a volunteer capacity.

Two key men in the budding Kennedy organization did not last the course. One was Peter Cloherty of Brighton, the ex-enlisted Army man who was recruited to help organize the inside headquarters. He recalled: "In the fall, he told me I'd done a fine job and he'd like to take me to Washington with him—but unfortunately I didn't live in the district. Our parting was an amicable one. He said he'd do anything he could to help me get a job with the state or city." But Cloherty recalled he already had a job offer—from the Curley forces. He went to the Boston Department of Celebrations (run by Curley's son, George) as a city greeter.

Jamey Kelley told us he asked Jack to try to get him a job as a U.S. marshal in Boston. But Jack either failed or didn't try. Eddie McLaughlin told us that Kelley was "*very* aggressive, an opportunist. He wanted to move in and knock everybody out. After the election, he lasted about three seconds. They had a big row." Kelley told us, "A lot of people couldn't take the Kennedy thing—working for them. They walked away. I got mad and went back to Railway Express." Later, James became involved in another Boston political machine and married a wealthy girl, Mary Cronin, whose father owned a department store.

The driver-valet George Taylor, the token black in the organization, also left. We found a couple of documents at the Kennedy Library that may explain why. The first was a bill ($10) from Dr. Benjamin Sachs, dated May 31, 1946, for "treatment" of George H. Taylor. The second, dated the same day, was a bill ($35) from a lawyer, Ray W. Guild, representing Taylor before the Boston Municipal Court. We could find no official records at the court to explain what this was all about; perhaps the charges (if any) were dropped. Peter Cloherty vaguely recalled a minor incident involving Taylor. He told us: "Taylor had a few extra drinks and got in some kind of fight." According to Taylor's slim oral history at the Kennedy Library, after the election he joined the Merchant Marine on account of his "asthma" and remained in it for the next seventeen years—to 1963.

The three Cambridge lawyers who had helped Jack—John Droney, Joe Healey, and Mark Dalton—did not expect, nor did they receive, any direct or indirect payoff for their work. Or so Dalton and Healey told us. All three remained in close contact with Jack, serving as a real "junior brain trust" on various legislative matters. The Dowd PR man, John Galvin, pitched in from time to time. All four would play important roles in Jack's 1952 Senate race.

Finally, Eddie McLaughlin told us, "One day Jack and I were having one of those chocolate ice cream sodas he so loved. Suddenly, apropos of nothing we were discussing, he turned to me and said, 'How about working for me in Washington?' I looked at him and laughed. Then I said, 'The two of us wouldn't last five minutes; one of us would go right out the window.' He said, 'Jesus, McLaughlin'—he was human, he swore like a longshoreman—'I'm not all *that* bad.' And I said, 'You're worse.'"

39

Indirect Politics

IN the 1946 elections, incumbents were being held responsible for the unsettled state of the economy. In Massachusetts, that meant Democrats. David Walsh's senatorial campaign had collapsed in a personal scandal. The Tobin-Dever ticket was running behind. James Michael Curley had a prison sentence hanging over his head.

Both the senior and junior brain trusts in the Jack Kennedy machine apparently advised that both Jack and the ambassador maintain a low profile in the fall campaign, which opened officially on Labor Day. Jack's seat was safe; his Republican opponent Lester Bowen was regarded as a curiosity, a political kamikaze. Why publicly commit Jack to Walsh, Tobin, and Dever, when disaster loomed so clearly on the horizon? There was nothing to gain and much to lose.

So it was done. The clips in the scrapbook show that Jack made a few obligatory appearances in the fall, but by and large, his political activities were what we came to think of as indirect. Some examples:

On August 12, 1946, on the second anniversary of Joe Junior's death, the Kennedys revealed that a "memorial foundation" honoring him had been established. Since none of the ambassador's financial records have been released, we could not ascertain how much money was put into the Joseph P. Kennedy, Jr., Foundation at its founding, or how much was fed into it in the coming years from exactly what sources, other than the Merchandise Mart. The foundation owned 25 percent of the Merchandise Mart, a huge source of revenue. As Koskoff points out, charitable foundations such as this one can be financially advantageous to the very rich.

In one document at the Kennedy Library, we learned a little bit about the personnel makeup of the foundation. The ambassador, of course, was the founder. Jack was named the first president. The other officers and directors were the ambassador's employees in the "New York Office": Edward E. Moore, John J. Ford, Paul E. Murphy, and James A. Fayne.

On August 12, the president of the foundation, Jack Kennedy, made the foundation's first, and most spectacular gift. He presented Archbishop Richard Cushing a check for $600,000. The money was earmarked (by the foundation) for a hospital for children. This gift—there had never been anything like it in the recent history of Boston—made headlines in the Boston newspapers.

The press, as yet, did not know that Rosemary was retarded, and the Kennedys were still going to extraordinary lengths to keep that fact secret. Cushing told reporters the hospital would be for "poor" children. In fact, as he later revealed in his oral history at the Kennedy Library, it was designed for "mentally and physically handicapped" children. Much of the Joseph P. Kennedy, Jr., Foundation money in the coming years would be channeled for that purpose.

It was not immediately revealed where the hospital was to be located. Ultimately, it was placed in Jack's district, on Warren Street in Brighton, opposite the Brighton High School. It was staffed by the Franciscan Sisters of Mary.

Inevitably, the foundation received thousands of requests for gifts and donations. Much of this correspondence has been opened to researchers at the Kennedy Library. In going through the file, we noticed that proposed projects within the 11th Congressional District got more than routine consideration. For example, in a letter dated December 2, 1948, from Jack to Paul Murphy in the New York office, Jack wrote, "This section is located in my Congressional district and I would like very much to have the request placed on file for consideration. . . ." As we saw, a substantial number of such requests were honored.

In his oral history at the Kennedy Library, Joe Casey, whose political career had been smashed by the ambassador in 1942, recalled these foundation gifts. He said they were "perfectly legitimate" and "laudatory," but they were also "political currency." Every time a gift was made, there was a ceremony, prominently recorded in the Boston papers. Every time a new facility, such as the hospital in Brighton, was established in the district, it provided not only help for the underprivileged in Jack's district, but also a place of employment for some of his constituents, and therefore a form of personal patronage, since the foundation undoubtedly had a voice (direct or indirect) in determining who was hired and fired.

The following year, August 12, 1947, on the third anniversary of Joe Junior's death, Jack, as president, donated $250,000 to various Boston charities. These included $100,000 to the Sisters of the Third Order of St. Francis for a parochial school, $50,000 for the Christopher Columbus Catholic Center (a boys' club, to be built in the North End), $50,000 to the Boston Children's Hospital and—perhaps to help offset the ambassador's rumored anti-Semitism—$50,000 to Associated Jewish Philanthropies. Again, the Boston papers were awash with the news.

In early September the VFW met in Boston, with Jack as chairman. This was a huge gathering—30,000 veterans, the Boston papers reported. Navy Secretary James Forrestal sent the battleship *Missouri,* on whose decks one year before Japanese officials had signed the official surrender papers. There was a mammoth parade on September 4 or 5.

As chairman, Jack was a highly visible figure during these goings-on. The scrapbooks are full of clips about him chairing the meeting, marching in the parade, speaking before various VFW meetings, committees, sub-committees, and local posts, which held countless receptions for the visiting firemen. Tobin and Curley and other Massachusetts political figures used these forums for political appearances. In a booklet by John Galvin, *Twelve Mayors of Boston 1900–1970*, we found a photograph of Jack, in uniform, sitting on a podium with Tobin and Curley. Jack seems ill-at-ease and looks sickly, almost skeletal.

On this occasion, the Joseph P. Kennedy, Jr., VFW Post held its most-remembered gathering. It was a large formal dinner in the Somerset Hotel ballroom. Jim Reed (since August 28 proud father of a girl Candice, for whom Jack was the godfather) was there, along with Eddie McLaughlin, who was being groomed by Jack to take over as the post's second commander. The featured speaker that night was Joseph P. Kennedy. No one who was present will ever forget his talk. Eddie, who introduced him, remembered:

> The ambassador gave this great, great speech. There was a press table, I remember, and he turned to the press and said, "Now, this is off the record." Then he stood there and told us most of the story of his life—all his business deals and so on. He was very, very candid about everything—talking as he was to a group of would-be businessmen on the way up. I remember one thing he said about some of his big stock deals. He said you couldn't do a lot of them anymore because the laws had been changed. But, all in all, it was a really inspiring talk.

During the VFW convention, Jack got into a terrific ruckus with the old-guard VFW leadership. It arose over a policy question concerning a proposed bill in the U.S. Congress to provide public low-cost housing. The need for housing for veterans was so acute that even archconservative Senator Robert Taft had put his name on the bill, then known as the Wagner-Ellender-Taft (or W-E-T) bill. The bill had been fiercely opposed by most conservatives and by the real estate lobby. Jack Kennedy very much wanted the bill passed, to help his constituents, especially the veterans, get housing. So, during the VFW Convention, he offered a resolution from the floor endorsing the W-E-T bill. The resolution was passed, even though the old-guard VFW leadership traditionally sided with the real estate lobby.

Subsequently, the newly elected VFW commander in chief, Louis Starr, held a press conference in Washington. During it, he claimed that the VFW had not known what it was doing when it passed the resolution. He claimed the acoustics had been poor. In the November, 1946, issue of the VFW house organ, *National News*, Starr published an article criticizing the endorsement of the resolution.

Jack wrote Starr a letter, published in the December, 1946, issue of *National News*, defending the legality of the proceedings. He went on to say that since the acoustics at the convention were the same for both the endorsement of the W-E-T resolution and for Starr's election, either both or neither vote should be retaken! Starr backed down. Changing his position, he urged Truman to call a special session of Congress for the purpose of passing the W-E-T bill.

All this VFW activity generated a lot of publicity for Jack. And, as we shall see, "housing" would become one of his principal issues.

On the weekend of Friday, September 27, to Sunday, September 29, 1946, The Choate School held a fiftieth-anniversary celebration. *The Choate News* for September 28, kindly furnished us by the alumni director, Edward Ayres, reported that more than five hundred distinguished alumni attended the gathering, including the governor of Connecticut, the president of Yale, and Jack Kennedy. Over the three-day period there were about forty brief speeches, toasts, and sermons. Saturday night, at the main banquet, Jack gave a brief speech that stirred up a lot of talk— and writing in *The Choate Alumni Bulletin*. His theme was that private prep schools, such as Choate, sent too few men into politics.

Writing in *The Choate Alumni Bulletin* in January, 1947, H. L. Tinker said:

> One of the most provocative things said at the Choate Fiftieth Anniversary was Jack Kennedy's challenge to the independent preparatory schools to produce more leaders in American political life. His challenge has caused us seriously to take stock, and from what we can learn, men in other schools have been giving it much the same thought. To be frank, he has put us all somewhat on the defensive. After all, if there is one thing that responsible teachers do try to do, it is to instill into their charges the responsibilities of full citizenship. We have tried to give Jack's words the honest consideration which they deserve. . . .

Tinker goes on for four long pages in his consideration. He grants "the truth of Jack's fundamental theses," and deplores it. Then he lists everybody from Choate he can think of in public life—Adlai Stevenson, Chester Bowles, George Jackson Mead, and so on. He goes so far as to list Morris Kerr, who served on "the Board of Selectmen in Winchester." He concludes with a plea for the alumni to write in and tell Choate what public service they had rendered—so the records could be brought up to date—and a bow to Jack: "We are grateful to Jack for placing emphasis on this problem. It has done us good, all of us. . . .

All this, of course, had nothing to do with politics in Massachusetts. But the Choate alumni were a distinguished group. Jack's challenge had the effect of keeping them stirred up for months and, of course, dramatically directed their attention to the fact that *he* had entered public life.

After that, Jack (judging by newspaper clips) campaigned only sporadically and when it was absolutely necessary. In early October his plans were interrupted by the dreadful news that Lennie Thom had been killed in an automobile accident. Kate told us:

> Lennie got out of the Navy in January, 1946. Jack telephoned and asked him to come to Boston and help in his political campaign, but I talked Lennie out of it. We went home to live at my mother's house in Youngstown. Lennie took a job with an insurance agency, and he also went back to Ohio State to get a masters degree in physical education, so he commuted back and forth from Youngstown to Columbus.
>
> On Friday night, October 4, he was on the way back to Youngstown with two other boys in the car, including my brother. Near Ravenna [just east of Akron] there was a blind railroad crossing. There were two trains a day, one in the morning, one at night. Lennie couldn't see it and ran into the engine. . . .

Lennie Thom died in the Ravenna hospital Saturday night, October 5. (That same day, in San Francisco, Red Fay married Anita Marcus.) Kate said:

> Jack called Sunday morning. One of Lennie's fraternity brothers had called him. He flew out the next day, Monday, October 7, and stayed with a neighbor. He was a pallbearer at the funeral Tuesday. He was a very great comfort to me, personally. He really helped me through it. His philosophy was the living go on living. There was much more to life. He encouraged me to go back to school after I had the baby and get into teaching. He said that Lennie's friends would be my friends for life. And in Jack's case, that was true. Right up to when Jack was killed. . . .

When he returned to Boston, Jack was in a somber mood. We found a notation dated October 9 on an invitation to speak later that month: "No political speeches this fall." But there was one date he could not duck: the Columbus Day celebration, October 12, a great Boston holiday for the

Italians. Jack marched in the parade and (according to a clip in the scrapbook) was toastmaster at a Columbus Day banquet.

Election day came on Tuesday, November 5. Nationwide, the Democratic Party was swamped and for the first time in years there would be a Republican Congress and a Democratic president. In Massachusetts, Walsh, Tobin, and Dever went down to crushing defeat. Henry Cabot Lodge defeated Walsh by 330,000 votes. Jack's opponent, Lester Bowen, polled 26,007 votes to Jack's 69,093. (Philip Geer of Boston, a Prohibition Party candidate entered in the race, got 1,036 votes. There were 9,237 blanks. Total votes: 105,373.) And now it was official: Jack was a Congressman-elect.

We could find only two notes of congratulations in the Kennedy Library. One was a telegram from London signed "Kay." It said, LOTS OF LUCK AND MESSAGES. We assumed it was from the tennis champion Kay Stammers. The other was a telegram from James Forrestal: DEAR JACK, CONGRATULATIONS. I AM DELIGHTED THAT YOU SURVIVED.

On Monday night, November 11, Armistice Day, Jack spoke in Charlestown at the Bunker Hill Post of the American Legion. It was the usual rhetoric: he would fight for labor in Congress, oppose Communism, work hard for the W-E-T Bill (or some form of it), try to make Boston a busier, better port, and so on. One of his Charlestown supporters, Mary McNeely, was in the audience. In her oral history she recalled, "He was going along fine, giving a good speech until he came to 'No greater love has a man than he who gives up his life for his brother.' Then he broke down and was unable to finish the speech. An elderly little woman, Mrs. Lillian Keeney, got up to carry on for Jack. While I played the piano, she sang 'Too-Ra-Loo-Ra-Loo-Ra.' And whenever I met Jack after that, he always asked for that. . . ."

There were campaign spending laws—of a sort—at that time, and so Jack made an accounting. The *New Bedford Standard Times* reported, "His coast to victory in the 11th Congressional District seat was a free ride, according to Congressman-elect John F. Kennedy. His report on file with Secretary of State Frederic W. Cook, stated he completed his campaign without spending a penny. . . ."

The *Salem News* of the same date reported Jack had "no contributions or expenditures."

40

A Secret Marriage?

FOR the first time in the twenty-nine years of his life, Jack Kennedy would now have a full-time job. He would report, fairly regularly, to two offices, one in Washington and one in Boston. This new responsibility brought on another need new for Jack: residences in both cities.

In Boston, Jack and his aides picked out an apartment in an older building near his Boston office and the State House, 122 Bowdoin Street. In 1974 the apartment was still being rented by the Kennedys—as an office, a fund-raising headquarters for the Kennedy Library. We went there for a casual inspection. The building was rather dingy. There was a small elevator. The apartment was far from pretentious: two bedrooms, a small living room and kitchen. Its acquisition in 1946 gave Jack a place to hang his hat and helped mute the criticism that he was a carpetbagger who didn't even have a legal residence in Massachusetts. To round things out, he got a Massachusetts drivers license, giving the Bowdoin Street address, and changed his voting registration to the same address.

Washington was a little more complicated. Eunice, whose social work had now evolved into a passionate interest in juvenile delinquency, decided to volunteer her services to the National Conference on Juvenile Delinquency, a semipermanent committee of the Justice Department. This meant that she, too, would be moving to Washington. It was decided that she and Jack would share a house. One of the Kennedy cooks, Margaret Ambrose, would also live there. Eunice would be Congressman Kennedy's hostess. The house would also serve as a headquarters for other members of the Kennedy family and close friends visiting Washington.

In late November Boston newspapers reported that Jack was in Washington "house-hunting." He picked out a three-story row house in Georgetown, at 1528 31st Street. It had a small, but attractive, patio-garden in the rear. He did not buy it. He signed a rental agreement for $300 a month with Gilliat & Co., according to a document we found at the Kennedy Library.

Jamey Kelley recalled that he went along on this trip. He said:

We had a terrible time trying to get back to Boston. We tried to leave on the Wednesday before Thanksgiving [November 27] but we couldn't get a plane or train reservation of any kind. Everything was booked. We couldn't even buy a stand-up train ticket.

While we were down there, Jack had seen some of his father's old friends, like Supreme Court Associate Justice Frank Murphy and Navy Secretary James Forrestal. Well, luckily, Forrestal and his wife were going up to Newport, Rhode Island, for Thanksgiving and Jack hit up Forrestal for a ride. I went out to the Anacostia Naval Air Station, separately, in a cab, but the Marines at the gate wouldn't let me in. This delayed the takeoff. Finally, Forrestal's limousine came tearing down to the gate and took me to the plane. Jack was furious, gave me a royal chewing-out, then introduced me to Secretary Forrestal and his wife and aides. Then we took off.

I remember that all the way up to Newport, Forrestal was talking to us about the threat posed by Communism—Soviet Russia. In Eastern Europe, Berlin, China. It was like an obsession with him. The Forrestals got off in Newport and then the plane took us on to Boston. And that was how we got home—in real style.

During November, perhaps on the way down to Washington, Jack stopped off in New York. He undoubtedly saw Torby (working for the Motion Picture Association) and he probably saw his good friend Flo Pritchett and others.

Inga Arvad's son, Ronald McCoy, said in our interview that at this time Jack also saw Inga, probably for the last time in his life. Around mid-November, Inga became pregnant; Jack may have caused it, Ronald said. He told us:

So two-and-a-half to three years ago I was home for a weekend from the university, and we were sitting at the table having dinner together and she said there was something she wanted to talk about. She'd never mentioned it. She didn't want me to talk to my father about it or to my brother about it, and that it wasn't a good thing to talk about because nobody would believe it. Even if they did it's nobody's business. That kind of thing, you know? And it was that . . . oh . . . she said when your father and I were married . . . what she said was . . . ah . . . your father thinks we've been married, let's say, twenty-three years. But . . . we've been married for one year longer than that. And I said so what? And she said that would mean that I was pregnant when I married your father. It came within like a week or two of having an abortion. She was going to have an abortion but found out she was a week or two too far into the pregnancy to do it—Be too much of a hassle. Then she said the thing was, you see the problem was, she

said I didn't know who your father was for sure, she said. I *really*
don't know if it was Jack or Tim. *I don't know.*
And . . . ah . . . I mean it really took the top of my head right
off. It wasn't the thing, well my father was either Tim McCoy or
Jack Kennedy and Jack Kennedy had been President of the United
States. That's not the way it was. It was just kind
of . . . ah . . . a lot of the things she had said over the years
then kind of fit into place . . . and . . . I'd always felt from talking to her that I pretty much understood how his mind worked. I
could understand the compartmentalization and stuff like that. I
could understand why he'd have to have it, too. It just put a lot of
things in place. It had me upset for a while, a couple of months.
You know, I didn't know and there was no way to find out. I
wasn't sure that it was important. It was just one thing
thrown. . . . It didn't make much difference as far as—it didn't
make *any* difference—as far as my feeling toward my father goes.
To me he's still my father. But it was a shock. It really was. And
also, because it's one thing when you're saying my father was
either Joe Blow or Frank Kaputsky. But when you say my father is
either Tim McCoy or Jack Kennedy, it makes you sound like a pre-
tender to the throne. . . . You know—the Prince of Wales or
something. It's something you don't talk about. . . .

Inga Arvad had a tendency to romanticize her background and asso-
ciations with the great and near-great; perhaps Ronald had inherited
this trait. Inga seems never to have told Jack—or anybody else—she
might be carrying his child. If she'd talked to anyone the rumors would
surely have spread like a prairie fire. As to Inga's and Ronald's credibili-
ty, there seems no point in adding to our earlier speculation.

Ronald told us that Inga married Tim McCoy on February 14, 1947, in
"upstate" New York. We checked the New York State marriage records
and found this to be true. They were married on that date in North Castle,
New York. Ronald told us he was born six months after the marriage
ceremony, on August 12, 1947.

After Thanksgiving, as Rose recounts in some detail in her book, the
Kennedys closed up the house in Hyannis Port and moved the staff to the
Palm Beach home. Jack, having nothing else pressing to do, must have
gone down to Palm Beach in early December for a month's rest.

By this time, Jack had many friends in Palm Beach, old and young,
male and female. He made the scene regularly at the Everglades Club and
other haunts. Among his friends in Palm Beach were the Cassini brothers,
Igor and Oleg. By this time, Igor was out of the Army (where he worked
on *Stars and Stripes*), had separated from the *Times-Herald* columnist

Bootsie (she got a Las Vegas divorce in August, 1947), and had a job with the Hearst newspapers, writing a gossip column under the byline Cholly Knickerbocker, which would soon eclipse Bootsie's in readership and importance to café society. Oleg, emerging as a dress designer, had married an aspiring film star, Gene Tierney, but now that marriage was shaky and they would soon divorce. The Cassini brothers were the darlings of the Palm Beach café society set.

One of the several girls Jack dated in Palm Beach over this Christmas was Durie Desloge. On January 20, 1947, the *New York World Telegram* gossip columnist, Charles Ventura, reported that:

> Palm Beach's cottage colony wants to give the son of Joseph P. Kennedy its annual Oscar for achievement in the field of romance.
>
> The committee says that young Mr. Kennedy splashed through a sea of 'flaming early season divorces to rescue its sinking faith in the romantic powers of Florida, The Moon and You.
>
> Worried dowagers were voicing the fear that the court bench had taken the place of the love seat in Palm Beach when Jack saved the situation by giving Durie Malcolm Desloge the season's outstanding rush. . . .
>
> Only the fact that duty called him to Washington . . . kept Jack from staying around to receive his Oscar in person, so it may be awarded to Durie. The two were inseparable at all social functions and sports events. They even drove down to Miami to hold hands at football games and wager on the horses.
>
> Durie is the daughter of the George H. Malcolms of Palm Beach and Chicago. She is beautiful and intelligent. Tiny obstacle to orange blossoms is that the Kennedy clan frowns upon divorce. Durie has said "Good morning Judge" with F. John Bersback. A similar situation in St. Louis with Firmin V. Desloge IV makes it two.

This silly story would, in later years, cause Jack a world of grief. It led, in a curious, somewhat complicated way, to rumors and then published reports that Jack had secretly married Durie and then divorced her (or had the marriage annulled), and the records had been expunged. We believe that none of this was true, but since the matter evidently fascinated millions, it is worth pausing to take a look at how it all got started.

Durie Malcolm was probably born in Chicago on December 30, 1916, daughter of Isabel O. Cooper and a man named Kerr. Her mother later married George H. Malcolm and Durie took her stepfather's name. On April 3, 1937, Durie married F. John Bersbach in Lake Forest, Illinois. They were divorced fifteen months later, July 15, 1938. The following January 2, 1939, she married Firman Desloge IV of St. Louis in Palm

Beach. They were divorced January 27, 1947. On July 11, 1947, she married Thomas Shevlin, Jr., at Fort Lee, New Jersey.

The Malcolms had a home in Palm Beach close by the Kennedy home. When Durie and Joe Junior and Jack were growing up there in the 1930s, they were good friends. Joe Junior and Durie dated before she married Bersbach and Desloge. The elder Kennedys knew Durie's mother and stepfather quite well.

Durie was an eleventh-generation descendant of a Dutch family, the Blauvelts, who migrated from Holland in 1638. In 1957 a Blauvelt family genealogy was published in Hillsdale, New Jersey. It was prepared by one of the family, Louis L. Blauvelt, who died at age eighty-two a year before his book came out. On page 884 of the genealogy there is the following entry:

> DURIE (KERR) MALCOLM, (Isabel O. Cooper, 11,304) We have no birth date. She was born Kerr but took the name of her stepfather. She first married Firmin Desloge IV. They were divorced. Durie then married F. John Bersbach. They were divorced and she married, third, John F. Kennedy, son of Joseph P. Kennedy, onetime Ambassador to England. There were no children of the second or third marriages. The only child of Firmin V. Desloge and Durie (Kerr) Malcolm (12,427) was:
> 12,642 Durie born _____, _____.

This entry, presumably compiled by the aged Louis Blauvelt, had several errors and omissions. He had reversed the order of Durie's first two marriages. He had misspelled Firman (as had the columnist Ventura). There was no mention at all of Durie's marriage to Shevlin. He had not yet got the name of the child born to Durie and Firman Desloge.

The entry went unnoticed for several years. Then in March, 1962, *The Realist*, an irreverent New York City satire magazine of small circulation, published the item in full, headlined: THE STORY BEHIND THE RUMOR ABOUT PRESIDENT KENNEDY'S FIRST MARRIAGE. It next turned up in a racist Alabama hate sheet, *The Thunderbolt*, under the headline KENNEDY'S DIVORCE EXPOSED. IS PRESENT MARRIAGE VALID? EXCOMMUNICATION POSSIBLE. Then it spread to other extremist publications and to the British press. On September 2, 1962 *Parade* magazine published a letter from a Palm Beach reader asking "once and for all, will someone please tell me the truth" about the rumors. Following that, the aging Walter Winchell asked in his column, "Why hasn't the White House debunked it?"

The White House had not debunked the story on sound public relations grounds: to debunk it would officially call attention to it. However, after *Parade* and Winchell, it could no longer be ignored. The White House categorically stated that Durie had never been married to Jack. The *New*

York Times, Newsweek, Time, the AP, UPI, the *Washington Post,* and other news organizations assigned dozens of reporters to comb through marriage and divorce records all over the East Coast. They found nothing. (Our account of this affair is based on research done for articles in the *New York Times,* September 18, 1962, and *Newsweek,* September 24, 1962.) The daughter of author Louis Blauvelt, Mrs. William Keys Smith, a teacher at Newark (New Jersey) Academy, told the *New York Times,* "It can be considered an error."

How had the error happened? The supposition was that Louis Blauvelt kept a filing system. When the Charles Ventura story about Jack and Durie appeared in the *New York World Telegram* in January, 1947, he snipped it out and put it in Durie's file. Nine or ten years later, when he was old and possibly a bit senile, he put Durie's entry together, misreading the Ventura story as a marriage.

The rumors persist, we discovered. During our interviews in 1973 and 1974, many asked us if we had "found out anything about the secret marriage." We had seen no reason to explore the matter—mostly because of the thorough research that had been done by others, but also because it simply never made sense. It would have been utterly out of character for Jack. Still—if the rumor still has life, and if we meant our book to cover every available detail. . . .

Durie Shevlin, who still lives in Palm Beach, had refused to talk to reporters in 1962 when the story first appeared. Perhaps now she would talk. We wrote her a careful letter, then telephoned. She was uneasy and didn't want to talk. But she said, "The story is absolutely false. I knew Joe Junior well. At Christmas in 1947—I dated Jack—but not much. We went to the movies a couple of times and down to the Orange Bowl game on New Year's Day in Miami with his father. That was all there was to it."

We routinely checked the marriage and divorce records at the Court House in Palm Beach. There is nothing about Jack and Durie, but the divorce records of Thomas H. Shevlin, the man Durie married in July, 1947, clearly show that he separated from his wife of eleven years, Lorraine, in February, 1947, and was "linked" with Durie shortly afterward in Cassini's Cholly Knickerbocker column. According to Lorraine's testimony, Shevlin was a playboy, a lush, and a philanderer. In the final decree, June 10, 1947, he gave Lorraine $18,000 a year "maintenance."

The chronology of all this seems to rule out time for Durie to have been secretly married to anyone. And again: in Jack's love affairs, one aspect seemed to stand out: his cool. He was a chaser, but a dedicated bachelor. He was just not the type to run off impulsively and secretly marry a twice-divorced woman when he was on the threshold of his political career.

When we were in Palm Beach interviewing Flo Pritchett's widower, Mayor Earl E. T. Smith, we asked him if he knew Durie and if he thought there was anything to the rumored marriage. He said he knew Durie "very well" and the story was "untrue." We asked Smith how such rumors got started. He said, "There were a lot of women who exaggerated their relationship with Jack to promote their own self-interests."

The Ventura story must have made it crystal clear to Jack that henceforth he would have to be more circumspect. It could scarcely have been helpful politically in the 11th Congressional District. While his constituents were shivering, huddled in crowded housing, out on strike, or job hunting, Jack was in Palm Beach and Miami, gaily squiring a two-time divorcée.

Surprisingly, there were almost no mentions of Jack in the gossip columns in the next few years that we could find. Perhaps the ambassador now hired public relations men to keep Jack's name *out* of the columns. In those days it was not an uncommon practice among the rich.

Part V
WASHINGTON

41

Going to Work

I~N~ 1947, as now, a Congress sat for two calendar years, usually in two formal sessions lasting (in those days) about six months, from January to July. There were usually several recesses, at Easter and other times, providing the members a chance to get home to their districts. During the formal sessions, a Congressman usually spent most of his time in Washington. At the close of each session, many divided their time between Washington and home districts. The business of Congress, conducted by paid staffers, continued all year long—committee hearings, investigations, service to constituents.

The First Session of the 80th Congress convened on January 6, 1947. It was a time of vast unease. The cause of the unease was still the same, Communism and the economy. But both issues had reached a crisis stage. Anti-Communist feeling (foreign and domestic) had not yet reached the hysterical level Joe McCarthy would later lead it to, but it was rising. The economy was still wobbling along uncertainly. There was rampant inflation.

President Truman's brief honeymoon with the American people was over. The Republican-dominated press was generally scathing. He was a hick, an ex-haberdasher surrounded by poker-playing, bourbon-drinking cronies. His public appearances embarrassed many. He spoke with a Missouri twang, punctuating his points with an awkward, hand-chopping motion. His wife, Bess, was dowdy. His daughter, Margaret, was making a fool of herself by trying to launch a singing career. Some of Truman's Missouri political friends had gotten into trouble, but he had stood faithfully by them, leading many to believe Truman was also corrupt. In this time of crisis, world and domestic, he did not appear to be the leader the United States needed—or wanted. Some of the men in Truman's cabinet, such as Navy Secretary James Forrestal, did not hold the president in the highest regard.

Now, for the first time in fourteen years—since January, 1933—there was a Republican Congress. The Democrats, who had been the minority party from Lincoln to FDR, were once again on the outside looking in.

505

Those Democrats who managed to survive the Republican sweep in November, 1946 (mostly very senior Southerners), surrendered powerful committee chairmanships to Republicans. The men they had appointed to key patronage jobs around the Hill likewise turned their responsibilities over to successors.

In the Senate there were fifty-one Republicans and forty-five Democrats. Thirty-six of the Senators were newly elected, including Henry Cabot Lodge, who had served there before. The two most powerful men in the Republican Senate were the sixty-two-year-old Arthur H. Vandenberg, of Grand Rapids, Michigan, and the fifty-seven-year-old Robert A. Taft, of Ohio. Vandenberg, a specialist on foreign policy, took charge of the Senate Foreign Relations Committee. Bob Taft, a specialist on domestic policy, took over the Senate Labor and Public Welfare Committee. The senior man, Vandenberg, held the honorary post of president pro tempore of the Senate, but Taft was the man in charge. He made most of the committee assignments and controlled the flow of legislation. He declined the post of majority leader, giving it to Kenneth S. Wherry, of Nebraska. The minority leader of the forty-five Democrats was the genial raconteur, sixty-nine-year-old Alben W. Barkley, of Kentucky, recently a widower.

The Republicans in the Congress considered they had a mandate from the people to fix the "mess" in Washington. To stop the rampant inflation, to check the power of big labor, to cut the growth of the federal bureaucracy.

In January, 1947, the new House of Representatives was composed of 246 Republicans and 189 Democrats. Among these were seven women, including Edith Norse Rogers, of Massachusetts. There were two blacks, Adam Clayton Powell, of New York, and William L. Dawson, of Chicago. The youngest Congressman was not Jack Kennedy, then twenty-nine, but George W. Sarbacher, age twenty-seven, a war hero and Republican from Philadelphia. (The minimum age requirement for Congress is twenty-five.)

For the past seven years, the most powerful man in the House, the speaker, had been the sixty-four-year-old bachelor, Samuel Rayburn from Bonham, Texas. Sam Rayburn, who was elected to the House in 1912, was a squat, taciturn conservative (who voted New Deal) and a master parliamentarian. In January he turned the speaker's job over to the senior Republican, sixty-three-year-old Joseph William Martin, Jr., of Massachusetts, another bachelor. Sam Rayburn became the minority leader.

Joe Martin represented a district near Fall River—Attleboro—a safe territory uninvolved in general Massachusetts politics. He was elected to the House in 1924, survived the Roosevelt sweeps of the thirties, and in

1940 became the House minority leader. Like his close friend Rayburn, Martin was considered to be a superb parliamentarian.

After Martin and Rayburn, the next most powerful men in the House were the majority leader and the majority and minority whips. The majority leader was Charles Abraham Halleck, forty-six, from Indiana, who had served in the House (with the exception of one term) since 1935. The majority whip was fifty-one-year-old Leslie Cornelius Arends, a banker from Melvin, Illinois, who had served in the House without interruption since 1935.

The minority whip was John William McCormack, of South Boston, then fifty-five. McCormack had come up through the Massachusetts Legislature and had served in the U.S. House continuously since his election in 1928. He had never been either an ally or an enemy to the Kennedys or Honey Fitz. For most of those years he had been Rayburn's political confidant and right arm, becoming majority leader in 1940 when Rayburn first became speaker. When Rayburn turned the gavel over to Joe Martin and stepped down to minority leader, McCormack was bumped one step down to minority whip. He was a happily married Catholic, but he had no children.

These men—Rayburn, Martin, McCormack, Halleck, and Arends— would find the U.S. House sufficient for their ambitions, and they would dominate it for the next two decades. But among the faces on the floor that January, 1947, were many who would soon move on. Among the older hands who would soon move up to the Senate: Margaret Chase Smith, of Maine; Lyndon Baines Johnson, of Texas; and Karl E. Mundt, of South Dakota (in 1948). Next: Everett M. Dirksen, of Illinois; Mike Monroney, of Oklahoma; and Estes Kefauver of Tennessee (in 1950). Then Henry M. Jackson, of Washington; J. Glenn Beall, of Maryland; Albert A. Gore, of Tennessee; and Mike Mansfield, of Montana (in 1952). And then: Clifford P. Case, of New Jersey; and Hugh D. Scott, of Pennsylvania.

Among the freshmen Congressmen that January, in addition to Jack Kennedy, there were six who would move to the Upper House—or beyond. They were: Richard M. Nixon, of California; George A. Smathers, of Florida; Jacob K. Javits and Kenneth B. Keating, of New York; and Thruston B. Morton, of Kentucky, who, after a roundabout route, was elected to the Senate in 1956. One freshman, Carl Albert, of Oklahoma, would remain in the House, to become speaker. Two others who later became counted as freshmen in the 80th Congress due to special elections or appointments, also went on to bigger things: Russell B. Long, son of Louisiana's notorious governor, Huey P. Long, age twenty-eight, was appointed Congressman, but in 1948 he moved up to the Senate. Lloyd M. Bentsen, Jr., of Texas, a twenty-seven-year-old Air Force hero, joined the 80th on the last day it sat. In 1970 he was elected to the Senate. In 1974 eight members of the 80th Congress were still serving in the Senate: Long, Bentsen, Jackson, Beall, Mansfield, Case, Javits, and Scott.

The Massachusetts Delegation to the 80th Congress was composed of seventeen members. In size, it ranked eighth, after New York (49 members), Pennsylvania (36), Illinois (28), California, Ohio, and Texas (each 26), and Michigan (20). It was led by the two Republican Senators Leverett Saltonstall and Henry Cabot Lodge, Jr. The fifteen Congressmen (ten Republicans, five Democrats) included two of the most powerful men in the House, speaker Joe Martin and minority whip John McCormack. It also included Christian A. Herter, who would become prominent in Massachusetts state politics and later be secretary of state under President Eisenhower. All in all, it was distinguished company.

In our interview with Billy Sutton, he recalled that he and Ted Reardon drove from Boston to Washington. Jack flew directly from Palm Beach, arriving on the night of Thursday, January 2. The Georgetown house was evidently not yet ready. They all checked into the brand-new Statler Hotel at 16th and K Streets. Sutton recalled:

> The next day, January 3, the minority whip, John McCormack, had called a caucus of Democrats. Jack got up late, and Joe Feeney, McCormack's administrative assistant, was calling and calling. Jack came down wearing a gray suit and black cashmere overcoat. His hair was tousled. He was well tanned. Ted and I were urging him to hurry, but he insisted on going to a drugstore for his two soft-boiled eggs and tea.
>
> We were in a panic, hurrying him. But then Jack said, "How long would you say McCormack's been in Washington?" I said, "At least twenty-six years." [Actually, it was about eighteen years.] Then Jack said, "I don't think he'd mind waiting another ten minutes."

When Jack got to the caucus, he learned, if he did not know before, that he had drawn two committee assignments, one routine, one exceptional for a freshman. The routine assignment was to the District of Columbia Committee, the twenty-five-man tribunal (fourteen Republicans, eleven Democrats) that served as the government of the District of Columbia, then a federal jurisdiction without a local mayor, or "home rule." The committee chairman for that Congress was the silver-tongued Ev Dirksen of Illinois, who had been in Congress since 1932.

The exceptional appointment was to the twenty-five-man (fifteen Republicans, ten Democrats) House Committee on Education and Labor.

That year, labor legislation was to receive very high priority, so the committee would be constantly in the spotlight, an important forum. Its chairman was forty-three-year-old Fred A. Hartley, Jr., of New Jersey, who entered Congress in 1929 at age twenty-six. When James MacGregor Burns interviewed Jack for his book, Jack could not recall how he got this appointment.

Jack's appointment caused surprise—and comment—in Boston. On January 17 Wiliam Mullins, the influential political columnist for Boston's Republican-oriented *Herald*, wrote, "Into this dangerous post the inexperienced Boston freshman has been cast and there are two views on the motive behind the assignment which he did not seek. One is that it was a hostile act designed to destroy him and the other was that it was a friendly act to give him a chance to show his mettle at the outset and thus make him or break him. . . . "

There was a third assignment for Jack which was also important. The House Veterans' Affairs Committee, chaired by a woman, Edith Norse Rogers, had formed a Special Subcommittee on Veterans' Housing. This subcommittee was composed entirely of war veterans. On January 22 Jack was asked to serve on this subcommittee in addition to his two primary committees. He did.

On his arrival in Washington, Sutton recalled, Jack was invited to appear on CBS and NBC network radio shows which were introducing new Congressmen. After the caucus with McCormack, Jack, Billy, and Ted went to the National Press Club to appear on a program arranged by Martin Agronsky. Among the freshmen Congressmen present was Richard Nixon, whom Billy had already met on the Hill. Nixon, too, had been appointed to the prestigious Education and Labor Committee (Nixon the junior Republican, Jack the junior Democrat). Sutton recalled, with a sense of history, "I then introduced Jack to Dick Nixon."

Jack was assigned office space in the Old House Office Building, a two-room suite, Room 322. Sutton recalled that it was "freshman row" and "about as far from the Capitol building as you could get." Republican Thruston Morton was across the corridor. Democrat George Smathers and a comer from South Carolina, an Air Force veteran named William Jennings Bryan Dorn, a year older than Jack, were nearby. So was the twenty-seven-year-old George Sarbacher from Philadelphia.

There was an immediate need for help—a bright, hardworking secretary who knew her way around the Hill. Billy Sutton recalled:

> We didn't have anybody, so I called Joe Feeney in McCormack's office and they sent us a gal named Mary McCarthy, who was hoping to get an appointment in the Foreign Service and then be married. So we asked for another gal and they sent Mary Davis, who overlapped with Mary McCarthy for a while.

Mary Davis was unbelievable. She could answer the phone, type a letter, and eat a chocolate bar all at once. She was the complete political machine, knew everybody, how to get anything done. She stayed six years, until Jack went to the Senate, and she was a godsend. When Mary Davis came in, you could have let twelve people go.

People were always trying to bad-mouth Jack and McCormack's relationship. It was not so. McCormack was a great help to us, a gracious, understanding man, the kindest man I ever knew in politics. Jack always referred to him, deferentially, as Mr. McCormack. Jack's mother was *very* close to McCormack, had great affection for him. If he'd been against us, he could have screwed us, but he never did. His office never once said no to anything I ever wanted, no matter how complicated. When we first got there, Joe Feeney took me by the hand and walked me all over the Hill, introducing me to all the key people. Then he gave us Mary Davis. . . .

We looked up Mary Davis who was, in 1974, administrative assistant to Congressman Benjamin Rosenthal, of New York, and a very important and busy woman on the Hill. We found Mary Davis everything Sutton had said: bright, wise, cheerful. It is probably no exaggeration to say that during the six years Jack spent in the House, she was his right arm, boss of the Washington Office, and chief organizer.

Mary was born in Washington, D.C., one of six children of Calvin C. Davis, an economist with the Federal Trade Commission. Her parents were older (thirty-eight and thirty-five) when they married. In addition to their own six children, they raised three others, nine in all. They all lived in a big brownstone house near downtown Washington. Mary was baptized a Catholic, attended parochial schools, was graduated from high school in 1936—a year after Jack was graduated from Choate. Then she went to a business school (taught by nuns) for a year. She loved horses, but the family could not afford to give her one when she was growing up. She made up for it later. In 1974, she had a full dozen stabled on a farm in Maryland and riding was her abiding passion.

After her schooling, Mary embarked on a full-time career and did not marry. She worked first for a Washington attorney. In January, 1939, she took a job on the Hill as secretary to an elderly Congressman from the Bronx, James M. Fitzpatrick. After that, she served two other Congressmen, Charles A. "Doc" Eaton, from New Jersey, and Charles R. Savage, from Washington state, who was unseated after one term, in November, 1946. This left Mary temporarily out of a job. Then she got a call from McCormack's office.

She told us:

I went in and talked to Jack and I liked him very much. He had just come back from the war, and wasn't in topnotch physical shape. He was such a skinny kid! He had malaria, or yellow jaundice or whatever, and his back problem, and he was rather lackadaisical. He wore the most godawful suits. Horrible-looking, hanging from his frame. He was not that actively involved then and was just getting used to being a member of Congress. He didn't know the first thing about what he was doing. And he'd never really been exposed to acquiring a staff before so he said when could I go to work for him? He said he'd pay me out of his own pocket—because he'd already used up all his official budget in Boston and Washington. [At the Kennedy Library we found some correspondence which indicated that Jack distributed his official budget among about six people, in Boston and Washington, then paid them an extra stipend from his own pocket.]

He offered me sixty dollars a week, which was really not that bad, but it was rather shocking to me at the time, knowing that he came from such a wealthy family. But he was a provincial New Englander and his father was the same. He'd say, "Mary, I can get any number of secretaries from Boston for sixty dollars." And I'd say, "But I'm not *any* secretary. I'm down here and I'm qualified and I have the experience, the background, and the talent." And he'd say, "We'll talk about it one of these days."

The Kennedy New York office was really the source of funding for the office. In those days Congressmen made twelve thousand dollars a year, plus a small expense allowance and they didn't have as many fringe benefits. So I was told that any expenses for Jack or the office were to be sent to Paul Murphy in New York. He had full charge of issuing checks and, of course, seldom questioned anything. Jack wasn't an extravagant guy. He lived very simply. In fact, he rarely had cash on him. I was the bank. It was, "Mary, can you lend me twenty dollars?" Or, "Mary, slip me a ten or a twenty?" and I'd wind up getting it back from Murphy. Most of the time he'd invite people to lunch or dinner and have no money and they had to pay. I would tell him he ought to carry *some* money, at least a couple of dollars, but it was too much bother. He'd always find some friend to pay for him.

While he was in the House he never did involve himself in the workings of the office. He wasn't a methodical person. Everything that came into the office was handed to me. I took care of everything. If I had any questions, I'd take them in to him at a specific time and say, "Here, what do you want me to say about that?" Nothing would land on his desk. I'd pin him down on the spot, get his decision, then do it.

One thing that really surprised me were his formal speeches. He wrote his own. He appeared to be such a disinterested guy, not involved, couldn't care less but then he'd say, "Mary, come on in." Then he would start dictating off the top of his head. The flow of language, his command of English was extraordinary. It would come out beautifully—exactly what he wanted to say. And I'd think, "This, coming from *you*?" I surprised myself, but I came to the conclusion that he was brilliant—the brightest person I've ever known.

For a while there were the four of us: Billy, Ted, Mary McCarthy, and I in the outer office. When Mary left, another girl came to replace her and so on, but Billy, Ted, and I stayed on until he went to the Senate. My desk was in the back, near the file cabinets. Ted was in front of me, then Billy. The only distinctive thing we had in the entire office was the coconut shell from the *PT-109*. It was in a plastic container. It went everywhere—and, of course, it was on Jack's desk.

When he first came, he'd never been out in the business world and his health wasn't that good. Joe had been killed and it fell to Jack to pick up the cloak and go into politics. He was sort of lost for a while. I don't think he really knew if he wanted politics—if he was going to remain with it—or what politics was going to do to him. Later, he grew to enjoy it.

He was always late, always in a rush. He was constantly traveling. It was a way of life. He—the whole Kennedy family—left clothes all over the place. He was constantly replacing or trying to retrieve his coats. He'd leave them, or his camera or radio, on a plane or on a pushcart someplace. He very rarely carried a briefcase in those days. Thank God! That would have been lost too.

He had no conception of the amount of work that came into the office. He had a very active district. Besides that, people all over Massachusetts and the United States wrote to him. Once in a while I'd get snowed under. He'd walk out and say, "Well, I'm taking off." And I'd say, "I just can't get all these letters done. I'm deluged. What am I going to do about it?" And he'd say, "Mary, you'll just have to work a little harder." And I was already working until seven or eight at night, taking work home, and working on weekends!

We asked Mary to give us her reaction to Ted Reardon and Billy Sutton. She said:

Ted was the quieter of the two and impressed me as being a very, very competent guy. A guy who had a brain but unfortunately he didn't use it that much. I used to get annoyed with him. He just wouldn't apply himself. Much of the time, he wasn't in the office. He'd say, "I'm going to the library," but he'd be off somewhere else. Much later, after Jack was killed and Ted went off on his own into federal service, he pulled himself together and has been doing a very good job. I think that's because he had to. It's unfortunate to my mind that years ago, when he started working for Jack, he didn't have that compulsion to do something. Because of the commitment Joe Junior had made to him, that he'd always have a cushion and be taken care of, he didn't have to. And it was a shame.

Billy Sutton? He was a delight. He lost his calling. He should have been on the stage or in radio or TV. He was the wittiest guy—funny, humorous. We called him the court jester. If Jack was down—needed to be bolstered—you'd say, "Billy, come in," and Billy would regale Jack with funny stories. He made the office a happy place to work: He could imitate people like a professional. He used to "do" [Congressman] Vito Marcantonio [of the American Labor Party, from New York City] so perfectly we'd break up. One of Jack's favorite stunts would be to get Billy to call George Smathers or somebody and pretend he was Marcantonio.

I'd been on the Hill for years and knew a great number of people. But Billy had a great ability for meeting people. He would buzz around the Capitol and he got to know everybody! It was good because if you needed anything, Billy always knew somebody. If he didn't know somebody, he soon would know somebody. And pretty soon everybody knew who he was, what he was, and whom he was with. He was a great asset.

During these early days in Congress Jack received some recognition which helped him politically and boosted his prestige on the Hill. In January he was named by the U.S. Junior Chamber of Commerce as one of the Ten Outstanding Men of 1946. We found evidence at the Kennedy Library which indicated to us that this coup was most probably engineered by the ambassador and his friends, notably a famous New York press agent of this era, Steve Hannagan.

It was not an easy honor to obtain. The Junior Chamber invited nominations from all over the country. They must have flowed in by the hundreds. A screening committee weeded out the unlikely bets, finalized a list of probably two dozen men, then passed it (and back-up material) up to a board of judges, composed of U.S. industrial leaders. No doubt at this point there was intense lobbying. The judges read the back-up material, then voted their choices, one to ten. The results were tabulated and the ten men with the most votes got the honor.

Steve Hannagan, who may have been in the ambassador's employ, lobbied the judges. A portion of his correspondence is on file at the Kennedy Library in a folder on this subject. He mobilized the ambassador's friend, the singer Morton Downey, to write a letter in Jack's behalf to one of the final judges, William M. Jeffers, president of the Union Pacific Railroad, who was a friend of Downey's and also evidently a friend (or client or both) of Hannagan's. On December 5, 1946, Downey wrote Jeffers a letter extolling Jack. On December 14 Jeffers wrote a "Dear Morton" letter in response, copy to Hannagan. On December 27 Jeffers wrote Hannagan that he had voted Jack number one on his list. Three days later, Hannagan wrote the ambassador this news and on January 2, the ambassador responded to Hannagan with an ecstatic telegram from Palm Beach: I SUPPOSE YOU DON'T HAVE ANYTHING TO DO WITH GUYS WHO DON'T GO THROUGH. YOU SHOULDN'T. YOUR FRIENDS CERTAINLY DO NOT. MY DEEP GRATITUDE TO YOU AND YOUR GO THROUGH FRIENDS . . . THANKS A MILLION AND HAPPY NEW YEAR.

There was more back and forth. On January 13 Hannagan sent Jeffers a copy of the ambassador's telegram. That same day, Jeffers wired Hannagan: OUR MAN WON. On January 15 Hannagan wrote Jeffers:

I was delighted to receive your wire this morning in the Joe Kennedy matter and I immediately called him at his home in Palm Beach. He was more than delighted. . . . He says you are quite a guy and that all of my friends are real loyalists. . . . He says he can't understand why he has missed you in all the years and I am going to arrange to have you together when we are all in the same territory sometime. Every good wish. Cheerfully. . . .

The final voting was as follows:

1.	John F. Kennedy	48.	
2.	Charles G. Bolte	45.	A New York veteran leader
3.	Harry M. Wismer	35.	ABC radio sportscaster
4.	Joseph A. Beirne	35.	Union leader
5.	John A. Patton	33.	Engineer
6.	Dan Duke	33.	Georgia politician
7.	Joe Louis	32.	Prize fighter
8.	Dr. Philip Morrison	31.	Professor of Physics
9.	Arthur M. Schlesinger, Jr.	29.	Historian
10.	Bill Mauldin	25.	Cartoonist

The news was released from Chicago, home of the Junior Chamber, on Sunday, January 19. It received wide newspaper publicity the following day. The *New York Times* carried it on page 11, noting that Jack received the award "for civic responsibility and fighting for veterans housing." On

January 22 the ten were honored at a banquet at the Morrison Hotel in Chicago, where Jack posed for a picture with the others present.

Sometime in late January, we believe, Jack, Billy Sutton, and Ted Reardon checked out of the Statler. Jack moved into his house in Georgetown with Eunice and the cook, Margaret Ambrose, bringing along Billy Sutton. The house soon had a new addition to the staff: a black valet, George Thomas, provided by Arthur Krock. George Thomas, in effect, replaced George Taylor, who had joined the Merchant Marine. (In his oral history at the Kennnedy Library, Krock said, "I never saw a Negro on level social terms with the Kennedys in all my years of acquaintance with them. And I never heard the subject mentioned.") Ted and Betty Jane and young Timothy moved into their own house.

Eunice, now twenty-four, was settling into her job as executive secretary for the Justice Department's Juvenile Delinquency Committee. The appointment had brought her considerable recognition. When it was announced on January 16, there was a story about it in the *New York Times* on page 20 the following day. On January 20 there was an INS profile on Eunice in Cissy Patterson's *Washington Times-Herald*. It said she had an office of her own at Justice, and "no marriage plans." *Newsweek* of January 27 carried her picture with the announcement. Papers in Massachusetts (the *Fall River Herald News* for example) also published the story.

We asked Billy Sutton why he moved in with Jack and what it was like living with the Kennedys. He told us:

> I did it mainly to save a buck. It was that or get a room someplace. I moved into a room on the third floor. Jack said it wouldn't be right if I just lived there free, like a public ward, so we agreed I would pay him two dollars a week! I don't remember he ever collected the rent, but that was the deal. I wasn't a peasant. They had this great, great cook, Margaret Ambrose. I ate my meals with the Kennedys. It was the best food in the world.
>
> Jack really had a bad stomach. He was on this Sara Jordan diet: cream of tomato soup, lamb chops, creamed chicken, et cetera. He didn't have an ulcer, but he was on an ulcer-type diet. He never ate anything like a ham sandwich or hot dog. They had this valet they got from Arthur Krock, George Thomas. Well, Margaret Ambrose would fix this really great bland lunch, a hot lunch, and George would get in the car and bring it up to the Hill every day. But Jack'd usually just pick at it—not really eat it—so I'd eat it myself.
>
> The house was fairly big and there were always people coming and going, like a Hollywood hotel. The ambassador, Rose, Lem Billings, Torby, anybody who came to Washington. You never

knew who the hell was going to be there but you got used to it. Jack and Eunice were always going off on airplanes somewhere. And Jack would always joke about me. He'd introduce me as Billy Sutton "of the Suttons from Boston." Then he'd say, jokingly, "Billy, please don't tell them how you made all your money."

I was concerned about the way Jack dressed. I had all his pink shirts, but his suits were horrible. He didn't care. He'd go on the floor of the House in khaki pants and sneakers! He had this old suit he had made in London in about 1939. It was worn out and much too small. I told him he had to get rid of it. It fit *me* pretty well, so he said he'd sell it to me for eleven dollars. Much later, he made contact with Sebastian's, a fine tailor in New York, and that's where he got his clothes. But he really didn't give a damn about clothes.

We were both bachelors then and we double-dated a lot. I got to know the gals on the Hill in the airline ticket office and places like that. Jack didn't drink, so mostly we'd go to the movies. The way he loved movies was something else. Always going to the movies. His favorite movie in those days was *Red River,* with Montgomery Clift. These dates were all pretty casual, never conspicuous. I remember once a girl said she'd already seen the picture we planned to go to. So Jack said, "Why don't you take this money and go see another picture and I'll meet you afterwards."

Of his dating, Mary Davis had this to say:

I don't know where the rumors got started that he was such a dater—a swinger. He couldn't have been less interested in girls, really. He dated very infrequently. He wasn't that interested in exerting himself. His idea of a big date was to call up one of the airline stewardesses and go to a movie! Margaret Ambrose would fix dinner for them, they'd go to the movie, then back to the house again where Margaret would have a little snack for them. That was his idea of a big date! There were plenty of girls who were serious about Jack. But he wasn't serious about them. He'd hit it off beautifully with girls, enjoy their company, but he wasn't ready—he'd not go beyond that.

Other friends had a somewhat different recollection of Jack's Washington dating. His Choate pal, Rip Horton, who visited Jack from time to time in Washington, told us:

I went to his house in Georgetown for dinner. A lovely-looking blonde from West Palm Beach joined us to go to a movie. After the movie we went back to the house and I remember Jack saying something like, "Well, I want to shake this one. She has ideas." Shortly thereafter, another girl walked in. Ted Reardon was there, so he went home and I went to bed figuring this was the girl for the night. The next morning, a completely different girl came wandering down for breakfast. They were a dime a dozen.

Tony Galluccio told us:

He was immature emotionally. He had no depth of emotion. The male side of the family were all like that. They came by it naturally—from the father, who chased anything in skirts. Girls would come around and Jack would get all excited. He was like a kid. He really liked girls. But it was just physical and social activity for him. He'd just keep moving. Italians get emotionally involved. But Kennedy never got emotionally involved. He'd sleep with a girl and then he'd have Billy take her to the airport the next day. Billy Sutton will tell you stories about that.

No, he wouldn't. Despite his falling out with Jack, Billy Sutton was the soul of discretion. He helped us tabulate a list of what we called Jack's "serious" girlfriends, but he would not talk about the one-night stands. Sutton had other things on his mind:

Football! If you could figure that out, you'd have the real key to his character. He really cherished this dream of being a great football star. He was always talking about Otto Graham of the Cleveland Browns and people like that. That's why he admired Torby and Whizzer White and Kenny O'Donnell so much, especially Torby. He had more admiration for Torby than anybody, and that went back to football at Harvard. And that was why he was always going over to the park in Georgetown to play touch—really brutal touch football games. I honestly think he'd rather have been a pro football quarterback than president.

Maybe it was because he himself was sick a lot then. Jack was in pain perhaps twenty-four hours a day, but I don't know that I knew it two hours a day. Once, I remember, we went up to Boston—we were always flying up to Boston—to the Bowdoin Street apartment. He got very, very sick. I never saw anything like it. The doctor prescribed this particular medicine which we got from a drugstore downstairs. Well, he had to take it every three hours. Bob Morey, the driver, was with us that night. So we had to try to stay awake and give Jack his medicine. I called the night man at the Bellevue Hotel and fixed it up so he telephoned me every three hours, right on the dot, all through the night. That way, we gave Jack his medicine. Then, the next day at a certain hour, he was okay. In fact, he was terrific. I never did find out what the hell was wrong with him.

The infusion of youth in the House of Representatives that spring, Sutton recalled, led to a minor change in custom. Jack, George Sarbacher, Jr., of Philadelphia, and another youthful Congressman, Marion T. Bennett, a thirty-two-year-old Republican from Springfield, Missouri, were so often mistaken for House page boys by the older members, that it was decided the pages must wear uniforms similar to those worn by Senate page boys. The uniform would be black tie, white shirt, blue serge suit—with knickers. In its issue of March 10, *Time* reported, "The pages rose as one boy. A uniform, yes. Knickers, never! The House yielded."

Jack Kennedy's life was becoming hugely complex, busy, and fragmented. He had an official and private life in Boston. He continued a social life, in New York, Palm Beach, and California. Now he began shaping an official and private life in Washington, looking up old friends, making new ones.

His appointment books—on file at the Kennedy Library—give a picture of his official or semiofficial Washington life. There were breakfasts, luncheons, cocktail and dinner dates (there is no way of knowing how many he kept) with officials of or lobbyists for veterans, housing and labor groups, and visiting Boston pols, seeking favors or the right connections. (Ted Reardon handled most of these visitors in the social sense.) There were invitations to black tie affairs at the homes of James Forrestal and the columnists Arthur Krock and Joseph Alsop; gatherings at the exclusive Chevy Chase and Metropolitan clubs. On February 18 Truman held a white House reception for new members of Congress. There were invitations to embassy parties and receptions.

However, Billy Sutton and Mary Davis told us that Jack found the official and semiofficial social life of Washington boring. He declined all but the most necessary invitations: a black tie affair at Krock's, for example. He and Eunice organized their own social set among the younger crowd in Georgetown. Some were old friends, some new. All were "bright" or "interesting" or "committed." They met for small dinner parties.

Among these—a constant fixture in the Kennedy's Georgetown House—was Robert Sargent Shriver, Jr. In 1947, Shriver, a thirty-one-year-old bachelor, held a unique position among the Kennedy friends. He was both an employee of the ambassador's and a suitor of Eunice's. Six years would go by before they were married. After that, of course, Shriver became one of Jack's principal political lieutenants in the 1960 campaign, director of the Peace Corps, ambassador to France and, in 1972, George McGovern's vice-presidential running mate.

In 1974 we interviewed Shriver, now a Washington lawyer with offices in the Watergate. It was one of the longest, most confusing interviews we have ever conducted. Shriver is a handsome, charming man, but one of the most disorganized we have ever met. Throughout the interview—it went on for five hours—he was constantly on the phone, constantly pulling visitors or office associates into his quarters (they sat in on portions of the interview), or digressing to extraneous matters. We asked him how he got involved with the Kennedys. He told us:

When I was at Yale, I met Kathleen, who dated a couple of fellows I knew quite well. After the war, I saw her again in New York at a party. She introduced me to Eunice. About that time—1946— her father had gotten together a lot of material on Joe Junior—diaries and stuff—with the idea of publishing it in *The Saturday Evening Post* or *Reader's Digest*. Eunice knew I was with *Newsweek*. Not long after that, Mr. Kennedy called and asked me to come over to the Waldorf Towers, the very splendid thirty-fifth floor, for breakfast. I read the diaries but they didn't seem publishable. They were sort of outdated, had no insights about prominent figures, and there was no color or hard news. I suggested he have them privately printed—for the family. So he said, "Okay, what do you want for breakfast?"

During breakfast he told me he'd bought the Merchandise Mart, but had no staff and asked if I might be interested in going out there to work for him. I'd never heard of the Mart, knew nothing about the real estate business, and had no idea of working for Mr. Kennedy. But I found him extremely appealing. He was very direct, very practical and down-to-earth. No pomposity. No effort at trying to impress anybody by his position. He didn't have staffs of people to call on. There were two people in the New York office. He had no overhead, no staff, no organization. His empire was in his head. So I went to work for him.

When I was heading for Chicago, I asked him what I should tell people I was supposed to be. He said I was his "personal representative," and "just keep in touch." There was a guy already there, an accountant, Wallace Ollman, who was the general manager, so I took the office next to his—Mr. Kennedy's office. I spent my time analyzing the operation—to see if it was going well. And I tried to help Ollman and his staff. Mr. Kennedy only came out there about twice a year.

After about eight months, Mr. Kennedy called me and said Eunice was going to Washington to work on juvenile crime in the Justice Department and would I please go to Washington, see what was going on and organize it. I didn't know a thing about juvenile delinquency. I put enough clothes in a suitcase for a week's stay, got on a plane, and flew to Washington and checked in at the Statler Hotel. The next day I went down to Justice to find Eunice. And I wound up staying in Washington for over a year.

It turned out Eunice had a job with no budget, no staff, didn't really have an office, and it really wasn't clear as to what her mission was. A national conference of juvenile delinquency had met and put out about eighteen task force reports on all aspects of JD. Her job was to implement all those reports. I can't remember exactly what we did, but I think we did pretty well.

I moved into a house in Georgetown on N Street with a couple of bachelors, Merle Thorpe, Jr., who was a classmate at Yale and Yale Law, and Walter T. Ridder, who was working as a correspondent for his family's newspaper chain. We had a good time. Eunice was living with Jack and they had a lot of dinner parties. That's where I first met Richard Nixon and Joe McCarthy . . . both young veterans. Nixon was a freshman Congressman, like Jack, and I saw him there several times. Joe McCarthy was a freshman Senator from Wisconsin, a colorful, dynamic, outspoken, frank, Irish-type fellow. It was natural for them—Jack and McCarthy—to be friendly. . . . It was an intelligent group. Young. Optimistic.

Another close personal friend of Jack and Eunice's in those days was a girl named Mary Pitcairn. We found her living in a lovely home in Princeton, New Jersey, where she gave us an interview. In 1951 she had married a lawyer, William Harding Jackson, who was a partner in the J. H. Whitney Company, and under Eisenhower, deputy director of the CIA. Then she married Wendell Davis, who died. A few months after our interview, she married the U.S. ambassador to Israel, Kenneth B. Keating, of New York City, who had been a freshman Congressman with Jack in 1947. Like other female friends of Jack's, Mary, in her fifties, was lithe and beautiful and intelligent. She recalled her meeting with Jack and Eunice:

I had an adorable little apartment over a garage in Georgetown. One of Sarge Shriver's roommates, Merle Thorpe, took me to dinner at Jack and Eunice's. And after that I became very close to Eunice and Jack. I was a bridesmaid in Eunice's wedding. She was highly nervous, highly geared, and worshiped Jack. I always thought she should have been a boy.

Jack was adorable, a very thoughtful, very sensitive man. I wasn't seriously dating him. I was seeing a lot of other people. You could have easily had a romance with Jack—I guess a lot of people did—but I was always on my guard. I always felt Jack was not ready to commit himself to any person; that his commitment would not be a profound one because he wasn't ready. He was flirtatious. If the lady or girl succumbed, that was part of it. But I was more interested in a serious relationship and I always knew in the back of my mind that he did not feel that way about me—or any of the girls.

I don't think Jack was ready for deep affection at this time. I don't think he was afraid of women. I think he was very idealistic—that when he made a commitment, it was going to be a romantic, idealistic one and in the meantime he was going to have light romances. And the young girls—the secretaries and the airline hostesses—they were safe grounds. They were not going to make intellectual or strong demands on him which he wasn't ready to fulfill. He was capable of it, but he was in the process of becoming a man, intellectually, in many ways. He was capable, but not ready for deep commitment, either politically or romantically.

He would come by, in typical fashion, honk his horn underneath my garage window and call out, "Can you go to the movies?" or "Can you come down to dinner?" He was not much for planning ahead. Sometimes I'd go down for dinner and he'd be having dinner on a tray in his bedroom and I'd have my dinner on a tray in his bedroom. He was resting, you see? The back brace and different things would be hanging around. Then he'd find out what was at the movies and he'd get dressed and we'd go to the movies. And I'd pay for it because he never had any money.

Mr. Kennedy always called up the girls Jack was taking out and asked them to dinner. He came down and took me to the Carleton Hotel—then the fanciest dining room in Washington. He was charming. He wanted to know his children's friends. He was *very* curious about my personal life. He really wanted to know. He asked a lot of personal questions—*extraordinarily* personal questions. And then—I'll *never* forget this—he told me a lot about Gloria Swanson, how wonderful she was and how he kept in touch with her. When he brought me home, he called her up from my apartment. She was at the Plaza Hotel in New York. He said I'm going to call her up and make a date for tomorrow night, or something. Which he did.

He did something that I heard he did to everyone. After dinner he would take you home and kiss you goodnight as though he were a young so-and-so. One night I was visiting Eunice at the Cape and he came into my bedroom to kiss me goodnight! I was in my nightgown, ready for bed. Eunice was in her bedroom. We had an adjoining bath. The doors were open. He said, "I've come to say goodnight," and kissed me. Really kissed me. It was so silly. I remember thinking, "How embarrassing for Eunice!" But beyond that, nothing. Absolutely nothing.

I think all this confused Jack. He was a sensitive man and I think it confused him. What kind of object is a woman? To be treated as his father treated them? And his father's behavior that way was blatant. There was always a young, blonde, beautiful secretary around. I think it was very confusing to Jack. When he did get involved with someone, what kind of a woman was she? Like his mother or like his father's girls?

And then his mother. I can't decide if she influenced the family or not. Of course, she never saw things or acknowledged things she didn't want to, which was great. I had the feeling that the children just totally ignored her. Daddy was it. I mean, I was the one who went out and picked her up when she was coming down to Washington for dinner. When the children went to Europe, Mr. Kennedy would come down to the boat with a couple of his Catholic legmen, but Mrs. Kennedy never did. At the Cape, Mrs. Kennedy was always by herself. You know that little house she had by the beach? She'd take her robe and her book down there. When she went to play golf, she'd go by herself. She did everything by herself. I never saw her walking with one of the children on the beach. . . . She was sort of a nonperson.

Mr. Kennedy did worry enormously about Jack's health. He was not well. At the Cape he rested an awful lot, in bed an awful lot. Mr. Kennedy was always asking him if he felt all right.

I used to go around with Jack when he gave political speeches. One night we drove over to Baltimore. He was to speak at the Congregational Church. He asked me to go in by myself—he didn't want to be seen bringing a girl to a political meeting—and sit in the back row and hold up my hand if I couldn't hear him. I had my hand up the whole time. He was the lousiest speaker! He just muttered and muttered. He was impossible! It really amazed me later on, how he learned to speak so well.

There were always a lot of Congressmen and Senators at the Kennedy house. George Smathers, Joe McCarthy. Eunice liked McCarthy and pushed him and always had him over. He would come with that secretary, Jean Kerr. I couldn't stand McCarthy. One night Eunice called and asked me to dinner, and came over to pick me up. I thought we were going to her house, but when I got in the car, she said we were going to McCarthy's—that he was going to cook a steak in his backyard. I couldn't go. I just couldn't go to that man's house.

Jack and Eunice had wonderful parties. We played a lot of games—charades, murder, sardines, twenty questions, and so on. I remember Claiborne Pell, now a Senator, who was in the State Department. Really amusing guy who used to wear a Sherlock Holmes outfit. And they saw a lot of the young crowd at the British Embassy: George and Patsy Jellicoe and a girl they'd known in London before the war, Dinah Brand. Dinah was then married to a really kooky American, Littleton Fox. She divorced him and married an Englishman named Bridge. Dinah would have made a wonderful wife for Jack. She was aristocratic. The Kennedys admired true aristocratic intellectuals and she was both. But . . .

Jack made many good friend friends on the Hill. But the Congressman he liked best, and became closest to in these years, was George Armisted Smathers, of Miami, Florida. He would be one of Jack's ushers in the wedding—the only politician so honored.

George Smathers was a tall (six feet, three inches) handsome "comer," then thirty-three years old, one of three children of a Miami judge who was also an Establishment lawyer. George went to public high school—Miami High—then to the University of Florida, graduating in 1936. At both these institutions, he was a star athlete (football, baseball, basketball), class or student body president, skilled debater, and a lady killer, known as "Gorgeous George" or "Smooch."

George went on to law school at the university. In 1939 he was appointed an Assistant District Attorney in Miami. During the war George joined the Marine Corps and served with a Marine air squadron in the Solomons. Discharged in 1945, George came back to Miami, and in 1946, ran and unseated a four-term Congressman, Pat Cannon. One of George's most ardent campaign workers in that race was Bebe Rebozo, a schoolmate from Miami High. Unaccountably, James MacGregor Burns (and others parroting Burns) described Smathers as a "bachelor" who accompanied Jack on dates in Washington in his early days in Congress. In fact, Gorgeous George had married a Miami girl, Rosemary Townley, before the war. When he went to Washington in 1947, his wife and two young sons, John and Bruce, went with him.

Smathers would go on to the U.S. Senate in 1950. In that body, he was known as a Southern conservative, whose Miami law firm represented big businesses—airlines, railroads, real estate developers—and Latin American interests. In 1968 Smathers declined to stand for reelection and thereafter concentrated his energies on his law practice, with offices in Washington and Miami. He and Rosemary divorced and George married a much younger woman.

We met Smathers at the Key Biscayne Hotel, where he maintains a permanent residence in a "villa" on the Atlantic Ocean. We found him at six-

ty-two graying but still handsome and athletic. (He is an excellent golfer.)
He spoke with a Southern accent, measuring his words carefully:

I'd met Jack's father in Miami at the Hialeah racetrack in 1946
when I was running for Congress, but not Jack. Right after the
Eightieth Congress convened, I met Jack. His office was near
mine. In those days he was a rather sickly fellow. In addition to his
bad back he was constantly plagued with colds and one thing or
another—constantly laid up. If you had to pick a member of that
freshman class who would probably wind up as president, Kennedy was probably the *least* likely. He was so shy he could hardly
tell you his name. One of the shyest fellows I'd ever seen. But we
had a natural chemical reaction. I liked him and he liked me. Our
offices were close by. We had a lot in common. We'd walk to the
floor together to vote, talking about legislation, events of the day,
girls, and so on. And he was always coming to Florida, so we'd
take those long, long plane rides together. Sometimes he stayed
with me—or I'd go up to Palm Beach.

He told me he didn't like being a politician. He wanted to be a
writer. He admired writers. Politics wasn't his bag at all. Joe Junior
was supposed to be the politician. When he got killed, the father
turned to Jack with some reluctance and said, "You're the one,
you're the next eldest and you're going to do it." So Jack found
himself running. He told me the agony he suffered in going around
sticking out his hand to people he'd never met, never seen, and
saying, "I'm Jack Kennedy. I'm a candidate for Congress." And
they'd look at him (and think) "Why, you're not old enough to be
the baby-sitter." It was quite an embarrassment to him in those
days, because he was very, very shy and diffident by nature.

Eunice was down in Washington with Jack. Of all the kids in the
family, Eunice was far and away the strongest minded. Sort of the
leader of the clan. Very tough when she wanted to be. Eunice
would have loved to be the one the father picked to run in the Eleventh Congressional District in 1946. If she'd been a little older, and
if it had been like today, when a lot of women are running for
office, I suspect the history of the Kennedy clan would have been
quite different. You might have seen Eunice as the first woman
Congressman from that district.

Jack was a very good student. He loved to read. He took rapid
reading courses. He knew a lot about economics—more than his
father's people gave him credit for. He had a very conservative
economic philosophy, which constantly surprised me not only
when we first met, but later on in the Senate. Sometimes the posi-

tions he'd take would be much more conservative than the positions I'd take. Of course he was getting a great deal of input from the father and the father's financial friends.

He admired his daddy very much. I don't know that he liked him a great deal, but he admired him for the things he'd done. He never said that in so many words, but if you were around him a good deal, as I was, you couldn't help but get the feeling that he admired his daddy's business accomplishments. But I'm not sure if he approved of him in some respects. Joe Kennedy was a hard-nosed fellow, ambitious, pugnacious. Bobby was like him. Jack was much sweeter, softer, thoughtful and tender.

During these early days in the U.S. House, Smathers also became good friends with Republican Dick Nixon. A Miami legend has it that it was Smathers who first introduced Nixon to Bebe Rebozo, and after that Bebe and Nixon went on to be best friends. Bebe even changed his political registration from Democrat to Republican. When Bebe organized the Key Biscayne compound, George's house (which Nixon bought) became one of the five structures comprising it. We asked George about the legend—and also if Bebe had met Jack Kennedy. He said:

I'll be very frank with you. I *thought* I introduced Nixon to Bebe. The way I remember it, in the winter of 1948 or 1949, Nixon had a bad cold. He was sneezing and coughing and I said, "You ought to go down to Florida and sit in the sun." I couldn't go, but I told him I'd fix him up with friends who could take him fishing and so on. So I called Bebe, a bachelor with a pad and boat, and told him to take care of Nixon. Show him a good time. But now, a lot of other friends of mine claim they introduced them—and I'm really confused about it. Nowadays, Bebe himself likes to think it was like the birth of Jesus to the Virgin Mary. Nobody introduced them. Nixon just appeared out of the clouds!

Later, Bebe met Jack. Jack liked Bebe. I don't know that Bebe ever took him out on the boat. Jack's family had boats in Palm Beach—bigger and better than Bebe's. Bebe was a Democrat in those days. He entertained a lot of Democrats down here—Lyndon Johnson, Dick Russell, Stu Symington, and so on. But, of course, Bebe and Jack were not good friends.

In Washington, and later in Florida, Jack became really good friends with one of my aides, Grant Stockdale, who was in my Washington office about a year. Grant was a really handsome, gregarious, outgoing type of guy—a poor boy from Mississippi who was a football star at the university of Miami. A very likable guy.

He and Jack had a lot of chemistry. Jack used to see a lot of him when he came to Florida, and, of course, in 1961, appointed him ambassador to Ireland.

Jack liked girls. He liked girls very much. He came by it naturally. His daddy liked girls. He was a great chaser. Jack liked girls and girls liked him. He had just a great way with women. He was such a warm, lovable guy himself. He was a sweet fella, a really sweet fella. It was very rare you'd see him get real tough and hard-boiled.

Smathers left an exceptionally good oral history at the Kennedy Library, from which we had taken extensive notes. Among the many useful items in this recollection, Smathers recalled the men in Congress in those days whom Jack most admired. What struck us was that all of them, like Smathers, were conservatives. In the Senate, Smathers recollected, Jack "admired Bob Taft the most." After Taft came the Southern conservative Richard Russell of Georgia, Lyndon Johnson of Texas, and Spessard Holland of Florida.

His relations with Nixon were "very cordial" but, Smathers recalled, "I think Nixon had a greater admiration for Kennedy than Kennedy had for Nixon." Smathers said Kennedy had known McCarthy "some time" before McCarthy became famous: "I don't know whether it was through the Catholic Church angle, or what it was, but I always had the feeling that Jack Kennedy was very sympathetic to Joe—not with what Joe was saying—but sympathetic to Joe as a person. . . . Jack liked him personally." On Mississippi's white-supremacist John E. Rankin, senior Democrat on the House Veterans' Affairs Committee: "Kennedy *liked* Rankin." Smathers recalled a time Rankin good-naturedly chewed them out:

Rankin said to us one day, "You young boys go home too much. I've got my people convinced that the Congress of the United States can't run without me. I don't go home during the session because I don't want them to find out any different. You fellows are home every week—you're never around here. You're always going somewhere. And your people are finally going to realize the Congress can run just as good without you. And then you're in trouble." We laughed—but I don't doubt that in some ways it was a very true statement.

42

The Red Menace

CONGRESS faced many controversial issues. Foremost among them was the question of subversion. To what extent had Communism penetrated the government and social fabric of the United States? The 80th. Congress decided the penetration was deep and dangerous. It declared war on Communism at home. It was a war that would gather momentum in the first session of the 80th and go on, building in intensity, for years. There is no need to rehearse this well-known history here, nor to list the men and women in all walks of life—but principally government service and the arts and entertainment—whose careers were shattered, nor the others whose reputations were made, by this tidal wave of anti-Communism. The question would dominate the Congress and the American people as Watergate dominated in 1973-1974. Even more than Watergate, it spawned seemingly endless and confusing Congressional investigations, federal and state trials, libel suits and other legal actions. It all added up to one of the most painful—and shameful—periods in U.S. history.

In 1952, when Jack Kennedy was running for the U.S. Senate, presidential candidate Adlai Stevenson asked a Massachusetts audience, "I wonder how many of you know that it was Congressman Kennedy and not Senator Nixon who got the first citation of a Communist for perjury?"

We'll say this: until we began this research, we certainly didn't know it. It is not part of the Jack Kennedy mythology. He did not boast of it in his 1960 presidential campaign, as Nixon did about the Alger Hiss case. In fact, we had never thought of Jack as a "Communist hunter." What was this all about?

It turned out to be a rather complicated story, barely touched on in the Kennedy literature. Almost everybody involved is now deceased, so we could get no firsthand recollections. We relied on some congressional documents, court records, and the *New York Times* and other newspapers.

Soon after his assignment to the House Education and Labor Committee, Jack met and became close friends with another freshman Congressman on the committee, Republican Charles J. Kersten, age forty-five, from Milwaukee, Wisconsin. Kersten was a lawyer, a Catholic, and a conservative. He was also good friends with Dick Nixon, the junior Republican on the committee. Both Kersten and Nixon were then educating themselves to the Communist conspiracy. One of their teachers was a Catholic priest, a labor expert, John F. Cronin, then assigned to the National Catholic Welfare Conference in Washington—a lobby for the Catholic Church. (As Gary Wills points out in his book, *Nixon Agonistes*, it was Cronin who first put Nixon onto the Hiss case.)

Charlie Kersten had a problem in his district. A large manufacturer, Allis-Chalmers, had had a strike on its hands for months. The leaders of the strike were said to be Harold Christoffel, thirty-five-year-old former president of United Auto Workers Union, Local 248, and its current president, the man who had succeeded Christoffel, Robert Buse. By March 1, 1947, Allis-Chalmers told newspapers, the strike had cost the company about $70 million. It had caused bitter controversy in Milwaukee. Allis-Chalmers wanted it stopped.

Kersten had information indicating that both Christoffel and Buse were Communists, or had been Communists. The word was that in 1941, Christoffel, then president of Local 248, had called a seventy-six-day strike against Allis-Chalmers, then engaged in war production. Kersten believed that this strike had been directed through the U.S. Communist Party by the Soviet Union, then allied with Germany. The purpose of the strike, as Kersten saw it, was to delay the completion of matériel which would be used for the military mobilization then in progress.

After the organization of the House Education and Labor Committee, the chairman, Fred Hartley, appointed a subcommittee whose purpose was to investigate Communist infiltration of labor unions. The chairman of the subcommittee was Charlie Kersten. The other two members were freshman Republican Thomas L. Owens, a forty-nine-year-old lawyer and labor expert from Chicago, and Jack Kennedy.

This little subcommittee seems to have directed almost all of its energies toward the Allis-Chalmers situation. It went after Christoffel and Buse hammer and tongs. Christoffel would argue later that its whole purpose was to break the current strike by defaming him and Buse.

By March 1, a Saturday, the subcommittee had information enough to pursue the matter before the full Labor Committee and had called both Christoffel and Buse (along with others) to appear at 10 in the morning. Christoffel said he was ill and could not make the morning session; he appeared in the afternoon. Although it was an odd time for a congressional committee to be meeting, fourteen of the twenty-five members showed up, constituting a quorum, which meant the committee was officially in business. However, as the afternoon dragged on, some of the fourteen drifted off—and this would become an important point in the legal hassle which was to follow.

We examined the published transcript of the committee hearings for that afternoon. Jack put some questions to the first witness, a union official, but when Christoffel testified, Jack was either not present or remained silent. The senior Republican and presiding committee chairman, Clare E. Hoffman, an experienced trial lawyer from Michigan, did all the questioning. He asked Christoffel if he was or had ever been a member of the Communist Party or the Communist Political Association or had worked with either of those organizations. To all these questions, Christoffel answered, "No, sir." At about 5 in the afternoon the committee adjourned.

The hearings resumed with Christoffel on Monday, March 3. According to the transcript, Jack asked sharp questions, showing he had done his homework. His questions seem designed to show that when Christoffel led his local on strike in 1941, he was being responsive to shifts in Soviet foreign policy. Christoffel denied all, and the matter ended, it seems to us, in a draw.

The Christoffel matter had so far generated little attention. On Sunday, March 2, the *New York Times* had a very brief story on page 44, with no mention of Christoffel's testimony. On March 4, at the tag end of a story on an impending telephone strike, there was mention that the committee would call the former editor of the Communist *Daily Worker*—now an ex- and anti-Communist—Louis F. Budenz. He appeared and testified that both Christoffel and Buse were Communists, that the Communist Party had ordered the 1941 strike, and that Christoffel had carried out these orders.

Immediately following the Budenz testimony, on March 13, Jack Kennedy rather precipitously asked the committee to recommend perjury indictments against Christoffel and Buse. Several of Jack's colleagues seconded the motion, but the presiding chairman that day, Republican Gerald W. Landis, of Indiana, ruled the motion "out of order at this time." This exchange was noted in the *Times* on March 14, on page 16, buried in an entirely different story headlined, POLICE ARE BLAMED IN LABOR RACKETS. On the weekend of March 15-16, Kersten and the subcommittee staff removed themselves to Milwaukee for further intensive investigation of Christoffel, Buse, and Local 248. Jack could not be present immediately. Monday, March 17, was St. Patrick's Day in Boston, a command performance. We found a photograph and a story in the Boston papers for Saturday, March 15, showing the arrival at Logan Airport of Senators Henry Cabot Lodge, Jr., Leverett Saltonstall, Joseph R. McCarthy, and Congressman Jack Kennedy. The story said all would be present that night for Boston's famous Clover Club dinner. Presumably they marched in the parades on Monday.

The subcommittee staff was busy in Milwaukee. On Sunday, March 16, the *Times* carried a full story on page 31, reporting that Christoffel had been fired from his job at Allis-Chalmers because of his testimony. (Buse had been fired previously.) On Tuesday, March 18, the *Times* reported on page 28 that Kersten and Owens had arrived in Milwaukee and the staff had demanded records from Local 248. On March 20, page 23, the *Times* reported Owens as saying from Milwaukee, "Falsehoods have been told here and we have proof of them." There was no mention of Jack Kennedy in any of these stories.

But Jack was there by March 19. The *Milwaukee Journal* of March 20 is crammed with stories about the subcommittee hearings, including two full-page picture spreads. There were photographs and drawings of Jack inside—and outside—the hearings, looking very somber and businesslike.

The Christoffel case dropped out of the news until late May, when the subcommittee filed its report. A front-page story in the *Times* on June 1 carried the meat of the report, which was signed by Kersten, Owens and Kennedy. It stated that, "At the direction of the Communist Party and for the purpose of carrying out its programs, Harold Christoffel called a 76-day strike at Allis-Chalmers" in 1941. There was "conclusive evidence," the report went on, that Christoffel "willfully and feloniously testified falsely" under oath about his past Communist affiliations before the full House Education and Labor Committee on March 1 and 3. The current strike, the report noted, was called by some "Communist inspired."

The Department of Justice took over from there. The subcommittee data was turned over to a federal grand jury. On July 23, 1947, the grand jury handed down an indictment of Christoffel for perjury. He was tried the following spring in Washington. On March 3, 1948, a jury found Christoffel guilty on six counts of perjury—for denying he was a member of the Communist Party and the Communist Political Association or that he supported those groups, and for denying he knew a couple of key Communists in Wisconsin.

Christoffel's attorney, O. John Rogge, formerly an assistant U.S. attorney general, appealed all the way to the Supreme Court on a technicality: that when Christoffel had denied being a Communist, etc., there was not a quorum present and therefore the committee was not officially in session. Hence no perjury could have been committed. On June 27, 1949, the Supreme Court upheld Christoffel 5-4, with the ambassador's (and Jack's) friend, Justice Frank Murphy writing the majority opinion. The majority also consisted of Hugo L. Black, Felix Frankfurter, William O. Douglas, and Wiley Rutledge. Justice Robert H. Jackson filed a very strong dissent from the majority opinion, joined by Chief Justice Fred Vinson, Stanley Reed, and Harold Burton. Jack joined conservative Republican Samuel McConnell of Pennsylvania in issuing a statement deploring the decision as "most regrettable" and a "travesty on justice."

Following the decision, in a Sunday piece on July 3, 1949, Arthur Krock attempted to give Jack and his disappointed colleagues a lift with a story headlined, PERJURY RULING STIRS DISPUTE IN THE CAPITOL. He pointed out the dangers of the decision, the main one being that most of the time that bodies met on the Hill, members drifted away, leaving only a few in official attendance. By the Court's reasoning, most of the business on the Hill could be deemed illegal or unofficial. But we could find no further evidence that the Capitol was stirred. There was no noticeable public outcry. The case dropped from sight for months.

Christoffel was retried in Washington in early 1950. On February 23 the jury found him guilty on five counts of perjury. After years of legal wrangling, he was sentenced June 23, 1953, to serve sixteen months to four years in jail by U.S. District Court Judge F. Dickinson Letts. He maintained to the bitter end that Allis-Chalmers had used Kersten and the subcommittee as a weapon to break the 1947 strike.

As we said, the Kennedy books have almost nothing about this case. The longest account we could find was one paragraph in the James MacGregor Burns book. Burns says that Jack's call for an indictment had been "hasty" but he had been "vindicated" when Christoffel was finally sent to jail. But: "Kennedy's remark about the Supreme Court disturbed those who saw in the courts the last bulwark against violation of due process."

Christoffel was really Charlie Kersten's quarry, and not Jack's. Kersten (and the subcommittee staff) did all the work, the hard digging that led to the hearings and the follow-up efforts to get the convictions. We could find no evidence in the files that Jack spent much time or effort on the case. It seemed to us that, at most, Jack merely lent his presence to the proceedings. Kersten let Kennedy demand the indictment. But it was Kersten's pressure and work that led to the conviction and to the settlement of the strike, the prime objective, we believe.

Thus when Adlai Stevenson reminded Massachusetts voters that Jack, not Nixon, was the first to get a Communist cited for perjury, he was stretching things a bit.

Paralleling the question of Communist subversion in the United States was the question of Communist aggression abroad. Some held that all of Europe and Asia were being steadily undermined by a Kremlin-directed policy of subversion and would soon collapse. They urged the United States to do something about it—to lend money or military supplies to the threatened nations. Others argued that if there were positive evidence of Soviet aggression, it should be laid before the United Nations; the United States should not take unilateral action that might provoke the Russians to war. The issue came to a head very early in the 80th Congress and led to Jack's first public break with his father on policy.

On February 24, 1947, the British Government informed the United

States that it would no longer be the sole reservoir of support for Greece and Turkey. It was costing Britain $250 million a year in direct and indirect costs and she simply couldn't afford it.

The Soviets, who had been granted certain naval-base rights in Turkey, appeared to be pressuring Turkey for larger concessions. In Greece, it was believed, the Soviets were directing a large guerrilla army seeking to topple the right-wing government. If all financial and military aid were withdrawn, there was danger that both these countries—dominating the strategic eastern Mediterranean—would fall under control of the Soviet Union.

The Greek-Turkish situation was Harry Truman's first real foreign policy crisis. After a feverish series of meetings with his advisers (notably the Washington lawyer Clark Clifford), feisty Harry decided the United States should intervene—give help. Not a loan, but an outright grant of money and military aid. It was a radical notion. Never before in peacetime had the United States done anything like it. It was the birth of the concept of foreign aid.

On March 12, at 1 P.M., Truman went to the House of Representatives to lay his plan before a joint session of the hostile 80th Congress. Bess sat in the House gallery. Speaking with what *Time* would describe as "newly acquired forcefulness," Truman asked Congress to vote $400 million for Greece and Turkey. The audience, which included Jack Kennedy in his back-row seat, was grave. Later, in a speech, Jack recalled, "Only twice did applause break out and then it rippled fitfully across the crowded hall of Congress and died. Reporters noted that never in recent history had a presidential message been received with such a deep sense of awareness of what that message might eventually mean to the security of this country and to the peace of the world." *Time* reported that Bob Taft, sitting in the front row, "yawned prodigiously" in the middle of the speech.

Truman's proposal came to be called the Truman Doctrine. The debate over it was bitter and vehement. Liberals such as Henry Wallace and Florida's Senator Claude Pepper opposed it because they did not want to prop up the rightist governments in those two countries or risk Soviet ire by such an aggressive move. Let the United Nations deal with the problem, they argued. Conservatives, bent on cutting the federal budget, opposed it as an expensive giveaway.

The issue squarely divided Jack and his father. Jack favored the Truman Doctrine; his father opposed it. The ambassador "went public" with his views, earnestly trying to persuade the Congress to vote down the doctrine, while Jack was publicly speaking in favor of it. The Senior Kennedy's stand evoked public countersallies from liberal-internationalists such as Harvard's Arthur Schlesinger, Jr.

The ambassador first surfaced with his views in the *New York Times* in a silly, verbose story written by Arthur Krock from Palm Beach on the day Truman addressed the joint session of Congress, March 12. Writing the day before, Krock said:

Ever since the perfection of the long distance telephone the number of men active in large affairs who spend much of the winter in this region has greatly increased, and the arrival of commercial air transport has added to their ranks. One of the aspects of American capitalism is that citizens who have attained great power and influence can continue to exercise both for days at a time in places distant from their normal headquarters.

An ambitious young American might very well conclude that a system which rewards hard work and native talent in this fashion before the end of the activity or influence of these self-made men—for nearly all are such—is worth striving to maintain and to share. . . .

Krock went on to draw a picture of Ambassador Kennedy, Bernard Baruch, and other others sitting around Palm Beach, pulling strings that moved the government in Washington. (In her memoirs of her father, Margaret Truman points out that Truman refused to see Baruch in this period. "I'm not going to spend hours and hours on that old goat, come what may," Truman memoed. But Baruch, or his ghost-writer Herbert Bayard Swope, made one memorable contribution to the times. On April 16 Baruch said, "Let us not be deceived—today we are in the midst of a Cold War." This phrase caught hold as firmly as Churchill's "Iron Curtain.") Krock described a "round table" which the ambassador dominated, setting forth his views on foreign policy. They were, basically, that since the United States already had $100 billion in short-term internal obligations, it could not possibly afford to finance resistance to other forms of government. The wiser policy, Kennedy argued, was to keep the American way of life as strong as possible and (in Krock's words) "permit Communism to have its trial outside the Soviet Union if that shall be the fate or will of certain peoples. In most of these countries a few years will demonstrate the inability of Communism to achieve its promises, while throughout this period the disillusioned experimenters will be observing the benefits of the American way of life, and most of them will then seek to emulate it."

In sum: isolationism. (Kennedy's views, as reported by Krock, were picked up and published in the *Time* issue of March 24. *Time* commented, "The argument had a faintly early-1941 ring.")

On March 27 Jack made his first major speech on foreign policy, before the Carolina Political Union at the University of North Carolina at Chapel Hill. On April 1 he inserted it in the *Congressional Record.* "I support the

President's proposal for assistance to the Governments of Greece and Turkey," he said. Directly opposing the views of his father, he assumed a tough-minded posture:

> Long a cornerstone of our foreign policy has been the belief that American security would be dangerously threatened if the continent of Europe or that of Asia were dominated by any one power. We fought in 1917 when it appeared that Germany would break the thinning lines of the French and the British and win through to domination of the European continent. We fought again in 1941 to oppose the domination of Asia by the empire of Japan. We fought in Europe to prevent the fall of Britain and of Russia and the consequent subjugation of Europe and Africa and the Middle East.
>
> The atomic bomb and guided missile has not yet weakened that cornerstone. We would still fight, I believe, to prevent Europe and Asia from becoming dominated by one great military power and we will oppose bitterly, I believe, the suffering people of Europe and Asia succombing to the false, soporific ideology of Red totalitarianism. . . .

He went on in well-reasoned, well-written prose to meet the main objections to the Truman Doctrine, stating that the aid would not increase prospects of war with the Soviets; the U.N. did not have the capability of dealing with the problem at that time; the doctrine would not necessarily prop up an "undemocratic and reactionary" Greek Government.

In sum: internationalism.

The ambassador turned to his old pal William Randolph Hearst to further spread his negative views on the Truman Doctrine. In an interview with Hearst columnist Frank Conniff, published in the Hearst newspaper chain on April 30, he said, "I decided to admit from now on that the term 'isolationist' described my sentiments perfectly. We never gave isolationism a chance. The 'interventionists' had their way and look what happened. I'm proud I warned against participation in a war which could only leave the world in a worse condition than before. . . . ."

On April 22, the Senate, guided by the work of the internationalist Arthur Vanderberg, passed the Truman Doctrine by a vote of 67 to 23. The House debated for another two weeks. On May 9 it voted 287-107 for passage, after a plan to give some money to Chiang Kai-shek had been tacked on. Jack voted for the doctrine.

In late April, Secretary of State George Marshall returned from Europe in a pessimistic mood. He thought the Russians were, as Truman quoted him in his memoirs, "coldly determined to exploit the helpless condition of Europe to further Communism." Marshall brought the grim news that all Europe, wracked by a terrible winter, was in economic chaos. It might

not even make it through the following winter. (On May 14 Winston Churchill asked, "What is Europe now? It is a rubble heap, a charnel house, a
breeding ground of pestilence and hate.") Marshall established a policy
planning staff, headed by the Soviet expert George Kennan, to come up
with solutions.

This body, working in feverish haste, produced a broad plan for Europe's survival. The heart of it was a scheme for massive foreign aid for
all European countries, including Soviet-occupied territory. Undersecretary of State Dean Acheson first broached the plan May 8 in Cleveland,
Mississippi. In a carefully detailed analysis of the world economy—and
the capability of the United States—he proposed that $17 billion in U.S.
funds be earmarked for Europe over the next four years.

Acheson's speech went almost unnoticed. The ambassador, for one,
must have missed it. On May 18 he sounded off in the Business Section of
the *New York Times* in a story headlined KENNEDY URGES U.S. TO CLARI-
FY POLICY. He was worried about what it was all going to cost and the
ability of the country to survive the giveaway. "The government must
honestly tell the people pretty soon what the overall cost of stopping
Communism abroad is likely to be. . . . Personally as I have said before
I believe our efforts to stem Communism in Europe with dollars will eventually prove an overwhelming tax on our resources that will seriously
affect the economic well-being of our country."

Arthur Krock brought it all into focus in a column in the *Times* two
days later, May 20. He reminded his readers that Baruch, Kennedy, and
others had been demanding a national "balance sheet" and a candid statement of what the United States intended to spend long-range. Now, said
Krock, Acheson had provided what they had demanded.

But the ambassador did not like the Acheson proposal either. On May
25 he published a long, windy article in the Hearst chain, urging a more
careful study. "The dangers at home," he wrote, "are far more real to
me. Concretely I regard as dangerous a public policy which rushes headlong into tax burdening expenditures abroad and does nothing to bring
about tax relief at home."

Truman now rolled out his biggest gun. On June 4, at Harvard to accept
an honorary degree, Secretary of State George Marshall restated the concept Acheson had broached in Mississippi. This speech did not go unnoticed. It electrified the world. Thereafter the concept, at Truman's insistence, came to be known as the Marshall Plan.

Now, a curious turn occurred in the ambassador's public life. In the
summer of 1947, Truman, dissatisfied with the slipshod overlapping structure of the U.S. Government, asked former President Hoover to head up
a special commission to study the government and recommend ways of
simplifying and streamlining it. The commission would be made up of
men recommended by the Executive Branch, the Senate, and the House.

Senate President Pro Tem Arthur Vandenberg picked the men the Senate would recommend. Among them: Joseph P. Kennedy, and Senators George D. Aiken and John L. McClellan, Dr. James K. Pollack, a political scientist from Michigan. House Speaker Joe Martin named James H. Rose, Jr., former executive assistant to FDR, Congressmen Clarence J. Brown and Carter Manasco. Truman named George H. Mead, Forrestal, Arthur Fleming, Dean Acheson, and Douglas Southall Freeman.

We thought Joe Kennedy's return to the federal government for the first time since 1940, was news of a sort and wondered how and why it came about. The ambassador's biographers pass over it rapidly. Whalen does not even mention it; Koskoff only fleetingly. The *New York Times,* which carried the commission story on page 1 on July 17, does not attempt to explain it. Nor did Krock or anybody else at a later date, that we could discover.

Senator Vandenberg was then leading the drive in the Senate for foreign aid. Had he invited the ambassador into the government to co-opt him out of his isolationist stand on foreign aid?

If so, there are some signs that it may have worked. In the *Times* of September 14 that year, Arthur Krock had a big story suggesting that Kennedy had changed his position. Krock wrote that Kennedy, "convinced now that the Government and the American people are determined on an economic aid program of some sort," had proposed a new idea: authorize only $5 billion for a one-year trial period, with the understanding that if some strict conditions were met, more money would be forthcoming. Two of the conditions: that Germany be allowed to reestablish its industrial production—short of a warmaking potential—and that the people of all nations work hard and long hours and try to stabilize their economies. Koskoff writes that the ambassador did not like the idea of excluding Spain (as was the plan) and that Jack disagreed with his father about reindustrializing Germany.

Truman had hoped to push the Marshall Plan through in the first session of the 80th Congress. But that was not to be. It was too radical an idea; the 80th was still in a doubting mood. A great many wanted to go to Europe and examine conditions firsthand after Congress adjourned. So, the matter was put off for the time being. A committee of members of the Cabinet and Senate, known as the Harriman Committee, was formed to make a detailed study of Europe's needs and the capability of the United States to help. And many members of Congress, including Jack Kennedy, began making reservations for passage to Europe for late summer.

43

Congressman

J ACK turned to the housing bills before Congress. Housing was a very
hot issue.

In his summary of Jack's House and Senate years, James MacGregor
Burns notes that one of Jack's most clearly discernible political traits was
his cool. He could not find a case where Jack had been emotionally or pas-
sionately committed to an issue. Intellectually yes, but not with the heart.
But the housing issue may have been an exception to this general rule. We
think Jack, having seen the miserable living conditions in his district in the
1946 race, had been genuinely concerned. In pursuing the issue, he took
some political risks.

To assist in formulating a campaign to mobilize public opinion in favor
of public housing, Jack turned to John Galvin, the PR man with the Dowd
advertising agency who had helped Jack in his House race. The Dowd
agency had been retained by Governor Tobin for his 1946 race for reelection and also had one or two state accounts probably arranged by Tobin.
When Tobin was swamped by Bradford, the Dowd agency fell on financial hard times. Galvin had gone to work as a PR man for the Massachusetts Federation of Taxpayers, a sort of consumer watchdog outfit. He
told us in our interview, "The housing bill was a very big issue. The housing crisis was worse in a way than the energy crisis today. Every veteran
was doubling up or living with his mother-in-law. You can't imagine the
conditions. It was *the* issue that was grabbing people. The newspapers
had all appointed columinists to write about veterans' issues and gave the
housing situation a lot of space. So Jack went after it."

In a series of speeches that spring, some of them inserted in the *Congressional Record,* Jack painted an alarming picture: During the depression years, 1930–1940, while the U.S. population continued to grow at a
substantial pace, the housing industry built only about 250,000 units a
year. The result was an annual shortage of about 600,000 to 700,000 units.
The existing housing was getting older every year, much of it falling into
the substandard category. During the six years of the war—1940 to 1946—
only a handful of homes were built for private use. Result: by 1946, the
housing shortage was acute; as Galvin said, a crisis of major magnitude.

537

At the beginning of 1947 there were 2.2 million married couples in urban areas doubled up in homes with other families, and about 300,000 couples living in hotels, rooming houses, tourists camps, or similar places. A disproportionate number of them were veterans. In Boston, for example, in July, 1946, about 42 percent of the city's married vets were doubled up. Studies undertaken in the Democrat-controlled 79th Congress had shown that to overcome the crisis, the country needed to build about 1.5 million new homes a year. But it was already clear when the 80th Congress convened that the housing industry—hobbled in many areas by antique building codes that prohibited cheaper, mass-construction techniques—could never meet the demand. Moreover, when price controls were removed from the housing industry, the cost of housing zoomed. Veterans could not afford to buy them.

The Wagner-Ellender-Taft Housing Bill, which became in the Republican 80th Congress the Taft-Ellender-Wagner Housing Bill, was designed to help overcome the crisis. It was basically a long-range program which would provide federal money to help low-income groups (including veterans) by (1) slum clearance and (2) construction of public housing units. Rent controls were still in effect, and the T-E-W Bill would continue rent controls on federally financed units.

There was much opposition to this bill in the 80th Congress. Conservative Republicans and Democrats opposed it on philosophical grounds. It was not the federal government's business, they argued, to house the less fortunate members of society; that was more New Deal socialism or welfarism. The real estate and home construction lobbies opposed it out of simple greed. For every public housing unit constructed, there would be one less private unit needed and therefore less profit for the industry. Finally, many Republicans believed the 1946 election had given them a clear mandate to cut the federal budget—*reduce*, not increase, federal spending.

As we have seen, since the VFW national encampment at Boston in September, 1946, Jack had been committed to the W-E-T or T-E-W Bill. Now his strategy was to push the T-E-W Bill through the reluctant 80th Congress. Galvin recalled:

Jack called me from Florida and asked if I could come down to Washington and work on the Housing Bill for about three months. My boss, Norman MacDonald, was very generous. He said, "Work out a deal; go down for two or three days a week but don't take money." So in the winter or spring of 1947, I would go down to Washington on the train—Kennedy paid for my transportation reluctantly, the way all Kennedys pay. I lived in the house with Jack and Eunice and that big Irish cook, Margaret Ambrose, who completely dominated the house and would not stand for any monkey business. No drinking. Not that there was ever any booze around anyway. She couldn't get up the stairs, but she was a marvelous cook.

I worked very closely at the office with Ted Reardon. Ted was a very bright and very talented guy. Very handsome, good athlete. But—awfully kind of beaten, you know? Really beaten by these people. He should have gotten out. But he never did. He began to goof off a little bit.

Mary Davis was the real worker in that office. Fantastic! She must have written ten million letters. And she just wanted to work and be left alone. Horses were her only interest. She used to ride all weekend and she'd get mad as hell at Kennedy if he came to town and wanted to get something done on Saturday.

And then there was Billy Sutton! He had a great deal of ability. He could get more done in Washington than Jack. He was always running around, dropping in people's offices, always on some Hill committee collecting for somebody who was sick. He was also very funny, a great imitator. I remember, late in the day, Jack would say to him, "Call Smathers and give him the Italian dialect." He'd call Smathers and give it to him and we'd all be on the telephone extensions laughing like hell. But Mary Davis never joined in those high jinks.

The Kennedys didn't handle Billy very well. I don't think Margaret Ambrose liked him. Eunice didn't either. She, or somebody, got teed off because she left her mink coat someplace—the Kennedys were always leaving things behind— and she couldn't recall where she left it, so Billy couldn't find it. Something minor like that.

Anyway, we formed a nationwide committee to promote the Housing Bill. Bob Wagner of New York [Senator Wagner's son], FDR, Jr., the war hero Audie Murphy, Will Rogers, Jr., Jacob Javits of New York, others. I'd write speeches, letters, and help set up forums and rallies and conferences to push the bill. And we'd see people, like Joe Martin, House speaker. I'd go up to the House Press Gallery and give out press releases. Then we'd set up speaking engagements for Jack up around Massachusetts and elsewhere. He was campaigning statewide. One of the first trips I took with him was up to North Adams over the Mohawk Trail in wintertime, which was just crazy; old roads, covered with ice and sleet.

Dave Powers helped a lot with the Housing Bill program in Massachusetts, setting up speeches, traveling with us. I remember once we wound up down at Hyannis Port. We were going out to play golf and then we thought we'd like to have a drink when we got back. So Dave asked the Kennedy chauffer, who used to drink

with us, "Is there any booze?" While all the Kennedys were nap-
ping—they're all great nappers—the chauffer checked and said
there was an almost-full bottle of Vat 69. So we looked forward to
this. But when we got back from playing golf, we found out the
ambassdor had flown off to New York and taken the one bottle
with him! And he didn't even drink!

Jack's opening shot was fired in Chicago, March 10, at a National Public Housing Conference, a forum Galvin had helped organize to debate
the bill. The New York Times reported the conference in a story on March
11, mentioning Jack. From his Congressional files, we obtained part of his
statement:

> Veterans need homes and they need them quickly. Upon the so-
> lution of this problem will depend much of our own future. Most
> veterans recognize the whys and wherefores of the housing short-
> age, but let us remember that *most* veterans are young men and
> have but one standard to apply to the current waste—the prodi-
> gious accomplishments of this nation in war. Any veteran who
> watched the American supplies pouring ashore on the Normandy
> beaches; who saw Pacific Islands cleared and air strips rolled out in
> four or five days; who saw the endless waste of war and the seem-
> ingly never-ending productivity that replaced that waste, is it any
> wonder that the veteran cannot understand why he is not housed?

As we noted earlier, the VFW leadership had at first opposed the
T-E-W Bill. Soon after the 1947 debate began, the American Legion also
declared against the bill. In his speeches, Jack attacked the "leadership"
of the Legion (as opposed to its "membership") as being tools of the real
estate lobbies which were fighting the bill. These attacks generated
further publicity. For example, on March 11, immediately following
Jack's speech in Chicago, he flew to Boston for another Galvin-organ-
ized housing rally in Boston's historic Faneuil Hall. The following day
the Boston papers were full of stories on the rally. They noted that the
American Legion had boycotted the rally, and that Jack had quoted the
Jesuit magazine America, which had described the American Legion
Housing Committee as "a legislative drummer boy for the real estate
lobby." The Boston Herald quoted the rally chairman, "Only one Congressman, Mr. Kennedy, has enough courage and shows enough interest
for the veterans living in trailers and half a garage to appear here tonight." The adjutant of the Massachusetts American Legion denounced
Jack as an "embryo" Congressman who did not know what he was talking about. This kept the stories in the newspapers for several more days.
    In sum, the newspaper space was considerable. Typical was a column

by Clem Norton, a Massachusetts political sage, published in the May 25, 1947 Lynn *Sunday Telegram*:

Watch this young fellow, Congressman John Fitzgerald Kennedy from Boston, for he definitely shows signs in more ways than one, of having moral courage, the most lacking thing in public life today. When he ran for office, I said to myself: "Well this young man, a rich man's son will just be a 'run of the mill' politician. He will get down to Washington and become a part of the social swirl. . . ." Recently he has been in a row with the American Legion over the housing question and came right out boldly with a statement that not one in a thousand politicians would dare to make. Here is one of the very, very few young men in the political life of our State for many years who has had the fortitude and the courage and independence to come right out and name names. To come right out and say that in his opinion the American Legion—on the national level—has been double-crossing the veterans on the housing issue. Do you know of any other politician, in any of the major political parties, who would have the courage to do that?

But this considerable effort was to no avail. The first session of the 80th Congress failed to report out a housing bill anything like the original T-E-W proposal. In the closing days of the session, July 24, Jack stood on the floor of the House, deploring the lapse. He accused the Republican Party of "crass ignorance" and "fraud" and concluded bitterly, "I was sent to this Congress by the people of my district to help solve the most pressing problem facing the country—the housing crisis.

"I am going to have to go back to my district Saturday, a district that sent probably more boys per family into this last war than any in the country, and when they ask me if I was able to get them any homes, I will have to answer 'Not a one—not a single one!'"

In the House in the next few years, Jack kept up the public housing campaign and his assault on the American Legion, even venturing so far as to say that "The leadership of the American Legion has not had a constructive thought for the benefit of this country since 1918."

At the same time, Jack began to take on "labor" as an issue. It would become his specialty. During his three terms in the House, he learned a great deal about it. When he moved on to the Senate, he continued to specialize in labor, and when Bobby came along, he, too, specialized in labor.

In the first session of the 80th Congress, Jack was mostly feeling his way on the issue, educating himself. It was an immensely complex field, entangled in federal, state and local laws and regulations. Apart from his sessions in Arizona in 1945 with Pat Lannan (when he read books on labor) and his contact with labor leaders in the 11th District during the 1946 campaign, Jack had had no "experience" in labor. He had had no close association with unions. He was not a lawyer.

The 80th Congress was a good place to learn about labor. Joe Martin, Bob Taft, and their Republican colleagues in the House and Senate had come to Washington determined to write a new labor law to replace the New Dealish Wagner Act of 1935. They believed the Wagner Act had given the unions too much power ("a despotic tyranny") and shackled management. After twelve years of the Wagner Act, they were going to swing the pendulum the other way. No other domestic issue, not even Communism, generated more heat in the first session. As a member of the House Education and Labor Committee, Jack had a front-row seat, leading to his most important vote in this three terms in the House.

Every legislator, it seemed, had his own ideas about a new labor law. In its issue of January 6, 1947, *Time* predicted that "In the first 48 hours probably a hundred labor bills will be dumped in the hopper." From January to April, both the Senate and House Labor Committees, presided over by Bob Taft and Fred Hartley, met day after day, amassing volume upon volume of testimony. The giants of big labor, Philip Murray (CIO), George Meany (AFL), Walter Reuther (UAW), Daniel Tobin (Teamsters), John L. Lewis (Coal Miners), James C. Petrillo (Musicians), Harry Bridges (Maritime), David Dubinsky (Garment Workers) and others, appeared before the committees to urge caution—and the status quo. They were dutifully heard and interrogated, but they changed few minds.

As Jack sat listening and reading, doing his homework, he became dissatisfied with the direction in which Fred Hartley and his Republican majority (including freshman Richard Nixon) were taking the House Committee. He thought that the bill Hartley was working toward went too far in favor of management. But, on the other hand, he thought the Democratic minority on the committee was going too far in favor of labor. In early April, as the time drew near for the Hartley Committe to report on the bill—with the usual majority and minority reports—Jack decided to get his views on record with a one-man independent report.

To help prepare this report, Jack called on two members of his Boston "brain trust," Mark Dalton and Joe Healey of Cambridge, both lawyers and budding labor experts. John Galvin, still in Washington working on the housing issue, was on hand to help. In our interviews, Dalton and Healey told us about going to Washington to prepare the report. They stayed at the Georgetown house with Jack. Healey remembered a phonograph playing, again and again "Younger than Springtime," a favorite song of Jack's from the Broadway musical *South Pacific*.

Dalton recalled one amusing moment in the feverish work:

We were dealing with some highly technical aspect of the report. Billy Sutton came in and said, rather sagely, "If you do that, you'll have to amend the Wagner Act." Jack dismissed Billy out of hand. What did *he* know? Later that night, Jack saw Sutton and asked, "What was that about the Wagner Act?" Billy said, "You have to amend it." Jack said, "How do *you* know? And Billy floored everybody with his answer: "I had lunch with Bob Taft today and he told me." And you know, he had.

Jack's report said, "Management has been selfish. Labor has been selfish." It warned the Republican majority that an overly repressive and vindictive labor law would set off a "tide of left-wing reaction" that might destroy the free enterprise system. On the other hand, he wrote, "Equally fundamental was the right of each individual union member to a square deal from his union." To protect the individual, he called for secret balloting in union elections and strike votes; free speech; modest dues; and other measures. The report was, as Burns points out, a plea for a moderate, middle-of-the-road bill which would contain safeguards for all three factions: business, unions, and individuals.

The House labor bill reported out by Fred Hartley's majority was a very tough measure. It banned industrywide bargaining, the closed shop, jurisdictional and sympathy strikes, mass picketing, strikes by government workers, and Communist officers in unions. Penalties were stiff: unions could be deprived of their bargaining rights for a year and were made suable; unlawful strikers could be deprived of their right to get their jobs back. In addition, it gave the president the right to obtain an injunction against interstate transport, communications, or public utility strikes. The minority report, offered by the Democrats, took exception to most of these provisions.

Bob Taft's Senate labor bill was not as tough, certainly not as tough as he would have liked to have written. New York's freshman Republican Senator, Irving Ives, a liberal on Taft's Committee, had formed a dissenting coalition of liberal Republicans and Democrats, forcing Taft to water down the Senate bill. *Time,* in its issue of April 21, reported, "For Taft it was one of the worst lickings he had ever taken." In what was to be a Taft-dominated Congress, Taft had failed on the key domestic issue.

The House bill came up for debate on the floor in mid-April. Jack had prepared a dissenting speech for delivery on April 16, stressing the points in his dissenting report. Sutton recalled in his oral history that it was Jack's "maiden speech" in the House. Sutton put the speech in his pocket and went with Jack to the chamber. Jack went on the floor; Billy took a seat in the visitors' gallery. When Joe Martin recognized Jack, Billy realized to his horror that he had forgotten to give Jack his speech. Sutton jumped up and ran madly to the anteroom, from which someone then carried the speech to Kennedy. The episode reminded Billy of the movie starring James Stewart, *Mr. Smith Goes to Washington*.

Jack's opening words were, "Mr. Chairman, it is my firm conviction that the House would be making a great mistake to pass this bill in its present form. . . . This grave error that the majority of the Committee on Education and Labor have made is that in seeking to destroy what is bad, they are also destroying what is good." He then went on to repeat the major points of his independent report.

Jack's stand got him a big press in Massachusetts. Most of the stories, brief and hastily written, did not go into the nuances of his dissent. They pictured him (accurately enough for an oversimplification) being against the Hartley Bill and thus pro-labor. Typical was the headline in the Hearst paper Boston *American*, April 15: KENNEDY DEMANDS REVISIONS OF DRASTIC NEW LABOR BILL.

The Hartley Bill passed by a stunning margin: 308 to 107. Ninety-three Democrats, mostly conservative Southerners, joined the 215 conservative Republicans to make up the margin. Jack, of course, voted "nay" on the roll call.

The bill led to the first public confrontation between Kennedy and Nixon. A couple of days after the voting, at the request of Democratic Congressman Frank Buchanan, from Pennsylvania, Jack and Dick Nixon went up to McKeesport, a suburb of Pittsburgh, to stage a debate on the Hartley Bill. Nixon remembered the trip in his book, *Six Crises:*

> I doubt if either of us, or those who were in the audience of 150 to 200 that night will recall much of what was said during the course of the evening. I was for the bill. Kennedy was against it. And we both presented our points of view as vigorously as we could. As far as the audience was concerned, I probably had the better of the argument because most of those present, as employees, tended to be on my side in the first place. After the meeting, we rode a sleeper from Pittsburgh back to the Capital. I remember that our discussions during the long, rocky ride related primarily to foreign affairs and the handling of the Communist threat at home and abroad, rather than the Taft-Hartley Act. I do not recall the details of our talk but of one thing I am absolutely sure: neither he nor I had even the vaguest notion at that time that either of us would be a candidate for President thirteen years later.

The Senate bill took longer to get to the floor for debate and when it got there the debate was dragged out by all kinds of maneuvering. Finally, in May, the Senate voted. The bill passed overwhelmingly: 68 to 24. Only three Republicans voted against it: Wayne Morse, of Oregon; George Malone, of Nevada; and William Langer, of North Dakota. New York's Irving Ives, still not satisfied that the bill was liberal enough, gave up and went along with the majority of his Republican colleagues.

The two bills then went to a conference committee to see if the gap could be closed. It was: with the House members giving way to the more moderate Senate version. On June 6 Arthur Krock wrote a column about the situation. He took a position remarkably similar to Jack's: a plague on both your houses. He gave Jack a pat on the back: "This correspondent today set out to find some member of Congress opposed both to the Hartley bill and the Taft-Hartley conference report and in favor of a Presidential veto, who . . . has anything but the *status quo* to offer as a substitute. He discovered that member in Representative John F. Kennedy of Boston, though doubtless there are others."

The final bill—called the Taft-Hartley Bill—was then resubmitted to the Senate and House for voting. On June 6 the Senate voted for it 54–17, including seventeen Democrats, mostly Southern conservatives. The House voted for it 320–79. Jack voted against it.

The outcry from labor leaders was deafening. They labeled it the "slave labor bill" and demanded that President Truman veto it. Among the thousands of voices raised against it, we noted with interest, was that of the NCWC—Father John Cronin's handiwork, we suspect. The NCWC claimed the bill played into the hands of the Communists. The Communists claimed it was a sellout to the reactionaries.

Harry Truman vetoed the Taft-Hartley Bill on June 20. The Senate and the House promptly assembled to override the veto. The vote in the Senate on June 23 (after a filibuster by Idaho's Democrat Glen Taylor and others) was 68–25, six more votes than required for a two-thirds majority. Henry Cabot Lodge was among those voting to override. The House voted to override by 331–83. Jack was among those who voted to sustain the veto. With that, the Taft-Hartley Act became law. Jack's votes—his first real liberal stand—were, of course, cast in the interests of his working-class district. They put him squarely at odds with his father, who had been ardently pro-Hartley Bill all through the debate.

Who really won? Nobody was quite certain. What was clear, however, was that the battle lines for the 1948 election had been drawn. That, at any rate, was the way *Time* saw it. In the issue of June 30, it blasted Truman for "flouting" the will of Congress and said his action opened the 1948 presidential campaign with a "hiss and a roar." It pointed out that Truman had "chosen the left side of the line"; that his position "squared exactly with the analysis of Lee Pressman, the C.I.O.'s able counsel, a communist-line leftist." Thus the level of public discourse in those years.

In the curious way that politics sometimes works, Jack picked up support for his stand on Taft-Hartley from an odd corner. On June 14 he traveled to New Bedford, a Republican stronghold, to address the Junior Chamber of Commerce. While there, he met Basil Brewer, then the owner-publisher of the *New Bedford Standard-Times,* and one of his chief underlings, Charles J. Lewin, both strong supporters of Bob Taft. In an oral history at the Kennedy Library, Lewin recalled that Jack had told them, "Taft is a surprising man. He is highly competent" and that the Taft-Hartley Bill, (which had just then emerged from conference), was "fairly reasonable." He meant, we suppose, better than the Hartley Bill.

Jack's comments about Taft and his bill fell on sympathetic ears in Brewer and Lewin. They liked Jack, Lewin recalled, because Jack liked Taft. Thereafter, Jack and Brewer began exchanging correspondence and Brewer talked with the ambassador, who also liked Taft. In 1952, when Jack ran against Lodge, this developing friendship would prove to be valuable to Jack.

At any rate, as the little side trip to McKeesport with Dick Nixon had shown, Jack now had a new issue firmly in hand. By taking an equivocal stand on Taft-Hartley, then voting to sustain the veto, he had granted himself the right in the future to plug for a better bill for all parties concerned. It was a pro-labor position that did not overly antagonize management or Taft supporters. In Washington that is called "statesmanlike."

In the spring and early summer, when the weather in New England moderated, Jack stepped up the number of weekend trips to Boston. According to his appointment book he was there almost every weekend, tearing around the state on speaking tours to veteran's groups, women's clubs, and Catholic societies. He was based at the Bowdoin Street apartment, where he had recruited the janitor, Joe Murphy, to prepare and serve his breakfast.

Dave Powers told us:

In 1947 Jack was the most sought-after Democratic speaker. Your governor was a Republican, your two Senators were Republicans, and more than half of your congressional delegation were Republicans. Many of the groups who were staging political rallies were now veterans' groups. In every town, a VFW or American Legion or AMVETS had sprung up. Jack was a veteran, so they'd say, "Let's get Jack Kennedy." Jack would try to get up here every Friday, Saturday, and Sunday to speak. Frank Morrissey or Bob Morey and I would go around with him. I remember he'd fly up on Friday. Then on Sunday night he'd take a train, The Federal, a sleeper that left South Station at eleven at night. He'd get a bedroom. When the train got to Washington, it just sat in the station and they'd let the passengers sleep in until nine or ten o'clock. Then he'd get up and go back to work on the Hill.

Many thought Jack Kennedy was already running for higher office. In our interview, John Galvin, who was close to Jack in that period, doing the PR on the housing issue, told us, "Jack was aiming for higher office. As soon as he was elected to Congress he started campaigning for the Senate. He was running. All the Kennedys were *always* running for the next job." Billy Sutton and Mark Dalton agreed. The Senate was already on Jack's mind. In his oral history at the Kennedy Library, Dalton said that after Jack, Dick Nixon, and George Smathers had become friends, they became friendly rivals; three "ambitious men all shooting for the future." The question, Dalton said, was "who was going to be the first one to make the Senate?" Billy Sutton agreed emphatically. "Jack told Smathers he thought it was advisable for George to go for the Senate and what inspired Jack to go to the Senate was that Nixon and Smathers went."

If this were the "plan" for these friendly rivals, the political situation for Nixon and Smathers was more or less favorable. In California and Florida there would not be another senatorial election until 1950, enabling both men to spend three years in the House (assuming reelection), making a name for themselves and a voting record that was broadly appealing in their respective states, followed by a year of hard campaigning. The only fly in the ointment was that Smathers would have to run against Claude Pepper, who had done more than any other man to start him on his political way. But that did not appear to daunt Smathers.

The situation in Massachusetts was not so good for Jack. The two Senate seats, held by the two Republicans Leverett Saltonstall and Henry Cabot Lodge, would be up for reelection in 1948 and 1952 respectively. From Jack's point of view, this was unfortunate. To make a run against Saltonstall in 1948 might appear precipitous. Jack would leave himself open to charges that he lacked political experience (only one session in the House) and that his father was simply buying him a higher office. Moreover, the Republicans now had control of the State House and the patronage, useful tools in a statewide election. The year 1948 would be a national election year and the pollsters were firmly predicting yet another Republican sweep (Taft or Dewey), which would help Saltonstall. Then, too, Jack liked Saltonstall and really didn't want to run against him, Sutton and others told us. But to put it off until 1952 meant waiting five long years in the House, then a run against Lodge, who was a formidable candidate—perhaps unbeatable.

Many of Jack's advisers (such as Sutton) believed that the best solution was for Jack to run against Governor Bradford, who was also up for reelection in 1948. There were rumors going around that Bradford was not in the best of health; he had collapsed at a banquet. (In fact, Bradford had Parkinson's disease.) Sutton felt that with all the Kennedy money and Jack's proven voter appeal, Jack could beat Bradford in spite of a nationwide Republican sweep. If Jack gained the State House in 1948, he could probably be reelected in 1950. That would give him four years' experience in the top political job in Massachusetts. Time enough to build a statewide political machine to bring to bear against Lodge in 1952.

There was much promise in this scenario. Yet it, too, introduced further complications. Jack would face Democratic rivals in the primaries in 1948—perhaps the unseated Maurice Tobin or the ambitious Paul Dever. Both Tobin and Dever had been popular votegetters. Both had political machines of a sort. Both could point to long years of experience in office. Finally, to beat Tobin or Dever and then Bradford, it was clear Jack had to begin his campaign right then, in the spring of 1947.

We imagine that Jack and his father and Cousin Joe Kane spent many hours in discussion about what course Jack should follow. But we could find no solid evidence that any kind of decision was reached. However, we believe, on the basis of our interviews, the contemporary Massachusetts newspapers, and the study of Jack's records at the Kennedy Library, that they decided to play it by ear, awaiting further developments. As Joe Kane knew well, in politics anything could happen. Men die, go bankrupt, get caught in corruption. The country might take a sudden turn away from Taft or Dewey, making Saltonstall more vulnerable. Meanwhile, the best course to follow was to build Jack's name statewide (and to whatever extent possible, nationally) without declaring for a specific office.

On his trips to Boston, Jack spent very little time in his Boston office, which was situated on the seventeenth floor of the Federal Building. In fact, we gathered the impression he went out of his way to avoid the office, leaving the work to the staff: Frank Morrissey, Joe Rosetti, and Grace Burke. Rosetti told us Frank Morrissey was often absent from the office, pursuing his private law practice or chauffeuring the ambassador around when he came to town. The heavy load fell on Rosetti and Grace Burke, who worked very hard, often late, and who maintained close communication with Mary Davis, Billy Sutton, and Ted Reardon in the Washington office.

Rosetti recalled, "I saw very little of Jack. He wanted to become a Senator from Massachusetts, that was his aim in those days. He'd come up for speaking engagements and occasionally dropped by the office to see how we were getting along. But he didn't stay long."

Both Rosetti and Grace Burke (in her oral history) recalled the "casework" load in the office was very heavy. Dozens and dozens of people descended on the office daily for help in getting jobs with the city, the state, or in the post office or the Navy Yard; or assistance in filing claims to the VA for disabilities or schooling; or with local welfare boards; and so on.

Often, Rosetti said, these people had been everywhere for help and came to their Congressman only as a last resort. But sometimes the "tales of woe" were "half-truths that you had to weed out."

Grace Burke recalled that once Jack scheduled two full days for seeing these constituents but after one day he gave up in despair and said, " 'Oh Grace, I can't do it. You'll have to call them off. . . .' He couldn't get used to the requests that they wanted. He didn't know so many people were out of work and all that sort of thing. . . . He didn't know there were so many poor people around."

Rosetti, who was still going to college at night, did not really like the work either. He told us, "Maybe I didn't have the political feel. I represented Jack in some Itlo-American clubs, some Catholic organizations and VFW clubs, but politics wasn't my cup of tea. No matter how many good things you did for Jack's constituents, the only thing they remembered is what you *couldn't* do for them. That irritated me a great deal."

The "street" character, Patsy Mulkern, hung out in the Boston office. Dave Powers recalled, "Grace Burke used to get a great chuckle out of him. Every morning he'd go down to the Congressman's office and get a crisp brown envelope. Then he'd walk up and down School Street like he was doing an errand for them. He was really, really strange."

Patsy Mulkern also hung out at the Bowdoin Street apartment and occasionally drove around with Jack. He recalled in his oral history:

> I drove him to the airport one day. I'd get him newspapers and candy—he was a big candy eater. So I walked to the ramp and gave him the papers, candy, and his briefcase. Then he said, "Pat, have you got any change?"
>
> My girl, Alice, worked at Liggett's. That day she had given me thirty-four dollars in an envelope to pay her bill at Gilchrist's. Like a fool, I gave Kennedy the envelope. He said, "I'll see you later." I said, "That's Alice's money." He said, "See you later." I got it back. It took a long time, though, and I thought I'd have to go to court. [In his oral history, Joe Leahy, of Somerville, recalled driving Jack to the airport. When they got there, Jack asked if he could borrow a nickel. Astonished, Leahy asked what he wanted with a nickel. "A Hershey bar," Kennedy replied.]

Occasionally, when Jack was jaunting around the state by automobile, Patsy would go along. He recalled that Jack, who would often take the wheel, was "a wicked, wild driver; the fastest; a wild man." They were always being stopped by State Police for speeding, but they were always able to talk their way out of a ticket. Every now and then they'd wind up at the Kennedy home in Hyannis Port. When he and Walter Powers and Jack went there on one occasion, Patsy recalled, Jack became furious:

"We didn't stop to eat. When we got there, I went out to the kitchen and started grabbing peaches from the icebox. Jack put on his slacks and he came down. He said, 'What are you doing?' I said, 'What the hell do you think I'm doing? I'm eating.' He said, 'My peaches!' "

Although Jack had studiously avoided becoming enmeshed in local Boston politics, in June, while the 80th Congress was still in session, he got himself caught in a trap.

After a year and a half of legal maneuvering, Boston's mayor, James Michael Curley, then seventy-three, finally ran out of time and appeals. On June 26 he appeared before Judge James M. Proctor in Washington, displaying doctors' certificates describing nine dangerous ailments, and pleaded for clemency. Said Proctor, "I think the defendant should be committed today." Curley replied, "You're sentencing me to death." U.S. marshals then took Curley to the federal prison in Danbury, Connecticut, to serve six to eighteen months.

In early July, John McCormack got up a petition to present to Harry Truman formally requesting an executive pardon for Curley on the basis of Curley's poor health. McCormack sought out the Democratic members of the Massachusetts delegation to sign it. This put Jack squarely in a dilemma. If he signed, he would, in effect, be endorsing Curley. If he did not, he was cautioned, he ran the risk of antagonizing Curley supporters in Boston—and in his own district.

Jack's advisers were divided. Many, such as Billy Sutton (and, we suspect, Frank Morrissey and Joe Kane) urged Jack to sign. The new breed, such as Mark Dalton, urged him not to. Said Dalton in his oral history, "I was furious that the older people had the nerve to jeopardize his career at the start of it." There was evidence that the ambassador urged Jack to sign. Charles Murphy, a political figure of the time, recalled in his oral history seeing Jack in the Bowdoin Street apartment, where Murphy had gone to urge Jack to sign. According to Murphy, the following exchange took place:

Jack: You know, McCormack was just here, read the petition again, and you know who sent him?
Murphy: No.
Jack: My father.

According to Joe McCarthy's account in *The Remarkable Kennedys*, Jack took great pains to find out the true state of Curley's health. He reached the same conclusion as Judge Proctor: Curley had no dangerous illness the physicians at Danbury were not capable of attending to. An argument could be made that he was better off, from a health standpoint, relaxing in a cell at Danbury rather than tearing around Boston going to political functions. He would not sign the petition. He was the only Democrat in the Massachusetts delegation who refused.

According to Burns, the matter came to a head on the floor of the House. McCormack, eyeing Kennedy, came over with his petition. There was a tense moment; then, according to Burns, Jack said the following dialogue took place:

"Has anyone talked with the president or anything?" Kennedy asked.

"No," McCormack said. "If you don't want to sign it, don't sign it."

"Well, I'm not going to sign it," Kennedy said.

And he did not.

Billy Sutton told us that the petition began, "Those of us who have served in the Congress with James Michael Curley. . . ." or some such wording, and that Jack begged off on the technicality that he had not served in Congress with Curley. Sutton believed Jack did not sign the petition primarily because of the long-standing feud between Honey Fitz and Curley. "If he had signed," Sutton said, "how would he face his grandfather?"

Kennedy's stand naturally generated big headlines in the Boston papers. In the July 13 *Sunday Herald* for example:

KENNEDY COURTS CURLEY VENGEANCE

DECLINES COMPROMISE WITH CONSCIENCE

IN TRADITION OF INDEPENDENT FAMILY

Thereafter, the story simmered along for days.

In any event, Truman did not honor the petition. He let Curley stay in the Danbury prison, where he continued to draw his $20,000-a-year salary.

Ordinarily, the president of the City Council, John B. Kelly, a Curley man then under indictment for graft, would have moved up to acting mayor in Curley's absence. However, the Republican-controlled State Legislature—spurred by Governor Robert Bradford—rammed through a number of special bills, one of which specifically ordered that the city clerk, John B. Hynes, be elevated to acting mayor until Curley got out of jail. Hynes served for about five months, until the day before Thanksgiving, when Truman commuted Curley's sentence to the time he had served. When Curley returned, Hynes reverted to city clerk. This exposure to the top job in Boston apparently whetted Hynes's appetite; in 1949, he would oppose Curley's try for reelection with startling results.

Jack's stand on the Curley petition would often be cited as one example of his "political courage"—and determination to disassociate himself from the crooked old pols of Boston. But had he run a serious risk of losing substantial support among his constituents? We doubt it. To be sure, many of the old pols (Patsy Mulkern, for example, in his oral history) registered displeasure and believed Jack had made a mistake. But, by 1947, these pols were a dying breed; Curley's voice an echo of another age. Our guess is that for every old voter Jack lost (if any), he gained one among the younger voters. And he may well have picked up some support among the Republican Brahmins that would be important when he made his decision to run for the U.S. Senate.

Between speaking engagements, Jack sandwiched in visits with his friends and Bobby, still at Harvard, and Bobby's friends, such as Kenny O'Donnell. Jack's close personal friends were pursuing their own individual goals. After one year at the Harvard Business School, Lem Billings told us, he "was going on thirty and got anxious." He gave up his plans for a master's degree and in June went to visit his brother Frederic, the doctor, in Nashville, Tennessee. He took a job in Nashville with the General Shoe Company (now Genesco) and after further schooling became assistant advertising manager. For the next four years he remained in Nashville and saw Jack only on his vacations. Eddie McLaughlin continued working at the Snyder Fuel Company and going to law school at night. In 1947 and 1948 he was commander of the Joseph P. Kennedy, Jr., VFW Post. The Dowd agency continued to do the PR for its programs; both John Galvin and Mark Dalton were also active in the post. Jim Reed was still at Harvard Law School. Jewel was now a homemaker, caring for their toddler, Candy.

On most of his weekends in Boston, Jack had dates for the theater, movies, or dinner. As Cis McLaughlin remembered, the gorgeous Filene's model, Pam Farrington, was still number one in Boston. But Billy Sutton thought that the ex-Navy nurse, Ann McGillicuddy, was number one. The other Navy nurse, Elinor Dooley, was no longer available. She had become engaged to a Navy doctor, Clyde Johnson Dawe, also stationed at Chelsea. According to a marriage license we found on file in Revere, they were married at Chelsea Hospital on May 2, 1947. Two months later Elinor resigned from the Navy.

That summer, Jack's good friend, the British tennis star Kay Stammers Menzies, was in the United States for the Wrightman Cup matches, which had been resumed after the war. She lost to her American opponent. She recalled, "I was in Boston playing a match. Jack rang me up and said he was coming to Boston that night and would I have dinner with him? He was very late. We went to some roof place for dinner and a little dancing. I remember he asked me if I'd like to see Cambridge and he took me in the car and drove around Cambridge and Harvard."

Jim and Jewel Reed recalled having Kay Stammers as a houseguest. Jim told us, "We were spending the summer of 1947 in a seaside cottage in the North Shore town of Beverly and I was commuting to Harvard Law School. Jack asked if he could come up for dinner and bring a girl. I said sure. So he drove up from Boston with this girl, Kay Stammers. I didn't catch her name when we were introduced. Later on in the evening I asked her if by any chance she knew Kay Stammers! We had a wonderful evening playing word games, which Jack loved. Kay was a *very* attractive girl. They were great friends." Jewel recalled, "Jack came up one night with Kay Stammers. I didn't have a car then, so I had to make do with what the grocery boy had brought that morning. I served chilled grapefruit for dessert, and, of course, Jack wouldn't eat it. He was terribly hard on a cook.

"Jim said he had to study, and I was left to entertain the two of them. We played a lot of sophisticated word games. One was Botticelli, which is something like twenty questions, but much more complicated, with challenges, counter-challenges and so on. Jack Kennedy hated the trite in games."

None of these dates, we surmised, was serious. At least, not from Jack's point of view. He was still resolutely dedicated to bachelorhood. By all accounts, the girl who stood highest with him was still Flo Pritchett, whom he saw in New York and Washington. But, as Flo knew better than anyone else, there would never be a marriage. Flo was not getting any younger. In Jack's appointment book for June 28, we found an entry in Flo's handwriting: "Flo Pritchett's birthday! SEND DIAMONDS." That day she was twenty-seven. Within a year she would be married.

The 80th Congress, first session, adjourned *sine die* (without fixing a date for further meeting) at 3:49 A.M., Sunday, July 27, almost a month later than the target date. Its chief achievements were support of the Truman Doctrine and launching the hearings on the Marshall Plan, demonstrating a remarkable ability to approach foreign affairs on a nonpartisan basis; passage of the Taft-Hartley Act over Truman's veto; and beginning the war against domestic Communists. The last produced few victories—or casualties—in 1947, but in coming sessions of the Congress the harvest would grow.

There were two other important achievements. After much stormy debate and dissent by the Navy, Congress voted to unify the Armed Services. It created a single Department of Defense and made the Army Air Corps into the Air Force, a "separate service" coequal with the Army and Navy. In September James Forrestal, who had done much to hold the admirals in line and push the bill through Congress, was named first secretary of defense. (By an executive order, which did not require Congressional approval, Truman also attempted to merge intelligence-gathering functions of the government by establishing the Central Intelligence Agency.) In addition, Congress passed a constitutional amendment limiting the presidency to two terms, and sent it along to the forty-eight states for ratification. (It was ratified in February, 1951.) At Truman's suggestion, the system of presidential succession was changed. Under the new law, in the absence of a vice-president the speaker of the House (an elected official) would succeed to the presidency rather than the secretary of state (a presidential appointee).

One big item the 80th failed to push through was the big government spending cut and, with it, a tax cut. Truman asked for $38 billion, the Congress trimmed about $3 billion, leaving about $35 billion, but this was mere bookkeeping; it was soon clear to all that federal spending would go on at $35 to $40 billion a year—or more. There was no way to make a substantial cut in the face of rampant inflation without reducing the military budgets to a dangerous degree. In the face of Soviet saber-rattling, few wanted to do that. Twice the Congress voted tax cuts and both times Truman vetoed them. The Republicans could not muster sufficient votes to override the vetos.

Jack strongly supported Forrestal's push for unification of the armed forces. He favored limiting the presidential terms to two and having the speaker of the House succeed to the presidency in the absence of a vice president. He opposed any tax cuts—and went out of his way to speak against a tax cut on the floor of the House. He opposed most proposed reductions in the military budgets, and generally supported the $35-billion-level federal budget.

He could be categorized, then, as a Truman Democrat, a consistent Fair Dealer. On the big issues of the 80th Congress—Truman Doctrine Taft-Hartley, tax cut, military expenditures—he and Truman saw eye to eye. Big labor counted Jack in its corner. In a CIO summary of this session, Jack was deemed to have voted "right" on eleven key issues, "wrong" on none.

In early August, after Congress recessed, Jack went to Hyannis Port for a vacation. The Boston newspapers tracked him down there for interviews—to get his views on the Congress. The stories indicated that he was dissatisfied with its work. He was particularly bitter about his failure to get a housing bill through Congress. He complained that veterans' priorities were "a joke" and blasted the committee appointed to look into the housing problem as "nothing more than a political sop." He was also angry that Congress had failed to pass a minimum wage. "To pay a man less than sixty cents an hour in these times is simply not justifiable," he said.

Some of Jack's biographers are critical of his performance in the first session of the 80th Congress. Leo Damore (*Cape Cod Years*), for one, describes it as "undistinguished." But contemporary observers in Washington and Boston thought otherwise. In a column published July 29, Drew Pearson assessed the new Congressmen and gave Jack high marks (along with Jacob Javits, John Davis Lodge, George Smathers, Carl Albert and Thurston Morton), The *Boston Post* reporter (and Jack Kennedy admirer) Robert L. Norton wrote on October 6 that Jack was "the outstanding veteran in Congress," adding, "He has won the respect of Congress as one of its hardest working and best informed members." The prestigious *Boston Post* political observer, James G. Colbert, remarked September 28 on Jack's "balance and mature judgment."

Our research indicates that Jack's staffs—Morrissey, Rosetti, and Burke in Boston; Mary Davis, Reardon, and Sutton in Washington—provided Jack's constituents with careful, conscientious and speedy service. The fact that Jack held himself aloof from the day-to-day casework, avoiding the Boston office, is not grounds for criticism. Intentionally or unintentionally, it was good administration, we thought, to delegate all this deadly routine. It gave Jack extra time to educate himself about Communism, labor, foreign affairs, and other important matters. And, it seemed to us that he was hardworking and well informed—doing his very best. In sum: off to an excellent start.

That fall, Massachusetts newspapers were full of speculation about Jack's future. Colbert in his September 28 column wrote that it was remarkable how, after less than one year in office, Jack was on everybody's list as a potential candidate for governor or Senator and that it was "entirely possible that he might seek higher office next year," running against Leverett Saltonstall for the Senate. Such a possibility was not so "remote" as some politicians thought, Colbert wrote. True, Colbert said, he was young but "You can mature pretty fast . . . looking down the Jap guns as Kennedy did" and he had "tremendous appeal for the younger voters." A story in the *Boston Globe,* July 31, quoted labor delegates as urging Kennedy to run against Saltonstall. There had also been some talk of Salty being made vice president, thus removing him from his Senate seat. Other stories (the *Worcester Sunday Telegram,* November 30, for example) speculating on the Democratic race for governor—would it be Tobin or Dever?—considered Jack as a possible candidate.

After just seven months in public office, Jack had become a political power in Massachusetts. A phenomenon.

44

The Health Question: An Answer

T ruman and Secretary of State George Marshall had warned the first session of the 80th Congress that Europe was an economic shambles in grave danger of being overrun by Communism. They had recommended the Marshall Plan, financial aid on a scale unprecedented in the history of mankind. Beyond talk not much had been done about the plan. One reason was that Congress itself wanted to take a firsthand look at Europe to see if the gloomy stories were true. That fall, after August vacation and some time mending hometown fences, Senators and Congressmen flocked to Europe in droves. The *New York Times* estimated that no fewer than 200 members of the 80th Congress went abroad.

The House organized a formal fact-finding committee of eighteen members (ten Republicans and eight Democrats) chaired by Massachusetts Congressman Christian Herter. It was called the Herter Committee. Among its members was the freshman Republican Dick Nixon. The committee departed the United States about September 1, then fanned out across Europe, interviewing statesmen, laborers—and Communists—in Britain, France, Italy, and Germany. Jack had not been appointed to this committee. However, he and his House Labor Subcommittee pals who had pursued Harold Christoffel and UAW Local 248 in Milwaukee— Charlie Kersten and Thomas Owens—cooked up their own European junket. The announced purpose: to study "labor problems in Europe" with special emphasis on Communist infiltration of unions.

The three began making plans for the junket in mid-June. They added an extra dimension: they would go to Russia for talks with Soviet officials. After much backing and forthing, on July 2 they obtained an appointment with the Soviet ambassador to apply for visas. On that day Jack was in Hyannis Port. Ted Reardon, according to a wire we found at the Kennedy Library, sat in for Jack. After due consideration, the Russians rejected the visa applications. The news of the rejection was released to the press in late July. It made headlines in the Boston papers.

During the planning stages Jack recruited his pal Pat Lannan to go on the junket as a "special assistant" to the subcommittee. Lannan recalled the preliminaries:

Jack was a great telephone caller. He'd get on the phone any time of the day or night and ask you a question. He used me as an adviser on economics. Once he called me at two o'clock in the morning and asked me how would I like to go to Russia. This sub-committee—Jack and Kersten and Owen—was going to Russia and the western nations of Europe. Jack wanted me as a technical adviser. I went back and forth from Chicago to Washington and we talked about it. I read everything on Russia I could find. But, finally, the Russians turned us down on the slender theory that they didn't have accommodations for such a dignified group. . . .

Jack applied for a new passport—his third. We found it in the Kennedy Library. It was issued on July 2, 1947. He was described as 6' 0'' tall with "brown hair and green" eyes. The joint chiefs of staff held up the passport until Jack provided details on his planned itinerary and needs in Germany, a military zone.

Evidently the four—or more—men involved in this junket planned to travel to Europe independently and meet someplace. We do not know how Kersten and Owens got there. From his passport—and Boston newspapers—we learned that on Sunday, August 31. Jack left Boston's Logan Airport "for Ireland" in an American Airlines overseas flagship. Pat Lannan would come later by ship.

From other library records we saw that Jack flew to Shannon, Eire, arriving September 1. His first stop was a prolonged social occasion: a visit with Kathleen and her English friends. They were then at Lismore Castle on the Blackwater River in County Waterford, in southern Ireland. The castle was built eight centuries ago by King John. It had once been the property of Sir Walter Raleigh. In 1947 it was owned by Kathleen's father-in-law, the Duke of Devonshire. By all accounts, it is an awesome structure, set upon a magnificent bluff.

There must have been a grand reunion with Kathleeen. Among her friends who were there were Sean Leslie, an Irish writer; Charles Johnson, later British high commissioner to Australia; Hugh Fraser; Tony Rossyln, then a Member of Parliament; Anthony Eden, later prime minister; and Pamela Digby Churchill, a beautiful red-haired woman, recently divorced from Winston Churchill's son Randolph; and others.

In 1974 Pamela was the wife of Averell Harriman. We found her living in Georgetown. Mrs. Harriman—now fifty-three years old, she told us candidly—might be thirty-five. She is beautiful and charmingly English. She was about twenty-six when she was at Lismore Castle that fall. She has lived an extraordinary life, crowded with momentous events, yet she remembered that time vividly. She told us:

I'd met all the Kennedys in London before the war. Kathleen

was about my age and we came out together the summer of 1938. After the war, in January, 1946, the first time I came to America, it was to visit the Kennedys in Palm Beach. I'd seen Jack but I did not know him well until that time in Lismore Castle. Though he was three years older, he always seemed so very young to all of us. In England we dated very much older men and Jack seemed, well, boyish. Skinny and scrawny, actually. Kathleen's kid brother. Not eligible, so to speak.

Jack was not feeling well. The others went off to ride and play golf and things like that. He had a bad back. Jack *always* had a back back, since I can remember. He wasn't playing golf. I didn't know *how* to play golf, so Jack and I spent a certain amount of time together.

One morning he said, rather quietly, rather apologetically, "Would you mind coming on an expedition with me to find the original Kennedys?" He'd done some research before coming over and thought his ancestors came from a place near New Ross, about fifty miles from Lismore. So we started off one morning in a station wagon Kathleen had had shipped over from the States, a marvelous thing. The height of luxury; nobody had ever seen one.

We drove over these terrible Irish roads and finally, after five or six hours, we came to New Ross and then went up a lane to a little village. Jack stopped the car and asked somebody where the Kennedys lived. And a very Irish voice replied, "Auch now, and which Kennedys will it be that you'll be wanting? David Kennedys? Jim Kennedys?"

Jack didn't really know. He explained about being from America and what he was up to. They told us to drive to a little white house on the edge of the village. We found the house. It had a thatch roof, and pigs, ducks, and chickens running in and out of the front door. A rather suspicious woman came out. Jack explained everything, but she didn't look at all convinced. She looked more and more suspicious, but she finally sent about a dozen little children (they all looked like Kennedys) up the mountainside to fetch her husband.

The husband came down. They were all very nice, but quiet and dignified—and unbelieving. They kept thinking we wanted something from them. I was very impressed. I would have expected them to think we could offer them certain advantages. They kept offering us butter and eggs, very difficult to come by in 1947. They never could figure out who *I* was. "Wife?" I'd say, "No, no." And they said, "Ah, soon to be, no doubt."

We had tea. Jack kept pressing on about his ancestors going to America and so on, trying to make the link. They said, well, they had an uncle who went to America—Long Island—in 1920 and made good. He had a roadhouse! Jack said he didn't think that was the one. He could never make the link, but he seemed to be satisfied that they were some relation.

Jack kept saying, "What can I do for you?" Finally they broke down and said he could do one thing: drive the children around the village in the station wagon. So we piled all the kids in the wagon and Jack solemnly paraded around the little village. Then we left.

I never figured out if Jack really thought they were relatives or not, but we'd gone so far to find them, I think he more or less gave them the benefit of the doubt.

When we got back to Lismore, we were late for dinner. When Jack told Kathleen about finding the original Kennedys, all she said was, "Did they have a bathroom?" We told her they did not.

James MacGregor Burns begins his book with a brief description of this visit, without mentioning Pamela Churchill by name. In a letter to Burns, August 25, 1959, on file at the Kennedy Library, Jack said he "figured" the Kennedys they found in New Ross were "third cousins" and that he had departed the village "in a flow of nostalgia and sentiment." He concluded, "This was not punctured by the English lady turning to me as we drove off and saying, 'Just like *Tobacco Road.*' She had not understood at all the magic of the afternoon."

Jack remained at Lismore Castle about three weeks. No doubt there was time for close brother-sister talk between Jack and Kathleen. She had a big secret to confide. According to Pamela, Kathleen was again madly in love with an Englishman. He was Peter Milton, Lord Fitzwilliam, a dashing, very rich sportsman with a stable of racehorses. Pamela said:

> Peter was married. So this was a *very* complex problem. Kick had already upset her family by remaining in England. She had a little house off St. John's Square. The English adored her and she had really made her home there, been with us through all the tough time of the war. Her father used to talk to me about it. He said she's crazy for living in England. Why can't she come home? And then with Peter Fitzwilliam on the horizon, they got much more upset.

We could find nothing on the record to indicate what Jack's reaction to this news might have been. His really close friends preferred not to talk about it. We doubt that Jack discussed it in any detail with them. No doubt it troubled him deeply. Kathleen was his favorite. If she persisted in this headlong affair, there was bound to be public scandal—and pain. Pain for all the Kennedys, and if Peter proceeded toward divorce, with the intent of marrying Kathleen, pain for many others. Then, finally, the prospect of a Kennedy marrying a divorced man, which would mean banishment from the Church and sacraments for life—and possibly complete ostracism by her parents.

Pamela had told us Jack had not been "well" at Lismore Castle. We believe that during his stay he became progressively sicker. At the Kennedy Library we found two items that indicated he urgently needed some kind of medicine. The first was a wire dated September 13, from Jack at Lismore to Ted Reardon in Washington. Text: GET TWO PRESCRIPTIONS OF DOCTOR SULLIVAN OF BALTIMORE FOR HERE. HAVE THEM FILLED AND GET TO PATRICIA [Patricia Kennedy, Jack's younger sister, we assumed] SAILING WEDNESDAY FROM NEW YORK. IMPORTANT. JOHN KENNEDY.

The next was a wire from Jack to Reardon dated five days later, September 18. Text: IF YOU DID NOT GET DOCTOR SULLIVANS TWO HAIR PRESCRIPTIONS TO PAT ON TIME GIVE THEM TO J. PATRICK LANNAN HOTEL PIERRE NEW YORK SAILING SATURDAY. JACK.

Another medical mystery. We could find no other evidence that Jack was seeing a Dr. Sullivan in Baltimore or that he required a prescription for his "hair." We guessed that since the wire would go through the House telegraph office—and thus become part of the public record—the message was some kind of code Reardon would understand. The prescription was probably for something more serious than dandruff, we thought. But what?

On or about Saturday, September 20, the day Lannan sailed from New York, Jack and Pamela left Lismore, drove to Dublin, and took a plane to London. We assumed Jack had plans to meet Pat Lannan in London, get his prescriptions, and meet Congressmen Kersten and Owens at a prearranged place (London? Paris?) toward the end of the month. Pamela had separate plans. She told us she was passing through London on her way to the south of France for another holiday.

According to Jack's passport stamps, he arrived in London on September 21. (En route he bought forty cartons of tax-free cigarettes, according to some documents we found at the Kennedy Library. Why, we do not know.) Pamela told us he checked into the Claridge Hotel. That very day, September 21, 1947, a ghastly chapter in the life of Jack Kennedy began. It is a story very few people know, and the few who do know avoid discussing it. The complete story has never before been fully documented and seen in print.

It began in an undramatic way. Once again Jack became ill. Pamela Churchill was probably the first to know. She told us:

> On the day we arrived in London, Jack called me up from Claridge's and asked if I had a doctor. He wasn't feeling well. So I

called my doctor, who was Lord Beaverbrook's doctor, Sir Daniel Davis. He's dead now. I asked him to go around and see Jack at Claridge's. He did—and put him straight in a hospital, the London Clinic. I was rushing off to the south of France. I had a wonderful housekeeper at my flat in London, old Mrs. Martin. So I said to Mrs. Martin, "Lady Hartington's brother is sick and in the London Clinic. The food is filthy there. Will you go around and take him his food?" So every day, as long as Jack was there, she took Jack his lunch and dinner. Jack always remembered Mrs. Martin. Years later, when he was president, he asked me about her one day and when I said she was still very much alive, he sent her a picture of himself—with a dedication.

Jack also telephoned his friend the British tennis star, Kay Stammers Menzies. In our interview, she told us, "I was going to have lunch with him at Claridge's. He called me and said he was ill. I asked what was the matter. He said he didn't know—but when he got out of bed he couldn't stand up. They carted him off to the London Clinic. I saw him at the clinic. I brought him a little bit of filet steak because he didn't like the clinic food. He was darned ill, terribly thin and not a good color."
Pamela Churchill:

A couple of weeks later I got back from the south of France. I saw Dr. Davis and he said to me, "That young American friend of yours, he hasn't got a year to live." It was the first time they discovered that Jack had Addison's disease. Well, the awful thing is, I didn't take it too seriously. It didn't distress me as much as it would have if an American doctor had said it. In those days, the British and American doctors had such absolute, opposite medical theories. And we were all so *young* and selfishly involved in our own lives. I don't think I thought about it too much. I didn't dwell on it.

As we shall see, when rumors circulated years later—in 1959—that Jack had Addison's disease, his aides, doctors, and Jack himself, denied it. Jack described his condition as a "partial adrenal insufficiency." In 1960, during the heat of the political convention in Los Angeles, aides of Lyndon B. Johnson, who was competing for the nomination, told the press Jack had Addison's disease and had been kept alive all these years by drugs. Again Kennedy's aides, including his doctors of that period and Bobby, Sargent Shriver, and Pierre Salinger, denied it was true. After the election, on November 11, Jack was asked by a reporter if it were true. Again, a flat denial.

In light of these and other denials, especially the statements from

Jack's doctors, we made every possible effort to confirm or refute the recollections of Pamela Churchill that it was here, in London, September, 1947, that doctors first diagnosed that Jack had Addison's disease. We spent weeks on this question alone, searching out old newspaper clips, exploring medical journals and textbooks on the disease, talking to Jack's aides and friends, and finally to his doctor of the 1947 period, Elmer C. Bartels.

Let us begin with a description—and a brief history—of the disease. For this purpose, we consulted three texts—the most authorative of the period when Jack became ill. These were: *The Adrenal Glands in Health and Disease,* by the endocrinologist Max A. Goldzieher; *A Clinical Study of Addison's Disease,* by Leonard G. Rowntree and Albert M. Snell of the Mayo Clinic; and *The Diagnosis and Treatment of Adrenal Insufficiency,* by George W. Thorn of the Harvard Medical School. The last work was published in 1949. Thorn was then one of the leading experts in the world on Addison's disease. We found his book, a highly technical work like the others, to be most helpful.

Addison's disease was discovered by a famous British physician, Thomas Addison, in about 1855. It is a failure of the body's adrenal glands. The adrenal glands, located above the kidneys, are vital to life. They produce hormones which regulate certain body metabolisms, fight infection and, in times of stress, provide extra strength. If the adrenals fail, a person can die of a simple infection. Addison reported the disease to be caused primarily by tuberculosis, which attacks the adrenal glands and finally destroys them. Years later medical research revealed that the adrenal glands could also fail through atrophy, a premature wasting away or degeneration not associated with tuberculosis. In 1949 Thorn reported that about half of all Addisonians he had treated were tubercular in origin, the other half atrophy.

Addison's disease is difficult to diagnose, especially in its early stages. The early symptoms are fatigue, general weakness, poor appetite, and weight loss. The late stages are nausea, vomiting, diarrhea, and circulatory collapse. The physician finds low blood pressure, soft pulse, poor heart tones, and generalized brownish pigmentation—a tanning of the skin, especially over exposed areas and points of pressure of the mucous membranes. Tiny "ink spots" are also noted over the body. Failure of the adrenal glands results in disturbance of salt and water metabolism, the utilization of body carbohydrates. Of importance is the body's loss of resistance to infection and power of immunity. In some instances physicians have confused the yellowish or brownish pigmentation of the skin with jaundice or malaria. But a well-oriented physician, combining all the symptoms, is usually not misled in his diagnosis for long. In recent years complex laboratory tests have helped to confirm the diagnosis of Addison's disease.

Addison's disease does not usually come on suddenly. As a rule, it is insidious in its onset with gradual development of symptoms—though, of course, there were cases that developed very suddenly, precipitated by a strain or infection. Goldzieher writes "The full-blown stage of the disease is usually preceded by a period of latency which may last for years." In its acute stage—known as an Addisonian crisis—the disease is unmistakable.

Addisonian crisis is usually brought on by some kind of provocation which demands hormones which are not forthcoming from the diseased adrenals, such as infection or excessive physical stress, shock developing (as for example, in an accident or a surgical operation), or by a loss of salt and water through strenuous exercise on a hot and humid day. The crisis is a serious condition for the patient. He usually feels dizzy, light-headed, unduly weak and fatigued; his pulse becomes feeble. There usually is nausea, vomiting, and then suddenly the body temperature becomes subnormal. In many cases, the patient becomes disoriented and lapses into a coma due to vascular shock with low blood pressure.

Fortunately Addison's disease is relatively rare. In the early days following its discovery there was not much anyone could do to treat it. It was considered a fatal affliction. As Thorn points out, prior to 1930 the mortality rate five years following the onset of the disease was 90 percent. In the early 1930s endocrinologists experimented with a high-salt, low-potassium diet, which was helpful. The mortality rate five years after onset fell to 78 percent. Then, in the later 1930s, endocrinologists probing the frontiers of hormone research began to extract, in a very complicated and expensive process, adrenal hormones (adrenal cortical extracts) from cows and hogs. Daily injections of these rare and expensive hormone extracts, which varied greatly in strength and stability, benefited the Addisonian patient and the mortality rate fell substantially.

In 1939 endocrinologists developed a synthetic substance, desoxycorticosterone acetate (DOCA), which, as Thorn states, "was found to possess cortical hormone-like activity." It was more active than the natural extracts. When taken in conjunction with regulated salt and potassium intake the new drug greatly reduced the mortality rate of Addisonians. Physicians developed a means of implanting solid "pellets" of DOCA in the muscles of thighs or the back—thus eliminating the needle injections and making the patient much more independent. With the administration of DOCA, Thorn observed, "noticeable lightening" of the complexion occurred during the course of prolonged treatment.

This is where it stood in the fall of 1947. If the patient survived the Addisonian crisis, he then went on injections of DOCA combined with regulated salt, water, and potassium intake. Afterward patients who could, received the DOCA implants, which eliminated the injections. The pellets (usually one to four) released the needed daily hormones as the body required. They had to be replaced, by a simple procedure, after about two or three months.

Even with these new drugs, the life of an Addisonian still required careful discipline. The patient had to avoid heavy stress or physical exertion and wide changes in climate. Female patients were to avoid pregnancy. Surgical procedures, even a tooth extraction, were considered risky. A minor infection such as a cold could precipitate a crisis and require hospitalization and careful medical management. Patients simply died of shock or infection. In sum, merely to survive required a restrained life and good medical care.

Returning now to Jack in the London clinic. Did he have Addison's disease, as Pamela Churchill told us, or a milder form of the disease—or something else? In our interviews with Jack's friends and aides, and his sister Eunice, we asked each if he or she could recollect an illness in London in September, 1947, or what had happened. Only one aide, Mary Davis, conceded a recollection of the incident and her memory was hazy. But she turned out to be helpful on one point.

We counted heavily on Pat Lannan, who, at the time Jack became ill, was on the high seas en route to join Jack in England for the trip through Europe. In his *Who's Who* listing, he writes that he was a "special assistant" to a subcommittee of the Committee on Education and Labor of the U. S. Congress "which traveled throughout Europe, fall 1947." Surely he remembered that Jack became ill and had to cancel the trip? He did not.

At the Kennedy Library we searched the files carefully during this period, looking for clues bearing on the illness or Jack's movements. We found one. It was a telegram from Ted Reardon to Jack in London, dated October 9: ANN LEAVING BOSTON TONIGHT OCTOBER 9 AT 9:20 AND ARRIVING LONDON VIA PAN AMERICAN FLIGHT 110 AT 4:30 FRIDAY AFTERNOON OCTOBER 10. EXPECTING TO BE MET AT AIRPORT. EXCELLENT FLYING WEATHER FORECAST OUT OF BOSTON TONIGHT.

In our interview with Mary Davis, she said:

> If I'm not mistaken it was the ambassador's secretary or Paul Murphy who called and told us Jack was so sick. We, of course, were not to publicize it. It was strictly between the offices. I don't remember my personal reaction to this, other than I probably wasn't that surprised. He really wasn't a strong person. He'd had all those illnesses and London, cold and dreary, isn't the best place, so I wasn't surprised.
>
> The Ann in that telegram was the nurse, Ann McGillicuddy. She was like a member of the family. A real nice girl. She knew his case. The ambassador and everybody wanted her over there.

We examined Ann McGillicuddy's naval records, which had been supplied us. She had been "released from active duty" on June 5, 1946. She returned to active duty on October 14, 1948. So in the autumn of 1947 she was a civilian. We thought she was probably a registered nurse in private practice in Boston. She would not discuss this—or her trip to London— but we thought the illness must have been severe if Jack had a special nurse flown over from Boston to London.

Kay Stammers Menzies recollected, "Yes, I remember that nurse coming over. She was an American. Jack didn't fly back. He asked me to go down to the Cunard White Star and book passage for him and the nurse. I booked a cabin for Jack and a cabin for the nurse."

We next turned to the scrapbooks of newspaper clippings. We saw that this particular illness had been well covered by the Boston papers. They reported that Jack was in the London Clinic, and that he sailed from Southhampton on the *Queen Mary* October 11. (Ann McGillicuddy must have barely arrived in time to sail home.) One paper wrote that Jack had been "a patient in the ship's hospital." The *Queen Mary* docked October 16 in New York. Jack's passport was stamped with an entry mark on that day, we noted.

The Boston papers continued to follow Jack's journey. An ambulance met the *Queen Mary* when it docked. Jack was wheeled into the ambuance, then taken to a chartered plane at LaGuardia Airport. The plane flew him to Boston where, the papers reported, he would be cared for by the doctors at the Lahey Clinic. Reporters were on hand when Jack arrived at the New England Baptist Hospital on a wheeled stretcher. A reporter who saw Jack described him as being "thin and wan."

One of Jack's friends of this period, Frank Waldrop of the *Washington Times-Herald,* had a distinct recollection of this high drama. In our interview, he told us, "He went to England on a trip. He got sick. The word was given out that he'd had some kind of attack from swallowing sea water and oil in the *PT-109* thing. I guess the truth was it was the onset of the Addison's. I know he was given extreme unction and brought off the ship on a stretcher and it was touch and go."

We knew from some notices in the Kennedy Library files and the appointment books that about this time Jack had fallen under the care of a new doctor at the Lahey Clinic. He was Elmer C. Bartels, the man whom we introduced earlier in the book in connection with the Lahey Clinic and Jack's "unstable back." Bartels was a thyroid specialist—a gland specialist with a great deal of expertise in endocrinology. We had speculated that if Jack had come down with Addison's disease, Bartels would have been the logical man at the Lahey Clinic to treat him.

As our interview with Dr. Bartels progressed, we drew closer to the subject warily, knowing how controversial the issue had been in 1959 and

1960. To our knowledge Dr. Bartels had never been interviewed by a journalist. We fully expected the usual "I can't discuss a patient's diseases," but to our surprise we found that Dr. Bartels was willing to talk to us about it. He said that he thought that the truth should now be made known. He told us flatly and unequivocally that Jack had been diagnosed as having Addison's disease in England and had been sent to Boston to continue treatment. It was not a "partial adrenal insufficiency," but truly Addison's disease. He went on:

He was not in the crisis stage when he returned to Boston, as he'd been on active treatment. I don't know what his condition was in England—just that they made the diagnosis over there. He had an episode of weakness, nausea, and vomiting, and low blood pressure, which led to the diagnosis. The reason you collapse in Addisonian crisis results from low blood pressure.

When you develop Addison's, there is loss of appetite, loss of weight, great fatigue. Pigmentation of the exposed areas of the body and hands. And the hair stays brown. That's the only *nice* thing about Addison's, your hair remains brown and doesn't turn gray. You always stay young-looking.

Without a functioning adrenal gland one is very sensitive to infection. It used to be fatal in the old days before we had adrenal replacement—hormones. The patient invariably died of infection—even getting a tooth extracted was serious.

I'm sure that's the first time Jack knew he had Addison's disease. There are certain tests one does to confirm the diagnosis, although the clinical history is quite definite. So on clinical grounds and laboratory studies it was confirmed that that was the problem. Addison's disease.

We wondered how long Jack had had Addison's disease. Dr. Bartels could not recall Jack's prior medical history. He could not precisely date the onset. Every case of Addison's disease is different.

If the cause of Jack's adrenal disorder was atrophy, then the dissolution had occurred gradually over a number of years. We thought that might explain various illnesses beginning with that severe illness in his fifth-form year at Choate, and the "jaundice" in September or October, 1935. Had he had a mild form of Addison's disease? Had doctors confused his "jaundice" for the pigmentation associated with mild Addison's? As we saw from the medical texts, a lingering adrenal disorder would explain his symptoms over the next few years: general fatigue, gastrointestinal problems and absolute inability to gain weight. Perhaps the gradual onset of Addison's had been triggered by the trauma of the back operation in June, 1944. During the 1946 campaign several workers had recalled Jack's peculiar "yellowish color." In a passing reference to Jack in its issue of April 14, 1947, *Time* described Jack as "still Atabrine-yellow from PT boat service in the Pacific."

Lacking Jack's medical records, all this must remain pure speculation, which Dr. Bartels, a precise man, refused to engage in. He said, "Addison's disease isn't a chronic disease in the sense that you have it for five years and then discover you have it. When you develop Addison's disease it's usually known within a year." But there remained the possibility that it came on very gradually with the atrophy of the adrenals.

Nor could Dr. Bartels recall the exact treatment he prescribed for Jack in October, 1947. We presumed it was the standard one, daily injections of DOCA for a month or so followed by DOCA pellets. Later Jack had periodic DOCA pellets implanted in his thighs—in the standard dosage for the Addisonian.

At that stage of hormone research there was on the horizon a new development that would vastly help the Addisonian patient. This was the new "miracle drug," the hormone cortisone. In April, 1949, an endocrinologist at Mayo Clinic, Philip S. Hench, announced that cortisone had been found successful in the treatment of patients with arthritis.

This news set off a great stampede for the drug. But it was scarce and terribly expensive. In response to the huge demand, pharmaceutical laboratories began producing it by various means. By 1951 it was available to all at a reasonable price—and in oral form. In the later 1950s the drug was further improved.

Since cortisone is fundamentally a cortical extract, endocrinologists knew it would also be beneficial to Addisonian patients. In fact, for them, it was also a "miracle drug." It would not cure the disease, but when used in conjunction with the implanted DOCA pellets, it would enable Addisonians, for the very first time, to lead fairly normal lives. They would still have to avoid trauma, such as an operation, but cortisone dropped the mortality rate enormously.

At some point Jack began taking cortisone, probably first by injection, then orally. Our guess is about 1949, when cortisone first began to be available. Bartels recalled that the Kennedys maintained safe-deposit boxes around the country where they kept a supply of cortisone and DOCA—so that Jack would never run out. Seven years after the onset of the disease, in 1954, Jack was receiving the standard treatment for Addison's disease. He had implanted DOCA pellets of 150 mg, which were replaced every three or four months. In addition he daily took 25 mgs of cortisone orally.

Thorn wrote that the cortisone treatment for Addisonians (usually with DOCA) had an almost magical effect. "The outstanding clinical findings," he wrote, "were those of markedly increased sense of well-being approaching a state of euphoria accompanied by a real increase in energy, concentrating power, muscular strength and endurance. There was a marked improvement in appetite and an increased feeling of warmth in the skin" and, as most patients discovered, cortisone markedly increased sexual desire. The original batches of cortisone had some uncomfortable "side effects," but these were relatively minor inconveniences. Cortisone gave the Addisonian life. Female Addisonians could even bear children without fear.

Beginning in 1947 at the London Clinic, and continuing to the time of our search, Jack and the Kennedy family, some of Jack's doctors, and some of his political aides engaged in a systematic cover-up of his Addison's disease. Although it takes us beyond the time frame we set for this book, we believe an examination of the cover-up worthwhile for several reasons. It tells something about political technique in mid-century America. It tells us something further about Jack and his father. Finally, it is a fascinating and moving story.

The cover-up began in October, 1947, when the Boston papers found out Jack was sick in the London Clinic. Jack or somebody decided to tell the press he had had an attack of "malaria," perhaps because his unusual pigmentation suggested malaria, or a side effect from Atabrine used to treat malaria, or because it could be related to his war service, like his back. The cover-up was launched with a statement from Jack given at the London Clinic to the Associated Press. The statement was published in the Boston *Herald* on October 7, 1947: "Congressman John F. Kennedy announced today that he was 'much better' after a month's bout with malaria and planned to sail for home this week. He is a patient at the London Clinic.

"Kennedy, who has suffered malaria since 1943, said the attack began while he was visiting Ireland, forcing him to abandon plans for a tour of France and Italy."

In the ensuing days, we noted, the other Boston papers, the *New York Times,* and *Time* magazine reported the illness as malaria contracted in the South Pacific during his PT service. The Boston and Washington offices were probably instructed to give this out as the standard line. In the Kennedy files we found several letters from Frank Morrissey in the Boston office in October, 1947, canceling speaking engagements for Jack. Typical was one dated October 21: "As you perhaps know, Congressman Kennedy suffered an attack of malaria while studying labor conditions in Europe. At present he is confined to the hospital and has been advised to give up all speaking engagements for the next few weeks."

The "malaria" cover story would come back to haunt them, but at first it succeeded splendidly. In the coming years it was trotted out as necessary to explain other hospital confinements—for example, in Okinawa in November, 1951, and in Washington in July, 1953. In the late 1940s and into the mid-1950s there was not even a hint in the press, anywhere, that

Jack had any disabilities other than his PT-connected back problems and malaria. He was not then a major political figure so the question of the exact state of his health was of little interest to the press.

Jack's unstable back continued to plague him during the late 1940s and into the 1950s. By 1954, seven years after Bartels began treating Jack for Addison's disease, the back pain was so intense Jack could barely walk, and then only with crutches. He was told by some medical authorities that a "double-fusion" operation on his back might stabilize it and enable him to function without pain. But because Jack had Addison's disease, the doctors at Lahey Clinic firmly opposed the idea of the operation. Bartels recalled:

> We didn't want him to be operated on. That's one of the problems of Addison's disease: the increased risk in an operation, even with hormones. The patient doesn't tolerate surgery well. We simply wouldn't do the operation in Boston. Ned Haggart [the back specialist at Lahey Clinic] recommended conservative treatment. Physiotherapy, exercise, etcetera. We didn't want him to have any stress other than what was positively necessary. We were not sold on the *need* for the operation.

This decision was surely not arrived at casually. The Kennedy family had been patients of the Lahey Clinic for almost thirty years. They were multimillionaires who gave generously for medical purposes. Jack was a famous person. Bartels and Haggart (and others at the clinic) would certainly not have wanted to lose him as a patient. If there was any doubt in Jack's favor—if he had had a "partial" adrenal insufficiency and stood a good chance of surviving an operation—we can't imagine why they would not have approved it. But they didn't.

Jack sought out new doctors in New York. Chief among these were Dr. Ephraim Shorr, head of the Endocrinology Service at the New York Hospital, Cornell University Medical College Complex, and an orthopedic surgeon; and Philip D. Wilson, at the New York Hospital for Special Surgery. Bartels recalled, "It was questioned whether it was absolutely certain that Jack had Addison's disease. I went down to the hospital in New York to see him before he was operated on. I stressed the increased risk of doing surgery on a patient with Addison's disease."

Jack entered a New York hospital October 21, 1954. He remained until February 26, 1955. When the operation was finished, the orthopedic operating team, headed by Philip D. Wilson, was proud of its work. Jack survived, though just barely. The team was anxious to get the word out to the medical profession that one could operate on a patient with Addison's disease. So they wrote a description of the operation that was published in the November, 1955, issue of the *Journal of the American Medical As-*

sociation Archive of Surgery. In keeping with medical tradition, Jack's name was not used.

This article, we believe, is conclusive proof, if more is needed, that Jack had classic Addison's disease. It is signed by his surgeon, Philip D. Wilson, and other members of the team: James A. Nicholas, Charles L. Burstein, and Charles J. Umberger. In a footnote they say, "Dr. Ephraim Shorr . . . provided advice in the management of this case." The team did not mince words about Jack's condition. They describe him as a man with classic Addison's disease, taking the standard treatment. Excerpts:

> A man 37 years of age had Addison's disease for seven years. He had been managed fairly successfully for several years on a program of desoxycorticosterone acetate pellets of 150 mg. implanted every three months and cortisone in doses of 25 mg. daily orally. Owing to a back injury, he had a great deal of pain which interfered with his daily routine. Orthopedic consultation suggested that he might be helped by a lumbosacral fusion together with a sacroiliac fusion. Because of the severe degree of trauma involved in these operations and because of the patient's adrenocortical insufficiency due to Addison's disease, it was deemed dangerous to proceed with these operations. However, since this young man would become incapacitated without surgical intervention, it was decided, reluctantly, to perform the operations by doing the two different procedures at different times if necessary and by having a team versed in endocrinology and surgical physiology help in the management of this patient before, during and after the operation.

The article goes on, in highly technical terms, to describe the operation which "was accomplished on October 21, 1954." It states that both a "lumbosacral fusion" and a "sacroiliac fusion" were performed "since the patient's condition remained good." The team was pleased. "The postoperative course was satisfactory in that no Addisonian crisis developed at any time during the next two months." Four months after the operation, in February, 1955, Jack underwent surgery again "for the removal of a Wilson plate which had been used in the spinal fusion as a form of fixation." Again, no Addisonian crisis. The authors concluded, "Though the patient had marked adreno-cortical insufficiency, though the magnitude of the surgery was great, and though complications ensued postoperatively, this patient had a smooth postoperative course insofar as no Addisonian crisis ever developed."

The postoperative complication referred to in the article was that which Bartels feared as much as an Addisonian crisis: a severe infection that nearly killed Jack. In a brief mention of the operation Rose stated, "He nearly died: he received the Last Rites of the Church." This occurred, she wrote, after the first operation. In his oral history at the Kennedy Library, Arthur Krock says that in that dark moment the ambassador came to his office at the *New York Times*. "He told me he thought Jack was dying and he wept sitting in the chair opposite me in the office."

By the time this operation took place, Jack was a popular United States Senator and the state of his health received more notice than during his younger days. The *New York Times*, for example, carried three brief stories on the operation: October 11 and October 21, 1954, and February 26, 1955. These reported his initial confinement, that he was scheduled for surgery, and that he had had spinal surgery and had been discharged. Each of these stories related his back problems to his PT service. But none mentioned the severe complications—that Jack had nearly died—or that he had Addison's disease.

We do not know how Jack or the Kennedy family reacted to the publication of the "medical history" in the AMA *Journal* in November, 1955, by his surgical team. No doubt they were disturbed. Within the field of endocrinology, Jack's case must have been well known. No doubt some doctors easily recognized him from the description. Now, here in the public record, was a full disclosure of Jack's Addison's disease and the precise treatment he was receiving for it. Any doctor or nurse or technician could have drawn it to the attention of a reporter. But Jack was lucky. In spite of the furor raised about the state of his health in 1959 and 1960, no reporter "discovered" the AMA article or linked it to Jack until 1961, after he was in the White House. Then, as we shall see, the disclosure passed almost unnoticed.

But, as James MacGregor Burns points out, in the mid- to late-1950s there were rumors in Washington that Jack had more than back trouble: incurable cancer, tuberculosis, or "some other serious malady." The ambassador became irate, Burns writes. He issued a statement (quoted in Burns) denouncing the "unfounded and disturbing rumors that are being circulated in Washington." There was still no mention of Addison's disease in the press.

In the years following the back operation, Jack's health improved greatly. He came under care of a doctor, Janet Travell, who would go on to the White House and become famous. As she describes in her book *Office Hours: Day and Night* she prescribed certain physiotherapy for Jack's back (the famous rocking chair) which, with the corset (never discarded), helped. Endocrinologists further improved the miracle drug cortisone, bringing out superior follow-on "relatives." We do not know exactly which of these drugs Jack took to supplement his adrenal output, but it is unimportant. Once he had recovered from the back operation, these drugs gave him the strength and stamina to seek the presidency.

In the late 1950s, as Jack embarked on that quest, "presidential health" arose as an important issue. It sprang from the fact that in September,

1955, Eisenhower had had a massive heart attack while in office and Nixon had very nearly ascended to the presidency. Thus, in 1959 and 1960, reporters began digging into the health of the various candidates, including Jack.

The digging must have caused Jack anguish. In fact, sustained by drugs, he was entirely qualified for the White House. He had plenty of vigor and stamina; the drugs did not impair him mentally. There was no reason, then, to think he could not live out two terms in the White House in relatively good health. But, as Sorensen points out in his book, Addison's disease had "a frightening sound to laymen." In the minds of many voters it would be considered a fatal disease and would disqualify Jack for the presidency. To concede he was being kept alive "on drugs" was not good either. Thus Jack was caught in a real dilemma.

He decided to tough it out—bluff his way through the reportorial digging. This required a number of delicate obfuscations. For one thing, the damning article in the November, 1955, AMA *Journal* was on the public record. At any time a reporter might find it. Thus it became necessary to concede some kind of adrenal disorder. For another, they had used the "malaria" cover-up. It, too, was on the record. A reporter might dig back through the clips and discover that all those years Jack or his aides had been lying to the press about his health, a matter as grave as the illness itself. Thus it was necessary to cover up the malaria cover-up.

From various memoirs and public statements Jack's aides issued, we deduced the medical public relations strategy was roughly as follows. They would continue to emphasize heavily the "malaria" and relate it to *PT–109*, but declare the malaria completely cured because a continuing case of malaria might disturb some voters. They would concede a minor adrenal disorder, emphasizing that many physicians could confuse such minor disorders with Addison's disease. They would prove that it was merely a minor adrenal disorder by pointing out that Jack did not then have abnormal pigmentation characteristic of classical Addison's. They would assert that the minor adrenal disorder arose from the shock and stress of the *PT–109* episode or the malaria—giving his adrenal deficiency a heroic air, as they had done with Jack's back.

Dr. Travell was named the chief spokesman to carry out the strategy. On July 21, 1959, she composed a medical statement for Jack. Parts of the statement appear in her book, parts in an article by Ernest Barcella on Jack's health in the February, 1961, issue of *Today's Health* (an official popular magazine of the AMA). Dr. Travell makes the important, though highly dubious, point that doctors often confused true Addison's with a minor adrenal disorder, and goes on to say that:

In 1943, when the PT boat which he commanded was blown up, he was subjected to extraordinarily severe stress in a terrific ordeal of swimming to rescue his men. This, together perhaps with subsequent malaria, resulted in a depletion of adrenal function from which he is now rehabilitated.

Concerning the question of Addison's disease, which has been raised. This disease was described by Thomas Addison in 1855 and is characterized by a bluish discoloration of the mucous membranes of the mouth and permanent deep pigmentation or tanning of the skin. Pigmentation appears early and it is the most striking physical sign of the disease. Senator Kennedy has never had any abnormal pigmentation of the skin or mucous membranes; it would be readily visible.

Senator Kennedy has tremendous physical stamina. He has above-average resistance to infections, such as influenza. . . .

There are three interesting obfuscations in the statement. Dr. Travell does not actually deny Jack had Addison's disease. It is implied, but not stated. Secondly, the pigmentation argument is irrelevant. The hormone drugs had long since reduced his abnormal pigmentation to an unnoticeable level. Thirdly, if Jack had "above-average" resistance to infection it was because he was continually on drugs designed to fight infection. But she avoids mentioning that he was on drugs, merely saying he had been "rehabilitated" from a "depletion of adrenal function." How she determined he had "above-average" resistance—what statistical basis was employed—remains a mystery.

The Travell "medical statement" was employed in response to questions from reporters about Jack's health. These questions now included specific rumors of Addison's disease. According to James MacGregor Burns, one of the reporters who first asked Jack about these rumors was Fletcher Knebel, then a Washington correspondent for Cowles publications, which included *Look*, for which Knebel wrote an occasional article. Burns reports that in response to Knebel's queries, Jack's office released the following statement, a classic expression of the medical strategy: "During the war I contracted malaria in the South Pacific, along with water exposure and a series of fevers. Diagnosis showed that this stress was accompanied by a partial adrenal insufficiency, though there was no tubercular infection or other serious problem. From 1946 through 1949 I underwent treatment for malaria—the fever ceased—there was complete rehabilitation and I have had no special medical care, no special checkup, no particular difficulty on this score at all. . . ."

Jack followed the same line. For example, Schlesinger reports that in mid-July, 1959, he had dinner with Jack at Hyannis Port and:

I asked him about the rumors that he had Addison's disease and was taking regular doses of cortisone for adrenal deficiency. He said that after the war fevers associated with malaria had produced a malfunctioning of the adrenal glands, but that this had been brought under control. He pointed out that he had none of the symptoms of Addison's disease—yellowed skin, black spots in the mouth, unusual vulnerability to infection. "No one who has the real Addison's disease should run for the presidency, but I do not have it."

At this same time—summer, 1959—James MacGregor Burns was concluding his research and writing his book. He, too, asked Jack questions about his health—particularly the Addison's disease. In response, Burns writes, Jack or his aides gave Burns a copy of the statement given Knebel and let him see the July 21, 1959, "medical statement" prepared by Travell. Based on these statements and "other sources," Burns, without identifying Travell as the author of the July 21 statement, quotes the Knebel statement—"a partial adrenal insufficiency" linked to the *PT-109*, then follows with:

> While Kennedy's adrenal insufficiency might well be diagnosed by some doctors as a mild case of Addison's disease, it was not diagnosed as the classic type of Addison's disease, which is due to tuberculosis. Other conditions, often not known, can cause inadequate functioning of the adrenal glands. As in Kennedy's case, this can be fully controlled by medication taken by mouth and requires a routine endocrinologic checkup as part of a regular physical examination once or twice a year.

As the preconvention infighting progressed in early 1960, other reporters were probing Jack's health. One was Jack Anderson, then a legman for Drew Pearson, who also wrote for the mass-circulation Sunday supplement, *Parade*. On April 10, 1960, Anderson published an article in *Parade*, "The Candidates—How Healthy Are They?" It was based on an interview with Janet Travell and, for the first time, introduced her name to the public. This article deals mostly with the history of Jack's back problem—from Harvard. Interestingly, there is no mention at all of Addison's disease or of an adrenal disorder. Anderson quoted Travell as saying Jack had "a better-than-average resistance to infection and astounding vitality."

As the Democrats were gathering in Los Angeles in early July, 1960, the state of Jack's adrenals arose again—this time forcefully and dramatically. On July 2, Harry Truman, who did not believe Jack should have the nomination, went on national television and asked if Jack really had the "maturity and experience" required of the presidency. Two days later, from New York, Jack appeared on national television to respond to the

Truman attack. In the course of defending himself he said the presidency demanded "the strength and health and vigor of . . . young men." Aides of Lyndon B. Johnson, who was then hotly contesting Jack for the nomination, interpreted this as a slur on Johnson, who had had a heart attack in 1955. On the same day Jack spoke, July 4, two Johnson aides, John B. Connally, director of Citizens for Johnson, and Mrs. India Edwards, a former vice-chairman of the Democratic National Committee, called a press conference and opened fire on Jack's health.

As reported by William H. Lawrence in the *New York Times* of July 5, Mrs. Edwards, a paid Democratic Party worker, said flatly that she had been told by "several doctors" that Kennedy had "Addison's disease." She added, "Doctors have told me he would not be alive if it were not for cortisone." She was revealing this fact about Jack, she said, because she "objected to his muscle-flexing in boasting about his youth." Mrs. Edwards and John Connally proposed a "health test" for all the Democratic contenders, Lawrence reported. Connally said he'd be "happy" to make available Johnson's medical records.

The Kennedy camp in Los Angeles was angry beyond measure, as we saw in various memoirs. Jack's press aide, Pierre Salinger, for example, wrote in his book, *With Kennedy,* that ". . . the accusation went beyond the latitude of fair play. . . ." Salinger, Bobby, and Sargent Shriver tracked down Dr. Travell by telephone to get her permission to release yet another medical statement which she and Dr. Eugene J. Cohen had prepared on June 11, 1960. Most of the key elements of this statement are published in the July 18 issue of *U.S. News and World Report.* They again make the point that Jack's resistance to infection was "above average" and write that, "With respect to the old problem of adrenal insufficiency, as late as December, 1958, when you had a general checkup with a specific test of adrenal function, the result shows that your adrenal glands do function."

In the press briefings, Bobby and Salinger gave reporters this new statement, referred them to the "full exposition" of the matter in the Burns book (actually the one paragraph we quoted, in which Burns writes that Jack did not have Addison's disease), then a supplemental statement from Bobby:

> John F. Kennedy does not now nor has he ever had an ailment described classically as Addison's disease, which is a tuberculose destruction of the adrenal gland. Any statement to the contrary is malicious and false . . . in the postwar period [he had] some mild adrenal insufficiency. This is not in any way a dangerous condition and it is possible that even this might have been corrected over the years since an ACTH stimulation test for adrenal function was considered normal in December 1958. Doctors have stated that this

condition that he has had might well have arisen out of his wartime experiences of shock and continued malaria. . . .

Pierre Salinger reports in his memoir that the press "shared his view" that the attack on Jack had been unfair. This was apparently so. In his *New York Times* story of July 5 containing the Connally–Edwards charge and the Kennedy rebuttal, Lawrence included both the Bobby statement and the Travell–Cohen statements, giving the Bobby statement precedence. He did not point out that whereas Bobby claimed Jack's adrenal function test of December, 1958, was "normal," Travell–Cohen had said merely that the test showed Jack's adrenals "do function." Lawrence also quotes the complete text of the Burns statement. A shirttail story from Washington quoted Ted Sorensen as saying Jack was "not on cortisone. I don't know that he is on anything—any more than you or I are on."

It had been a tense moment in Jack's political fortunes. But the strategy of obfuscation and half-truths worked brilliantly. Reporters considered the Bobby–Travell–Cohen–Burns statements as definitive. None dug deeper or seriously questioned the statements. Luckily for Jack the November 1955 AMA *Journal* article did not turn up at this point. Nor did any of Jack's other doctors step forward. In our interview Bartels recalled that he was annoyed by Dr. Travell's implied impression that Jack had better than average health (resistance to infection) and thought her statement "dishonest." He told her that she should concede Jack had Addison's disease, stating that with proper treatment there was no medical reason why Jack shouldn't be president. But he issued no public statement. After one day, plus a cursory follow-up in the news magazines, the story died.

Jack himself had never publicly spoken directly on the subject of his adrenals. It had all been done through his political associates—and here we include Drs. Travell and Cohen. But *after* his election he did speak out, during a press conference on November 10, 1960, at Hyannis Port. This is the way the *New York Times* reported it the following day: "When someone asked about reports circulated in the campaign that he had once suffered from Addison's disease . . . Senator Kennedy answered without hesitation.

" 'I have never had Addison's disease,' he said. 'In regard to my health, it was fully explained in a press statement in the middle of July, and my health is excellent. I have been through a long campaign and my health is very good today.' "

There the matter rested—for three months. Then, on January 29, 1961, in the *Binghamton* (New York) *Sunday Press*, a reporter, Paul Martin, Washington bureau chief of the Gannett newspapers, turned up the November, 1955 AMA *Journal* article. He speculated it must have been a description of Jack. But this important revelation caused no stir at all. By that time, the New Frontier was in full gear and Dr. Travell was the official White House physician. She was spoon-feeding the press misleading stories about Jack's health. None of the reporters in Washington followed up Martin's disclosure.

But in official medical circles the matter was not forgotten. Long after Jack's death, one physician, John Nichols, reopened the matter in the July 10, 1967, issue of the AMA *Journal*. Having done a little detective work, Dr. Nichols published excerpts of the three *New York Times* stories printed during Jack's 1954–1955 back operation, linking them to the November, 1955, AMA article. He stated the article *had* to be about Jack, and that he "accepts the clinical diagnosis of Addison's disease." Dr. Nichols went on to deplore the "concealment of the diagnosis," maintaining that Addison's disease "formerly fatal, is an honorable disease and is not a disease to be concealed." He argued that if the true facts in Jack's case were made known, it would be immensely encouraging to Addisonians. But this article made no impression in the press.

The following year, 1968, Travell published her book. One would have thought that after all the controversy in 1960—and now the challenge being raised by Dr. Nichols in official medical circles—she would have included a careful medical exposition of Jack's case, conclusively documenting her contention that Jack did not have Addison's disease, with the original London Clinic diagnosis, the Lahey Clinic follow-up diagnosis, and subsequent medical records. No such luck. She ducks altogether on this important point, stating that the "true facts" were contained in Burns (who had obtained his original "facts" from her). Then, as her final authority that Jack did not have Addison's disease, she quotes the Burns statement in full!

The other Kennedy books and memoirs by political aides are no less obscure and confusing on the matter. Rose, for example, discusses it not at all. Sorensen is most confusing. He *seems* to concede a cover-up, yet he does not actually say so, further obfuscating with this statement, "Instead of the term Addison's disease he preferred to refer to the 'partial mild insufficiency' or 'malfunctioning' of the adrenal glands which had accompanied the malaria, water exposure, shock, stress he had undergone during his wartime ordeal." Schlesinger wrote. "Then he was told that he had Addison's disease . . . and between 1946 and 1949 he went on a regimen of cortisone. . . . It developed later that he did not have Addison's disease in the classic sense. . . ." Most recently (1975), Ben Bradlee, in *Conversations With Kennedy*, wrote of Jack's White House years, "Kennedy's Addison's disease was always a mystery to me . . . he did take cortisone derivatives and when he did it often made his face fuller. Vain as always, it bugged him if he appeared a little jowly at press conferences, which he often did, not because he overate, but because he was taking some form of cortisone."

There was one final mention of Jack's adrenals in the medical journals. In 1972 the Kennedy family permitted a friendly physician, John K. Lattimer, to examine the autopsy photographs, X rays, and related materials barred from the public. The primary purpose of this new look was to quell doubts about the Warren Commission Report regarding the number of bullets fired, and so on. Lattimer published his findings (supporting the Warren Commission) in a thirty-page article in the May, 1972, issue of *Resident and Staff Physician Magazine.* In this article Dr. Lattimer gives the first official description of Jack's adrenals. He wrote: "The adrenal gland areas were well visualized on the x-rays of the mid-portion of the body and no abnormal calcification could be seen in those areas to suggest tuberculosis or hemorrhage of the adrenals. It is the author's firm belief that the President suffered from bilateral adrenal atrophy."

Like Dr. Nichols, Dr. Lattimer thought the full facts on Jack's disease should be published and recommended: "That for the benefit of other sufferers from adrenal insufficiency," some other doctors be authorized to describe the President's adrenal glands, "to demonstrate that even the pressures of the Presidency could be overcome by a man with this condition. . . ."

This was where the cover-up rested in 1973 when we interviewed Dr. Bartels. Having followed this rather complicated story to that point, the reader can now appreciate our surprise when Dr. Bartels revealed that the original diagnosis of Jack's malady at the London Clinic had, in fact, been Addison's disease, and that he had confirmed it himself. After our long discussion, only one point bothered him. He was not satisfied with Dr. Lattimer's conclusion that Jack's adrenals had been destroyed by atrophy. He said he would like very much to have a look at the autopsy records to see if the disease had in fact been caused by atrophy—or by tuberculosis.

After our interview with Dr. Bartels, we renewed our efforts to have Jack's official medical records opened up. Edward Kennedy, through his press aide, Richard Drayne, continued to resist, and finally to ignore altogether our various queries. In light of this, the reader can well imagine our further surprise when, during our interview with Sargent Shriver, he said:

What happened was that Addison's disease used to be fatal. But in that period, 1950 to 1960, treatment developed for the disease. If you had put out [a statement] that Jack Kennedy had Addison's disease, everybody would have said, "He's going to die." Therefore you had to explain what the situation was in such a way that was not dishonest but would not arouse a reaction that was dishonest in view of medical advances. So they said yes, he had a disability, but it was treatable.

Eunice has Addison's disease. She and Jack were physiologically alike. So I've lived with it for ten years. Seeing how it's treated and what its effects are. It's like being diabetic. As long as you have your treatment you are in no more danger than a diabetic is.

Some final thoughts on this matter: Now that Dr. Bartels has chosen to go on record with his diagnosis of Addison's disease, and now that a member of the family, Sargent Shriver, has conceded that Jack and Eunice, "physiologically alike," had both positively had Addison's disease, we would hope that Jack's other doctors would step forward and tell the whole story. Along with that, we would hope that Jack's full medical records—including the autopsy on his adrenals—could be made public. The only purpose served by keeping these records secret is to avoid embarrassment to those still living who participated, wittingly or unwittingly, in the cover-up.

Beyond doubt, the full story of Jack's fight against Addison's disease will prove to be a much more heroic tale than his service on *PT–109*.

Conclusion

W E continued our close scrutiny of Jack's life through the next six years: his full three terms in the House, his tough, hairbreadth, 1952 Senate race against Henry Cabot Lodge, his marriage to Jacqueline Bouvier in September, 1953. We learned many more fascinating new facts about Jack's years, but our confidence in our understanding of the overall picture waned. The onset of Addison's disease in September, 1947, had to be a profound turning point in Jack's younger years. It must have controlled or heavily influenced most of his major decisions, for example, whether or not to continue in the stressful business of politics; whether or not to marry and have children. He had to face the possibility that a minor infection not detected and treated in time could take his life. We saw, in fact, that this very nearly happened—on Okinawa in 1951 when Jack and Bobby were on a round-the-world trip. Bobby later reported in *As We Remember Him* that Jack's temperature reached 106 degrees and that medical authorities at the military hospital to which he was taken "didn't think he would live."

But the Kennedys and Jack's close friends and political associates were then, as now, engaged in a dogged, systematic coverup of the Addison's disease. As we said earlier, only one or two of them, notably Pam Churchill Harriman, would even concede he or she knew anything about the disease. The official medical records are closed. In the official and personal correspondence for these years at the Kennedy Library, we could find no reference to it. This meant that either Jack never referred to the disease in his official or personal correspondence, or that the library archivists are under instructions not to release letters or documents referring to it.

A case in point is the illness on Okinawa in 1951 that Bobby referred to. It was the worst medical crisis Jack had faced since 1947. We made every conceivable effort to research this trip that terminated so dramatically. None of the Kennedy books has anything to say about it (beyond Bobby's brief comment); not even Rose's memoirs. There was nothing at the Kennedy Library: no itinerary, no follow-up thank-you letters, no passport and, of course, no information on his hospital confinement. In our interview with Eunice, she could not recall the incident, she said. Patricia, who was along on the trip, refused to see us. None of Jack's friends or associates could—or would—recall anything about it. The Army medical records for the hospital on Okinawa are closed. The only added detail we could dig up came from Jack's physician of those days, Dr. Bartels. He told us that Jack had not been properly taking care of himself on the trip, that Jack came down with a severe fever. Bartels was called by the medical authorities on Okinawa. By telephone he prescribed penicillin and adrenal hormones. Boston newspapers, which reported Jack had "cut short" his trip "after being taken ill in Okinawa," probably encouraged by Jack's political aides, speculated the illness "may have been malaria."

Without question the onset of the disease had a dramatic impact on Jack's performance in the House. As we have seen, he got off to an extremely promising start in the first session of the 80th Congress, praised highly by national and Massachusetts political observers alike. However, after the onset of the disease it was a downhill slide. His rate of absenteeism was one of the highest in the House. He sponsored no legislation of note, led no noteworthy investigations after the Christoffel case. Looking back over those years, political analysts, somewhat baffled, would assess his House performance as "unspectacular" (Fletcher Knebel), "lackluster" (*Time*), and "undistinguished" (Ted Sorensen). But they did not know about Addison's, or if they did, it was not mentioned as a reason for his slide into mediocrity.

All these factors considered, we decided that after the onset of Addison's in September, 1947, it was impossible to stay close enough to the real Jack Kennedy to produce a complete narrative. After he entered Congress, the medical cover-up was simply too vast, too overwhelming. Our time and our resources—and our patience and sympathy—ran out. Perhaps at some future date, when Jack's friends and associates are willing to be candid about these years, we will return to the subject. But that is another story, another book.

What, then, emerges from these pages? What was Jack Kennedy really like in the period 1935–1947?

Jack grew up in the shadow of a domineering, unscrupulous, absentee father, a devoutly religious absentee mother, and a bullying sibling, Joe Junior. Yet Jack emerged from adolescence remarkably free of disabling neuroses. He carried the burden of his father's notoriety and wealth with evident ease. Money, or the accumulation of money or what it would buy, was apparently something he seldom, if ever, considered. He had no special possessions of his own: no expensive cars, yachts, airplanes, villas, paintings, or jewelry. Despite the illnesses assaulting him, he never whined, never surrendered. On the contrary, he refused to concede he was in poor health—to an extent that might actually be thought delusional. He had a razor-sharp wit and not infrequently made himself the butt of his own jokes. He was often in nightclubs and yet he seldom drank. With the pain he was forced to endure, we thought it was remarkable that he didn't dive into the bottle or drugs as did all too many of his café society contemporaries. He had an admirable sense of purpose about himself (as opposed to, for example, Nixon's megalomaniacal sense of destiny); a curious, inquiring mind that never stopped growing. Physically, in spite of his thinness, he was handsome and winsome, a fey, bawdy, charming young man, fun to be with. He was well informed on international affairs, politics, history (especially English history), sports (especially football), theater (especially popular Broadway theater), and the watering holes of the rich. He was, in these years, fundamentally a conservative in his ideology.

As the adage goes, you can often judge a man by his friends. That was one reason we gave so much of our time to describing Jack's friends, male and female. In these years, Jack had two distinct, compartmentalized (that is, nonassociating) sets of male friends: political associates and personal friends. Leaving aside the political associates (a special case), we see that most of his close pals—Lem Billings, Rip Horton, Charlie Houghton, Ben Smith, Torby Macdonald, Chuck Spalding, Red Fay, and Jim Reed—were remarkably like Jack, from the same Eastern prep schools (except Fay), and Ivy League milieu. They were bright, gregarious, amusing, and fun-loving. Most came from more financially modest backgrounds, but none sought personal gain through Jack's money. Most (five of these eight) were non-Catholic. Some were notorious womanizers. Most were athletes, with a compelling interest in sports. All were, in these years, conservative politically. None was "intellectual" in the strictest definition. Jack was the dominant figure of the group; the others were satellites revolving around Jack. Most were willing to do almost anything he proposed. All were intensely loyal to Jack.

And what of Jack's relationship with the opposite sex? Does it tell us anything about Jack in these years? We think it does. As Betty Spalding, Cis McLaughlin, Mary Pitcairn and others close to the Kennedy family in these years told us, there was clearly a strained, if not bizarre, emotional relationship between Joe and Rose Kennedy. And, as we have seen in Jack's letters to Rip Horton's first wife, Jane, and to Red Fay, Jack, in spite of all this religious indoctrination to the contrary, grew up with a chary, if not cynical, view of "love" and marriage. He worried how it might upset existing male relationships. He was, as Betty said, "emotionally blocked," incapable of a deep and lasting relationship with a woman. Many young men of those days grew up with similar reserve, but Jack's was, we believe, exceptional, perhaps extreme.

His outlook about women may have been affected significantly by his college-days love affair with Frances Ann Cannon. By all accounts she was an exceptional young woman: strikingly beautiful, intelligent, purposeful, a member of the Establishment society. Evidently Jack pursued her ardently—all the way to New Orleans for Mardi Gras, for example. Rose wrote her husband in 1940 that Frances Ann was the only girl Jack "really enjoyed going out with." Frances Ann rejected Jack, leaving him, as Rose wrote, "depressed that he let his girl get away." Did this rejection add a touch of the fear of rejection to Jack's well-learned cynicism toward women?

Whatever the case, as Jack grew to manhood, marriage was far from his mind—and would remain so until age thirty-six. As Jim Reed, Chuck Spalding, and Kay Stammers Menzies told us, and as Kick wrote in a letter to Jack in 1943, Jack had adopted the "British view" of women. That is, he enjoyed foremost the manly companionship of his male friends. Women were secondary and primarily sex objects. He relished the chase, the conquest, the testing of himself, the challenge of numbers and quality.

After Frances Ann Cannon, Jack appeared to avoid women who were "eligible" (acceptable to the family or his Church) for marriage. Like his father and Joe Junior, he was drawn to beautiful models or starlets in café society: Inga Arvad. Angela Greene. Bab Beckwith. Flo Pritchett. Pam Farrington. Four of the above five were divorcées, as was Durie Desloge, the Palm Beach girl whose relationship with Jack inspired the false rumors of a "secret marriage." Some had intellectual pretensions. All, beyond doubt, were fun to be with, *au courant*, sexy, vivacious. A great deal of Jack's time was spent in the pursuit of such women for pure pleasure—though his relationship with Inga Arvad at least, and possibly others, was touched by real fondness of a sort.

Jack, as we were told, relished his reputation as a ladies' man, both in these young years and (as everybody must know by now) in later years, including his married years and White House years. It is our inclination to find this womanizing unattractive—but it must be said that he didn't coerce or deceive any of these women, and judging from their loyalty to him, none of them felt damaged by their relationships with him.

In our years, Jack's chasing was significant in only one instance. That was the Inga Arvad debacle. Jack was lucky not to have been cashiered from the Navy over this affair. Had he been, there would have been no *PT-109,* and almost surely there would have been no political career—no presidency, no Kennedy Dynasty, and all the rest. He was lucky, too, that he inspired intense loyalty among his friends, male and female. Had the story of the Inga Arvad affair surfaced along Jack's political way, we feel sure he would never have been seriously considered as a presidential candidate.

Let us here recapitulate the other major omissions and distortions in Jack's public image.

First, the impression was given that Jack was a robust young man. As we have seen in countless examples in these pages, the exact opposite is true. His health, almost from birth, was disastrously poor. He was born with an unstable back which progressively deteriorated throughout his life, necessitating first a brace or "corset" and, later, two spinal operations. It is a distortion—or a downright lie—to attribute his bad back to either a Harvard football injury or the *PT-109*. Even if he had not engaged in these strenuous exertions, the back would have failed. Throughout his childhood, and especially during our period, 1935–1947, he was tormented by an almost continual series of illnesses, most of which we are unable to identify because the medical records are still closed. In his junior year at Choate, a "severe illness" significantly impaired his schoolwork. Another illness (or a recurrence of this one) forced him to lose a full year of college in 1935–1936. He was ill during many of his Harvard years. He collapsed in London in September, 1937. He was ill during the spring, summer, and fall of 1938. In 1940, after graduation from Harvard, Mayo Clinic physicians advised him to take another academic year off to recover his health. At the end of the year he was back in hospitals for extended periods. He did not pass the Navy physical by doing five months of back-strengthening exercises. His father pulled strings to get him by the Navy physical. After a mere six months of active duty, he had to request six months' inactive duty for health reasons. According to Lennie Thom, he arrived in the Solomons in poor health. Seven or eight months later, he was relieved of command of the *PT-59* on orders of a doctor, and wound up in a hospital in the Solomons. He spent most of his last year in the Navy—1944—in and out of hospitals and, finally, was surveyed out of the Navy because of his health. Again, in 1945, he returned to Arizona planning to spend a full year recovering his health. He gave that up—but again collapsed in London. In the fall of 1945 he faced another (unspecified) operation, evidently not performed. In his 1946 race for the House he was in constant poor health (and suffered severely from back pains), collapsing in the final Charlestown parade. In 1947 he again collapsed in London—with Addison's disease. It is a distortion—or downright lie—to attribute any of Jack's postwar illness (including the cover story "malaria") to his PT service in the Solomon Islands.

Second, the impression was fostered that Jack was a dedicated and brilliant scholar. Here again we believe the exact opposite to be true. At Choate he was clearly a sloppy, lazy, and uninterested student. At Harvard, he was more interested in athletics than scholarship until his senior year, when he turned with an uncharacteristic burst of energy to write his thesis. In this period he did not ever again demonstrate any large capacity for study. The thesis itself was mediocre. The book that emerged from it, *Why England Slept,* was the product of many hands: the embassy staff, faculty advisers, Arthur Krock, and Joe Kennedy. Its publication heightened the impression that Jack was a scholarly intellectual with a natural talent for writing. But, as we have shown, there is little evidence to support this.

Writing and scholarly investigations are disciplines that demand long, lonely, patient years of solitude and reflection. We do not think Jack was intellectually or temperamentally suited for either. He was not a reflective man. He was an activist, living life (like all the Kennedys) at a frenetic pace, racing for planes, trains, steamers, lunch, dinner, the theater. We could not possibly imagine Jack forswearing that life for one in the Ivory Tower. And, of course, he did not. He was certainly very bright, but he was a "quick study," not an intellectual or scholar.

His studies at The London School of Economics and at Stanford University are cited by some authors and journalists as further proof of his scholarly dedication. As we have seen, he did not even attend The London School of Economics. The ninety-day stint (always reported as a full semester) at Stanford was a lark.

In this same vein, the assertion by many authors that Jack Kennedy seriously embarked on a promising career in journalism in 1945, then rejected it for politics, is also clearly wrong. As we have seen, it was Jack's father who put this scheme in motion, a temporary assignment for Hearst newspapers to keep Jack's name before the public and get him credentials to travel in Europe. His five thousand words of journalism (this time without Krock's skillful fingers) was a dismal performance, on a par with the output of any cub reporter. He did not, as widely reported, brilliantly predict Churchill's defeat. On the contrary, he wrongly predicted Churchill's reelection.

Third, the impression was assiduously nurtured that Jack was a war hero. As we have recounted in no small detail, the evidence does not support the claim. Skipping directly to the Solomon Islands and *PT–109*, once again let us encapsulate the provable facts. Between July 15 and July 31, during about two weeks in combat, the *109* made about seven patrols. On none of these nights did the *109* have contact with or fire at enemy surface forces. On three nights, the *109*'s section was attacked by Japanese float planes. On one of these attacks two of Jack's ten-man enlisted crew were injured and hospitalized. On the night of August 1/2, going on her eighth patrol, the *109* was part of a fifteen-boat flotilla deployed to intercept a specific group of Japanese destroyers at a specific place. When the destroyers appeared, precisely as predicted, Jack failed to follow prescribed procedure, did not follow his section leader to attack. Moreover, when the section leader suffered a "flash" in his torpedo tube, drawing heavy enemy fire, Jack left him to his fate. Two or three hours later, when the destroyers returned, again as expected, the *109* had a second chance to attack. But this time she was carelessly disposed for combat. Two men, Harris and Johnston, were asleep; two others, Thom and Kirksey, were lying down on the deck—unalert. The radioman, Maguire, was in the cockpit, not at his radio where he should have been. In clear violation of standard combat procedure and common sense (as Jack later conceded in the classified PT newspaper), the *109* had only one of its three engines engaged. Although other PTs spotted phosphorescent wakes from a mile or more away, the *109* did not see an onrushing ship until it was on top of them. Two men died in the collision; two others were badly burned. All in all, the evidence to this point suggests that (as some expressed it to us) Jack Kennedy was far from being a PT hero.

Contrary to all published reports of the six-day survival episode (including that in Burns) prior to his inauguration as president, Jack did not "save" his crew. It is not true, as reported by John Hersey and others, that the PT base gave up hope and launched no rescue operation. The opposite is true. It was the PT base alert to—and continued pressure on—the coastwatcher Evans and his native rescue apparatus that ultimately resulted in the rescue of the crew. The famous coconut message was far less comprehensive and helpful than the message written with a pencil on very prosaic paper by Lennie Thom. The very existence of a Thom message was not made known until Jack was already in the White House. He surely saved one life—McMahon's—and he performed bravely, but more impulsively than intelligently and not in the least effectively, in making his nighttime swims for help. His failure to fire the Very pistol surely led to the men being "lost" for a week in the first place.

Each of the three officers on *PT–109* (Kennedy, Thom, Ross) was awarded minor medals for "heroism" for their performances during the postcollision and survival phase. As we have shown, there is good reason to doubt the authenticity of some of the medal citations. We do not understand why there are *two* extant citations for Jack's medal. The enlisted men, some of whom "saved" more men than the officers, received no medals.

As we have reported, it was wartime censorship and Joe Kennedy's contacts at *Reader's Digest* that were primarily responsible for Jack receiving so much credit during this episode. He was, in effect, a "manufactured" war hero. Here, we believe, the Washington Press Corps deserves a failing grade. It blindly accepted Jack's version of his combat record, or the incomplete, censored wartime accounts, with no independent investigation. It was not until Jack was already president that Robert Donovan told the full story, and even then he distorted certain portions of it to put Jack in a more favorable light.

Finally, there is this question: Do these omissions and distortions matter? We believe that they constitute overwhelming evidence that shrewd manipulation of the media can make a man president of the United States. We think that matters; indeed, that it says something important about the quality of our democracy. Journalists can, and should, be condemned for careless and sentimental myth-making and for living on handouts from public relations machines, to the neglect of original research and questioning. But there is a more difficult problem here, too, and that is that the American people seem all too glad to be given comic-strip heroes to believe in, and woefully unwilling to consider human complexity in the very human beings who want to lead them.

We think that matters a great deal.

Acknowledgments

Many People assisted us in our research. We would like to thank first the staff at the John F. Kennedy Library in Waltham, Massachusetts, where we spent two months, especially John Stewart, Joan Ellen Marci, Dona Smerlas, Allen Goodrich, and others who cheerfully bore our countless requests and questions and who made available the hundreds of documents, letters, oral histories, newsclips, and so on, which are quoted in our narrative. Since these items are clealy identified in our text, we did not feel it necessary to describe them again in notes or an appendix. With our description, the Kennedy Library archivists can produce the items in a matter of a few moments. The library staff, of course, cannot be held responsible for our interpretation of the material provided us, nor for any views expressed herein.

And Dr. Dean Allard and the staff of the Naval Historical Center in Washington, D.C. Dr. Allard provided us, or our daughters, Marie Louise Marvin and Sybil Blair, with U.S. Navy records on the operations of the Solomon PT-boat force and *PT-109*. Over the years, Dr. Allard and his staff have spent countless weeks researching Kennedy's PT service and have assembled all available information such as Action Reports into a handy portfolio. Dr. Allard is not, of course, responsible for our interpretation of these documents or of Kennedy's war record. In addition, Dr. Allard very kindly made available the papers of Admiral Alan G. Kirk.

And Mr. Gibson Smith, Modern Military Branch, National Archives. The logbooks for naval vessels are on file at the National Archives. Mr. Smith kindly provided us, or our daughters, the available logbooks of Jack's three commands, the *PT-101*, *PT-109*, and *PT-59*, and the logs of the U.S.S. *Rochambeau* and U.S.S. *LST-449*. In addition, he furnished our daughters with the logbooks of dozens of PT boats operating in the Solomon Islands in 1943.

And officials at three schools in which Jack enrolled. These are: Mr. Edward B. Ayres at The Choate School, Wallingford, Connecticut; Mr. G. Ashley at The London School of Economics and Political Science; and Mr. Harry N. Press, who, at the time of our research, was director of the

Stanford University News and Publication Service. All were helpful in providing documents regarding Jack's studies—or nonstudies—at these institutions.

And those friends, relatives, Navy buddies, journalists, and political associates of Kennedy's who granted us interviews. We tip our hat particularly to Dr. Elmer C. Bartels of Osterville, Massachusetts, who, for the first time, gave a candid and revealing account of Kennedy's Addison's disease, and to S. A. Dulany Hunter for his candid interview on Kennedy's service in the Office of Naval Intelligence. Wherever we have made use of material from these interviews, it is clearly identified and set off in the text. Again, we did not think it necessary to include a list of these interviews in an appendix or source note. They, of course, cannot be held responsible for our interpretations or views of Jack Kennedy.

And Scott Meredith and Jack Scovil, our literary agents, and Edward T. Chase, our editor. These three men stood firm during some grim and dark times in the preparation of this book. Without their faith, encouragement, and support, we could not have proceeded.

Finally, we wish to thank, from the bottom of our hearts, two very close and dear friends, Ted Drury and Julie Drury of Bethesda, Maryland. Throughout the researching of this book, and several previous books, they kindly and cheerfully put out the welcome mat, sharing their home and table with us, sometimes for weeks at a time. Without their unfailing hospitality and friendship, this book and others could not have been written.

Index

591

7738